Reviews

Odd word charm ...

                                                          ...unday

The aut⁺ ⁻ ... e and wit make light of the dullest subjects.

                David Spiller, *Times Literary Supplement*

This marvelously produced volume is a treasure by any reckoning.

                        The Indian Review of Books

Reading *Hanklyn-Janklin* you have the impression that some time ago at the turn of the century the English language in India sprouted off in a different luxuriant direction.

                        The Independent on Sunday

Written in dry, witty prose, this is a guide to the customs, rituals and other trivia that make India such a source of mystery...

                        The Times, London

In every respect the book is the essential companion for a griffin (a newly arrived European unused to the ways of the East).

                        The Independent

There is plenty here for Indians and foreigners to learn from.

                        The Hindu

To help travelers unravel the mysteries of sub-continental English....Nigel Hankin shares the knowledge he has accumulated during more than four decades in India.

                        Time Magazine

An amazing attention to detail and heart-tugging observations of Indian life.

                        The Indian Express

For a quirky account of Indian English get hold of *Hanklyn –Janklin*.

                        The Lonely Planet Guide to India

He (Nigel Hankin) displays a fluent familiarity with the current of Indian history, folk lore and social customs past and present: from sadhus to viceroys...

                        Jug Suraya, *The Sunday Times of India*

At its purest, Indian English also preserves an elegance that many Britons have forgotten.

                        The Economist

It is no mere glossary of Indian phraseology; it includes explanation of common rites, rituals, customs and festival of India.

Sharad Chandra, *Sunday Pioneer*

A ready reckoner to rumble-tumble jargon.

HT City

Hankin has done the Delhiwallahs proud...

The Statesman

Great fun to read, keeping one infotained for hours on end.

The Telegraph, Calcutta

A fun read and a neat update on Yule's *Hobson Jobson.*

Sunday Magazine

A resident expat's 'guide-wuide' to India.

Dilip Raote, *Economic Times*

The instant wordsmith's classic.

Bill Aitken, *The Pioneer*

...and so crams it like a curiosity shop, an indophile Disneyland.

India Today

A most helpful and informative book on the current status of "Anglo-Indian" words.

T' e Hindu (Madras)

Hankin has produced an Indian English dictionary.

The Week

Some people collect stamps...But half a century of word-collecting in the capital of India...have let Hankin produce a work of much more use and entertainment value.

Gillian Wright, *Biblio*

A treasury of Indian and Indo-British words

Chowkidar

Trust Nigel to have a word for it!

The Bexhill Observer

I am neither historian nor Indologist, but I have been a guest in the country since I first arrived uninvited in 1945, and at least in the later years of this period, I have tried to keep my eyes and ears open to what has been going on around me. I like to think I have read fairly widely and I have constantly badgered friends, casual acquaintances and even total strangers: Why? Why? Immensely helpful explanations have always followed, although sometimes – such is the diversity of India – one would be at variance with another: especially so with regard to food. No two cookery books nor housewives seem able to agree on the details of prepared dishes. Also, as everywhere, precept and practice can be worlds apart.

Nigel Hankin

Originally from Bexhill, Sussex, Nigel Hankin came to India as a Captain in the British Army in 1945 and has been here ever since. In the early days, he ran a mobile cinema, and then worked for many years for the British High Commission in New Delhi. Nigel is a well-known Delhiwallah, famous for his fascinating, insightful conducted walks of the city which include the bustling alleys of the fragrant spice market and a lonely graveyard for statues of the Raj. He used to courageously negotiate the madcap traffic of Delhi on an old Vespa but nowadays relies on the marginally less terrifying buses and auto rickshaws to get around. Nigel never married but is delighted to be able to have his tea and newspaper brought to him every morning by his old retainer who has been with him for over forty years.

On Nigel's walks:

It occurred to me that for him to now this labyrinth so well, he must have spent the past 40 years poking his head inside every doorway in Old Delhi. The same applies for his glossary (*Hanklyn-Janklin*)

Tim McGirk, The Independent on Sunday

A Tribute

I was lucky enough to go on one of Nigel Hankin's amazing guided walks of Delhi that, even for Delhiwallas, were full of surprises and occasionally, not a little politically incorrect. Later I was Nigel's point of contact for the 5th edition of his equally amazing book that epitomizes the wry humour, keen observation, openness and warmth hidden in this shy reserved man.

Long before I met Nigel, I hit upon the idea of producing a one page 'Puppy's Pedigree' to try to find a home for an Indian street dog. I used Nigel's definition of 'Pie Dog' in its entirety (to be thorough, I also looked up Hobson Jobson but found this to be dry and colourless.) Nigel's description of 'the ubiquitous, often ownerless, dog of all villages and towns' brought tears to the eyes of the future owner of my waif. Years later, when I met Nigel and told him that his definition of pie dog had helped find stray dog a home, it brought tears to his eyes too.

Nigel was always on the lookout for and delighted to find new words to add to Hanklyn Janklin. When I presented my brother-in-law with a copy of 4th edition of Hanklyn-Janklin he immediately dived in asking if it contained 'bowlie gilas', a term he remembered from his childhood in India. It did not. The 5th edition has it - 'In British days, table bearers' English for a finger bowl'.

Nigel was a maverick who lived life uncompromisingly as an Englishman, or rather an almost Victorian Englishman, in India. This also says much about the incredible land he chose to live in and which allowed him to exist - accepted for who he was, without being seen as an eccentric - as a part of its eclectic mosaic.

I regret that I allowed our friendship to unfold slowly rather than, in Indian style, taking him aggressively under my wing which he would probably have hated although I would have felt better!

The text on the back cover of the 5th edition of Hanklyn-Janklin was to read '2000 entries and growing with each new edition'. Sadly, those words had to be removed but in its present avatar, Hanklyn-Janklin will live on as a classic.

In today's often bland and uniform society, Nigel will be sorely missed.

Deborah T. Smith
Editor, Tara Press. New Delhi

NIGEL HANKIN

hanklyn-janklin

Tara Press

Nigel Hankin

Tara Press
Flat No. 6, Khan Market, New Delhi - 110 003
Ph.: 24694610; Fax : 24618637
www.indiaresearchpress.com
contact@indiaresearchpress.com; bahrisons@vsnl.com

2008

ISBN-13 digit : 978-81-87943-04-4
ISBN-10 digit : 81-87943-04-1

Cataloguing in Publication Data
hanklyn janklin
Guide to some Words, Customs and Quiddities Indian and Indo-British
Nigel Hankin

1. Dictionary 2. Anglo-Indian 3. Language 4. Customs
I. Title II. Author

Printed for *India Research Press* at Focus Impressions, New Delhi-110003

PREFACE

More years ago than I care to remember, a newly arrived doctor to the British High Commission in Delhi, Sidney Hamilton, gave me a list of some twenty Indian words he said he had read in his local English newspaper, and what did they mean ? His problem was nothing new: over 160 years ago Sir Charles Napier had a similar difficulty :

"1844, Headquarters, Kurrachee 12th February. The Governor unfortunately does not understand Hindostanee, nor Persian, nor Mahratta, nor any other eastern dialect. He, therefore, will feel particularly obliged to Collectors, sub-Collectors and officers writing the proceedings of Courts-Martial and all Staff Officers, to indite their various papers in English, larded with as small a portion of the to him unknown tongues as they conveniently can, instead of those he generally receives–namely Hindostanee larded with occasional words in English"

(Quoted from Hobson-Jobson)

I believe I was able to satisfy the doctor and from that short list Hanklyn-Janklin just 'growed'. So it follows that the compilation is really intended as background information for the stranger residing in India, to give meaning to facets of life which otherwise might seem perplexing; I would like to think that it may also be useful to those outside the country concerned with Indian affairs: if it can answer any questions of those who have been in India since birth, I shall be doubly rewarded. In general, headwords are those which have caught my eye in matter written in English–inevitably, largely from my home territory, north India. My choice has been subjective with a bias perhaps towards drawing attention to bonds of behaviour and language between India and Britain. My qualification for offering such information is not academic: although I have touched on both history and culture, I am neither historian nor Indologist, but I have been a guest in the country since I first arrived uninvited in 1945, and at least in the later years of this period, I have tried to keep my eyes and ears open to what has been going on around me. I like to think I have read, in English, fairly widely and, as do all foreigners, I have constantly badgered friends, casual acquaintances and even total strangers: Why? Why? Immensely helpful explanations have always followed, although sometimes–such is the diversity of India–one would be at variance with another: especially so with regard to food. No two cookery books nor housewives seem able to agree on the details of prepared dishes. Also, as everywhere, precept and practice can be worlds apart.

In the Introduction I touch on the difficulty outsiders can have in pronunciation when reading Indian words from roman script, particularly to know when to make the vowels long. I well remember at school how gleefully we used to mimic a geography master who always spoke of the Himāl-yar mountains : he never explained his reasons nor corrected our use of the English Hima-lay-as. It was not until I came here that I learned that he was better informed than we. I fear that errors must be lurking somewhere unperceived. If challenged, I shall only be able to repeat the words of Dr. Johnson who, when asked why in his dictionary he had defined postern as a horse's knee (see pastern in the OED), replied, 'Ignorance, Madame, pure ignorance.'

My reason for writing above '...in the later years' is the memory always with me of my insularity during my first months in Delhi. I then lived in an army mess not far from Birla House where Mahatma Gandhi held his daily public prayer meetings : not once in those months did I, nor as far as I know, did any of my friends, travel the short distance to see him, to receive his *darshan* a word, of course, that I did not know. The fact was that in the circle in which I then moved, regard for the Mahatma was not high. It was not until the morning after his tragic murder in 1948, when I did see his body on his funeral car and the tears in the eyes of the people lining the route to Rajghat, that I realised something of his stature in India: a realisation to be strengthened some hours later when I saw the Viceroy of only a few months before, after the sovereign, the holder of the grandest job in the still existing British Empire, but by then, in theory a constitutional Governor-General, Lord Mountbatten, seated not on a throne nor even on a chair as is provided for dignitaries at state funerals today, but on a carpet facing the cremation pyre in a dusty piece of scrubland by Delhi's river.

Why Hanklyn-Janklin? The words have no meaning of course, but I would like to think of them not as a plagiarism but as a resonant tribute to the much more accomplished commentator than I of 1886, Henry Yule, and his work on roughly the same subject, Hobson-Jobson. The commercial reason advanced by Colonel Yule for his choice has not escaped my notice: in a bookshop, a volume with a main title of a glossary of something is likely to be perceived as a textbook or, at least, not for the general reader. It also happens that jingle or echo words are quite common in Indian family speech; one may give a party-warty, where one may drink a whisky-pisky or a cup of chai-wai. If bored, one may move ass-pass (nearby) and read a kitab-witab.

Hobson-Jobson has been my bedside companion for at least four decades, always ready in a sleepless patch to entertain and inform. The Concise Oxford English Dictionary has been a constant helpmate, particularly as a guide to the provenance of English words, only occasionally needing to be supplemented by visits to the British Council Library, New Delhi, to consult the full version: in addition to the reference facilities so generously provided, I owe thanks to the Council staff at all levels for information and ideas. The appendices to the American Heritage Dictionary indicating connections between the Germanic tongues, including English, and Sanskrit have been drawn upon.

For advice on vegetable products with a commercial use, I have found invaluable the ten volumes of Wealth of India, published by the Council of Scientific and Industrial Research, New Delhi. My thanks also to officials of the College of Arms and of the India Office Library and Records, both of London; the Librarian and staff of the India International Centre Library, New Delhi. Individual thanks to Mr. Rahat Hasan of the British High Commission, New Delhi, for his help and to Babu Prabir Basu for his encouragement, advice and assistance. Especially, I express my gratitude to Babu Soumitra Basu M.A. for his interest and erudite information always to the point, as a search agent, for many years for the spotting and correction of errors.

NIGEL HANKIN
November 2007

INTRODUCTION

Each new edition of the English Oxford Dictionary (OED) indicates a greater number of words in English usage with a connection to the subcontinent, but the real number with a link is even larger than any figure quoted. Those mentioned in the workaday dictionaries as having an Indian background are mostly relatively recent accessions: many, commercial imports by the young East India Company, such words as dungaree, chintz, lac, lacquer and the pigment, lake were received in this way. More arrived as part of the vocabulary of returning travellers, particularly that of soldiers and administrators. A smaller number came via Portuguese and French. The process is a continuing one and no doubt the large resident Indian community in Britain will be adding their quota. (A widely used Indian English neologism now accepted by the OED is an antonym to postpone, prepone.)

It is interesting that while the earlier supplements to English often came in a corrupt form, words here labelled anglicisms, arrivals since 1947, particularly from Hinduism, are employed more or less in their original sense: words such as guru, gherao, nirvana, asana, avatar and mantra; also many terms from the arts and food. But the mass of English words having ties with the Sanskrit-based tongues of India are recognised only by etymologists: e.g. the origin of wheel can be traced into prehistory and be shown to share a pedigree with the Hindi chakra, meaning the same thing. Dictionaries tend to ascribe such terms to downstream sources such as Latin or Greek or the ancient Germanic languages. But to those with even a rudimentary knowledge of Hindi, syllables common to the English ignite, vomit, regal, charisma, maternal, paternal, double and their northern Indian equivalents, must seem more than just a coincidence–and they will be right. The roots of wheel and the other words mentioned are part of the Indo-European heritage that descended with the horse, from shared ancestors (usually known as Aryans) living in the Eurasian steppes perhaps in the 5th or 4th millenium BC. A conclusion first made public by Sir William Jones, a judge of the Calcutta Supreme Court, in 1786.

The roman spelling of Indian words has ever been a confusion (which might, perhaps, have been resolved had Mahatma Gandhi's suggestion of Hindustani in the roman script for the national language been accepted. On the other hand, Devnagri English—i.e. Hindi letters—has sometimes been adopted: (see the currency notes). In the 1930s, the British tried to standardize at least place names by producing a definitive list as used in the Survey of India maps and from much earlier there has been an all-India list of Post Offices. The transliterations were often some distance from reproducing local pronunciations and since 1947 there has been an attempt towards a more phonetic rendering; thus Poona has become Pune; Simla, Shimla, and Ootacamund/Ooty is now Udagamandalam: some of the more prominent changes have been noticed in this work. Madras as a name had an ethnic root thought inappropriate after partition, so the city became Chennai after a prominent local family of long ago. But the University continues (2004) the old name.

The first spelling of headwords is generally that used in Delhi, but even here, all is not straightforward, for press house-styles vary, The Statesman with its base in Kolkata often follows the eastern India ba sound in place of the Hindustani va: thus basant (the season, spring) as against the vasant of, say, The Hindustan Times: banbas (a forest dwelling) and not vanvas. As Europeans in roman script for Larka/Ladka - a boy; kara/kada - bangle; or gari/gadi-a vehicle, so Indians tend to find it hard to distinguish between the English v and w sounds. The background to this is that although the Devnagri script is often claimed to be phonetic, this is not invariably so; particularly the same character represents both wa and the more rarely used va, the name Rajiv a lotus - is pronounced as it is written in roman, but a musician can be announced on an English radio programme as 'the celebrated wiolinist'. Both k and q can represent the gutteral Urdu Ka–from Arabic–so the famous tower of Delhi may be written either as the Qutab or the Kutab Minar. For Urdu words beginning with zay, phonetically the roman spelling should be z/zee, but there is no z sound in Hindi, (although a Devnagri character has been modified to reproduce it) terms such as zamin (land) and zira (cumin spice) can be written and pronounced jamin and jira.

Writers frequently pluralise and anglicise an Indian singular noun in an English sentence simply by adding an s, so that one can meet in a Delhi newspaper a phrase like - an actual example this - the 'hawas of change' (hawa, wind : the plural is really hawaen). So normal is this practice that it has been used from time to time here in the text. Sh is Hindi as in Shiva, or the family name Sharma, particularly in the south, is often written with just a plain s, sometimes employing a diacritical mark, sometimes not. Shiva and Siva: Sharma and Sarma. In roman Bengali, s almost always represents sh. One and the same deity may be spelled Krishna, Krsna of Kishen. To help those unfamiliar with Hindi, where sh is pronounced, this has been adopted as the initial headword spelling, although other forms may be indicated as alternatives. Alternative spellings, together with words of possible interest mentioned in the text, are indexed at the back. Sanskrit words often end with an all-but imperceptible click. This is really a release of breath, known to phoneticists as a plosion: so uses like Ashok (sometimes Asok) and Ashoka, nirvan and nirvana, are equally frequent. In the south, Sanskrit terms are often suffixed 'am' and 'lam.

The most common difficulty for beginners pronouncing Indian words from roman spelling is to know which vowel to stress: absence of the stress (the system of doubling the long vowel is a help, but it is not always followed): or a stress in the wrong place, can completely alter the meaning. Some examples: shastra - scripture, shâstra - weapon: hâkim - Unani doctor, hakim - ruler or governor: haram / harem - a sacred place, women's quarters, harãm–unlawful, bastard: hal - plough, hâl - circumstances, state of health.

It has been thought helpful to indicate the language of a headword, but the labels, Hindi, Urdu or whatever, in some cases really reflect no more than Delhi opinion and the purist may find much to cavil at. A word said to be Hindi will often be found, with or without modification, in other north Indian tongues and, if Sanskrit-derived, sometimes in the Dravidian also. If of Arabic origin, a word can safely be labelled as Urdu, but if from Persian, even if used by Muslims and considered in Delhi to be Urdu, may really be a form of a pre-Islamic Persian word with an Aryan (i.e. Sanskrit-linked) background. The Punjabi vocabulary too has many Persian words.

In the text, words printed in bold type are also headwords in their own right: so bold type is the equivalent to the abbreviation q.v. Alternative spellings of headwords and words of interest mentioned in the text not being headwords, are listed in the index at the end of the book. Diacritical marks, although essential for pronunciation by those unacquainted with the language, are rarely used with roman script in Indian writing. Here, where thought helpful, long vowels have been indicated in headwords and in the text where a word appears for the first time in any one monograph / article / treatment. Words with a sh (as the English shut) pronuciation are frequently reproduced in roman by a plain s (Siva, slok for Shiva, shlok).

A/AH Phoneme Sanskrit
Of the Sanskrit alphabet, as with many others, the first sound and honoured on that account. In an **upanishad**, it is said "...the A sound is the essence of all speech". Appended to many Sanskrit words it gives cadence in delivery to spoken sentences: personal names will have a suffixed A: as **Ashok**/Ashoka, **Rām**/Rāma.*See also* Ahinsa.

AAGEY WALA *n* Hindustani
Man in front. On a golf course, an anglicism for the caddy walking ahead with the duty of marking the fall of the ball. Slang for a penis.

ĀBĀD *adj* Urdu From Persian.
Under Muslim administration, a revenue-paying settled area. Thence, inhabited, populated. Also a suffix added to form the name of a city or town, as in Allahabad, the city of **Allah**. (The similarity in sound and meaning with the English abode seems to be a coincidence). In a village setting, the abadi is the built-up area. Strictly, the Persian suffix ...istān also has the meaning of inhabited, but in usage has become the equivalent of land of ...as Pakistan, land of the pure; Uzbekistan, land of the Uzbeks; registan, land of sand, a desert (*see also* Stan). Abad can mean prosperity, as in the Urdu salutation 'khush raho, abad raho' (happiness and prosperity be with you).

ABBA *n* Urdu from Arabic
Father. A word from Aramaic to Greek: in English, abbot.
Amma: Mother

ĀBDĀR *n Urdu*
Lit. person in charge of water. In a **Mogul** palace, the official in charge of the drinking water, also alcoholic liquor. In a British household or club, the head servant; an alternative title to butler. In recent times an abdar has become a bartender. In the 18th and 19th centuries, the foreman of the natural icemakers. (On cold clear winter nights of northern India, a combination of low temperature and evaporation caused ice to form on shallow pans of water placed in an open space. The thin slivers produced were stored in deep insulated pits for summer use.)

ABHINAYA *n* Hindi
Acting: any acting on a stage or an equivalent. But the word is usually used in connection with the form of acting in classical dance drama. Dance abhinaya can be divided into nritta, conventionalised movements

1

of the body, limbs and hands (*see* Mudra) common in some degree to all the Indian dance styles; and nritya, movements and voice applied to tell a story; miming to give a particular meaning to a particular dance. It has been written '...the song should be sustained in the throat, its meaning must be shown by the hands, the mood or emotion by the glances and the rhythm marked by the feet...' In Bharatnatyam, for example, the complex emotions of the solo dancer neglected by her divine lover are expressed without words through abhinaya and, if competently performed, are understood by the discerning as if read from a text. (Most writing in English follows the spelling abhinaya, but in today's Hindi speech, the final 'a' of the roman spelling is not pronounced.) *See also* Natya.

ĀCHĀRYA *n Hindi*

 A person advanced in Hindu or Jain (see Jainism) learning and philosophy. A learned teacher, and in Jainism particularly, a leader close to the top of the hierarchy believed to have considerable spiritual insight. A founder of a school of thought.

A title of Oriental Learning (corresponding to a higher degree) awarded by Banaras (see Varanasi) Hindu University and several other universities. (A specialist in Oriental Theology may receive the title, Vedacharya.)

Designation of the Chancellor of the Vishva (*see* Vidya) Bharati University at Santiniketan (*see* Shanti).
A **brahman** family name.

ACHKAN *n Hindustani*

A tight-fitting knee-length coat with buttons down the centre front and a small upstanding collar closed at the neck. Similar is the sherwani (sometimes called the Lucknow, or Lucknavi; sherwani: lit. the name means of Sherwān, a province of Iran. But the Kushān rulers of the 1st century AD (*see* Greeks) wore very similar long coats); said by Delhi tailors to be longer than the achkan by a few centimetres and to be wider at the skirt. The sherwani is mostly worn by Muslim gentlemen, often in black, but perhaps, as for a wedding, in gold brocade. In white, with a rose in the button-hole, it was much favoured by Jawaharlal Nehru.

A longish white cotton garment, perhaps flaring out a little from below a **cummerband** at the waist and worn with white **pyjama** trousers, feet bare, a **puggri**, the traditional uniform of the bearer, was the now less often seen, chapkan. *See also* **Jodhpuri** jacket.

AD *v* Sanskrit
To eat. A verb linked via Latin to the English edible.

ADĀLAT *n* Urdu
A court of law: criminal or civil. The term is a relic of the Mogul and British administrations.

Jan Adalat: a people's court, as set up perhaps by a revolutionary group in defiance of the lawful civil government.

ADHIKĀR *n Hindi*
Authority, command, entitlement.

Adhikari: an official; a prefix normally indicates the particular service or branch. A rightful claimant. Family name.

ĀDIVĀSI *n* & *adj* Hindi
Lit. original inhabitant (it could be inferred from this, that today, mainstream India, the majority people, are interlopers maintaining a colonial style). Often referred to as a tribal. Non-**Aryan** peoples, mostly forest dwellers (vanvasi), largely, but by no means entirely, concentrated in the central Indian highland areas; whose once almost inaccessible mineral-rich preserves are now being increasingly penetrated by heavy industry and the general population. Tribal culture has been retained with some influence from Hinduism; more than one hundred years of effort by Christian missionaries has also left its mark.

 A very early Aryan term mentioned in the Rig Veda for the original inhabitants was dasa/dasyus, fem. dasi: later, dasa had the meaning of serf, slave (the word is still current, as in the personal name, Devdas – servant of God or Yesudas – servant of Jesus.) Another term for the tribal, nishāda, was originally unexceptionable, but later in Sanskrit a note of contempt came into the meaning.

The Constitution of India specifically requires special assistance to be given to the tribal peoples. Those qualifying were first listed in a government order of 1950 to be attached as a schedule to the Constitution. Hence the official collective designation, the Scheduled Tribes. To better protect tribals' interests, the central government may designate their homeland a 'Scheduled Area'. Within such an area, a state Governor may order that a particular Indian law does not apply, or issue special rules that do.

Well-known tribal groups are the Gonds of central India. It was they, occupying a portion of that segment of the original southern continent (which, after inching its way northwards across aeons of time, has become today's peninsular India (see Deccan), who gave their name to the whole, Gondwanaland.

Others are the Santyals/Santals of Bihar and West Bengal, the Bhils of Rajasthan and the Mongolian peoples (also those kin to the Khmers of south-east Asia) of the north-east frontier regions, where the adivasis form more than ninety per cent of the population.

General names for the original inhabitants of the central ranges of the sub-continent are Mundas and Austrics. Some words considered as Sanskrit today for food stuffs are thought to by others to have an adivasi background.

When **dalits** advance their claim to be the original inhabitants of India they do not use the term adivasis but take a root from Dravidia, mulnivasis, foundation inhabitants.

ADRAK *n* Hindi

The rhizome from a South Eastern Asia plant from which the fragrant edible spice, solid and powder, ginger, is obtained. The OED states the English name, via Latin, has a Dravidian origin.

AGARBATTI/AGARBATHI *n* Hindi

Thin bamboo slivers about 30cm long, covered with slow-burning incense. Much used in **Hindu** worship (Muslims also, especially Shias – *see* Sunni – often burn agarbattis at a mazaar – grave monument, *see* Dargah. A practice sanctioned by

custom but not by scripture). A more humdrum use is as a portfire by the careful when lighting Divali fireworks, where the greater the distance the less the danger from an unexpected explosion. Mostly made by cottage industries in Karnataka (*see* Carnatic). Strictly, agar is the aromatic resinous wood of a species of the aloe tree,  but today the incense is usually from an added paste of charcoal impregnated with synthetic perfume, Aloe vera. (The inner bark of the aloe tree, after a lengthy process, was once a writing material. Examples have been collected from Assam dating from the 7th. century AD.)

Dhoop is a word for incense that in many parts will include agarbatti, but in the north it means a soft, black, putty-like material which smoulders to give a fragrant smoke. Most dhoop today is synthetic, but vegetable aromatic resins have been used for thousands of years; the myrrh of the Bible, for example, from the Commiphora family of thorny shrubs (natural to the dry areas of India. *See* bedellium in the *OED*). Such gum resins continue to be sold in Delhi's bazaars under the name guggal and are used in worship (in Catholic churches, in censers) and for keeping away flying insects at night. It is said that smoke from some of the guggals, if inhaled, has properties similar to those from marijuana. Another aromatic balsam and Indian medicine from antiquity is spikenard, sold in the bazaars as jatamansi.

Joss-stick: an inappropriate English term for the agarbatti. The word is from Portuguese (Deos – God) corrupted through pidgin on the China coast.

AGHORI *n* and *adj.* Hindi from Sanskrit
In the original Sanskrit, without horror or fearfulness. A ritually unclean man. Sect of Shaivite *(see Shiva)* sadhus inhabiting graveyards and cremation grounds. Through such necrophilic practices as using a human skull (kapāla) for a drinking bowl, they aspire to attain mystic powers.

Kapalika; a weaver of a garland of skulls. *See also* Shakti and Tantra.

AHINSA / AHIMSA *n* Hindi
The concept of not taking life under any circumstances. Non-violence and compassion towards persons and animals. Probably a Jain doctrine originally, later adopted by Hinduism and Buddhism: certainly it was a very strong message of the great Jain teacher. Lord Mahavir (though many Tibetan Buddhists do in fact eat meat. Many Hindus Including brahmins practice animal sacrifice).

The word ahinsa is interesting as an example of the similarity between **Sanskrit**-based Hindi and English: a prefixed *a* or *an* imparting a negative quality. Hinsa, violence; a-hinsa, without violence; an-dekha, not seen, invisible. Ashok, without sorrow. In English, these privative particles (*a, an*) came via Greek, as in a-moral, a-gnostic, a-nonymous, atypical, a-mazon – without breasts. Un as a prefix, of course, is also linked to Sanskrit.

The prefix apā (Sanskrit and Hindi) adds a negative and antisocial quality to a word: eg. bhasha - language, speech - apābhāsha - obscene speech.

AHMADIYAS / AHMEDIS *n*
Members of a sect, an off-shoot from **Islam,** founded in Qadian, Punjab (hence the movement is also known as Qadiāna), in the 19th century by **Mirza** Ghulam Ahmad, who became its first Caliph (i.e., successor to the Holy Prophet, see Khilafat, an assertion regarded by orthodox Islam as grossly aberrant). (*See* Khilafat). He died in 1908. The sect moved to Rabwah in Pakistan at the time of Independence (*see* Independence Day) in the expectation of a congenial country, but where the members now find themselves disadvantaged as heretics. Ahmedis accept the preeminence of the Prophet Mohammed, but consider that their founder, as a reformer of Islam, was also sent

by God. A belief of the sect is that Jesus Christ is buried in a known grave in Srinagar, Kashmir.

A'IN-I-AKBARI *n* Persian

Lit. the secular regulations of Akbar, or the governance of Akbar. The famous third volume of a three-volume history of the early **Moguls,** the *Akbarnama* (*see* Nama) from Babur to the Emperor Akbar, written by Shaykh (*see* Sheikh) Abu'1 Fazl, a court official close to the Emperor, and illustrated with miniature paintings by court artists.

A'in-i-Akbari is itself in five books, which together give a detailed picture of the royal household and the rules for running the great departments of state, in circa 1590. A well-known translation into English is that of H. Blochmann, published in 1873.

AIR (A.I.R.) *n*

All India Radio. See also Akash and Prasar Bharati.

All India Reporter: a journal reporting legal judgements from the higher law courts.

AJVAN *n Hindi*

In English, ajwain. A plant of the parsley family originally from the eastern Mediterranean. The dried seeds are used for flavouring (similar to thyme) and in Indian medicine.

AKADEMI *n*

So frequently is this word coupled with Sanskrit branches of the arts (Sangeet Natak Akademi, Sahitya Akademi etc.), that one might suppose that it has Sanskrit roots and is not solely derived from Academus, the Athenian owner of the grove and gymnasium where Plato taught. In fact, as in all European languages, it has been adopted from the Greek for its implications of scholarship and meaning of an association of like-minded persons.

AKĀLI *n Punjabi*

From Akāl, the Eternal One, the Supreme Being, as worshipped by **Sikhs.** (A-kaal, without time and so, without death, everlasting: (*see* Ahimsa.) A devotee of **Guru** Gobind Singh and a strict and ardent follower of Sikhism. At one time, Akali was an alternative name for a **Nihang** Sikh, but since the formation of the Akali Dal and the taking over of some Nihang-controlled **Gurdwaras** by the **SGPC** in the 1920s, the term Akali has, in general, been a reference only to a member of the Dal.

Akali Dal: a political party claiming to represent the interests of Sikhs, particularly in the **Punjab**. Sometimes known as the Panthic Party (*see* Panth) and often referred to as the political wing of the SGPC. In the troubled Punjab of the 1990s, the Akali

Dal has split into a number of factions, each distinguished by the name of its leader.

Akal Takht: See Sikhism.

AKĀSH / AKAASH *n Hindi*
Space, the sky, the heavens. One of the five fundamental elements of the ancient world: the other four were tej, light and energy; jal , water; vayu, wind; and agni, fire. (See Havan)

Akash bel: lit. sky creeping plant. One of the Indian varieties of the dodder, of the genus Cuscuta. A leafless climber, parasitic on the crowns of trees and bushes, giving the hosts (which it may eventually desiccate) the appearance of being festooned with yellow-green string or spaghetti. The parasite has no direct connection with the ground and the local name follows from a belief that it must be sustained solely by the air or sky. It is considered by some to have medicinal properties useful against stomach disorders and rheumatism.

Akash Ganga : See Ganga

Akash Vani: lit. voice from the sky / space. The term, as used in a **Purana** story concerning the implications of **Krishna**'s birth, has the meaning of a divine prophecy: it was Rabindranath Tagore who suggested it, with its association of truth and reliability of the highest standard, as the name in

Hindi for All India Radio (**AIR**). The television branch of AIR is known as Doordarshan – a view from afar would be a free translation, but see Darshan.

AKHAND/AKHIL *adj Hindi*
The whole, complete; (khand, a division, a portion, a piece. A canto of a lengthy poem, as of an **Upanishad**. For a comment on the prefixed 'a', adding a negative to a (word, see Ahinsa). Akhand Bharat: all India. To some, this means the subcontinent, i.e. pre-independence India.

Akhand jyoti: a continuous (everlasting) flame, as on a memorial; or at the **Hindu** temple of Jwala Mukhi in Himachal Pradesh, burning natural gas.

Akhand path: a complete and continuous reading of the **Sikh** scripture, the **Guru** Granth Sahib, before a congregation, usually by a team of professional readers, or chanters, known as pathis (the **brahman** family name, Pathak, once had the same meaning, a reader, usually of scripture), each reading aloud for periods of up to four hours at a stretch. To cover the whole work takes about forty-eight hours. The akhand path ends with the **Bhōg**, the usual ending to any Sikh religious ceremony, after which **prasad** is generally distributed to all.

ĀKHĀRA / AKHĀDA *n Hindi*
Long ago, just an open space within

a village on which the community could hold ceremonies or games such as wrestling contests. Later, other meanings became attached to the word, such as the seat of a religious leader and his sect, or a gymnasium. Congregations of **sadhu** akharas with their **mahants** borne aloft with pomp and ceremony, are especially visible at the great **Kumbh melas**. A group of drummers before a procession may be termed an akhara. (A phenomenon largely of the 18th century was that of sadhu akharas engaging in mercantile business and of forming mercenary armies available for hire.) The most usual application of the word is to a club of traditional wrestlers and body-culture enthusiasts, both **Hindu** and Muslim, under a **guru** or **ustad** with some using the old bottle-shaped heavy wooden mugdar, the Indian clubs of Victorian Britain. An akhara can also be the meeting place itself, something of an open-air gymnasium complete with large mirrors; also the shallow pit filled with soft moist earth used for wrestling. Indian-style wrestling, kushti, is a popular sport, largely rural, with the top-class exponents (pehlwaans/pahlwans) eating special and expensive foods and enjoying tremendous prestige: it is said that to keep a wrestler is of the same order as keeping a pet elephant. After retirement, wrestlers often establish themselves as bone-setters

and massage experts.

An alternative word for a wrestling ground is vyayamshala / byayamshala, place of exercise (*see* Hanuman).

AKHRŌT *n Urdu*
The walnut. Kaghazi akhrot: paper walnut; the expensive variety, the shells of which are thin as paper and may be easily crushed in the hand. Looking like bundles of old leather straps, folded strips of walnut tree bark are sold in the bazaars of northern India for use as fibrous teeth cleaners, datoon. Particularly popular with Punjabis.

ĀLĀP *n Hindi*
In classical vocal music, a prelude or introductory piece without using words (see Rag) but observing all the strict rules.

ALLĀH / ILĀH *n Arabic*
Al Lah : in Islam the essential name of God with the definite article, The God. Illahi, of God. The term used for the premier deity of many of the Arab peoples even before the mono-theistic message of Mohammed: the

8

God of **Islam**, for whom any one of ninety-nine sacred attributes may be used as names, e.g. Rahman and Rahim, the Merciful, the Compassionate, human tenderness. (In India, as a term, **Ram** Rahim, has the meaning of Hindu-Islam understanding and fellow citizenship). A popular belief is that the one-hundredth attribute is known only by the camel, hence the air of superiority about the animal's curled lips. See also Khudah.

"Allah-o-Akbar", "God the most Great". The invocation (in Arabic, the Takbir) repeated several times at the commencement of prayers (*see* Namaz): or when killing an animal so that the meat may be **halal**.

Abdullah : a personal name. Abd-Allah: slave/servant of Allah. Allahabad: See Prayag.

ALLOPATHIC MEDICINE *n*
An expression of the 19th century originating in Germany for traditional medicine, in order to differentiate it from homeopathy. Homeopathy has a large following in India and the term allopathy is the usual one to describe Western, but sometimes called modern or scientific, medicine. In a country in which at least four major systems (Western, homeopathic, **ayurvedic** and unani – *see* Hakim) find adherents and the expression 'alternative medicine' is simply not apposite, it is clearly necessary when referring to medical care to distinguish the principles.

Hahnemann Store: a shop selling homeopathic medicines. Named after the founder of the system.

ALMĀRI / ALMĪRA *n Urdu*
Cupboard, wardrobe. The phonetic similarity with such words as algebra and alchemy would seem to indicate an Arabic origin, but in fact the term entered Urdu from Portuguese (almirio) which received it as a corrupt form of Latin. It became anglicised as almirah and is still to be found in the *OED*. As Hindustani, almari remains in current Indian use.

ALSTONIA SCHOLARIS *n Latin*
A forest tree from the south recently popularised in Delhi for lining avenues. White scented flowers from a cluster of whorled leaves. The soft timber has a trade name of white cheese-board. Once used for children's writing boards, hence the whimsical Latin name scholaris – of scholars. Alston was an 18th century Scots botanist. In Hindi, the tree may be called sapt patt/a or seven leaves, from an accepted story that each full leaf from one node has seven leaflets (in fact, there may be six or eight). In Indian medicine, it is believed that an extract from the bark, infused, will reduce malarial fever.
ALTOO-FALTOO *n* and adj.
Urdu

9

A bazaar colloquial expression for something to be thrown away. Useless, garbage.

ALŪ / ALOO *n Hindi*
The potato:first introduced in the 17th century by the Portuguese on the west coast under the name papata, the origin of batata (correctly, Portuguese for the sweet potato), now Marathi and Gujarati for the potato. In Hindi the sweet potato is shakarkand. Later, the British brought the tuber to eastern India where the Bengalis called it alu (**Sanskrit**, aluka, for a type of edible root) – the current name throughout northern India.

Alu Bokhara (from Persian): the plum.

AMALTAS *n Hindi*
Lit. orange-yellow colour.
The Indian laburnum tree, *Cassia fistula,* fistula being a reference to the long (some more than two feet – 30 cm), pipe-like, black seed pods. A forest and cultivated ornamental tree. The English name follows from the similarity of the flowers, an explosion of golden yellow in April and May, to the English laburnum. (There is usually a second flowering during the **monsoon**.) In **ayurvedic** medicine, a pulp of the seed pod is used as a laxative. (In the Western pharmacopea, the old-fashioned 'opening dose', senna pods, comes from a related tree of the *Cassia*

family. Leguminosa.) The seeds of the true laburnum are poisonous to man and cattle.

Some say that an early flowering of the amaltas indicates an early onset of the monsoon.

ĀMAN *n North East India*
Lit. winter. The most important of the three annual rice crops of Bengal; harvested between November and January, the equivalent of the **kharif** of northern India. The crop harvested between March and May is the boro (spring), the same as the **rabi**, and during the late **monsoon** period the third crop, the aush (autumn) is taken in.

AMAR *adj Hindi*
Negative death. (See Mar). Immortal, eternal. The word often forms part of a personal name.

Amar jyoti: an eternal flame. A flame of remembrance.

AMIR/AMEER/EMIR *n Urdu*
A Muslim chieftain, a commander. When used in English directly from the original Arabic, the spelling is often emir. A wealthy man: a com-mon Hindustani adjective for wealthy. In the 18th century an anglicised form of the plural, omrah, could be applied to an individual.

Emirate / Amirate: the territory ruled by an emir/amir.

Mir: diminutive of amir, common in India, particularly of the Sind (now Pakistan) chiefs. The respect shown to a **Sayid** may well include 'Mir Sahib' as a term of address. Title of respect accorded to male descendants of an Islamic saint. In the form Amir-el-bahr (Commander of the Sea), amir is the origin of the English naval rank, admiral.

Amir Khusro: see Tabla.

ĀMLA / AVLA / AONLA *n* Hindi *Embilica officinalis:* a shrub or small tree of the myrobalan family. The fruit is sometimes called the Indian gooseberry; but although in appearance it is similar to a large European gooseberry, it grows on smooth rather than prickly branches and is no relation. Highly astringent in taste, with a vitamin C content some twenty times that of the orange, the amla is used in preserves, pickles (*see* Chaat) and dried, in medicine for which it is powdered under the Sanskrit name of amlak(a).

AMRIT *n* Hindi from Sanskrit An example of the privative a (*see* Ahinsa) denoting the absence of a quality, in this case, mrityu, death, linked to the English word mortal. Sacred nectar of the gods: one who drinks of it becomes immortal. Produced, so the texts say, by the gods themselves, assisted by demons who had their own purposes in view, by churning the ocean. For a paddle, a mountain resting on the back of Lord **Vishnu** in the form of an underwater turtle; the tail and head of the king of snakes wound round, became the pulling cords. First came forth poison, sufficient to kill the whole world. To spare humanity. Lord **Shiva** drank the terrible liquid, but held it in his throat, which turned blue. Not all versions are the same, but in many a total of fourteen miraculous 'jewels' appeared: these included the moon; two wondrous trees; Airavat, the four-tusked elephant which became the **vahan** (vehicle) of Lord Indra; Kamdhenu, the ever-bountiful cow; and Sri (*see* Shri), or **Lakshmi**, born Venus-like from the foam to become Vishnu's consort. Last, a golden **kumbh** (pitcher) of amrit issued from the waters. The gods drank, but the vessel was seized by demons who made off with it (*see* Kumbh to continue the story).

A present-day amrit (known as panchamrit) used as an offering or a libation to the image of a deity, or for washing the feet of a particularly holy person, contains five ingredients – milk, **ghee**, sugar, honey and water. To Sikhs, amrit usually means water from the holy **tank** at Amritsar (*see* below), but for their initiation ceremony, the water is first sweetened in an iron container and then stirred by exactly five Sikhs using the short double-edged sword, the khanda; while verses from scripture are sung or recited (*see* Khalsa).

11

Amritdhari Sikh: a Sikh who has entered the community through the pahul (gateway, see Sikh) ceremony and received amrit consecrated as above.

Amrit, as a term, may be applied to speech (amrit vani) considered to be spiritually inspiring and is often used for a personal name.

Amritsar (sar a water body amrit-sarovar: pool of amrit); city of the **Punjab** taking its name from the tank surrounding the Harmandar, literally, the Golden Temple, no doubt, from the golden dome, *see* Har. The heart of Sikhism; from which follows another name for Amritsar, **Guru-ki-Nagri**, city of the Guru. It was founded by the fourth Guru, Ram Das, and was originally known as Ramdaspura. The land was granted by the Emperor Akbar and the foundation stone for the Harmandar Sahib was laid by a Muslim. Some Sikhs object to sharing the English word temple with religious buildings worldwide and insist that their most revered House of God be referred to only as the Harmandar Sahib.

Amrit darna - a stream of amrit. A name for the R. Ganga.

Fish Amritsari: a dish from the pre-Independence frontier ; cubes of fish marinated in **dahi** and spices and barbecued on a skewer as a **kabab**.

Amrit-vela: the time of nectar, when man can be close to God. The first light between dawn and sunrise. A time for mysticism and prayer, when the world is silent.

Charanamrit / charnamrit: lit. foot amrit. Water that has been poured over the feet of a revered person, or the image of a deity. Believed by some to have spiritually ennobling and medicinal qualities when taken as a drink.

AMU (A.M.U.) Aligarh Muslim University **(U.P.).**

AMŪL *adj Gujarati*
A form of the Sanskrit word amulya, meaning invaluable: but known to most housewives as the trade acronym for Anand Milk Union Ltd., for the goods of the Kaira District Cooperative Producers' Union, Anand, Gujarat.

ANĀNA *n*
The pineapple: introduced by the Portugues. The Indian name is from Central America. It is said that the fruit was much enjoyed by the Emperor Akbar.

ANAND *n Hindi*
Pleasure, happiness, bliss. The **Sikh** marriage ceremony (Anand Karij), to complete which the couple walk around the **Guru** Granth Sahib, four times in a clockwise direction.

Ananda: cousin and disciple of the **Buddha**. To a Buddhist, Anand carries a meaning of spiritual bliss. Frequently a part of a Buddhist monk's adopted name. An alternative Hindi word for happiness, also with the meaning of inner or spiritual contentment, is sukh.

Anand Marg: lit. the way of spiritual happiness, the blissful path. The name of a socio-spiritual organisation working for the betterment of mankind. Founded in 1955 in Bihar by Ranjan Sarkar, the Anandmurthi (head) of the movement, until his death in 1990. The organisation was banned during the Emergency and many of its leaders detained. It was alleged that some of the activities of the Marg are secret and based on violence and tantric (*see* Tantra) practices for which the avdhoots (lit. religious mendicants or messengers, the name used for the movement's **saffron**-robed workers) require weapons and human skulls; also unquestioning obedience to the leader is required from all members. The political wing is known as PROUT – Progressive Utilisation Theory – or Proutist Bloc. On the social side, the Marg is said to work for human betterment, the removal of caste distinctions and to run schools.

ANDH/ANDHA *n Hindi*
Lit. A condition of blindness. A term for a dust storm which in north India can reduce visibility to a few metres. Perhaps thanks to irrigation in Rajasthan now rare in Delhi.

ANGLO-INDIAN *n*
From early Victorian days until the 1920s, the term for a Briton with a permanent residence (until retiring age, India never had a large European settler community). Those whom Paul Scott in his India novels, written in the 1970s, sometimes called British Indians. It then came increasingly to be applied (officially, the change was at least a decade earlier) to a person of mixed blood hitherto described as Indo-Briton, Eurasian, or East Indian (East Indian as a term remains in use for a community of Christians of Portuguese connection on the Konkan coast between Mumbai and Goa) and even the always offensive, half-caste. (Another nineteenth century  and earlier anglicism for a Eurasian, particularly if he was employed as a clerk, was Cranny, derived from Hindi, kiraani, a clerk.) No less offensive was the vulgarity of quantifying the Indian blood in terms of the sixteen **annas** of the **rupee**: a person of eight annas in theory would have one Indian and one European parent, but in fact the qualification would be more likely to be based on skin colour than genealogy. Many Anglo-Indians, of course, are of Portuguese

descent, as shown by the prevalence of such names as Braganza, De Mello and Pinto. As a division within the community they have occasionally been given the names Luso-Indians. (Lusitania being Portugal) and **firangi.** Additional European blood has no doubt descended from the staffs of the French, Danish, Dutch and Prussian trading companies. Referring to Paul Scott again in the Raj Quartet, 'Anglo-Indian' is restricted to a person of British and Indian descent; for Indians with other European blood, he reverts to the older 'Eurasian' In the early years of the 19th century, some Britons were fearful of their offspring:wrote Lord Valentia in a report of about 1806, 'With numbers in their favour, with a close relationship to the natives and without an equal portion of that pusillanimity and indolence which is natural to them, what may not in time be dreaded from them.'

As a minority community it is especially privileged in that two of its members are nominated by the President of India to the Lok Sabha. The custom has been that these two members support the government in power.

The Constitution of India (1950) defines an Anglo-Indian as one born of a male parent of European descent and domiciled in India. The Anglo-Indian Association of today insists that for membership the male parent must be or have been English speaking – a qualification designed to make clear the distinction between themselves and **Indian Christians.**

The change in meaning of Anglo-Indian came at about the same time as 'native' ceased to be used for an Indian. (Again, officials pre-dated Europeans in general: Britons in India, particularly those not in government service, usually chose to refer to themselves not by nationality but as Europeans.) In the army, 'native' went out of use in the 1880s (In southern Indian English today "my native" can be an abbreviation for my native place or village). Another change occurring just after World War II, was the revival of the 16th century word, Asian, in place of the harsher sounding Asiatic of the British period (To zoologists, the Indian lion remains the Asiatic lion). A change not yet absolute, is the term for a person from Goa, the older noun, Goanese, is being replaced by Goan. Anglo-Indian can also refer to a word or phrase from Indian speech adopted, with or without modification (usually with: the expressions called anglicisms in this work), into the everyday English vocabulary of Britons resident in India. Most such words did not leave the country, but a goodly number travelled to the United Kingdom, there to enrich the English language.

Anglo-Indian press: a 19th century

term, a reference to English language newspapers published in India and owned by Britons. While generally supportive, the English papers could be critical of government and out of official favour.

Indo-Anglian seems to be used solely to describe a literary work in English by an Indian author: as a term it is of no recent introduction, for Mark Twain quoted it in 1897 (*More Tramps Abroad*).

Recently (1999), the expression Eurasian is coming into general use.

ANGREZ *n Hindustani*
An Englishman. The term tends to include all Caucasians, which must be vexing to some. By those unfamiliar with it, angrezi (adjectival and the language) may be called gitpit, lit. unintelligible speech.

ANICUT *n*
Ayacut: strictly, irrigated land, but the usual meaning today is of an irrigation canal in the south

English from Tamil. In south India, a dam or weir, but not applied to the high modern dams.

ANIL *n Sanskrit*
The wind. A boy's name.
As in English body language, flatulence.

ANJUMAN *n*

Persian Assembly, meeting, society. Mostly used in relation to **Parsi** *affairs.*

ANNA/ANN *n Hindi*
From **Sanskrit**. Lit. food, as in the name of the Goddess Annapurna (*see* Kali), the provider of food.

Ann-jal: lit. bread and water, a term for subsistence-level living.

Anndata: giver of food, a fulsome form of address to a benefactor, a master.

Anna, Coin in circulation prior to decimalization of the currency in 1957. One-sixteenth of a **rupee**. The fact of sixteen annas to the rupee was used to express proportion; a statement that 'this is only eight annas milk', could be an allegation that the specimen was fifty per cent water. Children in school had to be taught their sixteen times table.

Anna (**Tamil**): elder brother.

ANSĀR *n Urdu*
Lit. helper, from Arabic. A worker or auxiliary soldier for an Islamic cause. In the plural, a militia. The original ansars were the people of Medina, who accepted and supported the teachings of Mohammed, as opposed to the people of Mecca, who, in the first instance, forced him to leave their city, the Hijrah of 622 AD. See Calendars.

Ansari: a Muslim family name, particularly of the weaver community.

ANTICIPATORY BAIL *n*

A provision, unique in the world's judicial codes, of the **Cr. PC** of 1973, whereby in anticipation of a criminal accusation, a person may apply to a court for bail: if granted and the charge is made, he will be exempt from police custody. The reason for the provision is to afford protection against the laying of vexatious complaints: said to be a not uncommon practice, particularly amongst political opponents.

ANTAR *n Sanskrit*

In Hindi, antri. An internal thing such as the intestines. Via Latin appears in English as entrails.

ANTYODAYA *n Hindi*

Uplift of, or compassion for the lowest, meaning those at the bottom of society. A scheme for the step-by-step relief of rural poverty. First introduced by the Rajasthan government in 1977. In each village of the scheme area, annually, the five poorest families are identified and assisted with capital and practical help to rise above the poverty line, a line in monetary terms far from sharply defined. The UNDP suggests a level of income sufficient to provide for an adult a daily intake of 2,400 calories rural or 2,100 urban.

AP (ANDHRA PRADESH)

A state formed in 1953, the first to be created following Independence on a linguistic basis, from the twelve **Telugu** speaking districts of Madras, later augmented by the addition of nine Telugu **districts** from what had earlier been the princely state of Hyderabad. In the capital city, Urdu is a major language.

The name comes from a kingdom of Andhra, covering roughly the same area as today's state, established in the 3rd century BC.

APPROVER *n* English

Usual term in India for one who, although himself criminally involved, gives evidence in court for the prosecution of his associates: probably in the expectation of a pardon or of lenient treatment for his own complicity. One who 'turns state evidence'. Approver, as a standard English word, of course, is obsolete.

APSĀRA *n Hindi from Sanskrit*

A female spirit, said to be young and beautiful; in Buddhism (*see* Buddha) also known as Yakshini. For many centuries, a popular subject for sculpture particularly as water nymphs. *See also* Gandharva and Kubera.

ARAB / ABJA *n Hindi*

The numeral 100 crores, i.e., 1,000 million.

ARATI / ARTI *n Hindi*

16

Hindu adoration or worship, by moving a flame held in the right hand and, usually, a small bell in the left, in a circulatory way before an image or picture of a deity perhaps with words of praise, sung or chanted. In eastern India particularly, arati may be performed by a dancer holding, in each hand, a clay pot of smoking incense on hot coals. In a temple, arati will usually have a loud musical accompaniment: the striking of gongs, the beating of drums, the sounding of conches, and, if on the bank of a river, at eventide perhaps, the launching of tiny leaf boats on the darkening stream each with a burning wick.

With the object of invoking divine blessing for his commercial affairs, a shopkeeper may commence his business day by performing arati before the goods on his shelves and his cash box: to a lala material riches may be an indication of God's favour.

ARCH, THE n *English*
The curved spanning of a space in building construction, came rather late to India. Pre-Muslim construction used the trabeate beam supported by pillars. Within the complex and nearby, of the **Qutab Minar** of Delhi, the evolution of the arch is clearly seen. The arches of the great mosque (1198) are corbelled, that is, each stone on the way up slightly overlaps the one below: almost at the crown, two large stones lean together, almost but not quite the way of a keystone. The first true keystone arch in India can be seen a few hundred metres away in the ruins of Sultan Balban's tomb (died 1287). By the time of the Alai Darwaza (1311, the entrance to the enlarged mosque), the true arch with a keystone is commonplace. A little later, the stones of the arch are wedge shaped, so that the thrust of the building above is transmitted to the sides, with less than a true arch some of the thrust is taken by the centre.

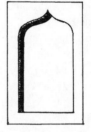 

In old city building one can often see cusped, or engrailed arches, in some cases these are purely decorative, pre-fabricated pieces supported at the sides and carrying nothing of the building load.

The Emperor Shah Jehan (17th. cent) sometimes decorated the crowns of his arches with the acanthus leaves of classical Corinth.

ARHAT / ARHANT n *Hindi*
One who is competent or qualified, especially in matters spiritual and philosophical. A title for the Buddha; master.

ARJUNA AWARDS : Annual national awards to outstanding Indian sportsmen and sportswomen. Named after Arjuna, great warrior and bowman, particularly famous for his dialogue with Lord Krishna at the battle of Kurukshetra (*see* Gita).

ARMY IN INDIA
In British days, a term covering the Indian Army (the successors to the Company's army, Indian and **Gorkha** soldiers with British and Indian officers), together with units of the British army temporarily in India (all ranks European). In addition, until 1858 the Company maintained six fusilier battalions of British soldiers (the Company's Europeans) for full-time service in India. The British Tommy in India in Kipling's ballad *The Widow at Windsor* (Queen Victoria) says "She 'as ships on the foam, she 'as millions at home, and she pays us poor beggars in red." Not in India she didn't, for no sooner were her redcoats on the troopship for the voyage east than their entire cost was charged to Indian revenue. Their role was to maintain the British presence and to provide men and material for British wars in Asia and, on occasions, outside. For a century and more India had been a wonderful base for the forces of the Empire, ready to serve anywhere in the eastern world at a negligible cost to the home government. But under pressure from the new advances of

democracy (*see* Dyarchy) things changed. From the 1920s Britain was forced to separate Indian from imperial requirements, so that Indian troops overseas in such places as Hong Kong, Singapore and in the Persian oil-fields, were paid for by Britain and from 1933 the Home Government paid £1.5 million annually for the maintenance of British troops. Also from Britain was the money required to modernise the cavalry regiments, from horses to armoured vehicles. Indian military expenditure during World War II other than for direct defence of the country was met by Britain: in 1946, £1,375 million was owed to India on this account at Independence.

Descriptive names of Indian military forces from history can be deceptive for the reference is more often to the employers than to the fighters themselves. The British Army in India was more Indian than European; the Company's Bengal Army contained few Bengalis; the regular troops of the later Marathas were recruited not from the **Maharashtra** highlands but from **Hindustan** and were often led by French and British adventurers; most of the guns in the **Sikh** state were served by Muslims.

Auxiliary Force (India) AF(I): a part-time Territorial force in which many of the volunteer Other Ranks were in fact potential officers for the regular forces (e.g. from col-

leges, business or railway operations). The pay was nominal and the
atmosphere that of a social club
(particularly with the Light Horse
units). Outsiders alleged that the
main classroom for military instruction was the bar.

BIA: British Indian Army. An
acronym appearing from the year
2000 or so.

ARSENAL *n English*
In the India of British days, this
Arabic-derived word had more the
meaning of a warehouse for military
stores than of the current factory for
weapons.

ARVI *n Hindi*
A vegetable somewhat similar to the
potato. The starchy tuberous rhizome
of a plant of the huge arum lily family. The English name is really from
Polynesia, taro. In the garden and in
the home the plant is cultivated for
its ornamental long-stemmed and
very large green leaves, resembling
in size and shape elephants' ears, a
popular name for it. To botanists it
is Colocaria esculenta.

Also termed elephant's ears are the
similarly shaped but more colourful
leaves of the caladium.

ĀRYA *n Hindi*
The Aryan people; also in Vedic
Sanskrit, as in many Indian lan-
guages today, noble, of high birth.
Early Sanskrit-speaking nomadic

peoples of Indo-European stock and
skilled in the use of the war-chariot;
with the horse generally considered
to have entered the subcontinent
during the period 1700 to 1000 BC
from the Iranian highlands – the
name Iran is itself a form of the
word arya. Solid evidence is slight,
but they are assumed to have overrun the **Indus Valley Civilisation**
and eventually to have fused with
the remnants: the non-Aryans with
darker skins and flattish noses becoming the **shudras** of the **Vedas**,
i.e., cultivators and labourers. (It
must be mentioned that at least a
few Indian scholars do not accept
this, but advance the theory that
the Aryans are indigenous and did
not enter India as conquerers. There
is no folk memory of an aryan
movement from elsewhere to the
tropical lands of India. The source
books of such conjecture there is,
the **Vedas** contain no reports of
such a migration. In fact, almost
nothing is known of the millennium
between Harappa and the historical
Buddha. The strongest refutation of
the indigenous Aryan comes from
philology, how else to account for
the fact of the early Sanskrit link-
age to European languages and, on
a different plane, the absence of the
domesticated horse in the Indus Valley civilisation. Untactful perhaps
to mention, but the highly desired
light pigment of so many north Indian brahmans has to be attributed.
Possibly the definitive answer will

be found from biotechnology, from genomes. Perhaps significant, Nirad C. Chaudhry pointed out that in early Sanskrit literature, nowhere is the sun mentioned as benign, but rather as terrible.

Aryavarta: land of the Aryans; the Indian subcontinent from the Indus to Bengal and south to the Vindhyas (*see* Dravidia and Deccan).

Arya Samaj: a reformist Hindu sect founded in 1875 by Dayanand Saraswati, a renowned Vedic scholar from Gujarat. He called for a return to the 'pure' Hinduism of the Vedas and rejection of the accretions from the **Puranas**. His vision was of a monotheism with no worship of images. Many decades before these became well-known causes, he called for equality of women with men, Hindi as a national language, uplift of those who later became known as **harijans/dalits**. It was a follower of Dayanand, Hans Raj, a penniless B.A. school teacher who in 1886, started, largely in the Punjab, the great memorial to his mentor, the D.A.V. school movement (Dayanand Anglo Vedic). Said today to number almost 700 institutions all over India. A footprint in the capital is the Hans Raj College of Delhi University.

ARYABHATA
Astronomer and mathematician who lived in the 5th century AD in what is now Patna. He is said to have recognised the movement of the earth around the sun and to have calculated the equatorial circumference of the earth to an accuracy of the equivalent of just 322 miles less than the figure of today. His name was given to India's first space satellite, launched in 1975. *See also* Zero. (A second but less known Aryabhata, also astronomer-mathematician, lived in the 10th century AD.)

ASH *n*
In Christianity, ash on the head is, or was, a traditional sign of penitence, believed to be pleasing to God: similarly, a Hindu undergoing penance (*see* Tapasya), may cover his body with fine ash. Ash, a substance purified by fire, is particularly associated with Lord **Shiva** (who, in one story, in anger consumed the deity **Kama** by a blast of fire from his third eye of destruction, and bathed in the ashes). He is spoken of as ash-loving and when depicted in meditation, (the Mahayogi, - See Yogi), is ash-covered: in emulation, Shaivite **sadhus** (*see* Lingam) apply ash to their bodies. In south Indian temples as a form of worship, ash may be poured over an image of Lord Shiva. The ash itself is usually grey in colour and is from burnt cowdung, perhaps with sandalwood ash or an aromatic substance added. Many believe that ash from burnt leaves of the bel tree (*see* Rudraksh) and, in particular, ash gathered from a cremation fire, is favoured by Shiva. Probably not today, but in earlier

times a youngish widow could have been required to be ash-covered – so as to make her unattractive.

In Hindi, there are a number of words for ash: rākh, bhasa/ bhasma/ bhasam and vibhuti/bibhuti/bhabūti. Vibhuti as a word is particularly popular in the south: there, Shaivite sect marks (*see* Caste Marks), often of powdered ash paste, are also known as vibhuti. Devotees will sometimes claim that an image or portrait of a deity produces ash (as a manifestation of the presence of God) from, say, the palm of a hand or from the forehead; a similar phenomenon is sometimes said to be observed when a photograph of a living person believed to be close to God is paid intense homage. In the home, ash is a popular cleaner for utensils, and is used by some for ritually cleaning the hands after a pollution.

ASHŌK/A *n* Hindi from Sanskrit An example of the privative a (see-Ahinsa). Lit. negative sorrow, i.e. without sorrow. A popular boy's name and particularly that of the great ruler of the Mauryan period, reigning from about 269-231 BC: strictly, his name as king was Priyadarshini – of gracious appearance.

Askok edicts: a series of governmental exhortations to good behaviour carved on polished stone pillars and on rock faces (the equivalent of a poster campaign) ot the Mauryan Period (3rd century BC) to the Guptas of 500 years later. Nine pillars have been traced in northern India – only two complete – in Delhi, brought there in the 14th century by the Muslim sultan, Feroze Shah Tughlak, but the Delhi rock edict is in its original site. It was only following the deciphering of the scripts in mid-19th century that the forgotten history of early Buddhism was rediscovered.

Ashok tree: confusingly, there are two if not three evergreen trees bearing this name. The traditional ashok, Saraca indica (also Ashok jonesia – after Sir William Jones, *see* Introduction – in the Roxburgh classification, little used today) is a red-flowered tree from eastern India, the south and Sri Lanka: associated with Lord Shiva and Krishna, sometimes called the Sita Ashok. This tree is rarely seen in the north (an ancient folk story has it that before it can flower, a virgin must kick the trunk or at least touch it with her foot). Also ashok trees, are two varieties of Polyalthia longifolia, evergreen trees with long shiny green leaves. The flowers and fruit are inconspicuous. One variety is bushy-topped, the other, steepled, tall and slender, sometimes dubbed the mast tree. Both make beautiful avenues. The leaves of the ashok are used in **Hindu** worship and are often hung over doorways to bless all

21

who enter. When young, the colour may be reddish being then short of chlorophyll.

Ashok Chakra: see Defence Services Awards.

ASHRAM *n Hindi*
Residential establishment maintained by a **Hindu** religious body, usually in connection with a temple or shrine; the retreat, the home of a **guru** and his disciples. Fairly recently, the word has been adopted by some Christian establishments, run on lines similar to the traditional Hindu ashrams.

An alternative meaning of ashram is one of the four abodes, or stages, of life enjoined by scripture for a **caste Hindu** (particularly a **brahman**). **Brahmacharya** for the student; grihastha for the householder and family breadwinner; vanaprasth (or vanvas / banbas) the retreat, literally to a forest, the sons having grown up and being able to look after the family and property (in the words of **Manu**, the law giver. 'When a householder sees wrinkles and grey hair on himself and also sees the child of his child, then let him go to the forest'). And finally, **sanyas**, complete renunciation of all wordly ties.

ASTH *n Sanskrit*
Bone. Linked to the European root for bone, oss, ost.

ASHTADHATU *n Hindi from Sanskrit.*
Lit. eight metals. In Hinduism, an auspicious alloy of gold, copper, silver, lead, iron, tin, bell-metal and another metal. Particularly used for icons. Some will wear a ring of the metal to ward off the evil eye.

ASHVAGANDH/A *n Hindi*
Lit. smell of horse (suggesting to some, the potency of a stallion). A highly regarded shrub, the source of an ayurvedic medical pick-me-up of the same name. To a botanist Ashvagandh somnifera : in English, winter cherry. The root twigs, powdered, are said to be a strong restorative in case of debility which, if necessary, will increase libido.

ĀTMAN / ATMA *n Hindi*
Soul, spirit, self. The indestructible spirit of God **(Brahma)** *within a person.* Says scripture "the soul is never born and never dies". *See also* Mahatma.

ATTA / ATA *n* Hindi
Wheat flour with much of the bran included. 'Brown flour' seems to be a fairly recent name; understood at least in **bazaars** where the foreign memsahibs do their shopping. Universally used in northern India for the making of **chapatis**: its importance to an average household may be gauged from the fact that at the time of writing, the minimum-size pack available from Delhi's Super Bazaars (government-

sponsored retail outlets for the less well-off) is ten kilograms.

ATTAR / ITTAR / ITR *n Urdu*
Perfume, traditionally the oils and distillates from strong-scented flowers absorbed in sandalwood oil. Nowadays, the fragrance may well be synthetic, with the sandalwood oil replaced by liquid paraffin. With synthetics, the scent is often strong – if not violent – to begin with, but soon evaporates. The spelling, itr, is closest to the original Arabic pronunciation: the **OED** mentions 'otto' as an alternative form.

Gulab attar / gulab-ruh (essence): possibly the most traditional and well known of all Indian perfumes, made from rose petals. The favourite of the **Mogul** courts. (Gul-ab, rosewater in Persian, is the origin of the European and American drink-word, julep.) *See also Khus.*

A production centre for attar and ruh is Kannauj in U.P. Much is consumed in **pan** and zarda.

Attardan: scent flask or phial, when finely made in silver, a collector's piece.

ĀVA
The ancient capital of **Burma**, a few miles south of Mandalay on a bend of the River Irrawaddy, and name of the Burmese kingdom until its subjugation in 1886 and annexation, adding

Upper Burma to the already British Lower Burma to become a province of **British India**. (Kipling's ballad. *On the Road to Mandalay,* refers to this episode.) The **Viceroy** of the day, on being honoured, chose as his style, the Marquess of Dufferin and Ava: a precedent perhaps, for Lord Mountbatten of Burma. (Four precedents from earlier ages were Lord Clive who took his title from his 1757 victory on the battlefield of Plassey; that of the Commander-in-Chief of the Company's forces in the northern war against the Marathas at the beginning of the 19th century: a campaign of much greater political significance for the British than the better known coincident battles of Arthur Wellesley in the south. In 1804, General Lake was created Viscount Lake of Delhi and Leswarree: Laswari, today's spelling, is a village south of Delhi and east of Alwar, the scene of the hard-fought final victory over the Marathas in November 1803. None of Lord Lake's three sons had a male heir and the title became extinct in 1848. Following the end of the first Sikh war, the British commander [and Governor-General] in 1846 was created Lord Hardinge of Lahore: this title is still in use. Sir Hugh Rose, a mutiny general, became Baron Sir Hugh Rose of Strathnairn and Jansi – the spelling of the time)

ĀVATĀR/AVTĀR/AUTĀR *n* Hindi
A word from **Sanskrit** meaning a crossing over, descended (from heaven) and made flesh. In Hinduism, an incarnation of a divinity (especially of Lord **Vishnu** in one of his many roles on earth). It is the stories of the heavenly deities as terrestrial beings that form much of the basis of popular Hinduism today. While Lord **Shiva** has a number of aspects on earth (*see* Nataraj, Bhairavi etc.) they are rarely described as avatars.

Male personal name, commonly with the spelling Avtar (close to the Hindi pronunciation, Autar).

AWĀMI *adj Urdu*
Of the people: the Urdu equivalent of the Hindi janta (See Jan). A word linked to ām, as *in* **Diwan-i-Am**. Awami often forms part of the name for a political party, particularly if there is a Muslim connection: The Awami League.

AYA RAM & GAYA RAM *n*
Haryānvi, from Haryana
Mr Ram coming and Mr Ram going. A colloquial reference to members of Parliament or state legislators who cross the floor, i.e., change political parties, for what are thought to be reasons of personal advantage. This is no recent tactic, a random sport of democracy; in Indian history a common cause of the rise and fall of princes has always been the defection of commanders and troops on a crucial battle-field.

AYAH *n*
Not an original Indian word, but by now domiciled for several centuries. From the Portuguese 'aia', a nursemaid, a female servant, particularly one who looks after children. A related word with the same meanings, also from Portuguese, but by way of China, is amah. From Hindi, the word can be naukrani.

AYUB
The Islamic form of the name of the Old Testament prophet, Job.

AYURVEDA *n Hindi*
A word with meanings 'coming from the Vedas' and 'knowledge for prolonging life'. The ancient **Hindu** systems of medicine and surgery. There is no single text, the Ayurveda, nor is the word even in the Vedas, but instructions for medical and surgical practice are to be found scattered throughout the sacred books; these were later extracted and compiled under the name Ayurveda. Today, over the length and breadth of India, it is probable that at least as many people have faith in ayurvedic remedies (supported sometimes, it must be admitted, by antibiotics) as in modern **allopathy**. But the fact remains that no scientific validatory tests of the many claimed miracle cures have been reported. As with the Islamic system (*see* Halim),

24

and allopathy before the 20th century, remedies are largely herbal (simples in archaic English) and dietetic: reliance is also sometimes placed on powders of jewels and valuable metals. The practitioner is a Vaid/Ved in northern India, like the title doctor in English, literally a learned man (*see* Vedas). In eastern India, a man qualified in ayurvedic medicine is often styled Kaviraj (lit. king of sagacity. In Sanskrit, the kavi is a man of insight, of special gifts; again, a man of learning). A number of universities offer degrees in 'Indian Medicine' but the majority of Vaids have less formal qualifications. A word from Sanskrit concerning Indian medicine is arogya, meaning freedom from disease. *See also* Allopathic Medicine.

AZAAD HIND FAUJ *n Urdu*
Lit. Army of Free India, the Indian National Army (INA). A force raised in Singapore during World War II, largely from Indian Army prisoners in Japanese hands. The name of its second commander. Subhash Chandra Bose *(***Netaji***)* remains greatly respected in India. The force the Springing Tigers, (from the Bengal tiger device on its flag) was first raised as The Indian Legion in South East Asia. Formed again as the Azaad Hind Fauj it fought as part of the Japanese army

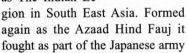

in Burma and just into north-east India for Indian independence (*see* Independence Day) from Britain. The records were placed in the National Archives in 1998. It has to be mentioned that at least ten thousand Indian soldiers, POWs of the Japanese, although treated very harshly, did not join the INA. *See also HIFS.*

At the end of the war some leaders were put on trial by court martial in Delhi's Red Fort on capital offences. But none was executed and all were released at Independence. On the trials, the Army Commander, Field Marshal Auchinleck, was reported to have commented "It is a poor specimen of humanity who does not want freedom for his country".

AZAAN *n Urdu*
From Arabic: lit. announcement. The Islamic call to **namaz** (the daily set devotions), made – from the door or **minar** of a mosque five times a day by the cryer, the muezzin/muazzin. (In a very large mosque, such as the Jama **Masjid** in Delhi, the call may be repeated inside to alert those assembled that the prayers are about to begin.) In the dawn 'cry', after the words 'Come to prayer' there follows the counsel, once, and then again.'Prayer is better than sleep'. The azaan is also a ceremony performed when a newborn child is only a few hours old; the Islamic word of God is spoken

into the baby's ear, if possible by its grand-father.

Murga azaan: (colloquial), the dawn cock crow.

AZADI *n Urdu*

Freedom. The word often refers to independence from Britain, achieved in 1947. See Independence Day.

Azad Kashmir: Free Kashmir. A term used in Pakistan for that area of the state of Jammu & Kashmir occupied by their forces. (Known in India as Occupied Kashmir or POK Pakistan Occupied Kashmir.)

B

BĀBA *n* Hindi

(In its adult applications, sometimes written and pronounced bawa'.) An affectionate and respectful term for an old man, particularly if a religious teacher: a grandfather and, equally, a young male child. But this last is not a natural Indian language use of the word, but is possibly adopted from the pronunciation of baby by **ayahs** with English families. (Meaning a boy : in the ayah's vocabulary, a girl-child was missy-baba. In today's Hindustani, where the boy is baba, the girl is often referred to as baby.) Baba is also a colloquial term of address between one person and another, man or woman, often with a note of exasperated affection.

Father in East India

Baba-Dal: see Nihang.

Baba-suit: a two-piece winter suit for a very young child.

BĀBU / BABOO *n Hindi*

Lit. an educated gentleman: once, a man about town, his style supported by landed property. A title of respect superior to **Shri** or Mister. Still employed in this sense amongst the **bhadralok** (gentlefolk) of Bengal and everywhere in north India by the humble, to those who seem to be their betters. Otherwise, mainly through European misuse, the word has come down in the world, so that to the anglicised, it now means a clerkly person with a superficial knowledge of dictionary English but no mastery of idiom (Babu English) and an exaggerated respect for the minutia of office procedure. Illustrating the inadequacy of this is a common Bengali style for their most revered man of the arts and Nobel prize winner, Rabindranath Tagore, Rabi/Robi Babu.

BABUL/KĪKAR/KEEKAR *n* Hindi

Names loosely applied to at least six species, of which *Acacia nilotica* (formerly, A. *arabica*) is the true babul, of the huge family (about eight hundred varieties, including the wattles of Australia, of which some twenty-two are found in India), of thorny acacia trees growing on dry scrub land. Also two varieties of the exotic but very similar Prosopis, correctly, jand in Hindi, the mesquite of Mexico, introduced by a raja about the end of the 19th century, with the same mimosa flowers. Of browsing animals, only the goat and the camel can ignore the spikes and find much sustenance from the small pinnate leaves. The pods are long and like a strip of medical tablets, each seed has its individual capsule. Those who wish to grow them, prefer to collect the seeds from goat pens, believing that the course through the animals' stomachs increases the likelihood of germination. The source of an equivalent to gum arabic (the gum arabic of Western commerce comes from a West African variety of the tree, *A. Senegal*): soft globules are exuded from cuts in the bark; these later harden so that they can be broken into clear amber crystals, known as gondh. All the barks yield tannin, but the best supply comes from A. catechu, khair, of which the red heartwood provides the astringent kattha, an ingredient of **pan**. Apart from their use dissolved in water as a mucilage, gum crystals are fried and enjoyed as crispy nibbles: Victorian cookery books for Britons in India suggested them as a locally available substitute for animal gelatine. Today the crystals are extensively used for making vegetarian jelly confectionery, food items, being added to chocolate, ice-cream and jam under a term such as 'permitted stabilizing agent'; beverages and pharmaceutical capsules. (*see* China Grass) As medicine, babul crystals are reputed to be of value to pregnant women. In autumn and much of the winter, the thorn acacias are covered with the fluffy yellow balls of mimosa.

Babul: (northern India) a father.

BACHAO *v Hindi*
An invocation to save, help. As in the political slogan 'democracy bachao'.

BADĀM *n Urdu*
The almond. Very popular in India on account of its believed great strength-giving properties. An essential item in the training diet of wrestlers. See Akhara, Heating foods.

BADLI *n* and *v Urdu*
Substitute, an exchange, a replacement: transfer (of a person from one appointment or place of duty to another). Particularly in Anglo-Hindustani, a substitute, a locum tenens', e.g. a domestic **sweeper** before going on leave may be required to produce a badli to do his work.

BADMĀSH / BUDMASH *n Urdu*
Rogue, ruffian, a bad character. In use, often coupled with **goonda,** a term with a somewhat similar meaning.

The prefix bad, from Persian, evil, in meaning is very similar to the English bad, but the roman spelling bud more closely represents the Urdu pronounciation.

Also from Persian into Urdu is the word lafanga, meaning an unprinciple character. With affection badmash may be addressed to a young child.

BAGASSE *n* English from French. In India, khoi the fibrous residue of sugarcane after crushing and extraction of the juice. It could be a raw material for paper manufacture or particle board, but in fact is largely used as fuel by the sugar processing units themselves, both large and small-scale.

BĀGH *n* Urdu from old Persian To a Muslim, the image invoked by the word is perhaps that of an idealised garden of fruit trees, watered by a stream, attendants, and four walls to ensure privacy: but in fact bagh is applied to any largish garden and even to public parks with little claim to being gardens at all. While the roman script spelling is almost always bagh, in devanagri (see Dev, especially in compound words and in eastern India, the form is bag (see IST Bagan-time).

Baghi: from Arabic, a rebel. In the British period a term sometimes given to one who objected in an overt way to the British presence. In referring back to such a person, the term today would be Freedom Fighter. The Chambal Valley **dacoits** have the local name of baghis – rebels. (But some would say tigers, *see* below.)

Bagicha: a small garden.

Char bagh: four gardens, the traditional symmetrical paradise-garden design from Persia. Used not only in ornamental grounds but also on carpets. (The **Koran** describes paradise as a walled private garden of delight with four streams, trees and flowers: its old Persian name entered Greek as paradeison, and English as Paradise.) Brought to India by the **Moguls**. (The concept is millennia older than **Islam**; says Genesis: 2/10: 'And a river went out of Eden to water the garden; and from thence it was parted and became into four heads.' For all that it can be termed Timurid style (*see* Moguls). The garden of Humayun's Tomb (1573) in Delhi is a good example: another is that of the **Taj** Mahal in Agra. In general, as landscapers, the Muslims took pleasure from straight lines, no curving paths or circular lawns. (In architecture also, aside from the dome and the arch, the squared form – the octagon – was preferred to the pure circle.) As the centuries passed, the channels became larger and the pools and fountains at inter-sections more elaborate, but the basic layout of formal symmetry remained throughout the Mogul period – it was continued, of course, in Lutyens' garden for the Viceroy's House (now **Rashtrapati Bhavan**) in Delhi of the 1920s.

Company/Campani Bagh: a garden set apart by the **East India Company** for the recreation of its European servants. The type of garden at the gate of which, so Indian historical memory now has it, were the words: 'No Indians or Dogs Admitted'. Where the gardens are now municipal parks, the old name often lingers on in popular, if not official, use. Hindi equivalents of bagh are vatika and uddayan. If designed to resemble a natural forest the word may be upvan.

In reports of the 1857 fighting, so and so bagh could be a reference to a palace or mansion set in a large garden or estate in the way that a similarly placed building in England could be known as The Park.

Bāgh (Hindi): a tiger.

Sometimes deified by villagers as Bageshwar – Lord Tiger (see Isa). The tiger has been declared India's national animal.

The Sanskrit word for tiger is vyaghra, also meaning best, preeminent. A connection perhaps to the western medicine for male potency.

Bagh as embroidery, see Phulkari.

Baghelkhand: a tract of **Madhya Pradesh** north and east of Jabalpur (earlier Jubbulpore), named after a tribe of Baghela **Rajputs**.

Gulzar and gulshan: words used in Urdu poetry for a pleasure garden.

BAHADUR *n* and *adj Urdu*
The brave one, the hero. From the Mongolian batur, a title of honour in the hosts of Chengis Khan. (The name of the capital of today's Mongolia, Ulan Batur, can be translated as Red Hero.) Brought to India by the **Moguls**, the title became the gift of the emperors and in their turn an award by the British Viceroys on behalf of the sovereign: Khan Bahadur to Muslims, **Rai** Bahadur to Hindus except those from the south who became **Dewan** Bahadur. Seemingly important people are sometimes addressed as **Sahib** Bahadur even today by humble folk. Frequently a part of Nepali, **Garhwali** and **Kumaoni** personal names: e.g., Shamsher Bahadur – heroic swordsman (shamsher, a name for a curved sword, as the claws of a lion – sher. Perhaps the origin of the English word scimitar, meaning an oriental curved sword). Particularly amongst its soldiers, the **East India Company** was referred to as Campani Bahadur.

BAHEN / BEHEN *n Hindi*
Sister. A title of affection and respect without necessarily any family relationship. Again as a gesture of respect, bahen may be suffixed to a woman's name when addressing her, or when referring to her.

Bahenji: Normally, as above (*see* ji). But as a noun used by the gilded youth of today, the meaning can be a scoff: a derisive word applied to a girl not accepting their free and easy mores, a **Gangaputri.**

Ben: Gujarati form of behen. But the Marathi bai on the other hand, is used not only in the sense of sister, but as a respectful suffix to a lady's name, particularly in western India and even in Rajasthan: as in Laxmibai, a popular and honourable epithet given to the scourge of the British at the time of the 1857 war, the Rani of Jhansi. Surprisingly perhaps, in context, bai can also mean a singing girl (*see* Dancing Girls) and a prostitute (baiji).

Bahen-chod: probably the most common Hindustani expression of abuse. An allegation that the person to whom it is addressed has an incestuous relationship with his sister. But generally, of course, this is no more intended nor accepted literally, than sexual suggestion in an English exchange of insults. Similarly, the words may equally be directed to awkward inanimate objects and situations. As used by the British, either through ignorance or bowdlerisation, the expression was usually rendered as barnshoot.

BAISAKHI / VAISAKHI *n Hindi*
By the **Hindu** solar calendar, the first day (Sankrant) of the first month (Chaitra) of the year. The day the sun enters the zodiacal house of Mesha (Aries) according to the Nirayana system (*see Uttarayana). But as a*
New Year's day it is little celebrated except by those of Bengal (where the festival is often a day or two later than in northern India) who exchange naba basha (New Year) greetings.

Mother **Ganga,** the river goddess, is believed to have entered Shiva's matted hair on this day on her way to earth: the happy occasion is celebrated annually by a multitude of Hindus offering worship to rivers. To Sikhs, Baisakhi is of two-fold significance: firstly because in order to foster unity in a growing but still thinly spread movement, the third **Guru**, Amar Das, decreed that his followers should assemble annually on the day and secondly, because it is the anniversary of the raising of the **Khalsa** by Guru Gobind Singh in 1699.

Since Baisakhi, unlike almost all other Hindu festivals, is based on the solar calendar (another exception is **Pongal**/Makara Sankrant), the date has a continuous relationship with the Gregorian: falling on the 13th or 14th April (*see* Calendars) and a day later in Bengal.

BAITHAK n Hindi
(Sometimes baithak khana.) A sitting place. In a dwelling house, the sitting room. Particularly in a village, in a largish house, the room or

place where, of an evening, visitors (male and of appropriate status) are welcome to sit with their host, to smoke the **hookah** and to discuss the affairs of the day. *See also Chaupal.*

A specified time when a family will be in residence to receive visitors in connection with an event: such as to receive condolences or congratulations. An "At Home".

A sitting, as in session of a conference. A classical music programme where, traditionally, those invited are seated shoeless on a cloth-covered and padded floor, legs crossed or tucked under, so that no feet are pointed towards the musicians or their instruments. (In a social setting, a seated junior's feet should not point towards a senior. In western surroundings to avoid this some contortion may be necessary. A Delhi ambassador visiting Pakistan was rebuked in the press for giving offence in that in a drawing-room armchair conversation with the Prime Minister seated opposite him, a published photograph showed the diplomat's feet apparently pointing in the direction of his host.) See Shoes.

An exercise particularly to performanced by wrestlers in order to strengthen leg and thigh muscles : squatting and rising to the feet with a swing of the arms over and over again.

BĀJRA *n Hindi*
A tall cultivated grass of the Pennisetum group (elephant grass is related): the pearl, bulrush, or spiked millet. A coarse grain grown as a **kharif** (autumn) crop mainly for animal fodder and for those who cannot afford the more popular wheat for their **chapatis**. Bajra, at the right season, can be readily distinguished in the field from the other common millet, jowar, by the bulrush shape of the grain spike.

Bajra: a boat; see Budgerow.

BAKSHEESH *n Urdu*
A tip for services rendered. A bounty added to an agreed payment. A free offering to a beggar: if demanded or requested, the Hindi bhik is more appropriate *(see* Bhikku). In English slang, baksheesh has become buckshi/buckshee, meaning free, without cost.

BAKSHI *n Urdu*
Like bahadur, a Mongol title from Central Asia: later, a Mogul designation, a paymaster, treasurer; the Mir Baksh *(see* Amir) was the equivalent of today's Accountant General, Defence Accounts, for his duties particularly related to military strengths and payments for troops claimed to have been mustered. North Indian (especially Punjabi) family name, deriving, no doubt, from the Mogul office.

BAKWĀS / BAKWĀD *n Hindi*

Bak – a gabbling, a jabbering. Nonsense speech, twaddle. Used as a harsh and possibly offensive judgement word. Carried to England, the origin of the word buck, for boastful or (slang) impertinent speech: 'none of your old buck'.

BAL *n Hindi*
Strength, vigour, power, potency.

BĀL *n Hindi*
A child. Balak: a boy child.
Bala / Balika: a girl.
Balkrishnan / Balakishen: the young **Krishna**.
Balkan: Children.

Balvadi: a rural or urban neighbourhood young children's centre, usually run by low-paid social workers. The name is literally child house. Vadi and bari (*see* Kali Bari) are the accepted transliterations in roman script in different contexts of the same Hindi word, meaning a house. (But sometimes also an enclosed space, such as a garden or orchard.) The Marathi form, wara/wada – a palace or mansion – is often met as a place name; even in Delhi, derived from the 19th century occupation by the forces of **Scindia**. An alternative word to balvadi is anganvadi (angan – a courtyard) with a similar meaning.

Bal/Balak Yesus: the Christ child.
Bal (Urdu): a hair, the hair of the head.

BALATKAR *n*
Hindi from Sanskrit. A taking by violence. Of goods, a city, a women in rape, etc.

BALUSTER PILLAR *n*
Baluster, an English word for an ornamental pillar having a bulge towards its base derived from the Greek name for the similarly shaped flower of the pomegranate. (Hence balustrade). The European design (perhaps seen in prints) attracted the interest of the Emperor Shah Jehan who used and reserved it for his imperial buildings. Eg. in his Delhi Palace (the Red Fort). The Urdu name for the pomegranate is anār and the flower anārkali. (Also anār is an ornamental firework burning in the form of a fountain.)

A motif from Greece also favoured by Shah Jehan was the bunch of acanthus leaves to be seen above the keystones of the arches of his imperial buildings.

BĀND/BĀNDH *n* and *adj.*
Hindustani
Closed, locked, discontinued. A tie, a knot. A general strike: a total shutdown of work.

Bandh: an embankment, a dam: often anglicised into **bund**.

Bandhna: to tie, to fasten, to pack. The English name bandana – handkerchief – originates from this verb.

In the traditional Indian process (bandhini), before dyeing, the cloth is tied or knotted tightly, so that the colour does not cover it evenly, leaving clear spots. Band, of course, has a common ancestry with English words for something tied – band, bond, bind, bend (as in sheetbend), bundle, etc.

Bandhna: Hindi. A cloth strip round a head often carrying a political message.

Bandgobi: lit. closed cabbage - a cauliflower. An unseemly bazaar term for a burkha wearer.

BANDAR *n* Hindi
A monkey, especially of the macaque  species: the common rhesus of the north and the bonnet of peninsular India. The grey, long-tailed black-faced group without cheek pouches, is known as the langur or **Hanuman** of which there are said to be seven sub-species. As colloquialism, the word bandar can be used to mean a European, qualified perhaps with the adjectives safed (white), lal (red), or **gora** (pale skinned). Also a colloquialism is a common name for a balaclava helmet: a monkey cap. No doubt due to a facial resemblance to the langur.

Bander (Urdu): a dock, a harbour. Also written bundar.

Bandergah: a harbour, a port.

BANDE/VANDE MĀTARAM
Sanskrit
Hail or salutation, to the Mother (see Vandana): to some, the Motherland of India; to others, the Mother Goddess of Bengal (*see* Durga Puja) and to others again, **Lakshmi**. A greeting and a battle-cry for those of all communities involved in the struggle for independence from Britain. The opening words of a poem of love for India (or Bengal) adopted as a hymn of liberty by the pre-independence Congress Party. Recognising it as an Indian Marseillaise, its singing was locally proscribed from time to time by the British.

The **Sanskrit** and Bengali words were in a novel Anand Math by Bankim Chandra Chatterjee (or Chattopadhyaya – *see* Rai) first published in 1882 and set to music by Rabindranath Tagore (an earlier score was by Hemchandra Banerji). It has become India's national song (as distinct from the National Anthem, *see* Jana Gana Mana) and is used daily to open the morning transmissions of All India Radio: but some non-Hindus object to its alleged sectarian connection. No less a very popular national song on patriotic occasions is Sare Jehan se Acha (Best in the World). Written in Urdu by Sir Mohd. Iqbal in 1902 for the freedom movement (in later life he did not use his British title).

Bande/Vande Mataram was the name of a political movement against British rule following Hindu discontent after Curzon's partition of Bengal in 1905. With the reunion of the **Presidency** at the Royal **Durbar** of 1911, the movement died but, of course, the freedom struggle continued under other names.

BANDICOOT *n*
An anglicism from the **Telugu** name for the rodent, pandi-kokku. A large and destructive rat (it can even get through a brick wall); of up to 1.3 kg in weight and almost a metre in length (half of which is tail): largely a parasite on man. Its presence can be detected by its large burrows and piles of soil in the manner of a garden mole. In north India the animal is ghus. See also Hafta

BANDOBAST/BUNDOBAST *n*
Urdu
An arrangement to do something: organisation, as in the English sentence: 'the police bandobast (on a certain occasion) was very good'. In the **Mogul** and British administrations, a land **settlement**.

BANGLA/BANGA/BANGIYA *n*
and *adj Bengali / Hindi*
Bengal (Vang, in strict but rarely used Hindi, particularly with reference to East Bengal, now Bangladesh. Once, today's West Bengal and the people living there had the name Ghoti): geographically largely the alluvial plain deposited by the two great rivers, the **Ganga** and the Brahmaputra. A person from Bengal; the Bengali language; adjectival for anything connected with Bengal.

Bangla: of Bengal, Bengal pattern. Name given by early Europeans to the low, single-storeyed residential buildings with thatched roofs – the shape was sometimes likened to that of an up-turned boat (*see* Basha) common in eastern India and anglicised and sent round the world as bungalow. As built for the English, at first the thatched roof remained, but it was often larger than the exterior walls by as much as five metres supported by columns so as to provide a shady **veranda**. Inside, ceilings were of stretched cloth – in order to catch foreign bodies falling from the thatch. The plinth level was usually nearly a metre off the ground. Later, roofs tended to become flat, perhaps of stone slabs resting on wooden beams, even if the walls were still plaster-covered, sun-dried mud bricks, an outside staircase gave access to the roof.

By mid-19th century, bungalow had come to mean any building not being a large mansion, set in a separate **compound**, used as European residential accommodation: in Indian English today, a bungalow is not necessarily single-storeyed. The typical bungalow of the British period in any part of India probably ceased to be built after 1945: at its best it can still be seen in British New Delhi, often within a garden compound of at least an acre in extent – in Kolkata, the description was a garden house. The main feature was usually a large windowless central room with a very high ceiling: light and air came from skylights high in the walls; cross ventilation from open doors on all four sides; in areas of winter cold, probably a fireplace. Smaller rooms with lower ceilings led off; if bed-rooms, each with its own bath-room with both an internal and external door – the latter for the **sweeper**. Wide verandas surrounded the house. The kitchen, with open cooking fires, was normally separate and at a little distance from the main building. The style perhaps owed something to a prosperous Indian home, with rooms opening on to a central courtyard, the angan, the centre of social life in a **haveli**. In addition, within the compound of a European bungalow, there were always a number of small houses (quarters) for the servants.

In Lutyens' New Delhi the size and grandeur of a government bungalow is scaled according to the rank of the occupant.

*Bangla **desh**:* country of Bengal. *Sonar Bangla:* golden Bengal. Names used by Bengalis for their homeland long before its division into Bangladesh and the Indian state of West Bengal. *Amar Sonar Bangla* – My Golden Mother, Bengal – is the title of a poem and song by Rabindranath Tagore, adopted as the national anthem of today's Bangladesh. Bangla is widely used in Bengal as a name for a colourless rice country liquor: also referred to colloquially as sonar Bangla.

Bangla (or turtle) *roof:* a form of rounded roof with cornices reproducing the curve, which first evolved in Bengal – perhaps as a thatch resting on bent bamboos, designed to cope with the region's heavy rainfall – and was later copied by both Hindu and Muslim architects all over India. In the north, usually in a small way for decorative effect over a kiosk rather than to cover a major building. (A fine example in Delhi is the marble canopy over the imperial throne in the Diwan-i-Aam of the **Mogul** palace of the Red Fort.)

Bangladaar: lit. of Bengal. As an architectural term, Bengal-style. A reference to the curved roofs and cornices typical of Bengal – but to be found, of course, all over India.

Bengal Light: from the end of the 18th century a blue signal flare made in Britain especially for marine use. The name was from its chief chemical, saltpetre from Bengal, a monopoly export to Europe, of the **East India Company** from 1758. Later, the Bengal flare could be of any colour with no Indian connection.

Bengal Cat: a breed of Bengal partly recognised by the Cat Fancy of the U.K. Claimed to be a cross between a leopard and the domestic cat. At a guess, the spotted leopard cat, Felis bengalensis, only a little larger than the home cat, would seem to be the likely ancestor. Said to be gentle, the male cat can weigh 9 kg.

Bengal Mud : a euphemism of the 19th century within the trade for opium, especially that exported to China.

Bong: used in friendly ribaldry, a modern sophisticated term for one from Bengal, but objected to by traditionalists.

Probashi: One from Bengal living outside his home state.

BANGLE *n*
The origin of this English word  is the western Indian bangri (Marathi), the coloured glass or metal circlet for the wrist, the joy of every woman other than a widow, often worn in clusters. In Hindi, the term is usually churi/choorie, but the steel bangle worn as by a **Sikh** is referred to by another Hindi word, kara/kada.

But this bangle is no ornament: in fact it represents a fetter, a curb; a reminder to the wearer that a Sikh should be restrained in the exercise of his senses.

Chūdiyan/Chooriwalan : bangle-wearers. When a reference to males an insulting allegation that they are as woman, effeminate. A riposte of course is that the macho sikhs are bangle-wearers. *See also* Raksha. (To most Western ears, the roman spelling 'kara' is pronounced phonetically, but to Hindi and Urdu speakers, the correct sound of the second syllable is one unknown to English; between *ra* and *da* and indicated in the Hindi script by a dot placed under the character for *da*. When transliterating to roman with English pronunciation, Indian writers may use *d* rather than *r*.) There are many similar words.

BANIA/BANYA/BUNIYA *n* Hindi A Hindu of the merchant class, **vaisiya** by **caste:** perhaps a village shopkeeper cum money-lender, perhaps a wealthy city entrepreneur. The term is of no great age, possibly all-India acceptance of the Gujarati vania (merchant) with the *v* (or *w*) sound changed to *ba* by Europeans and the tongues of eastern India, Often addressed as Lalaji (*see* Ji): Lala is a term of respect for a bania, but with a short a, a word of endearment for a boy child: particularly as an epithet for the young Lord Ram.

Pejoratively, bania can be used to imply a miser, or a person skilled at turning any situation to his financial advantage. (But says the bania "if the horse makes friends with the grass, how will he live?"). Other words with better antecedents as Hindi, for merchant and money-lender, particularly used in western India, are sahukar (anglicised into sowkar) and saudagar. Another Hindi word for a merchant, perticularly at the grocer level, is modi.

Banian/banyan: Anglo-Bengali forms of bania. In early Company days, bania/banian could be a reference to the script used by merchants in Gujarat: a form of Devanagri (*see* Dev) without the top line. In the 17th and 18th centuries, the **factories** of the **East India Company** employed banyans – as they were called – for their intimate knowledge of local mercantile conditions and usefulness as commodity brokers or agents. The practice continued in the 19th century in foreign-owned firms, where the banyan often carried great responsibility in the manner of the comprador of the Far East. Elsewhere than in Eastern India, the term for a similar English speaking intermediary could be dubashi – lit. two languages.

Banian/banyan: a cotton singlet. Once an anglicism for a thin cotton upper garment (perhaps what is today known as the phatua) seen by foreigners to be worn by bania merchants. By now, banian has been completely assimilated into Hindi. (More authentic Hindi for the singlet is the little used word ganji.)

Banyan-day: an anglicism of several centuries standing for a meatless day, or a day of austerity for any reason. (Vaishya merchants, then as now, were almost invariably strictly vegetarian.) The expression has been used by the Royal Navy around the world for almost as long as it has been used in India – Captain Cook, in his 1769 journal of his South Seas exploration, refers to banyan days.

BANJĀRAS *n Hindi*
A nomadic people from Rajasthan, but perhaps originally from outside the subcontinent: once specialising in the transport (by cart, pack-cattle and donkey) of foodgrains all over India; traditional suppliers to armies on the move, including those of John Company. Arthur Wellesley, later to be Duke of Wellington, in his south Indian campaigns against the Marathas *(see* Maharashtra) thought very highly of his 'brinjarries' as sutlers and a supply service. The scale of their operations at one time can be judged from a mention in the journal of Tavernier (a 17th century French traveller and merchant jeweller) of 10,000 pack animals in one caravan. With the coming of the railways, their employment as country-wide transporters was finished and many of them probably turned

to less acceptable occupations, so that by the end of the 19th century, they were numbered amongst the **Criminal Tribes**. The folk costume of the women includes pieces of mirror embroidered onto the fabric: the scintillation, it is said, inhibiting attack by wild animals. But really, like all tribals (*see* Adivasis), these travellers are expert in the ways of wild life and indeed have a reputation as skilled poachers. It is possible that their tribal name derives from ban/van, a forest, and could be translated as forest people. They are one of a number of Indian nomadic groups believed to be linked to the gypsies of Europe.

BANYAN *n*
Ficus benghalensis: a tree of the fig family, with growth of up to 31m in height. The circumference of the crown can measure 450m: the vast structure supported by roots dropping from the branches creating dark arches with sturdy props. The famous tree in the Calcutta Botanic Garden is a grove in itself, for it is said to cover almost 1.4 ha. with more than eighteen hundred descending roots. John Milton had read of the

tree in an Elizabethan botany book *Herbal*; in his 17th century *Paradise Lost,* he has Adam and Eve covering their newly re-alised nakedness by leaves '...broad as Amazonian targe' from:

"...The fig-tree – not that kind for fruit the quotation renowned, But such as at this day, to Indians known, In Malabar or Decan spreads her arms Branching so broad and long that in the ground The bended twigs take root, and daughters grow about the mother tree, a pillared shade High overarched, and echoing walks between: There oft the Indian herdsman, shunning heat, Shelters in cool and tends his pasturing herds..."

Birds and monkeys enjoy the fruit, which may sustain human life under famine conditions. In forests, the banyan and some other varieties of the fig family often start as parasites or stranglers on trees which are eventually throttled: a fig seed left by a bird in a wall crack, over the years can demolish a building, the swelling roots growing down, closely hugging every curve of the masonry and thrusting into every crevice. At no time does the banyan show bare branches, making it an ideal shade tree, even if the leaves are not 'as broad as Amazonian targe'. For this reason Emperor Ashok *(see* Mauryan Period) ordered it to be grown on roadsides to benefit travellers.

The name is an anglicism – as is the superfluous *h* in the botanical name – given by early Europeans who saw merchants (banians, *see* Bania) conducting their business under the tree in the market-place – as indeed they still do. A god-fearing merchant whose business is conducted beneath the banyan should abjure all sharp practice. In Hindi, the banyan has a number of names, one being bargad, bridegroom tree; some consider the tree to be the male partner of the female **peepal**; in fact, the two may well be planted as a pair. An alternative name from **Sanskrit** is bat/vat. It is this Sanskrit word for an enclosed garden and trees, as around Hindu and Buddhist religious buildings, where the banyan grows as a symbol of eternal life, that in South East Asia (*see Greater India*), has become the word for the sites themselves: e.g. Angkor Wat/Vat, in Kampuchea.

On one day of the year, particularly the full-moon day of the month of Jyaisth (May-June), married Hindu women worship the tree, and as a token wind cotton threads round the massive trunk.

Banyan days: see Bania.

BAOLI / BAWRI *n Hindi*
Northern Indian word covering a variety of masonry structures, both **Hindu** and Muslim, allowing a stepped access to water. The original concept was almost certainly Hindu, but most of the major examples now to be seen in the north are Muslim in origin, and date from the 13th century onwards. An impressive form is that of a deep

well, (sometimes, particularly in Gujarat and Rajasthan, very deep indeed, perhaps 60m) with flights of steps descending to the water, spanned by an arch or two to buttress the side walls: at least a few are the equivalent of an eight-storeyed building below ground. There may be galleries and chambers built into the sides, providing cool rooms in hot weather: if Hindu, there is likely to be decorative carving and possibly a shrine. Those most elaborately carved are probably to be found in Gujarat where they are termed, not baolis, but vav. At the opposite side to the stairway there is usually an inter-connected well-shaft of the normal type with arrangements at the head for bullocks to raise skin bags of water (mushak, *see* Musk) for irrigation. The term baoli is also applied to pond-like **tanks** with wide steps to the water and to small stone wall structures with water spouts for public use.

In Rajasthan the word for a stepped well may be bawari.

BĀPU *n*
A Gujarati family word for father. A term of affectionate respect given to an elderly man: the most famous example being perhaps **Mahatma** Gandhi, who was frequently addressed as Bapuji by his associates. Like baap, **baba** and **babu**, bapu comes from the **Sanskrit** vapra, also meaning father. A similar term in **Urdu is abba**.

Bapre bap: 'Oh Father' A common expression of wonder or anxiety: anglicised into bobbery, or bobbery bob.

BARĀSINGHA *n Hindi*
The widely used anglicised spelling of barehsinga – twelve horns, or tines, of antlers (srnga, horn, antlers in Sanskrit. Linked is ginger, horn-like tubers). A twelve-pointer, a royal stag. The great red stag of Kashmir, the hangul. Also the swamp deer of the **UP terai** wetlands, especially, these days, of the Dudhwa National Park and of **Madhya Pradesh** – where, in fact, they prefer dry ground. Both the barasingha of Kashmir and those of the plains often carry more than twelve points.

BARĀT/BARAAT *n* Hindi

Bar/var: a bridegroom. The groom and the party of his relatives and friends (Hindu, Sikh or Muslim) at the place of the wedding, perhaps to stay for a few hours, or in village society, more likely for a few days. The final few hundred metres to the bride-to-be are usually accomplished after sunset in considerable style (but the traditional Sikh custom – not always followed – is for the marriage ceremony to be held in the early morning, or at least before noon, so that the baraat arrives in daylight). But strangely, the groom,

who is considered king for the day, often appears a rather neglected figure riding a mare, a sword on his belt, at the tail of a grand procession headed by a strident brass band. In North India a small boy, if available, a young brother, rides pillion. But in a village at least, **a dalit** riding to his wedding could be considered to be acting above his station. Baraati: a member of the baraat.

Baraat-ghar (*see* Ghar): lit. a house for a baraat. A building and hall provided by a sect or group in a locality particularly to supply accommodation for baratis (who may have to come from a considerable distance) in connection with the weddings of members' daughters. An ashram may give the same facility. In a residential colony of government servants, a barat-ghar is sometimes provided for all at public expense. The halls can be used for the wedding festivities and ceremonies themselves, and indeed for other purposes also.

Barati : a member of a barat, so a member of the bride's party may be referred to as a gharati.

BĀRGĀDAR *n* Urdu
Barga/bargir: An administrative term of the Mogul period meaning an agreement. In Bengal today, a barga-dar is a farmer who has a share-cropping agreement with his landlord. A farmer in a small way.

As a military word (barghir, in Persian, a horseman) of the 18th and 19th centuries, in both local rulers' forces and in the Company's army, the bargirdar was a cavalry-man mounted on a horse (or camel) provided by the state or by a person (the silladar) who had contracted to supply an agreed number of equipped horsemen; a silladar could also be a trooper who rode his own personal animal.

In the 1740s, Bargis were Maratha horsemen who, with great cruelty, raided the wealth of Bengal – hence the Maratha Ditch of Calcutta: see Mulligatawny. (The origin of the word bargi as a raider was perhaps baghi, tiger – *see* Bagh.)

BARSĀT / BARSAĀT *n Hindi*
Rain. The rains, i.e., the monsoon period. Varsha has the same meaning in Sanskrit-derived Hindi.

Barsāti: a rain shelter, usually on the upper terrace or roof of a building, designed for night use, allowing a free current of air yet giving protection from sudden showers. With the sides enclosed, the barsati may become extra residential accommodation. Barsati can also mean a raincoat.

Geet *varsha:* following the searing heat of May and early June in the plains of northern India, songs both classical and folk welcoming the relief of the rains.

BĀRZIGĀR/BĀZIGĀR *n* Old Persian
Member of a gypsy-like tribe, probably of Rajasthani origin: traditional village acrobats, jugglers and musicians.

BASANT / VASANT *n Hindi*
One of the six seasons of the Hindu year: the two-month period of spring, the ritu-raj, the king of seasons. See Calendars.

Basant Panchami: a Hindu festival falling in January / February and, in northern India, considered to mark the onset of spring. Yellow is the predominant colour of villagers' clothes on this day, echoing the mustard plant (**sarson**) in full flower in the fields.

The day is also the annual festival, particularly celebrated in Bengal, of the Goddess **Saraswati/Saraswathi**, patroness of learning and inspirer of the arts.

Vasanti : the Goddess personifying the season spring.

BĀSHA/BĀSA w Bengali
The Bengali form of the Hindi vas / vasa (*see* Nivas): a dwelling house, a residence – equally, a bird's nest. A traditional Bengali, particularly if he has a share in an ancestral village property, may term his town house

a basha: in English, he may say it is his lodge, i.e. not his real permanent home. As used by Europeans, particularly during World War II, a basha signified a lightly constructed building with a straw, leaf or grass roof, such as provided temporary accommodation for the troops in eastern India. In the British army today, basha is still a word for a temporary shelter. Basha is a kin word to bari – *see* Kali Bari and Bal Wadi; also Bangla.

BĀSMATI *n* and *adj Hindi*
The long-grained, sweet-smelling rice particularly favoured for **pulao**. The best is said to be grown in the Dehra Dun district of **U.P.**, and to be in optimum condition for use one year after harvesting: an added advantage of age is that the older the rice, the shorter the cooking period. The long-grained Patna rice originated in Bihar, but the name is rarely used in India today: now, most Patna rice is grown in the United States.

Sela or golden sela, basmati: basmati (and other varieties also) treated by the sela process of parboiling (the term, although invariably used, is a misnomer, the part cooking is minimal), said to have been devised at Saharanpur, U.P. The paddy is soaked in water for approximately thirty-six hours and then dried in hot sand before milling. The advantage to the consumers is that some of the nutrition, particularly Vitamin

Bl – normally lost in milling – is absorbed into the grain. To the producer, advantage follows from a slightly increased moisture content (more mass) and more sellable rice because of less breakage in polishing. The final product does not have the stark whiteness of polished 'raw' rice, but a too obvious golden colour may be due to the use of a deleterious and banned coal-tar dye.
Export from India of basmati for the year 2005/06 is claimed to have totalled more than 1 million tons.

BASTI/BUSTEE *n Hindi*
Lit. a settlement. A particular residential area in an old town or village, usually of a humble nature e.g. the **chamar** basti, the dalits' quarter. The word is derived from the **Sanskrit**, vas, a dwelling and is not used in newly built-up districts.

BATIK *n*
Lit. drawing, painting: from the Javanese 'batik – painted.

A cottage industry craft of creating coloured designs and figures on cloth through a process of repeated dyeings, the parts not requiring a colour being protected by a film of wax: the wax is later removed with hot water.

BAŪL *n*
Bengali and Hindi pronounced ba-ul. The original **Sanskrit** *word has the meaning of eccentric, or possessed*

– in today's Hindi, it can mean just mad.

Baulani: a woman baul

Member of a village-based joint **Hindu** and **Sufi**-Muslim sect of Bengal (the Muslims are sometimes termed Aul – from auliya- *see* Chisti). Itinerant singing musicians, sometimes using running trains as stages, men and women: the men bearded, **saffron**-robed and carrying an ektara (one-string guitar) and perhaps a small drum, the duggi. The music is largely **bhakti**, devotional, on the theme of Radha and **Krishna**, something perhaps from the poetry of Jayadev (*see* Gita). At the same time, a musician may dance with ankle-bells jingling, sing, with one hand pluck the guitar and with the other, tap the drum tied to his waist. Bauls are casteless and anybody can become one after due study.

BAZAAR *n Urdu*
An area of retail trade, a market. The narrow streets of an old city lined with small shops. (A rural market held weekly or perhaps, monthly, is known as a hāt.)

Bazaari: coarse language (of the streets); a woman of the bazaar, a prostitute.

Chor bazaar: thieves' market. The place from where, so the story goes, one whose hubcap is stolen from his car in the morning, can buy it back the same evening.

Kinari bazaar: temporary stalls on the sides of a road, a street market. Kinari (Urdu) means edge or border; it can be applied to a river bank, a coastline, and in Delhi, Kinari Bazaar is the name of a lane in the old city specialising since **Mogul** days in selling gold and silver threaded lace (kinari and **zari**) borders, or anchal, trimmings for ladies saris. Also a word for a footpath street market is patri.

Lal bazaar (red bazaar): for 150 years a military anglicism for a brothel area. Particularly one to some extent supervised by the army for the exclusive use of its European soldiers; sometimes with the encouragement of the higher command, sometimes run covertly at regimental level against official disapproval. In the 19th century, as in Britain, arrangements were made to treat venereally infected women as compulsory inpatients in lock hospitals – the name derived, not as often thought, because the women, unlike men, were not free to leave until believed cured, but from the Lock Lazar House in 15th century London, which later specialised in venereal disease.

It must be noted that in West Bengal, Lal Bazaar is well known as the name of the building housing the headquarters of the Kolkata police: the equivalent of London's Scotland Yard.

Tehbazaari: lit. of below the bazaar. *See* Tikhana. Normally a reference to the collection by a municipal authority of ground rent from petty pavement traders.

Kala bazaar: the black market.

BAZAAR WEIGHTS *n*
The European term during the British period for the traditional Indian measures of weight. Rather surprisingly, as early as 1870, the Government of India acquired powers to introduce the metric system; with the seer, *(see below)* to be made the exact equivalent of the kilogram, as the basic unit. But the then **Viceroy**, Lord Mayo, was assassinated and his successors had no interest in going further. (A success that Lord Mayo did have, was the introduction of the metre gauge in the railways – *see Broad Gauge.)* The metric system only came to India with the passing of a new Weights and Measures Act, this time implemented, eighty-six years later in 1956.

Of the **bazaar** weights, the basic unit was the tola (from **Sanskrit**, tula, a weight, scales. See Tulādān), equivalent to 11.66 grams, the weight of a silver **rupee**. Five tolas made one chattak, sixteen chattaks one seer, and forty seers one maund

(the last word is an anglicism from the Hindi man/men, but the name and unit came originally from the Arab world). It may be noted that tola, particularly in rural UP and eastern India, can also be a small settlement area, part of a village, such as the dalit tola. The seer was a fraction over I kg and the standard (or railway) maund, 37.3 kg. In the bazaar, the seer was also used as a liquid measure, particularly for milk. The tradition continues, for in today's markets, a litre of milk is commonly referred to as a kilo: the maund as a name remains in use, particularly for wholesale vegetables, but is now the equivalent of 40 kg. The metric tonne is rarely heard of, the preferred large unit being the quintal – 100 kilograms – perhaps because of its eastern sound: quintal come from kintar, an Arabic word for one hundred units of mass.

Gold and silversmiths still use the tola: another goldsmith's measure is the rati/ratti, a poisonous shiny red seed with a black spot, from the climbing plant *Abrus precatorious* (sometimes known in English as country liquorice or jequirity). Each seed is believed to weigh exactly the same, 0.27 gm. The principle is not uncommon: for example, the origin of the carat as a unit of weight for precious stones was the uniform seed of a Mediterranean plant, the carob. Again, the old apothecary's smallest unit of mass, the grain, was once just that, the equivalent in weight of a dry grain of wheat.

BEARER *n* English
Domestic man-servant, a personal servant, a waiter (table-bearer). The word is said to have originated from the habit of the early Europeans in India employing their palanquin bearers (*see* Carrying Chairs) as body servants.

In the army, an assistant to an officer in battle. At home, a soldier-servant (a batman in English terms). Today, the word (Hindi from Sanskrit) may be sahayak. An orderly.

Church bearer: the man who looks after a Christian church building, but not having quite the status of a verger.

BĒDI/VEDĪ *n*
The khatri (see Kshatriya) clan of the founder of **Sikhism, Guru** Nanak, and the family name of those who claim kinship from him. The original Hindi name had the meaning of one who knows the **Vedas**.

Bedi/Vedi: a platform, an altar, the firm base on which a statue or an image, as of a deity, stands. As in Christianity, there is a tradition, by no means always observed, that the bedi should be so placed that a priest offering worship should face the direction of the rising sun, to the east.

BED TEA *n Hindi*
A particularly Indian-English expression meaning the cup of hot tea, plus perhaps a biscuit or two and the morning paper supplied at one's bedside as one awakes in the morning. A most welcome luxury.

BEEN/BIN *n Hindi*

The hollow dried gourd from which a reed flute of the same name is made: the been, also known as the punji, is the usual instrument of the snake charmer.

A serious employment for the snake charmer is to catch and remove a cobra at large in a residence.

BĒG/BAIG *n Urdu*
Once a courtesy (now a family name) added to the names of the descendants of the original Turki (Mongol) invaders of India, and particularly those of the **Mogul** house of Timur. The word from Turkey, bey, meaning a governor, a commander, has the same origin. Some with the name Beg/Baig in India, mindful of a Turkish background, prefer that the final g of the roman spelling be silent.

Begum/Begam: the consort of a Beg. While Beg as an honorific is no longer used, the title of his wife became usual for all Muslim married or widowed ladies of rank. Mogul princesses, compelled, as they often were, to remain single, were accorded honorary begum status: e.g. the Begum Jahanara, daughter of the Emperor Shahjehan. Nowadays, Begum is no more than the equivalent of Mrs or Shrimati (*see* Shri). A Muslim married lady of position, may be addressed as Begum Sahiba (*see* Sahib).

A Muslim courtesan of the Hindustani culture of the north (*see* Dancing Girls), will not normally consider herself a begum, but will add Jan after her first real or assumed name. (Jan / jaan as an Urdu word is really a term of affectionate endearment, such as lover or darling, but when used by a high-placed courtesan it is accepted as a title of respect far removed from mere lubricity.)

The Begums of Oudh: see Oudh. (Correctly, the plural of begum is baigmat.)

BEGĀR *n* Hindi
Lit. without reward or remuneration. Forced or impressed labour, with or without payment: to impress labour, except for reasons of state, is now an offence under the Indian Penal Code (*see* IPC). In early British days and until the mid-19th century, European travellers could be given powers to call on village headmen to provide porters for carrying themselves and their baggage. Associated with this form of begar was the ancient system of purveyance, under which travelling government officers were required to be supplied with fresh provisions and firewood by roadside villagers. In theory, all goods so delivered were paid for, but even in later British days, it was claimed that recompense did not always reach those entitled to it.

Considered begar today, is the custom whereby a tenant-farmer has to work an agreed number of days a year, without payment, for his landlord; perhaps on the latter's fields at harvest time or, on such occasions as a marriage, in his household.

Bonded labour: A social problem, mostly of the rural areas. A worker may undertake that in return for an immediate cash advance, he will give his labour (or that of his children) until such time as the advance is repaid. Since 1976, to receive a bond in such terms is illegal and as a civil contract it is unenforceable in law. However, to one very close to destitution, the system has an advantage: the person holding the bond and receiving the labour necessarily has to feed, house and clothe his worker. Abuse can lie in that the worker may be exploited long after (by any fair computation) the original debt has been discharged.

In politics, 'bonded labour' can be a contemptuous term for a group so beholden to a leader that, come what may, they must support him.

BENĀMI/BENĀM *adj* Hindi
Without a name, anonymous, Usually a reference to a transfer of property in which, by the use of false names, or 'front' men, the principals are concealed. In 1988, benami transfers of property (with certain exceptions within a family) were made illegal.

BEOPĀR/VYAPĀR *n Hindi*
Business, trading.

Beopar Mandal: an association of businessmen, traders. But usually not quite with the status of a Chamber of Commerce.

BĒR *n* Hindi
The jujube. The edible plum-like fruit, green through yellow to brown in colour, of a dry scrubland spikey tree (now also cultivated), *Ziziphus mauritiana*: available fresh in the **bazaars** in the winter months and dried or candied all the year round. The English name has its origin in classical Greek (the tree is also Mediterranean) and in the last century the fruit juice was used to flavour medicated gelatine lozenges.

BERM *n English*
A word much liked by the Public Works Departments (PWD) for the shoulders, or verges of a roadway. Seen in roadside cautions, such as 'Beware of soft berms'.

As a military engineering term, the narrow flat piece of ground between the base of a fortress wall and a ditch: normally exposed to covering fire from a bastion.

BĒSAN/BASIN *n Hindi*
Flour of the Bengal gram dal: cookery books in English may refer to it simply as gram flour. Particularly used for the batter in which vegetables are dipped before frying *(see* Pakoras) and also for many sweets.

BHADRALŌK *n Bengali*
The gentlefolk of Bengal, originally almost certainly the owners of landed property: those with a cultured middle-class background of a minimum of more than one generation, those who can expect to be addressed by the honorific **Babu**. The opposite to the bhadralok are the chhotalok, i.e., persons of no account. For the northerner, the equivalent but rarely used term is bhadrajān (bhadr, Hindi, of noble or gentle birth). Bhadralok is a reference only to males, the female equivalen is bhadramahila.

BHAGIDARI *n Hindi*
A sharing, a partnership. A term frequently invoked by Delhi's local government inviting the citizens cooperation in various projects.

BHĀGWAN/BHAGAWĀN *n*
Hindi
The Supreme God, but without physical form, the Lord. Used as a reference to the Almighty without

mentioning a particular name. (But the feminine form of the word, Bhagawati, is specifically Devi *see* Dev, spouse of Lord **Shiva**.) Also used as an honorific to a particular deity: Bhagwan Krishna, Bhagwan Buddh (*see* Buddha). Again, sometimes accorded to, or assumed by, living, popular **gurus**.

Bhagawan / Bhagavat: as above, but used less often, except in the form 'Shrimad Bhagawad Gita'. Male personal name.

Bhagwa: the colour **saffron**, orangered. The colour of holiness for the **Hindu** family of religions.

BHAI *n Hindi*
Brother. In general, family rela-tion-ships tend to be particularised in some detail, so that, for example, there are specific terms for cousins, male and female, indicating descent from the mother's or father's families. Yet brother (and sister) is frequently far from literally applied. It is often employed in the way preachers do, to include all mankind: politicians address their public gatherings 'Bhaiyon aur Behenon' – Brothers and Sisters. 'My brother' can refer to a friend or a man from the same village as the speaker. If pressed for a more precise relationship, the answer may be 'cousin-brother', meaning that the person spoken of at least comes from the same family. (All those

of one village may be considered to be one extended kin-group.) To indicate a sibling relationship, it may be necessary to say 'saga bhai' – real brother.

Used in a non-kinship situation after a man's name, or in the form 'bhai sahib, personal friendship, or a friendly overture is implied. Emphasising the goodwill, a vocative form, bhaiya (little brother), may be used. Brother in English is clearly linked to the Hindi word from Sanskrit with the same meaning, bhrata.

Bhai bandhu / bandhi: brotherly relationship, fraternal assistance. Often used to mean nepotism, or a similar improper assistance rendered because of an affinity such as caste, family or regional origin. A phrase common in this context, bhai-bhati-javad, meaning a system favouring a family group of brothers and nephews (a virtue here), is almost the literal equivalent of nepotism. Delhi clerks have been known to refer to the practice as the Principle of Relativity.

Sat bhai: seven brothers. The Hindi term for the babblers; birds met with in noisy family groups of between five and ten at a time, scuttling about in undergrowth and only flying with reluctance. To the British, they were the seven sisters. (They had a point, for the sexes are indistinguishable, except, presumably, to a babbler, and the family nests are a group responsibility with both males and females feeding any gaping mouth in a colony. As might be expected, they are regularly imposed upon by cuckoos.)

BHAIRAVI *n Hindi*
Form of vocal music expressing Hindu religious reverence, particularly sung in the early morning. *See* Rag.

Bhairav: an epithet of Lord Shiva in the role of the Destroyer. In this form he is often shown digamber (*see* Jainism), with ferocious fang-like teeth (when he may be described as being in terrific form) and his vehicle (*see* Vahan) a dog. From tantric association, liquor and meat may be offered as **prasad** in a Bhairon **mandir**.

In musical mode, bhairav is the early morning **rag** welcoming the dawn, darkness to light.

BHAKTI *n Hindi*
Adoration. In Hinduism, with little concern for philosophy, extreme devotion to a personalised god, particularly but not exclusively. *Lord* **Vishnu** in the forms of **Ram** and **Krishna**. A movement of ecstatic fervour, largely of the lower castes and women, to whom access to the **Vedas** and other sacred scriptures was barred by the **brahmans**, often focusing admiration on a particular living **guru,** even to the extent of

regarding him as a deity incarnate. A divergence from orthodox Hinduism on the part of the bhakt/bhakti/ bhakta/bhagat (one given to bhakti) being the belief that salvation can be achieved not through rites and ceremonies or rational enquiry, but more simply through devotion to the Godhead and one's guru. Devotees of the Western-based Hare Krishna Consciousness – ISKCON) can be said to practise bhakti.

Particularly in the really vigourous days of the movement (15th century AD, but the concept of bhakti is very much older), some Hindu bhakti saints, crossed the divide between Hindu and Muslim, making common cause with their equivalents in Islam, the Sufis, in the worship of the one eternal God. (Guru Nanak, the founder of Sikhism, was, of course, influenced by the Sufi perception of God.)

Desh Bhakti: devotion to one's country: the usual meaning is of patriotic songs.

BHAN *n Sanskrit*
A proclamation, an announcement. Linked to the English words ban and banns.

BHANDĀR *n Hindi*
A storehouse, godown. Often a large shop, an emporium. In a Hindu or Jain temple, a library: a storehouse for sacred texts and icons.

Bhandari: owner, or man in. charge, of the bhandar. A family name.

Bhandara : See Langar.

BHĀRAT *n Hindi*
The name of the country India: the alternative name mentioned in the Constitution, Bharatvarsh is **Sanskrit** for Land of the Bharatas, preeminent of the group of Aryan (*see* Arya) tribes settled in the **Punjab**, probably in the second millenium BC. So, strictly, at that time just northern India. When used today, the word Bharatvarsh often carries emotional undertones: meaning perhaps '...the sacred Hindu land of the sub-continent, from the Indus to the Brahmaputra Bharatvarsh was considered in ancient times to be part of an immense circular flat continent (dvip – island – in today's Hindi) known as Jambudvip – land of the jamun, see Lady Kenny. An Ashokan (*see Mauryan Period*) Buddhist rock edict in Delhi of the third century BC exhorts the people of Jambudvip to work hard for the common good. But for all its age-old cultural affinity, until recent times under foreign dominance, politically, the sub-continent has never been a nation state.

As told in the *Ramayana*, Bharat was the prince who ruled Ayodhya during the absence of his elder step-brother. King Ramachandra (Lord **Ram**).

Bharat Choro: the slogan 'Quit India'. In 1942, with the Japanese in Burma and requiring Indian co-operation for the war, Churchill sent a Mission led by Sir Stafford Cripps to offer full Dominion status after the war was won. The **Mahatma** described this as "an undated cheque on a crashing bank" and the offer was rejected. In August, the Congress leadership demanded that the British 'Quit India'. The Viceroy responded at dawn the next day by arresting the leaders including Gandhiji.

Bharat Darshan: a tour of India.

Bharat Māta: Mother India. An early concept of India personified and deified is that of Dharti Maa, the Earth Mother: *see* Shakti.

Bharat Natyam/Bharatnatyam: the classical dance style which evolved in **Tamil** Nadu as an act of worship in the temples of **Shiva**. The dance was always a solo performance, normally by a woman – traditionally, a **devadasi**, who accepted that eroticism was a god-given emotion as any other. Perhaps the first male to perform the Bharat Natyam was the famous Ram Gopal in the early 1940s in the role of **Nataraj** himself. The name derives from Natya *Shastra*, a massive treatise on stagecraft and the performing arts, compiled by Bharata, a sage, said by some to have been a historical person living in approximately the first century

AD, and by others to have been personally instructed by Lord Shiva on earth in the form of Nataraj, Lord of the Dance. But as a name for the dance style, Bharat Natyam dates only from the 1930s, adopted by middle-class enthusiasts anxious to distance the art from the less than respectable devadasis for whom the old name in Tamil was dasiattam – or the (temple) servant girls and so bowdlerised it. Now in the more liberal 2000s, at least on city stages, the traditional **shringara ras** is beginning to return. The original name for Bharat Natyam was sadir. The music is that of the **Carnatic**.

Bharat Ratna: Jewel of India. The highest decoration awarded by the state for public service. *See* Civilian Awards.

BHARO *v Hindi*
An imperative 'fill', load-up'. Often a slogan, an exhortation: 'jail bharo' – 'fill the prisons'. A call to large numbers to court arrest for a political purpose with an intention to embarrass the government.

BHAVAN / BHAWAN *n* Hindi
A large building: a mansion. The Hindi word sadan also means a building or home, both large and small.

BHETKI *n Bengali*
Estuarine fish of the perch family. Those from Bengal, caught in the rivers or cultivated in flooded paddy fields, are claimed to be the most tasty. By non-Bengalis, the fish may be referred to as bekti.

The word has a number of alternative spellings. Eg. Begti, Becti, in north India Vekti, in Victorian days the fish could benamed cock-up by Europeans.

BHIKSHU *n Hindi*
Sometimes written bikku. A beggar, particularly a respectable mendicant such as a Buddhist monk (of the Hinayana path, *see* Buddha) who, without a companion and carrying no money,  is required to beg for, but never demand, only sufficient food for the day's need. Feminine: bhik-shuni. For the common beggar, bhikari is the more usual word. Since the giving of alms (bhiksha) is a meritorious act earning approbation from God, it follows that a beggar is performing a public service by being available to receive a coin. Equally, to give when directly importuned, is considered a social duty, especially by **banias,** and a refusal is likely to be followed by misfortune; most bazaar shopkeepers have a supply of small change to toss to the numerous beggars who call on them during the day—as busy men, with many calls to make, each supplicant spends only a few seconds in any one shop.

To a Muslim, in Urdu, a beggar can be sawali, fakir (*see* Dervish), or Allahwala (man of God).

BHĪL/BHEEL *n*
Adivasi tribe of central India and Rajasthan.

BHŌG *n Hindi*
Sensual pleasure. **Prasad.**

To a Punjabi, especially a Sikh, the word has the meaning of the conclusion of any sacred text: or the closing part of a Sikh religious ceremony, such as a reading from the final chapter of the **Guru Granth Sahib,** perhaps a kirtan and a scattering of rose petals. In a busy **Gurdwara dera**, all within hearing of the sung and chanted text of the bhog, will stop work and stand reverently and silently. Following a death in a Sikh family, the bhog is the last of the religious ceremonies, normally held thirteen or fourteen days after the event and usually taking place between two and four in the afternoon. *See also* Akhand.

BHŌJPURI *n Hindi*
The name for Hindi as spoken in eastern **UP,** roughly the districts of Varanasi, Gorakhpur and into western Bihar. *See also* Purabiya.

BHOOSA *n Hindi*
Residue of grain and other crops after harvest, the straw and the chaff, and particularly the dried stalk of the mil-

lets, after cutting into small pieces use as animal fodder.

BHŌTIYA *n*
In **Sanskrit,** Bhot is the land of Tibet and the Bhotiyas its people: these meanings are the general usage of Hindi speakers today, except that bhotiya can equally be applied to Indians of Mongoloid features from the high **Himalayas.** Bhot was also the province of Tibet, the Buddhist country astride today's frontier between Uttaranchal and Chinese Tibet.

BHOWĀNI/BHAVANI *n*
An aspect of the Mother Goddess (*see* Shakti) in fearful or terrible form, worshipped particularly in times of aggression and the object of devotion by those of the **thugee cult:** spouse of Mahadev (Lord **Shiva**). The Mother Goddess in this aspect can be known also as Bhairavi and her Lord as Bhairava. *See also* Kali.

BHRĀSTATA *n Hindi*
A word from Sanskrit often used today (2003). Depraved conduct, particularly financial corruption. BHU / B.H.U.

Banaras (*see* Varanasi) Hindu University.

BHUJIYA *n Hindi*
Parched food grains: often served with drinks. Nibbles.

53

BHUMI / BHOOMI *n* Hindi
From bhu: **Sanskrit.** The earth,
soil, land.

Bhoodan: land donation. A movement started in the 1950s by Acharya
Vinoba Bhave with the object of collecting voluntary gifts of agricultural
land for distribution among landless
labourers.

Bhoodan yatra: a journey (usually
on foot, a padyatra) from village to
village by one such as Vinoba Bhave,
in connection with the bhoodan
movement.

Bhumidār/Bhaumihār/bhumia: a
generally prosperous land-owning
and farming class of eastern **UP** and
Bihar. Although **brahman** by caste,
they till their own land and exercise
no priestly functions.

Bhukamp: an earthquake.

Janmabhumi: land of one's birth,
motherland.

Bhumigat : a road or rail underpass, a
subway particularly for pedestrians.

Bhoomi puja: religious ceremony
invoking the blessings of the gods
before commencing a new use for
a piece of land, say, for building or
other projects.

Bhoomi putra: son of the land. That
is, native to a particular place or

state. In the English language, the
expression seems to be used more
often in South East Asia – where it
is a relic from the period of **Greater
India** – than in India itself.

Bhopal: once a princely state, now a
city in **Madhya Pradesh.** Originally,
the name was bhupal, a ruler's title
– protector of the land.

BĪBI/BEEBI/BEEBEE *n* Urdu
A middle-class housewife. A respectable woman. In the 18th century,
before the coining of memsahib (*see*
Sahib), the few European wives were
addressed as Bibi, or Bibiji (*see* Ji)
by Indians: itinerant vegetable sellers
and the like, may still use the term
today. The queen in cards.

Bibighar: (more likely to have been
written beebeeghar): an early expression with reference to a European's
house, meaning the separate quarters
occupied by the the master's Indian
mistress. Of the same period was
the term 'sleeping dictionary' for
the lady, from the undoubted fact
that from the propinquity, the sahib
would gain a useful understanding
of the local language, culture and
customs. By the 1850s, with the arrival of the memsahibs in force, the
bibighar had all but disappeared.

BĪDI/BEEDI/BĪRI *n* Hindi
The poor man's cigarette. Tobacco
dust poured into a small tube of a
rolled tendu/kendu leaf tied with a

cotton thread. The leaf is from a forest tree of the ebony timber and persimmon fruit family, *Diospyros melanoxylon*, with the properties of not  cracking when dried and the absence of a taste. The making is a cottage industry based in central India and in the South.

BĪDRI *n Hindi*

Metal handicraft work carried on in Bidar in Karnataka (see Carnatic) and, in a small way, in Lucknow. Table or pocket objects such as trays, cigarette cases, etc., made of a zinc alloy with a matt black surface and damascened with inlaid pieces of plate silver and silver wire.

BIGHA *n Hindi*

A measure of land area, equal to 5 / 8th of an acre: now officially replaced by the hectare which is 2.471 acres.

BIHISTI / BHISTI / BHEESTY *n Urdu*

Lit. man of paradise. From the Persian, bihist. (As envisaged by a desert Arab, abundant water is one of the assured delights of heaven.) Before the days of piped supplies, an essential domestic servant in every European household: the man who carried water from the well to the kitchen, the bathrooms and whenever it was needed. The water carrier, usually a Muslim, with his goat-skin leather bag (mushak – see Musk) as the tool of his trade, can still be seen in public parks in Muslim areas, advertising his presence on hot evenings by clinking together his silver drinking bowls. Also employed in building work and in street cleaning in the narrow lanes of the old cities. Once enlisted as a follower by the **Army in India** – commemorated forever in Kipling's ballad: '... The finest man I knew, was our regimental bhisti, Gunga Din'. In the army, the bhisti has been replaced by the pakhal, a metal tank slung on each side of a mule or camel, or by a tanker vehicle.

Operating at a higher social level than the bihisti, at a gathering a drinking water provider is the saki/ saqi, also a word from Arabic. In some settings of course, he will bring the wine cup. See Mushaira.

BILAIT/VILAYET *n* Urdu from Arabic

Strictly, the meaning is the centre of government of an empire, but sometimes, as in Turkish, a province. In British days frequently used by Urdu speakers when referring to Britain and corrupted by British soldiers in India into 'blighty'. The term became part of the whole British army vocabulary during World War One. Bilait can also mean a territory, a country, just foreign and even an estate.

Bilaiti pani: an obsolete expression for soda water (water from Britain). First advertised for sale in Calcutta in 1812. Nowadays, 'soda' is acceptable Hindustani. Pani is the same word for water as pawnee, as in the old English Nabob's (*see* **Nawab**) alleged order, "Fetch me brandy pawnee and wash the sweeper's daughter". The English word soda is also widely used for baking soda (Sodium bicarbonate).

BIMARU *n*

An acronym of today used by professionals concerned with human development for the block of largely agricultural states, Bihar, Madhya Pradesh, Rajasthan and Uttar Pradesh.

As a Hindi associated word, bimaru can be said to mean sickly.

BINDU *n Hindi*

A spot, a dot, **zero**, a round mark on a male forehead. A spot of light, compared by some to Lord **Shiva's** third eye, said to be capable of being induced in the brain behind the centre forehead, by intense personal **sadhana (Hindu meditation).**

In the context of tantra, the dot of the bindu can represent the life-charged original seed: semen.

Bindi: the feminine form of the word. The circular spot (traditionally) on a married woman's forehead:

it derives perhaps, from the blood smear once ceremoniously offered from a sacrificed animal to a bride entering her new home. (In places such as the **Garhwal** and **Kumaon Himalaya,** where animal sacrifice as Hindu ritual continues – but not at weddings – the blood **tika** for those taking part is still quite usual and, of course, as ritual in European bloodsports, it is not unknown.) Nowadays, the bindi may be little more than a beauty patch, painted with great care or bought readymade in adhesive plastic from the **bazaar:** worn by all at some time, married or single including Christians, but not Muslims and widows. A lady may well declare that without the bindi she is not dressed to go out. The fashionable will vary the colour to suit their ensembles, but normally it is red. *See also* Zero and Tika.

Similar in purpose to the bindi, but rarely seen today, is the ornamental tikuli. A small thin decorative disc, often of gold or silver, worn on the forehad using a fixative.

Generally, with many exceptions, Sikh ladies do not put on the bindi.

BIOSCOPE *n English*

This Edwardianism may still be heard in rural areas as, seemingly, a Hindustani word for the cinema. Also a bioscope is

a simple device used by travelling showmen to amuse, mostly, children. A large and impressive closed box on a stand with wheels, containing a record player and a paper roll of coloured pictures, probably cut from magazines. There will be two or three viewing ports in the front, capped when not in use. For a coin, a child looks through a window and to the accompaniment of loud film music, will see in a frame, the series of still pictures on the paper roll as it is slowly cranked by the operator from one side to the other. In an advanced technology model, a mirror may reflect sunlight onto the 'screen'.

BIRĀDARI/BARĀDARI *n* Urdu
Brotherhood: a patrilineal group; a sub-caste community, possibly endogamous so that marriage partners have to be found within the members' families. Often a reference to a council formed by the elders of a particular artisan or community group of an area: for example, of the tailors or of the Muslims, to regulate social or trade practices for the group and even, perhaps, to give instructions as to whom the vote should go in a general election. A member failing to accept the council's ruling for himself, or to enforce it on his family, could face ostracism and, possibly, expulsion. *See also* Panchayat.

BISMILLAH *n Urdu*
In the name of God'. An Islamic invocation spoken aloud at the be-

ginning of an undertaking. In full, 'Bismi'llahi-rehmant-rahim' (In the name of God, the Compassionate, the Merciful). The opening words of a literary work by a pious Muslim. By assigning a numerical value to each letter of the sentence according to its position in the Arabic alphabet, a total of 786 is reached. This figure is sometimes used as an abbreviation for the invocation itself: as on a personal letter, where a Hindu might use the devnagri character, **0m.** In acknowledgement of the goodness of God in providing 'the lesser creatures for man's sustenance, a shortened form of the Bismillah (In the name of God: God the Most Great'-*Bismillahi Akbar*) must be uttered at the killing of a living thing for food, so that the flesh may be **halal** (lawful for Muslims.) In the case of animals killed in hunting, the Bismillah must be said either as the gun is fired or when the animal or bird is seen to be struck.

The words of the invocation may be written and then sealed in small copper tube to be worn as a protective charm. Such an amulet may be referred to as a Bismillah (but the more usual Urdu word is taaviz).

The family ceremony with which a young Muslim child is first introduced to the writing of the alphabet, is often termed the Bismillah.

BISTAR/ BISTARA *n Urdu*

A bed, bedding. A valise or hold-all containing bedding for a journey. (But

correctly, the word for valise is bistarband.) Before the advent of **mofussil** hotels and tourist bungalows, say in the 1960s, a bistarband was an essential item for all well-found travellers in India.

BLEEDING MADRAS *n*

A handloom cotton fabric, the colours of which in an early shipment to the USA inadvertently had run one into the other. The mishap proved attractive to buyers and has since become – with fast colours – a manufactured feature of the cloth.

BLUE STAR

For some years previous to 1984 some **Sikhs**, both at home and overseas, had been claiming very vigourously that they were different from other Indians and that their homeland, the **Punjab**, within India, should have more autonomy. Others, more extreme, claimed they should have their own country, Khalistan (a term mentioned in the years running up to **Independence**, see Khalsa). Acts of terrorism had occurred, possibly planned in the centre of Sikhism, the Golden Temple of Amritsar. The **GOI** under Prime Minister Indira Gandhi, had not been able to suppress these and in June 1984 the Army were ordered to enter the temple. The

troops were badly informed about the position and on their march through the main gateway (Operation Bluestar) suffered heavy casualties. The reply was to bring in armour and the temple was secured. Unfortuantely, the killed and injured included men, women and children, pilgrims, who had been inside on their religious occasions (the day was a Sikh festival) and the damage to buildings was considerable.

Following the Prime Minister's assassination in October, over the next three days in Delhi and elsewhere, Sikhs say about 4000 of their community were murdered (Government figures are less). Sikhs term the slaughter, the ghalughara, genocide: other words are halaku (see Chengis Khan) and katle-ām.

BŌGIE *n*

Indian railway English for any rail passenger coach, with or without bogie-wheels, and a goods wagon with bogies.

BOHRAS *n*

Dawoodi Bohras, of Arab origin. A sect of Ismaili Shia *(see* Sunnis) Muslims largely of western India (and abroad) mostly traders by profession (bohra means trader in Gujarati). The sect's high priest, to whom members vow strict obedience, is known as the Syedna **Sahib** and his council is the **Anjuman**-e-Shiat-Ali.

BOLLYWOOD *n*
A word coined in the 1970s to describe Bombay's commercial film industry, which draws inspiration from America's Hollywood. Perhaps today the word should be Mollywood. *See* Mumbai.

BOMBAY DUCK *n*
Small sea fish (the bummelo). Fresh, it is gelatinous with a delicate flavour especially favoured by **Parsis** and Goans. But mostly it is sun-dried and spiced and used as a condiment. It has been said that the name is an anglicism from the **bazaar** cry in Marathi, 'bomil tak' – here is bomil. Today (2003) the delicacy may appear on a menu as Bombay Dak.

Bombay ducks: in British days and occasionally today, name used by Europeans in other parts of India for their compatriots living in Bombay. *See also* Mulligatawny.

BOMBAY HIGH
Name, probably coined by geologists rather than by mariners, for a portion of the continental shelf about 170 km west of the coastline at Bombay, below which oil has been found.

BOOTH CAPTURING
An aberration of the electoral process by which, generally at a rural polling station, a strong-arm group intimidates the officials and forces voters to hand over their slips to be marked in favour of a particular candidate and inserted in the ballot box. Of the same sort of shenigan, although without violence, is vote rigging.

BOREAT *n Hinglish*
A modern colloquialism for a bore, tedium, boredom.

BOWLI GILAS *n*
In British days, table bearers' English for a finger bowl.

BOX WALA *n*
Lit. a man with a box (*see* Wala). An English detractive term in the days of the raj for those in the second division of European civilian society (government officers formed the first), the businessmen. From a pretence of affinity with the itinerant trader who travelled from bungalow to bungalow carrying his wares in a large box. Within the businessman class there were also gradations: those in commerce, seniors in mercantile firms and bankers, for example, were of the highest status. Those whose firms were 'in trade', the business of retail selling, were inferior. Concern with some commodities conferred a higher social cachet than others: tea, for instance, ranked superior to coal or jute. In a large firm, a marketing manager was likely to be considered socially superior to one in production i.e., not employed in the factory. The reasoning, of course, reflected social origins in Britain: recruits to tea were mostly gentlemen amateurs, associ-

ated perhaps with landed acres, but skilled technicians were required for coal and jute.

A reference to a box wala today is unlikely to be pejorative: he may be expected to be an ultra-anglicised Indian in commerce, probably in a large foreign-connected mercantile firm.

BOY *n*

This anglicism for an adult man-servant is seldom heard now except, perhaps, in the south and occasionally in **Parsi** homes (but in their case, the origin may well have been the Bhois, traditional servants and **palanquin** bearers of western India).

BRAHMA / BRAHM *n Hindi*

The all-pervasive supreme power mentioned in the **Upanishads,** the power of the universe: said to be indescribable, having neither attributes nor gender. Referred to, perhaps, by the pronoun tat (that, *see* 0m). Also  known as **Atman,** but this word carries in addition the meaning of an individual's indestructible soul.

On another level, some identify Brahma as the masculine deity of the *Mahabharata* (*see* Epics), worshipped as the Creator of All, with **Saraswati** as his consort. Now

largely ignored, the only temple dedicated to Brahma as a deity is said to be that at Pushkar, near Ajmer in Rajasthan.

Brahmanda: The magesty of nature as exemplified by the abode of the Gods, the Himalaya. But see also Lingam.

Brahmotsavam (*see* Otsav): the name in **Tamil** Nadu for the annual festival observed by most large **Hindu** temples. Normally a ten-day period in the summer months previous to the solstice (*see* Uttarayana). But the deity honoured is more likely to be that associated with the temple than Brahma. This is the time when the huge temple cars (*see* Rath) and temple elephants are used in processions. In the north, such a festival is usually known as a **mela.**

Brahmrandhr: of all the body's orifices, the most noble, the aperture of Brahma on the top of the skull through which the spirit is believed to enter at birth and to leave at death. Anatomically, the aperture, under the name fontanelle, of course is a palpable fact only during the first few months of an infant's life. *See also* Choti. Even a basic Sanskrit dictionary will require two pages to define forms of this word. All Indian medicine recognises nine body apertures, but only traditionalists accept the tenth door dasami da - the brahmandhr.

BRAHMACHĀRYA/BRAHM-ACHAR *n Hindi*

Strictly, one whose life is solely dedicated to contemplation of Brahma: the stage of life of a model **brahman** youth (*see* Ashram) as a celibate student with his guru before marriage – which, according to the **Shastras,** should not take place until his twenty-fifth year. In practice, the word means celibacy, enjoined as the correct life-style of the student and the house-holder having once raised a family. Also for the serious **Hindu** religious neophyte, or for one wearing the kesri robe (*see* Saffron) combined, of course, with vegetarianism and ascetism in general. Probably, most male Hindus accept the theory that expulsion of the 'vital fluid' (semen) by any means is damaging to health and that through permanent retention it can be induced to rise to the area of the brain leading to extraordinary physical and spiritual powers. (*see* Hanuman and Yoga.) Following from a belief of a connection between the large toe and the sensory centre of the brain, in order to support his celibacy, a Brahmacharya may wear wooden sandals called kharaon, each with a wooden peg pressing on the big toe.

Brahmachari: one who practices brahmacharya; a celibate. Fem, brahmacharini. Brahmacharya ashram: *see* Shanti.

BRAHMAN / BRAHMIN *n Hindi*

Lit. one who knows **Brahma:** created, says **Manu,** from the mouth of Brahma himself, as the first-born and the possessor of the **Veda,** he is, by right, the Lord of this whole creation. A man conscious that he is closer to God than most other people. A member of the highest caste of Hinduism: traditionally with duties solely of priesthood, study and teaching. Also with traditional privileges. The roman spelling brahman more nearly represents the original **Sanskrit** brahmana and today's Hindi, than the commonly used form in English, brahmin. While brahmans still carry out their priestly functions and now study and teach in fields much wider than the scriptures, most have to work in the marketplace, rarely using their hands, but especially as clerks, government officers and lawyers. Generally they enjoy respect from non-brahmans on account of their birth and are addressed as **Pandit** or Panditji. But in the south, possibly owing something to a believed connection between brahmanical superiority and a northern and **Aryan** assumption of superiority, anti-brahmanism is a force. Except, perhaps, those from Kashmir, the **Himalaya** and eastern India, orthodox (kattar) brahmans are strict vegetarians. All brahmans are not equal in status: for example, archaraj – fire brahmans, also known as mahabrahmans – who have no priestly functions except the traditional rites at cremations, because of their duties, are barely accepted by other brahmans as full caste fellows. *See also* Caste Hindus and Nambudri. *See also Janeu.*

Beyond the Hindu and Indian connection, in English a brahman will be an intellectual and in the United States one may well meet a Boston brahmin, an intellectual particularly from New England.

Brahmani: the wife of a brahman. Anglicised to an adjective, brahmini is applied to three species of Indian birds: the brahminy duck (or ruddy sheldrake); the brahminy kite-hawk, scavenger of inland water and estuaries (believed by some to be the vehicle of Lord **Vishnu**, Garuda); and the brahminy mynah. About the only quality they share in common is a certain reddishness in colour. There is also the brahminy (or Indian humped) bull and, in England, brahma poultry, said to be named after the River Brahmaputra.

Brahmastra (Brahma's weapon): an infallible weapon which cannot be countered. As told in the *Mahabharata* (*see* Epics), this celestially guided missile was offered by Lord **Shiva** to a sage for use in the battle of righteousness against evil. A devotee must invoke Lord Shiva's assistance for each resort to it against a named enemy of **dharma**.

Brahman Hotel: see Hotel.

BRAHMA-SAMĀJ *n*
Reformist Hindu sect formed by Ram Mohan Roy in Bengal in 1837. No symbols or figures of deities are used in worship.

BRAINFEVER BIRD *n*
The hawk cuckoo, whose loud screaming call was said by the British to be 'brain-fever, brainfever' and by Indians, 'pee/kahan' (where is my love), is repeated ad nauseum all day' and through moonlit nights during the hot weather. Often confused with the other noisy member of the cuckoo family, the **koel**. The blue eggs of the hawk cuckoos are very similar to those of the common babblers (*see* Bhai) who frequently are imposed upon to be surrogate parents.

**BRANDICOAT/
BURANDICOAT** *n*
A hybrid English/Urdu military word of two centuries ago, which may still heard today, for a long heavy overcoat, a greatcoat.

BRINJAL *n*
An anglicism (originally from Portuguese) for the green, purple and white fruit, eaten as a vegetable, of an Asian species of the Solanum family – which includes the potato. The egg plant, or aubergine. The Hindi name is baingan / bangan. (The *OED* traces both words, aubergine and brinjal, through a lengthy chain to a Sanskrit original.)

BRITISH INDIA *n*
During the British period, the territory directly administered by the Government of India; about sixty per cent of the land area of the country, i.e., excluding the more than six hundred princely states *(see* Princes, Viceroy), but including **Burma** between 1886 and 1937. Until 1927, Aden, together with a few islands in the Red Sea, such as Socotra, were de facto part of Bombay Presidency. From 1795 until 1798 Ceylon (Sri Lanka) was governed from Madras and from then until 1802, when it became a separate Crown Colony, by an unworkable system of dual control of the Governor-General in Calcutta and the authorities in London. Until the separation of Burma in 1937 the frontiers of British India arced some 9600 kilometres (Curzon claimed 55 degrees of longitude) from Persia (Iran) in the west to Siam (Thailand) in the east, bordering on the way, Afghanistan, Tibet, Nepal, Bhutan, China and French Indochina (Laos). *See also Presidencies.*

India, of course, was never a British colony in the way that, say, Australia was. With exceptions Europeans did not migrate to India as settlers to make a new life. In India, the intention was always to work for a period and then to retire home with a competance – sometimes a very large one – but see European Cemeteries.

BROAD GAUGE *n*
The main trunk line system of the Indian railways, the width between the rails being 1.67m, similar to railways in Spain, Portugal, Brazil and Chile. (Britain uses 1.42m). This was decided when Indian railways were first proposed in the 1840s on the grounds that extreme stability was necessary to prevent wagons being forced off the rails by typhoon winds. Feeder lines and the whole system in Burma have the metre gauge: some rural and hill railways, the narrow at 0.76m and a few, just 0.61m. The plan now is to widen the more important metre gauge tracks to broad gauge. One hill line, that to Darjeeling, in 1999 was awarded the status of a World Heritage Railway.

The early railways in India were designed by British engineers, in 2000, it was reported that engineers from India are being recruited to build England's new electric west coast line.

BSF (B.S.F) *n*
Border Security Force. An armed police force of the central government, whose regular beat is the land frontiers of India.

BUDDHA *n* English
An anglicism from the **Sanskrit**, bodh, an enlightened one, perfect knowledge. (In Hindi, buddha means an old man), in context, an educated intelligent man; also buddhi: but in another sense, a buddhu

can be senile, an incompetent. By Indian tradition, there have been many buddhas before the historical Buddha: some believe there is still a Buddha to come, to be known as Maitreya. Siddhartha Gautam, the Buddha, was born in the 6th century BC, the son of an elected chief of the Hindu Sakya tribe of the area of today's northern Bihar (*see* Vihara). He lived the protected life of a young prince until learning of some of the hardships of the world. After reflection, he suddenly left his wife and young son, Rahul (a boy's name today) and became a wandering hermit. After years of austerities as a bodhisattva (an aspirant to the achievement of bodh: a human being nearing divinity) culminating in forty-nine days' deep meditation beneath a **peepal** tree close to Gaya in Magadh (Bihar), he received wisdom. Gathering disciples, for many years thereafter the Buddha preached his doctrine of life, a reformed Hinduism bereft of deities, priests and ritual: of simple goodness of man to man without violence. By overcoming all earthly desires and passions, **nirvana**, a stāte of perfecion and release from the cycle of birth, death and re-birth, could be achieved.

Following the Buddha's death the Church (the Sangha) grew in numbers and influence, initially during the period of patronage by King **Ashok** (*see* Mauryan Period), becoming the dominant religion in India, Sri Lanka and Burma. Monasticism; accretions and sects developed particularly the divisions known the Lesser and Greater vehicles : Hinayana (once a term of disparagement), also called Theravada, and Mahayana. The latter was followed in India and the former in Sri Lanka, Burma and in South East Asia, A third division, the Vehicle of the Thunderbolt, Vajrayana / Bajrayana evolved in eastern India spreading later to Tibet. Vajrayana shakti doctrines and their texts are also known as **Tantra**. As a popular faith, by the 9th century AD, following the vigorous Hindu revivalism of those such as Shankaracharya (*see* Math), Buddhism had all but disappeared from India: where pockets remained, as in the area influenced by the great monasteries, the invasions of the Muslims in the following centuries and the Hindu **bhakti** movements completed its decline. By the 18th century Buddhism had been forgotten; so great was the default of local information that early British scholars were seriously suggesting that the Buddha had been Egyptian or an Abyssinian. The holy shrines were deserted or taken over by Hindu priests with no knowledge of their origin – unhappily, some had become quarries for building material and, later of ballast for the new railways. It was not until journals of two Chinese Buddhist travellers to India of the 5th and 7th centuries respectively were found in China and published in translation in France in the 1830s, that the connection between Buddhism and India was realised and the significance of sites such as Sarnath (near Varanasi) and Sanchi (near Bhopal) came to be understood by archaeologists – but decades were to pass before many could be identified and protection given by the Government of India.

The source may have been unknown, but the gentleness, toleration and respect for life, both human and animal (*see* Ahinsa), the ideal of Hinduism, the Middle Path (neither extreme austerity nor gluttony in any aspect), surely owes much to the teachings of the prince known in Hindi as **Bhagwan**, or **Mahatma** Buddh. While Buddhism has comparatively few followers in the land of its birth (from the 2001 census, 0.77 per cent of the population), respect for its founder is high. Indeed, for some the Buddha has been embraced into the Hindu pantheon as an **avatar** of Lord **Vishnu**. *See also* Karma, Panchshil, Purnima, and Neo-Buddhists.

Budh/Budha: the **Hindu** deity of the planet Mercury. Budhwar: Wednesday.

Budhhu/Buddhi: a stupid person, man/woman. A dullard.

BUDGEROW *n*
Anglicism from bajra (Hindi), a pleasure boat. A heavy flat-bottomed **houseboat**, once used by Europeans for travelling on the Gangetic rivers, from Calcutta even up to Agra and Delhi. (At the time, the rivers had not been tapped for irrigation). The budgerow could be sailed, rowed or towed by men or horses from the river bank.

BUKHĀRI *n Urdu*
Charcoal-fed room heating stove, used in Kashmir. *See also* Kangri.

BULBUL *n Urdu*
A popular passerine bird, particularly beloved of Hindi and Urdu poetasters – which would appear to be the sole reason for sometimes terming it in English, the Persian or Indian nightingale: while it has a number of single note calls, it produces nothing in the way of a tune. There are four varieties of which two, with black crests a red patches under the tails, are well known. Jaunty, vivacious and friendly to man: frequently kept as pets and, sometimes, for fighting purposes. In the India Scouts and Guides movement, the Bulbuls is the name for the young girls' branch, known in the English original as the Brownies.

BUND *n Hindi*
An embankment, a dam, a harbour landing place. A more phonetic spelling would be baandh.

Contour bunding: ploughing on sloping land so that any single furrow remains at the same level, thus reducing the loss of top-soil from the action of storm water. Also, the construction of level embankments combined with the digging into hillsides to produce flat terraces for agriculture.

BUNK *n English*
A particularly Indian use of the word is for a petrol-pump or filling-station: derived, no doubt, from bunker, meaning a fuel store, e.g. a ship's bunker. While to 'do a bunk' – to abscond abruptly – is 19th century English slang, the use of the word as a verb, particularly by students, e.g., to bunk – to miss – a college lecture, is today's Indo-English.

BURFI / BARFI *n Urdu*
Fudge-like milk sweet, made from **khoya**. A similar sweet in eastern India, but using chhana (*see Khoya),* is sandesh. (In another context, sandesh can be mean a message.)

Very sweet milk based sweets are vastly popular, the usual word is mithai, or in purer Hindi, mist/mistan. Both terms are from Sans4krit.

BURJ *n Urdu from Arabic*
A tower (not being tall and slender, as a minar). A bastion or turret in a defensive wall.

BURKHA / BURQA *n Urdu*

Tent-like garment worn by purda-nash-in Muslim ladies to conceal themselves from head to foot when outside the seclusion of their  homes, or when likely to encounter an unsuitable male gaze. White for the traditionally minded, with a lace-covered aperture for vision – a style popular with old ladies. For the fashionable, tailor-cut in black or a quiet colour, often in two pieces with the eyes uncovered.

Somthing less than the burkha is the hijab. A cloth covering the head and uppert chest, but leaving the face exposed. *See also* Chaddar and Purdah.

BURMA
The British name for the country (largely the catchment area of the Irrawaddy River) to the east of India annexed by conquest by the Madras army, during the 19th century: Lower Burma and the port of Rangoon were in the **East India company's** hands by 1852. In 1886, the king of **Ava** (Upper Burma) was deposed and Burma became a province of India, as much as anything because of British disquiet at growing French influence, including a proposed railway linking Indo-China to Mandalay. The badge of the kings of Burma, a peacock with tail displayed, adopted for the

British Indian province of Burma, can still be seen in New Delhi, in Sir Herbert Baker's Secretariat complex. On the floor in coloured marble: below the dome in the entrance rotunda of North Block there is a **mandala** of the abbreviated heraldic insignia of the then twelve Indian provinces, including Burma. The royal throne was carried off to Britain, to be returned in 1948 by Lord Mountbatten as a goodwill gesture. Under the 1935 Government of India Act, Burma was separated from India but continued to share the same master in London, who became the Secretary of State for India and Burma. Communications with India were by sea, mostly through Rangoon, for mountain barriers prevented any rail or road connection.

As a name, Burma came from Mranmā, often pronounced by the Burmese, says *Hobson-jobson,* Bamma, the common word the various racial groups used to mean the people of the country. In 1990, Burma was officially renamed Myanmār. (At the same time, Rangoon became Yangdon, the original pronunciation.) In India, despite ups and downs, mostly a working understanding existed between Britons and Indians, which 'under different conditions has continued since Independence: generally, a similar rapport hardly existed in Burma and since its independence in 1948 the country has isolated itself (of course, the Myanmarese never took to cricket).

BURRA DIN *n Urdu*
Great Day. The name given by the humble, particularly those in contact with Europeans and who have witnessed the festivities, to Christmas Day.

CABIN *n* English.
A small compartment or office usually within a large building. for one, or at the most, two persons, especially if constructed of temporary partitions. A term no doubt brought ashore from shipboard.

CAFTĀN/KAFTĀN *n* Urdu
A loose fitting, long-sleeved garment with a waist girdle. From Central Asia and Turkey rather than India.

CALDIA *n*
A name contrived to cover both the inland port of Calcutta (now Kolkata) and 'the coastal harbour at Haldia eighty kms. downstream.

CALENDARS & ERAS *n*
Traditionally, like that of the Jews, the **Hindu** calendar is a lunar one, but a solar calendar came from the West early in the Christian era, brought by the Saka dynasties who had been influenced by Greek-Chaldean ideas, together with the signs of the zodiac and the seven-day week used for work-a-day secular affairs, in Hindi, the days are named after the same planets as in the West. Since then, lunar-solar calendars have been used: as with the Christian Easter, the dates of most festivals are determined by the sun for the season and the phase of the moon for the precise day, but others (e.g. Makara Sankranti: *see* Uttarayana) are related to the dates of the sun entering the zodiacal houses. In the Hindu calendar, the new day and date start at sunrise. For time purposes, each day and night was divided into four periods (pehar) of three hours, but this computation hardly exists today, although a vestige remains in the usual Hindi expression for the hours just after midday, dopehar – two periods. The lunar months begin on the day following the amavasya (day of the new moon, *see* Purnima). Of the two fortnights (paksh, in Hindi) in a month, Shukla or that of the waxing moon is the bright one and Krishna, or waning moon, is the dark one (Lord Krishna is dark in colour).

The Celts of Europe similarly divided their months and the Christian Easter day can be expressed as the Sunday following the fourteenth day of the moon's bright fortnight occurring immediately after the spring equinox. The year has twelve months (in Hindi, baramasa) with an extra leap month added from time to time to keep them in step with their traditional seasons.

In addition to the twelve months,

the year is divided into two ayanas (*see* Uttarayana), the northern and southern paths of the sun. Also six seasons, (sometimes termed the ritu **mala** – the garland of seasons said Kalidasa – periods of approximately two months each: spring, summer, the rains, autumn, winter and the cool season (Jan-March). The calendar from which the northern Indian Hindu feast days are calculated by the **pandits**, is based on a treatise *Surya Siddhanta* – sun knowledge – written soon after 500 AD: each year was intended to commence on the day following the spring equinox and each month on the day (sankrant / sankranti) the sun entered each of the twelve zodiacal houses (rashi, in Hindi). But as with all similar computations elsewhere until the 16th and 17th centuries, all the factors involved in arriving at a 'mean solar day' and a 'tropical year' were not appreciated: the Indian astronomers fairly accurately measured a 'sidereal year' – a difference of about plus 23.8 minutes from the more exact 'tropical year' in which the seasons stay in place. Over the centuries since the starting point in 285 AD, the difference has been so compounded that by this solar calendar (used in Punjab, eastern India and the south). New Year's day, Chaitra, falls twenty-four days (plus or minus one day according to local computation) after the equinox (*see* Baisakhi): the reason for the discrepancy between Indian and Western dates of zodiacal houses.

(In point of fact, neither Western nor Indian houses correspond any more to the constellations whose names they bear.) The error and its approximate dimension was recognised in India by at least the 10th century AD, but the **pandits**, then as now, did not want the trauma of a change: nirayana – without solstice – became the name of the system, and so it remains. *See also* Uttarayana.

To bring order into the chaos of at least thirty regional calendars, each to some degree at variance with the others, the Government of India in 1957 introduced a rational scientific all-India official calendar (Rashtriya Panchang), which has a permanent relationship to the Gregorian. Each month has either thirty or thirty-one days and the year begins (1 Chaitra) in accordance with Surya Siddhanta on 22 March (21 March in a Gregorian leap year). The era adopted was the one traditionally used by Indian astronomers, the Saka, commencing with the Saka kings of Ujjain, seventy-eight years after Christ: Saka 1925 corresponds, therefore, to 2003/04 AD. (Ancient Ujjain – or in Hindi Ujjayini – was a famous centre of astronomy: much later, for Arab mathematicians, the position of the city still marked zero degrees longitude.) But the pandits of northern India mostly prefer to use the Vikram Samvat (Vikram era), popularly believed to date from the Vikram dynasty, also of Ujjain, established one hundred and thirty years earlier than the Saka: so 2003/04 AD is 2060 Vikram. The Vikram is the official calendar of Nepal.

The Saka era is retained today, but the Panchang of 2006/07 AD gives preference as a name for the present era, beginning February 3102 BC, to the Kali era so that 2006/07 is dated 5106/07 Kali.

Hijrah/Hijri: the Islamic purely lunar calendar commencing with the departure of Mohammed from Mecca for Medina in 622 AD. The twelve lunar months total approximately 354 / 355 days: eleven short of the solar year, so that festivals move through the seasons, completing the cycle in about thirty-three years. A Muslim claiming to be a centenarian by his calendar, will still be three years short by that of the West.

A day runs from sunset to sunset and each month commences with the sighting of the new moon by at least two responsible observers (subject to a limit of thirty days to a month: a proviso more used in India than in Mecca with its rare cloudy nights). By the Muslim calendar, now in its 15th century, the year 1425 AH (Anno Hejirae, in the Latin of European writers) began in February 2004 AD. The first day of **Muharram** marks a new year, but no festival is observed, The calendar is only approximately the same worldwide, for each community decides for itself the occasion of sighting the important new moon: a moon seen in Delhi may have been obscured in Mumbai and Algiers. Thus, even in India, there can be regional differences, so that Muslim festivals are not always held on the same day throughout the country. As may be imagined, the conversion of a date in the Islamic calendar, say of two hundred years ago, with precision to the Gregorian, is a task of considerable complexity. But for most purposes, where an accuracy of plus or minus one year, according to the month of Muharram, is sufficient, there are simple formulae. AH x 0.970225 + 621.25 will give the year AD and AD – 621 x 1.0307 will give the year AH.

Jains date their calendar from the **nirvan** of Lord Mahavira, accepted to have taken place in 527 BC, on the dark night of no moon in the month of Kartik, the **Divali** of the Hindus. The year 2003/04 AD by the Jaini era, is therefore 2530.

The Buddhist era dates from the day of 'triple blessing' (*see* Purnima), specifically the day of Mahaparini-ravena (the starting of Eternity), the day the Master achieved nirvan: computed by Buddhists to have been that of the full moon of Vaisakh 544 BC so that for them the year 2547 began in May 2003 AD.

Parsis in India date their era from

the time in the 8th century when they migrated from Persia. Their New Year's Day falls in August: for them, 2003 is 1373. But Parsis who follow the ancient Iranian calendar observe the spring equinox (21 March) as the first day of a new year.

Sikhs have traditionally used the Vikram calendar, but following from the desire to have a separate identity, some Sikhs are advocating the use of the Nanakshahi Calendar. Solar-based devised by a Canadian Sikh, in which the festival dates remain the same in terms of the Gregorian calendar, every year.

CAMP *n*
Relic word of the 19th century still in use today. A senior officer travelling on duty away from his normal **station** (on tour, in official jargon), even if staying in a luxury hotel, may describe his location as 'in camp', or 'Camp' followed by the name of the place. But as a romance the custom can be said to be older than British days, for the **Moguls**, with the memory of their nomadic central Asia origin, sometimes referred to their battlemented palaces as Camp (**dera**, or urdu – *see* Khari Boli) so and so.

CAMPHOR *n*
This English word for the common aromatic substance, comes at second or third hand from the **Sanskrit** karpuram: either an oil or a white crystalline material, obtained (when not synthetic) from the leaves and wood of trees of the cinnamon family – those growing in Kerala are said to yield the best quality. (To the chemist, the camphors are a group of terpene oils.) In today's Hindi, while genuine camphor is kapur / kapuri (karphuri in Urdu), in common usage, the name is no less applied to the insect repelling napthalene 'moth balls'.

CANTONMENT *n*
From the French canton, a sub-division or corner of a country: mostly pronounced in India as 'cantoonment', often abbreviated both in writing and speech to 'cantt'. Military English expressions used since the late 18th century when the bulk of the Company's (*see* East India Company) army moved out of fortresses to largely undefended (as the troubles of 1857 proved) open areas at some distance from the cities. The cantonments provided relatively healthy living conditions where sanitation could be controlled and plenty of space for well separated barracks, parade grounds, messes and bungalows for the officers, a **bazaar**, a church and, as likely as not, a race course. These days, still a special township set apart for military use and administered under rules made by the Ministry of Defence. The north Indian word most often applied to such a township (although cantt. is widely understood) is the Hindi,

chhaoni: accepted as meaning an encampment, but derived from the Sanskrit chhadni, meaning shade, a common feature of the tree-lined roads of the average cantonment. In 19th century and earlier military English, to canton, as a verb, meant to station troops permanently in an area.

Within a cantonment, the soldiers' tents, huts or barrack buildings were usually put up in straight lines, hence a word for military accomodation (similarly, for the police), the lines. *See* Civil Lines.

On a flag, a canton is a corner, normally at the top next to the mast, on which a heraldic device, an insignia, may be displayed.

CARAVAN *n*
Anglicised form of the Persian and Urdu 'karvan', lit. a file of camels. A party of travellers on foot or on animals. Very similar in meaning and background is the Arabic/Urdu word, kafila/ cafila, which reached English as coffle, from lines of Africans roped together by Arab slave traders.

Caravanserai/Karavanserai/ Serai: an enclosed space where a caravan could find food and shelter for man and beast. Those on the **Mogul** royal routes (see National Highway) were particularly grand: many of their battlemented gateways still survive

today. Other serais are no more than place names. Perhaps the liveliest. description of a serai is to be found in the first chapter of Kipling's *Kim*. Less elaborate than the serai, and possibly without facilities for food, was the musafakhana/musafirkhana (musafa/musafir – Urdu – a traveller. Safa/safar – a journey: a word with links to the now English expression from East Africa, safari). Musafakhana today can mean a railway station waiting or **retiring room**. In Punjabi, a serai/sarai can be temporary accommodation, perhaps just one room in a gurdwara **dera**.

CARBORUNDUM *n* English
This composite word for an abrasive is carbon plus the **Tamil** karunda (corundum in English): a **Sanskrit**-derived term for the extremely hard material of gemstones, such as the ruby and the sapphire.

CAR FESTIVAL *n*
A reference to a journey through the streets by a deity in a temple car (see Rath), particularly that of Lord **Jagannath** at **Puri**.

CARNATIC *n*
The name the Muslims from the north, and in their turn, the early British applied (it could be said, misapplied) to the country below the **ghats** in south-east India. The fertile coastal plain averaging about 112 km in width between the sea and the hills (Eastern Ghats), from the River

Krishna (often written Kistna) in the north to Cape Comorin (*see* Kumari) in the south. The strip included the **Coromandel** coast. In the 18th century, the capital of much of the Carnatic was Arcot with its **Nawab** technically subordinate to the **Nizam** of Hyderabad. A descendent of the Nawabs of the Carnatic to this day (2004) uses the title Prince of Arcot, with no territorial powers.

The ancient Karnataka (or Karnatak) is the Canara/ Kanarese/Kannada speaking area of the southern Deccan, the country above the ghats, approximately the area of the present Karnataka state (in British and early post-**independence** days, the **princely** states of Mysore and Hyderabad, with portions of Madras and Bombay),

Kannadiga: a person from Karnataka.

Carnatic/Karnatic/Karnataka Music (the most common form is still Carnatic, but Karnataka is likely to find favour in future): the music of the south, as opposed to the Hindustani music of the north. Largely traditional devotional music and songs in praise of Lord **Ram**. The classical style developed by the **Telugu** composer, Thyagaraj, of Tiruvaiyaru (a village near Tanjore in today's **Tamil** Nadu). In recent years, young musicians have experimented with new compositions, not without some hostility from the purists.

CARRYING CHAIRS *n*
As elsewhere where roads were non-existent or unsuitable for vehicles with springs (the springless jolting and lurching bullock-cart must be as old as the wheel), so in India also, men with power contrived to be carried by men without, seated or reclining in various forms of litters. Some used by both Indians and Europeans during the past three centuries are mentioned below (occasionally, they can still be seen in use today. But the names were often local and in time even changed from one conveyance to another, e.g. jampan: *see below*).

Palki (or in the anglicised form, palanquin): originally a flat cushioned platform with carrying poles on each side: the occupant, either a man, or perhaps the image of a deity, sat above the shoulders of the bearers. Catholic Europe today may well carry the image of a saint in procession in this way and so does village India with a local deity, particularly in the **Himalaya**. In Bengal the palki was improved to become an all-weather wooden box just over two metres long and one wide; the roof curved and slightly overhanging the walls, there were curtained sliding-door openings on each side and racks and nets for necessities: sometimes even a slot for holding firm a **hookah** so that it could be smoked without danger of upset and fire from the rolling and pitching. The occupant, sitting or lying on a mattress and cushions, was borne a foot or so above the ground by four or six men with the single roof-level pole on their shoulders. Such a box, on long journeys, could be a traveller's ambulatory home for weeks on end. Over suitable portions of the route, skeleton vehicles pulled by ponies were sometimes provided; these would speedily convey a palki and occupant for a few miles: this was the palki-gharry. (Also a palki-**gharry** was the equivalent of a box-palki with permanent wheels: the driver sat on the roof.) *See also* Dak. In northern India, a hereditary group of labourers, the Kahars, for centuries specialised as professional porters and particularly as palki bearers.

Tonjon: anglicism for tamjharm. An open sedan chair, or palki without a roof. For city use rather than long-distance travel.

Dhooli: (an anglicism), dooli, dōly: from the verb, dōlna, to swing. Something equivalent to an up-turned string cot, suspended from the four corners to a single pole. Once required by the army for the sick and wounded, it is still in use today in villages for the old and infirm. Also traditionally by a bride on her first journey to her husband's home: so much so, that the car trip for a similar purpose to a prosperous urban home today, may be listed on the wedding programme as 'Doli'. A hanging meatsafe (or equivalent for a vegetarian household), suspended to discourage crawling insects, may be termed a doli. By extension, the word may cover any meat-safe or similar food box.

Dandy: a type of hammock or wooden-framed carrying chair, used in the hills slung from a single pole and carried by two or four men.

Jampan/Jompam/Jhampan: originally a portable chair slung on two poles, particularly used in what is now **UP** and the **hill stations**. The name was later transferred to a superior type of **rickshaw,** like a bath chair pushed and pulled by four men (jhampanis), if in private ownership, usually liveried: in places such as **Shimla** and Mussoorie, a few such rickshaws in poor order still remain. (Mussoorie – *see* Mansuri – supported its once somewhat rakish reputation, by providing two-seater curtained vehicles.) In Matheran, in the hills high above Mumbai, similar and no less ancient vehicles with the old English name of buggys, are in regular use.

Kandy: the cone-shaped all-purpose basket carried on the back in hill areas (as in pictures of tea picking), often containing a child or a small, light adult. In Nepal the word for the basket is doka.

CASH/KASH *n*
A one-time very low value coin of

south India. In the pre-**Independence princely** state of Travancore (now largely Kerala – *see* Malabar), 456 cash were the equivalent of one **British** Indian **rupee**. The word derives from kashya, **Sanskrit** for a seed used in weighing bullion (in the manner of the present-day rati: *see* Bazaar Weights). The Portuguese perhaps, took it from India to southeast Asia and also to China, where it became the European name for a small coin with a hole in the centre. Cash meaning ready money, entered English either direct from **Tamil** or via Portuguese.

A minor copper coin of the Mogul period was the dam: by the mid-18th century practically worthless. Hence a belief that the coin was the source of the English phrase 'not worth a damn' – some even ascribe its first use to Arthur Wellesley (*see* Tipu Sultan). Spoiling a good story perhaps, modern authorities do not accept an Indian origin for the expression. (However, dam as a Sanskrit prefix, meaning taming or suppressing, has an echo in English: a dam tames a river.)

CASTE HINDUS *n*
Caste: an attribute of the Hindu body acquired at conception.

Literally, all **Hindus** who are not outcaste (*see* Harijan): the **brahman, kshatriya**, complementary to each other; one with spiritual status, the other, the king, temporal; followed at a distance by the **vaishya** and at a distance again, the **shudra**: divisions as old as early **Aryan** society and believed by many Hindus to be divinely ordered: by others, to have been introduced by man with a social purpose. The chaturvarn – the four colours linked to the groups (in descending order) white, red, yellow and black. But in fact, normally a reference is intended only to the three upper groups, the twice-born (*see* Janeu), savarn – of one colour – and excluding the shudra.

Perhaps a refutation of the Western concept that the caste system entered India with the aryans, is the fact that today. Caste separation is very strong in the Hindu deep South where Aryans barely penetrated.

Caste in English comes from the 16th century Portuguese, who applied their word casta –from Latin meaning pure or chaste but in Portuguese, meaning lineage or breed – to the hereditarily mutually exclusive groups they found within Hindu society. In Sanskritised Hindi, termed varn-vibhag (colour division), but in common speech today, the word most likely to be used to cover each of the four main classes mentioned above is **jat.**

Hereditary occupation groups – frequently as exclusive as the main castes – are often called castes in English: for example, the goldsmith caste, the leather-worker caste, for which the literal equivalent in Hindi – the leather-worker varna – would be meaningless. These are sub-groups (**up**-jat), whose members may or may not be caste Hindus. (A parallel could perhaps be found in the medieval trade and employment protection guilds of Europe.) Nevertheless, to the traditionally minded, close social relations, and marriage in particular, outside one's sub-group, even although within the same varna, would be unthinkable. Hinduism does not encourage social mobility. The importance of caste in family life is demonstrated daily in the quests for marriage partners, lists published in every newspaper.

By precept, within **Islam** there is nothing equivalent to the caste system, but in practice, especially in rural areas, in Muslim social relations, the equivalent of **dalit** and **brahman** groups do exist. The Sadat (Sayids), **Sheikhs** and **Alvis,** those claiming Arab descent being the brahmans.

Caste Politics: a situation where one votes for one's caste fellow, irrespective of his political opinions or party. A trait on the increase in recent times and normally favourable to those low in society. In political election reports of today, the number of named castes, really social-economic groups of low status, can be seen to be very large.

Zoologists also use the word caste to distinguish the separate social groups in certain insect colonies such as bees and termites. The termites, for example, have soldiers, workers, queens plus fertile males and females who can leave at certain times to form a new colony.

CASTE MARKS
Although frequently mentioned by foreign authors, caste marks on the body do not exist in Hinduism (only in the very distant past did **brahmans** and **shudras** wear distinguishing marks). The writers are presumably misled by the **tika**, a spot on the forehead, and the tilak and sect marks (tilak can also be a facial mole), which may be assumed by any **Hindu**, on the forehead, upper arm and sometimes, the chest. These represent various groups, in fact, mostly brahman, especially those from the south and west. Much simplified, the two main types are those of the followers of Lord **Vishnu** who paint vertical lines on their foreheads, a V or a U said to represent the feet or footprints of Lord Vishnu (even a mark like a Shaivite **trisul** is Vaishnavi, the centre stroke, often in red, representing **Lakshmi** or Sri – *see* Shri), and the followers of Lord Shiva who have the tripundra–three horizontal bars – believed by some to represent the three syllables of the **Om** mantra. The Vaishnavi marks, generally known as naman, are usually of a white chalky substance

(Gopichandran) perhaps with a touch of sindoor (red, as above) and the Shaivite, of grey **ash** (vibhuti). A southern temple will sometimes have an elephant attached to it: in such a case, the appropriate sect mark will be painted on the animal's forehead. *See also* Tika.

CATAMARAN *n*

This English word for a two-hulled (nowadays, of course, also trimaran for three hulls) vessel originates from the **Tamil** name for a raft of three or four logs lashed together for inshore use off the South-eastern coastline. In Tamil, kattu means bound and maran (with the final a short), wood.

CATTLE *n*

Why do cows, even defying hot sun, choose to sit in the middle of a busy highway? A reason suggested is vehicle pollution. This does not bother cattle but flies are pestilential. Cows have discovered that flies are at their minimum at the divide of a main road.

CBI (C.B.I.)

Central Bureau of Investigation. A plain clothes police organisation of the Government of India.

CESS *n* English

A tax for a specific purpose, from the word assessment. Rarely used in English today but still common in India, with perhaps a prefix indicating the use to which the proceeds will be applied. First recorded use 1818.

CHAAT/CHĀT *n* Hindi

A spiced delicacy of cut fruit, tomatoes, cucumber, potato etc., with perhaps a touch of lemon: often sold by hawkers as a tasty roadside snack to be eaten from a fresh leaf with a sliver of wood. There is a connection with the verb chaatna – to lick (applicable to a food item, but not, say, to a postage stamp), to taste. Also connected is chatni, a smooth condiment sauce (tomato ketchup can be described as chatni). This word is the origin of the anglicism, chutney, meaning not a sauce, but a sweet or sour pickle of solid pieces of fruit or vegetables (e.g. mango chutney). In Hindustani, such a pickle would probably by termed an achar, a word originally from pre-Muslim Persian.

CHABUTRA *n* Hindi

A raised platform: as may often be seen in a garden, on which to sit and enjoy the evening air. In western India, a chabutra can be a pigeon loft or dovecot on top of a pillar.

CHĀCHA *n* Hindi

Uncle, correctly a father's younger brother, but as a customary politeness, used by young people to address any adult male with whom they wish to indicate respectful friendship.

Tau: uncle. Indicating a degree of respect to an elder. Lit. a father's elder brother. Tai-his wife.

Chachi: aunt, married to above.

CHADDAR *n* Urdu

A sheet, bed coverlet. Sheet-like upper garment either of cotton or in the form of a woollen shawl, worn over the shoulders by both sexes. By Islamic injunction, when outside her home, or in the company of males other than close relatives, a Muslim woman must cover her head, shoulders and chest with a chaddar (Roman script reports from Iran use the spelling chador). The wearing of the all-enveloping **burkha** is traditional for Muslim women in the subcontinent, but is not mandatory by scripture. A pall; a cloth usually of silk but perhaps of flowers strung together in the form of a net, placed over a Muslim tomb. (The provision of such a cloth is considered a pious and meritorious act: as a Catholic Christian may burn a candle to a saint in devotion or invocation, or to indicate contrition, so a Muslim may supply a chaddar for the grave of a pir – *see* Dargah. The ceremony of placing such a pall over the grave can be termed 'chaddar pōshi'.)

Name given to a large inclined stone in a **Mogul** garden (*see* Bagh), perhaps ridged or scalloped, down which a stream of water flows with a pleasing rippled effect and gentle music.

An 18th century soldier's term for chain-shot.

CHAGUL/CHUGAL *n* Hindi

A water container. To most Europeans, the canvas water bag. Being slightly permeable, evaporation from the moist outer surface cools the contents. When hung from a moving vehicle in hot dry weather, the water temperature, at least to a parched traveller, can seem almost that produced by refrigeration.

Chagul as a word has roots going back to the **Sanskrit** for a goat – the original bags, no doubt, were of goat skin (in Bengali, chagul means a goat): the change to canvas with its constant moist surface was possibly a military improvement of the British period. Outside the army, where it is still in regular use, the chagul is seldom seen today: but as a term it can be used for the particular type of water container often carried by wandering **sadhus**. An alternative name from sanskrit for an ascetics water-pot is kamandal.

Using the same principle for cooling as the chagul, the evaporation of moisture, are the traditional unglazed earthenware vessels: the matka (spherical, with a wide mouth to take a dipper), a word from the south is chatti for the same vessel. More or less similar is the ghara – also made in brass or copper, simply for storing water. There is the surahi, with a long neck, a small mouth or a teapot spout for pouring and perhaps a handle: the design owes something to that of a Persian wine jug – sura means **wine**. An old European word for a surahi rarely heard today was goglet, particularly applied to one made not from clay but of cloth covered metal, often silver, the name came from the Portuguese, gorgoleta. Yet another very ancient word for a waterpot is **kumbh**.

CHAITYA *n* Hindi
In pre-Buddhist times, a sacred place, a grove, grotto or mound of non-**Aryan** popular village animism. Later, with the coming of Buddhism, the repository of a sacred relic (**stupa**) and later still, the prayer hall (equivalent to the nave of a Christian church) of a Buddhist building. The Buddhist building as a whole.

Chaitya Arch: in Buddhist architecture, an almost horse-shoe entrance (but sometimes described as a peaked arch) to a cave shrine.Examples can be seen in the Ajanta Caves and, of today, as the entrance to the conference hall in New Delhi, Vigyan Bhavan. First seen from the Gupta period, derived perhaps, from bent bamboos. Another ralely used word for this arch is gavaksha.

CHAJJA *n* Urdu
A dripstone: a feature of early **Hindu** buildings widely adopted by Muslim architects from the **Sultanates** period onwards. Stone cornice slabs, overhanging in the manner of eaves, designed to shade walls and openings from the sun and rain. Some of those at **Rashtrapati Bhavan**, New Delhi (built for the Viceroys), extend about 1.5m from the walls, adding deep bands of shadow to the colours of the stone.

CHAKKI *n* Hindi

A small mill employing grindstones to which for example, people may take their own household grain for production of **atta** for their domestic consumption. (Those who can afford to do so, even when living in urban areas, tend to continue the village tradition of obtaining sufficient grain at harvest time to last the whole year, particularly those who hold the conviction that the wheat from their ancestral village is the sweetest in all India.) The motive power is either an engine or, in suitable areas, a water-wheel. In the home, a small hand-turned chakki (a quern, in English) may be used.

CHAKRA *n* Hindi

A wheel, a circle, a discus, a circular medal. The discus used as a weapon by, and hence a symbol of. Lord **Vishnu**. A cipher for the universe. (Philologians trace a connection, not readily discernible to the layman,

between chakra and the English word wheel; more easy to accept is the link with the Latin circus).

Ashok Chakra: the Buddhist spoked **Dharma** Chakra (Wheel of the Law). Found on many stone antiquities from the Ashok period and considered by some as a symbol for the Buddha and his teachings. Once seen most magnificently on the shoulders of four lions on the capital of a pillar at Sarnath, **UP** where it is known in **Sanskrit** as the dharma chakra dvaja (a standard, an emblem). The prayer wheels of Tibetan Buddhism are a form of the dharma chakra. These are drums containing written **mantras,** some hand-held and small, others, on roadsides are turned by passers-by, others, immense, may rotate continuously by the power of a mountain stream. The wheel and the squatting lions have been adopted as separate national emblems of the Union of India. (The architect. Sir Herbert Baker, used the animāls and small chakras, also on the capital, for his four Commonwealth pillars between the two Secretariat Blocks in New Delhi but placed the abacus carrying them below the ornamental petalled bell and not above as in the original.) The Sarnath column, one of many with animal capitals erected by the **Mauryan** empire, marked the site of the **Buddha's** first sermon. Luckily, perhaps, it was not unearthed until 1904: John Keay in his book *India Discovered,* quotes the words

of an early archaeologist who had excavated Sarnath in 1835: ". . . The remaining statues, upwards of forty in number, together with most of the other carved stones I had collected, and which I left lying on the ground, were afterwards carted away by the late Mr. Davidson and thrown into the Barna River under the bridge to check the cutting away of the bed between the arches." On the capital as it now rests in Sarnath Museum, the chakra is missing: it originally stood vertically, like a large stone medallion, on the shoulders of the four lions. (Only three are visible on the state emblem.) Small versions are below the lions and it is from these that it is reproduced on the national flag.

Ashok Chakra as a medal: see Defence Services Awards.

Pada Chakra: foot chakra. Believed to have been a mark of distinction on the sole of the right foot of the Buddha. A similar distinction of today, perhaps a lotus, can be seen on the stone footprints of Mahatma Gandhi at the site of his 1948 martyrdom in New Delhi.

Chhakra: a two-wheeled bullock cart. The origin, perhaps, of the anglicism 'hackery', in use from the 18th century to the 1920s: first, for a light two-wheeled cart for passengers drawn by trotting bullocks and then applied to a more ponderous vehicle for the carriage of heavy materials.

Sudarshan Chakra: see Vishnu.

Chhakra: a two-wheeled bullock cart.

CHAKRAVARTY/ CHAKRABORTI *n*
Now a Bengali family name (actually a title; the Delhi Telephone Directory lists twenty-one variations of the roman spelling) derived from the ancient Indian concept of a benign world ruler. Lord of the Universe, that is Lord Vishnu, ensuring prosperity for all: often written nowadays as Cakravartin. Strictly, the meaning is 'One who turns the Wheel' (of the world). Probably, the kings of the Buddhist **Mauryan** empire were the first to use the title. Title in Oriental Learning and Theology, corresponding to Doctor of Philosophy, awarded by Banaras Hindu University (*see* Varanasi).

CHALLĀN *n* Urdu
A delivery voucher, a treasury or bank receipt, a 'ticket' from the police for a minor offence. More formal than a **chit**. As a verb, to challan someone is to give him a charge sheet for an alleged offence.

CHALTA HAI *n* Hindi
Lit. "it moves". A common expression which sometimes finds its way into journalistic English "it will work", "it will get by", or "just about adequate".

Together with **sifarash** a facet of culture said to be inimcal to an Indian in world competition.

CHAMĀRS *n* Hindi
(The term can be chambhars in western India.) From chamra – leather, hide or skin. In northern India, with the highest concentration in the state of **UP**, the traditional leather workers; the cobblers, the flayers of dead animals and the tanners. These days, since there are far more of them than can be employed in connection with leather, the majority are village and urban general labourers. By birth, members of a Scheduled Cāste. The wife of a chamar, the chamari, is the age-old village midwife, the **dai**, whose clients will include **brahman** families. In the south, the **Tamil** word for the leather worker, the equivalent of the chamar, is chakkliya: rendered in 18th and 19th century European writing as chuckler. (But in the north, particularly in Oudh, a chakla was a division of a large estate [*see* Taluk] and the chaklidar, the superintendent and collector of rentals.)

Particularly in northern India, the chamars have their own historical patron, a **sant**-poet of the 16th century, Ravidas. In his, and their, honour, annually a large procession is taken out on the streets of Delhi City.

CHAMCHA *n* Hindi
Lit. a large spoon. A flatterer, a sycophant, a yes-man, a courtier.

Chamchagiri: flattery, sycophancy etc.

Chamach: a small spoon. An opinion expressed in Delhi these days is that not even a large spoon is sufficient to contain the flattery needed to appease the appetite of some in power and that a more suitable implement is the large ladle, the karchhi: leading to the term, karchhigiri. An English word of the same meaning – toady – has established itself in the common vocabulary, so the Hindustani abuse expressions, todi/tori and todi-baccha, lackey and son of a lackey.

CHANAKYA
Advisor-counsellor to King Chandragupta of the **Mauryan** empire (of appromixately the third century BC). Also known as Vishnugupta and dubbed Kautiliya (a word from Sanskrit meaning fraud, deceit, sharp practice.) Chanakya was the reputed author of the *Arthashastra/ Arthasastra,* a classical text on realpolitik in fifteen volumes for rulers on statecraft in all its aspects; economics, foreign policy and domestic administration including chapters on civil and criminal law. A forerunner by 1800 years of Machiavelli's The Prince; but some scholars aver that the work was compiled early in the Christian era. (*Artha:* wealth, gain, advantage in the widest sense, both in economics and in politics.)

CHĀND/CHĀNDR *n* Hindi
The moon. Slang for a bald head. Chandra was an early moon deity who drove across the night sky in a chariot pulled by ten white horses: *see* Soma. A relationship can be traced between the English candle and chandelier and chand in **Sanskrit**, meaning a shining object.

Chandni: moonlight (to be distinguished from chandi – silver. Chandi is also the name of an aspect of the Mother goddess – *see* Kali: sometimes one with Kali Maa, sometimes a separate goddess who adds her power to aid Kali). A smallish cloth canopy supported by poles, as over a bed. Usually, but not necessarily white. A popular boy's name, Shashi, also means the moon.

CHANG *n* Tibetan
Beer made from fermented barley.

CHAPĀTI/CHAPĀTTI *n* Hindi
Basic daily food of millions in northern India. A dough of cereal flour (sometimes from pulses or pounded roots) and water, shaped by hand into a circular disc of two to ten millimetre thickness: cooked on a hot curved griddle (a tawa/tava: northern village custom causes Muslims to use the convex side and **Hindus** the concave) and completed by being placed for a moment direct on the fire, so that it becomes puffed up by the remaining moisture turning into steam. In this condition, the chapati

may be termed a phulka (phulana: to inflate). *Chapati school of writing:* a term referring to the habit of some English authors writing about India – and elsewhere – of inserting in their texts as many local words as possible with the intention of adding ethnic colour.

CHAPPALS *n* Urdu

The anglicised form is chapplies. Open leather sandals as originally worn on the north-west frontier of pre-**Independence** India. In military English, frontier pattern. Nowadays, made in many styles and materials.

Hawai chappals: 'air-chappals'. Rubber and very light, the soles being sponge: flip flops, or bathroom chappals.

Kolhapuri chappals: leather with straps no more than the bare minimum necessary to hold the thin soles to the feet.

CHĀAPRASI/CHUPRĀSSI *n* Urdu

Lit. a badge wearer (*see* Chhap), from the insignia of his employer, worn either on his chest, or sometimes in very old and very grand offices, as a huge brass plate on a red sash. An office messenger, an orderly in government service. Also known as a peon (a word probably introduced by the Portuguese, but unlike in South America, without the meaning of a day labourer); but chaprasis tend to be employed within a building and peons are employed to take messages and run errands outside.

CHAR *n*

As in the World War II British servicemen's expression, 'char and a wad' (tea and a cake or bun). Like the word tea itself, a rendering of the Chinese character representing both the raw material and beverage. In Mandarin Chinese (*see* Mantra) pronounced cha; in the dialect of Fukien, tay. In north India, the word is chai, from where it entered the British military vocabulary as char.

It may be found in the OED in the correct form, chai.

The tea camelia tree is native to the wild border country between northeast India and China, and if it was the local inhabitants who discovered the pleasing result of infusing the dry leaves, the information travelled first to China rather than to India. Tea from China sent to Europe and North America was very profitable for the **East India Company.** It was British insistence on taxing the tea sent to their American colonies (the tax was later removed) that caused the colonists aversion to the beverage, which to a minor degree still remains.

Charwala/chaiwala: the owner of the roadside tea-stall (chaikhana). One who, in a humble way and with little equipment, provides to the weary a cup or glass of hot, sweet, but often smoky, tea; a cigarette perhaps, a rest and the chance for a gossip. (For the fussy, on request, the beverage will usually be served in an unglazed, disposable, earthware pot without a handle, the kulhar or sakora, straight from the kiln and thus uncontaminated. Such a pot may be mandatory for a known or obvious dalit who may be refused the more usual stainless steel beaker). In the **hills**, especially after a lengthy trek, a chaikhana under a rock by a path can represent heaven. Colloquially and in the appropriate context, a chai-**wala** can be a person 'in tea' in a far from humble way, as a planter or a merchant. *See also* Hazri.

Nabbe mil chai (ninety miles tea): as offered by a highway tea-stall, a claim by the owner that the beverage is so strong that it will keep a truck driver going for ninety miles.

Chai-pani: lit. tea and water. Tea and a snack. As mentioned by a petty official to a supplicant, a suggestion that a small payment would help to get a matter expedited: hence a euphemism for a bribe.

CHARITR *n* Hindi from Sanskrit
A person's behaviour, ways. Via Greek, cognate to the English word, character.

CHARKA *n* Hindi

A hand-operated village spinning wheel. This became the Congress party symbol after a campaign by **Mahatma** Gandhi to replace imported mill cloth by village homespun (*see* Khadi). 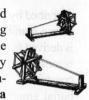 Charka: in Sanskrit, the word has the meaning of wheel. In ancient physiology it was applied to six centres or wheels of power within the body from the skull to the perineum where resides the Goddess Kundalini (see Yoga) normally dormant.

Ambar Charkha: an improved wheel, spinning four threads at a time.

Peti Charkha: box charkha. A portable spinning wheel in a case not more than six inches deep and about three feet in length: with the hand-turned wheel for turning the spindle parallel to the base. Designed for use by a traveller, a model favoured by Mahatma Gandhi.

A much simpler instrument form for producing homespun thread is the tikli, without the wheel, just a hand-held spindle.

CHARNOCKITE *n*
Geological term for distinctive coarse-grained stone mostly found in the Deccan and from early days shipped to Calcutta for building: also known as Pallavaran gneiss (from the Pallavaran Hills near Chennai)

described by petrologists as a hyper-sthene-granite. The name charnockite is derived from its use in the large octagonal mausoleum of Job Charnock, constructed in 1694 in the Calcutta burial ground that later became the churchyard of St. John's. Charnock is said to have founded Calcutta some four years earlier (*see* Kali). In New Delhi, large labelled specimens of charnockite may be seen in the geological **park** surrounding the **samadhi** of Indira Gandhi.

(Another south Indian granite named after a Briton is closepet. The connection is not direct for it comes from the place where it was first studied, near to the town of Closepet in Bangalore district of Karnataka [*see* Carnatic]. The town was established in 1800 by Sir Barry Close, appointed **Resident** to the Mysore raja by Arthur Wellesley following the downfall of **Tipu Sultan**.)

CHĀRPAI/CHĀRPOI/ CHARPOY *n* Urdu Lit. four feet. A string bed or cot: a very light, simple bedstead. Just four legs on a wooden

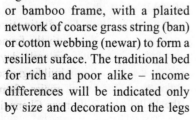

or bamboo frame, with a plaited network of coarse grass string (ban) or cotton webbing (newar) to form a resilient suface. The traditional bed for rich and poor alike – income differences will be indicated only by size and decoration on the legs

– such as silver plates on the feet for the wealthy. By custom, a person using a charpai will always lie with his head at the end opposite to the tensioning strings. When a cot is stood on end – a normal position by day in a household cramped for space – the tensioning strings must be at the bottom. A more formal word for a bed from Sanskrit, as for a wedding bed, is sayyal.

Particularly in a village, a charpai has uses beyond that for sleeping; it is a bench for friends at the **chaupal** in the evenings; on a cloth, grain is spread on it for drying in the sun, to the delight of the sparrows; it will be used as a litter on which to carry a sick person for medical attention -perhaps for many miles; and, finally it is needed as a bier to the cremation ground or **kabristan** (cemetery).

The Hindi word in place of charpai is khātia (probably linked to the origin of cot in English). A more formal bed, in Hindi, is palang – the root is the same as in palki/palanquin. *See* Hazri, Pan and Carrying Chairs.

Charpai bashing: British army colloquialism from the Indian barrackroom for sleeping, on a charpai.

CHARRI *n* Hindi
Ceremonial mace, particularly as awarded to winners of wrestling tournaments – because of its association with Lord **Hanuman**, the deity

of super-human strength. A walking stick. Also gada.

CHATAI *n* Hindi
Correctly, matting in a traditional Hindu home, woven from thin strips of palm leaves or bamboo: perhaps used when sleeping on the floor. The name has crossed over to the similar article made from plastic. Also large sheets of plaited palm leaves etc., used for temporary screens, or as roofing for huts.

CHAUDHRI/CHAUDHRY *n*
A village headman. Title of respect to a rural owner of land: in writing often abbreviated to Ch. In a city context, in recent years the title has been somewhat devalued by becoming a form of address to gang leaders. The wife of the Chaudhri is the Chaudhrain.

Once the title, now a family name, both Hindu and Muslim: in eastern India usually with the spellings Choudhri/Chowdhury etc.

CHAULMOOGRA *n* Hindi and Bengali Known to Western pharmacy as hydnocarpus oil. An old south Indian remedy for wounds and skin infections; adopted by **allopathy** for the treatment of leprosy, both by external application and by injection: now-a-days, replaced by sulphone drugs. The oil is pressed from the seeds of an evergreen tree found growing in the forests of the Western **Ghats**.

CHAUPAL *n* Hindi
Traditional place in a village, perhaps a raised platform outside a building or under a tree, where the elders sit in the evening and where public meetings are held. In a domestic setting, a space where outsiders can meet members of the family without entering the house.

CHAWL *n* Hindi
Usually pronounced chaal. A tenement building or group of such buildings: particularly in Mumbai.

CHEETAH *n* Hindi
The leopard-sized, rapid-sprinting, hunting cat of rough scrub and open grassland, where its advantage, its speed, over short distances greater than that of any other quadruped, could best be used. It is now extinct in India in the wild state (the last sighting was reported in 1968) but it is still found in Africa, the largest population being on the south-west in Namibia. From the 11th century tamed and used for the sport of coursing by princely India, particularly for bringing down deer and blackbuck: there is no record of the cheetah attacking man. The name was often misapplied to the leopard/panther (correctly, in Hindi, tendua).

The cheetah is reputed to be alone in that it is the only member of the cat family that can be tamed and trained to be useful to man, in that it was trained to run down deer but not to eat them. This is not strictly true, for the caracal (lynx) was similarly trained but only rarely in India since Moghul days.

The word cheetah (the female is cheethi) comes from the Hindi chhit, itself from the **Sanskrit** chitraka, meaning spotted or variegated – a leopard's coat carries rosettes unlike the spots of the cheetah. The English term for a variegated patterned cloth, chintz, derives from the same source.

In the 18th century the Governor of Madras sent a cheetah to the royal menagerie in Windsor Castle. An unsuccessful attempt was made to persuade it to attack an antlered red stag. The subject of a painting by the famous animal artist, George Stubbs, in about 1765. The original is now in the Manchester Art Gallery, but copies can be seen in Delhi in Maidens Hotel and Hyderabad House. (In Africa, it is said that the cheetah will not course an animal larger than the small impala antelope).

CHĒLA *n* Hindi
Disciple, follower of a guru, pupil. (Kipling's Kim described himself as the chela of the **lama**.) In **Islam**, the equivalent word is murid. Shagird (Urdu) has a smilar meaning, and is particularly used for the pupil of a guru or **ustad** (master) in music. The **Mogul** Emperor Akbar is said to have decreed that the word chela should

be used to mean a slave, rather than the more pejorative **ghulam**. (In old Delhi, there is still a narrow street, Kucha – *see* Gali – Chelan, the street of slaves.)

CHENĀR *n* Persian
The famous oriental plane tree of Kashmir, introduced by the **Moguls** from Persia. Many of the great trees so admired today were ordered to be planted in the 17th century by the Emperor Shah Jahan.

CHENGIS/GENGHIS KHAN
Tribal chieftain of the heartland of central Asia who, in 1206 AD, united the Mongolian people under standards of stallions' and yaks' tails and commenced a world-shattering outpouring of his mounted archers, until at the height of empire, the Khagan, or **Khan**, of Kharkoram controlled the land mass from the China coast to the gates of Vienna.

By 1215, Chengis had conquered north China and at his death in 1227, almost all Central Asia was his. In 1237, his son, Ogedei/Ogotai, as Khagan, sent his horsemen to ravage Europe: Moscow was sacked in 1238, Kiev a year later and Cracow and Breslau in 1241. Following Ogedei's death the same year, the Mongols withdrew from the west in a matter of weeks, never to return.

But under Chengis Khan's grandson, Huluku, the Khans scourged Iran and the Middle East, until in 1260, a Mongol army was decisively beaten by the Mamlak **Sultan** of Egypt. Under another grandson, Kubilai (Kubla) Khan, the Great Khan served, for some twenty years, by Nicole and Marco Polo (but *see Hobson-Jobson*), the Mongols occupied the whole of China. But creating his court at Pekin, Kubilai gave up the steppes and a nomadic life and became a Buddhist (his father and grandfather had been shamanists). After his death in 1296, the Mongol tribes once again went their separate ways and in 1368, the Ming dynasty took over China.

The connection of the Mongols with India was indirect; Timurilang, who invaded the subcontinent in the 14th century, had the blood of Chengis, and the first **Mogul** (or Mongol) emperor, Babur, was of the same line. (For a link between Timurilang and the British crown, *see* Koh-i-Noor.) The name of Huluku lives on in India today as an opprobrious Urdu – from Persian – word for mass slaughter, halaku

Timurilang is commemorated in Delhi by the name of a residential area north of the Civil Lines, at the place where he and his army crossed the river, Timarpur.

CHEROOT *n*
A small Indian cigar, particular one open at both ends. The word is an anglicism from the **Tamil** for the same article, shuruttu, meaning a roll. The tobacco industry is located in the south, especially in Andhra Pradesh and in the Tiruchchirrapalli (known to the British as Trichinopoly, or just Trichi) region of Tamil Nadu.

CHERRAPUNJI
The town in Meghalaya (*see* North East India) famed for its heavy rain, located on a scarp rising straight from the plains at the head of a north-south valley. A contender for the record of the world's wettest place, the annual rainfall averages 428 inches. (In 1861, 905 inches were measured and in 1876, India's heaviest fall ever in twenty-four hours, 40.8 inches.) For a period during the 19th century, Cherrapunji was used as a sanatorium (*see* Hills) for British troops, but the abnormal number of suicides caused it to be abandoned.

Cherrapunji is also locally well known for its coal measures of high grade anthracite.

CHETAN n Hindi
An awareness of. Chetan Rally: a public meeting, usually to inform people, usually of grievances.

CHETTIYARS/CHETTIS *n* Tamil
Popular name for a close-knit and

enterprising trading community, the Nagarathars, originally from Chettinad (Land of the Chettis) in **Tamil** Nadu. Staunchly Shaivite (*see* Shiva), the Nagarathars are businessmen throughout South India and many have prospered greatly, particularly in **Burma**. The word is derived from the Hindi, **Seth**.

CHHAKKA *n* Colloquiel Hindustani
The figure six. An ineffectual and incompetant person (male). One unequal to a task. Six refers to a clock face. Six is at the bottom and represents a drooping penis. An impotent fool.

CHHĀP *n* Hindi
A seal, a stamp impression. The origin of the English and pidgin English expression used generally in the East, chop, meaning an insignia: a trade or personal mark. *See also* Chaprasi.

Angutha chhap: the thumb impression; the signature of the unlettered on myriads of documents daily throughout India. Used more in the south than in the north, chhap can be a colloquial word for an illiterate person. Chhap can also mean the splashing sound of falling liquid.

CHHAPPAR/CHAPPAR *n* Hindi
A grass roof, a thatched roof. At a wedding ceremony, sometimes the canopy over the bride and groom is so termed.

CHHATH *n* Hindi
The sixth day of a lunar fortnight. An important festival of Bihar and eastern UP. Observed six days after Divali in which the rising and setting sun is worshipped, particularly in connection with a river.

CHHATRAPATI *n* Hindi
Lit. Lord of the Umbrella/Canopy. In antiquity, a white umbrella of state, swet-**chhatri**, formed part of a ruler's regalia, a symbol of royalty and of the protection provided by a ruler to his subjects: for ceremony, there could have been a triple umbrella – three canopies, one above the other on a single shaft. Often to be seen in a flattened stylised form (chattravali) in stone above Buddhist shrines. Today, a wife may be happy to describe her husband as her 'chhatra', umbrella or protector.

An ancient Buddhist title from a time when the universe was believed to be quartered by four great kings, before the concept of a single world ruler (*see* Chakravarty) of the Mauryan period. The Chhatrapati was the king of the west.

Assumed by Shivaji Bhonsle, the great Maratha leader, in 1674; the title remained in use with the family (subsequently the rulers of Kolhapur and Satara states) until officially recognised princely styles were abolished in 1973.

Chhatrapati Awards: made by the Maharasthra government to outstanding sportsmen of the state.

CHHATRI *n* Hindi
Umbrella, often part of ceremonial regalia. Parachute. Small stone kiosk normally roofed by a dome supported by pillars: used decoratively on the tops of Hindu, Muslim and **Sikh** buildings. A silver umbrella-like disc over the image of a Jain tirthankara or saint.

A built-up platform with a canopy, usually but not necessarily circular. (Although probably not via India, kiosk came into English from the Turki/Persian – and Urdu – kushk, a word with the same meaning.)

CHI-CHI *n*
An anglicism for the lilting form of English speeech, said by pre-**Independence** Britons to be characteristic of the Eurasian. Hence, a meaning of Eurasian.

CHICKS/CHIKS *n* Urdu
Large blinds, screens, of thin or split canes, one side is usually cloth covered: used to block apertures in buildings and to give shade from the summer sun while allowing a current of air, particularly on **verandas**. The word was perhaps brought from central Asia by the **Moguls**. An alternative name is jhillmil (jilmill to the British, a word also applied by them to slatted Venetian type wooden jalousies or shutters): meaning a twinkling, a shimmering, as sunlight reflected from a wind-blown lake (a jheel). From the effect of the rays coming through the fine spaces between the moving canes. *See also* Khus. Yet another term for the hanging light bamboo screen is chilman, from Urdu. Also a curtain or **purdah**.

CHIKAN/CHIKANKARI *n* Urdu
Also known as white embroidery. A Muslim household craft particularly associated with Lucknow, although it originated in Persia where the word means raised. Delicate white cotton embroidery on the finest muslin cloth, but nowadays coloured threads are often used and the embroidery is sometimes combined with printed patterns.

The name is also applied to the style of engraving on art brassware practised in Jaipur, in which floral designs in relief appear against a coloured lacquered background.

CHIKU *n* Hindi
The edible fruit of a Central American tree of the sapota/sapodilla/achras family: probably introduced together with the name by the Portuguese. Plantation grown, mostly in south India and Bengal. Egg-size, with a potato-like brown skin and soft brown, sugary flesh containing a little latex – the chicle of chewing gum. In some areas, the chiku is

known as sitaphal (the fruit of Sita, *see Ramayana*) – but in others, sitaphal means the custard apple or sharifa, and in others again, the yellow pumpkin.

Chico: British servicemen's slang for a young boy, a lad. Perhaps from a Spanish word having the same meaning, but not from India.

CHILGŌZA *n* Hindi
The small edible seed kernels of the chilgoza pine, a tree of the north-west **Himalaya**. Eaten raw or roasted, or powdered for use as a food flavouring. Also called pine-nuts and, sometimes, patience nuts because of the labour required for shelling from which in volume the gain may seem somewhat meagre: but it is said that for its size, the protein content is exceptionally high.

CHIMTA *n* Urdu
A pair of tongs as for kitchen use. Punjabi musical instrument particularly used for **Sikh** devotional music: metal circles fixed loosely to the two arms of metal tongs, which can be made to jingle in time with the beat.

CHINA GRASS *n* Chini-ghas in Hindi.
Indian household name for agar-agar: a substance prepared from marine algae and used in cooking as a vegetarian substitute in place of the animal-based gelatine. It is also of course the agar jelly used for the culture of bacteria. As a word, agar is of Malay origin. China grass is equally a name for a low shrub, grown for its long silky fibre remie in Malay and English used in textiles. *See also* Babul and Halal.

CHIPKO *v* Hindi
Usually met with in the form 'the chipko movement', or 'chipko-type agitation': a protest against the felling of trees. The name arose following an incident in 1973 in a **Garhwal** village when, in order to protect trees that were about to be felled, women put their arms around the trunks and refused to move. The word comes from the Hindi verb, chhipakna, to stick, adhere, to embrace. (The Hindi word for a **gecko** – chhipkali – is from the same root.) The Bishnoi tribes of the neighbourhood of Jodhpur in Rajasthan, who are strongly attached to nature, are similarly prepared to go to great lengths to save trees and animals from destruction. An alternative to the more common syndrome 'if it moves, shoot it: if not, chop it down'.

CHIRANJIVI *n* Sanskrit
An urbane expression of greeting, wishing the recipient a long and happy life. Gandhiji sometimes used the term to his correspondents in an abbreviated form, the initials CH.

Chiranyuva: The state desired by most, everlasting youth, Immortality.

CHISTI *n* Urdu
Order of Muslim mystics in the **Sufi**
tradition: followers of the teaching
of **Shaikh** Nizam-ud-din Syzi (or
Chisti) of Ajmer in the 15th century.
Nizam-ud-din Aulia of Ghiaspur
(now Nizamuddin, New Delhi) was
his disciple. (Auliya is an Arabic
honorific to these believed to be near
to God. The plural of Wali – *see*
Wala.) The order today has a large
number of followers, as may be seen
from the many thousands who attend
the **Urs** at Ajmer and Nizamuddin.
Chisti saints stress service to mankind and often carry the Persian title,
Khwaja – Lord.

CHIT/CHITTY *n*
An anglicism from chithi, a letter:
meaning an informal piece of paper
serving as a cash memo, a memoran-
dum, a delivery note, etc.

To receive, or give, a good (or
bad) *chit:* a reference to a written
commendation (or censure), or a
favourable (or unfavourable) report.
A clean chit: the equivalent of an
unblemished report.

Chitta (Fem. chitti) : bright, white
complexion.

CHITĀL *n* Hindi
The axis, or spotted deer. Largely
a forest animal still common in the
wild state. Sometimes confused with
the chinkara (Hindi), the Indian gazelle, an antelope of open scrubland

plain. The chital is highly prolific and
in no danger of extinction: apart from
man, its chief enemies are the tiger
and the **dhole**. *See also* Sneezing.
Related to the chital is the hog deer,
locally known as the para: a small
animal, the English name follows
from its habit of running with its
head down in the manner of a jungle
pig. The fawns may carry spots, but
not adults.

CHIT FUND *n*
A well-established system for personal saving originating over one
hundred years ago in rural south
India and now established all over
the country; sometimes organised by
major financial houses. Each person
in a group contracts to subscribe an
agreed sum of money, or amount
of a cormmodity such as grain, in a
number of instalments corresponding
to the number of members. Once
during the period of the fund, each
has the right to receive the total of
the instalments: this payment may
either be drawn for by lot or given
to the member offering the largest
discount. The discounts and sums
earned by investment are distributed
to the members as dividends. The
person administering the fund, called
the foreman, receives a commission, usually five per cent on each
subscription.

Well-run, chit funds help both the
very poor and the better-off to save,
but much depends on the integrity of

the promoter and difficulty may arise in collecting premiums from those who have already received the chit or chitty (kitty).

CHITTR/CHITTRAn Hindi
Illustration, sculpture in the round, painting, visual art.

Ardhchittr (half sculpture): bas-relief. Chittrkala: the art of sculpture, drawing and painting.

Chittrakar: the artist.

Chittrshāla: (the place of art), an art exhibition.

CHĪZ n Urdu
A thing, an item. A word adopted into colloquial English, the big cheese. *Pakka* chiz: the real thing.

CHŌBDĀR n Urdu
Chob, an ornamented ceremonial staff or mace, equally, just a watchman's simple stick. The chobdar carried a mace or silver stick before persons of rank, such as **Mogul** officers and seniors of the **East India Company.**

CHŌGYAL n
Adapted from chosgyal, a designation of the early Buddhist rulers of Tibet, the title of the princely rulers (except during the British period, when the style was raja and maharaja) of Sikkim. The state was absorbed into the Union of India in 1975.

CHŌKRA n Hindi
A small boy, usually of the urchin variety. Fem. chokri. Similar but less slighting as a term for a young servant boy is chotu.

CHŌLA/CŌLA
A **Tamil** dynasty of rulers based in Tanjore (Tamil Nadu, now Tanjavur) which, from the 10th century AD expanded a hitherto local fief into an empire covering the **Coromandel** Coast and also Sri Lanka. By naval expeditions in the 11th century, unique in India's history, parts of **Burma**, Malaysia and Indonesia were occupied for some time. In 1001, the great temple at Tanjore was completed by King Rajaraja: by the 14th century, once again the Cholas ruled little more than the country round their capital. *See also* Greater India.

CHOLDARI/CHOULTRY n Hindi
A small tent, or tent-like temporary shelter. But in the 17th and 18th centuries, the word seems to have been applied to more substantial buildings.

CHOLI n Hindi
A woman's upper garment: anything from the merest brassiere to a short-sleeved bodice leaving just an inch or  two of midriff bare. The style and

the name are said to have originated with the ladies of the **Chola** dynasty of the south.

CHOMŌLUNGMA *n* Tibetan Goddess Mother of the Country: one of many alternative spellings for the name used on the northern side of the Nepal-China frontier and by the Tibetan Buddhist **Sherpas** within Nepal, for the great peak named officially by the Survey of India in 1865 after their retired Director-General, Sir George Everest (Sir George, it is said, pronounced his name Eve-rest). In Nepal, the official term for the mountain is **Sagar** Mata, Mother of the Ocean. (8848m above sea level).

CHORTEN *n*
Tibetan roadside Buddhist shrine in Tibet and in the Buddhist areas of the **Himalaya**, containing bones or relics of a revered person. A Tibetan Buddhist **stupa**. While built in various regional styles, tradition – not always followed – requires that a chorten should have five parts, representing the elements: fire, earth, water, air and ether. When passing a chorten, always keeping it to their right, Buddhists like to pay homage by murmuring a **mantra**, such as '**0m** Mane Padme Hum'.

CHOTI *n* Hindi
An apex, a summit as of a mountain. But more usually as shikhar choti (top-knot), *see* Shikhara. In the the

south the word is churki. The uncut tuft of long hair sometimes seen on a shaven or close-cut scalp of a **caste Hindu**: left to protect the aperture of **Brahma**, through which the spirit entered the body at birth and will depart at death. Also the plaits of a girl's hair.

CHOWK/CHAUK *n* Hindi
Lit. the open space in a town caused by the meeting of four roads. An urban open paved  space; a road junction; a main street through a town.

Chowki/chauki: a small military or police post on a road. A small building or hut on a road-side where tolls may have to be paid. Said to be the origin of the English slang word for a lock-up or prison, chokey/ choky. In general use a similar word is naka/ naaqa, but, strictly, its meaning is of a check or control point at the mouth of a road. Also a chowki can be a rectangular stool or platform, on which to recline or sit cross legged: an asan. (At a grand Indian-style banquet, the VIP guests may be required to sit in a line just off the floor on low asanas. *See also* Yoga).

Chowkidar: man in charge of a chowki. A watchman. Man in charge of a **Rest House** or Travellers' Bungalow. In a village, assistant to the headman and part-time policeman. *See* Mahar.

Thanda Pani Chowkidars: British army Hindustani for that very superior regiment, the Coldstream Guards (thanda pani – cold water). Until after World War II, units of the Brigade of Guards never served in Asia: hence an army expression for an unlikely occurrence '. . . as rare as Guards' shit east of Suez'. It is said that the reason was that the Guards had always to be available for emergency ceremonial duties with the Sovereign in London.

CHUKKA/CHAKKA *n* Hindi
A circuit; a round, as in 'once round the block'. A period of play in polo. As an adjective, giddy (*i.e.,* one's head is going round). A wheel, the word is related to **chakra**.

Chakkajam: the jamming of wheels, circulation. In political agitation, the ploy of the blocking of roads or railways in order to prevent the movement of transport. (Jam, now Hindustani, is from English in the context of preventing movement by friction or by wedging). Similar in meaning is the slogan 'rail aur rasta, roko' – lit. rail and road, stop. Another political gambit designed to embarrass authority is for large numbers to court arrest and conviction, usually for public order offences, the slogan is 'Jail Bhāro' – Fill the jails.

Chukka boots: boots with tops reaching about halfway between the ankle and the knee: also known as **Jodhpur** boots, originally made of heavy leather and worn, supplemented with gaiters and knee protectors, for playing polo. These days, knee length boots are more usual fo the game, while chukka boots, of soft leather, have become casual wear.

CHULA *n* From Dravidian
A stove, a cooking place, fire place.

CHUMMERY *n*
Nineteenth century English expression particularly used in India for a bungalow shared by a number of Europeans (usually young and single), who also shared the running costs. To go chumming was to live in a chummery.

Use of the word seems to be coming back into fashion (2005). In south India a chummery can be the residential accommodation set up for their staff by software firms who may operate 24 hours a day.

CHŪNA/CHŪNĀM *n* Hindi
Lime, both as an edible constituent of **pan** and as in lime mortar. In connection with old buildings, usually a reference to stucco plaster which could be of remarkable whiteness, hardness and polish. It was even used for flooring; burnished by the passage of many bare feet it could wear to the gloss of marble.

CHŪT/CHŪTYA *n* Hindi from Dravidia.

Strictly, the female genitals. But the common usage, to be heard all the time on the streets, is as mindless abuse between one person and another. There is a specific meaning of a man who will stoop to any depth to obtain sexual relations with any woman, but in general, as with its no less vulgar English equivalent, use of the word can be intended to convey anything between friendly banter and extreme venom. *See* also Yoni.

CIDER *n*

In India, this English word has acquired the meaning of unfermented, non-alcoholic apple juice.

CIRCARS, THE *n*

Sometimes, the Northern Circars: lit. governments, see Sarkar, An old and long obsolete term for the coastal strip fronting the Bay of Bengal from the north of the once Madras **Presidency** to Bengal and controlled by a number of minor chiefs, or governments. Formerly in the possession of the Nizam of Hyderabad, and of France, who probably first used the name, the region came to the **East India Company** towards the end of the 18th century, and was incorporated in Madras: it is now part of Andhra Pradesh (*see* AP).

CIRCUIT HOUSE *n*

Government building providing comfort and amenities superior to a **Rest House** – but normally found only in administrative headquarters towns – for the temporary accommodation of senior officials and approved visitors. May be used by the public in some places. The name remains from British days from use by governors and other senior officers on inspection circuits of their **presidencies** or provinces.

CITY OF NINE GATES from Sanskrit

An expression used by Lord Krishna in the **Gita**, a reference to the human body, seven gates (openings) to the head and two to the trunk.

CIVILIAN AWARDS

The President and Government of India recognise exceptional public service with four awards:

BhĀrat Ratna (Jewel of India): exceptional public service of the highest order, or for the advancement of the arts or sciences.

When first instituted soon after **Independence**, the Padma (lotus) awards were simply Class I, II & III. The grades were later named as:

Padma Vibhushan (Special Ornament of the Lotus): exceptional and distinguished service in any field.

Padma Bhushan (Ornament of the Lotus): exceptional service in any field.

*Padma **Shri** (Lotus Honour):* distinguished service in any field. The Constitution forbids the conferring of titles, other than those of academia or of military service, on individuals. Some hold that the civilian awards contravene the spirit if not the letter of the Constitution.

CIVIL LINES

An open area of a town or city where, in British days, to escape the congestion and narrow streets of the old cities, the administrative offices and the residences of government officials were built. Also known to Europeans as the Civil Station, or just the Station: the natural habitat of the bungalow (*see* Bangla).

While prosperous merchants often owned property in the Civil Lines which they rented to officials, for themselves they generally preferred the togetherness of their city homes to the open spaces. But now-a-days, the old bungalows are coming down, the vast plots are being divided and subdivided again, so that all over India the Lines are losing their once distinctive appearance.

In the 18th century and for some decades later, in cities such as Calcutta and Madras, the British terms for the European and Indian residential areas were White Town and Black Town. The term Civil Lines rose from the need to distinguish the civilian area from

that of the military (*see* Cantonment), but of course the officers' bungalows were not in straight lines as were the barracks.

COFEPOSA

Conservation of Foreign Exchange and Prevention of Smuggling Act, 1975.

COIR *n*

An anglicism from Malayalam (*see* Malabar). Fibre from the flotation husk of the coconut, used for cordage, rough matting, etc: the Indian coir industry is centred in Kerala. (A coconut seed is designed to be dispersed by the sea and to land on a distant shore for germination.) The dried kernel of the nut, from which the oil is extracted, has the English trade name copra (from the **Tamil**, khopra, a word linked to the Hindi khopra, a skull. Also Hindi for a skull is kapal). Copra is on sale in the **bazaars** for use by housewives; grated, it produces desiccated coconut.

COLLECTOR

The government official in charge of adminstration in a **district** in some states. He also often holds the position of District Magistrate. In other states, his designation is Deputy Commissioner (*see* Presidencies). The term is a relic from early **East India Company** days, whose first essay into civil administration with English officers was the collection of the **diwani** (revenue) in Bengal in the name of the Delhi Emperor from about 1772. (From a few years before, some officers had been in the districts under the designation of Supervisors; but the early arrangements were subject to many changes over the years. In fact, it was not until after the upheaval of 1857 that the system became general, of one officer in a district representing all the departments of government.)

The **Indian Civil Service** head of a district in **British India** had. within legal constraints, almost absolute power and a tenure of many years: his main duties being the keeping of law and order and the maintenance of revenue. He was expected to have personal knowledge of most of the villages in his district and for this purpose spent much of the cooler months on tour: a saying was 'the tent is mightier than the pen'. He was strong in the knowledge that, within reason, whatever his action, he would receive the support of his colleagues in the provincial capital and, if necessary, in the Government of India. Not without reason could he be unofficially known in his area as Ziladish – Lord of the District. Since **Independence**, while the responsibilities are greater than ever and the administration vastly more complicated, with many agencies of government represented at district headquarters, the prestige of his office and his personal power base has

been reduced – democracy means local pressure groups, many with a voice and a power base in the state capital. The district officer of today is unlikely to remain in one appointment for a period of more than three or four years.

COME HITHER
The beckoning motion of the hand in summoning a person is worldwide: but there is a division between the fingers-down-pointers and the fingers-up-pointers. In India, fingers point downwards. To a Westerner, head signals can also appear contrary. A nod can be negative and a side-to-side motion, affirmative.

COMPETITION WALA *n*
A competition man. A **British Indian** term of the second half of the 19th century for those who entered the **covenanted** services through a public examination rather than, as prior to 1856, by private nomination.

COMPOUND *n*
In India, an anglicism for the area, including all buildings, enclosed within one boundary, usually a wall or fence. The word is said to derive from the Malay for an enclosure (or village), kampong.

COMPOUNDER *n*
English word once common but now less so in India for a person experienced in compounding, or dispensing, **allopathic** medicines.

Such persons, as did the apothecaries of England, often also gave medical advice. Compounders are now being replaced by more highly qualified pharmacists. See also IMS.

CONCH *n* English
In Hindi, *shankh/sankh:* the origin of the English word of the same meaning, chank. The volute (spiral) shell of a marine mollusc found almost entirely in Indian waters and fished for as a commercial catch mainly in the Gulf of Manaar (between **Tamil Nadu** and the island of Sri Lanka). Valued by **Hindus** as a sacred and ceremonial horn, producing a sound, resembling perhaps, the trumpeting of an elephant. Together with the **chakha**, a symbol of Lord **Vishnu**, but used to honour all deities. The call of the conch may sound a welcome to a personage, to signal an auspicious moment in a ceremony: traditionally, it was sounded in an army to order the commencement of a battle. In the central hall of the Delhi parliament, it heralded the midnight hour of 14/15 August 1947 and the rebirth of independent India. Bengali married ladies daily salute the sunset with three blasts and, almost certainly, will wear conch shell **bangles**.

The instrument is made simply by cutting the vertex of the spiral: the notes being produced through pursed lips, as with a bugle. By cupping the hand over the large flared opening,

the tone can be varied or muted: it is said that an expert can sustain the sound with one breath for more than two minutes.

Roasted and powdered (shankh bhasm: *see* Ash), the conch shell has a use in **ayurvedic** medicine.

CONSERVANCY *n*
The standard English meaning is of conservation especially management of natural resources, such as a river and its catchment area: but in the India of British days, and no less today, conservancy can mean sanitation. The reason is probably the military vocabulary of the last century. The conservancy cart (a honey-wagon to the British soldier, at least at the time of World War II), an iron tank on unsteady wheels pulled by a bullock, is for the collection of night-soil. The conservancy staff of a town is the corps of municipal sweepers.

In an official designation, such as Conservator of Forests, the word, of course, is being used in its standard English form.

COOLIE *n*
An unskilled labourer, particularly one who carries things: a porter. An anglicism (absorbed into Hindustani) which spread throughout the East and into parts of Africa: said to have originated from the **adivasi** Kuli tribals of Gujarat. Known to have often been applied from

the heights of white colonial superiority to Indians in general; it is not a polite word today; nevertheless, it is firmly entrenched in the vocabulary of middle-class India. Non-emotive words for a labourer are **karamchari** and **mazdoor.**

COORGI *n* English

A person from Coorg, a **district**, and distinct entity in Karnataka (*see* Karnatic),, situated on the Western **Ghats** and long a major centre of coffee growing. Those from the soil of Coorg really prefer to describe themselves as Kodavas. Prior to 1947, Coorg was a small enclave of British India surrounded by **princely** states: the name is an anglicised form of the Kannada word kodagu, meaning stepped. (In reply to a conjectural question, home to the corgi dog is Wales.) Kodagu is now often used for the region.

COOTIE *n* English

This slang word for a body louse or flea derives via the British army in India probably originally from kutu, Malay for a similar parasite.

COPPERSMITH *n*

An English colloquial name for the crimson-breasted barbet: a bird the size of a large sparrow, more often heard than seen. In the spring and hot weather, made conspicuous by its call, a monotonous tonk-tonk-tonk, continued for several minutes at a time, like a distant one-cylinder gas engine, or someone beating copper.

COPY *n*

The usual Indian English and Hindustani term for a school exercise book.

COROMANDEL *n*

An anglicism said to be derived from Cola Mandalam (*see* Mandal), the territory or country of the **Cholas/Colas**. The coastline of today's states of Tamil Nadu and Andhra **Pradesh** between Point Calimere (now Kadikharai in Tamil), at the head of the Palk Strait, northwards through Chennai to the mouths of the River Krishna/Kistna. To the British, the coastline of the **Carnatic**, in the 18th century dotted with European settlements: the Dutch in Masulipatam (now called Machlipatnam, in Andhra Pradesh), Negapatam, *Pulicat and Sadras:* the Danes in Tranquebar (now Tarangambadi, the original **Tamil** name); the French in Pondicherry; the name is from Tamil, Puducherry- new village : the Imperial Ostend Company (of the Germanic Empire) at Covelong; and the British, first at Fort St. David (today's Cuddalore), from 1691 until its capture by the French in 1758 and then in Madras. The name, the Coromandel Coast, later fell into disuse, but Coromandel has recently been revived in the corporate titles of some commercial and industrial projects of the region.

Coromandel screens: no connection with the Coromandel Coast. This term of the valuable antiques trade in Britain is the result of a misrepresentation by the **East India Company.** The screens of black lacquer (*see* Lac) with inlaid colour designs, were brought from China via Calcutta in the 18th century. The Company's London brokers, wilfully or by mistake, provided the fanciful Indian name.

COUNTRY LIQUOR/ SPIRIT *n*
Rectified potable spirit distilled from grain, fruit, palm sugar, **toddy**, etc. The strength is now much reduced by law, its one-time potency is perhaps indicated in the Urdu name arrack, derived from the Arabic word ar'q, meaning sweat. (Correctly, arrack is distilled from toddy only). Country liquor may be plain, or have spices or fruit flavourings added. Any India-made drinkable spirit not given a 'foreign' name, such as whisky, rum, etc. Also known as country, desi (see Desh), tharra, **theka**, and by the British many years ago, as just rack (dim. of arrack). An Indian spirit given the name brandy, whisky, gin, etc., is legally termed India Made Foreign Liquor, or IMFL. *See also* Theka; Wine.

COUNTRY MADE *adj*
A relic expression of the British meaning something normally imported (from Europe), but in fact made in India: deshi. Used today mostly in police reports, in connection ...with crude village-made arms such as the katta/katti - one-shot pistol or a dagger, see Country Liquor and Kattar.

Country born: pre-**independence**, as used by one Briton of another, a disparaging allegation that the person referred to was not merely born in India – for many of the most **pakka** of **sahibs** had been so delivered – but that his parents had been settled in India for a generation or two. Used in early **East India Company** days, the phrase most likely would have been intended to mean Eurasian (*see* Anglo-Indian).

COUPE *n*
In the old long-distance, non-corridor trains, a half first-class compartment with just two berths and a bathroom, complete with shower – a most necessary adjunct with non-sealed coaches which, in arid regions, moved enveloped in a cloud of dust. Providing the two occupants were congenial each to the other, a domestic, intimate way of railway travel. The coupe is not found in the new coaches of today. (Use of an acute accent over the final 'e' was unusual and the normal railway pronunciation was coop. The word came from a four-wheeled horse carriage for two of the same name).

Coupe. lit. cutting. English from French. A forester's term in India for a portion of land, the trees on which are intended for felling.

COURT OF PROPRIETORS
The body of shareholders of the **East India Company** (originally a General Court of Proprietors was a meeting of the body). In the early days at least, the Court could influence the Company's activities in India, but from the time of the India Act of 1784, its sole official function was to elect the twenty-four members of the Court of Directors, the committee in England governing India until the British government assumed full responsibility in 1858. *See* East India Company.

Before the introduction of competitive examinations in 1856 (*see* competition Wala), a valuable perquisite available to members of the Court of Proprietors was the power of patronage to Indian appointments.

CONVENTED adj. Indian English
As seen in a matrimonial advertisement, a plus-point for a girl who has been educated in a convent school and therefore may be expected to have a high standard in English. The background to the word is economy: newspaper notices are charged per word, convented is an abbreviation for 'convent educated'.

COVENANTED SERVICE
In the 18th century, the East India Company required a covenant from its European servants that they would not accept land or presents from the **princes**, of value in excess of £ 4000. In later years, they were also required to abjure private trade.

Service for the Government of India after 1858 on contract, or covenant, with the Secretary of State for India in the UK government: by members of the **Indian Civil Service,** the IMS, Indian Police (*see* IPS) etc. – the covenanted services. The concept and the term were also adopted by the major British firms in India for their expatriate managerial staff.

COW BELT *n*
A modern journalist term for the rural areas of, largely, the Indo-Gangetic plain, where development has been slow and where age-old Hinduism remains the norm and where, allegedly, the cow is revered more than elsewhere. The states of Bihar, U.P. and Madhya Pradesh. *See* Bimaru.

COW DUST TIME
(Go-dhuli). A village expression for that time of day (evening) when the cattle return from the fields, raising dust in the lanes. Twilight.

CRIMINAL TRIBES/CT *n*
Communities, mostly of tribal (*see* adivasi)) **harijan** status, often nomadic, illiterate and landless, whose

permanent livelihood was brigand-age and petty crime. Each group had a speciality, such as picking pockets, coining, highway robbery or burglary.

In British days, once a tribe was notified as criminal, all its members could be required to live in a settle-ment, or to be restricted to a particu-lar area: the children could be sepa-rated from their parents and placed in reformatory settlements. By 1952, the Acts authorising these repressive measures had been repealed and the description of a tribe as criminal no longer has any administrative or legal meaning. (But for an individual, the label 'Habitual Criminal' with certain disadvantages, can follow a specified number of convictions.) Amelioration of position of the ex-CT is now part of the general campaign to improve the lot of the Scheduled Castes (*see* harijan/dalit). But all have not given up traditional ways, for teams of five or six women together who once would have been described as from the CT, or, more colloquially, Crims, still pick pockets in the crowded bazaars of Old Delhi. Such groups can be under some surveillance by the police under the semi-official category of de-notified tribes.

Crim con: Amongst the top people (European) of the late Victorian and Edwardian periods, particularly it was alleged, in the summer capital, Simla, a colloquial expression and pastime. Dating from a legal term of 18th century England, criminal conversation, i.e. adultery.

CRORE/KRORE *n* Hindi
Numeral equivalent to 100 **lakhs**, or ten million. Written -1,00,00000 (one crore zero lakhs).

Crorepati: owner of a crore of **ru-pees**: term for a person considered to be very rich.

CRPF (C.R.P.F)
Central Reserve Police Force. An armed police maintained by the cen-tral government, available for service anywhere in the country. The force was raised just prior to World War II as the Crown Representative's Police, for exceptional duties within the **princely** states particularly in the then Rajputana, at the discretion of the **Viceroy**, the Crown Repre-sentative.

Cr. PC *n*
Criminal Procedure Code, or more correctly, 'Code of Criminal Proce-dure, 1973' (replacing the Code of 1898, which replaced the first all-India Code of 1882). A companion volume of jurisprudence to the Indian Penal Code (see]PC). Mandatory instructions on the manner in which the lower courts and the police are to carry out their duties in implement-ing the criminal law, dealing with civil commotion and so on. Some offences are qualified as 'cogni-

sable'; the Code lists these in a Schedule and defines them as crimes for which the police have powers to arrest a suspected perpetrator without a magistrate's warrant. *See also* Ilbert Bill.

CUMMERBUND/KAMARBAND
n Urdu

"Beware, ye Fair! ye Fair, beware! Nor sit out late at night, – Lest Horrid Cummerbands should come, and swollow you outright". A macaronic verse by Edward Lear, 1874.

From kamar, the middle, the waist. A girdle, a stomach cloth, a waist belt. A wide stomach sash worn by **khidmatgars** as part of their uniform (coloured canvas) and by gentlemen in evening dress (silk). Nowadays, the use of the cummerbund by servants is considered rather old-fashioned. The Hindi equivalent of the Urdu kamarband is the patka; this was really more of a sash, holding perhaps, a sheathed dagger: worn with the jama (*see* pyjama), the traditional long coat of Indian nobles. (For a Punjabi meaning of patka, *see* Puggri). A word similarly formed is bajuband (baaju/baazu, the arm), an arm-band: an amulet, or perhaps a jewelled ornament worn round the upper arm. *See* Koh-i-noor. A bajuband could also be a protective leather and steel cover, worn in combat on a sword-arm.

CURRY *n*

An anglicism from the **Tamil**, kari, a spiced and seasoned sauce; particularly one flavoured by the leaves of the karuveppilei plant – a Tamil name: it is not clear whether the plant is named from the sauce or the sauce from the plant. In north India, the same aromatic leaves, used both dried and fresh, are known as kari patta (curry leaves in the cookery books) or meetha neem (sweet neem). To botanists, the shrub or small tree, related to the citrus and the **bel**, is *Murraya koenigii*, honouring an 18th century naturalist born in Sweden, John Murray. Koenigin is a glucoside.

Generally, there is no dish in an Indian language called kari/curry. (But in Delhi there is a snack of this name: sesoned **besan** boiled with **lassi** and eaten with **pakoras** is traditional on Tuesdays and Saturdays – Hanuman's days). Spices, some pungent, some just aromatic, are used to give piquancy to a daily diet of cereals, **dals** and vegetables – most **Hindus** are vegetarian. Meat dishes for daily eating were introduced by the Muslims and are not native to India (but it is said that at least fifty animals are mentioned in the **Vedas** as being appropriate for sacrifice and no doubt, for eating) neither is the widely popular chilli, having been brought from Aztec America by the Portuguese in the 16th century. In the north, a hot savoury gravy-like sauce, ideally containing **ghee**, added to vegetables or into which a **chapati** may be dipped, will be termed tari, particularly as supplied to a customer in a **dhaba** (eating house). *See also* Haldi, Mirch.

Balti Curry: this popular mutton curry in Britain is unknown in today's India but it is certainly available in Punjabi Pakistan. The name is a sales promotional one with no connection with Baltistan, from where it may be alleged to have originated. An alternative derivation is that the iron vessel in which it is cooked, actually a karahi (see Prasad) may be thought to resemble a balti – a bucket. In fact, the word entered Hindustani from Portuguese.

Curry biscuit: see Pappadum.

Karhi: to the untutored ear, similar in pronunciation to curry. But, in fact, **besan** flour dumplings served with thickened and seasoned **dahi**.

Curry as an English word associated with food can be found far far earlier than from any direct import from India. The origin here was the Latin for leather, coriam. In English a horse may be groomed by using a curry comb.

CUSHY *n*
Meaning easy, pleasant: a colloquial anglicism from the Urdu adjective, khush - happy, pleased, good. The word is in the *OED.*

D

When a group of dacoits finally arrive at their nemesis at the hands of a police party, the bodies may be laid out for photographers in the manner of the bag at an erstwhile tiger shoot.

Daku: a thief, especially one using, or threatening violence. In criminal law, dacoity is robbery with violence by a party of four or more persons.

DA *n* Sanskrit
A gift, charity. Dan in Hindi. The Indo-European syllable with a link via Latin to the European words meaning donation.

DA (DA)
Dearness Allowance. A supplement to wages to compensate for a rise in the cost of living.

DACOIT *n*
An anglicism from dakait: a member of a gang of armed robbers. In rural areas, particularly in the ravine country between Agra and Gwalior to the south, the badlands of the river valleys of the Chambal and  **Yamuna**, dacoits may be termed baaghi, rebels, tigers (*see* bagh), but gang-leaders, although murderous enough on occasions, can be local heroes: God-fearing Robin Hood characters, who cock a snook at landlords and authority, but who support temples and assist the poor.

DĀDĀ *n* Hindi
Elder brother: paternal grand-father: gang leader. In Bengal, an affectionate suffix to a male first name.

In northern India, a way of addressing a person from another part of the country; the equivalent of stranger, or **Bhai Sahib.**

Dadagiri: hooliganism, gang-rule. Intimidation by a gang-leader and his men.

DAFADĀR/DUFFADĀR *n* Urdu
Lit. leader of ten. Military rank in the cavalry (Armoured Corps), equivalent to **Havildar** (Sergeant).

Originally, the title was used only in the Company's irregular cavalry units in which the silidari system obtained (see Bargadar).

DAFTAR/DUFTAR *n* Urdu
Lit. a stitched book, a register. An office. In Delhi, especially to the bus conductors, a term for the Central

Secretariat of the Government of India. Secretary to the ruler of a Rajput state (obsolete).

Daftari/Daftary: in the Mogul courts, the officer who carried the registers of the Emperor's correspondence and of payment orders on the imperial treasury. Today, the man who looks after an office in a humble way: an office keeper. A book-binder.

DĀHI *n* Hindi
Curds of milk: unflavoured yogurt. When served containing cut pieces of raw (particularly cucumber) or cooked vegetables and, perhaps, spices and salt, it is known as raita. (A rather special raita, sweet and sour can contain fine cut pineapple).

Dahi, with sugar, ice (if available) and water, makes the famous cooling drink from the **Punjab,** lassi, (before taking an exam, to cool his brain, dahi may be put on a student's forehead). In the south, lassi is likely to be seasoned with condiments and pieces of green chilli. **Kachcha** lassi: *see* Piao. In Western India, de-watered dahi beaten up with sugar, spices and perhaps, fruit pulp, will carry the name shrikhand, further south, rice may be added. In eastern India, mishti doi sweet dahi, is very popular.

An Indian housewife intending to make butter, will normally churn dahi rather than fresh milk. After churning, the light liquid remaining, the whey or butter-milk, perhaps seasoned or sweetened, makes a pleasant drink, chach.

In **British-Indian** cookery books, dahi was often referred to as tyre, an anglicism from the **Tamil** tayir for the same dairy product.

In India the English word curd/curds is often used for dahi. Strictly this is incorrect. Dahi is milk acted upon by an added bacterium (a starter), whereas curd should be milk coagulated by an added acid such as lemon juice. The usual word for curd is chhana.

Charan : a mixture of dahi, ghee, milk and honey, used as a lustration, for washing an icon or the feet of a revered person.

DAI *n* Urdu
A midwife. In traditional **Hindu** India, midwifery is an unclean employment: *see* Chamar. Nowadays, except perhaps in the most remote areas, the professional dai will have had at least some scientific medical training.

DĀK *n* Hindi
The **Mogul** system for carrying imperial despatches by relays of runners and horsemen. The name remains unchanged for the postal service of today, the mail. In the 18th and early 19th centuries, the British employed similar methods:

runners in stages of about eight miles each would carry the letters some seventy miles a day (In 2000 AD the postal harkaras – runners – are still in business, carrying the mail to villages where no vehicle can reach. Dak originally had the meaning of the staging place where the couriers changed and in a similar fashion to the English equivalent, post, became the name for the service. At first, only government despatches were handled, but in 1837 the mails became open to use by the general public with payment by postage stamps at an all-India uniform rate introduced in 1854.

Travelling Dawk (Dak): an expression of early British days before roads were good enough for light vehicles, meaning a long-distance journey of days or weeks in a palanquin (*see* Carrying Chairs), with changes of bearers arranged by the postal authorities: when everything went well, moving day and night, progress could be as much as ninety miles in twenty-four hours. Not only did men journey in this way, from the days before the Mutiny there are many narratives of young European girls travelling alone, or attended by just a single maid-servant, long distances across country in perfect safety. (But this was not always the case for Indian travellers: see Thug). Later, but still before the railways, speedy two-wheeled pony traps and four-wheeled carriages carried the mails on trunk

routes, the one or two passengers enduring extreme discomfort in a cloud of dust 'travelling dawk'. The service was often performed by private firms operating on contract. To make arrangements with an authority for a journey, the stages, the vehicles, the palanquin bearers, was 'to lay a 'dawk'. *Hobson Jobson* has a story that a newly arrived young officer, being posted 'up-country' and instructed to lay a dawk, had to request an explanation: '... for. Sir, you might as well tell me to lay an egg.'

Dak Edition (of a city daily newspaper): lit. a postal edition. One prepared so that, allowing for travelling time, when on sale at some distance, the date printed and the actual date will be the same. With airmail service between cities, the dak edition is now probably all but obsolete.

Dakgari (in connection with railways): a mail train (*see* Passenger Train).

Dakwala (correctly, dakia): a postman.

Dakkhana: a post-office.

Dak-Tar: Post & Telegraphs. (As

in 19th century English, the word for wire – tar – was adopted for the message by wire, the telegram.)

Dak-tikat (ticket): a postage stamp.

Dak Bungalow: a staging post, a European modification of the old **Hindu** idea of the panthshala (*see* Path, but note that pathshala means a school), or the Islamic serai (*see* Caravan) to provide basic accommodation for travellers. The bungalows were first constructed by the British, on main roads roughly a day's march apart, fifteen to twenty miles, for an overnight stay, by officials and worthy private citizens. Still providing good service, but since those travelling on government business have priority and appear to be myriad, worthy private citizens find more difficulty in gaining entry these days.

Bangy-dak: the bangy was an anglicised form of the Hindi word bahangi, meaning a single light pole, or even a cord, with an equal load suspended at each end and balanced at the centre on a man's shoulder. The bangy-dak was a system of conveying postal parcels in this way and the actual carrier was the bangydar.

Dhak : see Flame of the Forest.

DAKSHINA *n* Hindi
Originally, a gift by a pupil to his guru on the successful completion of studies. An offering to a **Hindu** temple or priest for some spiritual comfort received, or for the performance of a ceremony, or for religious instruction.
Vardakshina : see Dowry.

DĀL *n* Hindi
Usually written as dhal in eastern India. An important group of edible pulses such as the lentil (masur dal); the chick-pea (gram or channa dal); the red dal (arhar, but tuvar in the south); black dal (urad/urd); golden or green gram (mung) and horse gram (kulthi), The consumption of all pulses leads to digestion gas or flatus but it is claimed that mung is least productive in this respect. Correctly, a pulse from the fields only becomes dal after preparation for the kitchen, by shelling, cleaning and, perhaps, splitting. The English word for a pulse (from Portuguese), gram (but pronounced with a long a in India) is frequently used for the dals, although, specifically, it is applied to the Bengal, or channa dal.

At least one of the dals, khesari, is a near poison: it is grown for its hardiness, for the plant will survive even a severe drought. If eaten without an admixture of other pulses for any length of time, as it may be during periods of scarcity, paralysis and deformation of the legs (lathyrism, from the botanical name of the dal, *Lathyrus sativus*) can result. In the Bible parable of the good seed, when St. Matthew mentioned tares among the wheat, it is said that the reference is to khesari dal. In largely vegetarian India, it is the pulses which are the main source of low-cost protein for many.

Dal bhāt: Pulses and rice (bhat – cooked rice) prepared separately then mixed together: but the term can also mean a simple basic meal. (In north India, dal roti.)

Dal-Chini : See Tejpat

Dal: a group of persons united for a purpose, probably political as, for example, the Akali Dal, a political party of the **Sikhs**. From a **Sanskrit** term, dala, a military force.

DALAI LAMA *n*
Dalai (Mongolian) strictly means the wide ocean of the world. The spiritual leader of Tibetan Buddhism, or Lamaism. Previous to the Chinese occupation of Tibet, also the temporal head of state of that country. This title is little used in the Tibetan language: to Tibetans, their leader is the Gyalwa **Rimpoche.**

DALĀL *n* Urdu
An agent between buyer and seller, a broker. On the seamy side, a tout or pimp.

Dalal Street: the financial district of Mumbai (from a street name). Used in reports in the same way as 'the

City' or 'Wall Street'. In Kolkata, the equivalent is Lyons Range, rarely, but more correctly, Lyon's Range, the name of the building housing the Stock Exchange. (Thomas Lyon was a master craftsman of the **East India Company,** the probable builder of **Writers'** Building: range is an archaic use of the word meaning a lengthy building or line of buildings.)

Dalali: Commission due to a dalal for his services, brokerage.

DĀLI *n* Hindi
A token gift to a superior perhaps on a festival day: normally, in a basket or tray, sent with compliments. Traditionally of flowers, fruit and nuts or sweets. Regulations allow nothing more substantial to be accepted by government officials. In British times the word could be anglicised into dolly.

DALIT : See Harijan/Dalit

DAMARU/DUMRU *n* Hindi
Small waisted drum, held in one hand: as used by Lord **Shiva** (of whom it is a symbol) and today, by the monkey-man (the delight of children, the itinerant exhibitor of performing monkeys, which, seemingly, dance to the beat). By shaking and twirling, two knotted strings can be made to strike the skins.

Some believe that Lord Shiva's drum produced sounds that were the source of the vowels and consonants of **Sanskrit**.

DANCING GIRLS *n*
As with the singing girls – sometimes, the occupations are combined under the Urdu names, tawaif, baiji (*see Bahen*) or kothawali *(See* Kotha) – a class of trained artistes, usually Muslim, once providing private entertainment (*see* Nautch) in the palaces and mansions of the wealthy, and when famous, receiving substantial rewards. A part of the **Hindustani**  culture of north India. As might be expected, an element of the skilled courtesan was often present. Nowadays, while the true artiste may still be found, usually performing in her own salon, with prostitution illegal in many states, the terms dancing and singing girls may be little more than a cover for the other profession. A performance by singing and dancing girls is often referred to as a mujra. (In traditional Hindu society going back to ancient times, the accomplished courtesan catering for the wealthy, cultured and trained in the arts, as the geisha of Japan, was the ganikaa. The term today may mean no more than a **bazaar** prostitute. The dancing 'girls' sometimes seen performing behind the band in an urban wedding **baraat** will, in fact, almost certainly be dancing boys. *See also* Devadasi, Hindustan and Nautch.

DAND/DANDA *n* Hindi
A stick; punishment. See Lathi. In state-craft, danda raj, rule by coercion or force asignifying the use of coercion.

DANDI *n*
The place on the Gujarat coast to which in 1930, with the world press in attendance, **Mahatma** Gandhi led his followers on a twenty-four day, 388km, pad-yatra (journey on foot, see Yatra) to make a symbolic quantity of salt from sea-water and to pick up from the shore small pieces naturally crystallised. The **Viceroy** ignored the challenge, technical defiance of the then Salt Tax Law, for almost a month, but then non-violent pressure against a state salt works finally provoked from exasperated officials the reaction required to demonstrate government brutality, and the arrest of the Mahatma. At more or less the same time as the drama at Dandi, all over India, in street meetings, brine was boiled to make salt. There are no salt works in the neighbourhood of Dandi today. (2005).

Today, only remembered in the south, also in April 1930, was another non-violent salt march, 240 kms to the eastern sea coastline, led by the statesman, **Rajaji** (in 1948 to be India's only Indian Governor-General.) Here the government was a lot tougher, Rajaji was arrested and lathi charges were the norm. here too.

the marchers won a moral victory. Rajaji's coast destination had the name Vedaranyam which can be the name of the march today.

Shortly after the marches, salt production for personal consumption by coastal villagers was exempted from tax. The Salt Tax was a small impost paid by everyone from the highest to the humblest, centuries old and inherited from the **Mogul** administration. Even in ancient India, the production of salt was often a monopoly of the ruler. In 1903, Lord Curzon had wished to renounce the tax as a **Durbar** boon, but the Home Government had over-ruled him – the quantum was reduced in a subsequent budget. In 1927/8 it amounted to 0.03% of government revenue.

But in an an earlier century it had been of major importance. So much so that in the 1840s it had been thought worthwhile to plant and man a 2500 miles spiked-thorn barrier to fence off eastern India (high tax) from western India (low or zero tax). This ceased to be manned only in 1879.

The salt march was perhaps the Mahatma's greatest political triumph; it stirred the country as never before, made for excellent public relations the world over, and the impishness of it – the spectacle of an old man boiling a can of sea water versus the Empire – greatly embarrassed the government. Yet for all that, the

following year, that old man was received by the Viceroy, each toasting the other with **nimbu** pani (the guest adding salt to his from a small packet, saying it had been illegally made and had paid no tax). The same year in London, the Mahatma met King George in Buckingham Palace.

Even before the transfer of power, the Finance Minister, Liquat Ali Khan, in his budget of February 1947, abolished the salt tax.

DANGAL *n* Urdu
An Indian-style wrestling tournament or competition. *See also* Akhara.

DANT *n* Hindi from Sanskrit
A tooth. Cognate to the European language dental words received through Latin.

DARGĀH *n* Urdu
A building round or over the grave of a Pir, a Mùslim respected as one blessed by God (Allah-wali: close to God); particularly one within the **Sufi** tradition. Frequently, accommodation and **langar** (free food) will be available for pilgrims. The annual **Urs** (festival) at the **Chisti** dargahs, such as that at Ajmer, draw huge crowds of devotees from all over India. Something less than a dargah, perhaps no more than a grave

mound with a canopy, is the mazaar. Either may be the object of Muslim pilgrimage and may be referred to as simply a pir. (Pir can also be the day of the week, Monday, and in the original Persian, a respected elder, a spiritual guide.) In some cases, the grave of a pir can be an object of devotion to both Hindus and Muslims.

Ziarat/Ziyarat: a word from Arabic. Strictly a visitation, a pilgrimage to a revered Muslim's grave for devotion or intercession, but it has come to mean the grave monument itself particularly of a sufi, which may be a large shrine or no more than a roadside grave with a low boundary wall.

DARŌGA *n* Urdu From Persian Police officer in charge of a rural police station before the introduction of state police forces, provided for in the Police Act of 1861. Municipal superintendent as of, say, a market.

DARSHAN *n* Hindi
A sight, a view, an inclination towards God: the term includes an element of respect, deference, to the person or object seen. To a **Hindu**, the sight of a superior or a revered being (not necessarily a great one of the earth, the principle applies equally to one's parents or **guru** after an absence), can be received as a mystic gift to the soul. On the public appearance of any well-known and respected figure, people will travel long distances

and gather in possibly considerable discomfort, to gaze on the great man (or woman): if there is a speech, the actual words may well be casually received and part of the audience may leave even before the chief speaker has completed his oration, but no matter, darshan will have been given and received. Failing personal sight, contemplation of, and perhaps a **pranam** to, a revered person's image or picture, will be to receive his darshan, as will be a final glimpse of his body after death.The fullness of gratification an Indian can receive through darshan would seem to be unique in world culture.

Muslims, but to a lesser degree, have similar feelings, using the Urdu word deedar: except of course, concerning a representation of the deity, or of a prophet, which would be anathema, but the early morning routine of the **Mogul** emperors showing themselves to their subjects from a palace balcony or projecting oriel window, (jharoka, jharoka also is a grille-covered opening in a wall for a purpose such as air-supply or for covert observation) was a leaning towards the Hindu philosophy of darshan. The practice was discontinued by the orthodox Aurangzeb.

Priyadashni: usually translated rather crudely as just "good to see". A given name or description for a girl. The most famous recipient being its use as a title for Prime Minister Indira Gandhi.

DASTŪR *n* Urdu
Custom. The constitution of an organisation or of a country.

Dasturi: A payment, or deduction in some form, probably irregular by strict accounting standards: a payment with an element of bribery: such transactions being accepted by the parties as 'customary'. A commission allowed by custom.

Dastur: pre-lslamic Persian. Chief priest of a **Parsi** agiary (Fire Temple).

DĀUD *n* Urdu
The Islamic form of the name, David. Alternative and now more common spelling is Dawood.

DECCAN *n*
An anglicism from dakan, the Urdu form of the Hindi word, dakshin, south: itself from Dakshinapath, the whole of the peninsula south of the Vindhyas, as distinct from Aryavarta, the northern land of the **Aryans**. The British applied the term Deccan to just the plateau of the southern shield, part of the old continent of Gondwanaland (*see* Adivasis), which remains the current usage.

(In **Sanskrit**-based Hindi, the cardinal points are those of the early Aryans facing the rising sun. **Purabiya**, lit.

in front, east: pachami, behind, west: dakshini, to the right, dexter in Latin, south; uttar, the left, north.)

Deccan Queen: the express train of the Central Railway leaving Pune each morning down the Western Ghats to Mumbai (*see* Up Trains, Down Trains) and returning the same evening: the 193 km are covered in just over three hours.

Deccan Trap : the geological name for the lava cover overlying much of the far older Gondwanaland (see Adivasi) now forming the tableland of the Deccan. Moisture-holding black cotton-soil and flat-topped hills rising to a height of about 1200 metres.

DEFENCE SERVICES AWARDS
For bravery in the face of the enemy: 1. Param Vir **Chakra** 2. Maha Vir Chakra 3. Vir Chakra. Gallantry and self-sacrifice in the presence of the enemy: 1. Ashok Chakra 2. Kirti Chakra 3. Shaurya Chakra. Distinguished Service:
1.Param Vishist Seva Medal
2.Ati Vishist Seva Medal
3.Vishist Seva Medal.

Samanya Sewa Medal: General Service Medal awarded for active service under war or near war conditions.

DĒGCHI/DĒKCHI *n* Urdu
A cooking pot, a saucepan (normally without a handle). Through the

British soldier, the origin of the English word, dixie, meaning a camp kettle.

Deg/degcha: larger than a degchi, a cauldron. (To a Punjabi, particularly a **Sikh**, deg can be a synonym for food, or the **langar**. Antedating Napoleon's maxim, a Sikh **Guru** is said to have declared that military victory depended on both deg and tegh – food and sword. The Sikh king, Ranjit Singh, included the phrase on some of his coins.) Popular Hindi words for cooking pots are handa (large) and handi (small). Such utensils are valued articles in an Indian home with which the housewife likes to make a display: traditionally of brass for Hindus and copper for Muslims, kept highly polished and tinned on the insides. A status symbol in today's kitchen is undoubtedly shelves laden with expensive stainless steel. (In Urdu a handi can be a bell-shaped glass container, plain or coloured, suspended by three chains open-end up, to hold an oil or candle lamp. Popular in well-to-do Muslim homes and buildings in the 19th century and still to be seen today).

Degchi mirch: see Mirch.

DEKKO *n*
This English slang word for a look derives, via the British army, from the Hindi verb dekhna, to look, to see. But from a far distant past in Indo-European languages the linked Sanskrit dic sound (to show) appears in English via Latin in such words as indicate, index and vindicate. A word with the same meaning also used by the British army was shufti, not from India but picked up from Egypt and Arabic: spoken not as a verb but as a noun, "take a shufti".

DELHI
From time to time over several thousand years the region of Delhi has been the seat of rulers. Geographically, it is the point in the plains from where its deity river is obstructed by the Aravalli Hills and where she can be crossed on elephants and later by a bridge of boats (see Yamuna). The region is mentioned in the Mahabharat (see Epics, the citadel of the Pandavas was on the site of today's Old Fort.) Hindu rulers made it their centre and so did some Muslim sultans. Next, the Moguls and in 1911 King George announced that Delhi would become the centre of British rule under the name Imperial Delhi (later, simplified to New Delhi) situated in a Central Government enclave, Delhi Province, cut out from the Punjab and on the eastern river bank, from the United Provinces.

In 1992 following from the 69th. Constitutional Amendment, Delhi officially became the National Capital Territory, under a Lieutenant

Governor appointed by the GOI. Also supervisory powers were acquired over areas of the adjoining states, especially the satellite towns close to the border to be known as the Delhi Metropolitan area. Further afield, parts of the states of Punjab, Haryana, Rajasthan, Madhya Pradesh and Uttar Pradesh, the National Capital Region (NCR) are watched over by the NCR Planning Board. It has been estimated that the Delhi area by 2021 will have a population of about 22 million with the sattelite towns adding 8 million more.

DELHI BELLY

A stomach disorder sometimes afflicting newcomers to the capital: akin to Gippy Tummy of Egypt; the Rangoon Runs of **Burma**; Montezuma's Revenge of Mexico; the Turkey Trots of Istanbul and the Kathmandu Quickstep of Nepal.

As a pleasantry, Delhi Belly can be the increase of girth, of routundity, often observed on a diplomat after a year of the capital's social whirl.

DELHI ORDER, THE

The design by the builder of Rashtrapati **Bhavan** in New Delhi (Sir Edwin Lutyens) for an Indian rather than a classical capital for the head of his columns: a stone bell at each corner of the entablature. The order has been repeated on some other Lutyens buildings such as the National Archives and on the four baldachin columns supporting the now empty canopy that once covered the memorial statue of King George V at India Gate. Lutyens used the Delhi Order at least once in England in the chapel of Campion Hall, Oxford, of the late 1930s. Another Lutyens' peculiarity, employed in his landscaping in New Delhi as elsewhere, is the wide bands of steps with risers of only four inches.

DENTING

As an Indian-English term in connection with the body work of vehicles, not the infliction of dents, but their removal and the restoration of the surface. A craft in which many of those who practise it are highly skilled: their artistry perhaps owing something to the considerable demand for their services.

DEODAR *n* Hindi

Lit. tree of God, or a divine tree. The Himalayan or Indian cedar: found only in the western **Himalaya** and associated ranges, such as the eastern valleys of the Hindu Kush. A gigantic tree, sometimes living for more than 700 years. Deodar timber, being insect resistant, also has a life measured in centuries.

A fragrant oil extracted from deodar wood has a use as a perfume, and is also an insecticide.

DERA/DEHRA *n* Urdu from Persian
Strictly, an encampment as in the place name Dera Ismail Khan (Pakistan: the camp of the tribal leader, Ismail Khan). A word with several applications. A **Sikh Gurdwara** complex with administration and residential buildings. In the Sikh kingdom of Lahore, a military unit. The name of the town Dehra Dun (the roman spelling is an anglicism) follows from a gurdwara complex built in the Valley by the Emperor Aurangzeb in the 17th century. The collegiate building used by **Hijras** under a Guru is termed a dera. An equivalent word in Hinduism for dera could be **ashram**.

DERVISH/DARVISH *n* Urdu
Dervish, from Persian, is synonymous with faqir/fakir, from Arabic: an Islamic mystic who has given up the world to serve and understand God. Like the sadhus of Hinduism, who follow a parallel path, some are respected as blessed by God, some feared for believed super-natural powers: some are organised in orders (mostly the music loving **Sufis**). After death, the remembrance of a revered faqir may well cause men to build a **dargah** around his grave.

DĒSH/DĒS *n* Hindi
Country. One's native land. Also, in some parts of India, just a region.

Desi/deshi: adjectival, Indian and not imported. Regional. (But, applied to the arts, the meaning is usually rural or folk, as opposed to sophisticated or classical.) As with its anglicism equivalent of earlier years, **country-made,** so even today in some contexts, an adjectival 'desi' can convey an element of disparagement.

Desi ghee: milk ghee. No detraction here, since as a dairy product, milk or pure ghee is regarded as **superior** to its workaday competitor, vegetable ghee (**vanaspati**).
Desi liquor: see Country Liquor.

Desi wheat: the original strains of Indian wheat, excluding the modern high-yielding hybrid varieties. Similarly desi eggs: in the **bazaar**, the small eggs from traditional village free-run hens, believed by many to have more taste than those from the new hybrid layers. Desi tomatoes are globular compared with the more recently introduced plum-shaped ones (in fact, of course, all tomatoes are exotics).

The antonym of desi/deshi is *pardesi/pardeshi:* meaning foreign, a foreign country. Also meaning a foreign land and adjectival foreign, are the words videsh and videshi.

Deshmukh: chief of a desh (in the sense of a **district** within a Hindu kingdom): a term particularly used by the Marathas (*see* Maharashtra). Nowadays, a family name.

Sardeshmukh: head or chief of the deshmukh. Head of State: again a Maratha title; one held by Shivaji (*see* Chhatrapati).

Sardeshmakhi: a Maratha land revenue tax.

Deshvasio: countrymen (as in the form of address "Fellow Country-men".

DETENU *n* French
A person imprisoned by the Central or State Government under powers other than the normal criminal or civil law (*see* MISA). The old English equivalent would be state prisoner.

DEV/DEVA/DEO *n* Hindi
A major God, e.g., Lords **Vishnu** and **Shiva**. An honorific term of address to a respected person, especially in the form Gurudev.

Devalaya: 'place of God', a **Hindu** shrine or temple. *See* Mandir.

Devi: goddess. *The* Goddess (consort of Lord Shiva). The principle of the power of the Mother Goddess, **Shakti**. *See also* Tantra, Durga Puja. A way of addressing a married woman (Deviji). A girl's name.

Deota/Devta: a lesser divine being; a term not usually applied to a major deity.

Devasan: seat or throne of a deity, or of one respected as a highly spiritual being.

Devanagri: the phonetic script reading from left to right, in which **Sanskrit**, Hindi and Marathi (also Nepali) are written: and with variations, all other Sanskrit-based north Indian languages. (The script of Tibet is also derived from devanagri.) Believed by the traditionally minded to be the writing of the gods, devised by the Goddess **Saraswati**. A development, more or less completed by the 11th century AD, from the Brahmi script of **Ashok's** time (*see* Mauryan Period). A subsequent addition so that Persian-derived words could be represented phonetically, was that a dot could be placed below certain consonants to indicate an Urdu and not a Hindi sound. *See also* Sanskrit.

Devnagri characters strung together to represent a spoken sound, a syllabary. A knowledge of which begins Hindi scholarship.

Dev (often pronounced deo) is kin to words used throughout the Indo-European language group for a deity and to a Sanskrit root for God, div or dyaus (for dyauspita/devapati, *see* Vedas). Dyaus also had the meaning of refulgence, light as opposed to darkness, day as opposed to night: that God is light is a worldwide belief. *See also* Diya.

DEVADĀSI *n* Hindi
Lit. woman slave, or servant, of the
deity (*see* Adivasi). A long-lived
pre-vedic **Hindu** institution (found
in many ancient civilisations): the
dedication of females to the service
of a temple deity, dancing and
singing: particularly well established
in south India (*see* Bharat Natyam),
where, although an element of
prostitution might be present in the
background, devadasis could be
honoured by society as the exponents
of a continuous and highly skilled
artistic culture. Since the devadasi
is notionally wedded to an immortal
deity, she can never become a widow
(her position is sometimes termed
in Hindi, **akhand** saubhagyawati
– the fortunate Goddess, who will
die before her husband). It is no
secret that India's most famous film
play-back singer, a single woman
in the conventional sense, Lata
Mangeshkar, a star in her own right
with a career stretching back fifty
years, was born into a devadasi
family, and considering herself united
to a deity, wears the **sindoor** of a
married woman. (Almost all feature
films made in Indian languages
require about six songs from the
heroine: if, as frequently happens,
the actress has no skilled musical
voice, the words are provided for
her by a play-back singer while she
mimes on the screen.)

Although the devadasi custom
is now legally banned in almost
all states, it certainly continues:
particularly vigorously in the border
areas between Karnataka and
Maharashtra and in Andhra Pradesh,
where such women may be termed
joginis. There, according to reports,
girls, almost entirely from the **dalit**
community, are dedicated for life to a
Goddess, Yellamma, only to become
prostitutes in the city of Mumbai.
(Those dedicated to the Goddess
often wear a necklace of yellow and
white beads.)

A word used in the past in English
for a south Indian devadasi was
the French bayadere (of the same
meaning in that language): it is still
to be found in the *OED*, but probably
is rarely used now. Perhaps as a
Victorian euphemism, it was also
sometimes applied to the nautch, or
dancing girl, of the north.

Yogin/jogin: can mean a woman
married to a deity. *See* Yoga.

DHĀBA *n* Punjabi
Roadside stall serving cooked foods,
usually including egg and meat
dishes: often of a very tasty nature,
especially
when the
proprietor is
a Punjabi.
Quick service
is the norm,
all the items being prepared in full
view of the customer and of passers-
by. In a Muslim dhaba, a customer

may be asked 'burra ya chhota?'
– large or small?' A coded question
understood by habitues to mean
'Do you want buffalo beef (cheap)
or mutton (expensive)?' In a rural
setting, the **charpoys** ranged outside
are an invitation to passing truck
drivers to take a rest – and a meal.
See also Hotel.

DHĀM/DHAAM *n* Hindi
A residence, particularly of a **Hindu**
deity or of a person respected
because of a spiritual quality. A
Hindu shrine or major pilgrimage
centre. A 'house' of the one of the
four cardinal points of the compass.
See Deccan. See Garhwal.

DHAMAKA *n* Hindi
A loud noise, a crash, hullabalu.
As used by advertisers with a new
product, a sensation. An uproar at a
meeting, a noisy interruption of the
proceedings.

DHANDHA *n* Hindi
Ones occupation, craft, business.

DHANDHORCHI *n* Hindi
A private person's town cryer. In
an urban residential locality, a man
who can be hired to make a street
announcement by beat of drum,
perhaps of a strayed dog or cat, of
a public meeting, or something of a
more commercial nature.

DHANIA *n* Hindi
The coriander plant (*Coriandrum*

sativum): although from the
Mediterranean area, sometimes
termed Chinese parsley. As fresh
leaves, seeds, or as an aromatic oil,
dhania is an essential flavouring
and garnish to many Indian dishes,
both northern and southern. (In the
West, coriander may be used to
give an additional flavour to gin.)
The leaves are rich in vitamins A
and C. The **bazaar** vegetable seller
will often include a few sprigs of
dhania as a goodwill gesture with
purchases made from his stall. Of the
same plant family as the coriander
is the cumin (*Cuminum cyminum*),
of which the dried and powdered
seed-like fruit is widely used as a
condiment under the Urdu name of
jira/jeera/zira. An oil pressed from
the seeds is used in perfumery.

DHANYA *n* Sanskrit
Blessings, gratitude.
Dhanyawad: Hindi, an expression of
gratitude; thank you. Muslim thank-
you words are shukriya (Arabic) and
mehrbani (Persian).

DHARMA/DHARM *n* Hindi
The combined religious and civic
conduct that exalts the soul: duties
of an individual, anywhere. But
in practice almost certainly a –
reference to the accepted divinely
established code of behaviour for
Hindus necessary to hold a group
of people together and furnishing
an indication to the correct course
of action in a given situation (the

Sanskrit root word of dharm is dhri, meaning a support, a frame. "That which is established".) Appropriate to his station in life, the duties of an individual towards his religion, ruler and family and to others, as laid down in the Dharma **Shastras**. Yet Hindu society accepts that for a person already on a high spiritual plane, one regarded as close to divinity, the customary dharma intended to guide lesser men need not apply. To such a person, the divine intention will be apparent through his conscience, the voice of swadharma – self dharma. 'Abandon dharma and take refuge in me... ' said Lord **Krishna** to Arjuna in the **Gita.**

Adharma/adharm: without dharma (*see* Ahinsa.). Throughout Indian history, especially in the **Epics**, the theme of all stories has been dharma against adharma, righteousness versus evil.

Dharmachakra: the Buddhist Wheel of the Law. See Chakra.

Dharmaraj: see Yama.

Dharmashāla/Dharmsala: temporary accommodation, free or at low cost, for travellers, for pilgrims in connection with a shrine; when in a city, also used perhaps by wedding parties accompanying a bridegroom (*see* Baraat). Basically Hindu, but sometimes open to all: a dharmashala may restrict entry to persons of a particular caste group, or from a particular region. Usually managed by a trust as a charity.

Dharmyuddh: a war for dharma. The Hindu equivalent of the Islamic jihad, a holy war a just war.

DHARNA *n* Hindi
A peaceful protest by one person, a group, or groups, against a considered injustice, by remaining continuously for a considerable period – sometimes for many weeks – outside the factory, office, or home of the person who is thought to be responsible, or who can provide a remedy: or in any public place. Often combined with a hunger strike. The dharna is designed to shame the person against whom the protest is directed – or to punish him by burdening him with a sense of guilt.

Self-imposed suffering in order to force compliance with one's wishes is a traditional response to personal frustration (*see also* Tapasya). In the early 18th century, pressure could take the extreme form of, and as a final step, suicide, all performed at the door of the individual being coerced.

Alternatively, a **brahman** could be engaged to carry out a dharna on one's behalf. A sub-caste, the Bhatts, once specialised in providing this service. An extreme form of dharna reappeared in 1990 when a number of upper caste students in northern

India publicly burnt themselves to death as a political protest.

DHATŪRA *n* Hindi

A plant said to have been blessed by Lord **Shiva** and is particularly used in his workship. The botanical genus is Datura, of the potato family; ten varieties grow in India, including the one found in England (D. *stramonium*) , where it is known as the thorn apple – because, no doubt, of the spiky golf ball-sized seed case (in the USA, the name is jimson weed). All have attractive trumpet-shaped white flowers. The leaves, fruits and seed contain the depressive alkaloid poison, hyoscine – the weapon of the notorious English murderer of 1910, Dr. Crippen – and traces of atropine. Ground and given in food or drink, dhatura is sometimes used by thieves (known as dhatureas) to produce insensibility – an overdose will cause death – in their intended victims. But the toxicity is not that of the improbable libretto of the French opera, Lakme (*see* Lakshmi), set in 19th century India, in which the heroine commits suicide by nibbling a dhatura leaf. In both Indian and Western medicine, in England under the name stramonium, fumes from burning leaves of the plant have been found useful for the treatment of asthma. Hyoscine yields the sedative drug, scopolamine.

DHOBI/DHOBY *n* Hindi

A member of the Scheduled Castes (*see* Harijan) born to wash and press clothes. A washerman; his wife being the dhoban. As a colloquial anglicism, the word may be applied to the 'wash', collectively the soiled or cleaned articles (in Hindi, the noun is dhob). Traditionally, the dhobi had gold or silver rings in his ears, but this custom is not followed by the youngsters of today.

Dhobi **ghat**: the term originally referred to the separate place, a slope or steps by a river or **tank** where the dhobi worked at his trade. Nowadays, the name can be applied even to a municipally provided concrete sink.

Dhobi's itch: an anglicism for a ringworm-type skin infection, particularly of the groin and armpits under conditions of high humidity and temperature. Alleged to pass from one person to another through underwear mixed together by the dhobi: a route of cross-infection now thought unlikely.

Dhobi mark: an inconspicuous mark made on clothing by a dhobi in order to identify the owner. A European slang expression for a signature, or signed initials.

Dhobi nuts: *See Reetha.*

DHŌL *n* Hindi

Large double-ended drum, hung from the player's neck and played using sticks.

Dholak: similar to, but smaller than the dhol and sounded by the fingers alone.

DHŌLE *n* Hindi
The Asian wild dog; the red dog (the red killer of Kipling's second Jungle Book): in Hindustani, the jangli kutta – the feral dog, *see* Jungle. But dhole is the name used worldwide by zoologists. Dog-like in appearance, but its genus is Cuon and not Canis: for the reasons of an extra tooth in the lower jaw and in the bitch, teats extra to those of a true canine. Rusty red in colour, with the same dark bushy tail as the jackal, the dhole is a pack-hunting animal of scrub forest and open plains. Until fairly recently, in many areas the government paid a bounty for the tail of each animal killed.

DHŌTI/DHŌTY *n* Hindi
The traditional garment of the **Hindu** male, from the peasant to the raja and the **crorepati** – even the most Westernised will probably wear one for a serious religious occasion. A piece of cloth about 4.5m long, normally white (a **swami** may prefer **saffron** or pink) of any material from the finest muslin to the coarsest cotton, worn in many regional and sectional styles. Often said to be a loin cloth by English writers, this may be descriptive for a farm labourer, but as worn by, say, a Bengali gentleman, the dhoti will enclose his left leg to the ankle and his right to the calf.

The dhoti comes from the loom, ready-to-wear, conforming to the ancient preference for unsewn (unstitched, is the usual term in Indian English) clothing. Many Hindu temples in south India and some in Bengal require devotions to be performed wearing only unsewn clothing, thus ruling out underwear. Muslims, too, when on pilgrimage, are enjoined to wear two simple wraps, the ihram, rather than sewn clothes.

The word dhoti is also used to mean a woman's inexpensive workaday **sari.**

Less than the dhoti is the gamcha, a scrap of cloth used as a breech clout or a towel.

DHRUV *n* Hindi
One of the two geo-poles.

Dhruvya: polar.

Dhruvtara: the pole star. (For the 'pointers' *see* Rishi).

Dhruv or *disha suchak:* pole, or direction, indicator – a magnetic compass. The story of Prince Dhruva is told in one of the **Puranas:** after a long and greatly respected rule, on his death he was placed in the heavens as the pole star, ever after to be looked up to and to be a guide for all men.

DIGIT *n* English

This word in its sense of a finger or toe, particularly a pointing finger, is linked through the Germanic tongues and Old English, to the Sanskrit syllable, dik/dig, direction. *See* Dekko.

DIKSHA *n* Hindi

Initiation, consecration (*see* Janeu). *Dikshit:* an initiate (e.g., to an order of **sadhus**). A **brahman** subcaste name (often anglicised to Dixit: amongst brahmans, the Dikshits, originating from the Kanauj district of eastern **UP**, are considered to be somewhat superior.

DIL *n* Urdu

The heart : also the soul or spirit.

Dilkhush (adj): pleasing to the heart, attractive, charming. A frequent name for a house or a garden: for which the routine English translation is Heart's Ease.

DĪN/DEEN *n* Urdu

Religion, particularly that of Islam. A cry, especially a war cry, in support of the faith. A strict adherence to the shariah.

Din-i-illahi: the divine faith, the religion propounded by the Emperor Akbar, composed of elements from Islam, Hinduism and Christianity. It did not long survive the Emperor's death.

Din/deen in Hindi has the meaning of the poor, the humble. Hence the epithets for Lord **Krishna** (often used as personal names, particularly by Lalas – **Baniyas**): Din Dayal (Provider for the humble) and Deena Nath (Lord, or Protector, of the poor).

Deen Bandhu: Friend of the Poor. A title conferred on the Englishman, the Rev. Charles Andrews, by Mahatma Gandhi. C.F. Andrews, one-time professor of St. Stephens College, Delhi, was a supporter of the Mahatma of many years standing from their days in South Africa.

C.P. Andrews is commemorated in the name of a residential area of New Delhi, Andrews Ganj.

Din: Hindi a day.

DINGI *n* Hindi

A small boat, the equivalent of a dinghy. The English word comes from the Hindi, which itself comes from the **Sanskrit** meaning of a trough.

DIR (D.I.R.)

Defence of India Rules: issued under the Defence of India Act, 1962, *see also* MISA.

DISTRICT

The basic administrative unit of a state government in the countryside, under the charge of a Collector, or Deputy Commissioner (*see* Presidencies). Other traditional officers in the headquarters will include the District Magistrate (the office may be combined with that of the Collector), the Civil Surgeon (Chief Medical officer) and the Superintendent of Police. There will be a hospital, courts and, probably, a jail. In the Urdu of administration, the district is known as zila. From the mid-19th century in the newly acquired **Punjab**, the British recognised for administration the zail, under a tribal leader, the zaildar. A group of villages whose inhabitants were thought to have had an ethnic affinity, perhaps with a common ancestor.

See Collector, Parganah, Taluk.

General Police District: see Range.

DIVA/DIYA *n* Hindi
"God is Light".
The oil lamp unchanged in shape since at least the time of the **Indus Valley Civilisation**.
A small open cup of baked clay, with a lip for the wick: still used today for **Hindu** religious ceremonies.
When alight, the diya may be referred to as a deepak or deep. The wick should be home-made from wisps of raw cotton. (Owners of tall buildings in New Delhi often fancifully name their expensive and sun-blocking constructions 'deep': e.g. '**Akash Deep**' – light of the sky.) The multi-tiered, many wick'd tall, free standing temple lamps from the south, made of brass, bronze or even silver, are termed deepam: these are particularly used in the worship of **Lakshmi**.

The word diya and its connection with light, is linked to the **Sanskrit** and Hindi word for the deity, **deva**: the divine flame that illuminates the world. In Urdu, a similar lamp is the chiraagh, from Persian.

DIVĀLI/DEEPĀVALI *n* Hindi
See Diva. Deepavali (**Sanskrit**: line of lights). **Hindu** festival of lights and good cheer occurring on the dark night of no moon; preceding the amavasya (*see* Purnima) following **Dussehra**: (October or November). While a major holiday all over India, its significance in one part of the subcontinent is not that in another.

To the north, the myriad lights, fireworks and redecorated houses – Hindu homes have their annual refurbishing just before Divali – are the same as those in the city of Ayodhya (*see* Oudh) which welcomed the return of Raja Lord **Ram** and his wife, Sita, after fourteen years of exile. The lights and urban night-long cacophony of crashes and bangs are no less in honour of **Lakshmi**, who, after prayers to **Ganesh**, is particularly worshipped on Divali night. To those homes with lights the Goddess will bring good fortune throughout the coming year. New household utensils may be bought (strictly, this should be done on the previous day, dhanteras, the thirteenth day. Dhan – wealth, a reference to Laxmi). The **Vaisiya**, the trading community, open fresh account books, for to them Divali marks the beginning of a new year. For a prosperous twelve months to come, business must be done on the New Year's day: although a public holiday, most shops are open. Even the stock and commodity exchanges operate for a while in the evening for token trading. Although gambling is never socially respectable, on Divali day it almost achieves acceptability: good luck then is taken as an index of forthcoming commercial profit. The **bazaar halwais** expand their shops into the roadways and put on special displays, tier upon tier of sweets, for on Divali morning, friends and families give each other presents, especially decorated boxes of sweetmeats, and perhaps toys for the children, for above all, the day is a joyous and happy family occasion. **Sikh gurdwaras** may be out-lined with lights on Divali evening to commemorate the anniversary day of 1620 when the sixth **Guru**, Hargobind, was released from seven years' imprisonment in Gwalior Fort, by the Emperor Jehangir. Divali for the **Jains** is celebrated as the anniversary of the day (said to have been in 527 BC) on which their spiritual leader, Lord Mahavira, attained **nirvan**. Bengali Hindus have little concern with Lord Ram and with them, Lakshmi was especially worshipped fourteen days earlier, on the day of the full moon following Dussehra. For eastern India, the day is **Kali Puja**, devoted to worship of the Mother Goddess, consort of Lord **Shiva** in his role of the Destroyer. The fireworks re-create the battle of the Goddess against demons.

For those of the south, the story is different again. Here the day is Deepavali, one day earlier, honouring Lord **Vishnu** not in the form of Ram (Lord Ram's greatest triumph was the destruction of a southern ruler), but as **Krishna** at his moment of victory over the demon Narakasura. The celebrations begin before dawn: new clothes are put on and a social custom is that young brides with their husbands, return to their parents' home for the day. But **Tamil** Nadu does have a close connection with the all-India Divali festivities, for a small town in the state, Sivakasi, is the fireworks and matchstick capital of the country.

The two days following Divali (sometimes the second and third, the calculation is lunar) are also festivals. The first honours Vishvakarma, a deity mentioned in the **Puranas** as the mechanic of the gods, the master craftsman, the maker of special chariots and ornaments: he has been likened to the Roman God Vulcan. In north India, **mistri** (mechanics) of all skills offer worship in his name to their tools and take a holiday. It is hard to get a vehicle repaired or even a puncture mended on Vishvakarma day. But in the south, the worship of the tools of one's trade is more usual on Vijayadashmi (*see* Dussehra) and in eastern India Vishvakarma Puja normally fall some three weeks before Dussehra.

The second day following Divali is Bhai Duj: Brother Day (duj: second day of a lunar forthnight): a celebration in which sisters especially honour their brothers, particularly by applying the tilak (*see* Tika) to the boys' foreheads. One story is that **Yama** has promised long life to those who carry the tilak on this day.

DIWĀN//DEWĀN *n* Urdu
A word with a number of meanings and shades of meaning. In the original Arabic, a collection of papers, a register, particularly when relating to state revenues. From there to the revenue itself and to the revenue officials. (The French douane, the customs, is the same word.) A court of revenue, the benches in the court, cushioned benches: whence the English divan (also ottoman, i.e. from Turkey). Any court of government authority. In India, diwan may have the meanings of: chief minister in a **princely** state: sometimes, and more correctly, finance minister. Royal audience chamber: Diwan-i-Am, Hall of

Public Audience: (the term am is from Arabic, meaning the mass of people, and not from the ambi of Old Persian which in today's Hindi has become aam, the mango. Aam admi, the common man). Diwan-i-Khas, Hall of Special, or Private Audience: for those of high position. In *Mogul* days, the equivalent of a Ministry, a government office, e.g. Diwan-i-Mamalik: Department of Civil Justice. A collection of poems in one volume: particularly the total work of a poet. In **Sikhism**: a religious congregation. Hindu and Sikh personal name.

Diwani: state revenue. A civil, as opposed to criminal, law court. It was following the Battle of Buxar (October 1764) that the British obtained the right to collect taxes on behalf of the Emperor.

Diwan Bahadur: title of honour, *See* Bahadur. *See also* Nizam.

DŌAB *n* Urdu
Lit. two waters. Land between two rivers, as between the **Ganga** and **Yamuna**.

DOCTRINE OF LAPSE
A British extension to a **Mogul** principle that the succession to an Indian ruler was not valid until recognised by the suzerain power. Introduced earlier, but firmly applied only by Lord Dalhousie (Governor-General 1848-56), the doctrine

asserted that on the death of a ruler without legitimate natural heir, his state could be annexed to **British India**: the throne was not always allowed to pass to an adopted son. The doctrine was never enforced on the ancient dynasties, but only on seven states whose rulers in some way owed their position to British power; it was abandoned after the 1857 uprising, to which it had certainly been a contributory cause, engendering as it did, a feeling of outrage and insecurity amongst the princes.

DŌGRAS *n*
Hill **Rajputs**, a people strong in **Hindu** orthodoxy and claiming descent from the moon, to be found mostly in the Jammu region of the state of Jammu & Kashmir: their Hindi-based regional language being Dogri. It was a Dogra governor of Jammu & Kashmir on behalf of Ranjit Singh, the **Sikh** king of the Punjab (*see* Sher), who in 1846 became the first of the ruling **princely** dynasty of the state (until 1947), being charged by the British one million pounds sterling for the privilege, later reduced to £ 750,000. The inhabitants were not consulted and neither they nor some Britons approved. From this transaction of 1846, it followed in August 1947, Kashmir was not part of **British India,** so the the northern limit of the newly devised frontier between India and Pakistan was the Jammu & Kashmir border.

DŌKMA/DAKAMA *n* Old Persian
A squat circular tower, a 'tower of silence', traditionally used in western India by **Parsis** for the disposal of their dead. A body is left in one of many receptacles on the top of the tower by white–clad attendants accompanied by a white dog, who alone are permitted to enter (the dog, it is said, will give a sign if by mischance the body is not, in fact, dead. It can be that the dog will see the body in the building where the death occurred). On the tower, the flesh is stripped by birds, particularly vultures and in due course, the bones are placed in the central well. Dokmas are used because of a desire to pollute neither earth nor fire. No connection of course, but the vulture population of India is rapidly declining: research seems to have established that the cause may be the consumption of bodies of cattle which have received vetrinary injections inimical to birds. To prevent their possible extinetion a captive breeding centre for vultures has been set up in Haryana with at least some success. From 2006 the use of the drug, diclofenae, has been banned. In areas other than western India Parsis bury their dead.

DŌMS *n* Hindi
Members of a class of **dalits** who perform such services as removing carrion and dead bodies for cremation. Traditionally employed as public executioners and as attendants at

cremation grounds. Doms are also known as village level musicians and entertainers. One of the number of Indian tribal groups suggested as the forefathers of the Romany gypsies of Europe. (Some find the similarity between Dom and Rom significant – although the o in Dom has a long pronunciation.) The English word rum, in the sense of odd or strange, probably derives from dom/rom, a gypsy.

*Dom **Raja**:* honorific accorded to the hereditary chief of the Dom family, the custodians of the cremation **ghats** at **Varanasi**. He is reputed to be a very wealthy man since all who require fire for lighting a pyre from the sacred agni **kund** maintained by him must pay a fee.

DOOLALLY
British soldiers' slang for a mental disturbance, insanity. From Deolali (now Devlali), the military **station** on the **ghats** above Bombay where those due for repatriation on medical grounds awaited the troopship.

Doolally tap: also insanity. From the soldiers' pretended belief that just in case he who was to be sent home on mental grounds was malingering, a sergeant-major in the Deolali British Military Hospital 'tapped' the patient smartly on the head, so as to effect an undoubted brain injury. A more probable derivation is from the Hindi tap, meaning fever.

DORJI/DORGEE *n* Tibetan
A thunderbolt. Also the small symbolic representation, usually of brass or copper (vajra in Hindi). As an icon the dorji is said to represent the sudden illumination of the mind and spirit when struck by understanding of the Buddhist Truth.

Darjeeling: the name of this **hill station** of West Bengal is an anglicism from dorglin, place of thunderbolts.

DŌSA *n* Tamil
One of the breads of the south. Rice and dal flours, self fermented, in shape like a thin **chapati,** perhaps twelve inches or more in diameter. Cooked on a flat hot-plate so that one side is crisp and golden. Often served folded over with a vegetable filling (*see also* Idli).

DOSHA *n* Hindi
Lit. disorder. In Indian medicine (*see* Ayurveda) the humours or elements of the human body: vata (air), pitta (fire), kapha (earth). For good health, these must be kept in balance. An excess of one leads to disease.

DŌSOOTI/DŌSUTI *n* Hindi
Lit. dõ **sutra** – two threads (twill, the English textile is made in the same way). A coarse strong cloth, usually plain white, woven with double threads.

DOWRY *n* English

Dahez in Urdu (Hindustani)

In most of nature a father after procreation has no role and may even savage his children, but the human child is helpless for so long that the mother needs support from either the father or the tribe. If the father has the job a way has to be found to bind him to the mother for a period of years. Hence the world over of a ceremony of marriage: buttressed in India by the understanding that for a man without a wife, his **shakti** is incomplete (but a lifelong vowed celibate can be accepted and honoured on a spiritual plane). For the tribe to maintain itself and prosper the members cannot be permitted an entirely free choice of partners, instead these are selected by the elders if possible to enhance group (**biradhari**), or family, status (hypergamy) perhaps with little consideration for individual romantic feelings. This has been the position in Asia – and in Europe at the same level – for many millennia and generally still maintains in India. In early days in elitist families in the case of a desirable bride, gifts could be given to her family or to the girl herself to be her property (stridhan), but in a case of the girl "marrying up" the gifts might have to be the other way. This has become the custom today, right across the social spectrum without necessarily any "marrying-up", Hindu, Muslim and even Christian. (But in traditional Islamic culture, in marriage the

husband contracts to dower his wife, the mahr). So much so that the birth of a girl can be seen as a burden, leading in Rajasthan and elsewhere, to infanticide. An index to this feeling can be seen in a childrens' hospital ward where boys will probably outnumber girls. Although baby girls worldwide are tougher than boys, here infant mortality figures show that more girls die than boys. A needy mother putting a new-born girl "to sleep" may not be unprincipled, she has to consider the welfare of siblings. A Punjabi saying has it "Bringing up a daughter is like watering a neighbour's plant.

The inequality is now usually ascribed to foetal sex determination, but this is not entirely so. Figures from the 1836 Delhi City census.
show :

Muslim children Boys 10098
                 Girls 8890
Hindu children Boys 9866
                 Girls 7987

Many recognise that near obligatory dowry payments to the boy's family are objectionable: they are legally banned under the Dowry Prohibition Act of 1961. A few notices seeking marriage partners do specify "no dowry", but generally the practice continues as the norm, sometimes leading to tragedy for the bride. Each equally needs the other, but as elsewhere, the male has so dominated social culture that in practice the female may have to buy a mate. Social opinion, supported by demography, will perhaps effect a change. But the 2001 census figures have been a shock : culture can transcend income. In the age group 0 - 6 years, in prosperous Punjab there were 796 girls to 1000 boys, the widest gap in India. (Outlook Nov. 15, 2001.) One cause being the custom of bridegroom price descending to lower social levels. If the trend continues, it must be at some stage boys will have to bid for the girls.

For child marriage (see Sarda) dowry is not usually paid. A reason for the continuation of the illegal practice.

DRAGON KINGDOM

The Land of the Thunder Dragon, Druk Yul, the local name for the eastern **Himalaya** kingdom of Bhutan, the population being Drukpas people of the Dragon (the original inhabitants are the Lepchas, but now they are a minority in a number of other peoples of the Mongolian race, particularly the Nepalese and the Tibetans). Bhutan as a word probably comes from the Hindi **Bhotiya**, a noun and adjective loosely applied to mean the Himalayan frontier region.

DRAVIDIA *n*

An English form of the **Sanskrit** name, Dravida, for a kingdom in south India of the first millenium AD. It is only in the last one hundred years that Dravidia has come to mean the south as a whole, peninsular India, bounded to east and west by the sea. The part of southern India culturally influenced but not physically occupied by the Aryans (*see* Arya.). The limit of the Gangetic catchment area, the Vindhya Hills (Vindhyachal in Hindi: the hunting region, i.e. full of game animals) running approximately along latitude 23°N, is generally considered to mark the northern boundary. But the language divide from the north is further south, on the middle reaches of the River Godavari. Another sign of the divide is the price in a wayside stall of a cup of tea: unlike that in the north to the south it can exceed that for a cup of coffee.

Dravidian: noun and adjective, Dravir in Hindi. The Dravidians were the inhabitants of much of the Indian subcontinent before the Aryan invasion (in the opinion of some anthropologists, the Dravidians themselves entered India from outside in pre-historic times, perhaps from lands east of the Mediterranean, submerging earlier Austric inhabitants). In general, the people of the south, but unassimilated groups of Dravidians, some of the **adivasi** tribes, still remain in the northern part of India. The Dravidian languages have no natural affinity with the speech of the north, but many linguists affirm that they were current in the north long before the arrival of any form of Sanskrit. Today, of course, all have absorbed Sanskrit words (Sanskrit also it is said, has been influenced by Dravidian languages). In the **bazaars** of northern India, any southerner is likely to be termed a Madrasi. (Correctly and politely, the description would be dakkhani, a southerner.)

DRUMSTICK *n* English
An anglicism, particularly in the south, for the long (two feet or more), thin, but rigid as a drumstick, seed pod of a small feathery tree (*Moringa oleifera* – moringa is from Tamil meaning oil bearing). The pods are cooked as a vegetable and both the seed nuts and the roots yield a light oil; traditionally used by watchmakers under the name ben oil. Oil from the roots is said to have a pungency similar to horseradish. In parts of the south, the seed sticks are alleged to be abortifacient. In northern **bazaars** the green pods have the name phali. Also Sahjim.

DRY DAY
A day on which, by state government order, no alcoholic liquor may be sold by licensed outlets.

DUM DUM
A suburb of Kolkata, which gave its name to the soft-nosed expanding bullets, made in the **arsenal** there.

Designed by the British for use against the tribesmen on the north-west frontier, for whom, it was said, the jacketed bullet fired from the Lee-Metford rifle had insufficient stopping power. On hitting a bone, the dum-dum bullet flattened and the exit hole in the body could be the size of a man's fist: the use of such bullets in warfare was outlawed by the International Hague Conference of 1898. Earlier, as the base depot of the **East India Company's** Bengal Artillery, the **Cantonment** was notorious for Dum Dum fever (now known as **kala** azar). Today, the location of Kolkata's airport.

DŪN/DOON *n* Hindi
A valley between the main **Himalaya** range and the parallel line of hills, the Sivaliks, e.g. the Dun Valley, with the town of Dehra Dun (lit. the camp valley. *See* Dera.)

DUNGAREE *n*
This English word for strong cotton working overalls has an Indian origin in that dungaree cloth, the equivalent of today's denim or jean, was listed from the 17th century amongst the **East India Company's** exports from Bombay where, it has been suggested, a coarse variety of the material had a use as sailcloth: no textile called dungaree is made today. The name probably came from a low rocky hill and village on Bombay Harbour, soon to be the site of Fort Dungaree/Dongri, demolished in

1769 and replaced by Fort George, again to be demolished in its turn: but the name lives on as a Mumbai street, Dongri Lane.

DŪPATTA/DŌPATTA *n* Hindi
Lit. two leaves, or two widths. Anything from a large shawl to no more than a narrow scarf; the material may be thick and embroidered or so fine and glistening yet so transparent as to merit the epithet shabnam, morning dew. Traditionally worn by **Hindu** ladies, the dupatta was adopted by Muslims; now it is particularly popular in the **Punjab** (and by girl students all over India) as an extra chest covering or flung over the head, or to cover the face as a veil (ghunghat). Also known as a chunni. The literal meaning stems from the days when ladies were more secluded than now and required a robust cover (two leaves, or thicknesses, or double width, of cloth) between themselves and a casual male gaze. The dupatta can also be worn by men, although not common today; a band of folded cloth falling back and front from one shoulder. In the south, plain white with, perhaps, a gold border.

Some prefer a village name for the dupatta particularly used in central and western India, odhini/orhini (odhna/orhna, to cover – the body). Dating from approximately the same period as the dupatta and introduced for the same reason is the lehnga, a ground sweeping skirt tied at the waist with a tape or cord like the **pyjama**. For fine ladies, in glorious red, lavishly brocaded and embroidered, often using gold thread, **zari**, the lehnga today can be fitting wear for a society wedding.

Somewhat similar to the dupatta is the chunri: a very thin red cloth with speckles. Frequently an offering to a goddess, particularly some aspect of the Mother Goddess, or to a shrine dedicated to a **sati**.

DURAND LINE *n*
Following the advance into the **Punjab** in 1849, **British India** and Afghanistan shared a rather vague common border. In 1893, Sir Mortimer Durand, then Foreign Secretary in the Government of India, negotiated with the Afghans, and a firm frontier, the Durand Line, was agreed upon: now, of course, the frontier between Pakistan and Afghanistan. Sir Mortimer is probably better remembered today as the donor of a trophy for an all-India football tournament, the Durand Cup: first held in **Shimla** in 1888 and still competed for annually, but now in Delhi.

DURBĀR/DARBĀR *n* Urdu
In very old Persian, simply a door, an open door. To the Moguls, the court of a prince: a ruler making himself personally accessible to receive petitions from any of his subjects. The concept of this duty

of a king is equally Hindu. A levee: an audience reception in a **princely** state. The government of a princely state. Nowadays perhaps, the receipt by a senior government official at a stated time, of complaints from the public: probably termed a **janta**, or people's durbar.

In a military unit, a meeting of all officers and men, with the Commanding Officer in the chair, in which matters of domestic concern can be explained and problems discussed.

The Great Durbar, in British writing, usually refers either to that held by Lord Curzon in 1903, or that staged with even more glitter and pomp, by the King Emperor, George V, in 1911: both in Delhi. It was at this later durbar that the King announced the transfer of the capital from Calcutta to Delhi (*see* Patliputra). The following night, the P & 0 liner, the Delhi, ran aground on the African coast of the Straits of Gibralter. Foundation stones for Imperial Delhi' were laid by the King and Queen in north Delhi, later to be moved and relaid under the name commem-orative stones some six miles – in a straight line—to the south. Mischance continued with the issue of a commemorative silver **rupee** coin. The obverse showed the King wearing the Collar of the **Star** of the Indian Empire. Some alleged that an elephant on the Collar was in fact a pig – certainly

the animal's trunk was porcine – and an insult to **Islam**. The coin was hastily withdrawn. A relic of this durbar is still in service: in London's Buckingham Palace, a portion from the main red and gold pavilion or **shamiana**, forms a canopy over the thrones in the royal ballroom. No less a relic, of course, is the Crown of India, worn only in India by the King Emperor. The idea of the change was not new; as far back as 1829, the then Governor-General, Lord Bentinck, described the Agra-Delhi region with its monuments and stones of past and future glory, as the brightest jewel of his crown, where the Supreme Council ought to sit. Lord Bentinck liked the image, in 1814, when he was, through a quirk of the strategy against Napoleon, administrator of Sicily, he had reported that island as having the potential of being "after Ireland, the brightest jewel in the British crown". An earlier Delhi Durbar was that of 1877 – officialy designated the Imperial Assemblage – at which the princes paid homage to Queen Victoria (represented by her **Viceroy**, Lord Lytton) on her assumption in the previous year of the title Empress of India (Kaisar-i-Hind), thereby formally creating the British Indian Empire. The Urdu title, Kaisar-i-Hind came from the Latin Caesar, thence to Arabic and Persian. In Russian, **Caesar** became Tsar. The Sultans of Turkey once claimed the title **Kaisar-i-Rum** – Emperor of Rome. **Between** 1901 and 1939 that durbar date was celebrated with military parades (see Proclamation day). The final Imperial Durbar was held in Delhi's Red Fort by the then Prince of Wales in 1922. Imperial durbars were considered for both Edward VIII and George VI, but in one case the Abdication and in the other, World War II prevented any firm planning. (An imperial portrait of King George VI with the Viceroy's House, New Delhi, as background was commissioned from the artist, Gerald Kelly – later. Sir Gerald, in 1938.)

Durbari: one attending a durbar, a courtier, a sycophant: often used pejoratively.

Durbar Sahib: particularly a Sikh title for the Golden Temple complex of Amritsar (*see* Amrit).

In London, the Durbar Court is in the old India Office building in Whitehall (now refurbished and part of the Foreign & Commonwealth Office) designed for the holding receptions with Indian notables. Its first use was for a ball for the Sultan of Turkey in 1867. A curiosity of a nearby room, once occupied by the Secretary of State, was that it had two identical doors side by side so that two visiting princes of equal status could enter, neither having to give precedence to the other. (But see Right Hand Left Hand.) The building contains a number of artefacts retrieved from the offices of the **East India Company** in the City.

The barren amphitheare of the 1911 Durbar still exists and a small portion has been converted to a necropolis of the **Raj**. George V is there with four of his Viceroys and two Council Members. A visitor's fancy may evoke Shelley's Egyptian desert vision of 1818 "My name is Ozymandias, king of kings; Look on my works, ye mighty, and despair."

DUREE/DARI/DURI *n* Urdu
The the original meaning of the word was of, or by, the door (dar – a door. Persian. A current Western spelling, dhurrie, does not represent any Indian pronunciation of the noun). A cotton woven floor drugget or mat, almost any size, although a very large duree may be termed a shatranj unlike with a carpet, there is no backing, so normally both sides are the same. (shatranji chess player, Hindi.) The traditional use was as an individual sleeping mat on the ground or to cushion the rough strings of a *charpai*, cum cover in which to roll bedding during the day, or for a journey (*see* Bistar). In British days, the weaving of durees became a jail industry, and it was then that the size increased, sometimes sufficiently for one to carpet a large room. These day's durees made for export often have a wool mix and the talented designers may well have had an art-school training.

DURGA PŪJA *n* Hindi
Worship of the Mother Goddess, Durga, also known as Mahadevi (the Great Goddess) Mahashakti or just Devi, consort of Lord **Shiva** and patroness deity of Bengal (*see* Kali; Shakti): but also regarded by many with both the familiarity and the respect accorded to a mother or sister. In Bengal particularly, the Goddess also has the name Aparajita – the invincible one. The period of the annual visit of the Goddess to the plains, the married daughter visiting her parents' home, is celebrated in Bengal and by **Hindu** Bengalis wherever they may be. For them, the chief festival of the year, lasting from the seventh to the tenth day of the eleven days of the northern **Dussehra**: but in fact, in this season much of Bengal is on holiday for more than the four days (*see also* Puja). As with the story of **Ram** and his fight against Ravan, so the days of Durga Puja personify the fight of good against evil: the ten-armed Goddess – each hand holding a weapon – on her lion **vahan** fighting to victory over evil in the form of Mahisha/Mahishura, a buffalo actually encapsulating a demon giant, Sambha.

As Durga left Lord **Shiva** for a few days to visit her father's home, so today in Bengal married daughters leave their husbands and visit their parents for the annual festival.

Wherever groups of Bengalis find themselves, committees are formed months ahead to plan and collect funds for the celebration (Kolkata has at least two thousand such groups, Delhi about two hundred): neighbourhood **puja pandals** are constructed with a shrine for the goddess – usually an elaborate tableau of Durga slaying the demon, and of the figures of **Lakshmi**, **Saraswati**, **Ganesh** and **Kartikeya** – and probably a stage for cultural programmes and Bengali film screenings, often lasting the whole night. Each committee is in competition with others to provide the most lavish spectacle.

The images (pratima/protima in Hindi and Bengali) of the Goddess and of her children who flank her on each side, Kartikeya and Saraswati on her left and Ganesh and Lakshmi on her right, are believed to come alive on the sasthi (the sixth day of the moon: *see* Calendars), when the drummers with dancers bearing smoking clay incense pots, one in each hand and, if skillful, perhaps one clenched in the teeth as well, perform **arati** to honour her divine presence. The pratima are made afresh for each celebration, usually by professionals using sun-dried clay – there is a story that a small portion of soil from close to a prostitute's doorstep must go into the mixture: since all men entering cast aside virtue, the ground by the threshold must be rich in the commodity. In the final ceremony of the period, at sunset on Bijoydashami day (*see* Dussehra), the Goddess in all her finery and tinsel is taken to a river or **tank** (the visajan, the sending away, the immersion) and following **arati** to the accompaniment of drums, cymbals and dancers, there to dissolve, to be one with the water and to rejoin Lord Shiva on **Kailas**. For the Bengali, it is only then, at the moment of immersion, that the victory (vijay/bijoy) is complete and the celebration of Bijoydashmi can begin. Children greet their parents and friends each other, perhaps exchanging gifts of sweets. Some will buy a blue roller bird so that it may be released to fly to Lord Shiva with the news that his wife is on the way home. Possibly, adults, if on no other day of the year, will take a glass of bhang (*see* Indian Hemp), termed siddha.

Bijoya: victory. Particularly at this festival time, a title used by Bengali Hindus for their patronness deity. Durga/durg can mean a fort, especially in western India.

DŪRWAN *n* Urdu

A gatekeeper, particularly in eastern India. But their day is perhaps almost over, at least in the cities, for the elderly, drowsy and throat-clearing durwans and **chowkidars** are being replaced by young English-termed, uniformed security guards.

DURZI/DARZI *n* Urdu

A tailor. Frequently described as Tailor Master and addressed as Masterji. (A male school teacher, particularly in a rural situation, may also be dignified by the title Master/Masterji, even after retirement. The distinction may also be accorded to a village postmaster).

DUSSEHRA/DASSERAH *n* Hindi

Lit. tenth day. The tenth climactic day of the major Hindu festival of the year: an eleven day period from the new moon day of the Hindu month of Aswin (September or October). For nine days and nights (**Navratri**), far from his kingdom and separated from Sita, his wife. Lord **Ram** (*see* Ramayana) fasted and prayed to the Mother Goddess for strength (*see* Shakti) to overcome his southern enemy. King Ravan; but **Devi** was sleeping. Only on the tenth day (Dussehra/Vijayadashmi/ Bijoya-dashami) does the Goddess awake and grant to the Lord the power he is seeking: so ensuring his victory, that of good over evil. In eastern India and in Nepal, the festival is less concerned with the story of Ram and is more in honour of the Mother Goddess herself. In Bengal, and by Bengalis everywhere, it is celebrated with great enthusiasm under the name **Durga Puja.** In Nepal, where the festival may be referred to as Dashain, and in the **Himalaya** generally, animal sacrifice (balidan) is usual on Vijayadashami and the worship of the tools of one's trade - his weapons by the soldier, his vehicle by the truck driver. Tools and valuable possessions are also worshipped on this day in south India.

For the south, Vijayadashami is chiefly the festival of **Saraswati**, the Goddess of learning, the day on which young children particularly, seek her blessings and have their first taste of formal education – although a holiday, primary teachers attend school and make-believe classes may be held. In a temple students may lay their pens before an image of Saraswati. In Karnataka (*see* Carnatic), especially in Mysore, the goddess Durga is worshipped in great splendour – when Mysore was a princely state, it was believed that she was incarnate in the person of the ruling Maharaja during the period. The very name of the city, Mysore, derives from the Goddess' greatest triumph, over the evil buffalo, Mahishura.

In the north, the story of Ram as told in the *Ramayana*, from his exile, his victory over King Ravan of Lanka on his return to his kingdom, is unfolded in an eleven-night serial drama, Ram **Lila**; performed on thousands of stages in villages and cities, both by local amateurs and by professional groups known as mandalis (*see* Mandal). In addition to the day itself as a holiday, Dussehra as a word can mean the crowning event at major centres of the Ram Lila programme: the setting alight of gigantic effigies of King Ravan and his two brothers by fiery arrows from Lord Ram. The eleventh night of the festival, Bharat Milap, celebrates the return of Ram to his kingdom after the fourteen years of exile and his joyful reunion with prince Bharat, his younger brother, who acted as king in his absence. *See also* Divali.

Ganga Dussehra: see Ganga.

DYARCHY *n*
Rule by two, a term from the early Roman Empire. (The current English spelling, diarchy, is rarely used in India.) Usually a reference to the situation following the Government of India Act, 1919, of the British Parliament. The opposite side of the coin to the Rowlatt Acts (*see* MISA). The first hesitant devolution of power to Indian hands, whereby in the **provinces** (*see* Presidencies) and Burma, a limited but genuine system of responsible parliamentary government came into being with elected members and ministers (the voters were property owners). The ministers held such portfolios as health, education and agriculture (transferred subjects), while the frame of government, police, law and order, finance, remained under

the control of the Governor and his Executive Council, of which half the members had to be elected members of the legislature. (It was under this Act that in 1922 Jawaharlal Nehru was offered the position of Education Minister for United Provinces. He would not support the British and refused the offer). At the Centre, of the **Viceroy**'s Executive Council of eight members (including the Viceroy and the Commander-in-Chief), three had to be Indian. A parliament with two chambers and a majority of elected members was set up in Delhi, but overriding powers remained with the Viceroy, In addition, the princes were given a parliament of their own, the Chamber of Princes. (By 1919, the building plans for official Imperial Delhi had been finalised, so that the parliament buildings had to be added on one side of the otherwise symmetrical design, seemingly in the shadow of the bureaucrat-filled Secretariat blocks.) Dominion status, i.e. the same as enjoyed by the self-governing countries of Australia, Canada, New Zealand and South Africa, was promised as the object of British Government policy (pre-1931, the Dominions really had only internal self-government, otherwise they were subject to Westminster). Opening the new assembly in 1922, the Duke of Connaught, representing the King, said that the new reforms were the beginnings of **swaraj** (the Hindi word was used) within the Empire. Amongst Britons in India, the changes were dubbed the Montford reforms – a combination of the names of the London Secretary of State for India and of the Viceroy, Edwin Montagu and Lord Chelmsford. (It was Montagu who gave India unofficial Dominion status by including her in the Paris Peace Conference following World War I so that she became a founder member of the League of Nations.) That the assembly did have some clout was demonstrated in the early 1920s when Britain, and not as earlier, India, was required to pay for Indian forces used overseas for Imperial purposes. (*See* Army in India.)

The Government of India Act, 1935 went further along the same road and gave real powers to provincial governments to order their own affairs; with the Congress government coming to power in nine provinces – the reverse of the intended purpose of its architects, the British Conservative Party. British officials unwilling to accept service under elected ministers were sanctioned terms more favourable than normal if they wished to take premature retirement. *See also* Section 93 Provinces.

The 1935 Act set up the Federal court in Delhi with bewigged justices. No longer would there be appeals to the privy council in London. In 1950 the Federal court became the supreme court, without bewigged justices.

To complete the story. With a general election in 1946 (still with the 1919 limited franchise the Central Legislature (two houses) continued until Independence, when under the British Act as promised in 1942 by Sir Stafford Cripps and Churchill's war-time government, it became the Constituent Assembly (one house) and the Dominion Supreme Parliament. (Some find a clear distinction between the House sitting to fulfil each of the two functions). This position acquired Indian Statutory authority (again two Houses) on the formation of the Republic in January 1951. In practice, the system was then no more genuinely federal than it had been under the British.

DZO *n* Tibetan
Hybrid between a **yak** and a domestic cow.

EAR CLEANER, THE

An urban itinerant professional gentleman identified by his small red **puggri** into which are tucked his instruments: tweezers, probes and buds of cotton wool on wooden splints. He will attend his clients anywhere, on the roadside in the **bazaar**, in the shade of a park tree, or at places of work or homes: peering and probing into ears for wax and producing for inspection the evidence of his skill. But as with the providers of other personal services in the bazaar, such as the **bihisti** and the **maleesh wala**, public demand is no longer what it was and the trade of the kan mailiya/kan bhedi – the ear cleaner – seems to be a dying one.

EAST INDIA COMPANY

It began in 1600 with a group of two hundred London merchants, the London East India Company, being given, by Elizabeth of England, a charter to trade with the East Indies (roughly the region of today's Indonesia). A time when the world over it was considered perfectly normal for a powerful people to enter and to take over the land of those less

so. The first known Englishman to see India was Thomas Stevens, a Jesuit priest in the Portuguese service in Goa who arrived in 1579 and lived there 40 years. It is said that his letters to his father, a London merchant, aroused the interest in the East that led to the founding of the Company. It was to be eight years before a Company ship actually reached India, at Surat in Gujarat, thus defying a Papal Bull of 1502 appointing the King of Portugal 'Lord of the Navigation, Conquest and Trade of Ethiopia, Arabia, Persia and India'. (In their turn, the London merchants were to claim that they alone had the monopoly of trade with India and whenever possible, took punitive action against those they termed interlopers, those trading without Company authority.) The first **factory** was set up in Surat in 1612. In 1668 King Charles II leased Bombay Island (until then a Crown Colony with a royal governor: Charles had received it as part of the dowry of his Portuguese wife) to the Company in return for a loan and a rental of £10 per annum. Twenty years later, at least a foothold had been gained in Bengal. In 1698, a rival company, the English East India Company, was formed: the two combining eleven years later under the little-used title 'The United Company of Merchants of England Trading to the East Indies'. Later to be semi-formally styled 'The Honourable East India Company' or HEIC. The Company's military power over eastern India became

141

absolute following Clive's victory at Plassey in Bengal in 1757. (The field of Plassey is still marked at today's Palashi village by a British memorial.) Political and financial and, in fact, political, independence resulted from the Treaty of Allahabad eight years later. Following the Battle of Buxar (1764), with the grant by the **Mogul** Emperor of the right to manage and collect the **diwan** on his behalf, cash flow was assured and title to what earlier had been mere usurpation. In effect, without the machinery of administration, what had been grasping commercial concern became the State. The Emperor was to receive an annual payment of about twenty-six **lakhs** of rupees. (By 1857, when payments ceased, the sum was down to about twelve lakhs.) Previously, much of the trading purchases, largely textiles, had had to be financed by bullion imports from England; now these could be paid for with rupees obtained within India. The goods so bought could be sold in London at great advantage, for no compensatory payments had to be made to India. But expenses were high and for much of its existence the Company was close to bankruptcy, although many of its rapacious senior servants in India were making personal fortunes; such profits as there were, came more from the China trade than from India. The Company lost its monopoly in 1813 and by 1833, when its trading functions were abolished commerce had become little more than a method

of remitting funds to Britain (But *see also* Madak.)

After the rebellion of 1857, the inexpediency of the subcontinent being governed by Britain through the managing agency of a chartered company of share-holders, receiving by statute 10.5 per cent on their investment, could be ignored no longer: nevertheless, London required two governments and three Bills in Parliament to effect the change. In 1858, all Company property and authority passed to the British crown (an exception was the share capital). It has to be said that once past the very early days, the powers of the Company in governing India were never absolute nor free from supervision by the Home Government.

The 1773 Regulating Act of Westminster established some rules and in 1784, an official Board of Control was set up in London with authority to receive copies of all despatches to and from India. But to obtain a reply to an enquiry from either London or Calcutta could take up to one year, so in practice officials in India were fairly free to do as they thought fit. That the Company could still be independent was shown in 1844, when the Directors forced the dismissal of the Governor-General, Lord Ellenborough, against the wishes of Queen Victoria and the Board of Control. From 1858, the powers of the Crown concerning the Government of India were exercised through a Secretary of State in the home government (the cost of his establishment was a charge on the revenues of India until 1919 when the salaries of the Secretary and of his political advisors were paid by Britain, but not until 1935 was the full cost of the India Office in London assumed by the home civil service It is said that the proposal for the change was first made by M.A. Jinnah in the Legislative Council in 1913).

The 1853 Charter had no expiry date and the Company itself continued a legal existence from a City of London office: having once controlled all the wealth of the Indies, it was now glad of a government grant of £800 towards expenses. East India House in the City of London was sold and demolished in 1861; a memorial tablet marks the site to this day. The Company was finally wound up in 1874; in accordance with the 1833 Act, shareholders could receive £200 for each £100 of stock held or, alternatively, could accept an offer of an annuity, or further stock. The face value of the original stock, held by approximately 3,500 proprietors, was just short of £6m and the total compensation paid came to about £12.125m, debited to the Government of India. (If, by 1858, it had seemed an anachronism to many that the Government of India should have been run by a commercial company – albeit, at that date with few commercial purposes – elsewhere in the Empire the concept of administering a territory with shareholders in the background was to

continue for many years. The Hudson Bay Company [of Canada], it is true, lost its governing powers in 1860, but the Imperial British East Africa Company carried on until 1894 [Kenya and Uganda]; the Royal Niger Company until 1900 [West Africa]; the British United South Africa Company – until 1923 [Northern and Southern Rhodesia]; and the British North Borneo Chartered Company was superseded only in 1946.)

A popular story even repeated in reputable writings of today, is that the Company, wishing to destroy competition, cut off the thumbs of skilled Bengali weavers. Seemingly, there are a number of reasons to discredit the tale. The only time such brutality could have taken place was towards the end of the 18th century: a period when the Company had plenty of ill-wishers: e.g. the impeachment of Warren Hastings. There is no evidence that the story was seriously aired in Britain, there are no details of time and place in India. The Company was then earning money by exporting fine textiles from India. It is true that manufacturers at home wished to suppress imports of cheap Indian printed calicos, but the methods used were fiscal not butchery.

As a tradition, mutilation of hands an Indian background. In the Mahabharata (*see* Epics) there is the account of Ekalavya, a tribal prince and skilled archer. The hero, Arjun, also an archer and Krishna's non-violent chariot companion and questioner (*see* **Gita**). jealous of Ekalavya's prowess, caused the boy to cut off his own right thumb.

The builders/designers of the Taj Mahal, so a story goes, on completion of the monument, so that it could never be repeated, had their hands maimed by the Emperor.

EAST INDIAMEN *n*
Vessels built for and chartered to the East India Company's Maritime Service (not to be confused with the Company's Bombay Marine Service, the forerunner of the Indian Navy) carrying the Company's trade and servants between Britain and Asia. Their heyday was from about 1770 to the ending of the Company's monopoly of British trade with China in 1833. Built on frigate lines and operated from their base in the huge East India Docks in London, the ships served both naval and mercantile purposes. Their masters were almost princes, entitled to gun salutes and auxiliary naval rank. They, and all the ships' officers, profited from a privilege allowing them to carry a certain amount of cargo on their personal accounts. The lower deck seamen were exempt from impressment by the Royal Navy. But the very magnificence of the Indiamen counted against them as carriers of commerce, for their charges had to be high. The tendency was for private shippers, particularly the Company's servants who preferred to move their large fortunes made in India to the home country by way of trade goods, to evade the monopoly and to send their merchandise to Europe at lower cost by using shipping of other than British nationality.

EKADĀSHI *n* Hindi
One plus ten: for **Hindus**, the eleventh day of each lunar fortnight (*see* Calendars): i.e. the third or fourth day before both the full and new moons. The devout fast on these days (*see* Fasting); days particularly dedicated to the worship of Lord **Vishnu**.

EKKA *n* Hindi
A two-wheeled, single horse drawn passenger vehicle extensively found in **UP**. Lighter and higher off the ground than a **tonga.**

The ace in a pack of cards.

ELAICHI/ELACHI *n* Hindi
The cardamom seed capsule, grown as a plantation crop on the Western **Ghats** of South India and in parts of Bengal. With its pleasant aroma, it is often chewed to complete a good meal, or added to **pan**. The seeds may be used to flavour tea and have uses in Indian medicine and in perfumery. The burra/bara elaichi (large, black and strongly flavoured) is normally used whole in curries – where its beetle-like appearance can cause not a little disquiet to one meeting it on a plate for the first time.

EMERGENCY, THE *n*

The period between June 1975 and March 1977, when the then Prime Minister, Mrs. Indira Gandhi, ruled the country under the emergency powers of the Constitution (as amended by her government) and with the support of the bureaucracy suspended many of the fundamental rights of the citizen. Thus demonstrating that it was possible for a small unprincipled coterie to subvert the frame of the state they had sworn to protect. In the end the group deluded themselves, held and lost a genuine election and democracy returned. Many housewives remember the emergency as the time when labour unrest was firmly put down and when shop-keepers and even small bazaar vegetable sellers, were required to price their goods clearly. Within three years Indira was voted back to power.

During the Emergency, in 1975 the Supreme Court ruled that the government of the day does not have the power to abrogate the fundamental rights given to the citizen by the Constitution.

EPICS *n*

Usually a reference to two **Sanskrit** poems of great length and antiquity, the *Mahabharata* and the **Ramayana**. Accepted by millions of Indians as being both scripture and the early history of their countrymen: tales from these works, absorbed as children, form part of the cultural heritage of all Hindus. The background to the Mahabharata (the title can be translated as The Great Bharatas:

i.e. the great tribe of the Bharatas, *see* **Bharat**), a poem of 1,00,000 verses, is an eighteen-day civil war in which, so it is said, all the people of India took part, on the battlefield of Kurukshetra, about 160 km north of Delhi. (the Kurus were the people of a kingdom in the neighbourhood of Delhi). Many of the stories of this epic contrast rectitude with iniquity and contain discourses and homilies by the semi-divine heroes concerning man's social and religious duty, so that the work is widely accepted as a guide to **dharma**. The famous sermon by Lord **Krishna**, the Bhagavad **Gita**, is part of the *Mahabharata*. While possibly first told in the 3rd century BC, the present form of the poem was reached by 500 AD.

ERI *n* Assamese

A forest silk moth (now also domesticated) found mostly in Assam whose larvae do not require mulberry leaves for food and from which silk is obtained by non-violent means: the moth emerges alive from the cocoon. Unlike that produced by other silk worms, the thread is not a continuous filament, but short lengths of fibre: which are carded and spun in the manner of cotton. The fibre (originally imported from China) is considerably thicker than that from the mulberry-fed worm. The yarn – also known as eri – has a natural cream colour and is slightly more expensive than cultivated silk. Eri as a term is sometimes replaced by endi: a word used by a local people of

Mongolian origin, the Bodo/Boros. *See also* Tasar.

EUROPEAN CEMETERIES

Over the length and breadth of the old India, first the Company (*see* East India Company) and later, the British Government of India, provided the final resting places for their many European servants and their families who died in service. Many of them cut off when very young, as recalled by a Biblical text on a memorial in a Delhi city church, to a bank manager, his wife and five young daughters, 'Their sun is gone down while it was yet day". In old cemeteries, truncated or broken pillars may be seen as grave monuments, indicating lives cut short.) More than one thousand cemeteries, many with headstones and monuments commemorating names famous in British Indian history or connected with well-known events: such as the little group in Meerut Cemetery over the bones of those who died in the opening hours of the sepoy uprising in May 1857 (*see* First War of Independence).

Recalling a more recent mutiny, in Dagshai Cemetery (Shimla Hills), lay buried James Daly of the Connaught Rangers, the Devil's Own, who died by sentence of General Court Martial for his part in a regimental revolt in 1920: an echo of the troubles in far away Ireland. Since that date, no execution by the British army of one of its own soldiers has been carried out (In October 1970 James Daly was returned to his village in

Ireland). The records are now open to public scrutiny and some feel that his defence at the court martial was not what it should have been.) Why are so many Germans named on some British regimental memorials of the later Victorian years? The answer is that they were the remnants of an oddity, the British German Legion – so named by Queen Victoria – raised with a strength of about 8000 men for service in the Crimean War. Later in the 1860s they served in Delhi as the 109th. Regiment of Foot . Later again, they served in South Africa.

Cholera is seen as the great killer, for the stones catalogue the many hazards to European life until almost the end of the **Raj**. The cemeteries were a public charge (non-votable in the latter-day Indian Parliament) until **Independence** in 1947.

Thereafter, the UK government retained an official interest, but with funds for maintenance limited to the sum total of the capital and the interest therefrom, contributed by those who over previous years had endowed a grave monument 'for ever', in most cases with a single payment of Rs. 16.00.

In 2000 the position is that some four hundred once European cemeteries (now open for general Christian burial where needed and space permits) remain the theoretical responsibility of the British, although title to the land is still with the Government of India.

Of the four hundred, most, through voluntary effort by local Christians, are in reasonable condition, but a few are in poor shape. Those cemeteries which could not be kept up at all have been abandoned; in some, nature has taken its course; others, generally in towns, have become public parks. At least one in Delhi, that containing the graves of those who died in the 1857 fighting has been permanently occupied by squatters.

Other official cemeteries in India, largely but not entirely European are those beautifully maintained by the Commonwealth War Graves Commission, twenty-one grounds for Services casualties mainly from World War II (a few graves relate to 1914-18). The major sites such as Delhi and in the north-east, have the Lutyens' Stone of Rememberance. A ten-tons block crafted to mathematical precision carrying the biblical quotation chosen by Kipling "Their name liveth for evermore." On the stone the seemingly flat top is a portion of a sphere 1801 feet 8 ins in diameter, so that the vertical lines if extended would meet at a point that distance above. The cemeteries also have Lutyens', or that designed by his colleague, Sir Reginald Blomfield, Cross of Sacrifice.

Most British military dead not being senior commanders had no cemetery or marked grave but as war casualtied of the 19th and earlier centuries were left in unmarked pits on the battlefields.

EUROPE MORNING *n*
To the pre-**Independence** British, a long lie-in-bed in the morning: as opposed to their more usual adoption of the Indian custom of rising with the sun (the Laws of **Manu** require a householder to rise before dawn, '... one caught asleep by the sun rising or setting, if he does not penance, incurs great sin').

Europe shop: an expression dating at least from the 18th century. In a **mofussil** town or cantonment possibly the one shop that sold imported consumer items and food-stuffs – with their familiar and nostalgic trade names to the exile.

EVE TEASING *n*
A journalist's term of recent years for the harassment of a woman by a male in a public place, so as, at the very least, to cause her embarrass-ment. The legal offence could be that of using indecent language or of outraging the modesty of a female. The action is usually by youths – of-ten students – suggestive words or gestures to a woman or girl unknown to them, or perhaps straying hands in a crowded bus.

FACTORY *n*

A post and settlement of the **East India** and other trading companies in Asia. The British established the first of their Indian factories at Surat, on the Gujarat coast, in 1612. Surat is now (2005) claimed to be the diamond processing capital of the world. Approximately sixty others followed at other places and at least as many in other parts of Asia. *See also* Gaddi.

Factor: In the Company's service, once the person in charge of a factory; later, the designation of the rank immediately above that of **Writer**, with duties that perhaps had no connection with commerce. The general trading functions of the Company ceased in 1833, but the old rank designations (*see* Writer) continued in use for some years after.

FASTING *v*

Upvas in Hindi : a term from Sanskrit implying a condition of being so close to God that food is of no consequence. From Arabic, saum and in Urdu from Persian, roza. While not a belief unique to India – many Christian churches demand an empty stomach for the performance of some rites and enjoin annual Lenten austerities, some fast on the quarterly ember days – it is widely held by Indians, particularly Hindus (but not Sikhs), that asceticism in general and fasting in particular, is a virtue and a remedy for both spiritual and physical ills; that enjoyment of food is a sensual indulgence and that abstinence is pleasing to God. Many believe that to allow the stomach a regular twelve or twenty-four hour period without solid food, is beneficial to health. Many fast weekly (*see* Tuesdays), others on the day of the monthly amavasya (*see* Purnima), or on the two **ekadashi** days of the lunar months, and on certain religious festivals. On a different level, a pact may be made with the Almighty: a vow perhaps, such as '...if my son is cured of his illness/ passes his exams ...I will not eat meat/eggs again'; or '...for a year/or two days a week...'; or, '...I will not sleep on a comfortable bed, but on the floor...' Within a family, a member may refuse food in order to indicate sorrow, or frustration: or to cause another member to follow – or not to follow – a course of action. As the *OED* mentions, a fast is not necessarily absolute; for example, liquids may be continued. So it is that a fast can be prolonged for several months.

A fast to death is frequently threatened as a weapon of political coercion, to draw attention to an injustice. But, as when made within a family quarrel, a mediator normally appears and the threat is rarely carried to the extreme, even if the object is not achieved. A notable exception was the death of a politician which led to the formation of the state of Andhra Pradesh (*see* **AP**). *Also see* Dharma.

Very different is an accepted custom of the Jains. In Hindi, prayopasan, (or also from Sanskrit, santhara–a crossing over—the voluntary abstinence from all nourishment and liquids as an honourable way to cause the soul to discard the body. An irrevocable decision to fast to death. A revered Gandhian, Vinoba Bhave – not himself a Jain – chose this course in 1982 after an illness: his cremation was attended by the Prime Minister of India.)

Muslims in general do not fast as frequently as Hindus (but the Prophet himself fasted on many occasions and some follow his example). Most, of course, strictly observe diurnal abstinence during the month of Ramzan (*see* Roza.), even forgoing drinking water: hardship indeed when the period falls during the summer heat, especially in the north, with perhaps fifteen hours of sunlight. Shias (*see* Sunnis) also fast during the month of Muharram. *See also* Tapasya.

FATWA *n* Arabic and Urdu
From Persian: edict or judgement, issued on a Muslim religious matter,

normally by the ruler as **imam** of an Islamic country.

FERA
Foreign Exchange Regulation Act, 1973.

FESTIVAL SEASON *n*
An expression usually meaning the period from the end of September to early November, in which fall the major Hindu festivals of **Dussehra, Durga Puja, Lakshmi** Puja (in Bengal) and **Divali**.

See also Puja.

FIDAYEEN *n*
Arabic plural of fida, self-sacrifice: one dedicating himself to a cause, perhaps even to death.

FIR (F.I.R.) *n*
First Information Report. A record made in a register by the duty officer in a police station on information about an incident first reaching him.

FIRANGI/ FERINGI *n* Urdu
A European. The same word as the Moorish (*see* Moor) Frank. Obsolete today, but in the 19th century. A Briton might have applied it, as no compliment, to a Eurasian of Portuguese descent. In Urdu, the ex-

pression 'dai firangi', the European disease, also just the word firang, had the meaning of syphilis.

FIRMĀN *n* Urdu
From old Persian and connected to **Sanskrit**. A written edict, a permit, a passport. Normally issued by a Muslim ruler.

FIRST WAR OF INDEPEN-DENCE

Since the end of the British period, the official name in English for the largely military uprising of 1857 (as a serious threat to British rule mostly confined to the four hundred miles of territory between Delhi and Allahabad). To the British, the tragedy was the Mutiny, or the Sepoy Revolt. A descriptive epithet popular with writers was the Devil's Wind, a translation of an Urdu phrase said to have been used by a soldier defendant in a Lucknow court-martial of 1858. There is a story that the current name for the rising was used by an unconventional general of the time, Sir James Outram.

The causes of the alienation of the Indian army from the British were many and one certainly was a tenden-cy by evangelistic British officers to proselytize their men and at least the name of another, that was little more than the trigger setting off the revolt, the greased cartridges, is known to all who have heard of the Mutiny. In 1856, the standard muskets in India of both the British and the Indian

armies were barely changed from those used in 1815 at Waterloo. One improvement had been that it was no longer necessary to strike a flint to create a spark to fire the powder; this was now done by using a sealed percussion cap.

To load his weapon, a rifleman needed the cap, a paper packet of powder, a small paper or cloth patch to ensure that the ball fitted tightly in the barrel and the ball, plus of course a ramrod: all separate pieces. In the early 1850s, the British army introduced a new rifled musket, the Enfield (firing a 0.577 inch diameter bullet, still termed the ball) and at the same time combined the ball and the powder in one paper cartridge the earlier patch being eliminated by clinching the paper round the ball. The ball end was greased to help the cartridge move down the barrel in loading and it had been found that animal tallow gave good results. To load, the cartridge was torn open, either by the teeth or the fingers, to expose the powder to the flash from the cap; the whole was then rammed down the barrel and the percussion cap placed below the hammer. For testing, a few rifles and the combi-nation cartridges had been sent to India in 1853 and had been handled without comment by Indian soldiers. The same grease had been used by the Indian army for many years for greasing gun and cart axles, but of course, no contact with the lips.

The new weapons eventually arrived in bulk, were issued to British troops and it was intended that they should also go to the Indian army. The cartridges being locally greased by the **arsenals**; given that beef and lard would have been the cheapest animal fats, it is probable that in fact these were used: if so, the workers would have known and very soon, the troops. To a **Hindu**, both are grossly polluting and could endanger his caste privilege. To a Muslim, the pigs' lard would have been an abomination and sufficient to ruin his chances for attaining paradise. Authority fairly quickly realised the implications and ordered that the greased cartridges should be issued only to European regiments; Indian regiments were to have their cartridges dry and to grease them under their own arrangements using a vegetable oil or an unobjectionable fat. However, no explanation was offered to the sepoys nor any admission that an error, now rectified, had been made. From all the enquiries after the uprising, no evidence emerged that any Indian unit had handled the cartridges other than those which had taken part in the much earlier trials. The new rifles alone were given for practice drills, but by now such was the distrust of the sepoys of their British officers that they were suspicious even of the packets of powder which they had used for so many years without doubts.

So it was that the immediate cause of the Mutiny was the announcement at a garrison parade on 9 May 1857 at Meerut of the sentencing to imprisonment of eighty-five troopers of the 3rd Bengal Cavalry, a muslim regiment, seventy-four to no less than ten years. Their offence had been disobedience of military orders in that they had refused to drill with the ungreased cartridges (the ammunition was almost certainly blank and being marginally less in diameter than that with ball would not have required grease for easy loading). To compound their humiliation those sentenced had their buttons and badges stripped on the parade ground and their ankles fettered by British armourers, a process that took several hours in the sun of the hottest month of the year. The bloodletting in all its horror began there in Meerut the next evening.

Over the following months, gross excesses were committed by both sides, but the early brutalities of some of the sepoys later were more than matched by the vengeful retribution visited on them – and on others – by Europeans, both civil and military, unrestrained by any semblance of a process of law.

The British memorials (such as that on the famous Delhi Ridge) are still maintained: often with an advice reminding present-day visitors that the 'enemy' of the inscriptions no less died for their country. Those earlier termed 'mutineers' are now Freedom Fighters. (Also Freedom Fighters are those who suffered imprisonment in later years for offences in connection with the political movement against British rule. To the British of the time, they were terrorists if violence was used, or seditionists if they wrote or spoke.)

With peace restored and retribution reduced, perhaps for the first time was the realisation that Indians too had feelings to be considered and there was much British introspection into the reasons that had led many peasants to support their feudal masters but almost none into the occupation of India by the British. It seemed the most normal thing in the world. Since time began a dominant group had felt free to take over the territory of one less powerful.

Several years after the mutiny, a simple notion removed the need for a lubricated cartridge, The bullet was made with a hollow in the base: on firing, gas pressure expanded this so that it tightly fitted the rifle barrel. The cartridge diameter could then be slightly reduced allowing dry-loading without difficulty. Had this been thought of earlier, perhaps there would have been no War of Independence – but *see paragraph 2 above.*

Since the story has mostly been written by the British and surviving Indian participants wished to make their peace with the victors, even today it is hard to be sure of constructing an unbiased and objective history of the rising, particularly as seen from the losing side. A source of information for historians that does exist are copies of the ishtahar (Urdu from Arabic, public announcement) from those in rebellion.

Before 1857 there had been other Indian army mutinies, the most serious being at Vellore in South India in 1806, resulting in the deaths of fourteen officers and over one hundred European soldiers. The cause was, as later, was ignorance by the high command of Indian feelings. Orders had been issued that the sepoy's uniforms were to include European type leather stocks and trimmings. Highly ohnoxious to caste Hindus. The orders were later withdrawn.

FLAG OFF *v*
Originally, the meaning was literal, to signal the start of a race, particularly of motor vehicles, using a chequered red flat. Now, in Indian English, a media expression for starting almost any enterprise with nary a flag in sight.

FLAME OF THE FOREST
Butea frondosa (**Roxb**.) or, more likely today Butea monosperma. In Hindi, dhak, palas/palāsh or tesu. An insignificant untidy deciduous tree of poor scrubland. But in February and

March, often spectacularly in a drab landscape, it flames into a scarlet-orange canopy, or sometimes, a tall narrow jet of fire, each flower with a black parrot-beak centre. In forest economy, the tree has a number of uses; as a good fuel wood; a host for the **lac** insect; the tough leaves can be folded and pinned (using **babul** thorns) into cups and plates; oil is pressed from the seeds; and the stringy root fibres are made into rope. A fine bright yellow-orange dye comes from the flowers: for this purpose the dried petals are sold in bazaars, under the name tesu, on the days before **Holi**. The name, Butea, is a tribute to the 18th century botanist, the Earl of Bute.

Dhaka, now the capital city of Bangladesh (Dacca in British days), is said to be named after the dhak trees, but these are not common in the region today. The battlefield of Plassey, which firmly established British rule in Bengal (Lord Clive, 1757), received its title from a nearby village given the name of the palas tree.

FLYING FERRY *n*

A term from military engineering for a ferry boat with a running hitch to an overhead cable for crossing a small but fast-flowing river, moved solely by the power of the running water.

FLYING FOX *n*

A flying mammal. The large fruit-bat (an alternative name, but there is a smaller fruit-bat, a separate species), with a reddish, fur-covered body upto 33 cm in length and a wing-span of almost a metre. The name follows from the fox-like head with prominent ears and the coloration. Fortunately, the bat is purely vegetarian and is not a vampire. Flying foxes use their eyes for flying and do not have the 'echo-location' systems of the insectivorous species: unlike other bats they do not pass the daylight hours in caves or in dark old buildings but roost pensile in quarrelsome colonies in tall trees (one such colony has remained for many years in the heart of New Delhi). Not generally in India, except by nomadic gypsy-like people and those more sophisticated who may regard the meat of the flying fox as valuable for asthma patients, is the animal eaten, but in some parts, e.g. the Seychelles, flying foxes are regarded as table delicacies.

FOLLOWERS *n*

From camp followers. As a military term, the uniformed domestic staff of a unit: officially known as NCEs – non combatants enrolled. Men such as cooks, **dhobies** and the **sweepers**. Normally unarmed and untrained, in an emergency the followers have been known to become fighting men. Now, of course, much reduced, in the last century the number of followers in a British Indian field army was vast: in 1845, for example, the 9th Lancers rode to the **Sikh** war with a 'tail' of 3,000 civilians to service just over 600 soldiers.

FOREST REST HOUSE *n*
Temporary residential accommodation provided for forest officers on tour, often situated in a most picturesque spot: in the hills, its small red roof on a distant hillside is no intrusion on the landscape, but a welcome mark to the traveller, visible for many miles. May be used by the public with permission from the Divisional Forest Officer (DFO) concerned. *See also* Rest House.

FOUR TWENTY (420) *n*
A reference to that section of the Indian Penal Code (**IPC**) dealing with fraud. A 'four-twenty man' is a way of saying a cheat (in Hindi: char sau bis).

FRONTIER MAIL *n*
In the 1930s, (the first run was in 1928), one of the famous trains of the world, covering the 2335 km between Bombay and Peshawar (now in Pakistan) in about forty-three hours. As with other prestige trains, the name of the driver, almost certainly at that time of the Anglo-Indian community, would have been on the outside of his cab. First-class, four-berth compartments were furnished with easy chairs and a bathroom. Glass-holders and bottle-openers were screwed to the mahogany walls: a special compartment at the end of each coach enabled the sahibs' personal servants to be on call at stops – there was no corridor. Dog boxes were available in the guard's van. It was usual to dress for dinner in the restaurant car. But the dust could never be altogether kept out and air-conditioning, if any, was an ice-block in a tray on the floor below the fan where, additionally, it was useful for cooling drinks. An unofficial name, the P&0 Express, followed from an earlier train on the same route, so called because it connected at the dockside with the arrivals and departures of the weekly mail boats. (A companion train, from Bombay, the Imperial Indian Mail, provided the service to Calcutta; First Class only with accommodation for servants.)

The Mail continued its daily run to the frontier city, now Amristsar (*see* Amrit), a distance of about 1930 km, until August 1996. Tradition was then overthrown and the Mumbai-Amritsar train became the Golden Temple Mail. *See also* Passenger Train.

FRRO (F.R.R.O.)
Foreigners Regional Registration Office (Officer).

G

GADDI/GADI *n* Hindi

Lit., a cushion, a bolster. A ruler's throne: a guru's seat, perhaps on a dais: a saddle. (In the case of a Muslim ruler, masnad – lit. a support – is the more correct term; it generally means a cushion, a bolster.) To be on the gaddi/masnad is to be in a position of power. A Mogul term for the emperor's throne was aurang: hence the name of the Maharashtra city, Aurangabad – the town of the throne – known as Gurka until Aurangzeb, as Prince and Viceroy of the **Deccan**, made it his headquarters in about 1635. (An additional meaning of aurang was of a building for manufacture, or a warehouse: so the early **East India Company** word for their **factories** in their Persian – and English – correspondence was aurang.)

GADDIS *n*

A Hindu people who tend their large flocks of sheep and goats in the summer months on the high alps of the Chamba,

Kullu, and Kangra districts of Himachal Pradesh (*see* HP). The name follows from their homeland, the Gadderan valleys, not far from Chamba. The Bakriwals (goat people) of Kashmir are similar, except that they are of the Islamic faith.

GADIS/GARIA/ GUDAUYA LOHARS *n*

Lit. cart ironworkers, Gypsy-like Hindu itinerant blacksmiths, tinkers, who travel the roads of northern India in family groups, with their tools and homes together in brass decorated bullock carts. They are said to originate from Chittorgarh in Rajasthan.

GAEKWAR/GAEKWAD *n* Marathi

Cow Protector. The honoured epithet adopted as a title and family name by the Maratha rulers of the former princely state of Baroda. The story is of the great-grandfather of the 18th century founder of the house. Noticing some cows (gai – a cow) passing his small fort on the way to slaughter, he opened a side gate (kavad in Marathi) and defying the drovers, gave the cattle sanctuary within. Gaekwar can thus be literally translated as 'cow's gate'. Generally, the forebears of the great Maratha rulers were minor chieftains, who as successful soldiers had become generals and chieftains in the forces of **Chhatrapati** Shivaji and later, became princes with large territories.

155

At least within the state of Gujarat, of which it is a part, Baroda city has reverted to its pre-British name, Vadodara, a corruption of Vatodar – of the **banyan** tree.

GALI *n* Hindi
A narrow urban lane, admitting no vehicle wider than a cycle **rickshaw**. An Urdu word of the same meaning is kucha, originally a residential street. Both are common in street names in the old city of Delhi where public memory has it that a gali is wide enough only to admit a **palki** (palanquin) while a carriage can be driven down a kucha. Gali, in the sense of a narrow passage, is kin to the English gully and gullet, from old French: in English there is gargle and gargoyle. In Hindi, gala, the throat.

Andhi Gali: As in English a blind alley. A cul de sac. Another word for the same alley is nukka.

Gali (Hindi from Dravidian): abuse, invective.

GALIS *n* Hindustani
A pair of European type braces or trousers' suspenders. The term can only have been derived from the 18th century English and Scots words for the same article for a man's breeches, gallows or gallus: gallus, or galluses is still current in the rural United States, particularly for the sewn-on braces of overalls.

It can be said of course, that a gallows has a role in the suspension of objects.

GAMAN *n* Hindi
Sexual reproduction. A word from Sanskrit and, via Greek, linked to the English biology term, gamete.

GANDHĀRĀ
The region covered by the present Peshawar and Rawalpindi district in Pakistan and adjacent Afghanistan right up to the Russian border; the home of the Gandharas, an **Aryan** tribe listed in the Rig Veda (*see* Vedas), their name continues in that of the Afghan city of Kandahar. Centre of a civilisation, an amalgam of central Asian, Buddhist, Vedic and later, Greek, culture from about 600 BC until invasion by Asian Huns in 485 AD. Taxila/Takshashila was the capital city and university centre near today's Rawalpindi. Alexander the Great, in the course of taking over the Persian Empire of Darius, visited and reported on Taxila in 326 BC and from then with increasing effect until the early centuries of the Christian era, classical European and west Asian influences were strong, particularly in sculpture. *See* Greeks.

GANDHARV/GANDHARVA *n* Hindi
In **Indra**'s heaven, the gandharv were the male counterparts of the **apsara**. Celestial musicians and demi-gods. Assistants to the Lord

possessing melodious singing voices, a celestial chorus: sometimes given the adjective daivika/deviya – divine. The apsara and the gandharv were somewhat loosely attached to each other, so that today a man and woman by simply pledging to live together can be socially recognised as having undergone a gandharv form of marriage. (The full edition of the *OED* has an entry, glendoveer, a sprite: from a work by Robert Southey, early 19th century, poet laureate, 'The Curse of Kehana', 1840. Glendoveer is a corruption of gandharv.) Following from the musical interests of the gandharv, gandharv as a word can be applied to mean music in general: gandharv vidayāla (*see* Vidya) – a school of music.

GANDHI *n* Hindi from Sanskrit
A perfume maker or seller. A **Hindu Vaisiya** (merchant) and Parsi family name, in which case the pronunciation is Gāndhi.

GANDHIGIRI
A word coined in about 2006 and popularised in a Bombay film of that year to mean the ethos of Mahatma Gandhi and associated with his belifes and practices. The values by which he is remembered

Giri a word from Persian and Arabic meaning behaviour. In older and more formal Hindi the term will be Gandhi vadri.

GANESH/GANESHA/ GANPATI
A vastly popular folk deity, non-**aryan** and non-vedic, but absorbed into the Hindu pantheon as a helpful family God, and accepted by most as the son of Lord Shiva and Parvati. Usually portrayed seated, with the head of a one-tusked elephant and with a rat as attendant and vehicle (*see* Vahan). Although popularly referred to as a rat – an animal adept in overcoming obstacles in the way of getting where it wishes to go – and usually shown as such in icons, texts indicate that in fact the animal is the velvet-coated, beetle and cockroach eating, musk-shrew or shrew rat, chuchunder in Hindi. Partly from respect to Ganesh's companion, few Hindus will kill a mouse or rat, even when in a 'catch-em-alive' trap.
Like the Roman Janus (hence the month January) in Hindu prayer, the name of Ganesh is invoked before that of any other deity: the first day of the long period of **Ram** Lila is always Ganesh **Puja**. To some, Ganeshji is Siddhidatta, the giver of **siddhi**, the skill of bringing a planned work to a successful conclusion. He is the Lord of beginnings, his symbol, the **swastika**, is often used at the head of a written or printed work, particularly if of a religious nature. Ganesh is also the Lord of Learning and patron of

the arts. A story has it that he wrote down the Mahabharata (*see* Epics) from dictation by the poet Vyasa, breaking off one of his tusks for use as a pen. Ganesh is particularly highly regarded in Maharashtra and western India, where, from the day of Ganesh Chaturthi (August or September) he has an eleven-day festival of his own. As the remover of obstacles he is especially worshipped before starting a new venture or a journey, perhaps no more than the words 'Ganeshya Namaha' – 'Oh Ganesh, I salute thee' or bow down to thee'. Thanks, no doubt, to his ample tummy, an indication of prosperity, **Shri** Ganesh is considered to have a benign influence on commerce: merchants invoke his protection by finger-painting the swastika in red on their premises and cash boxes. To ensure his entrance to a house, mango leaves are strung in a **toran** (also a word for a ceremonial archway, tor in German), a festoon hanging downwards over the door. The reason is indirect and concerns the other son of Lord Shiva, **Kartikeya**, whose favourite food was the mango. Lord Shiva is believed to have said that Ganesh would not attend a function nor enter a home unless his brother was honoured there by mango fruit or leaves.

A one-tusked elephant is usually termed a Ganesh. (No tusks at all – a makna).

Ganesh's name is a form of Gan-**Isa**:

Lord of the Gana – the group of attendant dwarfs and devotees of his father. Lord Shiva. Similar is the epithet Ganpati – Chief of the Gana. Yet another epithet is Vināyak.

GANGA *n*

The Hindu Goddess personified in the River Ganga, by whose name the sacred stream has been known to Indians since late Vedic times (the first river to be held sacred by the Vedic **Aryans** was the Indus). An earlier name was Sursarita – the river of gods. There are probably at least one thousand others. To most, the running water is simply Ganga Mai – Mother Ganga; as a word ganga derives from **Sanskrit**, with the meaning of fast moving or flowing, indicating perhaps, a historical awareness of the river unlike that of mythology, earlier than that of the Goddess. But to the British, it was the Ganges: until the coming of the railways, a route for traffic between Calcutta and Upper India – the region now the state of Uttar Pradesh (*see* UP and Budgerow).

For some, the waters from heaven spring from the coiled hair of Lord **Shiva**, seated in meditation on Mount **Kailas**: an older story (from the Vishnu **Purana**), has the stream first issuing from the big toe of Lord Vishnu's left foot. But most accept the source as the snout of the Gaumukh (Cow's mouth) – or Gangotri – Glacier, at something short of 4300m in altitude, not far from the pilgrim centre of Gangotri in the **Garhwal Himalaya**. (A belief that the Ganga flows from Mount Kailas on the northern side of the main Himalayan range is not entirely fanciful. The river Ghaghara – the Gogra of British days – which joins the Ganga near Dinapore in western Bihar, does indeed rise in the Kailas region.) In its early tumbling through the hills, the Ganga bears the name Bhagirathi, after the king who through extreme **tapasya**, induced the Goddess to come to earth one **Baisakhi** day, by way of Lord Shiva's hair to cushion the impact of the fall. Only after combining with the Alaknanda, if anything the greater stream while still in the hills, does the river become the Ganga by name. As an icon she can be recognised by her vehicle (*see* Vahan) the susu, a Gangetic dolphin (but in eastern India, probably a crocodile — *see* Mugger), found from Allahabad down to tidal waters.

At the Bangladesh border, the main stream flows on as the Padma until, after joining the mighty Brahmaputra (the son of **Brahma,** one of the few Indian rivers deemed to be male. Another is to the far west, the Indus), it finally becomes lost in a delta before reaching the Bay of Bengal. But the Padma has never enjoyed the sanctity of the Ganga, for Hindus believe that

the Goddess leaves the main river and running south, once again under the name Bhagirathi, joins the Hooghly to meet the ocean below Kolkata at Ganga **Sagar**.

As major rivers go, the Ganga is not impressive, only about 2500 km in length, nor is it very old. E.M. Forster in A Passage to India, put it thus: "The Ganges, though flowing from the foot of Vishnu and through Shiva's hair, is not an ancient stream, Geology, looking further than religion, knows of a time when neither the river nor the Himalayas that nourish it existed, and an ocean flowed over the holy places of Hindustan." But from Hindu hearts, the Goddess receives an adoration and respect unique amongst the rivers of the world. A Hindu, wherever he is living, during his life endeavours at least once to merge himself with Ganga-Mai: if possible, at one of the great pilgrim centres that line her course. The ritual bath – Ganga **snan** – for the cleansing of sins requires the devotee to close his eyes, hold his nose, and immerse himself completely three times. For some, a **parikrama**, a round trip on foot on each bank (downstream on the left and up on the right: *see* Right Hand, Left Hand) between the source and the sea is a way of expressing devotion: others, particularly old people, take sanyas (*see* Sanyasi) and pass the final years of their lives as solitary hermits by the water. Since the banks are the best of all places on which to die, the stream has received the ashes of countless millions: Ganga prapti (to receive Ganga) is a euphemism for death. (Jawharlal Nehru in his will directed that he did not require any Hindu rites or ceremonies at his funeral – his wishes were ignored but he did request that his ashes be immersed in the Ganga at Allahabad: an atavistic recognition of the river as a symbol of Indian Aryan culture.) The divine and all-purifying water (Ganga jal) is sprinkled on brides and bridegrooms and is used to moisten the lips and ease the passage of the dying. (The equivalent in Christianity to asperging.) An oath or statement made over it is an assertion of truth before God. The water is widely believed to be bacteria free and antiseptic – but certainly this is not so in areas of high population and of industry – it is carried all over India by home returning pilgrims and professional vendors (*see* Kanwar). A good proportion of the business of pilgrim towns such as Hardwar (*see* Har) is the provision of copper containers for the moneyed – others make do with recycled glass bottles. Devotees on the banks will make offerings of coins, as do those crossing the water on a road bridge or by train – giving rise to the profession of others who pan the sands below.

"Jai Ganga-mai" is the daily call of worship but she is particularly honoured by two festivals; one is **Baisakhi** and the other occurs a few weeks later. Ganga **Dussehra** (or Dashami), the tenth day of the first fortnight – *see* Calendars – of the month of Jayasth, May or June, remembering the day on which after years of entanglement in Shiva's twisted locks, she finally reached the ground. The Ganga (like her Goddess sister, the **Yamuna**) is perennial: in spate during the **monsoon**, but even in the rainless hot season, melting snow on the high Himalaya ensures a constant flow – a natural bounty spilling over into many irrigation canals. A worry for the future is that the snows which feed the river in the hot months have been diminishing since the early 1990s. Year by year the permanent snow-line and glacier snouts have been receding: a facet of global warming.

Akash Ganga : a style indicating the river's celestial, heavenly, origin.

Gangaputri: lit. daughter of the Ganga. An approving epithet for a simple unsophisticated girl, believed to have no knowledge of the evil ways of the world: pure as Ganga water.

Dakshin Ganga: the southern Ganga, the River Godavari.

Dakshin Gangotra: South Gangotri. The name for India's first scientific settlement on Antartica. The new site is named Maitri.

160

GAON *n* Hindi

A village.

Gaonwala: a villager, a rustic (*see* Wala). Frequently used in English sentences in the same context is the Hindi dehati: strictly, a villager (dehat, a village, a rural area) but the intended message may be derisory, a country bumpkin, an unsophisticate.

Gaon Sabha: a village parliament. *See also* Gram and Panchayat. Since many village names are duplicated, its definitive address will be that of the post office that serves it: also normally required in the address will be the name of the **district** and state, facts verifiable from the all-India list of post offices.

GARH *n* Hindi

A fortified place, a castle. A suffix to a place name. From the same word in Sanskrit meaning an impediment to an advance, such as a fence, a wall, a ditch.

GARHWĀL

A hill area once of north-western **UP**, since November 2000 in **Uttaranchal** (In common usage, the name covers much more territory than the present Garhwal **District**) to the west of **Kumaon**, from the foothills right to the Tibet (China) border. The region contains a number of the great peaks and the sources of the **Ganga** and **Yamuna** rivers. To the pilgrims trekking the routes to famous Himalayan shrines, the area is dev bhumi – the land of the Gods, particularly of the char **dhām**, the shrines at Badrinath, Kedarnath, Gangotri and Yumnotri. Another name is Kedarkhand (so always spelled in roman script but the local pronunciation is Kerakhand – *see* Bangle), the territory of Lord **Shiva** which really includes the minor range, the Sivaliks and the **Dun** Valley.

Garhwali: a man from Garhwal and his form of Hindi speech.

GARĪB *n* and *adj* Urdu

Poor. From Persian in literary Urdu, the word may mean stranger, foreigner.

Garibi: poverty

Garibi Hatao: a political slogan, 'Away with poverty'. Similar in form is 'Bekari Hatao' (bekār, without work): 'Away with unemployment'.

GATE SYSTEM

Traffic control on narrow hill roads, under which vehicles are allowed to move in one direction only during specified times; each stage being controlled by a gate

GAUNA *n* Hindi

After a child marriage (*see* Sarda Act), the ceremony of sending the bride to her husband on her reaching either the legal age or as sometimes in villages, puberty.

GAUR *n* Hindi
The wild ox of south and north-eastern India: the largest bovine animal in the world, sometimes standing over six feet at the shoulder. Frequently miscalled the Indian bison (it is not a bison), the gaur has never been domesticated, but in the hills of the north-east, it does inter-breed with local cattle. The offspring, known as mithun and gayal, are highly valued.

Gaur, or Lakhnauti, once a flourishing city on the left bank of the River **Ganga** on the border of today's Bangladesh, the ancient capital of Bengal and, later, that of the Muslims in eastern India during the **sultanates** period.

Gaur/Gur as a form of sugar, *see* Shakkr.

Gaur : a north Indian **brahman** family name.

GAYATRI *n* Hindi
Strictly, a poetical metre: three lines, each of eight syllables. Also a name for the sun in feminine form. A morning **mantra**. A **Sanskrit** verse from the *Rig Veda* (*see* Vedas) addressed to the bedazzling sun-God, Savitra, Lord of the dawn and light – who became Surya in later Hinduism (Suraj, the sun): he who drives daily from east to west across the sky in a chariot pulled by seven white horses. The mantra is frequently uttered by **caste Hindus** (and forbidden to others) in religious ceremonies, and in particular, when standing in water – with palms together above the head in devotion to the rising sun (surya **namaskar**). It has been translated: 'Let us think of the splendour of Savitra that he may inspire our minds.' Perhaps the Sanskrit names of the rivers of the old India will be invoked: Ganga, Yamuna, Godavari, Saraswati, Namade, Indus and Kaveri.

The many Hindi words for the sun are often used as personal names. Popular ones for a boy are Ravi and Dinesh.

Sunday : Ravivar
In music, it is said that the Gayatri mantra is represented by the **rag bhairavi**, traditionally played and sung only in the hours from before dawn to well after sunrise, the period from darkness to light.

The first part of the Hindu cremation ceremony at the ground may well be the chanting by a woman of the Sanskrit **sloka** of Gayatri words in which the deceased asks for his/her lifetime sins, if any, to be forgiven: a verse acceptable to those of any faith.

Suryagrahan: a solar eclipse. A time of serious moment to many Hindus, for emanations from the covered sun can be held to be dangerous to man and beast. a belief seemingly supported by the WHO with warnings that the sun should not be viewed with unprotected eyes. For the duration some will retire behind closed doors and curtained windows. In a home, food may be covered with tulsi leaves.

GĀZ *n* Urdu
Measure of length, in recent times equal to the British yard now superseded by the metre.

GAZETTED HOLIDAYS
Public holidays as notified in the official Gazette of India: observed by all Central Government offices and, usually, but not invariably, by banks. The list for the year 2007 totals eighteen. Probably not more than two, **Independence** and **Republic Days**, can be described as truly national when, at least in urban India, almost all commerce except entertainment, catering, transport and other essential services, stops.

GAZETTED OFFICER *n*
Government officer, civil or military, whose appointment to his service is published in the official gazette. A commissioned officer. Officially, the designation was abolished in 1974, but it continues in everyday use.

GAZETTEER *n*
As descriptions of alphabetically listed place and feature names of the geography – in the fullest possible meaning of the term – of a region, gazetteers

had been privately published from early **East India Company** days, mostly compiled from travellers' notes and non-official sources. The first official gazetteer was the *Imperial Gazetteer of India* published in 1881 in nine volumes: a second edition in fourteen volumes appeared during the years 1885-87. A later edition of 1907-09 required twenty-five: four introductory volumes under the headings Descriptive, Historical, Economic and Administrative. The remainder were the gazetteer proper with the final volume an index. Entries, written by district officers on the ground, often in loving detail described the major physical features, the larger villages, towns, cities and **districts** of the whole of India and Burma and also the **princely** territories. The **Presidencies**, the provinces, and the larger princely states also issued local gazetteers. Under the title The Gazetteer of India. – Indian Union, a new series of the 1970s has been issued in four volumes. In addition, the states are publishing District Gazetteers.

GECKO *n* English
A species of the numerous lizard family: in India the name (of Malay origin) is applied almost solely to the small house gecko so often seen on walls and ceilings inside buildings, performing its useful service of ridding the world of objectionable insects without danger to the environment. Its unusual ability to walk upside down on a ceiling owes noth-

ing to so-called adhesive pads on the feet, but in fact is due to thousands of minute retractable hooks on the toes, with which a grip can be obtained on all but the most polished of surfaces. Its tail, like that of its cousin, the skink lizard, will re-grow if lost.

The gecko, in Hindi, chhipkali, is feared and disliked by many, from a folk myth that a poison deadly to man is contained within its body. (An even more exaggerated belief of medieval Europe was the acceptance of the basilisk, the cockatrice of the Bible: a lizard with a bird's tail, whose glance or fetid breath was sufficient to cause human death.) In English a lounge lizard is still a term of disrepute.

On the other hand, a large spiny-tailed urumastix lizard (a protected species) of the arid western desert is popularly believed to have valued medicinal properties: often wrongly termed an iguana – the iguana is not found in Eurasia – the local name is sanda/sande. Oil from the fat tail is thought to relieve rheumatic pains. Of greater renown, application to the appropriate place is reckoned to revive fading male potency and to prolong enjoyment. To obtain the oil, the sanda is killed and boiled in **bazaar** streets in front of gullible customers. Needless to say, the gross claims by the vendors, usually tribals – *see* Adivasis – are spurious. In parts of India the gecko has the name from the sound it makes, tik-tiki.

GEET *n* Hindi
A song, vocal music.

Filmi geet: the songs and music of the cinema, particularly of the Hindustani films produced in Mumbai and Chennai. A synthesis of Indian and Western styles: despised by classicists, filmigeet is the vastly popular folk music of today (*see* also Sangeet).

Geetkar: the song writer, *see* Kar.

GHADAR/GHADR *n* Urdu
Revolt, mutiny against a tyrant. An Urdu weekly paper published in San Francisco in 1913 for circulation in North America advocating freedom for India from British rule. The name was soon adopted by a militant anti-British group formed largely of Sikh migrants to Canada and the USA. The group was finally wound up in 1947 following **Independence**.

GHĀGRA *n* Hindi
Ankle-length skirt, usually highly coloured and sometimes embroidered, tight at the waist and requiring about five metres length of material: originally worn by Rajasthani and western Indian peasant women, now adopted by the world of fashion.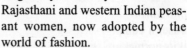

Ghagrawala (see Wala): the skirted ones, Indian and British nickname for the Scottish kilted soldiers of the Highland regiments: dating from at least the mid-19th century.

GHĀNI *n* Hindi
Also known as a kolhu crusher. The age-old village device for pressing oil from seeds, powered by a blindfolded bullock forever treading a circular path: the operator being the teli (oil-man). A heavy weighted pestle, almost a tree trunk, revolves in a roughly cone-shaped mortar fed with oil seeds. From the seeds crushed by the pestle, oil flows to the bottom and into a container; power ghanis are now in use, but seem likely to be replaced by the more efficient modern expeller and the large factory-like oil mill.

GHĀR *n* Hindi
A house, a residence, a home, in eastern India sometimes just a room.

Gharwala (*see* Wala)*:* the head of the household. Husband. Also a male living in the family home.

Gharati: see Barat

Gharwali: the wife of the gharwala. A housewife. A woman of the family.

Gharsansar: lit. the world of the house: a complete household, with all its normal inhabitants.

GHARRY/GHARRI *n*
An anglicism for gari/gadi (Urdu):

a vehicle, be it cart, car, truck, or wheel-barrow.

Railgari: a train. *See also* Bangle.

GHĀT *n* Hindi
In the 19th century and earlier, often written ghaut. Lit. a slope. Steps and platforms of a bathing place by a river or lake.

A landing place from river or sea. An escarpment, a pass through hills.

Ghat Section: on a road or railway in the plains, a portion with a steep gradient.

Eastern & Western Ghats: the word for the passes leading to the tableland of the **Deccan,** applied by the English to the lines of hills flanking peninsular India. Generally about 900m on the west, a lesser height on the east: but at their southern point of convergence, the Nilgiri Hills (*see* Giri), there are altitudes of over 2400m. *See* Dravidia.

Shamshan Ghat: Hindu cremation ground. Any proximity to a dead body requires a Hindu to bathe as soon as possible to remove the pollution: hence cremation grounds, wherever practicable, are located on the ghats of a river or tank. Also, of course, ritual may require that the body itself has a final bath (*see* Snan).

Bijli Shamshan Ghat: an electric crematorium.

GHAZAL/GAZAL *n* Urdu from Persian from Arabic
Strictly, a love poem addressed to a deer-eyed beauty, a girl. By Hindi speakers, the word is sometimes written gazal. A form of Urdu and Persian poetry with stanzas of almost any number of lines (but couplets are the norm and a ghazal with four line stanza is termed a rubai e.g. The *Rubaiyat* – plural of rubai - of Omar Khayyam), in which the words, perhaps with several shades of meaning, usually romantic and often erotic –with both boys and girls the objects of a largely unreciprocated devotion – are all-important. (Like sonnet in English, as a word, ghazal has amorous associations.) But verses should not always be read literally: for example, mashūk – beloved in male form – by custom in Persian and Urdu poetry could be used when the understood allusion was to the feminine mashūka. A disposition sometimes termed a sufiana). Originally recited or sung by courtesans with an accompaniment of harmonium, **tabla** and **sarangi** as part of the Hindustani culture of the Kotha (*see* Kothi), nowadays ghazals are mostly sung as lyrics with little evidence of a Persian background and are accepted by Hindus as a popular form of entertainment in northern India.

Ghazala: a girl's name.

GHĀZI *n* Urdu
(A phonetic spelling of the Arabic and Urdu word would be gaazi, but ghazi is the usual form in roman script.) A conqueror for the cause of **Islam**: a mere fighter could be termed mujahid (*see* jehad). A ghazi who dies in battle, said the Holy Prophet, is assured of paradise. To the British soldier on the Afghan frontier, the ghazi appeared to fight without regard for his own life: hence ghazi in army slang had the meaning of madness. As one of a Muslim ruler's titles, the word is often translated as 'Avenger for God', that is, a scourge on the backs of those not of the faith.

The first Mogul Emperor, Babur, assumed the title for himself in 1527, following his decisive battle with the Rajputs near today's Fatehpur (victory) Sikri.

GHEE/GHĪ *n* Hindi
Milk fat free of moisture and consequently, unlike butter in a hot climate, capable of being stored for a long period without deterioration. Usually prepared by sour-curdling milk and heating the solid to 110°C to boil off the water. Traditionally, aromatic leaves, such as those of the betel vine (*see* Pan), are added to give flavour and, some say, to improve the keeping qualities.

As a product of the cow, ghee is used for Hindu religious ceremonies and is believed to have many beneficial

– almost mystical – properties not possessed by vegetable oils. One being that food cooked in ghee, for example sweets, prepared and served by a lower caste, may be eaten by orthodox members of a higher caste without pollution: this would not apply to food made with water, such as a **chapati.**

The name, ghee, is sometimes misapplied to vegetable cooking oil (*see* Vanaspati and Desi).

GHERAO *n* Hindi
The act of surrounding. In the context of a labour/management dispute, the word has come to mean the coercion of an official by so encircling his office with a cordon of workers that he is unable to leave. A gherao may be continued for many hours.

GHULĀM/GULĀM *n* Urdu
A slave. (When written by Hindi speakers, the *h* is often omitted.) Domestic slavery has existed in India since antiquity as a part of well-to-do **Hindu** and Muslim culture, but not plantation or field slavery as elsewhere. Europeans used slaves about the house at least until the early 19th century (*see* Hobson-Jobson). Domestic slaves could be responsible and respected members of a large household with a loyalty and commitment to the interests of the family far greater than could be expected from a mere wage-earner. In medieval times as with the mamelukes of Turkey, some commanded military forces.

Although slavery became illegal throughout the British world in 1830, domestic slavery continued in India for many decades thereafter.

Ghulam Mohammed: Muslim personal name – the slave of Mohammed. Similarly, Hindus can be named as a servant or slave; e.g. Gopal Das, the servant of Gopal – Lord Krishna (*see* also Chela).

GHUNGHAT *n* Hindi
A face veil. Sometimes a separate piece of cloth, otherwise an end of the **sari**, the palla, flung over the head. In a **Bollywood** film, the height of eroticism is the hero lifting the veil of his bride on their wedding night. The rest is left to the imagination.

As a form of respect, a bride may wear the ghunghat in the home in the presence of the family elders.

GHUSL *n* Urdu from Arabic
Correctly, the ghusl is the bath obligatory for Muslims after certain body pollutions, but in India at least, the word is applied to any complete washing of the body.

Ghusl masnum: bathing required by the Sunna (usual, but not ritually essential. *See* Kor'an), as before the Friday congregational prayers. (The Holy Prophet is said to have remarked one hot day, that the smell arising from his brethren around him at prayer was not as sweet as it could have been.)

Washing of the face, hands, arms to the elbows, and the feet, the wazu/ waju, is obligatory before the prayers and, at least before the early morning **namaaz**, cleaning of the mouth and teeth. Also ghusl masnum is the ritual washing of a body after death.

Ghuslkhana: a bathroom. In a **Mogul** palace this could also be a private apartment close to the actual bathroom, wherein the ruler and his senior-most advisors would discuss affairs of state. *See also* Snan.

GINGHAM *n*
A now obsolete English word possibly from Malay. A light cotton cloth usually striped or checked.

GIRI *n* Hindi
A mountain, a hill, e.g. the Nilgiri Range of south India – the blue hills; so called, because, when seen from the plains, they often appear as through a bluish haze, but this is not a very ancient name.

Girijan: hill people. Used mostly for the aboriginal hill peoples (*see* Adivasis) of the south, particularly in Andhra Pradesh and **Tamil** Nadu. It is rarely applied to the people of the **Himalaya** (*see* Pahāri).

Girdhari: lit. he who carries a mountain. A name for Lord **Krishna**.

Giriraj: king of mountains, the Himalaya.

Giri: the kernel of a nut. Hence, with reference to nuts, shelled.

GIRJA GHAR *n* Hindi
Or simply, girja. A Christian church building. The Portuguese igreja, a church: modified perhaps, due to a confusion by **Hindus** on seeing in an early Catholic church an image of the Madonna and Child and assuming it to represent their well-known Girija, literally, 'born of the mountain', i.e. the **Himalaya**, an epithet for Parvati, wife of Lord **Shiva**, holding the baby **Ganesh**.

GITA *n* Hindi
A dissertation on **Hindu** spiritual matters or ethics, recited or sung (*see* Geet) by a divinity or near-divinity. There are many Gitas, but the word is normally a reference to the *Shrimad* (*see* Shri) *Bhagavadgita* (Song of thi Lord): probably the best known and most respected of all Hindu sacred texts – Forming part six of the Mahabharata (*see* Epics), it is a **Sanskrit** poem of some 700 verses, in which Prince Arjuna, one of the five **Pandava** brothers, seeks guidance on philosophy and **dharma** from Lord **Krishna**, his charioteer on the battlefield of Kurukshetra, (at no time was the chariot actually in battle, and Arjuna wishes to inspire Krishna to non-violence), between Delhi and the **Hills**. (Arjuna, mean-

ing white and shining in Sanskrit, passed into Latin as argentum, becoming the root European word for silver.) The Gita, in about 1784, was the first of the Hindu sacred texts to be translated into English. A girl's name.

Gitānjāli: the name given to a collection of poems in Bengali by Rabindranath Tagore, published in 1910. Although not exactly corresponding to the original, English editions with the Bengali name and sub-title 'An Offering of Song' (*see* anjali under **Namaskar**) followed, from Bengal in 1912 and from England in 1913 with an introduction by W.B. Yeats who also assisted the author with the translation – the quantum of that assistance has been a subject of debate ever since and this English version won Tagore the Nobel Prize for Literature in November of the same year.

Gitanjali Express: a train connecting Mumbai and Calcutta.

Gita Govinda: Song of Govind (Krishna as the Divine Cowherd). Composed by Jayadev of Bengal in the 12th century AD, a Sanskrit love poem: Radha and Krishna delighting in each other on both the spiritual and sensual planes – devotion to the Lord transcends conventional morality – so that the work has been termed the Hindu Song of Solomon. An early example of what later was to become the all-India **bhakti** movement. Touring players enacting the poetry of Jayadev (Krishnayattra – *see* **Yattra**) evolved into the jatra theatre of Bengal.

Gita Pāth: a reading aloud to a congregation of the Bhagavadgita, either the whole or a part.

As a revered book, the Gita is unusual in that it has a birthday, celebrated on the Ekadashi day of the month Pausa (December-January).

GOBAR *n* Hindi
Bovine dung, Processed Grass, Sundried and mixed with cut straw, used as fuel in all the villages in India as, for a long period, the buffalo chip was the fuel on the American prairie. A central government energy authority has estimated (1998) the total quantity as being in the region of 100 million tonnes a year. For storage, the cakes (upla) may be piled to make a circular or rectangular structure as high as three metres, known in the north as a bitora: the sides are mudplastered and the roof thatched. The whole not unlike a village hut.

For a Hindu, following ritual pollution, liquid cow dung is above all the purifying agent. A small quantity to be consumed.

Gobar gas: methane gas for use for heating and lighting produced by fermenting animal dung. Following the extraction of the flammable gas, the residual slurry has a high value as a crop manure.

GODMAN *n*
In standard English, a man of God from the Latin, *homo deus*. A saintly character: an epithet for Christ. In Indian English this has changed dramatically in recent years: in journalism to term a person (normally, a **Hindu**) a godman is to infer an allegation of charlatanism. (Dictionaries of today ignore this shade of meaning of the word, but the *OED* supplement of 1972 did quote just such a use, dated 1922.)

GŌDOWN *n*
An anglicism used throughout the East for a warehouse or storeroom. The original is the Malay word gadong, with the same meaning. In spoken Hindustani it appears as godaam, possibly picked up from the anglicism rather than direct from Malay.

GŌL/GŌLA *n* Hindi
Circular, spherical: a ball.

Goli: a small ball, a bullet, a medicinal pill. The origin, no doubt, of the not-quite-respectable English slang word for a testicle. (A popular, but surely apocryphal, story between the wars was that railway station vendors hawked a well known patent medicine with the cry 'Beecham Sahib's balls': a literal translation of 'Beecham Sahib ke goliyan' and that a disgruntled British pilot sky-writer

earned the sack from his employers by trailing the amended slogan in smoke for the world to see.)

GOMPA *n* Tibetan
Buddhist temple, monastery (or lamasery) or nunnery in Tibet and in the Buddhist areas of the Indian **Himalaya**, where the monk is a **lama** and the nun a jomu. Gompa is said to mean a lonely place: the **Buddha** was of the opinion that monasteries should be built far from worldly distractions.

GOONDA *n* Urdu
Hooligan, violent rogue. Goondaism. a commonly used anglicism for hooliganism, vandalism or in Hindustani, goonda-gardi. *See also* Zoolum.

GŌPI *n* Hindi
A village girl who looks after the cattle: the word is usually associated with the Krishna story. The boy cowherd would be gope or gopal (gao-pal – cow protector or friend, Rajgopal – royal cow protector. The English slang word, pal, meaning a friend, has probably been received from India via Romany). The local cattleman and milk-seller with just a few animals may be termed a gawala. Gopi, Gope, Gopal and Rajgopal are all popular personal names.

Gopal/Gope Ratna: see Krishi.

GŌPURAM/GŌPURA *n* Sanskrit
Hindu temple tower of a type found

mainly in south India: built from the 8th century AD onwards, usually over a gateway. Massive multi-tiered construction averaging 60 metres in height, topped with small domes: often gold-leafed sides covered with images. Worship of the gopuram is considered equivalent to worship of the deity to whom it is the threshold: in fact, until fairly recently in many major temples this was the only form of devotion allowed to the **dalit** community.

GŌRA *adj* and *n* Hindi
White : pale complexioned. A European.

Gora-log: white people, Europeans. A plain statement of fact no doubt, but during the British period, most Europeans expected to hear themselves referred to as the **Sahib**-log.
Gorashahi: white (i.e. European) rule. *See* Shah.

Ghora: a horse, a pony. Ghori: a mare.

GORKHA/GURKHA *n*
Correctly, a man of the hill tribes from the district of Gorkha in central Nepal, but in common usage, the term includes the Mongolian and **Rajput** hillmen of the western and eastern parts of the country who are recruited into the Nepalese, Indian and British defence services. The Gorkhas occupied the kingdom of Kathmandu in 1767 and took over the country. The Gorkha language, of the Indo-**Aryan** group, is officially known as Nepali, but used to be called Gurkhali. Gorkha citizens of Nepal are, of course, Nepalese, as are other peoples of the kingdom. Gurkha as a name is a corruption of gao-**raksha** – cow protector or keeper. Since 1947, the roman spelling of the word has been Gorkha, rather than the Gurkha of the British period. (However, one regiment, the 2nd King Edward VII' s Own, now part of the British army, has always used the form Goorkha for itself.) *See also* Line Boys.

It was in 1814 that the **East India Company** decided that the Gorkhas, who in the previous decades had occupied a lengthy strip of Himalayan India west from their frontier to the Kullu Valley, had to be evicted. From the fighting that followed their martial qualities were so appreciated that almost immediately they were recruited into the Company's army. Near Dehra **Dun** there is a war memorial of a type that must be very unusual; two columns, side by side: one in memory of the British who had died, the total included the General commanding, in an assault on a hill fort high above; the other has the words: "This is inscribed as a tribute of respect for our gallant adversary Bulbudder, Commandant of the fort, and his brave Goorkas, who were afterwards, while in the service of Rangit Sing, shot down in their ranks to the last man by the Afghan artillery."

Perhaps not quite to the last man, for there is a story that a young lad escaped to become, many years later, a much decorated Subedar-Major of the 2nd Goorkhas. For Ranjit Singh, *see* Sher.

The connection with the **Sikh** King of Lahore is that he also was impressed by the Gorkhas and needing hill fighters, he enlisted them for his hitherto unsuccessful attempt to capture Kashmir from the Afghans. He succeeded in 1819. Those who joined him being celebrated in Nepali song as Lahoria – a term still in use for those of the Kingdom who seek their fortunes in India.

As a memorial to a fallen enemy, the pillars near Dehra Dun may be unusual but are not unique. From World War I at Gallipoli is a memorial installed by Mustafa Kemal (later honoured as Kemal Ataturk – Father of the Turks) comforting mothers of Commonwealth dead "...wipe away your tears, your sons are now lying in our bosom and are at peace, having lost their lives in this land they have become our sons as well".

Gorkhas are frequently addressed as sathi-bhai: strictly, the meaning is of a close companion, but the sense is more that of the old English greeting, neighbour or more colloquially, mate. Fem. Sathin-bahen. (In recent years, sathin in India has been adopted as a

title by certain village-level female social activists often **dalits**.)

Ghurka (sic) bag: a proprietary name for an American-made high quality leather bag with no connection with Nepal. But it is claimed that the waterproof leather owes something to a type of English leather once specially tanned for use in India.

Gorkha hat: see Terai.

Gorkhaholic: A term used by Europeans to describe one of their number captivated by the Gorkhas beyond reason.

GŌSHALA/GŌSADAN *n* Hindi
A cowshed. A sanctuary for cattle maintained as a **Hindu** or Jain charitable act. *See also* Pinjrapol.

In eastern India a word with similar meaning and dairy can be khatal.

GŌTRA *n* Hindi
A word connected with the cow, but the accepted meaning is that of a clan or sept. A concept of **Vedic** days that all **caste Hindus** can be distinguished as descendants or followers of one or other of eight or nine rishis, or sages: each group being a separate gotra. (Over the centuries, the number has increased greatly.) The concept is still of importance, for, amongst the orthodox at least, it is held that marriage between persons of the same gotra is impermissible.

The classical Romans similarly had tribes practising exogamy.

GŌUS

The pre-history Indo-European term for cattle. Into Sanskrit as go and Hindi as gai/gao. Via the West Germanic languages it appears in English as ku/cow.

GOVERNMENT *n*

The Government of India, or of a state in the Union. Since at least 1774, the word has been used in English Indian writing without the definite article. Perhaps deriving from the **East India Company's** China connection, the British Government of Hong Kong used to refer to itself in a similar way.

G.O.I. /GOI: Government of India.

GRĀM *n* Hindi

Village: pertaining to a village. As the smallest unit of local government, gram includes a meaning in some ways equivalent to the civil parish in England.

Gram sewak (fem. sevika): village level social worker.

Gram Sabha: village parliament of the entire village population: its chief function is to elect the **panchayat** thus forming gram raj, village rule.

Gramdan: lit. village gift. A movement to persuade owners of land to give up some or all of their holdings in favour of collective village ownership. See Bhoomi.

Gram Udyog: village industry.

Gram as a pulse: *see* Dal.

Gramin: adj. pertaining to a village.

GREATER INDIA/FURTHER INDIA

Names given by historians to that part of south-east Asia (termed the East Indies and Indo-China upto World War II) in which Indian culture was dominant from the time of the early Christian era until submerged by the rise of **Islam** in the 14th and 15th centuries. Today's Laos, Cambodia/ Kampuchea (the latter name is itself Indian, said to be from Kambuja, an early town in the Punjab), Thailand, Malaysia and Indonesia. Except for a brief while under the **Cholas**, the **Hindu** and Buddhist kingdoms were not imperial extensions of political or economic power in India, but were set up by Indian travellers/ adventurers imposing themselves on local populations and by local rulers adopting the admired Indian way of life and beliefs.

The legacy today is the vast number of Hindu and Buddhist monuments of the period (e.g. the famous **Vishnu** temple of Angkor Vat in Kampuchea – *see* Banyan), the merged Hindu and Buddhist traditions still underlying much of the local folk culture (even of Muslims) and the **Sanskrit** base of many of the local languages. The emblem on the personal flag of the King of Thailand is that of a **chakra**. The religion of the island of Bali is still predominantly a form of Hinduism. But a much older connection going back into pre-history is the shared Austric language heritage of some of the **Adivasis** of India (particularly of the Munda group) with the peoples of south-east Asia.

GREAT GAME, THE

An expression used early in Queen Victoria's reign and immortalised over forty years later in Kipling's *Kim*, to describe semi-official adventures, often by individual army officers, amidst the emirates and khanates of Central Asia, to report on and if possible counter Imperial Russian expansion in the direction of India. It was said that the originator of the term was a Captain Arthur Connolly, for whom the game had a harsh finish in 1842 in Bokhara: capture and beheading. While the military threat was probably never so serious as thought by some – to mount an invasion across the inhospitable passes of the Pamirs and the Hindu Kush was beyond the powers of Tsarist Russia – a settled frontier was only reached in the 1890s with Russia just ten miles away from India at one point in Chitral (now Pakistan), with a buffer strip of Afghanistan in between. The China frontier was never firmly agreed upon, a fact which has caused trouble to India since **Independence**.

In Kim, of course, the term The Great Game, or just The Game, means

undercover work in India by the Intelligence Service, the British Raj at the level of state security.

GREEKS, THE

According to Herodotus, the first Greeks to see India were in the army of their General Scylax, in the service of Darius I of Persia, in about 517 B.C. The General sailed down the Kabul river and then explored the Indus to the sea. he returned to Persia via the Mediterranean coast, a journey of nearly three years.

After years of campaigning in Persia, the army of Alexander the Great, European and Asian Greeks together with local levies, crossed the River Indus in February 326 BC and so entered India. Six months later, the invading forces reached the River Hyphasus (the Beas of today's **Punjab**) near the mountains and would go no further, Alexander finally accepted the situation and, after building twelve huge stone altars (yet to be found), turned back and left the country in September 325 BC – a stay of nineteen months. Although garrisons were set up, apart from a few Greek colonies in what is now Iran and Afghanistan politically all trace of the Greeks was swept away within a few years. But in the visual arts – only sculpture, a few columns and coins have survived – Hellenic influences initiated by the first incursion and then later, more strongly and over a much longer period of time, by Greeks from Bactria in the 2nd century BC and from eastern Mediterranean lands in general, were to last for generations. Forcefully in the Buddhist sculpture of **Gandhara** (the descendants of the original Greeks soon became Buddhists) and of north-west India and less obviously elsewhere from the **Mauryan** empire to the post-Kushan period of the 10th century AD. To experts, the modelling of the four lions on India's national emblem, the **Ashok** capital (*see* Chakra.) is peculiarly Greek. (The Kushān rulers, Buddhists from Central Asia based in Peshawar, controlled a vast territory in Central Asia and in India down to Varanasi, from about the 1st century AD to the 3rd. Their best known sovereign was King Kanishka, sometimes considered a second Ashok. Many sculptures of their period using the spotted red sandstone of the locality can be seen in the Mathura museum.)

No less enduring than the stone sculpture has been Alexander's personal name, at least amongst Muslims: Sikander/Iskander derives from Alexander. Over thirty towns and villages bear in some form the name of the Greek (Post Office Guide), of which probably the most important is Secunderabad, the twin city with Hyderabad, capital of Andhra Pradesh (*see* AP), from Sikander Jah, an early 19th century **Nizam**.

Yavana: from Sanskrit. Strictly, the classical Greeks, the Ionians. But since those days the term has been applied to mean Muslims and Europeans.

GREEN WHISKY *n*
Also, thandai (coolness). Colloquial: an infusion of the cannabis narcotic, bhang (*see* Indian Hemp), In a similar vein, black gold may be a reference to opium (some Indian opium is black in colour). Particularly a drink of the **holi** festival. Thandai may also be a cool soft drink with almonds and rose water.

GRIFFIN *n* English
In the Indian context, since at least the 17th century, a term for a newly arrived European unused to the ways of the East, sometimes abbreviated to grif. Similar in meaning was the punning name, Tom Raw. These terms are not heard today. (In 19th century England, a griffin was a betting tip: later abbreviated to griff, a slang term for news in general, information.)

G.T. ROAD
The Grand Trunk Road, described in Kipling's Kim as "The Great Road which is the backbone of all Hind". "It runs straight, bearing without crowding India's traffic for fifteen hundred miles – such a river of life as nowhere else exists in the world." The British name for the metalled highway for vehicles constructed during the 19th century before the railways, which, section by section, was extended until it linked Calcutta with Peshawar. The alignment was, and still is today as part of the **National**

Highway system (N.H.1) roughly that of the Mauryan Royal Highway and the Sarak-e-Azam (State Road) of the Muslim period. Confusingly, a similar artery from Bombay, through Mhow, to join the original G.T. Road at Aligarh in **UP**, was also termed the Grand Trunk Road.

Grand Trunk Express: the long-distance train running daily in each direction between New Delhi and Chennai, taking just over thirty-six hours for the journey.

GTS (G.T.S.)
Great Trigonometrical Survey of India. The British, for military and revenue purposes, began mapping their new dominions almost as soon as they acquired them, but by the early 19th century the separate **Presidency** surveys still had not interlinked, In 1818, an all-India triangulation survey from one base-line supported by a few astronomical observations, the Atlas of India, was begun on a scale of 1:253440. On the ground, the project was the GTS, modelled perhaps on an earlier Ordnance Survey of Ireland. The base point for the triangulation for today's survey maps is a brass plate set in concrete near Kalyanpur, in Madhya Pradesh.

GU *n* Hindi from Sanskrit.
The English descriptive expression for a bit of a sticky mess (usually spelled goo), is surely a link to the Hindi gu derived from the Sanskirt gu, meaning excrement, or more cor-rectly, since gu is not a word used in polite Indian conversation, shit.

Sandas: latrine.

GUĀR n Hindi
The word is in the *OED,* defined as the cluster bean. *Cyamopsis:* plants of the pea family grown in dry regions such as Rajasthan. Flour made from the seeds is used worldwide as a stabilising and thickening agent in food processing, particularly in ice-cream: it also has a use in low-calorie, high-fibre 'slimmers' bread. Guar has many industrial application's especially in paper manufacture, and in medicine is known for some insulin-like properties. The major source to the world of guar is India.

GUEST *n* English
In northern India the common Hindu-stani word is mehmān from Persian. From Sanskrit it is atithi: thence the traditional hospitality expression "atithi Narayan" (see Vishnu) - the guest is God. (Mehmanawasi: Urdu, hospitality). Old time culture says that guests still present at midnight should be asked to stay the night. But courtesy is not unlimited, for an eastern India expression has it that fish and guests stink after three days.

GUJARS/GUJJARS *n*
Cattle breeders, settled as **Hindus** in the plains of northern India especially around Delhi: but throughout the hill regions of the northwest, Gujars may be found as Muslim nomads tending

herds of cattle and flocks of sheep and goats moving for seasonal grazing from one alp pasture to another – nomads, from the Greek nomas, a pasture. Under their ancient name of lbriya, their original home was Gujristan in the Georgian Caucasus – there are Gujars in the USSR with marked similarities to those of India – from where, it is suggested, they migrated to the subcontinent in about the 4th century BC: some taking up residence in the region covered by today's Gujarat.

GULĀL *n* Urdu
Originally a red flower, the name was applied to red powder, but now, particularly when associated with the **Holi** festival, gulal can mean powder of any colour used for throwing at, or more decorously, anointing, one's friends. (Gulal powder should be of vegetable origin, and traditionally was made from the flowers of the forest tree, the tesu. But these days, chemical colours are normal and even mica is added to give sparkle. As a word, gulal is linked to the European heraldic term for red, gules.) In eastern India, the word for the coloured powder is likely to be from **Sanskrit**, abir. *See also* Kumkum.

Note: gulel, a catapult.

GŪL MOHUR/ GOLD MOHUR
n
Anglicisms from the Urdu, Gul **Mor** (lit. peacock, or red peacock flower). A leguminous ornamental tree not to be found in the wild state, originating in Madagascar. Delonix regia, introduced into India in mid-19th century. Also known as the flamboyant and the flame tree. Covered with large flowers light orange to fiery red, in April/May and again, but less obviously during the monsoon in July, when the tree is in full leaf.

GUMBAZ/GUMBAD *n* Urdu
A dome as of a mosque or tomb representing, a Muslim or Buddhist may say, the vault of heaven. By the man in the street, the noun may be used as a descriptive word for any building with a prominent dome be it mosque, tomb, church or secular. The age old method of construction without using internal support is still employed today. On a circular base (the drum) bricks are laid on mortar; after a day or when the mortar is set the process is repeated, each horizontal ring overlaying the one below by a small amount, either increasing or decreasing the circumference until the final keystone disc is dropped in to close the top: the whole operation may require a number of weeks. Considerable ingenuity both technical and artistic, was shown in adapting a four or eight sided building to take the drum for the dome. (The buildings of Delhi's Qutab Minar complex and round about dating from the late 12th century form a museum of the evolution of the Muslim dome and arch in India.) As a rough guide to the age of a tomb or mosque it can be said that the higher the drum and

the more bulbous or onion shaped the dome the more recent is the date of the building. Domes resting on high drums became common in India during the 18th century, but were being built at least two hundred years earlier in Iran and Afghanistan, often with an outer skin of coloured tiles (the Timurid style). The usual, but not invariable, design in India, is for a mosque to have three domes over the western side; the largest placed centrally to indicate the kibla (*see* Mihrab) with a smaller dome on each side. From the mid-16th century double domes were being constructed (e.g. as with Humayun's tomb in Delhi) so that whatever the shape from outside the vision from the interior could be that of the hemispherical 'vault of heaven.' *See also* Masjid and Nawab.

It must be mentioned that the dome is not solely Islamic: centuries before Muslims began to build in India **Hindus** and Buddhists were constructing them for their temples and **stupas**. But, generally, such buildings had rigid proportions and alignments and the right angles of stone beams were preferred to rounded arches or domes for crossing open spaces. From the 17th century, the design for a **Sikh gurdwara** normally includes a large dome.

GUNGE/GANJ/GUNZ *n* Hindustani from Sanskrit and Persian.
A place for valuables. Metaphorically, a battlefield, ganj-i-shahidon (a

store of martyrs. In Delhi's Chandni Chowk, the **Gurdwara** Sisganj, the site of the martyrdom of the 9th **Guru**.) A grain market, usually wholesale. An earlier meaning was of a wealthy residential area.

Ganja: a bald head.

GUNGI GADIYA *n* Hindustani
A literal translation of the American colloquialism, a dumb doll. Said to have been applied to Indira Gandhi by the elderly politicians of her party who elected her to power, only to find themselves outwitted and ousted,
GUNNY *n*
This English word for **jute** sacking cloth (gunnybag) comes from the nowadays rarely used Hindi, gani, with the same meaning. (In north India at least, taat is the more usual Hindi term for sackcloth.)

Gunnies: the jute trade term for the cloth as an article of commerce.

GUN SALUTES *n*
In later British days, 118 ruling **princes** received gun salutes when visiting towns and cities in **British India** with military establishments and at the sea ports when leaving or returning: a privilege to which some attached great importance. (Not only the princes: in 18th century Calcutta, the Chairman of the Council was challenged to a duel because the guns of Fort William had not saluted the arrival of the aggrieved party.) The number of guns fired varied on a scale from

twenty-one (five rulers) to nine (thirty rulers). The **Viceroy** was honoured with thirty-one explosions and the number for the Imperial Royal Salute for the sovereign was one hundred and one. Even stone could be saluted: in 1934, in Great Place, just below the Secretariat blocks in New Delhi, an economy class statue – of limestone and not the more usual long lasting marble – of a previous Viceroy, Lord Irwin, was unveiled to the sound of thirty-one guns. Governors and senior British military officers also received gun salutes. In the late 18th century, loyal and patriotic toasts drunk at official entertainments, could be echoed from a cannon's mouth.

Salute states and nonsalute states: expressions indicating the relative importance of a princely state. The form of address 'Your Highness', was originally used only for rulers receiving a salute of eleven or more guns, but towards the end was extended to the nine gun salute rulers. Princes with thirteen guns or more had the title Maharaja, and those without salutes were Chiefs. Within their own states, rulers were free to award themselves as many salute guns as they wished.

GUP/GAP *n* Hindi

Gossip, rumour, hearsay.

Gupshap: tittle-tattle.

GUPTA PERIOD *n*

Roughly from 320 to 540 AD. A line of kings beginning with Chandra Gupta (not to be confused with the Chandragupta of the **Mauryan** Empire) centred on **Patliputra** (today's Patna). The Gupta Empire at its greatest together with its tributary states included most of the subcontinent from the Indus to Assam and Nepal. A period of the full flowering of Indian culture and said to have been one of great prosperity for all. Incursions of fierce Central Asian tribesmen Hunas or Huns, who destroyed but left nothing for posterity, had broken up the Empire by about 540 AD, but branches carried on a furthes 250 years.

While the boundaries are far from precise historians who mention medieval India are generally referring to the era of approximately one thousand years following the end of the Gupta period: say from 600 AD to the early years of the **Moguls** about 1600 AD.

GURDWARA *n* Punjab
Lit. the door/gateway to the Guru or, more fully to the House of the **Guru** and God. Sikh temple and important centre of **Sikh** community life. A gurdwara, as the presence chamber of the Holy Granth Sahib (i.e. the everlasting Guru *see* Guru Granth Sahib) is accorded the greatest respect. It is open to all, providing decorum is

observed; before entering shoes must be removed and the hands and feet washed: the head must be covered. It would be an act of gross sacrilege to carry tobacco in any form into a gurdwara. On entering and when just passing by on foot, a Sikh will usually indicate respect to the Holy Book within by touching the threshold with his forehead (matha-tekna to bow the forehead) or at least with his fingers. If in a moving vehicle his palms may be together at his forehead. From the 1920s until the dramatic military assault on the Golden Temple complex (*see* Amrit) in June 1984 there had been an understanding (but no statute) that the police did not enter a gurdwara on duty, but the understanding also was – by and large observed, at least until **Independence** in 1947 – that any person within a gurdwara who was wanted by the police, would be handed over by the management.

A particular gurdwara may be referred to as a taksaal, a mint: an accolade earned for it by its speaker or speakers, whose words on matters of the Sikh faith are likened to new coins from a mint. (Or, as could be said in English, in mint condition.) A major gurdwara is usually built in Rajasthani **Mogul** style with two or three storeys: overall there will be a single large fluted dome with perhaps, small domed **chhatries** on the roof corners. The ground floor will usually be clear except for a central platform for the Granth Sahib with a canopy overhead. There will be space for the Granthi and musicians, for the congregation standing and seated and room to allow a clockwise circulation, the **Parikrama**. There will be a small room, the Kotha Sahib, in which the scripture can be reverently placed when the building is closed at night. A word from antiquity to describe this would be tabernacle. In front of the holy Granth may be the large sword of state the two signifying spiritual and temporal rule (peeri and meeri. *See* Khalsa.) Some large Sikh temples like the most famous of all the Harimandir at Amritsar (the Golden Temple: *see* Amrit) will include a pool or tank (sarovar) perhaps with a cloistered surrounding walkway.

While every gurdwara does not have a **tank** or even a dome on the roof all are distinguished by a tall mast, the Nishan Sahib (the honoured mark – meaning a clear landmark for all to *see*), covered in deep yellow cloth (saffron) carrying the **Khalsa** pennant at the top and usually illuminated at night in the fashion of the imperial headquarters of the field camps of the Mogul emperors. Once the flag of the Sikh kingdom. (The pennant at the masthead of a gurdwara controlled by **Nihangs** may be blue and not the orange of the Khalsa.)

Almost all gurdwaras, the exceptions are the very small ones, supply basic accommodation facilities, including a minimum of two meals a day, without charge for travellers of all faiths provided the rules, especially the absolute ban on tobacco and liquor – are observed. *See also* Langar,

A gurdwara complex, including the langar, the administrative offices, residential accommodation and outbuildings, may be referred to as a **dera**, or **camp**. *See* SGPC.

GURMUKHI/GURUMUKHI *n* Hindi
Lit. from the mouth of the **Guru:** i.e. the word of God. The script, a variant of devnagri (*see* Sanskrit), in which the Sikh texts are written and also modern Punjabi – pre- **Independence**, Sikhs, Punjabi **Hindus** and Muslims mostly used the Urdu script for their correspondence. Gurmukhi was in use before the Sikh faith but it was the second Guru, Guru Angad, who adopted it for his writings and gave it its name. Nowadays, a non-Sikh may well term it Punjabi.

GŪRU *n* Hindi
The planet Jupiter and Guruwar, the day of the week, Thursday.

A teacher, a word charged with respect, in any sense, but particularly in connection with Hinduism and music, where, since there are no notational symbols, to progress with a classical style a guru is indispensible. As a guru is free to accept or reject a student and is unpaid but he may receive a gift, **dakshina** – the status of a guru is higher than, say, that of a salaried schoolmaster. Traditionally, the duty of a guru is completed by the initiation

(*see* Diksha) of his pupil. A **Hindu** spiritual preceptor: the director of an **ashram**, often a hereditary position.

*The **Sikh** Gurus:* the ten successive religious leaders of the Sikh faith – in roman script normally honoured with a capital G – from Guru Nanak, died 1539, to Guru Gobind Singh, died 1708. From the fourth, Guru Ram Das Sodhi, all were related. To the founder of Sikhism, Nanakdev (he never used the title for himself) as a word Guru represented the deity and not any living person. The often used Punjabi expression, "Guru Kirpa" can be freely translated as "thanks be to God" or "by the Grace of God". Images and statues of the Gurus are forbidden, but artists' pictures are everywhere. *See also* Guru Granth Sahib.

The spiritual quality of the first Guru flowed through the following nine, so Nanak may be used as a title. Guru Gobind Singh being referred to as Nanak Ten.

In Hinduism, once a disciple, known as **shishya** or **chela**, is accepted and receives initiation from his guru, the relationship is very close, each being committed to the other: but the ideal is for the student to revere and obey his guru as God. Such a relationship may be referred to admiringly as the 'guru shishya parampara' – the guru and pupil tradition (*see* also Gurukul). The Emperor Akbar ordered that his slaves should be termed his **chelas**). Most Hindus are convinced that at least some gurus have supernatural powers. The disciple is not necessarily a child or youth, he may well be a western type businessman, or senior government officer, who sits at the feet of his teacher only at intervals. By the laws of **Manu**, a son is enjoined to reverence his father as a guru. (To a European, the formality and deference customarily shown by a grown-up son to his father and even his elder brother and the distance between them, may seem excessive.)

Gurubani/Gurvani: lit. The words of the Guru. Particularly in Sikhism, the teachings of a Guru (as from the Holy Granth), in poetical form sung or chanted and accepted as the Voice of God.

Gurudev: a respectful form of address to a guru. An honorific accorded to a saintly and learned man, as, for example, Rabindranath Tagore: also, sometimes in irony, to someone who is far from learned or saint-like.

Gurpurb (Punjabi): lit. Guru's Day. Usually a reference either to the birthday of Guru Nanak (Kartik Purnima) or that of Guru Gobind Singh (December or January). Both occasions are lavishly celebrated by Sikhs: if street processions are taken out these may well be on the previous day.

Guru Purnima (Guru's Full Moon Day – *see* Calendars): the full moon day of the Hindu month of Asadh (June/July), an occasion when disciples and students specially honour

their teachers, the practice of Guru **Vandana**.

Gursikh: a Sikh who closely follows the precepts of the Sikh Gurus. An orthodox Sikh.

"Wahe Guru": in Sikhism, a term for God. Wah in Urdu is an exclamatory word of admiration, signifying excellence.

Sat Guru: the True Guru. Also a term used by Guru Nanak for God the Supreme God.

Guruwar : Thursday.

GURU GRANTH SAHIB *n* Hindustani from Sanskrit (Granth – like bible, a book, In Sanskrit the word comes from a knot, the knot that once held together inscribed palm leaves to form a book.) A respectful and reverential title in **Hindustani** for the sacred book of the **Sikhs**, also known as the Adi Granth - the original book: a book of peace and love for mankind. "None is our enemy, none is a stranger to us, we are in accord with one and all". (The Dasam Granth, on the other hand, the book of the tenth Guru, the work of Guru Gobind Singh, is a book to inspire soldiers and fighting men.) an anthology of devotional poems from the writings of the early Gurus and of praise and adoration of the bhagats (*see* bhakti), both Hindu and Muslim: compiled by Guru Arjun Dev in 1604. (Some of the compositions of Guru Teg **Bahadur** – *see*

Degchi – were incorporated later by Guru Gobind Singh.)

As a printed book, the 5,894 verses are invariably contained in exactly 1,430 pages: for reading, it is always placed on a cushion. The Granth Sahib is considered to be the Sacha Padshah/Badshah – true ruler, *see* Shah. An object paid deep reverence – but not worshipped – having a place of honour in every Sikh home: if possible in a separate room on a cushion, wrapped in a cloth when not in use, and with a canopy above or in a tabernacle known as the Palki Saheb the room may only be entered by a person barefoot and with the head covered. If carried in the street, a man barefoot goes before to sprinkle water, the Holy Granth itself will be on a small cot or on a special palki – *see* Carrying Chairs – on the head of a second: a third, also barefoot, walks behind reverently waving the chauri (*see* Yak), an ancient symbol of royalty, over the book: onlookers stand and offer respect. (for this sacred employment, the chauri may referred to as the chauri sahib). The tenth Guru, Gobind Singh, decreed that after his death, Sikhs should revere and bow to none visible save the Holy Granth, now known as the eleventh and eternal Guru. At a Sikh wedding, it is the steps taken together round the decorated Granth Sahib, in the place of the agni kund (sacred fire) of the Hindus, that make the couple man and wife.

Like Muslims with their holy Koran, Sikhs object to copies of the Granth Sahib being shown in Museums and exhibitions outside India. Not for reverence but to interest casual visitors.

The early editions of the holy Granth were handwritten on loose sheets, when bound together they could be known as bir, a Punjabi form of a word from Sanskrit to make strong, to fasten. An old copy of the Granth may be termed Bir to this day. To the chagrin of Sikhs, the original copy of the Granth Sahib is not in the Golden Temple but in private hands.

Granthi: strictly, an employee of a Gurdwara with the duty of reading aloud the Granth Sahib, but the title is sometimes used to mean a Sikh priest (mistakenly, for Sikhism has no priesthood).

GURUKUL *n* Hindi
Kul, **Sanskrit**: a residence, a family (there are other meanings also). A school in ancient India in which a small number of pupils of a guru lived as members of his domestic family, thus receiving constant personal attention and instruction: no fees were paid, but a parting gift, *see* Dakshina, was customary. In such a school, a boy would attain his second birth (*see* Janeu). The gurukul system today tends to be looked back on as that of a golden age of education, chiefly for the moral guidance believed to have been an important part.

GUWAHATI
The current roman spelling for the name of the town in Assam previously written as Gauhati.

GYAN/GIAN/JNAN *n* Hindi
Knowledge, learning.

Gyani: wise, learned. A learned man, particularly one with deep knowledge of the Sikh scriptures. An academic title the equivalent of a degree in oriental studies, awarded by certain **Punjab** and **Haryana** universities. Gyaniji: by custom, a polite form of address to a **Sikh**. Jnan is an alternative spelling in roman script, derived from the **Sanskrit** pronunciation of the word, jna—knowledge. (In English, linked to such words as gnostic and ignorance.)
Jnanyoga: see Yoga.

Jnanpith Award: an annual literary prize of Rs. 1,50,000 and a bronze replica of an 11th century temple statue to the Indian author of the most creative work in any one of fifteen languages (English is excluded). Selection is made at least five years after publication. The award is given by the Bharatiya Jnanpith (Institution of Indian Knowledge), a trust set up in 1944 with the object of the development of the literature, philosophy and culture of India.

GYMKHANA *n*
A Greek/English/Urdu hybrid word devised by British Victorians in India for the place, usually within a social club, where they exercised and played semi-enclosed ball games. It is said by some that the name is derived from the Urdu 'gendkhana', ballhouse. Later, a social club whose members, in theory at least, had an interest in open-air sports, particularly **polo**. Women, if admitted at all, might be restricted to a small area, sometimes colloquially and ungracefully known as the murgikhana – hen house.

Nowadays, an expensive social club, or, perhaps, just a medley sports meeting on horseback.

184

HABSHI *n* Urdu from Arabic

A term of the streets for a black African: considered as abuse by many Africans and at the least, pejorative by those using it, the word has a factual and straight forward background. At the time commerce between India and East Africa began (*see* Monsoon), the Habsh people occupied the coastal Horn of Africa (giving their name to Abyssinia) and the opposite part of Arabia across the Red Sea. The reason for the depreciation of the word probably was that until fairly recent times, many Habshis came to India as slaves. (The English word slave has a similar derivation via Latin. The Romans saw the Slav peoples of central and eastern Europe as captives.) In western India and in Hyderabad, a black African can be unexceptionably called a Sidi – a corruption, probably coined in the **Deccan sultanates**, from the Arabic **Sayid**. (A Spanish word for a chieftain, Cid, has the same source.)

HAFIZ *n* Urdu from Arabic

A guardian, a protector. To a Muslim, one of the attributes, or names, of God. A title for one who has memorised the whole of the Holy **Kor'an**.

Queen Victoria gave instructions that her **munshi** and Indian Secretary during the last fourteen years of her reign, Abdul Karim, as her protector, was to be addressed as Hafiz Abdul Karim. (Since Britons with Indian experience and also the Queen's household viewed the munshi with little enthusiasm, it seems probable that the suggestion for the honorific came from Abdul Karim himself.) *See also* Khuda Hafiz.

HAFTA *n* Urdu

Lit. a series, or a periodicity, of seven: hence a week. (From Old Persian linked to the **Sanskrit** saptah, a week and to the Greek hepta – seven – thence to such English words as heptagon, heptachy, hebdomadal.) The colloquial meaning is of a weekly or regular payment, normally made as a bribe. (The usual Urdu word for a bribe is rishwat, whence a term from Delhi's clerkdom for a small extra payment, vitamin R). A popular euphemism in government service for a bribe is upāri/upori, literally a supplement (in fact, to one's income). A similar word is ghūsa/ghoos (see Bandicoot). Among Muslims, hafta may be used to mean **Saturday**, in place of the Hindi (and **Hindu**) Sanichar, the last day of the Islamic week.

HAI-HAI *n* Hindi

A cry of grief; an interjectory lament; "alas", as on receiving bad news. A derisory shout following the name of a person or thing objected to by a group or public demonstration.

HAJ *n* Urdu

Lit. a setting out, a journey. The acts of faith at Mecca that are incumbent on every devout Muslim once in his lifetime (provided that his circumstances permit), during the five day period ending on the festival of **Id**-ul-Azha in the last month of the Islamic year, Zil-Haj. (A non-obligatory ritual performed at Mecca at other times is known as Umrah.) For the people of Arabia, the annual pilgrimage is far older than **Islam**, for it began, according to tradition, following the building of the House of God, the Ka'ba, in Mecca by **Ibrahim** and his son, Ishmael, now the centre of the Grand Mosque and the focus of worldwide Muslim prayers.

One undertaking the Haj will wear only the ihraam/ahraam, two pieces of unsewn white cloth. This garb may be assumed on setting out for Arabia.

Hadji (English form), *Haji:* a pilgrim performing the Haj. An honorific for one who has completed the Haj: on his return home he may prefix the word as a title for life before his name, and/or wear a green **puggri** – but this last is unusual in India. (Green is said to have been a colour pleasing to the Holy Prophet.) These distinctions are social customs but not Islamic law.

HAKIM *n* Urdu

With a long 'i' : strictly, a philosopher, but by common usage the word has come to mean a practitioner of Unani Tibb (from Ionian, of Greece), the traditional Islamic system of medicine. Also known as Tibb, Tibbia.

With a long 'a': a wise and just ruler (Arabic). Magistrate: the term is obsolete in India, but in Nepal the District Governor is still the Bara Hākim. The one who gives the orders.

HALĀL a Urdu

Lawful. Particularly as applied to meat that has been slaughtered in accordance with Islamic rites (*see* Bismillah). Pig meat can never be halal, nor flesh of a species which lives both on land and under water – such as the crab or the turtle. Of those under the water, only those manifestly fish are lawful. A substance such as animal gelatine–apart from water, the main ingredient of Western type table jellies–is behalal, not lawful. (The more usual antonym to halal is **harām**.) As an epithet for a man, halal has the meaning of one who follows closely the tenets of Islam.

HALDI *n* Hindi

The rhizome of turmeric (Curcuma), a relative of the ginger plant (in Hindi, adhrak). Requires cooking before use: pieces may be added to pickles, but mostly haldi is dried and ground to an orange yellow powder. By **Hindus**, the powder is considered auspicious (as of the colour kesri of gold and of the sun) and it can serve as an alternative to **kum kum** for ceremonies: the hands of a bride–to–be may be covered with haldi paste (often mixed with that of chandan – *see* Sandalwood), or even her whole body: similar attention may be paid to the groom. The reason possibly owing something to an additional belief that haldi lightens the complexion and softens the skin. As a condiment, it is added to all curries, it is the haldi that stains the clothes of unwary eaters: if washed, it may turn a deep red, the vegetable dye being reacted upon by the alkali of the soap. (But it is possible to be haldi spotted without ever sampling Indian food; in the shade of a garden tree one can be anointed by a curry partial crow perched overhead.)

In Indian medicine, haldi powder has long had the reputation of aiding the speedy healing of wounds. Industrially, haldi has a use as a colouring agent.

The botanical word for the genus. Curcuma, has a Sanskrit derivation.

HALWA *n* Urdu
Vegetables or fruit (particularly carrots – gajar halwa) cooked to a pulp in syrup with **ghee: suji** may be added. Karachi halwa is a clear stick-jaw jelly more often bought from a halwai than made in the home.

Halwai: the maker and seller of the halwa and other milk-based sweets, also of milk and **dahi**: often a very portly gentleman indeed. Since sweets are frequently offered to the deities, it follows that the halwai is usually a vegetarian: many would take exception to any meat or eggs being used or seen in his shop. In eastern India a confectioner may be termed a moira.

HAMAL/HAMALI *n* Urdu
In western India, a domestic servant; porter or casual labourer.

HAMMĀM/HAMĀM *n* Urdu
A Muslim enclosed bathing place using hot and cold water. A Turkish bath. The name is also given to the type of domestic bath water heater which uses a coke or charcoal fire.

HANGAMA : *n* Urdu from Persian
A commotion, a noisy disturbance by a crowd.

HANS/HANSA *n* Hindi
A goose (or a goose-like bird; a swan). In mythology, the vehicle (*see* Vahan) of both **Brahma** and of his consort, **Saraswati**, a bird of the land, the waters and the sky, with Mansarovar (*see* Kailas) as its natural habitat. Metaphorically, the bird can represent the sun or a man's soul.

Rajhans: a royal hans. An extra large goose, a gander perhaps or, as some say, a flamingo.

The hans has been a motif in **Hindu** design in clay, stone, metals and textiles for at least two thousand years: often appearing, it has to be admitted, most ungooselike, sometimes with a tail apparently borrowed from a squirrel. But the beak and the usually present webbed feet, can indicate the intention of the artist.

As an English word, goose has an Indo-European origin and is cognate to the **Sanskrit** bans (gans in Old High German).

HANUMĀN

Lit. he of the chin (hanu, a chin, in Hindi: actually a reference to his chin injured in babyhood). Commander of the army of the Vānars (the monkey people of the forest) of King Sugriv who helped Lord **Ram** to overcome his enemy. King Ravan of Lanka (*see* Shri) in the story as told in the *Ramayana:* an event commemorated particularly in the annual pageant of Ram **Lila**. Hanuman was born on a **Tuesday** (hence he is also known as **Mangal**) and is especially worshipped on that day, when large crowds flock to temples dedicated to him (Hanuman **Mandir**): to a lesser extent, he is also worshipped on Saturdays. His image, often in semi-relief on a stone slab, is always coloured vermilion (*see* Sindoor). The story is that Sita, the wife of Lord Ram, told Hanuman that she put red powder on the parting in her hair in order to please her husband:

Hanuman then decided to colour his whole body red in order to please Ram even more.

In the north, Hanuman is popularly believed to be a monkey (*see* Bandar) of the longtailed, blackfaced, greybearded langur species; but in south India he is identified with the bonnet monkey, a cousin of the northern macaque, the rhesus. Some accept Hanuman to be an **avatar** of Lord **Shiva**, the eleventh avatar of Lord Shiva and because he is said to have remained celibate all his life, brahmacharis revere him as their patron. Some **Hindus** may insist that no Hanuman icon is present in a connubial bedroom. Following from his celibacy, in Hindu credence, is his great strength: many who are physical cultural enthusiasts particularly swimmers and wrestlers, wear a red langot (waist cloth) for their exercises, to honour Hanuman and his mighty power. Again to honour Hanuman, a lady of strong convictions may wear no other than a red sari on a Tuesday.

Hanuman is also known as Lord Mahavir, the great hero, the brave one (not to be confused with Mahavira, the Jain tirthankara), and has often been called upon to inspire Indian soldiers before battle. At the same time he is cultured and is honoured as an expert in the **Sanskrit** language. Because of Hanuman and his army, few Hindus will wilfully harm a monkey, not even when a troop of them is damaging crops.

A story has it that Hanuman was the son of the god of the winds, Vayu or **Marut**, by a monkey mother; so yet another name for him is Maruti.

Hanuman Chalisa: twenty couplets (forty lines) in praise of Hanuman which may be sung or recited by a Hindu seeking the Lord's aid at a time of great distress or threatened danger.

Hanuman ring: a finger ring, often of copper, bearing an image of Hanuman, either embossed or engraved, indicating that the wearer has taken a vow of celibacy.

Bajrang: a strong frame, superhuman strength, used as an epithet for Hanuman. Bajrang A youth wing of the political party the BJP.

Bundi/Boondi: small crisp balls of sweetened gram flour, particularly made and sold on Tuesdays for offerings to Hanuman. As a general snack often added to raita, see Dahi.

HAR *n* Hindi
A name for Lord **Shiva**.
'HarHarMahadev': 'Shiva Shiva, great Lord', **Hindu** invocation and warcry of the Maratha armies.

Hari/Hare: originally, fiery, sunlike, golden (also green, e.g. **Haryana**). A name for Lord **Vishnu**. An invocation to him or in one of his various forms.

Hari/Har : *Vishnu and Shiva.*

Hardwar (Shaivite), *Haridwar* (Vaishnavite): Gateway to God. Pilgrim centre located where the River **Ganga** enters the plains; periodic locale for one of the great **Kumbh** parv (festivals). *Har Ki Pauri/Paudi:* the threshold to God. The most important' of the bathing **ghats** on the swiftly flowing river at Hardwar.

'Hare Krishna, Hare Ram : 'Oh Lord Krishna, Oh Lord Ram'.

Hare Har/Hari Har: a composite ShivaVishnu. Invoked in prayer and sometimes a single representation combining features of both deities may be seen.

Har/Haar: a necklace, a garland. A defeat. *See also* Lakh.

HARAM *n* Urdu
Pronounced with both a's short. That which is sacred: a sanctuary. As, for example, areas in the centre of Mecca and Old Jerusalem, from which non-Muslims are excluded. The sense of the word known best in the West, is used in Turkey and West Asia more than in India, where the equivalent of the women's section of a Muslim palace or large residence is the zenana (zan, Persian – a woman). Earlier, in

a Muslim noble family, the principal Begum (*see* Beg) could have also been termed the Haram. Separation of men and women has long been an Islamic way of life – copied in India by rich **Hindus** – but the haram, or zenana, was only possible for the well-to-do. The Western ideas of the glamorous and erotic 'harem', may have had a little, but not much, basis in fact. The haramsara, the residents of the haram, would have included the grandmothers, elderly aunts, young children and all the women of the family other than servants.

Harām/Haraam: Urdu: unlawful; i.e. against Islamic law.

Harām gosht: unlawful meat, e.g. pork, or meat from animals slaughtered without Islamic rites. *See* Halal.

Harāmzāda: lit. son of wickedness. A bastard. Used in general abuse.

Harāmi (noun and adjective): a rogue: unprincipled. Also naughty in a friendly way, as applied to a child.

HARIJAN/DALIT *n* and *adj* Hindi
Harijan. A term from scripture: lit. one devoted to Hari (God) or one particularly favoured by God. A Gujarati **bhakti** saint poet of the 14th century (one Narasimha Mehta), gave it a wider application to include those worthy but born outside **caste Hindu** society. In the early 1930's, **Mahatma** Gandhi accepted this interpretation and popularised it as being without obloquy to give self respect to people within the Hindu system but known as untouchable (achhut), beyond the four castes, the fifth group (panchama or avarn), the depressed classes, exterior castes and Scheduled Castes (*see* below). A shudra from whom the upper castes will not take water will be harijan. Also, the barbers, some artisans, landless labourers and at the lower end of the scale, the washermen (**dhobies**), the leather workers (**chamars**), the **sweepers** and others performing services considered by caste Hindus to be ritually polluting. With some versimilitude, at one time in South India (but probably not today) a harijan could have been the child of a **devadasi**: i.e., one married to a temple deity.

Such is the permanence of Hindu culture that the status of the outcaste continues the aversion that the almost prehistory Indo-**Aryans** felt for some of the local tribes they met and subjugated (*see* Adivasi): people of different habits from themselves with snub noses and of darker colour. These tribes were condemned to be hereditary performers of the more unpleasant but essential tasks and to have the minimum of social contact with those who later became caste Hindus. (As might be expected, the one context in which male caste Hindus have not invariably found the harijan to be untouchable, is that of extra-marital sex.)

Continental Europe also had its untouchables. One example is from the western seaboard, from Spain to Brittany, from the middle ages until the early years of the 18th century, members of a group, the Cagots, were socially ostracised and had an inferior legal status: any physical contact with them was considered defiling. Although Christians, both in church and in the graveyard, they were kept separate from others: but like the harijans, they were acceptable at popular festivals as musicians (*see* Pariah).

After **Independence** within the community many rejected the Mahatma's conferred euphemism as patronising and preferred the struggle epithet touching their own experience and used by their leader Dr. Ambedkar (*see* Mahar), dalit, meaning depressed, downtrodden, crushed. (A word with the same **Sanskrit** origin, dalia, meaning wheat grains crushed and broken for making porridge, indicates the significance of dalit). Reacting to pressure from those hitherto harijan, in 1994 the GOI ordered that the Mahatma's word would not be used in any official paper, to be replaced by Scheduled Caste. It is said that when Dr. Ambedkar used the term, he included all groups not being **caste** Hindus who felt crushed by society even if Christian or Bud-

dhist. Harijan is a word now rarely used. Also in 1994, the GOI rejected girijan - hillman, *see* Giri.

The expressions Scheduled Castes (often coupled with the Scheduled Tribes, *see* Adivasis), arose from a provision in the Government of India Act 1935, allowing the then 'depressed classes' special parliamentary representation, so that it became necessary to list the groups so entitled (this privilege continues, both in the central and in the state legislatures). It was done in provincial schedules (439 groups in all) attached to an order of 1936. The schedules, as amended from time to time, were later included in the Constitution. By 1984, the figure was 916, (It must be noted that the lists were separate for each province and so now remain for each state: some groups, particularly the Chamars and the Valmikis, appear in many lists, so 916 did not represent the 1984 all India total of the Scheduled Castes.) Scheduled Caste is a precise official term, but harijan was applied subjectively. Thus, while most, if not all harijans were of a Scheduled Caste, not all those of the Scheduled Castes were everywhere regarded as harijan: a profession that in one region carries an untouchable label, in another may not do so.

In recent decades it has been recognised that there are other groups at the bottom of the social scale who should be assisted to rise. Lists have been prepared state by state of such groups, termed Backward and Other Backward Classes (or SEBC Socially and Educationally Backward Classes); the word caste is not used since minorities not within the Hindu caste system are included; e.g. Christians. Government civil employment may be reserved to persons from such groups additional to the earlier reservations for the Scheduled Castes etc. in numbers so that the general competition open to all, is not reduced below 50% of the annual recruitment (Supreme Court ruling).

Similarly, places in colleges may be reserved for the SEBC's. It is known that some families from the listed groups have prospered and already enjoy income and social position well above their state average. Individuals from such families, the 'creamy layer', are to be excluded from the concessions. The terms used are not easy to define strictly and objectively. and probably impossible on an all-India basis, so that to establish whether or not a particular person is entitled to privilege can be hard. Today (1996), in some states the total percentage of reservations for those thought to be entitled to assistance has risen well above the fifty limit of the Supreme Court.

From the descriptive term Backward Classes/Castes inevitably the unofficial corollary Forward Classes/Castes (FCs) has come into use.

In spite of the generally used designation given by the Mahatma, some caste Hindus do not accept that the dalit is close to God: in fact, his position may be thought to be one of considerable distance, the result of divine rejection for a transgression against **dharma** committed in a past life. From this orthodoxy an extreme opinion follows that to improve the lot of the untouchable is to thwart the will of God.

The practise of any form of untouchability or discrimination against dalits (approximately one Indian in seven) in a public place is a legal offence and it is official policy to assist the community to obtain education and other than traditional employment. As elsewhere, so within the Scheduled Castes there are gradations: while the sweepers and the leather workers were generally content to accept the term harijan as applying to themselves (some adopted it as a family name), others, as they rise in the world, for example many shudras, carpenters, and the more prosperous washermen – particularly if they have been reborn as dry cleaners may prefer to forget their background.

Contrariwise, some low privilege groups not traditionally regarded as untouchable, may endeavour to get themselves included in the schedules in order to benefit from employment and educational advantages offered by the government. In the changed conditions of today, the necessary new working relationship between the dalit and the caste Hindu is not always easily achieved. In a village community, savarn farmers may still be dependant on the dalit, who now with the alternative of work in a town, may be able to bargain for wages. A rise in status and prosperity by those hitherto at the bottom, together with a new awareness that as citizens they too have rights, can only be resented by those who found useful a pool of cheap and compliant labour, as also by a group a step up in the social : scale which feels its position of slight dominance threatened. A response can be a bloody pogram. An illegal discrimination that still can be found particularly in the south, is in a tea-shop where separate glasses may be mandatory for use by dalits. Even in Delhi a Caste Hindu Shopkeeper my baulk at receiving a payment from the hand of a dalit, but require the cash to be placed on the counter. Against some dalit groups is the fact that although hand scavenging of non-flush dry latrines was banned by law in 1993, in the absence of any alternative method, the practice is still (AD 2002) widely used.

There is clearly potential for conflict of interests between the 1950 Constitution, guaranteeing legal equality for all and a caste Hindu population accustomed to several thousand years of socially accepted hierarchy stemming from birth and a scale of contextual criminal law pun-

ishments favourable to **brahmans**. (*See* **Manu**). That the traditional law is still there was indicated tn a case reported in 1991 from a village about 112 km south of Delhi. An eighteen year old harijan boy was alleged to have been too friendly with a **Jat** girl. By judgement of an unofficial Jat panchayat, the boy, his friend and the girl were hanged from a banyan tree: the girl's father was said to have consented to her 'execution'.

The Harijan: a weekly journal edited by Mahatma Gandhi during the periods 1933-34, 1946-48. It ceased publication in 1955.

Bahujan: mankind, the commonality, the people. In this sense the word is used in the motto on the logo of All India Radio. In recent years, a political meaning is foremost, the working people, the toilers. Adopted by the dalits for a political party. The Bahujan Samaj Party (BSP), to include all those who feel exploited by caste Hindus.

Subaltern Classes : a recent descriptive term from sociology for those of the lower levels of Indian Society.

HARTĀL *n* Hindi
Lit. a shop closing. A refusal to work, normally as a protest or as coercion. But mostly, it is applied to the closing of shops and **bazaars**: by the merchants themselves rather than workers. A **bandh** has a similar but

wider meaning covering all forms of commercial and industrial activity: a general-strike of workers probably called by political leaders.

Hartal, a mineral, *see* Orpiment.

Bhukh Hartal: a hunger strike.

HARYĀNA *n* Hindi
Lit. a condition of verdure, greenery. A state to the west of Delhi, formed from the partition in 1966 of the then **Punjab**: but the name is the traditional one for the region. (One of the prestige regiments of the British Indian army in the middle years of the 19th century, was the Irregular Corps, the Urrianah Light Infantry. During the **First War of Independence**, they held the Kashmiri Gate, from the inside, at the time of the British assault on Delhi.) In Hinduism, hariyali can mean the fertile green covered soil of Mother India.

HATTI *n* Punjabi
A shop: often seen as a notice such as 'Kapur di Hatti', Kapur's Shop.
Hat/Hatt n Hindi: in rural areas, a **bazaar** held not daily, but at regular intervals, perhaps a weekly market.

HAVĀLA/HAWĀLA *n* Urdu
A legal term from Arabic: a reassignment of debts from one party to another. In Hindustani, money or property placed in the custody of a trusted person: a trust. Earlier, particularly in western India, often

a euphemism, a reference to the transfer of funds in the black market between a foreign currency and the **rupee**.

In the 1990's, the word aquired an all India use, meaning an undercover payment, sometimes very large, often but not necessarily in foreign exchange, to one with political power in the expectation of favours. A corrupt practice.

HAVAN *n* Hindi
Also known, from ancient Persian, as hom/homan. Lit. a fire sacrifice, a fire offering. **Hindu** ritual from Vedic days (*see* Vedas) invoking the  intervention of the gods for a specific purpose: a ceremony conducted by a priest before the sacred fire personifying the God Agni, which, acting as a messenger carries the offering, the prayers or, in the cremation ritual, the human spirit, to the heavens and the gods. Agni is present at almost all Hindu rituals in the form of a flame, perhaps a **diya/diva**.

Agni is usually shown as having two heads and his vehicle (*see* Vahan), is a ram. Such English fire words as igneous, ignite, are linked through Latin to the **Sanskrit** ag, fire. Those who worshipped Agni cremated their dead, as, of course, do Hindus today. (During part of the bronze

194

age, say, 1000 BC, the custom of cremation spread westward across Europe and reached even Britain – but the habit of burial reasserted itself later – a supposition is that cremation was carried by waves of migrating **Aryans**.) It is respect to Agni which makes traditionalists reluctant to extinguish a domestic fire in the hearth or to douse the hot ashes even when, as in a high wind in a community of grass huts, there can be a danger to life. Again, some will not blow out a small lamp flame, particularly if it has been used in a **puja** ritual, for breath can carry a drop of saliva, a highly impure substance; nor may it be snuffed between finger and thumb. The procedure would be to wave the lamp in the air until it goes out, or to make a current of air with a cloth. (Since saliva is such a pollutant, it can be imagined with what horror some view the European custom of moistening the gum of postage stamps and envelopes with the tongue: i.e. sending one's saliva to a correspondent. A **Sikh** pathi (*see* Akhand) when reading aloud from the **Guru** Granth Sahib, will often have a cloth in front of his mouth to remove the chance of a drop of saliva falling on the holy book.) **Manu**, the law-giver, implies that it is impious to warm one's feet (ignoble parts of the body – *see* Shoe) at a fireside. The strict will not allow a child to blow out the candles on a birthday cake.

Havan/Hom **Kund**: the small pit in which the ceremonial fire burns, the focal point of the Hindu marriage ceremony. The fire is witness to the bond. (Focal point is a pertinent term, for the ancient Romans also greatly respected fire and to them the word focus had the meaning of the central point of the home, the everburning domestic hearth.)

In Vedic times, the priest who tended the fire and made the offerings was the agnihotri: the word is now a brahman family name. *See also* Yagna.

HAVĒLI *n* Urdu from Persian.
An enclosed space. A large residential building now becoming rare. A joint family ancestral home forming one economic unit. Residential buildings grouped around a court or lane with a common entrance and owned by one family. Originally, for security, blank walls to the outside world and a defensible gateway.

HAVILDĀR *n* Urdu
A military and police rank equivalent to sergeant, but in some police forces, the designation of a three-striper is Head Constable. The literal meaning of the word, from Persian (*see* Zamindar), is the holder of an office of trust. The title, like constable in English, was once that of a rather more senior officer than today, e.g., the commandant of a fortress could well have been styled the Havildar. In the cavalry and mounted units, the equivalent rank is daffadar.

HAYAT *n* Urdu
From Arabic: life, as in hayat baksh, life-giving. The name of the Emperor's private garden in his palace in Delhi (the Red Fort).

Hayatt: as of the hotel chain. No connection with the Arabic word. The story is that the name was that of the first guest to check-in at the opening of the new hotel in New York.

Abhayat: Arabic, "Water is life".

HAZOOR/HUZOOR *n* Urdu
Your honour, your honourable presence. A form of address probably considered somewhat servile today.

Hazoori: sycophancy. *See* also ji.

HAZRAT *n* Urdu
Lit. Majesty, presence (in the sense of an august personage), Muslim title of honour and respect accorded to a person 'of the Book' (*see* Kitab)., one considered to be a prophet of God or a saint, e.g. Hazrat Mohammed or Hazrat **Isa** Masih (Jesus Christ), or for a place with Islamic sacred associations, such as the famous mosque of the Dal Lake in Srinagar, Hazratbal, the repository of a relic of the Holy Prophet himself, a strand of hair. (Although bal means hair in Urdu, in this instance the word is Kashmiri for a place – Hazratbal – the revered place.)

HAZRI *n* Urdu

Lit. presence, attendance, muster. With a police connection, hazri can be the daily reporting of one with a criminal record (*see* Criminal Tribes) to a police station. In British days the word acquired the meaning to Europeans and those associated with them, of breakfast (the usual north Indian word is from Persian, nashta, – light meal, refreshment).

Chhota-hazri: again an anglicism – small breakfast. Early morning bed tea, plus, perhaps, a biscuit. The expression is now on the way out, being replaced by the literal 'palang chai' – bed tea (*see* Char). A British army term for morning tea, gunfire, followed from the early morning time signal gun in **cantonments**.

Many years ago in a British Indian household, a breakfast side–dish could well have been a complete cooked ham, to be carved by a guest in the way he liked. All guests were not skilled with a carving knife and the end result could be a ham with fuzzy irregular edges. The host might then order the joint to be neatened, meaning that it should be recut so as to present a smooth clean surface for slicing. The verb is to be found in the **OED**.

Jalpan : A snack, a small breakfast. Strictly little more than water with perhaps a piece of **gur**, or a batasha (see Prasad), sustenance. Also a term for a small payment with perhaps an element of bribery.

HEATING FOODS
Euphemism for foods thought to enhance sexual strength and passion (heating) in the human body, chiefly animal protein and eggs. The reverse is achieved by cooling foods, mostly vegetable, but not entirely almonds (**badam**), for example, are thought to be particularly invigorating. The theory comes from ayurveda (*see* Ayurvedic). The Chinese, Malays and some other Asian peoples, similarly categorise their food and drink. Those who wish to lead a godly and contemplative life are recommended to avoid heating foods: in general, they are considered ill-advised for women and firmly to be avoided by widows.

A Vedic classification, still accepted by some, divided food into sattvik, rajasik and tamāsik. Sattvik (satv, pertaining to purity, righteousness and virtue) foods are simple, natural and vegetarian: such as dairy products, honey, **gur**, vegetables – excluding garlic and onions and, some will aver, exotics like the chilli and tomato – fruit and cereals. Rajasik (of the good things of life, pertaining to kingship) items are high protein: fish, eggs, meat and wines. Tamasik foods (tamas, darkness and ignorance) are forbidden to all **caste Hindus**: beef, village pork (but wild boar is sometimes included in the rajasik category, particularly by **Rajputs**), fish without scales (e.g. eels) and spirits. In these days, some consider any convenience

food out of a tin or packet to be tamasik. *See also* Panchama.

HĒNNA *n* Urdu and English
Pronounced in Urdu as in the original Arabic, heena. A shrub (*Lawsonia*): the leaves, dried and sold in the **bazaar** as a green powder, after mixing with water make a reddish dye about an hour after application, also called henna. Mostly used for decorative purposes on the hair, hands, nails and feet. It is widely believed that henna painted on the soles of the feet will cool the body in hot weather. In Bengal and eastern India a similar belief is attached to alta, a bottled red liquid traditionally prepared from the waxy secretions of the **lac** insect. Intricate designs traced on the hands are particularly popular in Rajasthan, especially for weddings. The designs may be freepainted by a professional or, more likely these days, produced within the family using thin plastic stencils. The colour takes at least ten days to fade.

Hindi speakers usually use the word mehndi from Sanskrit for the same dye, Mehndi can also mean the ceremony preceding a wedding in which the hands and feet of the bride-to-be are decorated with henna patterns. As used in the Bible (Song of Solomon 1: 14) an obsolete English word for henna is camphire.

Kali mehndi (black mehndi): in effect, a black hair dye. Black dye combined with mehndi, available in both powder and liquid form: said to restore a youthful appearance and to cool the head. (And not only for humans: in rural India allegations are sometimes made that a farmer with cattle for market is not above using hair dye on older beasts to make them appear young and sleek.)

HIFS *n*
'Hitler Indian Forces'. An acronym used in the Indian army at the close of World War II in connection with returning Indian prisoners of war from German hands, meaning those who were considered to have; changed sides or in some way to have assisted their captors. Similarly JIFS, 'Japanese Indian Forces'. *See also* Azad Hindi Fauj.

HIGH COMMISSIONER
In India, usually a reference to the title of the diplomatic representative of one government to another, both being members of the Commonwealth of Nations: an indication of their rather special relationship. In this context, it seems to have been first applied to the agent of Canada in London in 1880: as the two governments were each headed by Queen Victoria, the title of Minister or Ambassador would have been inappropriate. India has had a High Commissioner in London since 1920 (his duties were nonpolitical before **Independence**). In London, some differences exist between the honours paid to a High Commissioner and to an Ambassador (e.g. a High Commissioner on presenting his credentials to the Sovereign is conveyed to the Palace by a vehicle from the Royal Mews with four horses, while an Ambassador has to be content with but two). In New Delhi no distinction is observed. The Indian High Commissioner in London today still uses as his office the building designed by Sir Herbert Baker in 1930.

Elsewhere in diplomacy, following from its service to the Allies in World War I, India was a founder member of the League of Nations with an Indian representative in Geneva. But, naturally enough, he had to put forward the views of the then GOI.

HIJRAS/HIJDAS *n* Urdu
Lit. impotent ones. An alternative term from Arabic (khunsa) is khusra; hermaphrodites (Hermes plus Aphrodite). Male transvestites living a tribal and group life in communities found all over India, with an accepted – if only with an amused tolerance – place in society. (In  some areas, particularly rural Gujarat, they receive considerably more respect: some see them as embodiments of the Goddess **Durga**, whose blessings are to be

sought and whose curse is anathema.) Popularly believed to be eunuchs, by no means all are emasculate. Many, known to the community as **zenanas**, are in possession of all their faculties, although some may not be fully developed. A child of indeterminate sex, considered a **pariah** by society and parents, may find a refuge of sorts within the collegiate life of a hijra group, led by one known as the **Guru**, Some, more akin to the western pattern, driven by who knows what urges, may live a double life: a normal worker by day and as a transvestite by night. In recent years there have been allegations of youths being first befriended by hijra gurus and later forcibly castrated, so that they have little alternative but to join a group. Hijras/zenanas often live in association with normally dressed males of the Mirāsi sect (Muslim musicians, singers and dancers of low social status).

A group (toli) of transvestites may appear when a family moves into a new house: at a wedding or at a home on the birth of a child, particularly when male, offering blessings and congratulations (badhai), clapping their hands in rhythm and singing songs of joy, sometimes to the considerable embarrassment of the family, to depart only after receiving a payment considered adequate (the fee for a girl is less than for a boy). Other groups visit the bazaars, chant blessings, clap hands and demand alms from shopkeepers: few refuse

to pay up, since none wishes to be the object of a full volume flow of gutter abuse from the party of these counterfeit viragos and many will consider it particularly inauspicious to be cursed by a hijra. On city roadsides in the evenings, couples or individual hijras can sometimes be seen offering their services to those who can find satisfaction from a fantasy woman.

Recruits, both **Hindu** and Muslim, adopt female names and insist on being treated as women. They sometimes go through what, within the community, is treated as a marriage with a Mirasi 'husband'. It is these Mirasis who serve the hijras by carrying out essentially male duties, such as burial or cremation arrangements, which accounts for the public belief, having never noticed a hijra funeral, that the rites are secret.

A word from the bazaars for a hijra is chhakka, lit. the number six. The analogy is via a clock face and is phallic: the figure six is at the bottom and the hour hand in that position can be said to be flaccid, impotent. The term can also be used for a generally incompetant person. Chhakka can also be a six as in cards, dice or cricket.

In the south, from Tamil, the word for a hijra is ali.

HILLS, THE
A high altitude area but unlike the high mountains, reasonably

accessible as a place of escape from the summer heat of the plains. In the days before air conditioning for the wealthy, to spend six or seven months of the hot weather in the hills was normal for all Europeans who could afford the time: if the **Sahibs** had duties to keep them in the plains, then their wives and children had to go alone. European schools were in the hills, with a single annual session normally, from early March to end November. Earlier, the **Moguls** had discovered the delights of Kashmir in the summer, but many of the hill **stations** of today were first developed as sanatoria (as they were then called) for British troops following the discovery during the Nepal war (1814/16) of the health restoring benefits of their situation. (Those on sickleave in the hills, particularly officers, were sanatorians.)

For almost a century prior to World War II, officials moved to **Shimla** during the summer (the first Gov- ernor- General to make the journey was Lord Amherst in 1827) but the annual migration as routine for the major part of the Government of India, from **chaprasi** to **Viceroy**, at first from Calcutta and then Delhi, did not begin until the time of Sir John Lawrence (1863). But perhaps it was not roses all the way: com- mented Field Marshall Lord Roberts (Forty-one years in India), "At the best, one gets very tired of the hills by the close of summer". The provincial

governments also had their winter and summer capitals, as did some of the **princely** states.

Geographically, the hills was a subjective term: to the people of the north and the wealthy everywhere, they were the **Himalaya** ranges; to those of the south, the Nilgiris (*see* Giri), particularly the summer capital of the old Madras **Presidency**, Oo- tacamund (or Ooty), now renamed, Udagamandalam; to **Bombay Ducks**, a place like Matheran high on the Western Ghats, or Mount Abu in Rajputana (*see* Rajput), people from the old Central Provinces would go to Pachmari (Madhya **Pradesh**).

The bungalows with their English country names and garden flowers are still there, memorials to Victorian Britons: those who can, the sahibs of today, still visit the hills in summer, probably in numbers more than ever before, but for much shorter periods, often for no more than a few days at a time. No longer are the central and the state governments able to afford two capital cities. (An exception is the government of Jammu & Kash- mir, which in part still moves be- tween Srinagar and Jammu.) Shimla, once deserted in winter, remains the state (**HP**) capital the year round.

Winter line: a European term of those northern hill stations from which the plains arc visible to the south (e.g., Mussoorie, but not Shimla). During the winter months, for some time after the sun has set well below the western horizon, as seen from the hills there is seemingly a straight line below which darkness is complete over the plains, but above which a colourful twilight still illuminates the atmosphere. In summer there is no sharp division, but a graded diminution of light to dusk at plains level. A reason, perhaps, is that in summer the sun sets further towards the north and sinks out of sight at less than the near right angle of the winter so that twilight lasts much longer.

HIMĀLAYAS

An anglicism: the Hindi name for the region, Himalaya (with the first a pronounced long), lit. the place of snow, mutated to an English plural. The great high barrier wall, the northern boundary of India separating the **plains** from the Central Asia plateau – causing the **monsoon** rains to give life and prosperity to the south but the partial desertification of Tibet. Also known as Himal-**pahar** or Hima Pahar – snow mountains – and Giriraj – the king of mountains. The mystic home of the **rishis** and of the gods, the Hindu Mount Olympus, Vaikunth to Vaishnavites (*see* Vishnu) and Swarg (heaven) to Shaivites (*see* Kailash). The range upon range of hills, including Everest, the highest mountain of the world, running roughly west to east from Afghanistan to the Indian frontier with **Burma**, where the general direction abruptly changes from north to south.

Geologists say that the plate carrying the Indian plains is moving northwards and that the distance between Kanyakumari and a fixed spot in the hills is decreasing by two cms a year so that earth tremors can be expected in the future.

Himsagar Express: see Sagar.

HIMROO/HAMROO *n*

Handloom silk brocade woven into cotton, mainly produced in Aurangabad **district** (Maharashtra): a special quality being that both sides are identical.

HIND/HINDI/HINDU *n* & adj
Urdu frum Persian

To the early Persian empires, words relating to the lands to their south-east, beyond the barrier of the mighty Indus. Geographical terms meaning the territory of the Indus River, Sind. (In Persian the s sound became h). From more recent times, Hind became a reference to India as a whole as in the slogan "Jai Hind". Queen Victoria used the word in her Urdu title "Kaisar-i-Hind" - "Empress of India": see Viceroy. Hindi refers only to the Sanskrit-based language of northern India and Hindu only to a person of the Hindu religion. None of the three is to be found in any Indian classical text.

Hinduism has no known founder

whose doctrines could bind his followers: no definitive Holy Book, nor an undisputed authoritarian hierachy to pronounce heresy on any particular theory. It is more than a religion, it is an identity, a way of life, the product of more than four thousand years of man's intellectual effort, of the deities and moral and social codes of the early **Aryans** and folk beliefs of gods and godlings of the myriad peoples of the subcontinent. All combining, yet somewhere retaining their separate identities and, by some at least, all perceived as aspects of a single Supreme Godhead. But with diversity there is a clear thread uniting, say, the Hindu fisherman of the south, the learned **pandit** of Varanasi and the **Rajput** soldier. Yet to put it in words seems a task beyond even the government, for when required to say who is a Hindu, their answer was to define who, of the citizens of India, is not. Hindu is not an original Indian word, but early Persian for the peoples of Sindhu (*see* India). Only with the coming of the Muslim invaders did the word begin to acquire its religious connection. But in law today, the matter is not entirely one of faith. Article 25 of the Constitution of India affirms that a Buddhist, Jain, or **Sikh** is to be considered a Hindu. In 1955-56, in the Hindu Code (*see below*), parliament stated that a Hindu is anyone not a member of a Scheduled Tribe (*see* Adivasi), nor of a foreign' religion (Muslim, **Parsi**, Christian, Jew etc.), unless it is proved that such a person cannot be governed by Hindu law or custom. It is sometimes suggested that Hinduism is not an appropriate name for a religion, and that the faith of those who adhere to the brahmanic **dharma**, more correctly could be termed Brahmanism (*see* Brahman and Sanatan Dharma); but change is unlikely. Today, many Sikhs repudiate the legal position that their faith is a sect within Hinduism: they remember the words of their founder, Guru Nanak, "I am not Hindu, I am not Muslim". Hindu philosophers may perceive their religion as but one road of many to a single Godhead, but this is not the understanding of the multitude to whom it is an exclusive social and cultural way of life: to many of them, other faiths in India are an intrusion. (The Constitution declares India to be a secular state wherein all may worship as they choose some will affirm that secularism is a European concept alien to India)

Hindutva: the Hindu ethos, the characteristics of a an ethnic Hindu community. Hinduism. Including perhaps a chauvinistic conviction that Hindus should be in a dominant position in their homeland. A gut feeling that the country must have a national culture and that only that of the majority religion can be acceptable. Hindutva as a word is more often used by politicians than semanticists. Some declare it to mean no more than the quality of Indianness deriving from domicile in

Hindustan. Others, stridently affirm that those with a faith centred outside the country cannot be nationalists. Such aggressive Hindutvi may be termed prakhar Hindutva.

As Hindu revivalism, some date Hindutva to a very popular dramatisation of the **Ramayana** (Plus some interpolations) broadcast over many Sunday mornings by the state television network from January 1988.

The term Hindutva seems to have been coined by V D Savarkar in 1920 and became the title of his book published in 1923. The volume is regarded as Holy Writ by the organisation which followed from it, the **RSS**.

HINDU CODE *n*
A reference to a series of Acts passed in 1955-56 with the intention of modernising and codifying Hindu personal law, perhaps as a step to a single all India family code. The Constitution directs, as a goal, a uniform civil code (UCC) for all, but like the British earlier, governments since Independence have found that to codify the gamut of customs and *lex loci* (law of the place), many held with religious fervour, governing family relations for the peoples of India, is just too hot a potato to handle. The following measures are usually considered to encompass the Code: Hindu Marriage Act, 1955; Hindu Succession Act, 1956; Hindu Adoptions and Maintenance Act, 1956; Hindu Minority and Guardianship Act, 1956. In an

earlier day, the first British attempt to set down Hindu law was 'The Gentoo Code' of Nathanial Halhead, published in 1776. (Gentoo was a 17th and 18th century anglicism for Hindu from gentio, Portuguese for heathen. The word remains in use for a species of penguin.)

HINDU GAINS OF LEARNING ACT 1930
An Act designed to ensure that property acquired by an educated person (as the result of his education) in a Hindu joint family, remains, if he so desires, his personal and not joint property, even though the family may have paid for his education.

HINDUSTAN *n* Urdu
Lit. the land of the Hindu: from early times, the Muslim name for India. Nowadays, to some the whole country, but to many, the word carries the meaning of the Gangetic plain alone, the cradle of Hinduism and the Hindi language, excluding Bengal and eastern Bihar. To the British in Bengal before the advance into the **Punjab**, the territory somewhat vaguely described as 'up country'.

Hindustani: a person from Hindustan. A popular *lingua franca* a mixture of Urdu, Hindi and English words: but this everyday speech is increasingly being called Hindi – or perhaps, when English words are numerous, sometimes in a form peculiar to India, as in the conversation of, say, a Delhi government clerk, Hinglish. *See also* Khari Boli.

Pre-independence both Jawaharlal Nehru and Gandhiji supported Hindustani as the national language a golden mean between Hindi and Urdu. A sweet mingling of the two: but this was not to be.

Hindustani culture: usually a reference to the composite Hindu and Persian Muslim areas of understanding of the upper classes in northern India wherein each could participate and perhaps influence the arts of the other: sometimes termed the Ganga-Yumuna tehzib (the culture of the two great rivers and particularly of Lucknow: a combination of dignity and warmth of feeling.) For example, Hindustani music, the classical music style of the north, as opposed to the **Carnatic** style of the south, is considered to have been influenced by Muslim contacts. And in fact, many of the leading exponents of Hindu music were Muslims; Hindus could enjoy Urdu poetry (*see* Mushaira and Ghazal); city night life could be shared (*see* Dancing Girls). But since **Independence** in 1947, the tendency in each community has been to reduce contacts and to ignore the other. (A classic evocation of Hindustani culture is the 1905 novel by Mirza Ruswa The Courtesan of Lucknow, Umrao Jan Ada, translated into English by Khushwant Singh and M.A. Husaini.) Until recently,

professional Muslim musicians (as a class, Rababis, players on the rabab, a sitarlike, stringed instrument from Persian Mogul days) were occasionally used in Sikh gurdwaras for kirtan and still are in gurdwaras in Pakistan.

HING *n* Hindi
Asafoetida: a waxy latex with a strong smell obtained from the living roots of a number of species of the ferula family, grown in western and central Asia. Hing sold in India is mostly imported: used as a condiment and in Indian medicine. That sold in the bazaars is alleged to be heavily adulterated with gum arabic (*see* Babul). The English name is from a particular ferula variety, *assafoetida*, *assa* from the Persian for mastic, and *foetida* linked to fetid – stinking.

Some will say that burning hing in a room will clear it of mosquitoes.

HIP *n* English
As in hip pocket. With English speakers, in the singular a euphemism for buttocks: in street Hindustani (*see* Hindustan) used with no euphemistic intent. Wrote Nirad C Chaudhry (Continent of Circe) "...it is a common experience to see peasant boys uncovering themselves and waving their hips at a passing train and its passengers." As can be imagined the local meaning associated with hip did little for the status of those uncon-

ventional Europeans who appeared in India in the 1960s, the hippies. (In Sanskrit there is also a link between hip and buttock, the word kati can apply to both).

Again, a term in English for the buttocks, nates, from Latin and anatomy, can be shown to be linked to a **Sanskrit** word with the same meaning, nitamb – in Sanskrit, also the beauty of a curved slope of a mountain-side or of a river bank. But a word from Persian, batakh, has the meaning of duck.

HOBSON-JOBSON *n*
Title of a famous glossary by Henry Yule, of **Anglo-Indian** words and phrases, unique in style, erudition and, above all, readability. First published in 1886, with a revised edition in 1903. In the book, Hobson-Jobson is said to be the English soldiers' version of the cry 'ya Hasan, ya Husain', uttered by Shia Muslim (*see* Sunnis) processionists at the time of **Muharram**.

The glossary was reviewed in April 1886 for his paper by a twenty-one year old reporter of the daily *Civil & Military Gazette* of Lahore (total editorial staff two), one Rudyard Kipling: "...unless we are much mistaken, it will take its place amongst the standard works on the east; and will pass, gathering bulk as it goes, from decade to decade". Prescient, but understated: the edition of 1903 did contain added material and the

volume, still in print, has entered its second century as a work of reference. The reviewer took Henry Yule to task for his contention that there is no contemporary evidence for the story that the doomba (doombur in *Hobson-Jobson*), the fat-tailed sheep of the Punjab and Afghanistan, pulls an attached cart to support its gross tail: Kipling asserted that such a ram with just such an appendage could be seen on the streets of Lahore.

Since *Hobson-Jobson* supplies none, a few biographical details of the main author will not be out of place (his collaborator, Arthur Burnell, Ph.D., C.I.E., of the Madras Civil Service, has had little notice other than the tribute paid to him in the preface to the work. Once known for his **Sanskrit** scholarship, at his death in 1882 he had completed only a little more than half of his translation of the Laws of **Manu**).

Colonel Sir Henry Yule C.B., K.C.S. I. served in India from 1840 to 1862, first as a military engineer (at one period, he was Executive Engineer at Roorkee for the building of the Ganges Canal) and then in general administration, mostly connected with public works. The design of the marble screen of the 1857 Memorial Well at **Kanpur** (now in the **Cantonment** churchyard) was his, and although construction work did not begin until some years after he had left India, the existence of today's metre gauge railway system (*see* Broad Gauge) is in part due to his advocacy. Following his retirement, he was appointed a life member of the Council of India in London. (An advisory body to the Secretary of State for India. Since the statutory term for a Member was ten years, a special Act of Parliament was required to sanction the appointment.)

In his later days. Col. Yule became a prolific writer, the list of his publications (but many are no more than pamphlets) runs to over 175 titles. He specialised in the study of early travellers in central Asia and his two volumes on the journeys of Marco Polo have been the definitive authority on the subject (but today, scholarship is raising doubts that Marco Polo went to China at all). The Latin dedication of *Hobson-Jobson* to G.U.Y. is to Sir Henry's elder brother. Sir George Uday Yule, C.B., K.C.S.I., also of the Indian service who died only days after it was written in 1886. A younger brother, Robert, was killed in the fighting at Delhi in 1857 (*see* First War of Independence. His name is among those on the 'Mutiny Memorial' there: 'Lt. Col. R.A. Yule, 9th Lancers'). Sir Henry received the K.C.S.I. in 1889, the year of his death.

HOLI *n* Hindi
A major and the final festival of the **Hindu** annual **calendar**; an occasion unique for colour and exuberant gaiety: when all, master and servant, **brahman** and **harijan**, male and female, forget their everyday separateness. When role reversal and horseplay at home and in the streets become the order of the day or, as it should be, half the day.

Holi can mean a number of things according to one's Indian viewpoint, but underlying all is the licence of the vernal fertility festivals of the Indo-Europeans – Holi is ignored in the **Dravidian** south. The spring lupercalia and bacchanalia of the Romans, the pre-Lenten carnivals of the Latin world and jollifications on the village green of the traditional English May Day. In India, the festival was originally in honour of **Kama**, the God of Love: later, at least in the north, Kamadev was forgotten and it may be claimed that the fun echoes the sport of the youthful **Krishna** with the village girls on the banks of the Yamuna. To this day, nowhere in India is Holi celebrated with more zest than in Braj (*see* Janmastami) the region of Mathura/Brindaban, although no particular deity is worshipped.

For many, Holi starts quite late on the night of the full moon in the Hindu month of Phalguna (February or March). Bonfires will then be lit (at an auspicious moment as decided by the **pandits**) in the streets to symbolise, some will say, the destruction by fire of Holika, a female demon. Others say the fire represents the sunshine that is needed by the tumescent grain in the fields: others again, the burning of evil. There will be much drumming music and ribald horseplay and, at least for a few, strong liquors or hemp derivatives (*see* Indian Hemp). To the purist, this night celebration by the light of the full moon alone is Holi, Holi dahan - the holi fire. Next morning, dhulandi for those in north India, is for everyone. The elderly and respected may receive no more than a decorous pat on the forehead with the traditional red coloured powder (**gulal, in some parts abir**) from their children and friends: younger people are more likely to end up thoroughly coloured and doused with colour water from a squeeze-bottle or handpump (pichkari). To be so decorated is no outrage but a mark of community acceptance and goodwill: to be ignored by one's neighbours on such a day would be a sign of rejection. Muslims and Christians - and Europeans - frequently join in. But there is another side: bands of young hooligans may roam the streets throwing colour and worse on complete and unprepared strangers: in the past, such actions have resulted in bloody riots between communities. It could be that as part of a fertility festival, the throwing of colour began as a tribute to the soil (dhul/dhool, dust in Hindi), the Earth Mother, the action of raising a handful of dust to one's own or another's forehead (*see* shakti).

The accepted custom is for the fun and games to stop by noon, when all should return home for a bath and change of clothing but inevitably some are tardy in observing the ceasefire.

In eastern India and in the Mathura region, either coinciding with dhulandi or, sometimes, the day before, dolyattra (dol - a swing: *see* dooli under Carrying Chairs; also Yattra), celebrates the childhood village play of the very young Krishna. Small box-like shrines supported by a long pole carried on the shoulders of many men are taken in procession (the yattra) round a locality. The shrine contains images of the young boy and his playmate, Radha, sitting together on a swing.

HOLKAR
The family name of the Maratha rulers of the former princely state of Indore.

HOOKAH/HUQQA *n* Urdu
Water bowl tobacco pipe, with the mouthpiece at the end of a tube, sometimes flexible, sometimes a hollow cane, perhaps five feet in length. The smoke from a rather special to-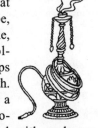bacco, sweetened with molasses and often spiced, on top of burning charcoal or cowdung, to cool and clean it is sucked through water with

a bubbling gurgling sound (hence an English name, the hubble-bubble, but strictly this applies only to the small handheld types as does the Hindustani equivalent term, gurguri). It is rarely smoked in the south. Europeans, men and the occasional woman, enjoyed the hookah until about the 1820s, using a snake (the flexible smoke-pipe) of anything upto three metres in length (if coiled in spiral form, the tube could be termed the **jalebi**): at least some Britons took it home with them when they retired.

In rural India, a hookah may be smoked in turn by members of a peer group sitting together (*see* Baithak): the mouthpiece being touched only by the fist closed into a tube, never by the lips. A social boycott of a person can be termed 'hookah pani **bandh**': meaning that no one may offer the man ostracised the smoke of a hookah nor water to drink.

The bowl of the hookah, usually of burnt clay, holding the coals and the tobacco, is known as the chillum: the word can also mean a type of minihookah, held in one hand, with usually a coconut shell for water container, the original hubble-bubble: this is really the instrument referred to by English romantic novelists as the narghileh/nargile (nargil, Persian for coconut).

Hookahbardar (lit. the hookah carrier): the servant who tended the hookah using a variety of instruments devised for the work, tongs, cleaners and probes, often finely decorated. In a European household, when the master went out to an evening entertainment, the hookahbardar was included in the invitation, even to the Governor-General's house: Such a specialised domestic is unlikely to be found today.

(Commenting in about 1840, a visitor wrote. "Every horse has a man and a maid to himself – the maid cuts the grass for him: and every dog has his boy I enquired whether the cat had any servants, but found she was allowed to wait upon herself; and as she seemed the only person in the establishment capable of so doing, I respected her accordingly." *Letters from Madras* – Anon.)

Forms of the hookah were in use before the 17th century introduction of tobacco, for the enjoyment of opium and cannabis (*see* Indian Hemp).

HOOPOE *n* English
Hindi : hudhud. An insectivorous bird of Africa, Asia and Europe. Reddish, with black and white zebra stripes on the back and wings. A conspicuous crest and a long curved break. The English name from Latin as in Hindi, is from its call. Mostly seen solitary on a lawn stabbing at the ground for its food.

HOSE TOPS *n*
A pair of short woollen tubes, socks

with no feet. An economical device of the British *Raj* to give troops and police wearing shorts and boots, the appearance of stockinged legs without the, nowadays forgotten, problems of sock darning.

HOTEL *n*
Any establishment, even a roadside stall, open to all and serving meals.

Military Hotel: a discreet advertisement that egg and meat dishes will be available.

Vaishnavi Hotel: vegetarian food only (sometimes emphasised by the notice 'Shuddh Vegetarian' – pure vegetarian), possibly omitting even onions (*see* Lahsan). In a **brahman** hotel, a brahman can expect to be served vegetarian food without risk of ritual pollution, i.e. the cooks should be brahmans.

HOT-WATER BAG *n*
The homely rubber hot-water bottle.

HOUSEBOAT *n*
In India, the equivalent of a European residence semipermanently moored to the bank of a Kashmir lake: built on a wide hull with square ends and an open deck on top.

To be able to live in Kashmir, despite the ban imposed by a 19th century Maharaja (still in force in the 1990s) preventing non-Kashmiris

owning immovable property in his state, Europeans began improving for themselves the traditional crude living space on the local work boat, the doonga/dūnga – a word related to **dingi**. A step further, taken in late Victorian times, was to design boats solely as residences.

HOWDAH *n*
The anglicised form of the Urdu haudaa. A contrivance more elaborate than the commonly used pad for riding on an elephant. Anything from a small upturned **charpoi** to an elaborately decorated box with upholstered seats and a canopy to provide comfort and/or, prestige.

In the army, in the old north-western India, the word also applied to litters for carrying the sick and wounded slung on the sides of a camel.

HOYSALA
Family name of one of a number of Hindu dynasties in the medieval **Deccan**, largely today's Karnataka. Chiefly remembered for the exuberant decoration of their temples, said to have been about 700, of which 80 remain, the dynasty was terminated by Muslim **sultans** of the 14th century.

HP (H.P.)
Himachal Pradesh: lit. the snow mountain state. (A–chal – no movement, see Ahinsa, a mountain. The Himalayan state with **Shimla** as its chief town and administrative cen-

tre. In British days part of **Punjab** Province: the state was established in 1948 by the amalgamation of a number of small **princely** enclaves of the Shimla Hills: it reached its present size and importance following the major reorganisation of the Punjab in 1966.

Handpractice: i.e., masturbation.

HUKM *n* Urdu from Arabic
An order, a command. Like **Sarkar** in Hindi, a form of address to one of high rank, or at a lower social level, from a workman to his master.

HŪNDI *n* Hindi
In a sale of goods, a user's or buyer's bill, due for payment after a fixed period (usance): issued by a bank or clearing house acting as guarantor to the seller.

In south Indian temple, a box or chest for receiving offerings to the temple deity.

HŪR/HOOR *n* Urdu
From Arabic, meaning gazelle-like (eyes). The celestial maids of the Islamic paradise: ever youthful, ever virginal. In the next world, to be at the service of the pious and dutiful Muslim of this. Plural, huri (the English word, houri and alas, whore).

HYDEL *n* Abbreviation of hydro-electric, electricity produced by water-power.

IAS (I.A.S.)
Indian Administrative Service, The successor service to the **Indian Civil Service**. The cadre of generalist officials running the bureaucracy of India both in the Central Government and in the states. Many senior appointments in the states e.g. **District** Collector/ Deputy Commissioner in the rural areas – are reserved by statute for members of the IAS: they work to the orders of the state governments, but as members of an All India service they are also responsible to Delhi, thus providing a basic unity of government throughout the country. In general their ethos remains that of the ICS, but unlike the earlier service, they have to share power with elected representatives whose survival depends on the ability to perform favours for constituents.

IBRAHIM
Islamic form of the name Abraham (*see* Kitab). When a reference to the patriach is intended, an honour such as **Hazrat** may be prefixed.

ID/EED/EID *n* Urdu
An Islamic festival. (The Turki word

bayram/bairam, used in Iran and Turkey but rarely in India, has the same meaning.) Compared to, say, Hinduism, **Islam** has few general holidays; there are really only two major festival days, ld-ul-Fitr and ld-ul-Zuha. In the Muslim **calendar** the first day of a new month normally follows the sighting of a new moon (subject to a limit of thirty days in a month). Thus there is often some uncertainty before the event about the date of any forthcoming festival in terms of the Gregorian calendar.

Id-ul-Fitr: festival of the breaking of the fast. The chief day of rejoicing of the Islamic year, commencing when the Id moon is sighted at sunset marking the end of the month **Roza**/ Ramadan/Ramzan, the four week period of daylong asceticism and beginning the new month, Shawwal. It is at this time and on the day following (by the Gregorian calendar) that Muslims greet each other and non- Mulims greet Muslims with the invocation *Id mubarak ho* – 'may the festival be auspicious for you'. New clothes are worn. Strictly, fitr means alms: on this day a Muslim is required to pay the zakat (two per cent of his annual income) either to a central fund as in an Islamic state, or as a voluntary personal distribution for the benefit of the poor. Since Id-ul-Fitr is a day of celebration, sweets may be distributed, so a bazaar name for the festival can be mithai Id (sweetmeats Id) Also zakat can be the sharing of food with the hungry.

Id-ul-Zuha: feast of the sacrifice. Also known as Bak'r Id and, in Arabic, Id-ul-Azha. A day when even the very poor eat meat. Popular belief (without, however, Koranic authority or any known statement by the Holy Prophet) is that the feast is a commemoration of the test of Ibrahim's (Abraham's) faith, part of the combined heritage of Muslims, Jews and Christians. The story of God's instruction to Ibrahim to sacrifice his son Ishmael/Ismail according to the **Kor'an**, or Isaac as named in the Bible. (The Arabs consider themselves to be the children of Ibrahim, through Ishmael.) While Mohammed may or may not have intended the festival to mark this story, he did instruct his followers to offer animal sacrifice (qurbani/kurbani) on this day, the tenth of the month of Zulhijja, to mark the ending of the **Haj** ceremonies.

Traditionally in India, cattle (bakr – cattle in Arabic) were sacrificed on Id-ul-Zuha (the **Mogul** Emperor ceremoniously cut the throat of a camel, to a salute from a cannon), but nowadays, goats and sheep have taken their place; only healthy animals without blemish are acceptable and they are usually especially fattened and washed. When bought in the **bazaar**, prices are high and it is not considered seemly to bargain for an animal intended for the Lord.

A less generally celebrated festival (but in recent years it has been made a **gazetted holiday**) is Id Milad, the same day anniversary of the birth and death of the Nabi (nabi, Arabic and Hebrew: a spokesman of God), the Holy Prophet. An occasion for congregations to hear addresses on the life and mission of Mohammed and special songs of praise.

Idgah: a place for Id prayers. Usually just a high wall with a **mihrab** and **mimbar**, built on the western side of open ground (often located on the western side of a town or village), for the purpose of permitting the large Id assemblies (jammat) to offer congregational prayers, for which the average mosque has insufficient space.

Idi: of Id. Especially an Id gift.

Id Milan: Usually an Id gathering at which guests exchange greetings with each other and the host.

IDLI *n* Tamil
As the **chapati** is to the north, so the **dosa** and the idli is to all south India. A dough of rice and urad **gram** flours, allowed to stand for some hours (often overnight) and so rise by self-fermentation – no yeast is added. Made into thin circular cakes and steam cooked. Often a breakfast dish, eaten with chutney (*see* chaat) and sambar (arhar **dal** – tuvar dal in the south – and vegetables, seasoned with tamarind). Often served with

sambar is vada (pronounced wara *see* Bangle – or, as often in the north, bara), ring doughnuts of rice flour or, perhaps, again arhar dal.

IJMA (I.J.M.A.)

An acronym, Indian Jute Manufacturer's Association.

Ijma (Urdu): a judgment or considered opinion of a council of *ulema* (men learned in Islamic faith and law). A consensus.

ILBERT BILL

The draft of a minor legislative measure put forward by the Government of India in 1882 by the then Law Member of the **Viceroy**'s Council, Courtenay Ilbert. But such was the totally unexpected hostility of the European community, that the distrust, the animosity, the dichotomy between liberal principles exalted at home and personal feelings on the ground in India, so exposed the raw edges between Briton and Indian that the episode is even today cited as a horror story in the context of Indo-British relations. Some opponents percipiently observed that to remove all European privileges could only lead to the departure of Britons from India. The bill (officially known as the Jurisdiction Bill) eventually became law as the Code of Criminal Procedure Amendment Act, 1884 (*see* Cr. PC.).

Criminal courts administering English law had been established by Royal Charter in the 18th century in Bombay, Calcutta and Madras wherein, since 1857, Indian judges and magistrates as Justices of the Peace, without controversy had exercised jurisdiction over Europeans. Elsewhere, Britons on criminal charges could only be tried by their own countrymen: a privilege sometimes referred to as their personal law (on the civil side, other communities had – and still have–their personal laws). By 1882, there were a number of **covenanted** Indian judges and magistrates in the **districts** and the Viceroy (the liberal Lord Ripon) agreed that their status should not be less than that of their British colleagues: hence the proposal, approved by the home government, that the new and first all-India Cr. PC. should be amended to allow Indian judges judicial powers over Europeans anywhere in **British India**.

The administration in general considered they were bound by Queen Victoria's Proclamation of 1858 pledging freedom for all qualified Indians to enter her service, irrespective of race or creed. But not so non-officials. European hostility was immediate, especially from the rural tea and **indigo** planters, with rough vituperation and abuse of Indians in speeches and in the English press almost of the level of the mutiny twenty five years earlier. The **GOI** was forced by pressure from Britons both at home and in India to allow a

European British subject before an Indian judge on a criminal charge, no matter how trivial, the right to claim trial by a jury of which at least half the members had to be European. (By a legal definition of 1872, European British subjects included any British subject, even if not of European origin, from any of Her Majesty's territories outside India: also Americans.) In cases involving the two races, the results were not always happy for justice: in a country district European non officials were few (officials were excused jury service) and a jury perhaps could be empanelled only from friends of the accused with similar interests. It was not until 1923 that the distinction between Briton and Indian in the criminal courts was almost abolished: the remaining difference being that Indian magistrates of the second and third class (very junior indeed) could not try European British subjects for offences for which the maximum penalty was in excess of a fine of Rs. 50.

Visitors to Shimla who stay in the up-market guest house, Chapslie, will be in the one-time residence of Sir Courtenay Ilbert.

IMA (I.M.A.)
Indian Military Academy, Dehra **Dun.** The training centre for the production of army officers.

IMĀM *n* Urdu
Originally in Arabic, the one in front, i.e. the leader of congregational prayers. But the meaning today is much wider and can include the ruler in an Islamic country; a leader in Islamic theology or law, the head of a sect, particularly one of Shia Muslims (*see* Sunnis) : e.g. the holder of the the hereditary title the Agha Khan is the imam of the **Ismaili** sect. (Shias, but not Sunnis, often consider their imams to have a measure of sacerdotal authority.) Leader of congregational prayers. The person in charge of a mosque (*See* Masjid).

Shahi (royal) Imam: Certain mosques in major cities were built by the **Mogul** emperors who personally appointed their imams: such a mosque may still carry the title of Shahi Masjid and the imam – now usually a hereditary appointment – will be known as the Shahi Imam. The Shahi Imams of the Jama Masjid in Delhi, a royal mosque, have always been descendants of the first imam summoned from Bokhara by the Emperor Shahjehan in the 17th century.

IMĀMBĀRA *n* Urdu
Building in which Shia (*see* Sunnis) Muslims gather at the time of **Muharram** to hear readings and discourses relating to Husain and others: the prime example being the great Imambara at Lucknow.

IMPEYAN PHEASANT *n*
Sir Elijah Impey, Chief Justice of the

Calcutta Supreme Court at the time of Warren Hastings (late 18th century) introduced to his coverts in England certain brightly coloured Himalayan pheasants to which his own name was given (*see full OED*): Lophophorus impejan. The word common in the Himalaya for any pheasant is monal and the impeyan monal has a particularly metallic refulgent plumage and crest: the bird is found at 2500m. Another local name for the now protected bird is danphe.

IMS (I.M.S.)

Indian Medical Service. In British days, the cadre of military medical officers, both Indian and British, who served not only the Indian armed forces but also filled the senior civilian medical and public health appointments of the central and provincial governments: the chief medical officer of a **District**, the Civil Surgeon, would almost certainly have been an IMS officer. (Rather surprisingly, ex officio, he could also have been Superintendent of the local jail, and, occasionally in this employment, as when he had to arrange a hanging, at odds with his Hippocratic oath.) The service was disbanded in 1947. Similar to the IMS was the Indian Medical Department (IMD), an economy service staffed by Licenciates of Medicine, the majority of whom were Anglo-Indian whose qualifications were less than full medical degrees and whose military rank was that of Warrant Officer or

Viceroy Commissioned Officer (*see* Junior Commissioned Officers). Their fore-runners in the 19th century had been Apothecaries (their title and rank, again equivalent to Warrant Officer); their services had gone far beyond mere compounding of medicines. During World War II, senior IMD officers were eligible for full commissions. The IMD was also disbanded in 1947.

INĀM *n* Urdu

A reward from a superior to an inferior: a tip. A prize.

INDEPENDENCE DAY

15th August. A national annual holiday celebrating the day in 1947 on which India once again became an independent country governed by those of the majority culture. By many of those personally involved, those who left their homes to cross a suddenly devised frontier, the trauma of the birth of the new India is still referred to as Partition – but the term is rarely used in Pakistan. (In the early years of the last century, a reference to partition probably concerned the 1905 division of Bengal into **Hindu** and Muslim majority provinces by Lord Curzon, rejoined in 1912, to be divided once again in 1947. The 1905 division, known as the Banga bhanga – the breaking of Bengal – was bitterly resented by the Hindus resulting in increased agitation against British rule which was certainly one of the factors which led to the transfer of the capital to Delhi a few years later, and eventually to the near extinction of Calcutta as a national political centre.) The British official expression, the transfer of power, neatly encapsulates the fact that while the faces at the top changed, the process of government continued much as before. Perhaps India was fortunate in that the political party taking over, the Congress, had so developed that it was truly national with a highly respected and popular leader with strong support throughout village India, thus providing stability during the formative years of the new republic. This was not the situation in all the newly created states of the period. (Some say that the form of the new state had little to do with India's traditional institutions and culture but was basically western. Dr. Ambedkar, founding father of the Constitution remarked in Parliament in 1948, "Democracy in India is only the top-dressing on Indian soil which is essentially undemocratic".)

Independence, in India first seen as possible and inevitable following the defeat of Europeans in 1942 by the Japanese, was simultaneous with the division of **British India** into India and Pakistan at Delhi - midnight of 14/15 August 1947. (Pakistan is considered to have been de facto founded a day earlier, with the installation of the first Governor-General of the new Dominion by the **Viceroy** on 14 August.) All treaties between princely

India (*see* Princes) and Britain were unilaterally abrogated at the same moment. The Union Jacks were lowered as usual at sunset on 14 August, and the flag of new India was raised on the same masts the next morning. An exception was in Lucknow; here for the previous ninety years, uniquely in the British Empire, the Union flag had remained at the hoist day and night, commemorating the siege of the Residency in 1857 (*see* First War of Independence). Paeaned Lord Tennyson "...and ever upon the topmost roof our banner of England blew". There, the flag was lowered at 8 p.m., the mast taken out and the socket filled with quick-setting concrete. The flag is now in Windsor Castle. While the decision to make August the month of Independence was a political one. Lord Mountbatten, the last Viceroy, has been reported as having said that he chose the 15th for the sentimental reason that the date was the second anniversary of the surrender of Japan, the ending of World War II (*Mountbatten and the Partition of India*, Vikas, 1982). It was said at the time that midnight was appropriate because astrologers were of the opinion that while 14 August was an auspicious day, the 15th was not. By the Hindu **calendar**, midnight and the hours till sunrise were still part of the equivalent of 14 August.

Partition came by an Act of the British parliament with the concurrence of

Indian leaders, but within less than a year, Prime Minister Jawaharlal Nehru was perhaps having second thoughts. In July 1948 – he was reported to have said "We consented (to partition) because we thought we were purchasing peace and goodwill, 'though at a high price. I do not know now, if I had the same choice, how I would decide." It is somewhat ironic that fifty years on, of the three countries resulting from the religious division of the sub-continent, that with the largest Muslim population is still India.

Again fifty years on, Britain is blamed and sometimes vilified for partition as being part of some imperial design. The division was certainly advocated by Mountbatten, but it is sometimes forgotten that there was an alternative. The British Labour government had firmly stated in February 1947 that come what may all British responsibility for India would cease in or by June 1948. Thereafter the people of India would make their own arrangements.

With hindsight, it can be said that Partition came about because the Congress government in U.P. from 1937 onwards did not work hard enough to convince the feudal Muslim landowners and peasants that they would receive a square deal under a permanent Hindu majority government.

INDIA *n*
The original Aryan immigrants into the northwest gave a **Sanskrit** word meaning an area of water, Sindhu, to the land near the coast and to its great river (today, of course, Sind in Pakistan and the river Indus. In recent years, the several hundred kilometres of the Indus within India before the Pakistan border, has been unofficially named the Sindu with Leh as its chief town.) Greek and Roman geographers picked up the sound and called the region Indos/Indus.

Persians (and from them, the Arabs) termed it Hind: in Old Persian, a Sanskrit *s* sound often became *h*. From just the north-west, the name spread to include the sub-continent and beyond to other regions further east (collectively, the Indies). Now Southeast Asia. European cartographers of the 15th and 16th centuries, for the sub-continent itself used the Latin term 'India intra Gangem' – freely translated as 'India of the Ganges'.

Indian: about one hundred years ago, it was written in *Hobson-Jobson:* "We use the adjective Indian, but no modern Englishman who has to do with India ever speaks of a man of that country as an Indian." That, of course, is not so today but there is still no language that is referred to in English as Indian. *See also Bharat.* By no means all English nouns qualified by India or Indian have an association with the subcontinent. For example: Indian corn, Indian bread, Indiana, Indian file, Indian hemp (as a fabric), Indian summer, all came from the Americas; Indian ink and paper from China and Japan. But the latex for India rubber in the 18th century came from Assam, from a fig tree, *Ficus elastica*: now mostly seen as an ornamental house plant, the rubber plant. By strange transposition of significance, in English from the 19th century, Indian as a word acquired a meaning of a European permanently residing in India. In the same period, one born of the country was a native: at first the term was often descriptive and no more, but soon a notion of inferiority was included. *See also* Anglo Indian.

India Pale Ale (IPA): a light beer brewed in Britain in the 19th century with qualities claimed to make it particularly suited for shipment to and for consumption in India–the hops content was higher than for UK use. It is still brewed but is no longer shipped to India.

INDIAN CHRISTIANS

Defined in the Government of India Act, 1935, as a person not being European nor *Anglo-Indian*, professing any form of Christianity. (Some Christians of the Roman Catholic persuasion tend to regard the term Indian Christians as applicable only to 'Mission Christians': i.e. in their opinion, low caste converts by Protestant missionaries.)

Rice Christians: an epithet some-times applied to Indian Christians, being a free translation from a **Tamil** expression, an allegation that they or their forbears adopted Christianity in order to benefit from the food/rice and jobs believed to be in the gift of foreign missionaries. The term was certainly not always deserved, for until government intervention in 1851, a Muslim or **Hindu** convert under customary law forfeited all rights to family property. (Similarly a rice soldier was thought to have joined the army for food rather than patriotism – but hunger has ever been a recruiter for all volunteer armies.)

Rice Christians with the same background may nowadays be pronounced to be milk powder Christians.

INDIAN CIVIL SERVICE (ICS)

First traders, then administrators, the civil servants (a term to distinguish them from their military colleagues) from 1765 were in **convenant** with the Company, able to add HEICS (Honourable **East India Company** Service) to their names, but they did not become Indian Civil Servants until the Bombay, Bengal and Madras services disappeared in the late 19th century. From 1858 to 1947, the Civil Service of India (the official designation) was the body of officials, both British and Indian (the first Indian member joined in 1863), who, in covenant with the Secretary of State for India (a Minister in the British Home

Government), maintained the Government of India. (It has been said that they were in no sense servants, they were the Government. The description 'the steel frame' was probably first used by the British Prime Minister, Lloyd George, in a parliamentary speech in 1922.) A member could be referred to as a Civilian, an Indian Civilian (irrespective of race), or just a Civil. By World War II, when recruitment of Britishers was suspended, (the last intake had been in 1941), out of a total strength of 1,299, 540 were Indians. In 1946, fifty-four European recruits were accepted for the service, but with the rapid developments of the time, they never arrived in India.

An Act of the British parliament of 1870 authorised the setting up of the 'Statutory Civil Service': entry was to be by nomination and it was intended for the sons of Indian nobles and educated landed gentry. Members were eligible to hold posts previously reserved for the ICS. The scheme came into operation in 1878, but was abandoned eight years later after sixty members had been recruited. Whatever the reasons for its demise, it is unlikely that it received much support from the senior service.

In the 1930s Jawaharlal Nehru is said to have declared "...it is essential that the ICS and similar services must disappear completely". But in 1947 when the British left (with a very few exceptions), the Indian members of the ICS continued in power much as before but in tandem with their successor generalist bureaucrats of the Indian Administrative Service (*see* IAS) and working, of course, to elected Ministers. Nehru's Home Minister and 'strong man', Sardar Patel, said "This Constitution (of India) is meant to be worked by a ring of services which will keep the country intact". By 1980, the last of the ICS had retired and soon after the acronym ICS became no more than a reference to the joint public examination for entrance to such services as the IAS, the Indian Foreign Service and the Indian Police Service.

In Britain, the service and the other Indian civil services, are remembered by a tablet in Westminister Abbey unveiled by the Queen:

> Here are Commemorated the Civil Services of the Crown in India. Let them not be Forgotten for they served India well what does the Lord Require of thee but to do justly and to love Mercy?

The Biblical text is abbreviated from some words of guidance by the Prophet Micah.

INDIAN HEMP *n* English
Cannabis sativa, the hemp plant. Lawfully cultivated in certain controlled areas for the production of its fibres and oil seeds. (Hemp produces one of the strongest natural fibres

known: the word for the fabric made from them, canvas, derives from the Latin, cannabis.) The plant grows wild over much of India, the leaves are sometimes eaten fresh or added to cooked vegetables to relieve – an enquirer may be told – aches and pains. Under the name bhāng (sometimes just **sabzi** – the vegetable), the dried leaves and flowers are compressed, either to be eaten as pellets or added to milk sweets, or after conversion to a paste, to a drink (*see* Green Whisky). A preparation of bhang, flour, ghee, milk and sugar, takes the name majun. Amongst orthodox **brahmans**, to whom alcohol is anathema, and other caste **Hindus**, particularly those dedicated to the worship of Lord **Shiva**, the use of hemp narcotics has always had at least some social acceptance - one name for bhang is shivabooti (Shiva's herb) - and in the West, once but not today, it was a constituent of that general panacea, Chlorodyne. Cannabis, medically a depressant, has a traditional use in Indian pharmacology, in both the **Ayurvedic** and Unani (*see* Hakim) systems. In the home, only at **holi** may a popular milk and flour based sweetmeat patty, the gujjia, be laced with bhang powder.

Traditionally, wrestlers have taken bhang to reduce pain.

Processing the fresh sticky flowers containing resin from the female plant in the same way as the leaves, results in a more potent narcotic, ganja, mostly used as an additive to tobacco. On bruising, the flowers, young leaves and stems exude a very small quantity of a resin which can be collected: this separated resin has the name charas (hashish). 'Eh, charas -pinewale' (Oh, smoker lit. drinker, of hash), can be a **tonga** driver's abuse to one slow to get out of his way. In Nepal hash can be known as kali. Much of the hemp grown in India is of high fibre quality but is low in the active narcotic ingredient THC (tetrahydro-cannabinol) and so produces a rather poor hashish – with the exception of some from Kashmir and the uplands of Kerala. Also produced in Kerala, it is alleged, is the refined and vastly more expensive hash oil.

Intoxicants, a term which includes the minor hemp narcotics, are generally controlled not by the **Government of India,** but by the state governments, largely through excise rules. The sale of taxed bhang to persons over twenty-five is permitted in most states. In **Punjab**, and, no doubt, elsewhere, cultivation of the hemp plant on land attached to religious institutions and the production of taxfree bhang for use on the premises, can be specifically sanctioned. Recently, the law has been changed: control of hemp products still rests mainly with the state governments and the position of bhang is unaltered, but the Central Government's

'Narcotic Drugs and Psychotropic Substances Act' (NDPSA) of 1985 greatly increased the penalties for improper production or possession of ganja and charas. (On conviction, a sentence of up to five years imprisonment can be imposed for ganja: for charas, the mandatory minimum sentence includes imprisonment for ten years. The penalties are much less for holding a 'small quantity' for purely personal consumption. For really serious drug related offences there is provision for the death penalty, but this is never mandatory.) In the west, cannabis is less and less being seen as a dangerous drug.

Note that bhang (short a) from Sanskrit can mean a division, a splitting, destruction.

It was Arabic that gave the English language 'hashish' for the dried and powdered hemp leaves and also the associated word 'assassin' from a particular group of hash eaters. Bhang, as a word, travelled with soldiers returning to Britain to appear as in the slang expression for one heavily drugged or sedated, 'banged up to the eyebrows'. From the Americas, came the Spanish word marijuana. *See also* Madak.

INDIGO *n* English and Portuguese Nil/neel in Hindi, from **Sanskrit** – blue. (The English name for the tree and colour, lilac, is a corruption of Hindi word nilak – blueish. Aniline derives from the Sanskrit, via Arabic – al nil.) To the Greeks, indikon – Indian, the origin of the English term. From the days of Egyptian mummy wrappings to the introduction of coal tar dyes, the fibres of the indigo plant, after being steeped and fermented in water, were a source of deep blue colour, although the ancient Mediterranean world considered it inferior to the much more expensive animal dye from a type of male murex snail (the female snail produced royal purple for the roman emperors). It is now known that both as a colour and chemically, the vegetable and animal blues are identical. The name indigo covers both the plant and the pressed blocks of blue powder.

Although indigo had been grown in Bengal and in today's Andhra Pradesh since time immemorial it was in the 18th century that, copying from the French in the West Indies, its cultivation as an export plantation crop was sponsored by the **East India Company**. The actual growers were small farmers with their own land under contract, perhaps not always voluntarily negotiated, to European 'planters', who controlled the '**factory**' and the rates paid for the raw material. (Factory was the word used, but this was little more than a shed or two and a series of large masonry cisterns in which the fibres were steeped and fermented, from tank to tank the liquor was concentrated to a paste which could be sun dried and cut into blocks. The remains of these sturdy masonry works, with their sluices, can sometimes be seen today in rural fields – agricultural archaeology.) Indigo made fortunes and a good life for many Europeans, it is said that a period of particular prosperity was that of the American Civil War with its consequent demand for blue for the northern uniforms but with the invention of the chemical colours in Germany their world began to come to an end in the first decade of the 20th century, although some struggled on until the 1920s. (Their decline could have been said to have been a turn of the wheel, for it was the introduction of indigo from the East in the 16th century that killed the European woad industry.) Indigo is still produced today albeit in very modest quantities; there are some who require natural vegetable colours and not chemical synthetics. Unlike the untreated effluent from a chemical dye works that from a works using vegetable dyes is not ecologically objectionable. Since the colour is stable, it is particularly used by pathologists for staining sections for microscopic examination. Exports in 1995 were about 4 tonnes to Britain, 5 to Germany and about 2.5 to the US: in its heyday, India exported about 8,000 tonnes annually.

Neelanchal Express: the train linking Delhi and **Puri** in Orissa. Although the state was a territory famous for indigo production, the neel in this case is the blue of the Bay of Bengal and the literal translation of the train name is the ocean border express.

Nilam: the blue jewel stone, the sapphire. For some, a highly auspicious stone bringing good fortune, even a kingdom, but for an unlucky few, wearing the sapphire can only lead to poverty. Also from Sanskrit for the stone is the name Shanipriya (beloved of Shani, see Saturday), to which perhaps, is linked the English word, sapphire.

Nilkanth: bluethroat. The bluejay (or Indian roller bird). Also an epithet for Lord **Shiva**. Within Islam the bird may be considered the guardian of King Suleiman (Solomon) and hence, blue is an auspicious colour.

See also Madak.

INDRA/INDER *n* Hindi
To the early **Aryans**, as indicated in the **Vedas**, the powerful warrior king and leader of the gods in battle, with command of thunder, lightning and of the rains: thunderbolts (vajra) were his weapons. A popular god whose blessings were frequently invoked for the good of the crops, but now, seemingly, little worshipped. His **vahan** (vehicle) was an elephant, Airavat by name. He is sometimes shown as having eyes all over his body (hence an epithet, the thousand-eyed one): to the early Buddhists he

was Sakra. Indrani, a girl's name today, was his wife.

Indra had the reputation of enjoying sensual pleasures and is believed to have become jealous of the powers acquired by ascetics on earth through **tapasya**, and on this account is said to have had the habit of sending **apsaras** (the celestial damsels of his court) to distract pious men from their devotions.

A **Hindu** male personal name: also in the form Mahindra/ Mohinder (Great Indra).

Gajendra: a compound Indra and his elephant (gaj).

Indradhanush (lit. Indra's bow): the rainbow.

Indrajaal (Indra's net): magic. The Hindi equivalent of the Urdu word, jadoo.

Indry: the senses, the organs of sense particulary the genitals.

Indrajit: conqueror of the senses. A personal name.

INDUS CIVILISATION
Also described as Indus and **Saraswati** Valley and also as Harappan. Generally considered to be pre-**Aryan** (*see* Arya) and possibly **Dravidian**; a civilisation existing during the 3rd and 2nd millennia BC,

with highly developed agriculture and brickbuilt cities (notably the now archaeological sites at Harappa on the River Ravi near Montgomery, and Mohenjodaro/Moenjodaro in Khairpur District, both in Pakistan): more than one hundred sites of towns and villages have been identified, some beyond the Indus drainage area in the **Ganga** basin to the east of Delhi. An important recent discovery of an urban centre, rivalling it is claimed, Harappa, is Dholavira in Gujarat's Gulf of Kutch. Little is known about the people, but they clearly had strong civic authorities and may well have been the first in the world to have made use of the cotton plant: their pictographic script, found on large numbers of clay tablets and seals, has yet to be deciphered. It seems that some features of later Hinduism were present, e.g., respect for the **peepal** tree and use of the **trisul** symbol.

The cities were thought to have been overrun by invading Aryans towards the end of the second millennium BC. But this is now controversial, for no firm archaeological nor other evidence has been found of any major conflict and at least some modern Indian scholars are of the opinion that the people of the Indus Valley culture were themselves Aryan and that the cities collapsed following a natural disaster. Delhi's a National Museum supports this perception by giving an aryan title to the Harrapans, they are now said to be of the Indus **Saraswati** civilisation, suggesting a link to the Vedic deities. A feeling with some Indian historians is that too much of today's understanding of ancient India has a colonial bias which needs to be corrected.

INNER LINE

A boundary running approximately parallel to the frontiers of India (the Outer Line) with Tibet (China) and north-west **Burma**: the territory between being termed a 'Protected Area'. In British days, taxes were not collected and administration, if any, beyond the line was very light: then, as today, the line could not be crossed without government permission, one of the objects being to protect the generally unsophisticated local inhabitants from exploitation by those from the plains.

Between the Inner Line and the rest of India is a belt of territory, a Restricted Area, to enter which foreigners require permission. Such permission is easier to obtain than for crossing the Inner Line. *See also* McMahon Line. :

INQILĀB/INQALĀB *n* Urdu from Arabic

Lit. Upside down, change. Frequently shouted as a political slogan meaning revolution, e.g., *'Inqilab Zindabad'* (long live Revolution).

INSHALLAH. Exclam. Urdu from Arabic

"God willing. If Allah permits."

INSPECTION BUNGALOW *n*

A government bungalow, often in an out-of-the-way place, offering temporary accommodation for officials visiting, say, a canal or bridge works. May be used by the public with permission from the controlling authority. The Military Engineering Services (MES) bungalows, however, are normally reserved for those connected with the Defence Services.

INTER-DINING

There are two meanings to this expression, contrary in spirit. The eating together of those of one religion with another, **Hindu** with Muslim: one Hindu caste with another: a crossing of barriers. Within Hinduism the expression may be applied to sub-castes who may eat together, each of the other's food, without risk of ritual pollution: commensality, a measure of equal caste status.

IPC (INDIAN PENAL CODE)

A clause of the 1833 Charter Act of the British Parliament, instructed the **East India Company** to bring order and a common code for Indian and European alike, into the confusion of the criminal law in **British India**, then an amalgam of English common law, Company Regulations enacted separately by each of the three **Presidencies** and traditional Indian law. A Commission was set up in 1834 with Lord Macaulay, the Legislation Member of the Governor–General's Council, as President. Owing not a little to the Code Napoleon, the draft was ready by 1837, but it was 1860 before it became law as the Indian Penal Code and two years later before it was enforced together with the Criminal Proceedure Code. Although amended many times, Macaulay's drafting together with the Proceedure Code remains the law under which crime is defined today. (Exceptionally, the IPC does not apply within the State of Jammu & Kashmir, which retains its own penal code.) *See also* Cr. PC.

IPS (I.P.S.)
Indian Police Service (in British days, just Indian Police). A cadre of Government of India **gazetted** officers. Considered superior to the state police officers who, normally, do not serve outside their home states and whose junior ranks are not of gazetted, or commissioned, status.

IRISH BRIDGE *n*
A causeway, normally with a dry surface and culvert below for a small stream, but over which flood waters can flow without damage to the roadway.

ISA *n* Urdu
Islamic form of the name Jesus. Although the word is Arabic, it is cognate to the **Sanskrit** Isha/Eshwar/Ishwara, meaning supreme Lord or

Master: frequently used as a Hindi suffix to indicate divinity. Particularly applied to Lord **Shiva.**

Isa Masih: Jesus Christ. Masih is a common family name for non-Roman Catholic Indian Christians. The word is linked to the Hebrew Masiah, the Messiah. *See also* Hazrat.

Isai/Isia: Christian.

Nazarene : English (see OED). Freely used as Hindustani for a Christian in the 18th and 19th. centuries.

ISABGŌL/ISUBGUL *n Hindustani Plantago ovate* a plant of West Asia and western India: its crushed seeds have been recognised by Indian medicine for centuries as a useful household emollient laxative and are now exported to the United States and Europe under the name of psyllium for their cholesterol reducing properties. The plant also has a commercial use similar to **guar**, as a stabiliser for ice cream and chocolate.

ISHĀQ Urdu
The Islamic form of the name, Isaac. Those conversant with Arabic tend to the pronunciation Iss-haq.

ISLĀM *n* Arabic
The word used by Muslims for their religion: meaning submission to the will of the one God, with the Holy Prophet, Mohammed, as the final and

greatest of His teachers on earth. In English, it also means the Islamic countries and the world population of Muslims, the equivalent of Christendom. To orthodox **ulema**, an Islamic country is one governed in accordance with Islamic law and custom: in which church and state are one and in which no individual can question any facet of holy scripture and where, unlike in Christendom, God does not share jurisdiction with Caesar. Such a government may be termed '**nizām**-e-Mustafa': administration by the Prophet, a standard not necessarily met by all countries with a Muslim majority. The words Muslim/Moslem and Islam derive from the Arabic assalam submission *see* Salaam. Musalman, a Persian word, is often used by Muslims for themselves, with Musalmani as an adjective and also having the specific meaning of circumcision – except that to a Punjabi, not being a Muslim, Musalmani may well mean a Muslim woman. (The more formal word in India for circumcision is sunnat – the custom, the tradition. Strangely, the one fact concerning Muslims known to all outside the faith, circumcision, is not mentioned in the **Kor'an**. This now essential excision is based on a tradition that Mohammed was born as if already circumcised and that he had expressed an opinion in favour of the operation. Also, in Jewish tradition, the Patriarch **Ibrahim**/Abraham, as a sign of his Covenant with God, was circumcised.) Muslims dislike the term Mohammedans applied to themselves, seeing an implied analogy with Christians, who may be said to worship Christ: in Islam, the Prophet is revered, but worship is reserved to **Allah** alone. All the world's Muslims are united by the battlecry down the ages 'Allahu Akbar' – God is Great – and what are sometimes called the Five Pillars, or Principles, of Islam. These are: the Arabic statement of basic belief, the Kalma/ Kalima/Shahadah 'La Illahu illa: Mohammed Rasula llah' – 'No deity save Allah: Mohammed is His Messenger'. The Salat – the five daily periods of prayer: the Saum or **Roza** – the Ramzan fasting. The Zakat ' – the Tax, *see* Id. And last, the **Haj**, the once in a lifetime duties in Mecca. Muslim scholars and the elite use an Arabic word to describe the world community of Islam, ummah (or in the plural form, ummat), the faithful the followers. Two other words for the community from Arabic are quom/quam and ahl, which can also mean a nation: for in theory, but not in practice, pan-Islam is the rule, with no national frontiers between the Muslims of the world.

The moon is mentioned in the Kor'an many times and the calendar is regulated by its phases (in poetry, a pretty face is traditionally likened to a full moon) but it does not have the significance in Islam imputed to it by the West (e.g., as in the expression, 'the Cross and the Crescent'). The reason the crescent moon appears on a number of national flags is simple history. It was the city symbol of Christian Constantinople previous to the conquest by the Turks, whose **Sultans** continued its use as their own – thus inspiring the bakers of 17th century Vienna to make their bread rolls, the croissants, in the image of the quarter moon on the standards of Suleiman the Magnificent whose forces had been repulsed from their city gates. But it has to be said that in at least one instance, Muslims them selves accept the crescent as representing Islam, Islamic countries tend to regard the reversed emblem of the Swiss Republic as sectarian and prefer that the Red Cross agencies within their states should operate under the title and sign of the Red Crescent.

Although small incursions by sea in the 7th century AD (*see* Moppila) first brought the faith to India (it is said that the first mosque in what is today's Kerala was built during the lifetime of Mohammed himself), it was not until a century later that a permanent foothold was gained through an Arab invasion along the Makran coast route into Baluchistan and Sind. But the flood of Muslim conquest came from another direction, over the north-western passes from Afghanistan and later from Central Asia. The way shown perhaps by Mahmud of Ghazni, who in

a series of seventeen incursions into India over twenty-six years from 1000 AD, wrought great destruction. Thousands of temples were looted including the very large and famous Shiva temple at Somnath (today, the Hindu name Somnatha is often used) on the Saurashtra coast. After this raid Mahmud is said to have returned to Ghazni with over six tonnes of gold. By the early 1300s, invaders had permanently occupied all north India (save for the deserts of Rajasthan) to the Bay of Bengal: with the rulers of Delhi claiming suzerainty. The trauma of the overrunning of **Bharatvarsh** and of the iconoclasm of some Muslim rulers still lingers in the Hindu folk memory of today. For a country under Muslim domination for a long period (six hundred years), India was unique in that Islam as a faith was never accepted by the majority of the population.

Throughout the Muslim period, only the Emperor Aurangzeb could in fact consider himself master of almost all India even to the deep south: but by the year of his death in 1707, the decline had begun and from then onwards, Muslim authority withered, until in later British times, vestiges remained only with the Nizams of Hyderabad and a few **princely nawabs**. After 1937, several elected provincial governments were Muslim and in 1947, two Muslim majority parts of India separated eventually to become the Islamic republics of

Pakistan and Bangladesh. From the census of 1961, of a total population of about 439 million, Muslims numbered about 46 million (10.47 per cent): in 1981, the total was 684 million and the Muslims about 76 million (11.11 per cent). From the 1991 census (excluding the state of Jammu & Kashmir), Muslims formed about 12.12 per cent of India's population. *See also* Azaan, Bismillah, Raj, Kor'an, Masjid, Namaz, Shariah, Sufi, Sunnis.

ISMAILI

Shia (*see* Sunnis) Muslim sect following the revelations of the 8th century saint and direct descendant of the Holy Prophet, Ismail lbn Jafar al Sadik. Their religious buildings, used, for example, for Friday prayers, do not have the name **masjid** (mosque) but are known as Jama **Khana** – a collection, or meeting house. In general, the Ismailis are a wealthy mercantile community, but pockets of peasant agriculturists exist in the mountainous country straddling the Pakistan-China border.

It is a sub-division of the Ismailis, the Nizaris, whose leader is the Agha Khan (a Turkish title from Arabic, the Commander of Khans). In the 19th century, Queen Victoria gave the rank and style of an Indian prince to the then Khan, in his later days a staunch supporter of the British **Raj**. The present **Imam**, Prince Karim, has been granted the style of His Highness by Queen Elizabeth and that of His Royal Highness by the late Shah of Iran.

ISPAT *n* Hindi
Steel.

IST (I.S.T.)
Indian Standard Time. Five and a half hours earlier than GMT. Official time for all India, but 'mean', or average sun-time, only at the intersection of the Indian central meridian (82°30'E) and latitude 32^0 11' N. (The latitude of Ujjain – *see* Calendars – at a point about 240 kms. east of Jabalpur.)

On a day when 12 noon IST is the correct meridianal time on the line 82°30'E, local noon time expressed in IST in **Mumbai** will be approximately 1239 hours: in Delhi 1221 hours: in **Chennai** 1209 hours: in Kolkata 1137 hours and in Dibrugarh (Assam) 1110 hours. But these times are only occasionally precise, for the actual moment of the sun's daily zenith can vary from month to month from IST local noon. (Eg. on 11 Feb 2005 Delhi's midday was 1235 IST).

IST was authorised for use by Lord Curzon from January 1906, but as in other things, he was many years ahead of his contemporaries. For almost half a century thereafter, Mumbai, for example, remained thirty nine minutes behind standard time. It was not until the radio and air-transport age of the 1950s that a single time zone for the whole country became a meaningful convenience. During the later British years, IST was often referred to as railway time, for the reason that it was used for the all-India train time-tables.

A rather special time of the British period (it may even still exist in odd corners) was GT, or garden-time, or bāgan time (*See* bāgh). In north-east India it was necessary for the managerial staff of a tea-garden to be at work before dawn. By having a local time, say, one hour later than standard time, having to rise at 5 a.m. seemed slightly more acceptable than the true time of 4 a.m.

Weather time : by international agreement a world weather dav runs from 12 midnight GMT/UT. The Indian equivalent being 0830 IST. It is from this hour that synoptic observations (precipitation, maximum/minimum temperatures etc.) for the 24-hour Indian weather day are registered.

ISTIBLE n Hindustani
Seen on old maps as a word for stable. **Hobson-Jobson** writes that this is direct from Arabic and is not a corruption from English.

IZAT *n* Urdu
Honour: a good reputation: amour propre. That respect in which a man would wish to be held by his neighbours.

———————

J

JACARANDA *n* Brazilian Indian
This mimosa leafed tree is a native of
Argentina with smoke blue flowers
appearing in April, Judas-tree like,
on otherwise almost bare branches:
the falling azure bells from a group
of trees may so carpet the ground as
to remind the expatriate Briton of a
bluebell wood in spring. A second
flowering often occurs during the
late **monsoon** period, but since the
tree is then in full leaf, the effect is
less spectacular.

JACKAL'S WEDDING
Translation of a village expression
for an occasion when it is both rain-
ing and the sun shining.

JACK FRUIT *n*
From the tree *Artocarpus integra*,
related to the breadfruit of southeast
Asia and, more distantly, the fig
family. The English name follows
from the Portuguese jaca – itself
a corruption of chakka, the Malayalam name. To the layman, the
jack seems to be the largest fruit
in the world, weights of up to 27
kg. have been claimed (but to a
botanist an even heavier pumpkin
is also a fruit). So great that the
clusters cannot be carried on the
branch tips in the usual way of a
fruit tree, but hang direct from the
trunk and even from exposed roots
at ground level where, it is said,
they are much enjoyed by jackals.
Another oddity is that a fruit is the
total of the fruits of a whole flow-
erhead fused into one. Natural to
the south, but cultivated in Bengal,
the skin of the jack is green yellow
in colour (when ripe) and closely
covered with short spikey stubs. It
has many uses; the readily edible
part is the soft flesh surrounding
each seed – the seeds themselves
can be eaten after roasting. Sold in
the vegetable markets of the north
(often hard and green) under the
Hindi name of kathal.

JAGANNĀTH
Lit. the Lord of the Universe: also
known as Purushottam. The pre-
eminent deity of
Orissa and great-
ly respected by
Hindus all over
India: a manifes-
tation of Lord **Vishnu**. The deity,
with his brother and sister beside
him, is represented by a roughly
carved wooden image in the great
13th century temple, the **Shri Mandir** at Purushottampuri (Puri) on the
Orissa coast. Only **caste Hindus**
may enter the temple: all dalits and
non-Hindus are excluded.

All three images are anthropomorphic, requiring to be daily roused, bathed, dressed and fed at frequent intervals: every twelve years or so, the Lord acquires a new body, cut from a **neem** tree to which a temple search party is said to be divinely directed. Annually, in June or July, for the **rath** festival, the images spend nine days away from the Shri Mandir and are taken in procession (rath **yatra** – car journey) a short distance along a wide straight street to another temple. New vehicles are made every year; that for Lord Jagannath being fortyfive feet high with sixteen wheels, each seven feet in diameter. It is this huge temple tower pulled by hundreds of devotees, with implications of irresistible advancing power, that is the origin of the word juggenaut. Although never as frequent an occurrence as popular legend has it, at least into the 19th century, the occasional pilgrim did indeed throw himself beneath the crushing wheels. Yet another English word derived from Jagannath is the cotton fabric jaconet (the material was originally made in the Puri region).

JAGĪR/JAGHIR *n* Urdu
In years gone by, the grant by a ruler to an individual of the right to collect revenue from a tract of land, either for state purposes, such as maintaining troops, or taxfree, for personal support. More recently, an estate or piece of land granted by the state for service rendered. In Mogul days at a higher level than the jagir was the mansab, often conferred by the emperor personally: the holder, the mansabdar, had more responsibility and could be required to attend at court.

Jagirdar: holder of a jagir.

Jagirdari: the system of land grants by a ruler for purposes of state. Feudalism. The management of a jagir.

JAGRĀTA/JAGRĀN *n* Hindi
An awakening, a vigil, a keeping awake. Often a reference to a night-long devotional congregation at a **mandir** or at a temporary street  shrine: in north India a popular act of worship to the Mother Goddess in one aspect or another.

Jan Jagran: people's awakening. A term often used by politicians.

JAI/JAYA *n* Hindi
A slogan: triumph, victory, all hail. Jey would more accurately represent the north Indian pronunciation, as in the original English spelling of the city name, now Jaipur, Jeypore. In eastern India, joi/joy would be a phonetic representation.

Jai Hind: victory to India, hail to India. A patriotic salutation perhaps first used as a greeting in the Indian

Legion in Germany during World War II (*see* **Azaad Hind Fauj**) now often employed at the end of a political speech. Also the final adieu at the conclusion of each day's programme from an All India Radio station.

The order of words may be reversed as, for example, the acclamation '*Mantri Sahib ki jai*' – all hail, or glory to, the Minister.

Jai Mata Di: Punjabi. Hail to the Mother Goddess. As a slogan often seen on vehicles in north India. Usually as a tribute to Vaishno Devi of Jammu.

JAINISM *n* English
A faith of antiquity, even older than the **Vedas** and much older than its greatest leader, saint and historical figure, Mahavira, whose life was approximately contemporary with the Buddha, that is, in the 6th century BC. Theoretically, all Jains (the word comes from jina, a conqueror – of the senses) are members of an order of monks and nuns: some are cloistered, most are laymen, whose lives on earth, if the correct path is followed – a course considered impossible for a layman – will eventually lead to **nirvān**, release of the soul. For Jain monks and nuns (**muni** and sadhvi), the practice of extreme austerities (*see* Tapasya) is sanctioned, even to suicide by self-starvation (prayopasan: *see* Fasting).

Jainism and Buddhism have a number of similarities but the former is much the older: both faiths were founded in the same region, Magadha (*see* Patliputra), with princely ascetics as leaders; both reject the concept of a Godhead, a Supreme Being, both lay stress on non-violence to any living creature and both were possibly protestant movements against brahmanical superiority; both repudiate the authority of the Vedas and from the beginning both desired that the priesthood should not be distant from the laity – in both, laymen may enter the cloister for short periods.

Today, practical differences from Hinduism are few, Jains follow Vaishnavi **Hindu** domestic customs, revere the cow and observe caste distinctions, and in law are considered to be within the Hindu fold. A Jaina **mandir** normally contains more space for congregational meetings than its Hindu counterpart and, especially in Rajasthan and Gujarat, much of the stonework is marble. Traditionally, Jain laymen are traders and merchants – often very wealthy – concentrated on the western side of India, but in recent times have also entered industry.

Jainism is divided into two main sects, the Digambara and the Swetambara, and each is further sub-divided. Digambar literally means 'the direction of the sky' (*see* Digit), i.e., nothing: idiomatically meaning naked. Often translated as skyclad. The word is occasionally used as an epithet for Lord **Shiva**. Apart from some doctrinal differences with the Swetambara, the monastic Digambara believe that in order to win salvation, it is necessary to give up all worldly ties and goods, including clothing: Digambara monks may sometimes be seen striding along a road shielded to some extent by clothed followers, completely nude, but others in public do wear a scrap of cloth. Laymen of either sect are not distinctive in dress. The Digambara believe that the achievement of nirvan is not possible for women and hence do not admit them to the monastic orders: all Jain nuns are Swetambar and clothed in white. A strong feature of the doctrine is **ahinsa**, respect for life, both human and animal: for this reason Jain farmers are rare, if any, since for some agricultural operations, e.g. ploughing, the chances of causing injury or death to a living creature are high. Some strain their drinking water, and (Swetambara) even the air they breathe with a mouth and nose filter to avoid taking in some tiny animate thing: some also gently sweep a path in front of them so that no insect may be crushed underfoot. Obviously, all Jains are vegetarian; the strict amongst them neither cooking nor eating after dark in case, unseen, an injury be done. Jains feed animals – even ants and as charity, run many animal hospitals (*see* Pinjrapol). While where there are Jains, there will be Jain temples,

their major sanctuaries are frequently constructed on wooded hills far from towns: often groups of small shrines, each containing the image of a tirthankara. One of the twenty-four 'ford-makers' or guides of Jain tradition, who assist others to cross the rivers of rebirths and finally, to reach nirvan. Each has his own emblem or symbol, mostly animal (*see* Vahan),, by which to the knowledgeable, his image may be identified. The tirthankara did not follow one another in immediate succession: it is said that there was a period of 250 years between number twenty-three, Parsvanathan, and the last, Mahavira. On South Indian hilltops, especially in Karnataka, there are a number of colossal rock-cut images of the saint Gomateshwara (a saint, not a tirthankara). Standing nude, motionless in deep meditation – as is proved by the creepers climbing up the body – the one at Shravana Belgola is said to be the second largest monolithic statue in the world, the first being that of Ramases II in Egypt.

Bhagwan Mahavira, the last and most revered of the tirthankaras (his emblem is a lion) attained nirvan in 527 BC, some thirty years before his physical death from self-starvation: a greatly respected form of suicide – *see* Fasting. *Also* Shrivats.

JAIPHĀL *n* Hindi
A tree of the myrtle family, native to the Moluccas but cultivated in a

small way in south India. The seed (also jaiphal) is the nutmeg of the kitchen: the spice, mace, is made from the seed's aril or outer skin and is sold in the **bazaar** in the form of the dried and flattened red and orange petal-like heads: the bazaar name is javittr. Both nutmeg and mace are used in **ayurvedic** medicine as a specific for stomach disorders. In Britain, nutmeg has long had a place in many folk remedies and is said to be aphrodisiacal. Recently, it has been found to have mild hallucinatory properties.

JALANDHAR

The present day spelling of the name of the **Punjab** town written in British days as Jullundur. It follows from a connection of the **doab**, the region between the rivers Sutlej and Beas, with the minor deity, Jalandhara, the son of the ocean and Goddess **Ganga**.

JALĒBI/JALĒBYAN *n* Urdu from Arabic

A sweetmeat. Made by extruding whirls of **maida** and **besan** with, these days, at least a little baking powder, into hot fat. The fritter–like curlicues are then steeped in syrup; best eaten fresh and hot. In the old city of Delhi, some prefer their jalebis with sweetened milk and no syrup. The jalebi is considered commonplace and is not usually served to wedding guests nor placed in presentation sweet boxes.

Metaphorically, jalebi may be applied to a thing complicated and difficult to unravel: a jalebi mind is that of a person whose thoughts are jumbled and not 'easy to follow. A firework that ascends in a spiral of sparks is termed a jalebi.

JĀLI/JAALI *n* Hindi

Lattice-work: a metal grill, stone tracery. From jaal, a net or mesh. An Urdu word from Persian is jafri, light wooden trellis work, perhaps used with climbing plants as a screen.

JALLIANWĀLA BĀGH

Jallianwala Garden: a national shrine in Amritsar (seeAmrit). As an enclosed open space on **Baisakhi** day of 1919 (later sometimes referred to as Lulluhan Baisakhi – blood bespattered) the scene of a tragedy when soldiers under orders fired 1,650 rounds within ten minutes, stopping only when ammunition was finished, into a crowd at a peaceful political meeting held in defiance of military orders (martial law had not been declared). Official figures of casualties were 379 killed and 1,200 persons injured; figures from Indian sources were considerably higher. An act as unsettling for the raj as the mutiny of 1857. Disturbances in Amritsar ceased but continued for several weeks after in the Punjab.

Queen Elizabeth visited the Golden Temple in Amritsar in 1998 (not the

Bagh). Although nothing was said, the visit was accepted by some as an act of contrition for 1919.

It was a time, the aftermath of the Rowlatt Acts (*see* MISA), of much civil unrest in the Punjab. **Mahatma** Gandhi had not been permitted entry into the Province, and several Europeans had been murdered in the Amritsar region. The officer in charge of the troops, Brigadier-General R. Dyer, afterwards stated his justification for the action was his perception of the need to intimidate the population and to demonstrate that military instructions could not be defied with impunity. The immediate result was all that the Brigadier expected: disturbances in the Punjab ceased, but over the years the slaughter and the callousness with which the army had ignored the injured, was disastrous for the government. Much Indian opinion that hitherto had been, on the whole, well disposed towards the British, was alienated for the remaining years of the **Raj**. Later in 1919, Amritsar was host to a session of the All India Congress Committee, attended by over 50,000 party members. The Mahatma, who was present, commented that Plassey (*see* East India Company) had laid the foundation stone of the British Empire, but Amritsar had shaken it. Brigadier Dyer was officially held to have used excessive force and was removed from army employment: he then resigned the service. The House

of Lords accepted a motion that he had been unjustly treated. In 1922, in a London libel action, a majority jury decided that the 1919 Lieutenant Governor of the Punjab, Sir Michael O'Dwyer, an outspoken supporter of Brigadier Dyer, had acted correctly; at second-hand the verdict was considered a vindication of the Brigadier, who died five years later.

During the Battle of Britain in 1940, few noticed the trial and subsequent execution of a Punjabi, Udam Singh, a mona (clean-shaved) **Sikh**. (As a word and name, udam derives from **Sanskrit**, udyam, a striving, an enterprise. In today's Punjabi, in roman the name almost always written Udham). The Sikh had been found guilty of the shooting in London in March of the seventy-five year old Sir Michael O'Dwyer. The murder had been requital for Jallianwala Bagh. Receiving a martyr's welcome, in 1974 Udam Singh's remains were returned to the Punjab. It is not certain that the full story is known, particularly of the background of Udam Singh, for although his trial was held in open court, the record and relevant papers remain (1990) unavailable for public scrutiny.

Brigadier Dyer was never court martialled, but he was compulsorily retired under a cloud. His rank of Brigadier General was temporary only). Nevertheless, Dyer is always referred to as Brigadier General or

General and on his death in 1927 was accorded a general's funeral procession in London. Eleven generals were present, but no band or gun salute. The body was cremated. In many ways Dyer had been an efficient officer who had earned many encomia, but he had also been described as a loose cannon-a marine term from wooden ship days, meaning a gun not fully secured to the deck and thus in a storm a danger to all.

JAL TARANG *n* Hindi
Lit. water waves. Xylophone type musical instrument, consisting of some fourteen round ceramic bowls containing water, arranged from the right in ascending order of size in a semi-circle round the seated player. The cups are struck with small wooden rods, like drumsticks. Generally used for classical rather than light music. But tarang, a word from Sanskrit, has a meaning of joy and rapture.

JĀMDĀNI *n* Urdu
Superfine cotton muslin with woven brocade designs; once made as a luxury for the **nawabs** of Lucknow and Dacca (now Dhaka in Bangladesh: but in general, such muslins are still described as Daccai – of Dacca).

As a word muslin comes from Mosul in Iraq. The fineness of the Dacca muslim may be judged from an early 19th century report that one pound

weight of cotton yarn was found to be two hundred and fifty miles in length.

JAN *n* Hindi
The people, the public in general, the masses. Janta, the adjectival form. Jan, as a **Sanskrit** root in connection with procreation, is linked to such English words as genitals, generate, genus etc.

Jan jagran: see Jagrata.

*Jan (*Urdu): *see* Begum.

JANĀB Urdu
A term of respect. Sir, Your Eminence. Today, the equivalent of Mr., or from Hindi, **Shriman**.

JANA GANA MANA Sanskrit-based Bengali
The opening words of the Indian national anthem: an invocation to the deity praying for blessings on the country. Words and music by Rabindranath Tagore (since its adoption as the national anthem the music has been so arranged that it can be played without difficulty by military bands, including those of other nations), The first line was translated by the author as 'Thou art the ruler of the minds of the people.' The work is said to have been composed at the request of Dr. Besant (*see* Theosophy), as a stirring hymn for her youth movement and was given the title 'The

Morning Song of India'. First used as an anthem (in a Hindustani translation) by the Indian National Army (*see* Azaad Hind Fauj and Netaji) in Singapore during World War II. The song's political geography is that of pre-**independence Akhand Bharat**, for Sindhu (present-day Sind, in Pakistan) is mentional as part of India. *See also* Bande Mataram. Jana Gana Mana is not the only national anthem to be composed by Tagore; that of Bangladesh, 'Amar Sonar Bangia' – My Golden Bengal, is also from the pen of the Master.

JANAM DIN *n* Hindustani
A birthday. In Indian custom, the day of one's birth is one's first birthday (but some count their years from the estimated date of their conception. Others, if born on a festival day, or a certain phase of the moon, may consider that day each year as their birthday, regardless of where it may fall in the Gregorian and national **calendars**).

Janam utsav: a birthday celebration or commemoration.

Janam patri: the horoscope prepared at a child's birth. Usually accepted as the equivalent of a birth certificate.

JANEU *n* Hindi
Waist-length loop of three strands, the sacred thread or **sutra**, traditionally worn by male **caste Hindus** (in a different form also by **Parsis**, but

with them by both boys and girls) next to the skin over the left shoulder. **Manu**, the lawgiver, said that the thread should be of cotton for **brahmans**, of hemp for **kshatriyas** and of wool for **vaisiyas**. These days, few other than brahmans regularly wear the janeu. The thread is treated with great respect: to avoid the chance of soiling during easement, it may be looped round the ear and is removed during sexual congress.

The **sanskar** (upanayana/ upayana ceremony) of receiving the janeu and a personal **mantra** from the **guru** may take place at the agni **kund** (sacred fire, *see* Havan) and is traditionally held at the age of seven, eleven or fifteen years, but now it may be delayed until marriage. Until it has been performed, a boy is technically a **shudra** and cannot take part in ceremonies reserved to the upper castes, neither can he hear nor study the **Vedas**. The upanayana is considered to be a rebirth, so thread wearers are often known as dvija from Sanskrit, lit. 'twice-born'. Or **diksha**, the 'initiated one.' (Applied to the janeu ceremony, diksha could be translated as a consecration, a consecration to the acquisition of sacred knowledge): terms more often used with reference to brahmans than to the other two castes. The words could also be applied, say, to a businessman who, resigning from his previous way of life, is received as a **sanyasi**. In irony, the term twice-born was sometimes applied in British days to members of the **ICS**, who were thought to consider themselves a superior caste; their rebirth having occurred when they joined the service. Some achieve a third initiation, trija or thrice-born.

A thread ceremony is also connected with the arts, in which a student of say, classical music or dancing is accepted by a guru. Again the personal mantra is given by the guru but in this case, the thread is likely to be placed round the pupil's wrist.

JANMĀSTAMI *n* Hindi
Lit. birth on the eighth day: in the Hindu lunar month, astami is the eighth lunar day (but sometimes the ninth, by Western solar reckoning) of each of the light and dark fortnights (*see* Calendars). Janmastami normally refers to the festival of the midnight birth of Lord **Krishna** (attended like that of Jesus, with special astral effects) on the astami following the full moon of the month of Shravan (August/ September) of the northern Hindu **calendar**.

In the south, the day may be known as Gokulastami (Gokul was the village where Krishna passed his childhood), or Shri Krishna **Jayanti**. The twelve hours before the birth moment make a day of fasting and prayer,

particularly for ladies: Vaishnavi (*see* Vishnu) temples are decorated and midnight may be signalled – as on the festival day of Mahashivratri (*see* Shiva) – with the sound of **conches** and fireworks. In homes and temples, tableaux (jhanki) and representations of incidents in the life of the infant Krishna are made and adored (a parallel, perhaps, with the Christ child's Christmas crib), possibly with offerings of milk, malai (cream) or **dahi** to delight the baby.

As might be expected, the festival is observed with particular fervour in the Mathura region, traditionally known as Braj/Vraj, the locale of Krishna's birth and childhood, where locals associate particular sites with the **Krishna lila**. By some in Braj, worship of Radha as a divinity is no less than that offered to her Lord.

JAN SARVAI *n* Hindi
Lit. Peopl's Hearing. Particularly in Rajasthan, an organised concept supported by the state and UNICEF. A public meeting attended by senior government officials at which women of rural districts and small towns can express their problems and at least sometimes, obtain redress.

JANTAR MANTAR *n* Hindi
Said to be derived from the words yantra and **mantra**, the magic aids to Hindu meditation: mystic diagrams (yantra can also mean machinery and instruments) and

incantations (*see* Tantra). The popular name for the five yantrashāla (place of instruments), astronomical observatories with giant masonry gnomons with calibrated scales for shadow readings and other devices, set up by Sawai Raja Jai Singh, the 18th century savant ruler of Jaipur for comparison purposes, first at Jai Singhpura - then a village a few kilometres from Delhi, now in the heart of New Delhi - and later at Mathura, Ujjain and Varanasi. (The Jaipur Durbar owned much of the land on which central New Delhi was built between 1912 and 1931; hence the significance of the Jaipur column in the forecourt of today's Rashtrapati Bhavan).

In the Jaipur ruler's title, Sawai has the meaning one and a quarter. The prince had come to the gaddi as a teenager and the story goes that the Emperor Aurangzeb was so impressed by the boy that he dubbed him one and a quarter of a man. The term thereafter was used by the Jaipur rulers as a title.

Jantar as a word can have the meaning of amulet.

JĀSOOS *n* Urdu
A spy: a police plain clothes detective.

JĀT *n* Hindi
A tough breed of agriculturists covering **Haryana, Punjab** and western UP. Perhaps originally immigrants from central Asia: before **Independence,** Jats could be **Hindu,** Muslim or **Sikh,** but most of the Muslims are now in Pakistan. Jatni, a Jat woman. Following from the weakening of **Mogul** power in Delhi, in the early 18th century a Jat chieftain and his sons carved out a state based on their fortresses at Deeg and Bharatpur (both south of Delhi), for a time probably the most powerful in northern India, The state remained in being (Bharatpur) in a truncated form until the dispossession of the **princes** after Independence.

Jāt/Jāti: a term connected to jana, to be born. Community or clan, members of which are of the same caste or subcaste. As a general expression '... of the same jat', could be taken to mean of the same type or kind.

Jāt-bhai, Jāt-wāla: jat-brother, jat fellow. Of the same caste or group.

Jāti dharma: the laws of caste (*see* Caste Hindus).

Neechi jāti: lit. inferior caste. A commonly used expression meaning the Scheduled Castes (*see* Harijan/Dalit).

Jatā/Jātaa (Hindi): long matted hair, perhaps coiled on top of the head, as worn by Lord **Shiva** in his role of the great **yogi,** or by a **sadhu.** Very different to the well-groomed long hair of a **Sikh.** *See* Jute.

JĀTHA *n* Punjabi
In rural **Punjab**, a citizens' group, a roving band, probably armed if only with **lathis**, a posse. Equally, a group of peaceful **Sikh** pilgrims to a religious shrine.

Jathedar: the leader of a jatha. Nowadays, a political leader anywhere in the Punjab may style himself Jathedar.

JATROPHA *n*
Jatropha curcas: a small tree of the sub-tropical Americas but established throughout the warm parts of the world providing highly regarded folk medicines. Recent tests have shown oil from the seeds to have diesel-like properties for use as a sulphur-free vehicle fuel. The cake left after crushing is a useful fertilser. In India the plant grows well on scrub land, is drought resistant and the oil has a promising future as a bio-diesel. It is said (2005) that the Northern Railway is planting jatropha in a big way on the spare land alongside its many thousands of kilometres of track.

JAU *n* Hindi
Barley.
Jau ka pani: lit. barley water. A colloquial euphemism for beer.

JAUHAR *n* Hindustani
A word from Old Persian and Arabic meaning a precious stone, a jewel. Jauhari, a jeweller. Often seen in the

Gujarati form, zaveri/javeri. Once solely a profession, now adopted as a family name by jewellers: Zaveri **Bazaar**, the famous business centre of jewellers in Mumbai. A linked word is jawahar, also meaning a jewel: Jawaharlal, a personal name for a boy – loved jewel.

An esoteric meaning of jauhar (also in the form jauhardar) is that of waved steel, lines of natural damascene caused in the forging of high grade weapon steel, as seen in dagger and sword blades. A graining on the surface, known as watering in English.
To a **Rajput**, jauhar – a precious thing – can have the metaphorical meaning of courage, bravery in battle, and; particularly, the custom of chivalry that when in a situation with only the options of a dishonourable surrender or death, warriors would don **saffron** coloured clothing and against hopeless odds, enter the fight. If the man did not return victorious, their ladies would commit mass suicide by fire–jauhar–rather than fall into enemy hands.

JAWĀB Urdu from Arabic
An answer, a reply.
In Islamic architecture, and elsewhere, a feature repeated for symmetry. The best known example being at Agra. On either side of the Taj are similar buildings, that on the west side, with the **qibla** arch being a mosque. That on the east side, the

jawab, is for balance and can only serve a secular purpose.

JAWĀN *n* and *adj.*
Old Persian into Urdu, now accepted as Hindi. Linked to the Sanskrit jiwan/jivati – full of life.

A youth, especially an idealised vision of a heroic member of the defence services in the lower ranks. Sometimes, with extra emphasis, naujawan a young man in the prime of youth. The English word juvenile is cognate, via Latin.

Jawan (adjectival): young, youthful – boy or girl.

JAYANTI *n* Hindi
Jaya – a victory. A celebration, particularly a birth anniversary of a person or institution.

Swarna Jayanti: Golden Jubilee.

JEHĀD/JIHĀD *n* Urdu From Arabic.
Lit. an effort, a striving. The struggle of a man with himself against Satan in order to follow the true path of **Islam**. A war fought by Muslims against non-Muslims: particularly enjoined by the **Kor'an** as a duty for advancing the cause of the faith or for repelling evil threatening a Muslim country. A jehad would be declared as such by the spiritual and temporal leaders of the state. Those who fight in a jehad have the

title of mujahid: the Arabic plural is muhajiron, but media in India use muhajideen.

JEMADĀR *n* Urdu
Lit. one in charge of a jamat, a small body of troops, or of an office. The junior most **Viceroy** Commissioned Officer (VCO) of the British Indian army (the equivalent rank today is Naib **Subedar** *see* Junior Commissioned Officers). Nowadays, the word is most likely to refer to a **sweeper** (his wife being the jemadarni) to whom in the fashion of **mehtar** it was awarded in irony. See also Thug.

JEWS
Jews from the Arabian peninsula established two communities in India early in the Christian era: that of Kochi (earlier known as Cochin), Kerala, it is claimed began in the 1st century (there is firm proof of its existence only in the 8th), but its earliest synagogue, still standing, dates from the 14th. The Mumbai Jews (the Beni Israel, the Sons of Israel) are thought to have arrived from Yemen in about the 6th century, AD.

The usual term for a Jew is from Arabic, Yehudi.

JHĀL *n* Hindi
Heat. Especially with food. As with condiments. eg. chillies. A strong hot taste. pungency-

Jhalfaraizi: a word from British days for the sahibs: an alfresco dish. Perhaps from left-overs of mutton from the day before. A lamb curry served with rice-

JHĀRKHAND

Lit. a tract of forest. The plateau (also known as Chotanagpur) once covering parts of the states of Bengal, Bihar, Orissa and Madhya Pradesh. An area of forests and coalfields having a large tribal population (*see* Adivasi): particularly, Jharkhand is the home of the Santhals.

In November 2000, Jharkhand was formed into the 27th state of the Union of India with Ranchi as its capital city.

JHATKA *n* Hindi

(*Jhat/Jhatpat:* instantly, suddenly). A shock, a jerk. Meat from an animal killed in accordance with sacrificial **Hindu** or **Sikh** custom: that is, the head severed at one stroke. For Sikhs, preceded by the declaration of faith "Sat Sri Akal": by the rules of their church, the only meat permissible. *See also* Halal.

JHEEL/JHIL *n* Urdu

A lake: but sometimes, especially in connection with shikar (shooting), the word is used for an area of little more than marshy ground.

JHOOLA/JHŪLA *n* Hindi

A swing: a swinging couch: an infant's hammock or swinging cradle. A swaying suspension bridge as constructed over Himalayan rivers: the most famous example perhaps, being the **Lakshman-Jhoola** over the River **Ganga**, near Rishikesh.

In village India the sport of girls and young women particularly during the rains and the month of shravan (July-August) with the play known as Shravan ka jhoola.

JHUMING/JHOOMING

An anglicism from jhoom, Arakanese (*see* Mugg) for a cleared patch in the forest, a field. The term signifies a primitive system of shifting cultivation (slash and burn): exhausting the fertility of a piece of land – usually in forest country – and then moving on. Still the agricultural practice of some tribes in north-east India, particularly in Arunachal Pradesh and in tribal forest areas elsewhere. In Orissa, the practice carries the name poda and in English, swidden.

JI *n* Hindi

An affirmative yes in reply to a question. A syllable suffixed to a person's name or designation; particularly used in speech, in northern but not in eastern India conveying a gesture of respect to the person referred to (**Ram** Singhji, **Havildarji**). Some Indian children may even address their parents as Daddyji, Mummyji. Names from western and eastern India may have ji permanently added (Morarji, Shivaji and Mukherji). Said to derive from **arya**, which became ayja/ayji in the common tongue, and then just ji.

Ji-hazoor: a response "Yes Sir". As a noun, a yesman, a sycophant. Similar in meaning is Han-ji or ji-han.

JILDI/JILLO

British Army slang: quick, get a move on. From the Hindustani, jaldi: hurry, quickly.

In the British army version of the game bingo/housey–housey, five number was always called as 'jildi' or 'jildi five'.

JIRGA *n* Pushto

Traditional council of elders in the village and tribal society of the British Indian North Western Frontier Province (NWFP), bordering on Afghanistan (now part of Pakistan).

JISM *n* Urdu from Arabic

The body. The Hindi equivalent is deh.

JIZYA/ZIZYA *n* Urdu

The poll tax levied in an Islamic state on non-Muslims, in return for protection by the state and exemption from military service.

J.J. COLONY *n*

Jhuggi Jhopri/Jhompri colony: a residential area, usually of squatters, within urban surroundings, of improvised and temporary huts, made, perhaps, from dried mud, old tin sheets etc., a bidonville, a slum. (But not all JJ addresses are not so depressing: some, after a formal layout of streets, allocation of plots and a decade or so of work have developed into prosperous small housing estates with **pukka** two and three-storeyed buildings, of which at least some will have a car at the door. The plot allottees, with some assistance, will have themselves constructed their residences with controls limited to plinth size and do not wish to lose this privileged position: so the colony remains nominally 'JJ'.

Literally, a jhuggi is a village grass hut and jhompri, a small house, a cottage: forms of the word used in **Mumbai** and **Maharashtra** are jopad/zopad, with zopadpatti meaning a collection of zopads, a slum. In Kolkata, the term is likely to be bastee/bustee.

JODHPURS *n* English

Riding breeches, especially close-fitting between the knee and the ankle. The name derives from their Indian homeland, the once **princely** state of Jodhpur, now a **district** of Rajasthan.

From the same region and also jodhpuri (of Jodhpur), is a jacket, a short tight-fitting coat with buttons down the front and closed upstanding collar. May be of almost any material from woollen homespun in the hills to silk or sharkskin for fashionable evening wear. Particularly worn by government officers, after Independence, so much so as to be almost a uniform. To Indians, the coat is sometimes a 'bandgala', meaning closed neck in Hindi. It enjoyed a Western vogue during the 1960s under the name Nehru jacket, revived again in the 1990s: the Prime Minister did not himself wear the style, but he did favour the type of coat from which it evolved, the **achkan**/sherwani of the Muslims and the jama (*see* Pyjama) of the Hindu.

(Bandgala can also be a scarf or a muffler. *See* Gali.)

Jodhpur boots: see Chukka.

JOHN COMPANY
Said by the British to have been an Indian term for the **East India Company**, but perhaps the people were saying 'jahan/jehan', or world, campani. To this day, in hill villages and in Nepal, silver **rupee** coins of the British period, worn as ladies' ornaments or a rupiya haar – rupee necklace, are still termed campani rupiya. In many towns, the municipal gardens originally laid out for the recreation of the Company's servants, to old inhabitants may even now carry the name from generations past, campani **bagh**.

Company art: term for miniatures painted by Indian artists during the early 19th century, particularly for European officials of the Company: usually scenes from Indian life with the traditional folk element modified by Western techniques. Such miniatures were often sent to families in England, in the way today people send photographs. *See also* Pahari Paintings. Some artists specialising in birds, animals and plants had a very high competence.

Jan Company: a European name for the Dutch India Company.

JŌTEDĀR *n* Hindi
From jot, cultivation (also flame, *see* Jyoti) one connected with land. A landowner, particularly in eastern India.

JOWĀR *n* Hindi
The great millet or sorghum: most of the Indian jowar is of the darra/durra group. A coarse grain largely grown for human consumption as a **kharif** (winter) crop: in planted areas, second only to rice. One variety, *sorghum subglabrescens*, is known as milo. *See also* Bajra.

JUGALBANDI *n* Hindi
Lit. a pair, a couple. In music, a duet

of two instrumentalists. The word
has links to the English conjugal:
or jugate, as applied to a coin or
postage stamp, meaning bearing a
pair of heads or figures.

JUGAR *n* Hindi
A recently popular word meaning
a way of getting something done
informally, perhaps irregularly,
through someone who has influence,
a fixer. may be with an element of
bribery.

JUNGLE/JANGAL *n* Hindi
Like 'forest' as used in the Highlands
of Scotland, not necessarily meaning
heavy tree cover. Any uncultivated
land from rough scrub on the edge of a
town to thick mountain woodland.

Jungli/Jangli: wild, as in nature. A
person without manners or refinement. As used by the British, jungly
could describe compatriots of **sahib**
status whose work was in far away
places, such as survey officers, geologists, bridge builders and foresters,
who had little opportunity, and sometimes little inclination, to practice the
social graces expected for European
community and **station** life.

Similar in use to jungli in today's
Hindi is barbar. A disparaging word
for a rustic and uncouth person. The
original **Sanskrit** word meaning a
man of mean and unpleasing habits, a non-Aryan, through Greek is
linked to barbarian in English.

**JUNIOR COMMISSIONED
OFFICERS** *n*
Army ranks between the NCOs,
and fully commissioned officers. In
later British days known as **Viceroy**
Commissioned Officers (VCOs)
– once, they had been simply Native
Officers, then in the 1880s, designated Indian or **Gurkha** officers. In
ascending order of seniority, the
designations are: Naib **subedar**,
Subedar, Subedar-Major. In cavalry/
armoured regiments, Risāldar is used
in place of Subedar. (Risāla, a troop
of cavalry.)

JCOs are saluted by their juniors in
rank and a limited number towards
the end of ' their service, receive
honorary (full) commissions. Earlier,
the rank of Naib Subedar was known
as **Jemadar**.

JUTE *n*
The English word comes from the
Bengali name for the fibre jhoto,
itself from **jata, Sanskrit** for matted long hair, as of Lord Shiva, or
of some **sadhus** (a hank of jute
resembles a braid of hair). *See* also
Jat and Gunny. Peasant weavers in
Bengal had used the jute fibre – really the outer sheath of the plant
stalk for centuries for homespun,
but as a major cash crop and textile
industry jute was first developed by
Europeans during the early years of
the 19th century as a cheap substitute
for hemp. Soon, every sack in the
world started in Bengal and wars

anywhere, meant good business for the British – particularly Scottish-owned mills.

JŪTHA *adj.* Hindi
Unclean or defiled food or drink as by being a left-over from another's dish. (But between husband and wife, or mother and child, nothing is jutha.)

JUTKA *n* Urdu
Two-wheeled, covered, single-horse drawn vehicle popular in south India in place of the tonga of the north. There are no seats: passengers sit cross-legged on the (usually) carpeted floor. The vehicle is really a horse drawn-bullock cart: getting in and out is no easy matter for the non-athletic.

JYŌTI *n* Hindi
A small flame, as from a wick, a light used for a devotional or ceremonial purpose.

Amar Jyoti: an eternal flame, as, for example, the one burning at the memorial to India's war dead, at India Gate, New Delhi: also the – Jawahar-Jyoti, the flame in memory of Jawaharlal Nehru, India's first Prime Minister, perpetually burning at Teen **Murti** House, New Delhi.

Jyotilinga: 'Light of Lord **Shiva**' (see Lingam). Name given to twelve sites in India, where Lord Shiva is believed to have appeared on earth as a shaft of light, a flaming lingam. One of the sites, **Varanasi**, is on this account sometimes termed the 'City of Light'.

JYŌTISH/JYOTISHA *n* Hindi
Jyotish in the original **Sanskrit** a word covering both astronomy and astrology as departments of the one faculty. The jyotisha (astrologer) is consulted as a matter of course by those with worries: for advice about auspicious times for ceremonies, for commencing business ventures or journeys and for the preparation of the very important janam patri (horoscope amongst other things, the equivalent of a certified date of birth) based on the lagna (the rising constellation in the eastern sky) at the moment of birth of every **Hindu** child. Parallel European belief appears in the English word disaster, from Latin (a malevolent star. Going further back into history there is the Sanskrit di-astr - two stars. The collision of two stars, a bad omen for mankind.)

From the doctrine of **karma**, a Hindu knows that his present is influenced by his past lives, but that timely corrective action can sometimes mitigate what could otherwise be calamity. It makes sense therefore to consult the professional expert in such matters.

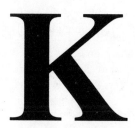

K

KABĀBS/KEBĀBS *n* Urdu from Arabic

Kebabs in English. Pieces of meat and vegetables roasted together on a skewer (seekh but direct from Turkish, sheesh), or by a soldier, perhaps on the point of his sword. Sometimes termed even today as **laskari khana,** or camp food. The simplest form of meat preparation for a traveller who, with little or no equipment, has to cook on a roadside fire.

Shami/Sami kababs: kababs made from cooked and seasoned meat ground or pounded into a paste (these days, more likely to be machine minced), before shaping and roasting on the seekh.

Shaslik: a word now sometimes used in superior hotels for diced meat kababs. It has no local connection, having arrived via the continental style of cooking from Russian Georgia: there it simply means cooked meat.

Kababi/Kababchi: the professional maker and seller of kababs.

KABADDI *n* Hindi
An ancient seven-a-side village team game (it is claimed that even Lord **Krishna** played Kabaddi): also known as hu-tu-tu. A sort of prisoners' base in which the raider has to hold his breath while continuously chanting 'kabaddi kabaddi'.

KABAL/KAVAL TOWNS
A collective name for the chief cities of Uttar Pradesh from their initial letters: Kanpur, Allahabad, Benaras/**Varanasi**, Agra and Lucknow.

KABĀRI/KABĀDI *n* Urdu
From Kabr/kabad: scrap, junk.
The welcome itinerant gentleman who pays the housewife cash for what otherwise would be thrown away: old newspapers, empty bottles, tin cans etc.; a scrap merchant. (The streetwise seller will be aware that the kabari often has two different tariffs, the higher rate per kilogramme being when his own scales and weights are used and the lower when using those of the household even when stamped by the Weights & Measures Authority.)

Another Urdu word with a generally similar meaning but particularly applicable to waste paper, is raddi (worthless) and its merchant the raddiwala. In Delhi and probably elsewhere, a class of tribals (*see* Adivasis) from eastern **UP,** mostly women, visit homes of-

fering cheap steel cooking pots etc. in exchange for old clothing: known colloquially as the bartan wale (utensil people – *see* Wala).

KABRISTĀN/QABRISTĀN *n* Urdu
The place of graves (*see* Sthan *Kabbr Qabbr.* a grave). A cemetery, usually either Muslim or Christian: outside Western India, **Parsis** tend to bury their dead, and there are at least a few Jewish cemeteries. By custom, Muslim dead lie on their sides facing Mecca: hence, in India their graves are dug approximately north-south (head to the north). If a memorial is later erected (orthodox **Islam** frowns on such monuments, on the grounds that a heavy masonry tomb cover could prevent the body from rising at the trumpet blast on the Day of Judgement. The Emperor Aurangzeb followed this precept. It was said at the time that his grave monument, near Aurangabad in Maharashtra, cost Rs 4). For a female the top will be flat, but for a male, the top will often, but not invariably, have a ridge, a few inches wide, lengthways down the centre: this is sometimes colloquially known in Urdu as the kalamdan – pen box. Other Urdu tomb words are mazaar, makbara/maqbara (usually applied to a large mausoleum, where, strictly, the maqbara – a word from Arabic–is the grave or the grave chamber itself) and **gumbaz**/gumbad, a mausoleum with a dome, *See also* European Cemeteries ; and Dargah.

KABULIWALA *n* Urdu.
Man from Kabul. Once, an itinerant moneylender of small sums, from Afghanistan, or at least a **Pathan**. The Kabuliwala of today is a pedlar, particularly of **pistas** (pistachios and other dried fruits and nuts).

KACHCHA/KUTCHA/ KATCHA *adj* Hindi
Immature, incomplete, temporary, uncooked, unripe, rough and ready. A slight variation from kachcha is the folk word used all over northern India for underwear shorts, kachchha—few non-Indians will notice in speech the distinction between a final single *h* and a double *h* sound. The formal pleated dhoti worn by the deities in iconography may also be termed a kachchha (underwear in Hindi is janghiya, but is sometimes advertised in the **bazaars** as wearunders).

A Punjabi word for underwear, chaddi, has entered Britain with the millennium and in an anglicised form, chuddies, seems likely to be accepted as Indian English for underclothing.

Kachcha food may be uncooked food, but the words also carry the meaning of food not cooked in pure milk ghee (*see also* Pakka).

Kachcha food may be raw or insufficiently cooked, but as a sign in a butcher's shop, the meaning would be a claim that the meat sold is from tender young animals. (In similar vein in the concupiscent language of the bazaars, a blossoming young girl may be described as kachchi.)

Kachcha house: one built not of masonry, but of shortlife materials, such as sundried mud.

Kachcha road: one without a permanent hard surface.

Kachcha sharab: freshly distilled spirits, not matured. Normally an illicit product consumed within hours of its distillation – sometimes with disastrous results.

Kachcha koyla/koila: charcoal. (Another name for the product, lit. woodcoal, is lakri ka koyla.)

An idiomatic use is the phrase ka- chcha kan–weak ears: meaning somewhat hard of hearing, or one susceptible to gossip.

KĀFAN *n* Urdu
In Islam, the covering cloth, the shroud, for the dead. A guess might link the word to coffin, but the *OED* ascribes a Greek origin, meaning a basket, to coffin and coffer.

KAFIR *n* Urdu
Lit. the coverer, one who covers or hides... the existence of God. An Islamic pejorative epithet for a non- Muslim or for a Muslim who is thought not to be a true believer.

The word is connected to the Arabic kufr, to hide the truth or to blaspheme. Under Islamic law, as with the Mosaic (*Leviticus* 24:16), blasphemy requires capital punishment. In English writing, the spelling is usually kaffir.

Kafiristan: (*see* **OED**). Territory in northwest Pakistan and across the frontier into Afghanistan whose inhabitants accepted **Islam** some centuries later than did their neighbours, thus earning the name Kafirs, or infidels.

Arabs referred to a negro African as kafir (plural, kofra) and in the 18th century, via Portuguese, the term came to English in India as coffre/caffre particularly meaning an African slave.

KAHWA/KEHVA *n* Urdu
Coffee, from Arabic. The English word is from the Turkish form, kahveh. But in Kashmir, karveh can be tea, often of the green variety flavoured with cardamom (*see* Elaichi) and perhaps **zafran**, made strong and sweet in a samovar. The coffee bean probably first came to the southwest coast of India in the 17th century, perhaps brought by Arabs from Mocha (Moka) at the entrance to the Red Sea and before the century was out the British were successfully cultivating the bushes in the Telicheri region of today's Kerala.

KAILĀS/KAILĀSH *n* Hindi

It is not to be wondered at that the early **Aryans** on first seeing the awe-inspiring peak upon peak and range upon range of the High **Himalaya** should have decided that here, where heaven and earth met, was the home of the gods, swarg, later particularised as the summit of a lone peak, seen as if rising from a large lake, the source of the great rivers of northern India, Meru, the axis of the world. This belief became known throughout Asia and was accepted as scripture by the **Hindus**, Buddhists and Jains of India. Later, the snow-covered peak became specifically the home of Lord **Shiva** and of his consort, **Parvati**, 'the daughter of the Himalaya' and the name changed to Kailas/Kailash (in **Sanskrit**, a word for rock crystal) . Some view it as the vishvalinga – the **lingam** of the world – a tribute to Shiva. To Tibetan Buddhists, the deity of the mountain is Demchok, like Shiva, the wearer of a garland of human skulls. Also in the Kailas region was placed the golden city, Alaka, of the Lord of the North and of wealth, **Kūbera**.

It was the 19th century before Europeans discovered that Kailas was a geographical fact, a peak 6714m in altitude located on the Tibetan side of the main Himalayan range some 112 km in the direct line northeast of the trijunction of India, Nepal and Tibetan China: to this day, the mountain is said to be unclimbed. The great rivers, the Indus and its tributary the Sutlej

– flowing to the Arabian Sea and the Tsangpo (lit. the river of Tibet), in India to become the Brahmaputra (the son of **Brahma**) flowing east and then south and then south through some of the most inaccessible gorges in the world to the Bay of Bengal, originate in the area. The **Ganga**, of course, does not; but water from the Kailas region does in fact form part of the sacred river, via the Karnali, which through deep gorges in Nepal, meets the Ganga near Dinapore in western Bihar. Only slightly less sacred to Hindus than Kailas, is Manasarovar or Lake Manas, lit. the lake of the mind. The story is that at the request of some **rishis** worshipping Kailas and short of water, God created the lake by an effort of will. Bewick's or tundra, swans (species of the Arctic and Central Asia), are sometimes seen there: the origin perhaps of the Hindu stories about the semi-mythical **hans**. (When on water, the Asian swan – a small number winter in Britain – carries its neck almost straight, not with the S bend of the European species.)

To Hindus, a circuit on foot (*see* Parikrama) of either the lake (80 km) or the peak (45 km on its lowest and easiest track) is the equivalent of an act of devotion to Lord Shiva in person: Tibetan Buddhists also make devotional circuits. For a plains-man from India, even today such a parikrama is no mean feat, given the altitude (that of the lake is just short of 4572 m) and the remoteness of the region.

Kailas: the largest and most elaborate of any rockcut temple in India. Dedicated to Lord Shiva, construction began in the 8th century AD, and probably continued for several centuries thereafter. Part of the Ellora group of temples cut from the living hillside, not far from the town of Aurangabad, in Maharashtra.

KĀJAL *n* Hindi

A black ointment, a mascara applied round the eyes of women and children as a specific against eye
  troubles and to enhance beauty: sometimes used by bridegrooms. (The original reason for the practice was probably to make a child unattractive to evil spirits.) Made in the home from lamp carbon mixed with mustard (*see* Sarson) or castor oils. Known also as kohl (from Arabic). Similar is surma, said to be powdered antimony, applied dry with a rod. But, in fact, much of the **bazaar** surma is made from the heavy cubes of galena (so termed by Pliny in the first century AD), lead sulphide: as such, prolonged use on the skin could be a health hazard. The best surma is said to be made in Bareilly, **UP**.

A town in Idaho (USA) has the name, Galena: there the mineral is a by-product of silver mining.

In the original **Sanskrit** kajal(a) was the colour black, as used in art painting. Kajal, kohl, black colour particularly used to beautify the eyelids, and surma (from Persian, powdered lead sulphide, claimed "to excite the lustre of the eyes") are often described in Indian English as collyriums (collyrium as a word for an eye-salve is almost obsolete in Britain).

In the south, under the Tamil name anjanakal, the powdered metal may be added to hair oil.

KĀJU *n* Brazilian Indian

The cashew: a South American tree cultivated in the coastal districts of southern India: both the tree and the name (caju) were introduced by the Portuguese.

Botanically unusual, in that the nut containing the seeds (the cashews of cocktail parties) appears to be an exterior appendage at the tip of the fruit. In fact, the pear shaped so called fruit, the cashew–apple, is an enlarged stalk, and the true fruit is the seed case (from which can be obtained a commercially valuable oil. Cashew Nut Shell Liquid or CNSL).

A spirit distilled from the fermented fleshy stalk, a speciality of Goa, is known as feni or cashew. (There is also a coconut feni.)

KĀKA *n* Marathi

Elder brother. Term of respect used before the name of a leader from **Maharashtra**.

Also and more generally used, to avoid mentioning names, for one who gives assistance in illegal transactions.

In Hindi: paternal uncle. In Punjabi: of brothers, the youngest or, perhaps as kake, a young man, a youth.

KĀL/KALAM *n* Hindi
Time in its infinite passage. Age, period.

Kalchori: a thief of time, a time–waster.

Kaliyug: The fourth age (the present) of the **Hindu** world. A time of sin and sorrow. *See also* Manu.

KAL *n* Hindi
Both yesterday and tomorrow: the distinction being clarified by the context and the verb. English speakers translating their thoughts from Hindi on occasions may confuse the two. Using the same time principle, the term for the day before yesterday and the day after tomorrow is one, parson: lit. from Sanskrit, on the other side of.

KALA *n* Hindi from Sanskrit from Dravidian.
An art or skilled craft. In bygone centuries, artifacts made by com-

mercial industry for daily use were no less kala.

Kalakar: an artist in the widest sense, including a writer and a puppetteer. Skilled performer. In the south, a **Tamil** form, Kalaingar/ Kalanyar, may be prefixed as an honorific to an artist's name. *See also* Kar.

Kala Vedi: particularly in the south, a centre for the study of and the teaching of the classical arts.

Lalit kala: fine arts (as in Lalit Kala **Akademi**, New Delhi).

KĀLĀ *n* Hindi
Black or dark.

Kala Azar: lit. the black (deadly) disease. A blood infection causing long duration fever, enlargement of the liver and spleen, emaciation and finally, death. The disease is one of potentially lethal fevers transmitted by the sandfly under the medical name of leishmanias. Once known as **Dum Dum** fever.

Kala Bazaar: the black market, meaning a source of goods where with an element of illegality and because of short supply elsewhere, enhanced rates have to be paid. (Similarly black money, earned by corruption or evasion of governmental controls.)

Black in the sense of anti-social is no modern use of the word. In the

Mahabharata (*see* Epics) the term krishna dhan (lit. black wealth) applies to means obtained through unseemly ways.

Kala Pani: lit. black water, a phrase meaning the ocean. Traditionally, owing to the difficulty in remaining free from ritual pollution, and equally important, being seen to have remained unpolluted, upper caste Hindus did not readily cross the kala pani, nor leave the confines of India. A brahman who did so could find himself outcasted on return. However, after a purification ceremony, pani patya, all could be well. Previous to World War II, kala pani could refer to a sentence of life imprisonment: usually served in the Andaman Islands necessitating transportation or a century earlier to Penang (see Presidencies) across the Bay of Bengal.

KALAM *n* Urdu
A pen, or a thin brush used for line work.

Kalamdan: a penbox. (As a *colloquilism* with a Muslim grave monument, *see* Kabristan.)

Kar-i-Kalamdani: the papier mache work of Kashmir. So called because the first articles made, when the craft was new from Persia – but originally from China – were penboxes.

Kalamkari: Lit. brush (or pen) work. Practically a generic term (once Persian, now adopted into Hindi) for any hand drawn or block printed coloured designs, or story illustrations, on cotton cloth: vegetable dyes should be used. The art possibly began with the hangings the **Moguls** liked to use to decorate interiors of their **shamiana kanats** (walls), displacing the much older patchitr (cloth pictures). Before the days of mill cloth, kalamkari and chintz (*see* Cheetah) had the same meaning to European cloth merchants who imported from India. (For the hundred years, upto the early 19th century, India was possibly the greatest textile exporting country in the world. But Indian cloth was highly valued long before that. Writing of the value of wisdom, said Job in the Bible [Job 28:15 & 16, Duai version from the 4th century compilation of St. Jerome], "The finest gold shall not purchase it, neither shall silver be weighed in exchange for it, it shall not be compared with the dyed colours of India".)

Kalamkari is still popular on walls as home decoration and can sometimes be seen ornamenting curtains and bedcovers with the name palampore – a term anglicised from palang posh, literally, bedcover.

KALAN *adj.* Urdu
Great, large: in an old northern city may be suffixed to the name of a building or street to indicate importance.

KALASH/KALASA/KALAS *n*
Hindi
Like **kumbh**, a word now out of
fashion for a waterpot, a pitcher. In
architecture, a reference to a decorative feature, either in stone or in
gold-leafed metal, a spherical – occasionally slender, waterpot at the
summit of a **Hindu** or Jain-temple,
a mosque, tomb or kiosk. Perhaps
as many as seven (the **Taj** Mahal
has three over the great dome), usually in diminishing order of size, up
to the finial (a point, a **trisul**, or a
crescent moon lying on its back).
The symbolism was once that of
the horn of plenty, an overflowing
vessel, both of material goods and of
qualities of **dharma**. Old Buddhist
shrines may have something similar,
but the shape is flatter, almost disc
like, perhaps again seven in number,
here the representation is of the state
umbrella (*see* Chhatrapati).

KĀLI
Consort of Lord **Shiva** in his role
of the Destroyer. The all powerful
Mother Goddess of Bengal: sometimes called Mahakali (Great Kali) or
Kali Maa (Mother Kali), also Chandi.
or Shyāma - the dark one. The city
of Calcutta, now Kolkata began as
a settlement around two villages on
the east bank of the river, one of
which had the name of Kalighata
or Kolikata. While it is agreed that
this village gave its name to the
city, it has been in dispute almost
since the days of Job Charnock (*see*

Charnockite) whether the village
name was in honour of the ghat of
Kali or whether it (Kolikata) was a
reference to the trade of limeburn-
ing carried on in the neighbourhood
(in Bengali, koli can mean lime and
kata a kiln). Certainly in Bengali, the
pronunciation of the city's name has
always been Kolkata and on New
Year's day 2001 the change was
authorised by the GOI.

Considered the most terrible
and potent **shakti** figure, Kali is
worshipped daily in **Hindu** homes in
eastern India and particularly on the
night of Kali Puja, known elsewhere
as **Divali**. Many believe that worship
of Kali requires blood, so animal
sacrifice, usually of goats, in her
honour is commonplace. (Inevitably,
associations have been suggested
between worship of the Goddess
and the acts of bloody violence that
all too often erupt in Bengal.) The
Goddess is often depicted as being
black in colour and wearing a garland
of the heads of vanquished demons
(traditionally, nothing else), with
her tongue out and, sometimes, one
foot off the ground. An alternative
portrayal explains this: showing Kali
with her right foot on the prone body
of her husband, Lord Shiva. The story
is that on one occasion, Kali was
very angry, so angry that the gods
had to send for Shiva to try to calm
her: finding no other way, Shiva lay
on the ground. Kali in her rage put
her foot on the body of her Lord.

When she realised the enormity of her offence, in expiation she stood still with her tongue out and her right foot in the air. But whatever the image, the Bengali worshipper is most likely to regard Kali as the benign Mother Durga, the protector: or as Annapurna, the provider of food grain.

Kali Maa has at least ten different forms or manifestations: one frequently seen in **tantric** icons is that of Chinnamasta. The Goddess, seated on a lotus, has cut off her own head and is depicted with gouts of blood issuing from her trunk, one being caught by the lips of her severed head. Below, a couple, Kamadev and his wife, Rati, are engaged in coitus.

Kali Bari: the House of Kali (*see* Bal). The community and social club (usually together with a Kali temple) set up wherever in the world a group of Hindu Bengalis may find themselves.

KĀLIGHĀT ART

A style of miniature painting (usually about 28 cm by 23 cm., but some were larger for binding in folios) originating in and around the Kalighat temple in Calcutta and in production throughout the 19th century for local patrons. Boldly drawn with bright colours and with obvious European influence the paintings were distinctive from

Company Art (see John Company). Often satirical caricatures of both Indian and European ways the paintings were also bought by Europeans. Rudyard Kipling presented his father's collection to the Victoria and Albert Museum in London.

KALINGA *n*

A kingdom approximating to the modern state of Orissa. Annexed to the **Mauryan** Empire of **Ashok** in about 260 BC.

Kalinga Prize: an international annual award of £1000 by UNESCO for an outstanding contribution to science; funded in 1952 by a gift from an Orissa industrialist.

KĀLOO/KĀLIYA *n* Hindi

Lit. dark complexion. When the reference is to, say, a tropical African, regarded as racially offensive.

KALIYUG *n* Hindi

The fourth age (the present) of the Hindu cosmos. A time of sin and sorrow.

KALPATARU *n* Hindi from Sanskrit

The Biblical trees in the Garden of Eden, the Tree of Knowledge and the Tree of Life, have their counterparts in other parts of Asia. In Indian mythology, the Kalpataru is the wish-fulfilling tree (the name is often assumed by lotteries). Seemingly of the fig family, but far from specific in botanical terms: depicted on carpets, textiles and marble screens, its branches support fruits, birds and animals galore.

KĀMĀ *n* Hindi

Sensual pleasure, enjoyment. In ancient **Hindu** society freely acknowledged to have an important place in life but only within the limits imposed by **dharma**. If things are a little more strait-laced today, the change, at least in part, stems from the ethos of prudery of the Victorian British accepted by the Indian middle classes.

Kamadev: the Hindu God of love. Portrayed as a youth riding a parrot (hence in graphic art and in verse, a parrot is a symbol of sensual love), Cupid-like, carrying a bow and arrows. His wife is Rati, which, as a word has come to mean sensuality, especially extreme female passion. The deity also has the name Madan. Rat in Sanskrit can mean lustful, but if there is a connection to the English rut it is not noticed by the dictionaries.

Kamadev may be referred to as **Chiranjiv**, the long-lived or immortal one.

Kamasutra/Kamashastra: a manual of correct and advantageous behaviour for the householder, largely but not entirely in a sexual context. Compiled by Mallanaga Vatsyayāna in about 450 AD of the **Gupta** period for the wealthy man-about-town, the work is a useful social commentary on the times: the relatively recent illustrations frequently included with modern editions are usually historically and textually irrelevant. "The Kama Shashtra Society of London and Benares" was a society of two members. Sir Richard Burton and his collaborator, Foster Arbuthnot, both at one time in India Government service. The Society was devised to conceal the pair as translators and publishers of Eastern books such as Kamasutra (1883) and, from Arabic, to give its correct title, "The Book of a Thousand Nights and a Night" (ten volumes), which, at the time in Britain could have been held to be have been obscene. Possibly, the obfuscation served its purpose for no prosecutions followed. The English editions of Kamasutra available today are, mostly Burton's translation and scholars claim there are many errors and omissions from the original.

Kama also has the meaning of work, employment and function; but in these senses, the less Sanskritised form, kam, is more usual in speech and roman spelling.

"Kam Chhor": from kam chhorna. An exhortatory "abandon, leave work" A strike, a **hartal.**

Nishkam: Action without a selfish

purpose, distinterested service for others. An ideal of Hinduism.

KAMRA *n* Hindustani
A word from Greek and the Portuguese that has become the pan-India accepted term for a room. So much so that many cannot even suggest an alternative from an indigenous root. Such a word is kaksh, from Sanskrit, more often used in a literary way than in speech. In eastern India, ghar may be a room.

Other words from Portuguese completely at home in Hindustani are **ayah**, almirah, **balti**, kamiz (shirt), sabun (soap), towelia (towel) and **mistri**.

KANĀT *n* Urdu
Canvas or cloth wall of a tent or **shamiana**, or just a cloth screen or wall to make an enclosure: bamboo staves are sewn in every twelve feet or so. When supplied by a **tent house** the kanats are decorated and multicoloured.

KANCHIWALA BOTAL *n* Hindustani
Lit. glass marble bottle. A bottle for fizzy drinks sealed by the inside gas pressure forcing a glass ball against a rim in the neck: invented in England in the late 19th century by a Mr. Codd. In Britain today, a Codd bottle can be a collector's piece but in Delhi's **bazaars** they continue in regular use for sweet drinks and soda under the short name, kanchi. The design, apart from the hygiene angle. which counted little in Victorian England, is most efficient. Opening is by pressing the ball into the retaining neck cavity, thus releasing the pressure: something more is needed to prevent the ball from once again closing the neck when pouring — two small nodules on one side of the chamber take care of this. There is a story that Mr. Codd's mineral water was not highly regarded by Victorian beer drinkers, hence the colloquial disparaging expression of today 'a load of old Codd's wallop' – meaning 'no sense at all' (Brewer's Phrase and Fable').

A Punjabi word used in Delhi for a glass marble, banta, can also be a name for the bottle, empty or full.

KANDY/KANDI *n* Hindi
Cone-shaped basket carried on the back with a supporting strap round the forehead. Mostly seen in hill regions: for tea picking for example, and for such loads as firewood, small children and even. sometimes, an old lady with her legs overhanging the rim.

The same word assimilated into south Indian English usually spelt with a *c* candy – has a meaning closer to that of its **Sanskrit** origin – khand, a portion. a division — is a measure of volume (cotton) and of weight (coffee).

KANGRI/KANGDI *n* Hindi
Small portable stove, burning
charcoal, for room heating or for
warming food at the table – as with
a chafing-dish. In Kashmir, usually
a small wicker bound clay pot, also
using charcoal: in winter carried
in the hands or else close to the
skin as central heating below the
pheran – the loose robe worn by
Kashmiri men and and women. A
custom which sometimes leads to
skin cancer. Another word used in
the north for a small charcoal stove,
for both room heating and cooking,
often no more than an open metal
box, is sigri.

KANJI/KANGEE *n* Hindi
A soft drink made in the home:
vegetable juices, especially from
carrots, and fruit juices, seasoned.
Popular in army messes. In the
last century, a similar word, an
anglicism, conji from Tamil was
much used. Boiled rice water, a
nourishing gruel for the sickroom
or of poverty. For the **dhoby**, a
useful starch.

KANKAR *n* Hindi
Gravel, particularly nodules of
limestone found in some soils, used
for rural road surfacing. Useful for the
same purpose is muram/moorum, a
reddish gravel from decayed igneous
rock. An international term for the
kankar nodules is calcrete. Burnt in
a kiln the kankar is used to produce
quicklime.

KANPUR
The spelling and pronounciation of
the name of the **UP** city known to
the British as Cawnpore: at one time
a great textile production centre,
hence an epithet 'the Manchester of
India'. Also famous for its leather
industry.

KANS *n* Hindi
Sacharum spontaneum: a tall grass
of the sugar cane family, with feathery flowering tops (pampas grass)
in the late summer and autumn.
Particularly grows in sandy riverine
country in late summer and autumn.
See Khadar.

KANTHA *n* Bengali
A decorative and long-lasting quilt
or floor rug made in Bengali homes
(especially by old grandmothers as a
gift to a newly married couple): the
sewing together and embroidering
of pieces of cloth, salvaged perhaps
from worn **saris** and **dhoties**.

KANWĀR/KUNWĀR *n* Hindi
Rajput title, son of a prince. Within
a family, sometimes used as an honorific for a son.

KanwĀri/Kawari: in north India a
male devotee of Lord **Shiva** who, to
acquire punya (moral and spiritual
merit) volunteers to carry under ritual
conditions jars of **Ganga Jal** long
distances for delivery in an assured
undefiled state to faraway temples.
The name comes from the kanwār, a

bamboo pole resting on the shoulder (kandha) from each end of which is slung a light cane frame supporting a matka (see Chagul) for the revered water. The whole decorated with coloured paper and cloth.

It is in the month of Shravan (July/ August) that the kanwaris gather at Hardwar (see Har) and as they return they are at their most visible in Delhi, some barefoot - but this is less common today - wearing red breech-clouts, on foot hurrying on their way to temples in Rajasthan, Punjab and Haryana, where the water will be used, particularly by women, for the important Shravan **purnima** worship of Shiva. It is esential that the vessels never touch the ground nor rest on any object: it is said that they move without stopping (with relays of bearers) for as many days as may be necessary. (Others say the kanwaris have the ability to sleep standing up with their load in place.) In some areas arrangements may be made for suspending the kanwars overnight without pollution and for the entertainment of those thus honouring God.

Other professional carriers are the kahars: even today they may be found in old citys employed in the traditional way, carrying a bride in a covered dooli or palki (*see* Carrying Chairs).

A group of kanwaris causing a traffic block on a busy highway can be agressive. A sentence of greeting rather than abuse is more likely to open a way for a car "Bam Bam Bhola Nath". The word also may be Written as kawaria.

KAPAS *n* Hindi
Raw unginned cotton, as picked from the fields.

KAPOK *n* Malay and English
Tree cotton. A very light silky fibre (botanically, *pappus*) covering the seeds (to aid wind dispersal) of the simul, or silk cotton, tree. (The Hindi name and that of the botanical genus, *Salmalia*, derive from the **Sanskrit** term, salmali. The cotton itself is known as binaula.) Traditionally used in Indian homes for stuffing pillows: now also used commercially for sleeping bags and quilted clothing. On account of its waxy glossy coating, the fibre is said to be vermin repellent.

True kapok comes from Indonesia, but the Indian floss is particularly buoyant in water and is therefore favoured for lifebuoys and similar equipment.

Britons sometimes called the simul the PWD tree (Public Works Department), for the saying was that if engineers had to design a tree, the silk cotton is what they would produce: when young, each symmetrical group of branches coming off a straight trunk at the same height and at regu-

259

lar intervals. Nearer the ground, the trunk is covered with spikey nodules to discourage trespassers (with age, the shape changes, the spikes disappear and massive trunk buttresses are formed).

KĀR/KAAR/KRI *n* Hindi
Lit. a hand. A **Sanskrit** and Old Persian syllable relating to manual work, or to performance of an art; appears in a number of guises, either as a prefix or a suffix to many compound words; also in the form **Kriya**. A link can be traced between such English 'doing words' as create and crew and the Sanskrit syllable, kri.

Bekār: without work, not required, redundant, useless. *See* Garib.

Karkhana (*see* Khana): an industrial factory. Equally, as in the karkhanas of the **Mogul** Emperor Akbar, an atelier, a place where an artist may produce a miniature painting or other unique object of beauty.

Karigar: skilled workman, mechanic, craftsman.

Karmik: workman.

Kar-seva: work service. The giving of labour without payment by both men and women of all classes for a community purpose. Much of the work in connection with the construction of a **Sikh gurdwara** and later on with its day-to-day running,

is karseva. *See also* Karamchari: Karma: Karta.

Kalakar: artist (*see* Kala).

Kalamkari: pen work.

Geetkar: song-writer.

Dastkar: hand worker, an artisan or handicraftsman. But dastakhat – signature. Dastakhati – signed, accepted, or passed. In early **East India Company** days a 'dustak'/'dustuck' was a signed pass allowing the Company's goods to move in Bengal without paying the **Nawab**'s taxes, (a privilege frequendy misapplied by Europeans to their personal internal trade.)

Kriti: a work of art or literature.

KARAMCHĀRI/KARMCHĀRI *n* Hindi
One who does things, a worker. An employee, a member of the staff: normally, an artisan, or unskilled as in safai-karamchari (cleaning employee; *see* Sweeper), but the word can be applied to the highly skilled as, for example, a member of the crew of an aircraft.

KARISHMA *n* Urdu
A word from Persian used by both Hindus and Muslims to mean a miracle or benign divine action. Closely linked to the classical Greek *kharisma* with almost the same meaning, grace or favour

from a deity. In English the noun is charisma.

KARMA *n* Hindi

Strictly, karma/karm means just actions or deeds, but the word has come to be used for the principle that through many lifetimes, as one sows so shall one reap (karma phal: fruit of karma). Fate: one's destiny according to one's good or evil actions in this and in former lives, for which the more appropriate Hindi term is samsar/samsara. A doctrine shared with Buddhism (*see* Buddha) that a man's spirit (jeeva/jiva) is immortal, but that with close adherence to the tenets of **dharma** according to one's position in life perhaps after many births and deaths, perfection may be achieved and the hitherto endless cycle broken to achieve **nirvana**, the merging of the soul with **Brahma**, the Godhead.

From the belief that actions in this life can affect one's circumstances in future lives, it follows that one's present, the result of conduct in lives already completed, is beyond one's immediate control.

Karma bhumi: the place of one's actions; one's native place.

Karma Yoga: performance of duties to a high standard without thought of reward. One who does this.

KĀRTA *n* Hindi

Head of a Hindu undivided family, or the person who conducts business on behalf of such a family. The man of action.

KARTIKEYA

Commander of the gods in fighting demons: sometimes called the God of War. Also known as Skanda: in Nepal as **Kumar** and, in the south, as Subramaniya/Subramaniam/ Murugan. Son of Lord **Shiva** and brother of **Ganesh**. Usually portrayed as a youth, sometimes with six heads (representing the six seasons of the Indian year), riding a peacock named Mayur/Mayura (*see* Mor) and perhaps holding a **shakti** (sword). In the north, Kartikeya is little regarded (but some give him a thought on the full-moon day of the **Hindu** month named after him, Kartik: *see* also Purnima). In the south, where his identity has fused with the youthful pre-Hindu fertility god, Murugan, he is highly popular.

Contrariwise, in Maharashtra, the deity is considered to be a misogynist and women are not allowed entry into his shrines.

KARVA CHAUTH *n* Hindi

In northern India, the twelfth day before **Divali**, on which **Hindu** married women fast (*see* Fasting) and pray for the long life of their husbands. Following a sight of the rising moon soon after 8 p.m., a meal may be taken, for which the wife perhaps, will wear her original wedding **sari** and jewellery.

KASIDA *n* Urdu
Cottage industry embroidery of Kashmir. Fine kasida, particularly on shawls and saris, has no 'wrong' side.

KATHA *n* Hindi
Katha, lit. a story. Katha-**kirtan** is the age-old one-man village entertainment, perhaps still to be found. The kathak (or kathakar) holds his audience with narration (often on a religious theme) acting the voices of many characters; songs, music and even a dance or two. The stories are romantic, of the love of **Radha** and **Krishna** and of kings and princes. Within Sikhism, the kathakar can be a rural preacher, particularly one who vividly illustrates his talk with stories from scripture.

Centuries ago in northern India, groups were formed with individuals providing the narration, the music, the dances: such groups also carried the name kathak. Like bharatnatyam of the south. performances were mostly given in temple surroundings. But later, the palaces and courts of the **Moguls** adopted, and adapted, kathak. Girls (see Nautch and Dancing Girls) wearing jingling ankle bells (payal, or ghunghroo. Since the feet are an ignoble part of the body, see shoe, traditionally, gold, a sacred metal, is not used for ankle or toe ornaments) entered the previously all male troupes and entertainment rather than **Hindu** worship became the purpose. The change was com-pleted in the 19th century courts of the **Nawab**-kings of Oudh: the style as it evolved there is that of today.

Quick movement and action is the hallmark of kathak dancing. The Muslim influence is probably strongest in the Lucknow schools and least in the gharanas (*See* Rag) of Rajasthan. In general, kathak is more folksy and far less esoteric than the formalised dances of the south.

The coloured 'comic' books of today for children, in which the story is told by illustrations and dialogue, are known as chittr (picture) katha.

KATAR/KATTAR *n* Hindi
A weapon often mentioned in police reports of mayhem. A smallish dagger, often of village make.

As seen in princely arms collections, the kattar/kattara can be more refined. Two steel bars giving protection to the forearm joined by cross bars for gripping.

Kattar (adjectival) : strict Hindu orthodoxy.

KATHAKALI *n* Malayalam from Sanskrit
Lit. story play. Classical dance style from the **Malabar** coast in Kerala: dramatic dancing with larger than life characters: kings, princes, sages and villains. based on the ancient temple worship theatre of the region, Koodi-

yatam. Traditionally performed only by male **brahmans**, but a few women exponents are now being accepted. Headdresses are high, costumes and makeup elaborate: green faces for the heroes, red for violence and black is associated with evil. A performance can last the whole night.

Older than kathakali is kutiyattam/koodiatam (kuth meaning theatre), the temple-theatre Sanskrit dance drama with stylised body gestures and movements conveying precise meaning until recent times solely to Brahman audiences (congregations might be a better English term for what is a spiritual exercise). Stage props are few and for lighting, the oil-fed deepam (see Diya). Some parts, but not all, are played wearing the elaborate head make-up of kathakali. A sūtradhār (interlocutor) may explain the action in Malayalam.

The art, said to be of over one thousand years ago, is now being revived and may well be recognised by UNESCO, like a heritage building, worthy of international protection and support as an exceptional part of all humanity's cultural past. Kutiyattam in Kerala is traditionally performed by two caste groups, over generations, temple servants, the Chakyars (male) with the Nangiyas (female parts and male drummers). Few skilled Chakyars are left but others are learning the art. Performances may take place anywhere with a spiritual ambience.

Also from Kerala, but less well known, is the style Mohiniattam. Danced bv a girl, originally a **devadasi**, as part of the ritual in Vaishnavite temples. (Lord **Vishnu**, in order to destroy a demon, once took the name and form of a maiden, Mohini.) Now enjoying a revival after a period of decline. Mohiniattam is a gentle, sinuous dance with a clear sung text.

KATHIAWAR
A peninsula jutting into the Arabian Sea north of Mumbai between the Gulfs of Kutch and Cambay also known as Saurashtra (one hundred states). Politically part of Gujarat. Of religious significance to **Hindus** on account of its association with Lord **Krishna**. The peninsula contains the last natural habitat of the maneless Asiatic lion, the Gir Forest. In British days, Kathiawar was known for its tangle of **princely** states, about 220 in all, mostly small, some no more than a single village: one princedom, said to have been the smallest in India, covered less than a square kilometre.

Kathiwar Horses: See Marwari.

KATHPUTLI *n* Hindi
Lit. wooden doll. A puppet.

Kathputliwala (see Wala): the maker and professional exhibitor of puppets. Most puppeteers originate from **Rajasthan**.

KATRA *n* Hindi

In an old **Mogul** city of north India, a small enclosed area of humble homes round an open court: just single or doubleroom quarters with a common water-source and toilet facilities, as in a slum close or court of Victorian London. For protection at night or in time of public disturbance, the single narrow entrance can usually be closed. In Mogul town planning, katras were provided for specific service groups, such as the **dhobies**, or for traders in one type of commodity. With tenancies often hereditary and rents that cannot be increased, the owners may now receive no more than a pittance for a valuable piece of city estate, so it is understandable that maintenance is often minimal.

KAVERI

The Karnataka and **Tamil** Nadu river rising in Coorg and flowing east to the Bay of Bengal. Sometimes termed the **Ganga** of the south. Known to the British as the Cauvery.

KAYASTH/KAYASTHA *n* Hindi

A **vaisiya** sub-caste: traditionally, the scribes, the writers employed as clerks, lawyers and bankers. Some kayasth family names of northern India: Bhatnagar, Mathur, Saxena Srivastava and Verma. Amongst Bengalis and the peoples of eastern India generally, where **kshatriyas** are not to be found, the kayasths rank second only to **brahmans**.

KĀZI/QĀZI *n* Urdu

A judge in Islamic law. Traditionally performs the Muslim wedding ceremony: i.e., is the official witness to the contract (nikah) between the parties. The nikah is normally purely verbal, but an opinion is being expressed within the community that it should be a document.

KEDGEREE/KIDJEREE *n*

An anglicism from the Hindi word khichree/khichri/khichdi: rice cooked with pulses and spices. Europeans frequently include fish. An expression meaning a mixup, a hodgepodge. A form of kedgeree made for European children by Indian cooks was pish-pash, for which the rice was boiled practically to a paste, like ground rice. (The **Sanskrit** root word, pish, meaning pounded, appears in English in such words as pestle, piston.)

To European residents of 18th and early 19th century Calcutta, kedgeree was also the corrupted name of a village (Kijari) on the right bank of the Hooghly close to the sea. Here was a settlement and landing place off which ocean vessels for and from Calcutta would lie to take on and discharge passengers and urgent cargo. Fast rowing pinnaces would carry mail and European newspapers to the city (68 miles distant). It was largely eroded by the sea in the 1830s.

KEEMA *n* Urdu

A dish of chopped-up meat: mince.

KENDRA *n* Hindi
Centre, geometrically and as an institution: e.g., **Kala** Kendra–Arts Centre. Indian television (Doordarshan – *see* Akash) terms its studios, kendra.

Kendriya: central.

Kendriya **Sarkar***:* central government (the Government of India). Both Kendra from Sanskrit and the English word centre share a common root.

KESRI/KESARI *n* Hindi
Lion.

Bharat Kesri: Lion of India All India wrestling title. With the title is awarded a silver gurj – a mace.
Kesar, and kesri as a colour: *see* Saffron.

KHĀD/KHAAD *n* Urdu
Manure: chemical fertiliser: compost.

KHADAR/KADIR *n* Urdu
Sandy riverine country, particularly in western **UP**, covered with a coarse grass (*see* Kans) up to ten feet tall, providing cover for wild pig: the venue for Tent Clubs, or associations for the sport of pigsticking.
Kadir Cup: an all-India annual pigsticking competition held near Meerut. 'Heats' of four or five 'spears' ride to flush a boar, whereupon follows a hazardous – both for the horsemen and the boar – chase at high speed of the wildly jinking 'tusker' through the khadar.

KHĀDI *n* Hindi
As **Mahatma** Gandhi envisaged it, cloth woven by hand from yarn village spun also by hand. Strictly, this remains the definition, with cloth handwoven using machine-spun yarn termed handloom: but in retail outlets, the distinction may be blurred. Khadi is mostly of cotton, but may be of wool or silk, even a cotton-synthetic fibre mix if handwoven, can claim to be khadi. Cloth produced in the smallscale sector of the textile industry on small power-assisted looms can be sold as handloom. The Mahatma derived the name from khaddar, a traditional village word for homespun, and strongly supported its use, both in order to revive village weaving and to reduce cloth imports from Britain: no less from a conviction that simple and unadorned clothing was best for everyone. (Strictly, khadi is the village name for the pit in which a weaver seated at ground level at the loom places his legs and feet. *See* Khud). It was in the 1920s that the wearing of khadi became almost obligatory for serious members of the Congress party, a political gesture. Jawaharlal Nehru termed it 'the livery of freedom'. Today most followers of Gandhian ideals continue the practice. *See also* Khud and Swadeshi.

Khadiwala: a wearer of khadi (*see*

Wala). A social worker, a politician. Alas, sometimes spoken in irony or even opprobriously, meaning one who, while wearing the uniform of Gandhian simplicity, is thought to have a material outlook on life distant from the Mahatma's ideals.

KHADIM *n* Urdu from Arabic
A member of the administrative staff of major Islamic shrine (Masjid or Dargah).

KHĀKI *n* English
Khaak (Urdu) – dust or ashes.
As a colour for British military uniforms, khaki came into use at the time of the 1857 uprising. At the siege of Delhi, regimental commanders had noticed the dust coloured uniforms of some of the irregular corps from the Punjab (particularly of the detachment of the Guides who had adopted it in 1848) and in the urgency of the times without seeking higher authority had been able to make the change from the traditional but dangerously conspicuous red coats of their men.

KHALĀSI *n* Urdu
A seaman (originally from the region of Chittagong, now in Bangladesh): particularly on small coasting vessels. Away from the sea, a porter, a labourer who carries things: a tent pitcher.

KHĀLSA *n* Urdu
A word from Persian: pure, unalloyed as if controlled by God. A military fraternity (the **Dal** Khalsa) of **Sikhs** raised in 1699 in what is now the shrine of Anandpur Sahib (Punjab) by **Guru** Gobind Singh to fight **Mogul** persecution: he gave it the battle-cry 'Raj Karega Khalsa' – the Khalsa shall rule. Today the body of orthodox Sikhism: those Sikhs, both male and female, who have entered the community through the pahul (gateway) ceremony. Other terms meaning the community as a whole are sabat khalsa and sangat. Sangat, a kin word to **sangh**, can also mean the congregation for a Sikh religious occasion. The khalsa emblem, the khanda, often seen in connection with Sikhism and always on the yellow pennant flying high on a mast outside a **gurdwara**, is a depiction of the **chakra** (chakkar, in Punjabi) as a weapon, supported **trisul**-like by two curved swords (tegh) and upright in the centre, the straight two-edged sword, originally from Rajasthan, the khanda itself, a symbol of the **kshatriya**, the soldier.

Khalisthan: Land of the pure, God's country. Today, a term with a political background for a homeland for the Sikhs.
Khalsa land: a revenue term in **princely** India for land, the tax from which supported the ruler. In British India, khalsa (or khas, meaning special, important) land was owned by the state. (The administrative word for much of the public land in Delhi today is nazul/najul [Urdu,

from Arabic], escheat or confiscated. An example of the permanence of officialese, for some of the land had first been nazul as the personal royal estates of the Moguls which, following the **First War of Independence**, in 1858 had been confiscated by the British Government of India. In this way the great Delhi monuments such as the Royal Palace, the Red Fort, Humayun's Tomb and the Qutab Minar came into public ownership.)

Diwan-i-khas: in a princely court, hall of special audience. *See* Diwan.

KHĀN *n* Turki

Central Asian word for a chief, e.g. **Chengis** Khan – universal leader. Later, a Muslim leader or ruler of a small Islamic state. A popular Muslim personal name, especially for **Pathans**.

Khanate: an anglicism for the area ruled by a khan.

Khan-i-Khanan: Khan of Khans, **Mogul** title of honour.

Khan Sahib: title of honour in British days, awarded by the **Viceroy** to Muslims. A respectful, if fulsome, form of address to an influential Muslim. As maharaj to a cook, or mehtar to a sweeper, an ironic salutation to a Muslim in a humble position.

Khanum: wife of a Khan.

Khan as an inn, *see* Khana.

KHĀNA *n* Urdu (from Old Persian)

A building, a place. Suffixed to a noun, khana means the building associated with that noun. For example, **chai** khana, tea-stall (*see*  Char): ghar khana, dwelling house: **musafir** khana, travellers' rest house: murgi khana, hen-house.

Khana (Hindi, but really Hindustani. The pronounciation of the kh is less guttural than with the word in Urdu): food, a meal. Better Hindi for a meal, a dish, food, is rasoi.

Burra khana: a celebratory feast.

Khana khana (first as noun, then verb): to eat a meal.

Khan-pan: lit. food and water, sustenance. As a bazaar convivial expression, intimate friends who eat and carouse together.

Khan – from the same Persian root. In the Levant and Middle-East, an inn or serai (*see* Caravan).

Khan, Hindi: mine, quarry.

KHĀNSĀMA *n* Urdu

Earlier a house steward. Nowadays more likely to be the cook in a European household. The word derives from the grand official in a **Mogul** palace, the Khan-i-Saman – Chief of Stores.

KHARI BOLI/ KHADI BOLI *n*
Hindi

Lit. the standing or upright speech: the straight speech of soldiers, i.e. without circumlocution. A colloquial language appearing in the 13th century in Muslim occupied northern India, being the **Sanskrit**-based regional dialect of the **Hindus** modified by the Persian/ Arabic/Turki of the rulers. An alternative reason for the name, ascribed to Hindu poets, is that they found the foreign words stiff and unrelaxed, so they termed it the standing speech. In the course of time, by the accretion of further Persian rules and nouns (specially technical words), but not verbs, Urdu, then also known as Hindustani, evolved. A form of the Persian script was used nastalique – which itself was derived from Arabic letters – a script so complicated that even in the 2000s, type fonts for it hardly exist and Urdu books and newspapers are often first written by hand and are then printed by a photo or lithographic process. As a word, Urdu comes from Central Asia, Mongolian and Turki, meaning an encampment and, by association, the fighting men who lived in such an encampment – it entered English in the 16th century from Russia as horde. The Golden Horde, a term for the Tartar invaders of that country for one hundred and fifty years from the 13th century onwards – and the speech of soldiers: a link language. The original meaning survives in place names, such as Delhi's Urdu **Bazaar**, the camp or soldiers' bazaar, in the Old City. Nowadays, chiefly because of the script, Urdu, sometimes Urdu zaban, the Urdu tongue, is considered the language of the northern Indian Muslims and it is the official language of Pakistan. Roman Urdu was the very successful – in its day – invention of the **British Indian** army: the writing of the common language for troops from all parts of India – Hindustani, *see* below, in roman script. **Mahatma** Gandhi suggested that roman Urdu would have made a good all- India script and lingua franca for everyone.

The original khari boli, rejecting the more intrusive Muslim forms and going to Sanskrit for its technical words, became Hindi written in the Devnagri script (*see* Dev). But not until after 1947 did Hindi enthusiasts resolutely attempt to remove Persian forms and English neologisms. Persian administrative and legal terms are still part of common speech throughout India, even in the south, established there by centuries of Muslim rule followed by the British who accepted the vocabulary as Indian English. Today, Hindustani means the mixture of

Urdu, Hindi and English, as spoken by, say, a Delhi clerk. Punjabi is still full of Urdu terms.

KHARĪF *n* Urdu
Arabic for the southwest **monsoon**. In India, the winter agricultural crop, normally sown towards the end of the monsoon and harvested in November or December. Mostly rice and the millets, but also maize, oilseeds, sugarcane and groundnuts. *See also* Rabi.

KHARĪTA *n* Urdu
Embroidered or decorated bag enclosing a document from a ruler, or one important person to another. Later, the document itself.

A formal notification from the **Viceroy** to a ruling **prince**. May be used today to convey a formal invitation, as to a grand wedding.

The message itself could be referred to as a paigam, a word from Persian, or if from the Emperor as the asahi paigam - the royal message.

KHATA *n* Tibetan
The white scarf necessarily presented to dignitaries of Tibetan Buddhist culture on formal occasions.

Hindustani: Khata a ledger account.

KHHATA *adj n* Hindi
Sour, acid in taste. Khatta metha : Sweet and sour.

KHATRA *n* Urdu
Danger. As in a warning notice.

KHEDAH *n* Hindi
The operation of trapping wild elephants using tamed elephants called khunkis, by encircling a wild herd and driving them into a stout enclosure. Both a **princely** entertainment and a method of obtaining working elephants (they rarely breed in captivity). But the demand is now very low and their capture from the wild is generally banned all over India.

KHIDMATGĀR *n* Urdu
Khidmat – service. A servant, a lackey. As used by the British, the reference was usually to a table bearer. In this sense the word is rarely heard today, but in a Muslim, or Muslim Gandhian, context, a man can be spoken of as a Khuda khidmatgar – a servant of God.

KHILĀFAT *n* Urdu
Pertaining to the succession from the Prophet Mohammed and the spiritual leadership of **Islam**. Once exercised by the Caliphs of Baghdad and latterly by the **Sultans** of Turkey: with the ending of the Ottoman Empire, in 1922, the khilafat ceased to exist.

In English, while the ruler is the Caliph (from Khalifa, the Vice Regent of the Holy Prophet on earth), in Arabic, the institution is the Khilafa, so correctly transliterating, the word should be Khilafat and not Khalifat as is often seen.

At a more humble level, a master of a trade or a leader, particularly of a group of wrestlers, may be referred to as a khalifa.

Khilafat movement: an anti-British agitation of the period 1916-24 in support of the Turkish Sultan, the Khalifa. Largely Muslim, but at one stage the cause was strongly championed by **Mahatma** Gandhi and the Congress Party – some allege, more for its potential nuisance value against the government and the opportunity to have a common platform with Muslims, rather than because of empathy. Orthodox Islam in India during World War I when Turkey was an ally of Germany, did not accept the Sultan as an enemy: after the War, the British inspired peace treaty, which stripped the Sultan of his temporal role as guardian of the Arabian holy places, further alienated those of the faith. The issue died in 1924 when the Turks themselves under the leadership of Kemal Ataturk abolished the Caliphate and exiled the Sultan: in New Delhi today, Ataturk has a prominent street named after him.

KHILĀT/KHILLĀT *n* Urdu
From the Arabic, khil'at. As a mark of honour, a coat (sometimes a complete outfit) ceremoniously presented by a ruler or nobleman to an inferior in rank: the distinction was increased if the garment had been personally worn by the donor. In addition, perhaps a horse or elephant, a sword, or a money payment. (Gifts of other than clothing could be termed peshkash.) But there was more than just a simple gesture of esteem. By a ruler, the gift of clothing particularly, symbolised a recognition that both giver and recipient formed one whole, each dependant on the other. *See also* Naz'r, Siropa.

KHĪR/KHEER *n* Hindi
A sweet milk-based puree of a cereal, fruit or vegetables, often garnished with dried fruit and nuts, and perhaps a covering of silver leaf (warq) beaten so fine and gossamerlike as to be edible. Rice khir is specially popular: traditionally it is the first dish offered by a bride to her new in-laws. Punjabi villagers are said to make a rice khir, to be offered to a shrine or holy **tank**, of the first milk given by a cow or buffalo. In north India, it is claimed that the best is prepared in **vaisiya** homes.

KHŌJA *n* from Persian
Shia (*see* Sunnis) Muslim trading community of the **Ismaili** sect: concentrated in the Mumbai area. The Muslim leader and first Governor-General of Pakistan, Mohammed Ali Jinnah, was from a Khoja family. A eunuch.

KHOYA/KHOA *n* Hindi, Punjabi
Lit. lost. Milk with the fluid quickly

evaporated (lost) so that only a thick paste remains. The paste is moulded into large round cream coloured cakes which dry further into a cheese-like consistency: khoya is the base for many Indian milk sweets, notably **burfi**. But in eastern India, for such sweets as the famous Bengali rasagolla, chhana is preferred: this is the light spongy residue from curdled milk: *see also* Panir. The rasagolla (roshogolla in Bengali, lit. sweet ball) is a ball of white chhana steeped in hot syrup.

In Delhi, a common word for khoya is mava.

Rabri, eaten as a sweet dish, is milk slowly concentrated and sweetened: a product not unlike condensed milk from a tin.

Rasmalai: an upmarket confection: the rabri thickened to a dough and fashioned to a circular disc. Served swimming in a thickened milk syrup. Very very sweet.

KHUD/KHADD *n* Hindi
A ditch or a deep pit: it is possible that it was the pit below the hand loom that gave the name khaddar (*see* Khadi) to village made cloth. In the **Hills**, a ravine, a steep slope. 'To go over the khud', a common anglicism meaning to leave a mountain road in a vehicle (usually in an accident) and to Khud race: a military physical sport in the Hills, a

running competition up and down a steep slope. The **Gorkha** battalions were always said to excel in such contests.

KHŪDA *n* Urdu from Persian
Persian word for God.

Khuda Hafiz : "May the Almighty protect you" An Islamic invocatory farewell.

KHUN *n* Urdu from Persian
Blood.

Khuni: bloody as in Delhi's historical Khuni Darvaja-Bloody Gate. A Hindi word for blood is lahu/lahoo.

KHUS/KHAS-KHAS*n* Hindi
From Old Persian, khashkhash. Sweet-smelling grass, *Andropogon muricatus*, the roots of which yield an essential oil (vetiver in English, via French from a **Tamil** word meaning root) used in India as a base for perfumes and, at least occasionally, as a flavouring for **sherbets**. It has also been used since ancient days in **Hindu** ritual: a **brahman** may wear an amulet of the grass while performing **puja**. Some headpriests of Vaishnavi temples (connected with Lord **Vishnu**) to which entry is normally restricted to **caste Hindus**, when under pressure from the civil authorities, will sometimes allow **harijans** to enter provided a kanthi (a necklace: *see* Tulsi) of the all purifying khas is worn by each.

Khas-khas tatties (tatti, in Hindi) is the name for the hanging screens made from khas roots matted together: placed across open doors and windows and kept moist, a current of air through the screen will produce not only a cooling effect but also a fragrance within the room. Early Victorian ingenuity used the grass in the thermantidote: a large box containing paddles cranked by a servant – sometimes bullock-power was used, with a system of gears as with a Persian wheel so as to propel air through wetted screens. An improvement was for the impeller to be moved by air rising with the heat of a paraffin lamp: leading in turn to the desert cooler, with electric fan and water pump. These devices of course, depend on low humidity, so generally are ineffective for cooling during the **monsoon**. *See also* Chicks.

Khas khas can also be the name for the poppy seeds used as a garnish for buns and breads, particularly **nan.**

KHUSH *n* Urdu
Pleasure, sweetness in life. As in Persian, so in Urdu.

Khushboo: pleasant smell, fragrance, perfume.

Cushy: colloquial military English from India and into English from the time of World-War 1. Meaning easy, pleasant, a word to be found in the

OED (as an Anglo-Indian term its use pre-dates World War I)

KHŪTBAH *n* Urdu
The sermon or oration delivered before the regular prayers in a mosque (*see* Masjid) particularly before the important weekly Friday congregation (usually at 1 or 1.30 p.m.); in a city at the Jama **Masjid**. In **Sultanate** and **Mogul** times of turmoil, the khutbah was sometimes of constitutional significance, since in an Islamic state, a prayer for the ruler must be included, thus indicating recognition of a particular person as the legitimate temporal and spiritual sovereign.

KIMKHOB / KINCOB *n*
Embroidery worked in gold or silver thread on silk fabric. The word is an anglicism from kamkhwab (Urdu from Chinese via Persian).

KIPS *n* English
A word of the leather trade, covering all bovine hides, unlike in Europe where the term covers hides from immature animals only.

KIRĀNA *n* Hindi
Dry fruits, nuts, spices etc. Groceries. The traditional neighbourhood gro

cery shop: usually family-run.

KIRTAN *n* Hindi
From sankirtan, an assembly for the purpose of group singing or chanting

of bhajans (hymns) or devotional folk songs, either **Hindu** (*see* Bhakti), **Sikh** or Christian: there is often a leader and chorus and perhaps an accompaniment of cymbals, Participants, particularly women, appear to achieve moments of religious ecstasy perhaps with eyes closed.

In the **Punjab**, the hymns themselves are also known as kirtan, and in connection with Sikhism, often as shabad/shabd kirtan, meaning that the words are scripture or from the **Gurus** and God. The singer of kirtan is the kirtankār (*see* Kar).

KISĀN *n* Hindi
A farmer: an owner or occupier of a small holding.

KISMET *n* Urdu
In Islam, a person's destiny or fate. Luck.

KITĀB *n* Urdu
A book.
Kitabi: from Ahl-e-Kitab, People of the Book. A Muslim expression for those of the Islamic, Jewish and Christian faiths who share a common heritage of many of the Old Testament stories, of prophets and others such as Adam, Noah, Abraham and Moses: and of beliefs such as a final Judgement Day to come when God will reward the faithful and punish sinners. According to the

Kor'an, only food prepared by those to whom the scriptures were given (i.e. Jews, Christians and Muslims), is lawful to be eaten by Muslims.

Kitab Mahal: lit. a book palace. A fanciful but not uncommon commercial name for a bookshop.

KOEL *n* Hindi
A bird of the cuckoo family – a **Sanskrit**-based Hindi name for it is parbhrit, one brought up by another, a foster-child. The male is glossy black with red eyes: present in gardens the year round, but only during the hot weather it is distinguished by its shrieking call rising to a crescendo, commencing about one hour before dawn and at intervals throughout the day (and even at night when the moonlight is bright). A village story has it that the bird can only drink from falling rain and that it is calling to speed the onset of the monsoon. For the rest of the year it is largely silent. His wife, the kokila, utters only an occasional kik-kik: her plumage is brown, speckled with white.

KOFTA *n* Urdu
A ball of minced meat or vegetables. Usually met with in a kofta curry. An elaboration, is the nargisi (narcissus) kofta: hardboiled eggs inside kofta meat balls (curried scotch eggs, in fact). The name is from the resemblance of the white and yellow egg to the narcissus flower.

Mincemeat is named (Urdu) from Arabic Kima/Keema.

KOH-I-NOOR/NŪR *n* Urdu
Lit. 'mountain of light' (nur - light, refulgence). A diamond with a long – but disputed history: said to have been found with a weight of over 700 carats in the Golconda mines near Hyderabad. In the 15th century, a large diamond was in the possession of the **Sultanate** of Delhi. Captured by the (then) Prince Humayun (*see* Moguls) it was given to the Persians. Thence again to Hyderabad and back to the Moguls in Delhi. There, in 1665, a French professional jeweller, Tavernier, saw and weighed (270 carats) in the royal treasury, a stone he called The Great Mogul Diamond. From Delhi it fell to Nadir Shah of Persia (who gave it the name, Koh-i-Noor) when he sacked the capital in 1739. Next, to the Afghans, from whom it passed by coercion to Ranjit Singh, of the **Sikh** kingdom of Lahore. In 1849, together with the **Punjab**, it was acquired by the British (it was adjudged to be state and not the personal property of the Maharaja). The weight was then 186 carats.

The Governor-General, Lord Dalhousie, caused the jewel, unlike the rest of the property of the Sikh state which passed to the **East India Company**, to be surrendered to Queen Victoria. The popular story that the Koh-i-Noor was carried and forgotten in the waistcoat pocket of an official, John Lawrence, must be without foundation. At that time it was not a single stone but was set between two smaller diamonds in an arm ornament (baajuband, *see* Cummerband), which is still in existence. The evidence is that it was delivered direct by the Indian custodian to a Dr. Login who had been appointed to take over the royal **toshakhana** (storeroom for valuables). He handed it to Lord Dalhousie who, in a bag tied to his waist, personally carried it to Bombay. From the port it went by warship to England.

When opening the Great Exhibition in London in 1851, Queen Victoria wore a light circlet crown and in her hair the uncut Koh-i-Noor: three years later, its former owner, Prince Dalip Singh, the deposed Maharaja of the Punjab, then living in England, was allowed by the Queen to handle it once again – since its size had been reduced by cutting to 106 carats, he can hardly have recognised it. In an apparently spontaneous gesture, he formally presented it back to the Queen. His suavity perhaps hid other emotions, for in private he was said to refer to the Monarch as Mrs. Fagin. The issue, of course, was that which every erstwhile **prince** since **Independence** has had with the **Government of India**, the position of the ill-defined divide between a ruler's personal property and that of his state. There is a story of a decade

earlier that when on his deathbed, Maharaja Ranjit Singh had wished to present the Koh-i-Noor to the **Jagannath** temple at Puri. he was told by his treasurer that it was not his to bequeath. In fact, it could be said that for much of the jewel's history, the principle of ownership has been that of 'to the victor, the spoils'. The diamond is now part of the British regalia, set as the central gem in the Queen Mother's crown: to be seen, together with Ranjit Singh's armband in which the great stone is a replica, in the Tower of London.

The Koh-i-Noor is not the only stone from the Punjab with the British Crown, for in 1851, from the jewels shown in the Great Exhibition (the diamond was already hers) as a gift from the East India Company, the Queen chose the Timur Ruby (352 carats): so called because, of the six sovereigns' names engraved on it (including the Moguls Jehangir and Shahjehan), that of Timur (Timuril-ang – *see* Chenghis Khan) is the first. It had been one of many gems encrusting the famous Peacock Throne when captured by Nadir Shah in 1739 and, like the Koh-i-Noor, taken to Persia. From descriptions, it seems the throne was a small platform with legs of solid gold and a canopy on which stood a large jewelled peacock with a gold body, a monstrous ruby with a pendant pearl on its breast and a sapphire studded tail (*see* Mor). The most recent engraved name on the ruby is that of Ahmed Shah Durani of Afghanistan, who died in 1772. Ranjit Singh obtained the stone at the same time as the Koh-i-Noor : he used it as an ornament to the pommel of his saddle. (Gemnologists regard the Timur Ruby not as a true ruby but as a red spinel.)

Since the British left, both India and Pakistan have asked for the Koh-i-Noor and there has also been an unofficial claim from Iran.

KOI/QUOI HAI
Anybody there? The call with which, in British days, masters were alleged to summon their servants. Hence the anglicism 'an old koi hai', a noun with the meaning of a long- term European resident of India.

KOIL/KŌL
Ancient **Hindu** name for the present-day Aligarh town in western **UP**. In the late 18th century, Aligarh referred to the nearby French-built fortress, the major stronghold and base of Maratha power in northern India until its assault and capture by Lord Lake's army in 1803 (*see* Ava) followed by destruction of the interior: now no more than impressive moated walls enclosing the University botanical garden. Of the headquarters buildings of **Scindia**'s French commander, General Perron, not a trace remains.

Koil : a bird, *see* Koel.

KONKAN
The coastal strip south of Bombay to Goa: the land between the Western **Ghats** and the sea. Above the ghats is the tableland of the **Deccan**. Konkani: the regional language.

KORĀN/QURĀN *n* Arabic
In India, often spoken of as the Kor'an Sharif, the noble Kor'an. The Muslim sacred book written in the Arabic language: and separated into one hundred and fourteen chapters or surah. The title has the meaning of recitation or reading, and derives from the origin of the work, the recitations of the eternal Word of God by the Angel Gabriel to the Holy Prophet, Mohammed, some in Medina and some in Mecca, over a period of twenty-three years. Says the work itself: "... the words of thy Lord have been completed and perfected and there can be no change in His words and He is all-hearing and all-knowing..." Translations, of course, are available, but since the text was revealed in Arabic, many Muslims consider that rewriting it in another tongue is irreverent. Muslims and Arabists claim that it is impossible to convey the beauty and meaning of the original in translation. The book is always treated with the greatest respect , and in the Muslim home, care is taken that no resting person's feet lie towards it – in point of fact, Indian tradition requires regard for all serious books: a schoolboy putting his texts on the floor may well be reproved by his elders for his lack of respect. A copy of the scripture that has become damaged by some mishap or just through age and constant use, must not be kept but should be disposed of with reverence, by such means as interment in a Muslim cemetery – *see* Kabristan. This is the reason for the displeasure sometimes voiced by Muslim divines at the news of a page from, say, a historical and valuable Kor'an being exhibited to the public in a non-Islamic country.

By the 7th century AD, there were large numbers of Jews and Christians in South Arabia, particularly in the region of Medina: most Arabs of the area, although the majority were idolators, would have been aware of the Jewish and Christian stories. This, perhaps, is the reason for the fact that the revelations of the Kor'an have many parallels with the Talmud. **Allah** is One with Jehovah and the Old Testament Prophets and Jesus Christ (the latter received as a miraculously born Servant of God, but not as His Son), are mentioned only with respect. Like parts of the Old Testament for the Jews, the Kor'an sought to regulate the daily lives of Muslims. It provided safeguards for the interests of women where none had existed before: all intoxicants were forbidden (some followers had arrived at congregational prayers too befuddled to take part). But as a social, civil and criminal code, it was insufficient, when, following the death of Mohammed, **Islam** expanded many hundredfold to include other than the Semitic people (descendants of Shem, a son of Noah: mainly the Jews and the Arabs), races with diverse backgrounds. Out of a total of some 6,200 verses, less than 300 are concerned with legal matters and less than 90 with personal law. For further guidance the sayings and actions of the Prophet, as remembered by those who had been close to him, the **Sahibs**, were drawn upon and eventually written down to make a companion volume second only to the Kor'an, the Sunna (the Arabic word means custom or tradition: the recorded actual sayings of Mohammed being termed Hadis/Hadith – the spoken word). Compiled from both is the **Shariah**/Shariat, the worldwide Muslim law: civil, criminal and religious.

KŌS/CŌSS *n* Hindi
Measure of length: approximately 3 km. Used today only in rural India. The original **Sanskrit** word had the meaning of a shout and so, a calling distance. (Even today in rural India things are not all that different; the smoking time of a cigarette can be a unit of distance, so that a certain point can be said to be, say, as far as three cigarettes.)

Kos minar: **Mogul** period 'milestones'. Pillars about 7.5m in height on the imperial trunk routes to mark the kos. They can still occasionally be seen from today's **national highways**, looking like large sugar castors.

KŌTHI *n* Urdu
A large house, sometimes a palace, as in King Kothi in Hyderabad, once the residence of the **Nizam**. For a mansion to be a kothi, technically at least one upper storey is necessary,

but by the humble addressing a '**sahib**', the latter's home, however modest, is likely to be referred to as a kothi. As an alternative word for a mansion, even Urdu speakers may use the Hindi deorhi/dehri: the deorhi-**zenana** being the part reserved for women. (Strictly, deorhi means just the entrance, the threshold, perhaps the area where business is discussed with visitors of lesser importance.)

Kotha: a large room, or set of rooms, on the upper floors of a building. The salon of a singing or **dancing girl** at the top of her profession.

Kotha Sahib: see Gurdwara

KŌTWĀLI *n* Hindustani
The original word was the Hindi kot, a fort, a citadel (the root, meaning a shelter, appearing in English in such words as dovecot, cottage and

coterie), still a part of many Indian place names. The commander was the Kotwal, or Kotpal in Hindi. The **Moguls**, in official Urdu jargon, termed the main police station in a city or town, the kotwali and its master, the city administrator and chief magistrate, the Kotwal. Kotwali remains in use in India, but the Kotwal as a designated official no longer exists. His duties, of course, are now largely accomplished by the myriad officials of a municipal corporation. Almost the last Kotwal of Delhi, immediately before the 1857 uprising was the grandfather of Jawaharlal Nehru, India's first prime minister.

Kotla: an obsolete Muslim form of kot; particularly used in the times of the Delhi **Sultanates** for a fortified palace. Kushk of the same period had a similar meaning.

KOURI *n* Hindi from Dravidia
The highly glossy shell of the small marine mollusc, the cowrie – the English word is from the Hindi – used since ancient times throughout Asia and Africa as minute units of money. **Hobson-Jobson** said that in the mid-19th century, 5,120 cowries were the equivalent of one **rupee**.

Cowries are available in the old **bazaars**, but their use these days is often for gambling: as counters representing money or in a game such as that in which wagers are laid on the number, out of five to be thrown on a table, that will land flatside down. Also they may be powdered for use in medicine. A necklace of cowries may honour a favourise cow.

As a picturesque turn of speech, kouri is employed in many Hindi phrases implying extreme poverty, low value and miserliness.

KRĀNTI *n* Urdu
Revolution

Kranti Dal: Revolution (political) Party.

Kranti Divas: revolution day, a day of struggle. A slogan for a day of political demonstration.

KRISHI *n* Hindi
Krish, a plough, Agriculture, farming.

Krishi Bhawan: the building in New Delhi housing the Ministry of Agriculture. The name may be used to mean the Ministry.

Krishi Pandit: title awarded to outstanding farmers by the Government of India. (Similar awards are Udyan Pandit, for excellence in horticulture, including fruit growing: and Gopal/ Gope Ratna [*see* Gopi] for outstanding dairy cattle husbandry.)

KRISHNA/KRSNA/KISHEN
Lit. black, dark: one of the many epithets for Krishna, Shyam, has the

same meaning. According to some, the eighth, to others the ninth, or even the tenth, **avatar** or incarnation of Lord **Vishnu**. Briefly, the very involved story of which there are several versions, known to all **Hindus** from their mothers and grandmothers, and accepted by millions as holy writ, is as follows.
King Kansa, of the city of Mathura, a tyrant and actually a demon, had heard that the eighth child, yet unborn, of his cousin, De-  vaki, wife of Prince Vasudev of the **Yadava** clan, would kill him: Herodlike, the king resolved to kill the infant first. Lord Vishnu was told about this and, as protector of the earth, decided that he himself would become the eighth child. Vishnu/Krishna, a very dark baby usually depicted in blue colour, soon after his midnight birth (*see* Janmastami) with his elder brother, Balaram, was sent to safety in the home of Nanda, headman of Gokul village, in the Vrindaban/ Brindaban/ **Madhuban** forest on the bank of the River **Yamuna** (then the R. Kalindi), not far from Mathura. There the young Krishna (Balakrishna) grew up, learning to look after the cattle: although full of childish mischief, he also showed his supernatural powers, helping the villagers in their calamities and in foiling the murderous intent of King Kansa.

A comely youth, Krishna aroused desire in the hearts of the village women (gopikas, *see* **Gopi**), which he either chastely or unchastely, according to one's reading of scripture, returned: his particular love was for Radha. (In some versions, Radha is Krishna's wife, in others, she is already married. Some will say that sensual descriptions of such events, no matter how vivid, are but symbolic of a woman's spiritual desire to merge with the godhead and are no more to be taken literally than an affirmation by a Christian nun that she is a bride of Christ.)

With manhood, Krishna returned to Mathura, slew the tyrant and moved with the Yadava tribe to Dwarka, on the Gujarat coast. There he lived as king, went through the second great romance of his life, his marriage to Rukmini following an elopement (against her will she had been betrothed to another): he killed more demons; married an incredible number of wives; and, finally, reunited with Lord Vishnu following an earthly death, Achilles-like from an arrow wound in his one vulnerable spot. his heel.

Probably in India generally and certainly in the north Krishna is the most worshipped of all Hindu deities: many see him not merely as a form of Vishnu but as the Lord of the Universe himself who came to earth in human form (in the life of

Krishna, and in his claim – accepted by many – to be *the* deity, there are a number of parallels with the Christian story). He is not, of course, a Vedic deity and his absorption into popular Hinduism is relatively recent. He achieved mass adoration in the 13th century AD, the time of the Muslim occupation of Bengal, of the beginning of the **bhakti** movement and of the sensual but spiritual bardic poem, **Gita** Govinda. Some scholars locate the origin or the legends not in the Mathura region but amongst the tribals of the country that is today's Andhra Pradesh (*see* AP): certainly his dark colour and peacock headdress would suggest a tribal origin.

For many centuries the story of the romance between Radha and Krishna has attracted the arts at all levels, remaining a constant theme of musicians, painters, poets and dancers. In his village, watching over the cattle in the fields, the youthful Krishna played the flute, as do his counterparts today: a favourite pastoral image depicts him with the murli/bansari/venu (venu, bamboo in Sanskrit) a transverse flute to his lips. (The phallic symbolism has not escaped modern notice, particularly as the instrument is traditionally played only by males.) The name of the Lord is a popular one all over India for Hindu boys, sometimes in the form Kanhaiya and since Krishna once assumed the likeness of the Goddess **Kali**, occasionally it is given to girls as well. *See* Bhakti, Gita, Janmastami, Puranas, Vishnu.

Krishna's city has been, and still is today, a centre for pilgrimage. Ptolemy, in his geography of India, published in about 151 AD, gave it the epithet 'Mathura of the Gods'. In days of the later **Gandhara** kings and for centuries afterwards, it was the workshop of Asia for the production of sandstone images – mostly on Jain and Buddhist themes – prime examples of which can be seen in Mathura's famed museum. In 1760, the great temple, said to have been built over Krishna's birth-place, was replaced by a mosque by order of the Emperor Aurangzeb, and for a while the city was officially known as Islamabad. To the British, it was Muttra. In the country round Mathura, (Braj, see Janmastami), worship of Krishana probably exceeds that of Ram and the Hindu greeting of Ram Ram may be replaced by Radhe-Radhe.

Krishna fig: Ficus krishnae (in Hindi, makkhan katori – *see* Thali). A variant from the **Banyan** tree. A small portion of the leaf at the back, close to the stalk is doubled, forming a pocket or cup. The Hindi name follows from a story that the baby Krishna hid butter (makkhan) stolen from the kitchen in the leaf cups (katori).

Vasudev, Manmohan. Names for Lord Krishna. If playing a flute, then perhaps Venugopal.

KRIYA *n* Hindi

Kirya in Punjabi. An action, a function. See Kar.

A word with a number of meanings but most often some form of **Hindu** funeral ritual, in particular a family religious ceremony held in the afternoon, often at 4 p.m., usually on the thirteenth day after the death of a member (hence the ceremony is sometimes known as terahwan – the thirteenth). Some believe that the rites are necessary to allow the spirit to achieve peace and to leave the place of death. If the death was that of the head of the family, it may be that at the Kriya the eldest son will undergo the **puggri**/pagri rasm (turban ceremony), at which he will be offered a turban by (usually) his wife's relatives, in token of his new responsibilities. An earlier funeral observance can take place, but these days not necessarily on the fourth day (chautha), when the ashes will be collected from the cremation site: with Punjabis, a rite known as the uthala/uthaoni is often associated with the chautha, after which the relatives are free to resume their normal occupations, but **Hindu** tradition calls for this on the tenth day.

KRUR *Adj.* Sanskrit and Hindi Crude and Cruel. The English Words are linked via Latin.

KSHATRIYA *n* Hindi
A word from **Sanskrit** for a member of the **Hindu** warrior caste, from which rulers normally came. At some periods accorded status higher than the **brahmans**, sometimes just below. A successful warrior of low caste, or even a tribal (*see* Adivasi) who became a chieftain of any consequence, could often acquire honorary kshatriya status: thereafter his line would be accepted as of the soldier caste. **Rajputs**, of course, are Kshatriyas. With Bengalis and the peoples of eastern India generally, there are no kshatriyas. **Gorkha** hillmen of the caste can be known as Chettrias.

See also Caste Hindus, Kayasth, Rajput, Shah.

In **Punjabi**, kshatriya is khatri, somewhat nearer to the original Sanskrit, khatriya. Over the centuries Punjabi khatris have left agriculture and have taken to commerce, so 'that a **Sikh** who announces he is a khatri, is advertising that his family are of the prosperous business class. (All Sikhs regard themselves as fighting men.)

KUBERA
The **Hindu** God of wealth. Misshapen in body, certainly a dwarf and perhaps, a hunchback: (Kubbar, a hump on the back) : always sculptured with a large protruding stomach. The Keeper of India's northern ranges with his city near Mount **Kailas**. His attendants are the supernatural yakshas and yakshinis – *see* Apsara.

(Appropriately, a massive stone yaksha and attractive yakshini may be seen as dwarpal and [fem.] dwarpalika [dwarpal, a watchman or door-keeper] guarding the vaults of the Reserve Bank of India in New Delhi.)

KUCHIPUDI

A village in Andhra Pradesh in which evolved a classical dramatic dance style possibly based on the still older yakshagana (*see* Udipi). At least from the 15th century AD, itinerant teams from the village have performed stories of the deities **Vishnu** and **Krishna**. Traditionally, the cast was solely **brahman** male and the language was **Telugu** and **Sanskrit**. Since the 1950s, girls play leading roles and purists allege that the style is no longer unique.

KUKRI *n* Hindi

Lit. curved. An anglicism from khukri, a word connected with khukna, to wind in the way of a hank of cotton thread and so, curved. In roman Hindi the spelling should be Khukri, as it was in the name of the naval vessel INS Khukri, lost in the 1971 war. A sharp, curved lopping blade with a handle, used as a general tool and weapon, principally by the **Gorkhas** of Nepal, but also by other **Himalaya** hillmen. Carried sheathed from the belt.

(A popular saying that the blade cannot be returned to its sheath without having drawn blood, is not true.) Near the handle, on the cutting side, is a small almost circular recess, with a central style. This represents a Shivalinga (*see* Lingam) in a yoni: also, it is said to assist the balance of the blade as a weapon.

A giant-size kukri, about a metre long, and used two handed, is kept for the ceremonial beheading of male buffaloes on such occasions as Vijayadashami (*see* Dussehra).

KULFI *n* Urdu

A form of ice-cream known in India as far back as the first **Mogul**. Sweetened milk, boiled to remove much of the water (*see* Khoya) and then frozen in metal cones, the kulfi, immersed in an ice-salt mixture. **Pistas** are often added. Served with faluda, a kind of sweet spaghetti.

KULPATI/KULAPATI *n* Hindi

Kul, Sanskrit, family.

In Vedic days having the meaning of head of the family or tribal group: now, Vice Chancellor of a university.

KUMAON

An area of 21,000 sq km in the **Uttaranchal Himalaya** comprising the districts of Naini Tal (the chief town), Almora and Pithoragarh.

Kumaoni: the people and language of Kumaon.

KUMAR *n* Hindi
A bachelor, a youth. (Literally, celibacy is implied.) A personal name. sometimes with the meaning 'son of...'. In writing, to begin a name, may be abbreviated to Km.

Chir Kumar : a confirmed bachelor.

Raj Kumar: a prince. A personal name.

Kumari: a daughter, a title of respect for an unmarried girl whose virginity is taken for granted.

Kanya Kumari (Virgin Goddess, or princess): the southernmost tip of mainland India, a place of pilgrimage for **Hindus** since time immemorial. The Goddess, Kumari, was a form of **Durga** made manifest as she bathed at the point. The temple there is dedicated to her and it was an anglicised form of her title that gave the British name. Cape Comorin. (Marco Polo, in 1295, referred to the Cape as Comari – the Venetian was on a voyage at the behest of the Great Khan of China with the duty of conveying a Chinese princess to Persia, but *see* **Hobson-Jobson**.) The southernmost tip of the Union of India is Indira Point, 6°N, on Great Nicobar Island: earlier known as Pygmalion Point. *See also* Kartikeya.

Sharwan Kumar : a son partienlarly obedient to his parents

KUMBH *n* Hindi
Lit. water pot. *See also* Chagul and Kalash.

Kumbh Mela (or, in better Hindi, Kumbh Parv – the Kumbh Festival): after the **amrit** or nectar produced by the-gods from the churning of the sea had been placed in a golden kumbh, it was seized by asuras (demons; in some texts the asuras were equated with non-**Aryans**) who made off with it. In their flight, drops of the ambrosia were spilt at four places, Prayag (Allahabad), Hardwar (*see* Har), Nasik and Ujjain: first said to have been organised by Sankaracharya (8th century AD, *see* Math), since when immense gatherings of ordinary **Hindus** and of the religious orders have been held at these holy places at regular intervals. At the Kumbh, one of the great festivals of India, can be seen the enormous unchanging compass of Hinduism, not merely of the unsophisticated, but equally of those who in other contexts would be seen to be both wealthy and worldly: spiritual exaltation sufficient to cause multitudes, pre-dawn on a near freezing winter morning, to bathe in the Holy **Ganga**. To a non-Hindu at least, grotesqueries abound: if not the ropetrick, that other delight of the cartoonists, the **swami** on a bed of spikes (thorns) is a reality. Separate from the sleaze so attractive to the media are the myriads imbued with the conviction that Ganga **snan** at this place and time will give them good standing in this life and in their next.

A major, or purna (complete/ full) Kumbh Mela, occurs approximately every twelve years linked to the cycle of Jupiter and takes place at one of the four sacred places as decided by the **sadhu** orders. The occasion is astrological, for the Allahabad Kumbh, the coincidence of the sun entering Capricorn with Jupiter entering Aquarius, it always includes the auspicious day and moment in January of the **uttarayana** when all must bathe. The Hardwar Kumbh occurs some three months later in the year when the sun entering Aries and Jupiter entering Aquarius coincide. The main bathing day here is **Baisakhi**. An Ardh (half) Kumbh takes place every six years and a smaller mela after three years. On each of the sites when there is no major mela, a Magh (January) Mela is held.

Kumbh/Kumbha: the water pot. The Hindi name for the sign of the zodiac, Aquarius.

Purna Kumbh: lit. a full pot. The equivalent of a cornucopia, or horn of plenty, a decorative symbol of Indian art from antiquity for the good things of life.

Kumbhar/Kumbhkar/Kumhar: the maker of fired clay kumbhs, the potter.

KUM KUM *n* Hindi
Red powder used for the **tika** on a forehead and elsewhere where the colour is required by **Hindu** custom. The base powder  should be the auspicious **haldi**, (turmeric) and perhaps sandalwood powder. *See also* Sindoor.

KUMQUAT *n* English from Chinese.
A minature (golf ball size) orange. In Rashtrapati Garden where the trees abound, known to the malis as China orange.

KUND *n* Hindi
A pool, an artificial lake, a **tank**.

Agni Kund: depression or pit in which a Hindu sacred fire burns, as for a marriage ceremony or **havan**. A relic of Vedic Hinduism when fire was the centre of worship. *See also* Yagna.

Kundalini: *see* Yoga.

KUNDAN *n* Hindi
Gold wire. Jewellery from **Mogul** times. Diamonds and semi–precious gemstones crafted together into usually a flat ornament using pure gold wire: a glittering multicoloured piece.

The craftsmen may be seen in the

narrow lanes of Delhi's old city, first embedding the stones in a block of **lac**: mostly they are Punjabis, both Hindu and Sikh, of the Jariya community.

KURA *n* Hindi
Rubbish, particularly household rubbish. In a domestic setting, taken to the tip (kuradan or dhalao) only by the sweeper.

KURSHI NASHIN *n* Urdu
Lit. one who sits on a chair. During the British period at least into the 20th century, to avoid embarrassing situations, district authorities issued 'Kurshi Nashin Certificates' to Indian gentlemen, meaning that the holders were of position in society and were entitled to a chair when calling on a British officer. Such certificates were sometimes framed and exhibited by those who had received them as evidence of status and respectability.

KURTA *n* Hindi
Loose knee length shirt without collar. But sometimes tight fitting at the neck. Normally worn outside the **pyjama/shalwar**. Somewhat similar to the kurta, but reaching below the knees and even to the ankles, is the angarkha (Urdu): traditionally a Muslim male formal court costume, frequently with a low U-neck. No buttons in front. Almost transparent, also worn by court dancing girls.

Kurti: worn shorter than the kurta.

KUSHAK *n* Tibetan
In Buddhism, a person who receives enlightenment and whose spirit, after bodily death, instantly passes into another body for future service on earth. Head **lamas** of major Tibetan Buddhist monasteries are usually considered to be kushaks.

KUSHT *n* Hindi
Leprosy.

KUSUM *n* Hindi
A fatty oil pressed from the seeds of a sub-Himalayan tree of the same name (*Schleichara oleosa*): in English known as the **lac** tree, the Macassar tree, and the Ceylon oak. The oil (Indian macassar oil) is used for hair dressing and in medicinal skin application. In Victorian England it was the reason for the name of a cover on the back of a chair at head level (still to be seen in India), the antimacassar.

In **Sanskrit**, kusum means a flower.

KUTCHERY/CUTCHERY *n*
From the Hindi, kachahree, a law court. The word was used by the **Mogul** administrators from whom it passed into Indian official English as cutchery, meaning an administrative office, particularly that of the **District Collector**. At one time it could equally have been applied to a mercantile office, but this use has been obsolete since at least the end years of the 19th century. In the south, kutchery/cutchery can be used

in **Tamil** to mean a performance of **Carnatic** music.

KUTH *n* Hindi
Saussurea lappa. Plant containing essential oils and small amounts of alkaloid narcotics grown commercially in the hills of Kashmir and Lahaul (Himachal Pradesh). The root is exported to many eastern countries under the trade name of costus: it may be burnt as incense, or in powder form, smoked as a cheap substitute for opium.

KUTĪR *n* Hindi
A cottage. A small residence in a rural setting.

KWASHIORKOR *n*
A word imported from Ghana (W. Africa) for a childhood condition associated with poverty, ignorance and malnutrition in regions of high temperature and humidity: a malfunctioning of body chemistry still not fully understood. The literal meaning of the word is 'the deposed one', a reference to a child displaced from its mother's breast by the ar-rival of a younger sibling. Following weaning on food deficient in protein and calories, and possibly, contaminated with fungal toxins, the child may suffer from a distended stomach, oedema (swelling) of the limbs, loss of hair pigment and retarded physical growth. While the causes appear to be similar, kwashiorkor is distinguished from marasmus, a general wasting away of body tissue. Another nutritional deficiency disease with a non-Indian name is beriberi: caused by the absence of vitamins (particularly of the B group) in the diet. Beri is Sinhalese (*see* Singh) for weakness and the sense of the expression is the cry of a sufferer: "I cannot do anything because of exhaustion".

KYANG/KIANG *n* Tibetan
The long-haired wild ass (the world's largest) of the high Tibetan plateau and of the adjoining Ladakh region of Jammu & Kashmir in India. A social animal living in herds of several hundred: locally protected by a certain amount of religious (Buddhist) veneration.

LA *n* Tibetan

A crossing point such as a high pass in the Himalaya in India close to the Tibetan frontier. Eg. The Rohtang La at the head of the Kullu (previously, Kulu) Valley. Also used for a mountain pass in the same region is the word jot/joth. In Tibet itself la can also refer to a crossing point of a river, a ford.

Ladakh (the largely Tibetan culture territory of the state of Jammu & Kashmir): a corruption of the Tibetan La-dag–land of high passes.

*Shangri-L*ā: anglicised form of the name Shamba La given by an early 19th century Himalayan traveller and Tibetan scholar, the Hungarian Count de Korus, to the pass leading to a mythical valley in Tibet where all lived in bliss and peace.

LAC *n* English

A reddish, scaly, resinous secretion by the minute female lac insect of the coccidea family; scale insects: cochineal dye comes from another insect of the same group. The insects feed on juices from twigs of bushes and small trees and immure themselves in a protective incrustation which also forms a brood chamber for the young. The incrustations, sticklac, an animal thermoplastic, are collected by forest dwellers, and after cleaning and crushing become seedlac: the base material of lacquer, sealing and seal wax – the quality for this is improved if mixed with rosin–and, once but not now the base material of the world's gramophone records. In film-thin sheets, lac becomes shellac, perhaps with added vegetable copal gum, used for French polishing. Craftsmen use it for making coloured bangles and as a temporary mastic for holding small pieces when making jewellery ornaments. It has a use in electrical insulation and, recently on an experimental basis, as capsules, for oral medicines. The insects are cultivated to some extent and sticklac is a forest crop over much of central India: India at one time was the main supplier of lac to the world: production in 1998 was said to have been about 3000 tonnes. A red dye (the origin of the artists' English colour term, crimson lake: more recent shade terms, such as purple lake, are imitative) can be made from it, *see* Henna. Lac dye is considered particularly suitable for use on silk. These days, natural lacquer, especially in **Burma** and Japan, is mostly made from vegetable resins.

The words carmine and crimson derive through a lengthy chain from a **Sanskrit**/Old Persian name for an insect. In early Sanskrit, kermi referred to an insect of the scale/aphis group (*see* kermes in the *OED*) the dried bodies of which give a red dye. As an English term, lac derives from the Hindi name, **lakh**, the numeral one hundred thousand; said to be an allusion to the immense number of insects required to produce a useful amount of the material.

Lac tree: see Kusum.

Lac wax: a high grade hard wax made from lac, used for polishes. A substitute for the much more expensive carnauba wax from Brazil, even to give a shine to apples.

LADIES' FINGERS *n*
The English name for the ripe seed pod of a species of hibiscus (*H. suculens*) when used as a table vegetable. Rich in vitamin A and pectin. An alternative name in English is okra (from West Africa) and in Hindi the word is bhindi/bhendi. Bhindi as a flowering tree, *see* Peepal.

LADY KENNY/LEDIKENI *n*
Like the sandwich and the pêche Melba, a food preparation named for a person. A sweet of Bengal said to have been invented by a confectioner for presentation to the first Vicereine (*see* Viceroy), Lady Canning: the period must have been between 1858 and her death in Calcutta in November 1861. To a non-Bengali, the black ball-shaped syrupy confection is very similar to that known as the gulab-jamun in northern India (gulab is rose and the jamun is a small black fruit of the myrtle family), except that in the Lady Kenny there should be a sultana in the centre and the outside is dusted with dry sugar: the sweet is frequently confused with the Bengali pantua, for which the ball should be smaller with a flavour of elaichi (cardamom) and without the dry sugar coating – but as with all made up dishes, the definitive version is hard to establish. Grown in the south there is a fruit, golf ball size, with the name gulab-jamun or rose-apple.

LĀHSAN *n* Hindi
Garlic.
As in the West, where garlic has rarely been acceptable at top tables, so in India the cloves have been deemed suitable only for **shudras**. Manu forbade **caste Hindus** to eat garlic and even the onion. Nevertheless, garlic is used extensively in Indian dishes.

LĀKH *n* Hindi
Numeral equivalent to one hundred thousand.

Lakhpati: person with a least one lakh of rupees (occasionally lakhier).

Naulakha: strictly, an object valued at nine lakhs of rupees. Often used as the equivalent of priceless, especially when the reference is to jewellery. In the form naulaka-haar (an invaluable necklace – haar, a necklace, a garland) the subject of many folktales of princely derring-do. Kipling used such a story for the 1891 novel *The Naulahka* (the spelling was the choice of his American collaborator who, had he lived long enough, would have become Kipling's brother-in-law). Kipling named his own Vermont (USA) home Naulakha, derived, no doubt, from his memory of Lahore, where a marble pavilion built at a cost of Rs. 9,00,000 by the 17th century **Mogul** Emperor, Shah Jehan, popularly has the same name, Lakh as a animal resin: *see* Lac.

LAKRI *n* Hindi

Wood, timber.
If not today, then at least until after world war II, a British army nickname for one whose surname was Wood.

LAKSHADWEEP *n*

One lakh islands: a misnomer. A group of islands – but not to the total of one hundred thousand – within the Union of India lying approximately three hundred kilometres off the Kerala coast. Previous to 1973, the group was named the Laccadive, Minicoy and Amindivi Islands. Earlier part of **Madras Presidency**, the islands are now a **Union Territory**. Geologists say that the islands, together with the Maldives to the south, below the coral which cov-

ers them, are a continuation of the Aravali range of Rajasthan. (The Aravalis, the degraded remnants of a mountain system, rise from the river at Delhi to about one hundred metres then run south west to Mount Abu in Rajasthan with peaks of 2600 metres. The Aravalis are much much older than the **Himalaya** and once bordered the sea.) The population of the island group is over ninety per cent Muslim.

LAKSHMAN/LAXMAN REKHA

n Hindi
A line, actual or imaginary, the crossing of which may have serious consequences: while the parallel is not exact, a Rubicon. The figure of speech derives from a story in the *Ramayana*.

During his exile, Lord **Ram**, his wife Sita and his brother, Lakshman, were living in a forest hut. One day, Sita noticed a golden deer (actually a lure, sent by Ram's enemy, King Ravan) and implored her husband to get it for her. Ram left to chase the deer, leaving Lakshman to look after Sita. An urgent call for help was heard from the forest, seemingly in Ram's voice. Before departing, Lakshman had encircled the hut with a line on the ground, saying to Sita that on no account was she to cross it. Ravan appeared in the guise of a yogi (*see* Yoga) asking for food. Sita could not refuse a holy man, crossed the line, and was abducted.

LAKSHMI/LAXMI/LAKME

Hindu Goddess of good fortune, wealth, prosperity, protector of the home: and in an earlier age if not today, of both male and female beauty: wife of Lord **Vishnu** and like her Lord, she appears in many guises. In some texts, Lakshmi was born from the churning of the ocean (*see* Amrit) and in others, from divine parents on land. She is particularly worshipped on the occasion of **Divali** and weekly, on Fridays. Bengal celebrates Lakshmi **Puja** on the full moon day following **Dussehra**. The Goddess is often shown as emerging from a **lotus** (hence, also called Kamla/Kamala, or Padma/Padmini) attended by an elephant as her vehicle (*see* Vahan) but in another aspect, she uses a white owl. For the purpose of worship, some hold that a coconut can represent an image of Lakshmi. Gold is said to be a token of her bounty, so to earn her good wishes, every Hindu woman – and many a man tries to wear at least a touch of the metal. Her devotees may refer to her as Mahalakshmi (Great Lakshmi) and she is also known as Sri. (The Devnagri character – *see* Sanskrit – for **Shri** is also a symbol for Lakshmi.)

Particularly in eastern India, in her aspect of prosperity, Lakshmi is thought to be represented by rice. To ensure her continued goodwill and family well-being, in the domestic kitchen the rice-bin must never be completely emptied. At least a few grains must always remain.

Popular opinion has it that Lakshmi and her sister goddess, Saraswati (*see* Basant), the patroness of learning, do not get on well together. The result for mortals is that if one smiles on a particular person, the other will frown: so that one can receive the gifts of either wealth or learning, but never the two together.

Both Lakshmi and Kamla are popular girls' names. Another name for Lakshmi is Indira - note, the second i is pronounced short.

*Lakshmi Vilas/Lakshmi Vilas **Mahal**:* often a name for a princely palace. A statement that every comfort and luxury will be found within.

Grihalakshmi: a term honouring the Lakshmi of the family home, the housewife.

LALIT KALA AKADEMI *n*

Lalit (Hindi): elegant, graceful. Set up in 1954, the national body for the promotion of fine arts. Annual awards are made and the **Akademi** sponsors at three year intervals, an international arts exhibition, the Triennale.

LĀMA *n* Tibetan

A title in Tibetan Buddhism: strictly, one who is accepted as being in at least his second incarnation, a

teacher of Bud-
dhist philosophy.
But in fact, the
honorific is usu-
ally accorded to
any well-respect-
ed senior religious
of the Mahayana

Path (*see* Buddha). A Buddhist monk
of junior grade would not normally
be considered a Lama.

Lamasery: a term for a Tibetan Buddhist monastery. Of European coinage, possibly derived from Lamaserai
(*see* Caravan), but more probably, a
gallicism (lamaserie), an invention
by French missionaries. Local names
are *gompa* and **vihara**.

LANGAR *n* Hindi (Hindustani)
From **Sanskrit** and Old Persian,
meaning a free kitchen. Probably
best known as a community kitchen
within the dera (*see* Gurdwara) of a
Sikh temple, from which all, rich and
poor, Sikh and non-Sikh, **brahman**
and **shudra**, may eat the same meal
sitting together without payment.
(Sikhs are not usually vegetarian but
only vegetarian food is served in a
langar so as not to cause difficulties
for those, Sikh and non-Sikh, who
are.) Since Sikhs accept that food
and water belong to the Lord, so
the langar is sometimes called the
Temple of Bread: it follows that for
a visit heads are covered and feet
bare. As an institution, the Sikh langar was established by **Guru** Amar
Das (16th century) to ensure that the

Hindu dharma requirement of caste
exclusiveness for meals was not carried into Sikhism and to inculcate the
virtue of charity. This enlarged on a
practice of the first Sikh leader, Guru
Nanak, who fed all without distinction from his home kitchen. Those
who wished to meet Guru Amar Das,
even the Emperor Akbar, had first to
eat in the langar. (But the concept
was not solely Sikh, for at least a
century before the time of Guru
Nanak, Muslim Sufis [*see* Bhakti]
had introduced an intercommunity
and intercaste kitchen, also termed
langar. Today, a langar is usually a
part of a Muslim **dargah**.)

High and low of the Sikh community, men and women, consider it
a privilege to labour voluntarily in
the langar (**Kar** Seva), especially on
feast days when the work is hard-
est, and to contribute money and
materials, as indeed they do also
in the gurdwara itself, if necessary,
in the most menial of jobs, including handling and ensuring the safe
custody of worshippers' **shoes**. Food
prepared in a gurdwara langar can
itself be known as langar.

Some Sikhs aver that two things
have kept Sikhism a living brotherhood throughout the centuries,
sangat (*see* Sangh, regular congregation in gurdwaras) and pangat;
pangat being a line, the seated line of
people, Sikh and non-Sikh, receiving
food together. As in a large Delhi

gurdwara, to see several thousand people, Sikh and non-Sikh, men, women and children, seated in lines on matting, quietly waiting their turn to be served quickly and efficiently by volunteers, is most impressive. (Also panghat is a village well-head, where housewives gather and, so the songs say, boy meets girl.)

Outside the gurdwara and dargah, the word langar may be used for any kitchen where food is prepared in large quantities (not being for sale), as in the army or, say, for public relief in a disaster area.

The word langar can also mean two different things with a similar purpose: a ship's anchor and the stone and rope used to prevent, say a horse, from straying. The link, of course, is that a heavy stone and rope may be used as an anchor (a killick in English) for a small craft.

A non-Sikh feast – or just a basic meal – normally for the poor given to celebrate a special occasion, may be termed bhandara.

LĀNTĀNA *n* English (Hindustani)
A coarse shrub of the subtropical world, a scourge of many parts including India, but also cultivated into an attractive garden plant flowering most of the year. A bunch of florets makes the round flower head with colours from deep red, to pink, orange and white.

In the wild state, a curse, the seeds are poisonous to cattle but harmless to birds. The plant can grow in vast clumps smothering all below, even young trees.

A Latin name for the plant was horride, from an objectionable smell from the green leaves.

In India the plant has been declared a deadly weed in certain forest areas and various methods of biocidal control are being attempted, none immediately highly successful. But against certain insects a lantana extract has been found to be an effective organic pesticide. Lantana is immune even to severe drought. It is said that an extract from one variety, Lantana camara, can be used to control cotton pests.

LASCAR *n* Hindi
An Asian seaman. The lascar boatswain being the **tindal**. A meaning now probably obsolete is that of a gunner's mate or a civilian working as a labourer with an army.

Lascar comes from a Persian word for soldier, lashkari (whence also, via Arabic, the East African equivalent of **sepoy**, the askari). English probably received it from Portuguese, meaning an Indian soldier. Today, Lashkar survives as the name of the **cantonment** at Gwalior, and in British days it was a term on the North West Frontier (now in Pakistan) for a group of tribal raiders.

LĀT/LATH *n* Hindi

An obelisk, a column, a free standing pillar, as for example, that which originally carried the Ashok Lion capital (*see* chakra). Also Hindi, stambh/stambha has a similar meaning: the lat or stambh would often carry, especially when before a temple, a dhvaja (a symbol placed on high for all to *see*), of a deity or person or animal; still a not uncommon feature of **Hindu** and Jain temple architecture.

A lat known to all India and to most metallurgists the world over, is the Iron Pillar now in the mosque of Delhi's **Qutab Minar**. Its length, including about fifty centimetres below the pavement, not plinth, level to the top of the ornamental capital (a separate piece) is 7.16 m. The weight is estimated at about 6 tonnes. Its construction is of very pure hot-hammered iron. Modern technology has dated it to the 4th/5th century AD. Corrosion over 1600 years is seen at the top where water can accumulate in a slot perhaps intended to hold the dhvaja, an animal standard (emblem) and on the below-ground bulbous base, on the shaft it is minimal. All evidence of the skill of the **adivasi** cottage-industry iron workers of the time. The provenance of this very important Vishnu stambh of the **Gupta** period and how it came to be set up where it is, probably centuries later, is still a matter of conjecture amongst experts.

As in the English expression, a pillar of the establishment, so lat can be applied to a person, the man at the top, a lat **Sahib**, in this case, originally a mispronunciation of Lord Sahib. In the British period often used with reference to the Governor of a Province, or the Governor-General. (The last was usually Mulki lat Sahib, Lord of the Country: and the Commander-in-Chief, the Jang-i-lat Sahib, Lord of War.)

A linked word is lathi, a stout bamboo pole (from what is usually said to be the male plant – this is a misconception, bamboo culms are not sexually distinct; almost solid bamboos are from a separate species to the largely hollow or light ones). About six feet long, sometimes with the heavier end brass capped. Carried by villagers as a staff (and sometimes as a weapon) and used by the police for crowd dispersal and riot control, e.g. a lathi charge. A milder weapon similarly used by the police is the light cane.

Lathia: a man carrying, or wielding, a lathi.

LAUNG/LAVANG *n* Hindi
The clove.

LEKHPĀL *n* Hindi
Lit. a writer. A village **patwari**, or keeper of the records. An accountant.

LICHI/LYCHEE *n* Hindustani

The litchi. Edible fruit of the nephellium tree, a native of south China. Trees are orchard grown and the plum sized fruit has a tubercled red skin with juicy white flesh: a single black polished seed in the centre. Pronounced in India as leechi although the word was originally Chinese, lychi. Also of the nephellium family and similar, but not identical, to the lichi is the rambutan of southeast Asia,

LILA/LEELA n Hindi

The play, the sport, of the gods which may, as with the Greek deities, involve the lives of mortal men. A **Hindu** religious story acted as a drama. For example. **Ram** Lila, the story of Lord Ram performed on a stage. *See* Dussehra.

Ras Lila: a dance performance associated with the **Krishna** story, actors depicting events from the life of Lord Krishna, particularly his bucolic games with the **gopis**: usually, but not necessarily in the form of a circular dance. Such dances are particularly performed in the Mathura region (*see* Janmastami) and often are really an act of devotion to Krishna by both dancers and the reverential audience and not simply entertainment. Traditionally, the dancers should be brahmin boys only.

LINE BOYS n

A term of British days for **Gorkhas** not from Nepal but born and brought up in the family quarters of the Gorkha regiments of the Indian army, or in the Gorkha settlements which grew up round the regimental centres. The term was slightly pejorative, in that as recruits, such Gorkhas were thought to have acquired undesirable **bazaar** habits absent in those straight from hill villages.

LINGAM/LINGA/LING n Hindi

Strictly, lingam is the **Tamil** form of the **Sanskrit** word, where its original meaning was of a symbol, a device: ling/linga in Hindi. A penis, particularly the phallic emblem of Lord Shiva as creator: the Shivalingam. Occasionally explicit but usually seen as a squat stone cylinder (the meatus is never indicated) placed within the **yoni**, the vaginal symbol of female power (**shakti**), and no more recognisable as a carnal object than a maypole on an English village green or a horseshoe over a cottage door. Worship is offered by abhishek, pouring cooling water or milk over the stone: in a temple an arrangement is often made to allow a constant drip of water. (As an oblation, abhishek has many applications, as in the consecration of an image of a deity, in the sprinkling of Ganga water round a body on a cremation pyre, or the equivalent at the installation of a ruler. A male personal name). A small egg-shaped stone, all white or all black, polished from a hill riverbed, may serve a household for a Shivalingam: or it may be termed Brahmanda, the egg of **Brahma**, the self-created (swayambhu in Hindi) cosmic egg antedating Shiva, representing (Genesislike), the original matter floating in an infinite sea from which the universe was created. (Some of these egg-shaped stones were taken to Victorian England – where, presumably, their **Hindu** significance was unknown – and there used as hand-coolers. Held for a few moments, a sweaty palm would be cooled before shaking hands with an important person.) A cosmic egg, a Brahmanda, forms the stone top just below the opening bronze lotus of Sir Edwin Lutyens' Jaipur Column, in the forecourt of New Delhi's Rashtrapati **Bhavan** (*see* Rashtra and Star of India).

In Bharatnatyam (the dance of Shiva), the lingam is symbolised in the samyukt **mudra** (gesture) of the right hand with thumb vertically upwards on the open palm of the left.

Lingayat: member of a strictly orthodox (except that caste distinctions are not observed) sect of devotees of Lord Shiva. Mostly to be found in the south, where many live in **maths** (monasteries). Distinguishable by a small personal lingam (istalingam Sanskrit, beloved as a family deity) in a casket carried round the neck. The **sadhu** branch is usually **ash**-covered.

Vishvalinga: lingam of the world, a term for Mount **Kailas**.

LODGE *n*
In Eastern India, the normal meaning attached to this English word is that of a boarding house. Such establishments, with basic but what are advertised as homely amenities, are common in the region and can be found elsewhere, owned by Bengalis catering mainly but not exclusively to their own community. In recent years, the Tourist Departments have acquired the term so that residential accommodation of a standard superior to that of a rural **Rest House**, but not quite that of a hotel, may be described as a Tourist Lodge. In the south, lodge is common as part of the name of a small residential hotel.
Viceregal Lodge: in later British years, the name for the **Viceroy**'s summer residence in Simla (now **Shimla**). *See* Rashtra.

LŌG *n* Hindi
People, in a group with something in common (be it only that they are waiting for a bus), as distinct from the public as a whole. A group that could be referred to as 'hum log' – we people.

Bandarlog (in Kipling's stories of the Indian jungle): monkey people.

LŌK *n* Hindi
Lit. one of the three worlds (trilok) into which **Hindu** cosmology divides the universe: **akash** lok (or parlok), the heavens: patal lok, the underworld: prithvi lok, the earth. The

world of a god, gods, or of a cosmic authority e.g., Indralok, the world of (i.e., ruled by) **Indra**: Chandralok, the world of the moon (*see* Chand). Lok also has the meaning of the people of the earth, humanity.

Lokmanya: Marathi title of respect – 'approval of the people'.

Lok Nadi: world's river, or humanity's river, an epithet for the River **Ganga**.

Lokpal: protector or the people. An Ombudsman, (a word from Sweden, a grievance man) with the duty of investigating maladministration and injustice by the central government at ministerial and senior officer level. The Lokayukt has similar duties but operates with a state government.

Lokpriya: 'beloved of the people', an honorific. Similar is Loknayak (*see* Naik) 'hero' or leader of the people'.

Lok Sabha: House of the People. The lower, but more powerful, house in the central parliament in Delhi.

Lok Sevak: Servant of the People.

Loktantra: people's system, democracy (*see* tantra).

LOO/LU *n* Hindi
Warm air, warm wind. By Europeans, the word is particularly applied to the hot (42°C and above) dust-laden westerly wind which blows across northern India from late April until replaced by the easterly **monsoon** current of mid-June.

LOOFAH *n*
An anglicism from luffa (Arabic and Urdu), the vegetable sponge vine of the gourd family growing wild in the Indian plains. The familiar loofah sponge is the fibrous network of the fruit after the pulp has rotted away. The uncultivated loofah from the countryside may be considered rough for personal use, but it is excellent for household purposes or for cleaning the car.

LOOSEWALA/LOOS-WALA *n*
An anglicism from the 19th century, particularly used in military circles, for a man of loose character, of lax morals: applied more often to Europeans than to Indians. While loosewala was still in use during World War II by British servicemen who had been in India, a secondary meaning of the term had died out: that of a person temporarily without a posting or appointment, i.e., at a loose end.

LOOT *n* and *v* English
The word has been accepted with its meaning unchanged from the Sanskrit original: the verb lutna, to steal taking advantage of public commotion and absence of law and order.

Loot was never a legal perquisite of the British army in India but at least until the end of 19th century so it was regarded, by both the soldiers and many officers. Distinct from loot was the prize fund money from the sale of public property acquired by the winners of a military engagement and legally distributed in proportion to rank to officers and men, the Commander's share was usually one eighth of the total.

Lut: plunder, booty.

Lutera: a looter.

LŌTA *n* Hindi
Round metal pot (once of brass or copper, but nowadays often stainless steel) for carrying a liquid: if of the capacity of a teacup or less, the usual word is lotiya. The Muslim lota normally has a spout for pouring.

LOTUS *n* English
To the classical Greeks, the lotus was not necessarily a water plant but in Indian English the name is used solely for the water-lily, particularly the *Nelumbo nuficera,* sacred lotus, Chinese water-lily. Padma (**Sanskrit**), kamal (Hindi). Aquatic plant with leaves and large flowers generally standing well clear of the water – unlike the lotus of the Nile Valley, Nymphaea, the common waterlily whose leaves float on the surface – found throughout India upto 1550m. White or pink scented flowers. The young leaves,

flowers, seeds and seedpods, stalks and rhizomes all are edible. At least the seedpods and the stalks (kamal kakri) can be found in most vegetable markets. The seed of a variety with purplish leaves, roasted or parched, in the manner of popcorn and looking like small puffy fungi, is sold in spice markets under the name makhana: as a dish, Dal Makhani. To the Greeks, the lotus-eaters were in a happy state of euphoria: less felicitously, there is no evidence that such is the consequence today. The small blue lotus from Sanskrit may be termed pushkar or rajiv.

The pink lotus (**Brahma** kamal) appears in almost all **Hindu** and Buddhist art as a symbol of purity and beauty, to suggest divine origin and association with the sun, water and fertility. Brahma, creator of all, emerged from a golden one thousand petalled lotus which itself grew from the navel of Lord **Vishnu**. Even Muslim mosques and tombs, particularly if dating from the **Sultanates** period, originally perhaps, due to Hindu builders, usually somewhere include the lotus motif as decoration.

The image of the lotus is a popular one when naming Hindu children. Abji (lit. born of water), Arvind, Kamal, Kanji, Niraj, Padam, Pankaj, Pushkar, Rajiv and Saroj for boys. (Prime Minister Rajiv Gandhi was actually Rajivaratna (from Sanskrit, jewel of the blue lotus) *See* Vakaar. For girls, Kamal (and hence **Lakshmi**), Nalini, Padma, Padmini, and Sarojini. All have the meaning of the flower. (Muslims do not name boys after flowers, nor girls after the Hindu associated lotus. In roman script, the Muslim male name, Kamal, may appear to be the Hindi noun, but the word is really Urdu, Kamaal/Kamāl, meaning a miracle or excellence.)

Lotus Awards: a series of annual awards by the Government of India for merit in various branches of cinema film production.

Lotus position (padmāsan): in **yoga**, the seated position appropriate for deep meditation (**samadhi**) and control of breathing. Legs crosslocked so that the body is unlikely to overbalance, soles of the feet uppermost. A padmasan (lotus seat) is also the oval or circular plinth decorated with lotus leaves, often used as a base for Hindu and Buddhist sculpture, in iconography signifying perfection.

LOVE English
Via the Germanic languages and Latin, a link can be seen between this word and the **Sanskrit** lobh, desire, wanton eagerness. Similarly libido.

LUDDOO/LADDOO *n* Hindi
Sweetmeat. Normally of **gram** flour (but almost any flour may be used), fried and then mixed with syrup, sometimes powdered coconut is added: fashioned into the shape and size of a golf ball. A rather special luddoo is the motichur (lit., pearl powder) in which the particles are dusted, a fine powder.

The luddo is a humble sweet but from tradition it has a place in celebrations far beyond its intrinsic savour. If a person is due congratulations, a gesture will be to offer him a luddoo, or even to place it in his mouth: luddoos may then be distributed to the company. But it has to be admitted that sometimes more up-market sweets may be substituted being still referred as luddoos.

LUGAI *n* Hindi
A term of low respect for a woman : possibly even for a wife.

LUNGI *n* Urdu
Piece of white or coloured cloth, about one metre by two, worn by men (also by women in **Burma**) in the fashion of a **dhoti**, but not tucked between the legs. Pleated and folded and worn perhaps a bit higher on the leg (particularly by Muslims), the lungi is known as a tehmad or tehband. A similar piece of material with a similar name may be worn as a head cloth. In the south, dazzling white, waist to ankle like a sarong, is the mundu: in Kerala, perhaps a name from Malayalam, the veshti.

M

MACHĀN *n* Hindi

A platform above the ground, often no more than an upturned **charpai** fixed in a stout tree from which animals may be observed or shot: or constructed from rough poles in a field of ripening crops, on which somebody sits hoping to scare away predators. For sporting purposes, to attract the big cats, either a live or dead bait (perhaps, a half consumed earlier 'kill') can be placed below the machan. An alternative, unlikely to be seen today, was the battue, a method certainly as old as the Muslim **Sultans** and the **Moguls**: an ever-decreasing circle of beaters and elephants would be formed round a large tract of country, in which everything that moved would be driven towards the spears or guns. But normal **shikar** during the later days of the **Raj** was not like this: more common was the party of one or two guns on the machan with just a few beaters placed to persuade a single beast to move in a desired direction.

For tiger shikar, the machan has to be about four metres off the ground, for (tigers have been known to jump and claw their way to almost that height). In British days, a **Viceroy**'s machan was no village bedstead (it was practically obligatory for a Viceroy, whatever his sporting inclinations or abilities, to shoot at least one tiger during his tour in India). He could expect a stout, spacious and carpeted platform, a parapet all round, cushioned seats and a thatched roof: for some distance around, all forest undergrowth would have been trimmed and an appearance by an animal of appropriately Viceregal size was all but a certainty. Tigers were also killed from the backs of elephants. (Allegations were not infrequent at the time, that special tapes for measuring Viceregal tigers were available to Maharajahs: these, if compared with a more workaday instrument, would have indicated an eleven-inch foot.)

The highly organised shoot is a thing of the past - and some were indeed highly organised: many princes had a department of state, supported by the man-power of the royal army as beaters, for the sole purpose of managing shoots for themselves and important guests. Now, only the occasional tiger, officially proscribed as a maneater, may legally be killed.

MACHCHARDĀNI *n* Urdu

A mosquito or similar net. (Machchhar, a mosquito or gnat.)

Colloquially in English spoken of as a mozzy net.

MACHĒRY

18th century name for the territory that later became the **princely** state of Alwar, southwest of Delhi, now a district in Rajasthan: from the original village estate of the rajah. The region was also sometimes called Mewat, particularly by Muslims.

MADAK *n* Hindi

Almost crude opium paste balls of about a centimetre diameter, sold by the government to registered addicts. Occasionally smoked in the Chinese fashion, but more likely to be taken in a drink, or just placed under the tongue. Minute quantities may be given to very small children to quieten them. Opium in a purer and stronger form is known as chandu.

Opium has long been the monopoly of the government and once was a major item in funding the commercial operations of the **East India Company**. Export of the drug to China (together with raw cotton) paid for that country's tea carried for sale in Britain. It has to be admitted that as drug-pushers, first the Company and then the British Government, in their trade with China, were the best organised and most ruthless of all time. It is recorded that in certain years 1/7th of government revenue came from the opium trade. Exports to China in 1896/97 were about 62,000 chests of 140 lbs each and in 1903/4 the figure was 73,000 chests. Opium then began to be grown in China and exports from India decreased annually until after World War I when the trade was stopped by the League of Nations. About all that can be said in extenuation of the commerce in early days is that Victorians at home regarded laudanum (liquidified opium) as a panacea, a sort of aspirin, a pain-killer for adults and a soothing mixture for their babies.

Such is the legacy of history, that even today the responsibility for control of growing the white flowering poppy with its jumbo seedpods, production of opium, its export for pharmaceutical purposes and licensed sale in India, remains with the Ministry of Finance: the making of opium is still largely concentrated where it was in Company days, the Government Opium and Alkaloid Works, Ghazipur, **UP**. (There is only one other authorised plant, in Neemuch/ Neemach, **Madhya Pradesh**). While the government is the only legal buyer of raw opium, it is frequently alleged that at least some producers earn large sums by diverting part of their crop into black market channels for illegal processing into morphine and heroin.

In the 1980s, as part of the youth drug scene, opium crudely processed into a form of heroin known as smack, or brown sugar, became illegally and relatively cheaply available in the **bazaars**. In general, the penalties on conviction for improper possession of processed opium are more severe than those for forms of Indian **hemp**.

MADĀRI *n* Urdu
A Muslim community of street entertainers with a tradition going back to **Mogul** days. Jugglers, conjurors and animal trainers of monkeys and sloth bears (not cows or elephants). With animals they are particularly visible on main roads leading to tourist centres such as Agra. Also a word for an itinerant animal showman is qalandari: in the original Persian a member of an order of **dervish**.

MADHUBAN *n* Hindi
Lit. forest of honey. Traditionally, the forest near Mathura where the youthful **Krishna** sported with the gopika.

Madhubani: there are several villages of this name in Bihar (*see* Bihar), one of which, in the northeast, part of **Maithila**, has achieved fame through a local folk art of the women painting on the interior walls of their homes. Often illustrations of incidents in the **Ramayana** or of stories from the region itself: prominent is the tota, the parakeet, the symbol of romance (*see* Kāma). Today, the distinctive paintings are still almost entirely produced by the village women using local-made bright colours, but on

paper and cloth as a home industry. Also from Bihar are folk motive embroidered quilts, sujani.

MADHYA PRADESH *n* Hindi
The middle state. The region traditionally known as Madhya **Desh** or Madhya **Bharat**. Formed in 1956 largely from the Central Provinces and the Central India Agency (of princely states – *see* Resident) of British India. The administrative capital is Bhopal. *See* Bhumi. The part of the state south of the River Yamuna, once a galaxy of minor princedoms, had the name Bandelkhand.

In Nepal, the Madhya **Desh** is the terai plains area where most of the people are of Indian origin (i.e. non-Mongolian), Much of it was gifted to Nepal after the **First War of Independence**.

MADRAS
In August 1996 the Government of **Tamil** Nadu decided that a 'foreign' name, a form of the name of one of two villages, was not good enough for their capital city. When the British built Fort St. George in 1639, it lay on the coast between Madraspatnam and Chennaipatnam. The former name is part Urdu and part Tamil and could mean, the village of the Madras' (madrasa, Urdu, an Islamic college or school). Of the other village, the Chennai were a local ruling family. Over time, the villages were engulfed by the new city with the

name Madras (but officially, for a long time, Fort St. George).

The Tamil Nadu government changed the city's name to Chennai in 1996 (The state name had changed to Tamil Nadu in 1969).

MADRASA *n* Urdu from Persian
An Islamic school, often attached to a mosque with divinity very much part of the curriculam. Traditionally, supported by the state or a wealthy individual. At an elementary level can be the maktab, teaching little more than the holy Koran. Residential and of a higher status than the madrasa is the khanqah.

Madari: plural of madrasa.

MĀHA *adj*. Hindi
Great or supreme: normally used as a prefix in compound words. The equivalent of the English magn, as in magnate or magniloquent, derived from the Latin magnus, in turn linked to **Sanskrit**. Two connected Hindi adjectives with a similar meaning, but not used in compounds, are mahan and mehat.

An Urdu adjective for great, grand, magnificent, is alishan.

MAHABŌDH SOCIETY
Founded in Calcutta in 1891, an association with branches all over India (and elsewhere) to further the interests of Buddhism. The society is responsible for the management of the Buddhist shrine at Sarnath. *See* Buddha.

MAHĀJAN *n* Hindi
A merchant in a big way, private banker. Also a village moneylender. Family name.

Particularly in Gujarat, a profession or merchants trade guild, or even a workers' union.

MAHAL *n* Urdu
A palace, or very large building, in **Mogul** days particularly one reserved for a senior queen or **begum**. A large estate. Under **Mogul** administration, a number of villages could be grouped to form a mahal (or **pargana**). Continued into British days, the meaning was of a single tax-paying unit of one or more villages.

A queen: following from the lady being ' ...of the palace'. Now probably almost obsolete, but with a derivation similar to its use for queen, so in noble Muslim families, mahal also has the meaning of wife. *See* Taj.

Rang Mahal: in a mansion or palace a room or separate pavilion intended for amusement and frivolity: at least in the popular mind, often with an associated element of eroticism.

MĀHANT *n* Hindi
Head priest of a large **Hindu** temple.

Head of an order of **sadhus**. Also the owner of a Hindu temple property, not necessarily a man of spiritual quality himself.

MAHAPALĪKA *n* Hindi
Municipality. A form of urban local government less than a **Nagar** Nigam (city corporation).

MAHARĀSHTRA
Lit. Great Nation. The more southern of the two states formed in 1960 from the division of the British created Bombay **Presidency** into the ethnic and linguistic states of the Maratha and Gujarati peoples: **Mumbai** is the capital city. Added to the state was the Marathi speaking portion of princely Hyderabad and Nagpur district from the old Central Provinces (now **Madhya Pradesh**).

The homeland of the Maratha people on the **Deccan**, approximately covering the triangle, Nagpur, Belgaum and **Pune**. Further south, one reaches the country of the **Dravidian** languages. In the 18th and early years of the 19th centuries, when the Maratha power under its **saffron** flag was at its height, most of the heartland of India (including Delhi and the **Mogul** emperor) was controlled – at least nominally from their centre and base, Pune, but in fact, the great Maratha chieftains, the Confederacy, the Rajas of Nagpur, Gwalior, Indore and Baroda, did not always act in concert. *See also* Chhatrapati and Peshwa.

This was the time in northern India that Hinduism became resurgent and grand temple building began once again. Going back to prehistory the time of the **Epics**, a maharathi, without necessarily any connection to Maharashtra, was a military commander of 11,000 archers. In Hindi today, a term for a successful commander can be marathi. The south-central region of the state, covering some eight districts has the name Marathwada.

MAHĀRS *n* Hindi
Members of a Scheduled Caste (*see* Harijan/Dalit) mainly of western India. Traditionally, the Mahars were village watchmen and messengers, being paid in shares of the village produce. The Law Member of the Viceroy's Council 1942, the framer of India's Constitution, 1950, and leader of the untouchables (he did not like the term harijan). Dr. B.R. Ambedkar was born a Mahar.

Until the 1890s and strict implementation of the British theory of the martial **classes**, Mahars were recruited into the Bombay Army (*see* Presidencies). In today's Indian Army, there is a Mahar Regiment.

MAHATMA *n* Hindi
Lit. Maha-atma (*see* Atman) great soul or spirit. An honorific for a Hindu saint, a learned **brahmacharya, sadhu** or ascetic. The most famous example being Mahatma Gandhi on whom the title is said to have been

first conferred by Rabindranath Tagore. But there is much evidence that this was not so and that in fact the title was used when Gandhiji was still in South Africa.

MAHĪLA *n* Hindi
A woman: pertaining to women.

MAHOUT/MAHAVAT *n* Hindi
Person in charge of an elephant, as driver and keeper. To control his beast, he will carry a spiked iron goad, the ankush in Hindi. His mount is the hathi (Hindi) or fil/pil (from Arabic. On old Delhi maps, a fil khana is an elephant stable). A word derived from Sanskrit for an elephant is gaj or, sometimes, honouring **Ganesh**, gajraj. *See* Raj. In chess, hathi is the castle, rook.

Gajendra: elephant ruler, often a personal name.

MAHSEER *n* Hindi
India's chief sporting fish. Salmon size of the barbel group, with twelve sub-species: found mainly in Himalayan waters, but also in some of the major rivers of the plains. The name is an anglicism from mahasir: large head.

MAHURAT *n* Hindi
From mahurt, Sanskrit, a moment of time, a period. In Hindi, an astrological auspicious time. Lit. an auspicious time to commence an undertaking,

Usually refers to an inauguration ceremony of an enterprise, conducted with **Hindu** religious rites.

Moorat Trading: a reference to the special-sessions of stock and commodity exchanges on **Divali** night: the auspicious commencement to the financial community's New Year. *See* Calendars.

MAI/MAA BĀP *n* Hindi
Lit. mother and father. A villager's submission that the person so addressed is considered to have the powers (and obligations) of parents, in relation to the speaker.

MAIDĀN *n* Urdu
A large open ground or common, in or adjacent to a built-up area: suitable for public meetings, games and entertainments. A battlefield. A plain. In a north Indian language, to express a need to visit the maidan (or the jungle) is a euphemism for a requirement to defecate.

Maidan-men hun/hain: lit. as in English, in the field or competition. To be a candidate.

MAIKHANA *n* Urdu from Persian
In an urban Muslim setting, a tavern dispensing liquor, these days possibly illegally. Traditionally, a convivial meeting place for Urdu poets.

MAITHILA / MITHILA
The northern part of Bihar and the

districts now just across the Nepal frontier, the Tirhut area: a tract renowned in ancient days for learning and culture, and more recently, for **indigo.**

Maithila/Maithili: the form of Hindi spoken in Maithila.

Maithili: an epithet for Sita, wife of Lord **Ram**. Her father, Janaka, had Mithala as his capital city.

MAITHŪNA *n* Hindi
Lit. coitus. Usually a reference to a temple statue of a couple in overt sexual embrace: prakriti, the way of nature. In all agricultural cultures the world over, ritual coupling has been an invocation to the gods to give rain to fructify the earth to ensure a plentiful harvest.

Mithuna: a human couple. The zodiacal symbol for Gemini, the Twins. An icon or temple sculpture of an amorous couple without overt eroticism.
Hasta Maithuna: masturbation.

MAJLIS *n* Urdu
An assembly, a parliament: normally with a Muslim connection. Shia Muslims (*see* Sunni) term their congregational assemblies majlis. The original Arabic meaning of the word was the tent in a desert encampment, or the room in a house, where visitors were received and the affairs of the day discussed.

MĀLA *n* Hindi
A garland, a rosary, a string of beads. The placing of a garland, sometimes floral, sometimes of shining tinsel, sometimes even of currency notes, round a person's shoulders is a particularly Indian way of offering respect (for the garland as an insult, *see* Shoes), If the personage is not present, the offering may be made to his picture or to a statue. Although Lord **Krishna**, whatever his activity, is often depicted as seemingly permanently wearing one, nowadays it is expected that the recipient of a garland will remove it from his neck shortly after its presentation. A rather special type of garland is the veni, a ring of flowers placed round a lady's hair bun. Another name for a fresh flower ornament, worn either in the hair or as a wrist bracelet, is gajra. Mala can be a girl's name. Also a girl's name and a garland is maneka.

Malakar: the maker of garlands.

Gendamala: the popular everyday floral garland of french marigolds. This plant, *Targete patula*, an exotic from Mexico, is widely cultivated as a commercial horticultural crop, both for the flower heads of the auspicious colour and as a source of perfume oil – genda **attar.**

Japmala: Sanskrit, see Mantra. The use of a string of beads as a rosary for

305

devotions in India, by Hindus, Jains and Buddhists goes back almost to prehistory. The practice travelled to the Middle East and from there was adopted by the Christian Church, in a minor way even before the Crusades. There are regional variations, but the generally standard Vaishnavi rosary has 108 beads while that for Shaivites has 50. *See* also Rudraksh.

Jay/jaimala: a victory garland. A symbolic award to the winner of a competition, particularly one of music or poetry: an equivalent to the laurel crown of ancient Rome. Just before the wedding ceremony, the garland of honour and homage placed by the new bride round the neck of her husband, to be.

Noton ki mala/haar (*see* Lakh): a garland of currency notes. Usually a gift to a bridegroom or to a politician for election expenses.

Ritu Mala: the endless garland of the seasons: the Hindu year. *See* Calendars.

Vanmala: forest garland. A long string of leaves and flowers strung along a road or over a gateway.

Volumes of a book in similar format. A series to complete a work, may be termed a mala.

MALĀBAR *n* Hindi
'Land of Hills'. The ancient country of Kerala, bordering the Arabian Sea, almost on the extreme southwest coastline of India. In British days, the Malabar **District** of the Madras **Presidency**, now part of Kerala state. (From Kerlam – land of coconuts. Kairali, adjectival, of Kerala.) Malayalam, of the **Dravidian** group, with a large Tamil and **Sanskrit** content (the latter perhaps introduced by the **Nambudaries**), is the regional language. The script, however, is quite separate from that of Tamil. It may be noted that as an English word, Malayalam is a lengthy palindrome.

HMS Malabar: there have been no less than seven vessels of the Royal Navy with the name: the first being a 54-gun East Indiaman purchased from the Company in 1795, and the last, a stonefrigate, the Navy depot in Bermuda in 1919.

MALBA *n* Hindi
Brick or stone rubble. Often seen as an invitation 'Dump Malba Here'. A request for hard-core fill for a depression in the ground.

MALEESH/MALĪSH *n* Urdu
Massage. Also known as champi (Hindi, pressing: the origin of the English word shampoo. Strictly, champi refers to head-massage only).

Maleeshwala: the itinerant **masseur**

who walks the streets and urban open spaces with his 'cruet-stand' of oil bottles and a grass mat for the comfort of his clients. His street-cry is 'Malish, champi, tel-malish' (massage, head-massage, oil-massage). As he rubs coconut-oil into the skin, he is said to be giving an oil-bath. But the status of the street masseur is rarely that of the professional wrestler who turns to massage and bonesetting when his fighting days are over: his clients visit him, often from long distances (*see* Akhara). Used metaphorically, maleesh can mean flattery. See Sarson.

MALI *n* Hindi
Lit. garland-maker. A gardener. His wife is the malin.

MALIK *n* Urdu
Originally a king, the Queen being malika/malka (but mallika is a jasmine-like flower). More recently, title for a chief inferior to a **khan**, particularly in the northwest of pre-**Independence** India. Head of a **Pathan**/Pakhtoon khel (tribal clan) or village. Honorific for a Muslim land-owner of substance.

Malik: a title for the Almighty used by Muslims. A landlord, proprietor, owner: the lady is malkin.

MALKHĀNA *n* Urdu
Lit. goods house. A store room. In a police **thana**, the room where recovered property, or confiscated goods, are held in safe custody.

MALL, THE
In Britain days normally a wide straight road, the principal road in a **cantonment** used by troops for ceremonial parades and in many military stations, so it is today. The name derives from a similar street in London leading to Buckingham Palace.

MANCH *n* Hindi
Lit. a dais, stage or platform: but as with platform in English, manch is often used to mean the policy or programme of a political group. A political party.

MANDAL *n* Hindi
An association, a group, of people with a shared interest. A circle in a sense of a zone of authority: e.g. post-office mandal, or rationing mandal or zone.

Mandala: a circle. A symbol for the universe. A completed series as in the ten mandala (books) of the Rig Veda. A Hindu or Buddhist circular picture or geometrical patterns within a circle – when, as in the Tibetan Buddhist Himalaya, painted on a ceiling, a consecrated (*see* Tanka) mandala confers blessings on all who pass below: or a yantra (*see* Jantar Mantar or Tantra), a diagram representing, perhaps, the cosmos, designed to give visual focus for meditation. In Vedic architecture, a building plan based on the perfect square, indicating the four cardinal directions. In eastern India, the Mandalas are a class of near subsistance farmers or labourers, generally considered to be **dalits**.

MANDĀP/MANDĀPA *n* Hindi
That part of a **Hindu** temple building intended for worshippers, the equivalent perhaps, to the nave in a Christian church: the main shrine often being a small dark room accessible only to the priests. A small canopy under which a Hindu ceremony, such as a marriage, is performed. A pavilion, as used in an exhibition. (The name of the capital of Nepal, Kathmandu, comes from Kathmandap – wooden temple hall.)

MANDI *n* Hindi
A commodity market, possibly selling on a wholesale basis only.

MANDIR *n* Hindi
In the original **Sanskrit**, a residence, a palace, an abode. (Mandira - a stable). From the last few centuries, the meaning of an abode of a deity, a Hindu or Jain temple has predominated. Many believe that in order to avoid misfortune, every inhabited locality must have a devalaya, or place of God. The **shastras**, particularly the Shilpashastra and the Vastushastra, codify the shape and form a Hindu temple should take: an east-west axis with the main entrance porch or hall, the jagmohan, leading to the **mandap** facing the east, the rising sun, is usual. From a small shrine to the vast complexes of the south covering many acres, almost

every feature has a symbolic reason. The purpose of the whole is to honour the resident deity and to provide space for a devotee to offer personal worship (for many, a **darshan**, a sight of the image, the making of a gesture of respect such as the **namaskar** and a token offering of a flower or a coin, is sufficient. Except perhaps with **bhakti** groups, worship in a Hindu temple is rarely congregational. The deity, represented by an elaborate sculpture, or just an unusual stone or baulk of timber, will normally be installed below the architectural centre, the main **shikara**, in a small dark chamber, the garbagriha, lit. the wombhouse.

There are few really old major Hindu temples in north India: most were destroyed by Muslim rulers, some, several times, e.g. the Vishvanath **Shiva** mandir in **Varanasi**. This was demolished more than once by the early Muslims, rebuilt bv the Muslim Emperor Akbar, demolished again by Aurangzeb and replaced by a mosque and rebuilt again in a corner of its original site by **Holkar** of Indore in 1777. No less, Muslim rulers did accept that they needed support from their Hindu subjects and providing the mandirs were not overtly anti-state such rulers could make grants to Hindu establishments.

MANGAL *n* and *adj.* Hindi from Sanskrit

The planet Mars. Auspiciousness,

well-being. A name for Lord Hanuman.

Mangalwar : **Tuesday.**

"Apko, mangalmai ho!" On a festival occasion, "Happy greetings to you!" Mangalik/Mangala: one born under the influence of Mars.

Mangal Sutra: the lucky, or auspicious, thread (see Shastras). A low necklace of beads or threads presented by a husband to his bride and worn as an auspicious and sacred symbol of marriage. An old traditon probably rarely followed today, was that the beads, should be threaded by a devadasi, one whose husband being a deity, can never be left a widow. A custom is that black and gold should form the necklace in the proportion of two to one. Should windowhood occur, the mangal sutra is removed.

MANGAS *n* Marathi *and* Telugu
The origin of the English name mongoose. The small agile animal of the civet family famed as a killer of snakes, believed by many in India to have an immunity from the venom: an alternative belief, equally mistaken, is that the mongoose knows of a herbal antidote to snake bite.

The names of most of the Indian animal characters in Kipling's Jungle Books are Hindustani, but that of the mongoose, Riki Tiki Tavi, is onomatopoeic, from, said the author, the animal's warcry as it scuttles through the long grass, 'rikk-tikk-takki-tchk'. The plural of the English word is usually accepted to be mongooses.

In Hindi the name is newal.

MANGLIK *n* Hindi
One whose birth horoscope indicates a strong influence by the planet Mars. It is frequently held that for compatibility, one manglik should marry only another.

MANGO *n* English
The mango, of the same family as the pistachio and the cashew (*see* Kaju), probably originated in the mountainous forest country astride the northeastern Indian border with Myanmar (**Burma**). As a jungle fruit it was almost inedible but with at least 3,000 years of garden cultivation it has been so improved that it has spread round the tropical and subtropical world and earned the common epithet of the 'king of fruits' – in the 4th century BC, the soldiers of Alexander's army reported their delight at their discovery of the crop. Within India there are said to be five hundred distinct and named varieties but except for a few developed abroad, the seeds of the improved trees do not reproduce the characteristics of their parents, so vegetative propagation is usual, normally by grafting while still at the seedling stage.

The **Sanskrit** name, āmr/āmbi (aam

in today's Hindi) travelled to the south to become mangkay (mang fruit) in **Tamil**, to south-west India to become manga in Malayalam and to South East Asia also as manga in Malay. All authorities agree that mango in English came from the Portuguese manga, but opinions differ regarding the Portuguese source: some say it was from Malay; others, for the reason that it is thought that the Portuguese landed on the **Malabar** coast before that of South East Asia, that the source must be Malayalam, or at least, Dravidian. For aam from Arabic, see Dewan.

Aam Papad (*see* **Pappadam**): a thin cake of sun-dried mango pulp with sugar added as a preservative. Sliced and enjoyed as a sticky confection the year round.

Amchur: lit. mango powder. The green fruit flesh, sun dried and powdered : used for flavouring or as a condiment.

Mango showers: a term of the British period, largely of south India. Rains in March and April, a time when the mango is in flower or the fruit just setting. If accompanied by high winds, considerable damage can be caused to the crop. But even at the best of times, of the many flowers on a spray, only one or two form fruit.

MANGROVE *n*
Correctly, one species (*Rhisophora*) of tree growing in the mud of estuaries, or on tidal shores and creeks along parts of India's tropical coastline, perhaps in a tidal forest. The tree has the ability to thrive on saline water: it may well appear to be on stilts, as for support but minimising the effect of wave pressure, the lower trunk and some of the branches may drop aerial shoots, in the way of the **banyan**, to form rooted props. Its bark is rich in tannin; in the leather trade, solid tannin made from mangrove is known as cutch (another form of cutch comes from the wood of the same tree as the kattha used in **pan**, the Acacia catechu).

In practice, the name mangrove is applied generally to all thick woody vegetation growing under swampy tidal or semi-tidal conditions.

The world's largest mangrove forest is the Bengal Sunderbans, (named after a variant mangrove, the sundari, found there) the swampy delta of the Ganga and the Brahmaputra rivers. Declared a tiger reserve in 1973, a national park in 1984 and a World Heritage site in 1987. It is also recognised as a World Biosphere Reserve. The Indian side contains some fifty-two villages.

A mangrove forest can protect a coastline under typhoon conditions. As a word, mangrove has no Indian connection. Grove can only be English man possibly from South America via Portuguese..

The Sunderbans cover an area of more than 10,000 square kms of which more than half are in Bangladesh.

MANI STONES
English name for the mounds of engraved (**Om** Mani Padma Hum and the Wheel of Life in particular) flat stones found, alongside paths and at the entrances to villages in areas of Tibetan Buddhism, such as Ladakh. Occasionally, those stones form 'mani walls' of almost a kilometre in length: petrified invocations added one at a time over the centuries. The custom is for a passerby, as for any object of devotion, to keep them on his right hand side. *See* Right Hand, Left Hand.

Mani - Tibetan from **Sanskrit** : a precious stone, jewel.

MANSURĪ
From the Hindi, mansur, the bush or small tree of *Coriaria nepalensis*, growing throughout the **Himalaya**. The fruit is edible, the wood good for small polished boxes, and the leaves useful for tanning. Mentioned here because the name is the local one for the **hill station**, of which the anglicised form is Mussoorie.

MANTRA/MANTR *n* Hindi
Linked to man/manas (see Kailash) : the mind, the perceptive heart, the soul. **Hindu** or Buddhist incantation: a verbal (but may also be written) charm. A **Sanskrit** sacred formula,

word or phrase from the Vedas, or just a single syllable repeated over and over again, as the words *Ram* or **Om** may be printed endlessly on a pilgrim's **chaddar**. Used in prayer, to be effective the mantra must be chanted word perfect by a **brahman**. 'Uttering a mantra creates loving devotion to God.' 'A seeker after truth believes that the mantra he utters and the divinity he calls upon, are identical...' Comparable perhaps, with the biblical, "In the beginning was the Word, and the Word was with God, and the Word was God.' In this instance, a reference to Jesus Christ, but to the non-Christian Jews, the meaning would have been of the power of God. It is believed that a mantra for one's personal use cannot be acquired from reading, but must be received verbally from a respected **guru**. The quiet murmuring of a personal mantra to oneself, as just a name of God, over and over again, can be known as jāp/jaap. *See also* Gayatri, Janeu, Tantra. Used in a political context, mantra may mean 'no more than an empty slogan'. Mantra as a word has been included in the OED.

MANTRĀLAYA *n* Hindi
Lit. place of incantations. A Ministry (of the government).

Mantri: a minister in the central or a state government.

Pradhan Mantri: Prime Minister.

Up Mantri: Deputy Minister.

Mukhya Mantri: Chief Minister (of a state). As a word, mantri entered South East Asia with the acceptance of Indian culture there in the early years of the Christian era (*see* Greater India): the Portuguese heard it as 'mandari' and applied it, as did the English in their turn, to senior government officials in the region and, later, in China; so, mandarin. (*See* Narangi)

MANU/MANAVA Hindi from Sanskrit
In Hinduism, the progenitor of the **Aryan** peoples: the first man of the human race, set up by **Brahma** to be king over his fellows. (If the word manu/manava is not the direct origin of, it is certainly linked to, the English man/mankind.) Manu is also the teacher, the lawgiver of each age, the era. The present time being the **Kaliyug**, a period of sorrow, lasting some 4,00,000 years – there are still over 3,94,000 years to run.

The current lawgiver, Manu Vaivaswata, whose title is attached to the Laws of Manu (Manava **Dharma Shastra** or Manu Smriti), is considered to be the source of the divinely revealed code, in twelve lectures, of the duties of priests and kings: also the rules for religious, domestic and social behaviour for each of the four **castes** and for their relations with those termed 'chandala' and 'mlechha' (*see* Panchama), the dalits of today who may object to his

commendation – such as the installation of his statue in a law court. For **brahmans** in particular, there are even detailed instructions regarding matters of personal hygiene. Compiled by an unknown author early in the Christian era, many brahmans today continue to regard much of the code as valid and as far as possible endeavour to regulate their domestic lives by its precepts. The law expounded is contextual and not of universal application. Thus to bear false witness is condemned and is punishable, but when a truthful declaration could lead to the death of a **caste Hindu**, then falsehood should be spoken, "for (in such a case) it is better than truth."

In medieval and later times, in England also the principle of privilege for the top people applied: in matters of civil law, the educated (not necessarily clerics) could claim 'Benefit of Clergy' and exemption from the jurisdiction of the ordinary courts.

First translated and published in English by Sir William Jones in 1794 (the year of his death), Sir William always transliterated Manu as Menu. Sir William, polymath and Judge of the Bengal Supreme Court, had been searching, and had learned Sanskrit for the purpose, for an authority on which to base Hindu criminal and civil law so that jurisprudence would not have to rely solely on court **pandits**. "The Institutes of Hindu Law"

(Jones' main title for the work), it is now known does not have the authority attributed to it by foreigners, but the clarity of its expression greatly appealed and it was quickly accepted as a much needed guide to Hindu culture.

MANZIL *n* from Arabic
In a building, a storey, a floor.

MAPPILA *n* Malayalam
Often Moplah in English writing. A Muslim people of Arabian origin living in **Malabar** descended from settlers who entered India long before the Muslim invasion of the north, *See also* Zamorin. It was, perhaps, the Mappilas who introduced and set the standard for making coffee in south India, good coffee is rarely found in the north.

MAR/MOR/MRTA Sanskrit
Death. The root sound linked via Latin to such English words as morbid, murder, mortal.

MĀR *n* Syriac
Title accorded to the bishops of the southern Indian Syrian Churches – whose members are sometimes known as St. Thomas Christians. Established, many believe, by the Apostle St. Thomas as a missionary in Kerala in 52 AD: it is also believed that the Saint was martyred in **Chennai** twenty years later. Be that as it may, there is no historical evidence that the original Syrian Church was in existence on the **Malabar** coast earlier than the 5th century AD. Now much divided by schisms, the Syrian groups (the Eastern Churches) over the years have been, to some degree, in communion with the Church of Rome. Mar, in old Syriac, is a form of address to an educated man. The head of the Syrian Church in India has the title Catholikos of the East.

**MARATHWĀDA/
MARATHWĀRA**
That part of **Maharashtra** centred round Aurangabad, Deccan. Previously part of the princely state of Hyderabad (the **Nizam**'s Dominions).

MĀRG *n* Hindi
A road, a highway, a route.
Margi: a traveller on a path. Often used metaphorically, e.g. **Anand** Margi, a happy traveller.

In Kashmir, a high altitude pasture, an alp, e.g., Gulmarg. From the original **Sanskrit**, marg/marga can also carry the meaning of the arts, classical music, culture. Hence the aptness of the acronym of the founders of the well known magazine devoted to Indian culture. Modern Architects and Artists Research Group – MARG. Occasionally seen is another Sanskrit word for an avenue or street, vithi.

MARTELLO TOWER *n English*
One would not expect to find maritime relics of the Napoleonic wars 1400 kms from the sea in Delhi, yet four such monuments still (2003) exist.

In 1818 the city walls were reinforced by the British and in order to give covering fire to the curtain walls, outwork gun-towers were constructed. The design copied from a tower encountered in Corsica at Cap Mortilla in 1774 which proved to be a hard nut to crack. (Admiral Nelson, then a young officer fighting on land, lost an eye there). A round tower with a central gun on the roof mounted on a pivot: quarters for the crew and magazine were below. These towers were built in numbers on the south and south-east coasts of England from 1804. Elsewhere in the British world, over one hundred towers were built. In Delhi, the tower to the east of the Delhi Gate is still in reasonable condition and in the 1857 fighting, the tower off the north wall was effectively used against its builders.

MARTIAL CLASSES

Hindu belief has always accepted that one caste, the **kshatriyas**, was better suited than the others to supply fighting men. Towards the end of the 19th century, British military opinion was, in spite of much historical evidence that in fact there was little, if any, difference, that the men of the north, in general, made better soldiers than those of the south and of Bengal. In the 20th century until World War II, the martial classes was the term for the **jats** who received preference in recruitment for the fighting units of the Indian army. Those which had rebelled during the Mutiny naturally were excluded: those favoured were mainly **Pathans** and Baluchis from what is now Pakistan. Jats and Jat **Sikhs**, Punjabi Muslims, Marathas, **Rajputs** and the hillmen, Kumaonis, Garhwalis and **Gorkhas**. Men with a rural background were sought after: quick witted townsmen were never popular. With the expansion of the army during World War II, new regiments were raised from all over India: but even today the old regiments retain their traditional patterns of regional and class recruitment.

MARŪT *n* Hindi

A storm godling, one of the attendants on the great Vedic God, **Indra**: said to number 180, or 48, and by some, just seven.

MARWĀRI *n* Hindi

A person from Marwar, an old name for a tract in Rajasthan with its capital at Mandor, close to present day Jodhpur. Marwar can be translated as the region of death, a reference to its unproductive desert. From this area, a closely connected community of small moneylenders and traders spread all over India: these merchants, many of whom are now extremely wealthy industrialists, have the reputation of being particularly astute in commerce. It has been said that at least half of the private industry in India is now controlled by Marwari families. (Surprisingly perhaps, some of the leaders of this highly orthodox Jain and **Hindu** community strongly supported **Mahatma** Gandhi and the social changes he advocated.) Nowadays, the term Marwari is often loosely applied to anyone from Rajasthan who has succeeded in business outside his home state.

Marwari: the regional dialect of the area of Jodhpur, in which otherwise English and Hindi-speaking merchants are alleged to discuss business when in the presence of outsiders.

Marwari Horses: cavalry horses bred in the Marwar district of Rajasthan and able to stand the heat and shortage of water in the desert. Like their cousins from **Kathiawar** and Kutch, distinguished by ears that curve forward and together, so that the tips may touch.

MASĀLA *n* Urdu
Spices, condiments. A mixture, even wet cement. Dry cells. As with spice in English, so the word masala is often metaphorically applied to piquant situations, conversation and writing. But a Hindi film described as a masala film would be understood to contain a bit of everything: popular music, violence, sex and humour.

Garam masala: hot or special spices (but not necessarily extra pungent). A mixture of at least five condiments, often compounded to complement particular dishes and normally, powdered, packaged and ready to use. Curry powder. It was the demand from Europe for spices that alone made autumn-killed meat still palatable in winter (and the desire to cut out the Venetians and the Genoese, then the Mediterranean middlemen in the trade from the east) that caused 15th century Portugal to send their mariners to find a way to the Indies round the southern tip of Africa.

Augmenting the uses of the word is the recent **bazaar** derogatory term 'masala aam' (masala **mango**): applied to mangoes picked green from the tree and ripened for the market by artificial means.

MASĀLCHI *n* Urdu
Mashal – a torch. A linkman: the torchbearer who, after dark, lighted the **Mogul** nobleman on his way, whose descendants should surely be those who carry gas chandeliers on their heads in a wedding procession. In fact, the masalchi became the man who tended oil lamps in a large house, and with the coming of electricity, just the odd-job worker in the kitchen: the grinder of the **masalas,** the peeler of vegetables, the washer-up.

MASJID *n* Urdu from Arabic
Lit. place of prostration. (A 'devout Muslim, kneeling, will touch the ground at least once with his nose and forehead in the course of each of the

five daily oblig-
atory prayers.
See Namaz.)
A mosque, an
enclosure for

Islamic congregational prayers. (As
a word, the Arabic masjid was first
corrupted by the Spanish and Portuguese, then via Italian and French,
it became the English mosque.)
Architecturally an elaboration on
the pattern of the first masjid of all,
the open space in which people
gathered next to the Holy Prophet's
house in Medina.

In India, usually an open court (in the
south, especially in Kerala due to frequent rain, mosques are usually roofed)
for the congregation with the magrib,
the western side, also the side nearest
to the Holy City, Mecca containing
the **mihrab** – arched niche – and
the **mimbar** – pulpit steps –covered.
(Words for this covered portion,
sometimes called the prayer chamber,
more often used by those who describe
mosque architecture than those who
visit mosques for worship, are iwan/
liwan: derived from the Arabic aiwan,
meaning a roofed court in a large
building.) Covered side cloisters are
termed dalān. (In a northern old city
residence, a largeish reception room,
by the main door, may also be dalān).
Over the western side there will be a
dome or domes (*see* Gumbaz): but
in Kashmir, domes are rare. There,
a wooden pitched roof, perhaps one
or more, rising one above the other

in the local style, is usual. Normally
there will be water arrangements for
the essential ablutions (*see* Ghusl)
– if these should be in the form of a
small pool, it is a source of clean water
and not a tub into which feet etc. may
be dipped. Decoration is restrained,
abstract designs (arabesque), verses of
the **Kor'an**, or some of the attributes
of God (*see* Allah), cut in stone using
graceful calligraphy (stone-cutting
for such a purpose itself being a form
of worship, echoing the Christian
monks' belief '*laborare est orare*',
to work is to pray, and calligraphy in
one of the many decorative scripts has
long been regarded as a fine art by the
Muslim world). Representations of
neither man nor animal are permitted
(for over one hundred years from 730
AD, Christian Byzantium similarly
banned human and animal forms as
church ornament and before **Islam**,
Judaism had the same interdiction),
but flowers are sometimes seen and
in fact, mosques and tombs in India
are often ornamented with the **Hindu**
lotus motif and, over the dome just
below the finial, the Hindu **kalash**
(water-pot).

If funds permit, there should be at
least one **minar**, to allow the voice
of the muazzin (the crier, *see* Azaan)
to be heard as far afield as possible
– but nowadays, of course, even in
villages, electronic amplification has
come to his aid. (In many countries,
a mosque with a single minar is not
unusual: Indian mosques almost

invariably have either none or the symmetry of two. An exception, perhaps, is the famous 13th century Qutab Minar alongside its mosque in Delhi.) Male Muslim travellers may usually rest and stay overnight within the cloisters of a mosque.

Juma/Jama/Jami Masjid:
English forms of the Arabic term Al Masjidu'l Jami, the assembly, or collecting, mosque. The chief mosque of a town or city in which Muslims collect for the important Friday midday prayers and **khutbah** (sermon). Juma as a day of the week, in Urdu day of assembly) is a reference to Friday and **namaz**-e- juma, the Friday prayers.

MAST/MUST/MASTH/ MASTHI/ MASTANA *n* Urdu
Adjectives and nouns to describe a carefree person with no thought for the morrow, perhaps an eccentric joy in living, also a wanton person. A condition of intoxication from drugs or alcohol; or sexual excitement. But, not always, for equally, delight, enjoyment, devoid of fleshly sensuality. In respect of male elephants and camels, the approximately annual period (musth in English), similar to the rutting season of the deer family: but in elephants the connection between mast and mating is not as direct as with deer. Mast occurs usually in the winter, but most elephants are conceived in the hot weather at about the beginning of the rains. When in mast, elephants are dangerously dif-

ficult to handle and in this condition owners, who are responsible for any damage their beasts may do, normally keep them firmly shackled.

A word from Arabic and Sufism (see **Sufi**) and then into Urdu, bindas, with a meaning somewhat similar to masth-a carefree person - has recently (2006) become popular with young people.

Mastani: the feminine form of mastana, a courtesan.

MATH/MUTT *n* Hindi
Monastery for **sanyasis**. The four great maths established by Shankara/ Sankara (also known as the Adi-Shankaracharya, the original Shankaracharya) in the 8th century AD at **Puri**, Badrinath/Joshimath in the **Himalaya**, Dwarka on the Gujarat coast and Sringeri in the south, have long been the centres of **Hindu** orthodoxy. The heads of these four Shaivite Maths, still known as Shankaracharyas, in some ways can be considered as the cardinals of Shaivite Hinduism. (Some claim that a fifth major math, that of Kanchi in Tamil Nadu, was also founded by the original Shankaracharya.) With the followers of Lord Vishnu, priests of the status of the Shankaracharyas usually have the title Jagatguru or world teacher.

MATHĀDI *n* Hindi
Term used mostly in **Maharashtra**, for porters and casual workers,

particularly those who carry head loads in connection with the goods transport industry.

MAULĀNA *n* Urdu
Title of respect accorded to a reputed Muslim scholar.

MAULVI/MOULVI *n* Urdu
A Muslim title of academic orthodoxy in Islamic studies, awarded following (in India) a course in a seminary (*see* Ulema) lasting some fourteen years. The title has two degrees: Maulvi Alim (senior) and Maulvi Fazil. In fact, however, any scholarly, pious and bearded Muslim may be honorifically addressed. as Maulvi – or Maulana – Sahib. (The Prophet Mohammed is said to have commented that the learned and pious should invariably be bearded.)

MAUN *n* Hindi
Silence. Speechless, particularly when by a self-imposed vow, perhaps as a **tapasya**.

Maun Vrata: a vow of silence for a specific period, perhaps of hours or even of days.

MAURYAN PERIOD/ EMPIRE
Considered to have been roughly between 320 and 180 BC. The first Maurya, Chandragupta, rose to power in **Patliputra** shortly after the departure from northern India of the Macedonian, Alexander (*see* Sikander). The humanistic person-

ality of Chandragupta's grandson, King **Ashok**, still shines today in folk memory and for historians alike. The Mauryas were the first to leave reasonably accurate records. At its height, the Mauryan Empire covered most of today's Afghanistan, Pakistan and all India, except Kerala and **Tamil** Nadu. While the state supported Buddhism, it is probable that the mass of the people followed their traditional faiths. The last but one Maurya ruler, Byhradratha, in about BC 180 was murdured by a commander in his army who considered that buddhist ahinsaa was endangering the nation.

Following the Mauryas came the Sungas/Shungas, a relatively short and little known Buddhist dynasty ending in 78 B.C.

MAYA *n* Hindi
An illusion or delusion. Often a reference to the doctrine of the 8th century philosopher, Shankaracharya (*see* Math), that the world and all in it, is unreal: the only reality being **Brahma**.

God's will: the power of God. A name for the Goddess Lakshmi, hence maya also has the meaning of wealth. But in the *Mahabharata* (*see* Epics), Maya was the creator and chief of demons.

A girl's name.

MAZDOOR *n* Urdu

A porter, a labourer. The word is without the taint of past colonial associations, such as possessed by the now old fashioned anglicism equivalent, **coolie**.

Safai mazdoor (also safai *karmchari*); cleaning worker. A modern descriptive designation, rejecting the irony of **jemadar** (leader of men) and **mehtar** (prince), for that still irreplaceable employee, the **sweeper**.

MAZHABI SIKHS *n* Persian
Converts to Sikhism (*see* Sikh) who were originally outcaste **Hindus** (*see* Harijan/Dalit). Although **Guru Gobind Singh** decried social distinctions (three **shudras**, a **brahman** and a khatri *see* Kshatriya were the Guru's disciples who together formed the first **Khalsa**), a measure of disability still exists, particularly when the low caste convert remains in his original village: he may be denied, for example, the courtesy title of **Sardarji**.

Also, groups of **dalit** background, who regard themselves as Sikhs, but with observances away from the mainstream, do exist.

A particular group of sweepers (the Churas) retrieved the head of Guru Tej Bahadur after his execution by Aurangzeb and on that account were admitted to the Khalsa by Guru Gobind Singh and honoured with the title Mahzabi – faithful, select. During the 1857 troubles they were recruited into the army as Pioneers and were highly regarded by their British officers as being both staunch fighting men and efficient sappers.

McMAHON LINE
Frontier of India from Bhutan eastwards into **Burma**: agreed with Tibet (but not China) at the Simla Convention of 1914 (Burma was then a province of India), of which the chairman, Sir Henry McMahon was Foreign Secretary to the **Government of India**. Since its occupation of Tibet. China has not recognised the Line as the international boundary and even the Line's actual position has been a matter of frequent dispute – in that remote region, it was never marked on the ground during British days. In September 1959 Prime Minister Nehru admitted in Parliament "...in some parts. it was varied afterwards by us, by the Government of India".

MEAD *n* English
This old-time word for a honey-based drink entered English from Greek but it can be linked to the Sanskrit madhu meaning honey or, as madh, an alcoholic drink.

MEENA/MINA *n* and *adj.* Old Persian and Sanskrit

The word has several meanings; the colour blue, blue lacquer or enamel (and by extension, any decorative enamel work, meenakari – using fused salts on metal, often gold or silver). Blue tiles or glazed colour work (also meenakari) as on the **gumbaz** (dome) of a mosque or Muslim tomb: a glazed decorative goblet or wine flask.

Ladies only, as in meena **bagh** (or **purdah** bagh): a garden reserved for ladies and young children, the only males present being aged **malis** (gardeners).

Meena Bazaar: a bazaar selling trinkets and fancy goods of interest to ladies; in **Mogul** times, a bazaar set up for the purdanashin (secluded) princesses of a palace zenana.

In **Sanskrit**, min means a fish and minakshi, fish-eyed: usually applied as a compliment to a girl with pleasing oval and perhaps slighly slanted eyes. Often portrayed in an exaggerated form in 17th and 18th century miniature paintings. Minakshi/Meenakshi was a wife to Lord **Shiva** and is highly regarded in the south as a goddess. The great temple at Madurai is dedicated to her. Meena, as a **Hindu** girl's name of today, is a diminutive of Minakshi.

In astrology, mina is the equivalent of the Western zodiacal house, Pisces.

MEH/MIH Sanskrit
The root sound concerning mensuration with links to Indo-European languages. In English, words such as measure, dimension, metric, menses, mean.

In Hindi, measurement can be a word such as mikdar.

MEHFIL *n* Urdu
Normally, an assembly for a Muslim type entertainment, of Hindustani music and **ghazals**, singing and **dancing girls**. Also, as in mehfil **mushaira**, a gathering of poets to recite their works to each other and to an audience.

MEHTAR *n* Urdu
A prince. An honorific once accorded in irony, now an accepted designation for a sweeper. (Such titles are quite common: the cook is addressed as Maharaj, the tailor as Master, the potter sometimes as **Prajapati** and the sweeper. in addition to Mehtar, may be **Jemadar** – leader.)

Mehtarani: the sweepress.

MELĀ *n* Hindi
From the root 'mil', meaning meet or unite. A fair: an open air gathering with entertainments and things to eat and buy. Often held on the occasion of a religious festival.

MEO *n* Urdu
A Muslim peasantry living to the southwest of Delhi, in **Haryana** and Rajasthan.

METHI *n* Hindi

The herb and the spice fenugreek. The widely used aromatic seeds have a bitterish flavour and a high nutritive value. It has recently been claimed that methi will reduce human blood glucose and also cholesterol.

METROPOLITAN *n*

Title from the Greek Orthodox and Eastern Churches previously assigned to the Bishop of Kolkata as head of the Church of England in India – at one time his province covered the territory from Afghanistan to Australia. In 1930, following an Act by the British parliament, the Church of India, soon to be the Church of India, **Burma**, Ceylon and Pakistan, was formed, free to govern its own affairs, not subordinate to but still in harmony with the Church of England for the statutory duty imposed on the Government of India, that of the provision for Anglican worship for their European servants, remained. For some years previous to **Independence**, many of the episcopal and missionary Churches in India (including the Anglicans but excluding the Church of Rome) had considered that the issues dividing them reflected their origins in Europe and had little relevance to India. A Church of South India uniting them was formed in 1947 and a Church of North India in 1970. In 1978 a Joint Council of the Churches of North and South India and of the **Mar** Thoma Church (of South India) came into being. Although historically the

Mar Thoma Church had connections with Rome, today the three Churches are members of the world Anglican community.

Metropolitan as a title was first: used in India by the Syrian Christians of **Malabar**: in the early centuries their Archbishops had, in theory, all-India jurisdiction with the Latin title of *Metropolita Indiarum*. The Metropolitan is still the designation of the leader of the Mar Thoma Syrian Church. The ' Churches of North and South India are each headed by a Moderator elected by the controlling Synods for a period of three years in the north and for two years in the south.

During the British period, the Metropolitan, his bishops and the chaplain clergy were a charge on public revenue: also the Anglican cathedrals, many church buildings and almost all **European cemeteries**. In general, the pastoral duties of the official clergy were confined to Europeans and Anglo-Indians: Indian Christians were mostly evangelized by and ministered to by the unofficial missionaries.

MEWĀR

Old name for the tract in Rajasthan much of which later became the **princely** state of Udaipur. The rulers (Maharanas) of Mewar were of the highest rank of **Rajput** princes and were famous for their resistance to **Mogul** pressures. One particular scourge of the Muslims at the time of the Emperor Akbar, Rana Pratap, has become a folk hero. Recently, an imposing bronze statue of him, riding his equally well-known horse, Chetak, has been erected outside the Kashmere Gate, Delhi.

MIAN *n* Urdu
A respectful term of address to a Muslim, or by which a wife may refer to her husband. A suffix added to the name of God (**Allah** mian), or to a man's name to indicate respect.

MIHRAB/MEHRAB *n* Urdu
Lit. an arch. A niche or an arched recess in the western (in India) interior wall of a mosque (*see* Masjid) or **idgah**: in a large mosque there may well be a number of such recesses, with that in the centre the most prominent, indicating the qibla/kibla, a word from Arabic meaning an object in front of one. Says the Lord in the Holy Kor'an of those at prayer. "We see thee often turn about thy face in the heavens we will surely turn thee to a qibla thou shalt like. Turn, then, thy face towards the sacred mosque" (at Mecca). The first qiblah was in Jerusalem, but dissensions with the Jews over the recognition of Mohammed as God's Prophet, led to the change to Mecca in the lifetime of the Prophet himself. The orientation is very carefully calculated: for example, the faces of the north and south interior walls of. Aurangzeb's

Pearl Mosque of the royal palace (Red Fort) of Delhi are slightly at variance with the exterior of the same walls which conform to the general building line. On an Islamic prayer rug (in Urdu from Persian, Jai' namaz – lit. place of worship, *see* Azaan *and* Namaaz), a mihrab is woven into the design (the type of arch may indicate to the oriental carpet expert, the place of origin). In use, the rug will be positioned so that the arch points to the qibla.

Within Islam, the term qibla may be used as a form of address to a respected person, such as a teacher or even one's parents.

MIMBAR/MINBAR *n* Urdu
A pulpit. The block of three or four steps in a **masjid** or idgah (*see* Id) from which the congregation is addressed: from their viewpoint, located to the right of the central **mihrab**. Sometimes, the uppermost step is not used, speakers deeming themselves unworthy to follow the Holy Prophet who himself spoke from the top of a similar block; some indeed speak from the floor and do not use the mimbar at all. (In Egypt and West Asia a mimbar may well be a much larger and taller structure.)

A rostrum, a reading desk.

MINĀR *n* Urdu
In the original Arabic, manar/manara, once a tall tower which, in the man-

ner of a Greek phāros, carried a fire to guide shipping (naar: fire or light) or, inland, after-dark travellers to a desert settlement: an encampment of the **Mogul** emperors when on tour was similarly marked, a lamp or fire in a bowl on a tall mast, which was fulsomely termed, the **akash diya** – the light of heaven. Later, such towers as part of a mosque were built in India from the Mogul period and used by the muazzin (see Azaan), the crier. In Persian and Urdu, manaar became minaar and in English, minaret. Any tall tower is likely to be called a minar: e.g. the Qutab Minar near Delhi. (In Arabic, qutab means pivot or axis, so that the name of the original builder of the Qutab, Qutab-u-Din Aibak, could be translated as Pivot of the Faith, a man of exemplary piety, Aibak –although a commander and viceroy on behalf of his master, Mohd. bin Sam of Ghor, was technically a mamlak or bond-slave.)

The site of the Delhi minar is of world heritage class and a must for the visitor to the capital: firstly just to see the pillar itself, 12th. century AD. 72 metres in height and then a second technical wonder, a wrought iron pillar almost alongside, of the Gupta period, 5th century AD., 7.2 metres in length, including that underground. A high phosphorous content has ensured a minimum of corrosion.

Minar Express: name for a train running between Mumbai and Secunder-abad, close to Hyderabad, the city of the Char Minar, a building with four minarets, adopted as a municipal symbol.

MIRCH *n* Hindi
The word is derived form Austric days (*see* Adivasi). Sensation on the skin: burning, tingling.

Fruit and seeds of three basic plants, of which there are many varieties, adding a pungency to food. Two are natural to India, the third is the chilli (an Aztec name from Central America) introduced by the Portuguese in the 16th century. Some will say that the pungency flavour of the chilli is distinct from that of the pepper and give it a name of its own, teekha.

Kala or gol mirch (black or round pepper): the pepper-corn. One of the ancient spices of the east, traded from south India to Mediterranean lands when even Rome was young. Picked as a green berry from a vine (*Piper nigrum*) of the same family as the betel (see Pan) which, when sun-dried and ground, produces black pepper, or if the dark hulls or skins are first removed, white. Pepper of the highest quality may have the name Tellicherry/Tellicheri: once an export shipping port of the **Malabar** coast and still a major wholesale market.

Long peppers : (in Hindi, pipli or pippali natural to India and exported to Europe since Roman days. The Sanskrit name, pippali, is the remote origin of the English word, pepper) : the sun-dried fruits of a perennial climber. Piper longum. In appearance like brown dried catkins or mulberries. Powdered and used as a spice and, together, with the root, in Indian medicine to produce salivation.

Chilli : lal mirch (the red chilli) and hari mirch (the green chilli). A plant of the capsicum family from tropical America bearing small pugent and nutritious green pods, probably introduced, like the tomato and the potato, by the Portuguese. (The pungency, capsaicin, is concentrated in the inner wall and varies greatly from one variety of the plant to another.) The pods change to bright red when dried. Dried Indian chillis are powdered for use as a condiment (red, or cayenne, pepper. The name is from French Guiana), usually more pungent that the paprika similarly made from the Central European chilli.

Assam mirch: the name in north India for a variety of chilli with very small pods of about two centimetres in length, but extremely pungent. Elsewhere the name may be longi and in east India dhandi. Similar to the bird or tabasco chilli.

Simla mirch: **bazaar** name for the large fleshy green capsicum, low in pungency but rich in vitamin C. Sometimes called bell peppers.

Degchi/degi mirch: cooking spice.

Chilli powder made from a variety of pods such as Kashmiri mirch, with very low pungency : used as a red colouring agent in food preparation rather than as a condiment.

MIRIAM Urdu
The Islamic (and Jewish) form of the name Mary.

MIRZA *n* Urdu
In Arabic, a term of respect for one of high birth and education. A Turki title of honour carried by the princes and **khans** of the Samarkand regions and by the **Shahs** of Persia. Adopted almost as a family name by the princes of the **Mogul** dynasty in India. As an honorific it was awarded by the Mogul court to some of the nobles of **Oudh** and even to some **Hindu Rajput princes**, notably to the Jaipur-Amber family.

Son of a Muslim nobleman, Today, a Muslim family name of those claiming descent from the Mogul princes: also sometimes used by followers of the **Ahmedi** sect.

Mirza coat: short and cotton-quilted, during the northern winter particularly worn by Muslims. Such coats are said to have been introduced from Afghanistan and central Asia by the Moguls (Mirzas). In battle, heavily quilted coats could be worn to give some protection against arrows and sword thrusts.

MISA (M.I.S.A.)

Maintenance of Internal Security Act, 1971. A much amended Act, permitting the central and state governments to imprison an individual for a certain period without judicial process or review and without necessarily informing the person concerned of the reason for his detention. In some form or another, such powers have always been with the Government of India from the earliest British days. Still often mentioned are two Acts of 1919 coupled with the name of Mr. Justice Rowlatt, who was later knighted – a High Court judge from Britain appointed chairman of a committee to consider means to contain violent agitation, following the automatic lapse of the Defence of India Rules with the ending of World War I. The Rowlatt Acts, particularly the authorisation of internment without trial, angered Indian public opinion (*see* Jallianwala Bagh), which felt that wartime cooperation merited a better reward. In fact, the extra legal powers were not used at the time.

MISTRI/MISTRY *n* Urdu, from Portuguesc

An artisan, a mechanic. In 16th century English, mystery had the meaning of one's craft or indentured trade. An unskilled labourer man or woman, can be beldar—bel a spade.

MITTAKSHARA/MITAKSĀRA *n* Hindi

One of the two leading books on Hindu civil law written in **Sanskrit** during the 12th century AD: the other being Dayabhaga. These two authorities governed family law, particularly in matters of inheritance, at least until modified by the **Hindu** Code of the 1950s. Dayabhaga is followed in eastern India and Mitakshara elsewhere, The former recognises the head of a joint family (*see* Karta) as sole trustee and division only takes place on his death or removal. Under Mitakshara, sons and grandsons may under certain conditions, receive their share of property before the death of the head of the family.

MITHUN/MITHAN *n* Tribal name.
Semi-wild animals (*Bos frontalis*) of the hills of north-east India, **Myanmar** and Malaysia: hybrids between the wild **gaur** and domestic cattle. They run freely in the jungle but, in India at least, have recognised owners. Possession of a number of these animals is a status symbol amongst the tribesmen: but they are used solely for ceremonial sacrifice and meat.

MLA (M.LA.)
Member of a Legislative Assembly : i.e., of a state parliament, a **Vidban** Sabha.

MŌCHI/MOOCHI *n* Hindi
A leather worker; if a **Hindu** then normally a **Chamar**.

The shoe-maker: the cobbler, the shoe-repairer, who goes from door to door or sits by the roadside awaiting customers. Exceptionally the mochis of Gujarat, particularly of **Kathiawar** and Kutch, the Rabaris - and their families are well known for fine embroidery, especially for sheeshadari, mirror-work: once a village fashion now sometimes adopted by grand ladies. Small circles of thin light-catching mirror-glass of not more than half an inch diameter, embroidered onto garments.

MOFUSSIL *n* and *adj* Urdu
Lit. beyond the four walls (of a city). Distant from the big cities, particularly the **Presidency** capitals on or close to the sea coast (Mumbai, Kolkata, **Channai**). Up-country, rural. The word is rarely used today.

MOGULS/MOGHULS/MU-GHALS *n* Urdu
As in medieval Europe, so too in northern India the name given to the nomadic horsemen of the Mongolian steppes, the Mongols, was one of horror. Incursions by Tartars of the tribe of **Chengis Khan** first occurred in mid-13th century (at that time the Mongol Khans had not been converted to **Islam**) but were driven back by the Delhi **Sultanates**. The names Mongol and Tartar, as perceived in Europe, were really synonymous, inhabitants of the Asian land mass north of Tibet between the Black Sea, China and the Siberian northern coastline, Tartary. In fact, the Mongols were a pastoral group of tribesmen occupying the heartland, of whom the Tartars were a small unit. Those who became known as Mongols, or Moguls, in the Indian context were actually Turks – as were most of the earlier **sultans** – people speaking the Turki language with a homeland in today's southern Russia on both sides of the Oxus river and generally north of the Caspian Sea: those of the country, Turkey, are one branch of a widespread family. Another group, on becoming Muslims, adopted the name Uzbeks. A serious foray into India was mounted by Timurilang (of Mogul descent, also written Tamerlane, Timur and Temur, but having Turki customs and language), who sacked Delhi in 1398 and then withdrew. It was his descendants, the House of Timur, seven generations later who gave India the line of seventeen Muslim emperors from Babur in the 16th century to **Bahadur** Shah 'Zafar' II, who, exiled to **Burma** by the British after the mutiny, died in Rangoon in 1862. (Zafar, meaning victory, was the Emperor's pen-name as a poet.) The later kings of the dynasty preferred not to be reminded of marauder ancestors (although mong in Central Asian tongues had the meaning of brave) and described themselves as Moguls and not Mongols – in no Indian pronunciation of

the name is there an aspirated 'h' sound, but from time to time from the 16th century onwards, the English spelling has been, and usually still is in India, Moghul: yet mogul is normal in a purely English use, as for example, film mogul. Babur had no such qualms: he was happy to go to war under the same standards of stallions' tails as Chengis Khan and claimed that north India was his by right, by virtue of Timurilang's brief occupation five generations earlier: indeed some of the Sayyid sultans (*see* Sultanates of Delhi) who followed that incursion, described themselves as Timur's Viceroys.

Mogul period: 1526-1857. The latter date perhaps requires an explanation. For most historians, the Mogul era ended in mid-18th century with the rise of first the Maratha and then the British powers; for some, earlier, with the death of the last 'Great Mogul', Aurangzeb, in 1707, following decades of profitless campaigning in the south which left the treasury empty. But eleven sovereigns followed, almost each with diminished power and dignity, until in the end the realm had shrunk to no more than the **khalsa** land and the royal palace – the Red Fort–in Delhi. But for all that, while the British had paid no more than a simulated courtesy deference to the occupant since the early years of the century and by 1857, Bahadur Shah was simply their pensioner King of Delhi, the **sepoys**

in the uprising marched to him as the legitimate ruler of **Hindustan** – a course of action not envisaged for a moment by those in command in nearby Meerut, the scene of the outbreak of the conflict, hence the lack of active pursuit. Formal recognition by the British of the Delhi emperors had ended in 1834 when the Company ceased to mint coins in the name of Akbar Shah; but he was never deposed and following the recapture of Delhi, the authority of the Company in arraigning his successor before a military court on a charge of raising rebellion, could only have been that of force majeure or conquest. The sole freely negotiated transfer of power by a Mogul sovereign to the British was that of the Emperor Shah Alam in 1765 by which he permitted the Company to collect revenue in Bengal on his behalf, since he was unable to collect it himself because of intransigence by his nominal satraps, the **nawabs**, and from which Rs 26 lakhs was to be remitted to him annually. See Diwan and East India Company. Today, still a symbol of nationhood and sovereignty, on the 15th of August each year, the high wall of the once royal palace is the venue of the official ceremony of the **Government of India** commemorating freedom from British rule in 1947.

Moglai: an adjectival reference to the Moguls or the Mogul period. Particularly used today in connection with the Muslim style of food preparation.

Mogul-e-azam: the Urdu term for the Head of State.

MOHALLA *n* Urdu
In **Mogul** days and after, in an old northern Indian city, a group of residential lanes with but one narrow entrance, closed in time of trouble and at night by the gate-keeper and even on hot afternoons when all within could be expected to be sleeping. The gate may still be there, but it will be rarely closed and there will be no keeper. A small territorial unit of municipal administration, a ward.

Mohalla (Punjabi): a procession.

MOHUR *n* Urdu
Gold coin of the **Mogul** period: also known as ashrafi/asharfi (ashrafi – plural of sharif, noble, distinguished. Term for Muslim aristocracy in Mogul days. The common people were the ajlaf.) In modern times, gold mohurs bearing the effigy of Queen Victoria were struck in India almost to the end of her reign, to be replaced by the British gold sovereign as legal tender. But like the nominal guinea in Britain, the mohur continued well into the 20th century as the unit of currency in which professional fees, such as those of barristers, were expressed. In **princely** Hyderabad, ashrafis continued as the **Nizam**'s gold coins until quite recent times.

Today, the mohur is likely to be no more than an official seal, or just the imprint of a rubber stamp.

MŌKSHA *n* Hindi
The state of being released from the **Hindu** birth-death-rebirth cycle. The condition of final achievement for man, the personal attainment of which is the aim of Hindu religious endeavour.

Mukta: one who has acquired moksha. In Sikhism, a mukta can be one who died for the faith, a martyr.

The word **mukti** has the same meaning: also that of the more secular freedom.

In Buddhism (*see* Puddha), the state of perfection and consequent release is known as nirvana.

Aldous Huxley used the word Moksha as the title of his book published in 1975.

MŌMIN *n* Urdu
Strictly, a true believer in **Islam** in Islam, as in the Arabic title, Amir-ul-Momin–Commander of the Faithful. But in India the title has come to mean a Muslim weaver, a member of the occupational group of handloom workers, particularly in eastern India: as a class within the Muslim community, considered to be backward. Up to the early years of the 20th century, the weavers were known as Julaha

and were alleged by British officials to be particularly bigoted.

MONEY PLANT *n*
One of a large family of lofty climbing vines from the tropical rain forests of Asia and Central America. *Pothos aureus* (in 1737 Linnaeus took Pothos from a Sinhalese word meaning ivy); *Epipremnun aureus; Scindapsus aureus* (Greek for ivy-like); devil's ivy and, when variegated, marble queen; all are names for the money plant. Associated are the philodendrons and monsteras of the Americas. In India, grown in almost every home and office in pots and plain water jars, as a trailing plant with small glossy green leaves, both for decoration and from a half-held folk belief that money will flow to where it is looked after – with the proviso that the specimen must have been obtained other than by paying for it. These beliefs, owing nothing to religion, and the universally used English name – seemingly, there is no Indian language equivalent – are of unknown provenance. It is also cherished under the same name in West Africa. (In England, money-plant is an alternative name for the cottage garden annual of the Luparia genus, honesty.)

In pots and jars indoors and in gardens as ground cover, the leaves of the money-plant are small, but when it is allowed to follow its nature and grow vertically on a tree, even in the north the change can be spectacular: leaves as much as ten inches across. But the vine never flowers in India and only rarely elsewhere.

MONSOON *n* English
In the early days of the Graeco-Roman empires, West Asian merchants and mariners, centuries before they became Muslims, using Alexandria as their entrepot, were eager to carry the goods of the East to the rich markets of the West: live animals and birds, precious stones and ivory, rice, ebony and teakwood, textiles and, above all, spices. It was they who discovered the convenience of the winds over the Arabian Sea: from May to October winds from the south-west would give them a good passage to the **Malabar** coast in India and then from December to March there would be a change to the north-east to blow them home again. (On the other side of India, similar circulation of the winds over the Bay of Bengal gave Indian mariners access to the markets of South-East Asia.) The time to set out they called (in Arabic) 'mausam', the season – the word much later anglicised into monsoon. (Nowadays, in Hindustani mausam also means the weather: e.g. Mausam **Bhavan**, the name for the office building of the Meteorological Department in New Delhi.)

The summer westerly winds blowing across the Arabian Sea continue over the subcontinent bringing moisture to the south, centre and west. But in northern India, much of the rain comes from the opposite direction: winds travel round the peninsula and enter eastern India from the Bay of Bengal. It is this easterly current, glancing off the **Himalaya** (causing a narrow low pressure belt the length of the Gangetic plain parallel to the hills, known in the north as the monsoon trough, or the axis of the mon-soon), which in general is the channel for the region's rainfall (but a deep depression from the east when over north-west India, in fact can attract the west coast branch of the monsoon). The 'onset of the monsoon' is a term of the meteorologists meaning the date on which the monsoon rains commence in a given area (usually, towards the end of June in the Delhi region): but since the rain is only incidental to the wind, it could perhaps be more rational to date the onset from when the moist monsoon current from the ocean firmly establishes itself – often accompanied by cumulus clouds and, perhaps, near darkness at noon from what are termed pre-monsoon showers. In Delhi, usually soon after mid-June.

For a long time, the reasons for the great continental air movements were thought to be the extreme temperature and consequent pressure differential between the cold winters and hot summers of the vast area of central Asia (the heavier the winter snowfall on the Himalaya ranges and the Tibetan plateau, i.e., the colder the spring, the less the following monsoon precipitation) and also the difference in air temperatures over the land mass and the ocean. But recent research has shown that these are only two of many influences, some of which occur well south of the equator. It has been said that the stimulus for the global circulation of winds is to be found in the Pacific Ocean. A correlation has been definitely established between low pressure in the equatorial South Pacific region and high pressure – and no rainfall – over the Indian sub-continent. A factor affecting the date of the onset of the rains is the position of a region of low pressure which constantly circles the globe at the equator, with a cycle of about forty-five days. Some find the cyclic variations in the solar radius to have a significance. The more the monsoon is studied, the more complicated and less understood the mechanism appears. Science has yet to offer any firm rebuttal of the widely held contention that the vagaries of the rains are the caprices of the Vedic deity, mighty **Indra**.

By mid-September in the north, normally the monsoon current will have faded out, but on the east coast, the season of the heaviest rain is then about to begin. The winds back from the south-east to the north-east (becoming the N.E. Trades, or the N.E. monsoon) and from the

Bay of Bengal bring heavy rain to coastal Andhra Pradesh and **Tamil Nadu**. This is when typhoons (*see* Toofan) usually strike, sometimes disastrously.

While the flow of the monsoon in north India is always from the east, local storms being cyclonic – an anti-clockwise circulation in the northern hemisphere – can approach from any direction: in other than the monsoon months, a switch from the prevailing westerlies to an east wind, together with a rise in temperature, is also an indication of rain on the way. The northern Indian winter rains (January/February: about ten per cent of the monsoon fall) come on an east wind. The reason for the about-turn is usually a low pressure disturbance moving into the region from the north-west. The common north Indian word for the monsoon is barsaat – the rain: but a **Sanskrit**-based Hindi term is sometimes used, varsha, or, more formally, varsha ritu, the rain season. Every June, throughout the country, in the cities and in the fields, all eyes watch for the build-up of the towering cumulus clouds that will bring rain and relief from the searing dry heat of the hot weather. But no less today than it has been since India was first populated, the timely arrival of a copious monsoon is of far greater importance than of merely lowering the temperature. Good rains put cash into the vast countryside and the

whole economy benefits. Everybody, including the government itself, will have more money to spend. At one end, the sale of aircraft seats will boom, so will vehicles, and at the other, makers of the cheapest cotton **dhoties** will see their sales graphs rise. If Egypt is the Nile, so India is the product of the approximately one hundred days of the south-west monsoon: a village saying has it that famine is as near as a failed monsoon. In an England situation to be under a cloud or to see a cloud on the horizon can be inauspicious: not so in India.

MOOLAH/MOOLA *n* English
This colloquial word for money, cash, at a guess will have more than a coincidental link with the **Sanskrit**-derived Hindi, muliya, meaning cost, value or wages. But all authorities insist that the origin of the English slang is unknown, merely saying that it first surfaced in the USA in the 1930s.

MOOR *n* English
A Muslim: a word (derived from the country of Mauritania) replacing the earlier Saracen (although Islamic architecture in India, meaning domes and arches rather than the trabeate beams of the non-Muslims is still described as Saracenic). Moor went out of use in India during the early 19th century. At one time, the Urdu language was termed Moors.

Older than Moor was the English application of Turk to all Muslims. The Anglican Book of Common Prayer in the Collect for Good Friday, calls on the Lord to 'have mercy on all Turks and Hereticks'.

In Indian history writing, a Turk is not nessarily one from today's Turkey. As with Delhi's Turkman Gate, the reference is to Turkistan (today's Turkmenistan), but many of those of Turkey may have a far background in Turkistan. An ancient Persian word for the trans-Oxus region is Turān so in English from the middle ages we have Turāni/Turānian (see OED) for the non-aryan nomads of central Asia.

MŌR *n* Hindi form Pali
The peacock. India's national bird. Respected in almost all villages as a bird of happy
omen; as the vehicle (*see* Vahan) of **Kartikeya** (for some, also of **Saraswati**) and also because of its association with Lord **Krishna** during his time in the **Madhuban**. In painting, accorded an accessory role second only to the **lotus**. Nowadays, the bird is protected by law. The period of maximum pavonine splendour is that of the **monsoon**, the breeding season, a time when insect food is freely available. It is then that, particularly on a day of light rain, the cocks may be seen dancing, or prancing, with

all plumage displayed to impress and attract the hens.

Morchhāl: ceremonial emblem of a Muslim ruler, particularly carried in state processions of the **Mogul** period. A cone-shaped bundle of peacock feathers with the handle at the base, in appearance like a lengthy shuttlecock: later adopted by rural magnates, both Muslim and Hindu. Now often carried as a staff of office by the ojha; an exorcist or shaman, one who cures disease by charms and spells.

Morni: peahen.
The Moguls used a Persian word for the peacock, taus. Hence takht-i-taus, the famous peacock throne of Delhi's royal palace, *see* Koh-i-Noor. In Hindi from **Sanskrit**, the bird is mayur, a name reflecting perhaps, the morning and evening shrieking cat-calls, 'may-urr, may-urr'.

Mayur-asan: a yogic posture (*see* Yoga) in which the body, parallel to the ground stomach downwards, legs wide apart, is supported by the palms of the hands only.

Peacock chair: a light grass-cane or wicker-work chair with a large high back in the shape of a peacock's displayed tail.

Peacock flower: see Gul Mohur.

MŌRCHA *n* Hindi

Originally a military term, fortifications, the front line. Now more likely to be a reference to a political front. A movement for political agitation. A march, by followers of a political party for a political purpose.

MŌRHA/MŌNDHA/MAURA *n*
Hindi
Maur: wickerwork: a light round stool or chair made of dried reed-cane, with woven string seat. A centre of the mohra industry (sometimes written moda) is east of Delhi at Garmuktesar, the crossing of the River **Ganga** and a source of riverine cane.

MUDRA *n* Hindi
A body pose or posture. An ancient Indian symbolic gesture by the hand and fingers, as seen in classical sculpture: in ritual and yog-asan (*see* Yoga) used as an aid to meditation. One of twenty-four basic gestures in **Hindu** classical dancing each with a clear meaning for the expert. (But the dance expert, when referring to a hand gesture as part of **abhinaya**, usually prefers the term hasta – hast: the hand.) But even the curling of the tongue may be referred to as a mudra.

Technically a mudra but not employed in classical dancing, is the finger gesture taught to young children – and, at least in a jocular way, often carried into adulthood – to indicate a need to urinate, a little finger extended as far from the hand as possible.

Samyukt Mudra: using two hands together, e.g., the gesture of greeting and farewell, the namaste (*see* namaskar). In today's Hindi, mudra also has the more mundane meaning of money. A die, seal or stamp.

MUFTI *n* Urdu
A Muslim expert in Islamic law. The word is acknowledged to be the origin of mufti in English (meaning civil clothes for one normally in uniform) but there seems to be no explanation for the transition.

MUGG/MAGH/MUGH *n*
A class of Buddhists and **Hindus** (often with the family name of Ba-rua – pronounced Baroi in Bengali) from Chittagong and Dhaka (previously, the spelling was Dacca): both are now in Bangladesh and from the neighbouring Arakan region of **Burma**: traditionally considered by Europeans to make the best cooks in India for English-style dishes. It has been alleged that in earlier days the Muggs were sea pirates who were forced to seek a living ashore by the British: another allegation, no doubt totally unwarranted, was that as cooks they had not entirely set aside some of their earlier maritime habits.

MUGGER/MUGGER MACH *n*
Crocodile. Three species are found

in India, with numbers much reduced in recent years: the gavial (from the Hindi gharial), up to nineteen feet in length: the marsh crocodile, up to twelve feet: and the estuarine crocodile, a monster of up to thirty feet. The word mugger is an anglicism from the Hindi, magar (magarmach, lit. crocodile-fish) , meaning the marsh crocodile. The gharial, with its long narrow jaws, is so named from a round knob, in shape like a small waterpot (ghara, in Hindi), often seen on large males at the extreme upper tip of the snout. Found only in the sub-continent, it is fish eating and does not attack man: but the now rarely seen estuarine crocodile can be savagely aggressive.

MUHARRAM/MOHARRUM n
Urdu

The word can be loosely translated as 'the sacred month' (see Haram). The first month of the Islamic year (Muslim chronology dates from the 1st of Muharram 622 AD – see Calendars). On the tenth day (Ashura/ Asura), Shia Muslims (see Sunnis) commemorate the deaths of two grandsons of the Prophet Mohammed. Principally, the martyrdom in battle of Hussain, the third Caliph (see Khilafat) in Shia eyes, at the hand of Yasid, the seventh Caliph of the Sunni, at Karbala in Iraq, in 680 AD: and secondly, the death by poison of his elder brother, Hasan, the second Caliph according to Shia opinion and the fifth according to Sunni. In many Indian cities, mourning passional processions particularly in Lucknow known as Azadari, are taken out in which zealous participants flagellate themselves or rhythmically beat their chests to express mātam (mourning grief), sometimes to the extent of causing bloody abrasions, crying 'Ya Hasan, Ya Husain' (see Hobson-Jobson). Tall bamboo and paper structures, tāzia, from the Arabic word for condolence, said to be replicas of the tombs of the martyrs (often red for Hasan and green for Husain), are carried or trundled or trolleyed as part of the procession to a local burial ground given the name of Karbala. These tazias as part of a Muharram ceremony are unique to the subcontinent. Also carried in the procession may be alams, replicas of the standards borne by Husain and his relatives in the battle: these are not destroyed but are used year after year: particularly in Hyderabad, the alams may be made of sheet metal. On the fortieth day following the main Muharram procession, on a smaller scale than before, tazias may again be taken in procession to the Karbala burial ground. See also Imambara.

For Sunni Muslims, the day is not necessarily one of mourning, for there is a tradition that it was on the tenth of Ashura that God created Adam and Hawwa (Eve) in the celestial Garden of Paradise: it was only after the Fall that they were ejected to earth.

MUKTI *n* Hindi
Freedom, liberation, (For the specifically **Hindu** religious meaning, see Moksha).

MULETHI *n* Hindi
Liquorice root: the English name is from old French for a sweetmeat made from juice from the root. In India an ayurvedic medicine for coughs taken as a powder or as juice.

MULKI *n* Urdu
Lit. of the country. Particularly in the former **princely** state of Hyderabad (now largely Andhra Pradesh, *see* AP), a term for a long established resident,who received privileges denied to newcomers.

MULLIGATAWNY *n*
An anglicism from the **Tamil** equivalent of pepper-water, molagu tunni: also called rasam (*see* Ras). A form of highly seasoned vegetable soup served in south Indian homes to be added to rice as part of a main meal. In the north, in south Indian restaurants, it may be served in a glass as an appetising drink. In other north Indian restaurants, mulligatawny can mean a **dal** soup flavoured with **tamarind** to indicate its southern origin, containing a little rice and garnished with fresh limes.

Mulls: a name once given by Europeans elsewhere in India to their compatriots living in the then **Madras Presidency**, from the southerners'

alleged partiality for mulligatawny at its fieriest: an epithet corresponding to the Ducks of Bombay (*see* Bombay Duck) and the Ditchers of Calcutta – from the Maratha Ditch, an old defence work of their city against marauding Maratha horsemen. (Another colloquialism for the Britons of Madras was 'the Benighted', expressing as an exaggerated pleasantry a common British belief that of the three Presidencies, that of Madras was a backwater: but it has to be said that until the opening of the Suez Canal in 1869, it was Bombay that was out of the mainstream.) Perhaps things were rather relaxed: the Madras army, it is true, denied the south to the French, but from the early 19th century there is a story that orders had to be issued to commanding officers that they should not conduct early morning parades from their bungalow verandahs clad in night attire.

MŪLTĀNI MITTI *n* Hindi
Multani earth : known in English as fuller's earth. An absorbent clay, largely hydrous silica of alumina, used in refining oils, both mineral and vegetable. Mined in Rajasthan and Madhya Pradesh and from small deposits over much of India. A conjectural reason for the place name is that the earth was consumed in quantity in Multan, now in Pakistan's Punjab, for degreasing (fulling) the raw wool used in the local textile industry. The clay absorbs colours

well and since antiquity has been used in central Asia and China for ceramics, particularly to make cobalt blue glazed tiles and pottery. So in India since the first century AD. Today, both Jaipur and Delhi made blue pottery is popular.

As a cosmetic aid to absorb oil, a mudpack of the mitti may be applied on the face. Also to the body to prevent or reduce prickly heat.

As imported from Germany the name is tonsil.

MUMBAI *n*

In a naming ceremony held in January 1986 by the Mayor, the city previously known to the world as Bombay was renamed. Mumbai follows from the patroness deity of the one-time islands, Mumba-devi. (Mumbai has always been used in Marathi and Gujarati.) The Portuguese had a fort there over a hundred years before the British arrived in about 1662 and the British name for the settlement was probably an anglicised form of the Portuguese Bom Bahia – a good bay. (Actually, the British were aware of the local name when they took over the islands, for some of their William and Mary coins of the late 17th century carried the mint designation in the Persian script as Mumbai. Considered a crown colony and not, as elsewhere in India, territory administered in the name of the Mogul emperor, Bombay had British

royal coins earlier than Madras or Calcutta.) *See* East India Company. Years after the mayoral ceremony, reiterated in an announcement by the State Government in 1995, the change of name has now received general acceptance.

Brihan Mumbai: Marathi from Sanskrit, brihat, great. Greater Mumbai.

MUNDAN *n* Hindi

(Mund, a head: mundmala, garland of heads – *see* Kali and Shiva).

Mundan means the shaving of the male head: a custom observed by some following the death of a close relative (tradition, in such circumstances, also calls for the removal of a moustache). In a mundan ceremony, a boy, usually aged about three years, has his baby hair shaved for the first time (but leaving, perhaps, the **choti**): often held outside a temple or on the banks of a river. Muslims also have a ceremony (akika/aqiqa) for young children in which the boys' heads are shaved: if means permit, a goat may be sacrificed. On the **Haj**, before donning the pilgrim's robes, a male Muslim traditionally has his head shaved.

Munda/mundan/mundoo: a young servant lad.

Mundu (Malayalam) : a white sarong worn by males. Waist to ankles.

MUNG PHALI *n* Hindi
Lit. a **dal** seed-pod. The ground-nut (peanut): an exotic from the Americas.

MUNI *n* Hindi
Lit. the silent one. An ascetic, one who has withdrawn from the world: frequently used to refer to a Jain monk, particularly one whose learning is thought to be profound.

Sakyamuni: the muni of the Sakyas (the tribe to which the **Buddha** belonged). A title for the Buddha.

MUNIM *n* Urdu
Book-keeper, treasurer, accountant. Also from Persian, but little used today, with a similar meaning is khazanchi.

MUNSHI/MOONSHI *n* Urdu
Correctly, a writer, a secretary. As used by Europeans, a language teacher, particularly of Persian or Urdu.

Munshigiri: clerk's work (slightly pejorative).

MUNSIF *n* Urdu
Small causes judge in civil law. A Mogul administrative title that continued through the British period and remains in use today.

MURABBA *n* Urdu
Fruit, or sweet vegetables such as the carrot, cooked whole and steeped in syrup. A conserve or European jam.

MURGA *n* Urdu
From the Persian murgh, a cockerel: as, for example, murga masala – chicken curry. 'Make a murga': an imperative to  a child, a traditional school punishment. He would be expected to squat on his hands, cross his arms and grasp each ear lobe between a thumb and forefinger, a gesture of shame. In this position he should beg forgiveness for his transgression.

Murgi: a domestic hen.

MURTI *n* Hindi
A three-dimensional representation in any medium, of any size, of deity, man or animal. A statue, a figurine, a rock carving, an image in a temple or church.

Trimurti: three figures. Normally, a statue or picture with three faces on one head, often representing the trinity of the pre-eminent deities of Hinduism (or, as some **pandits** would assert, the three aspects of the One God), **Brahma, Vishnu** and **Shiva** (or Shiva under the name Mahesh or Rudra). When designed to show Shiva as Mahadev, the Supreme God, the three faces represent different aspects of the deity: probably the best known example is the rock-cut bust of Shiva at Elephanta, in Mumbai Harbour. The term Trimurti may also be used in the abstract as a reference to the Godhead.

Teen Murti House: in New Delhi, the post-**Independence** residence (previously that of the British Commanders-in-Chief) of Prime Minister Nehru and now a national museum. From the World War I memorial outside, bearing the effigies of three Indian cavalrymen.

An alternative Hindi word frequently used in eastern India for an image used in worship, is pratima.

MUSA *n* Urdu
The Islamic form of the name Moses.

Mus/moosa: Hindi: a word with a **Sanskrit** root and connections in European languages, a mouse or rat.

MUSHAIRA *n* Urdu
A gathering of Urdu (*see* Khari Boli) poets under a Mir-i-Mushaira (Chairman and Master of Ceremonies) who commands a recitation by placing of a candle (shama) flame before the chosen versifier. The audience, which may number several thousand, has a participatory role and will show appreciation of well-turned lines by calling for repetition and by exclamations such as 'Wah, Wah!' (Excellent, Excellent!) A popular

entertainment on festival days in northern India and elsewhere where Urdu is well known; continuing, perhaps, from evening to dawn. Some allege that the subject matter is overly jām and saki – the wine cup and its bearer—perhaps a loved one. A similar gathering of Hindi poets is known as a kavi **sammelan**.

Nazam: a poem, from Arabic.

MUSK *n*
This English word for the perfume base once exported from India in large quantities comes, through Latin, from the **Sanskrit** mushka – a scrotum. Musk is the dried and powdered contents of a gland, having, perhaps, the appearance of a scrotum, a small pouch found below the abdominal skin with a duct to the exterior close to the genitals of the male musk deer. The scent from this has remarkable powers of diffusion, even when diluted to the extent of 1:3000. Its purpose to the animal is probably to mark territory. There is a folk belief, quite unproven, particularly strongly held in Japan, that musk is a powerful aphrodisiac. The home of the small animal is the Himalayan tree-line and into Central Asia as far as Siberia. Commercially, it has been exploited for its pod almost to extinction in the wild state, but there are musk farms in China having the technique of extracting the scent without killing and in India also a beginning has been made on similar lines by the forest

departments of Himachal Pradesh and Uttaranchal. Although hornless, the musk deer is extraordinary in having two elongated tusks.

In today's Hindi, musk is known as kasturi: with a use more in ayurvedic medicine than for perfume, but the Sanskrit metaphor continues as the Hindustani word for the brown leather pouch-like bags used for hauling water from a well and as carried by the **bihisti**, mushak. (Kasturika, Sanskrit for musk, passed to Greek as kastur and thence to zoology as castor, the scientific name for the beaver genus, rodents with anal perfume glands.)

Musk melon: so called from its tawny wrinkled skin. Kharbuja in Urdu: originally from the region of Iran and Afghanistan. Sown in winter in specially manured (compost) trenches and pits in the dry sandy river beds of northern India, with the juicy fruit harvested between April and June before the **monsoon** rise of the water. The seed kernels, dried and crushed, have a use in **masalas** and sweets, particularly **ladoos**.

Musk shrew: or ground shrew: Sometimes musk-rat in English, but the grey furred animal is no rat but an insectivore, a cousin to the mole. Chuchunder in Hindi, the vehicle of Lord **Ganesh**. The word, musk, follows from two scent glands: these long snouted animals are rarely welcome in a home, but they do serve the useful purpose of eating cockroaches and other insects and are hostile to rats.

MUTTON *n* English
Within the subcontinent, goat-meat is reckoned as mutton. (Sheep and goats, of course, share common ancestors: today, in the high Himalayan wild state the distinctions are largely of behaviour and habitat. Even taxonomists sometimes disagree as to whether a particular sub-species, such as the bharal or blue sheep, should be ovis or capra.)

As a dish, true mutton is bhera/ bhed.

MYNAH *n* Hindi
The south Asian starling. A family of pigeon-sized birds, vivacious and closely associated with man over all India. Often kept as pets (one variety is adept at mimicking the human voice). Brown in colour with yellow beaks. White patches on the wings. Omnivorous. In hot weather beaks can remain open.

MYTHOLOGICAL *n*
Indian English for a film dramatising a **Hindu** religious story: often a tale from the **Puranas**. Also known as a dharmic film (*see* Dharma).

NĀG *n* Hindi from Sanskrit
A venomous snake, particularly a cobra. The English name is from Portuguese, Cobra capella, a snake with a hood.

Nagini: a female Cobra.

NAGAR *n* Hindi
Town or Suburb.

Nagar Palika: the Municipal Committee of a small town. (Lit., palika means a feminine guardian: see Gopi and Kubera. The feminine form is required because as a noun, nagar is of the feminine gender.)

Nagar Mahapalika: Municipal Committee of a large town, not being a city.

Nagar Nigam: City Corporation.

Nagara: large kettle-drum.

Nagari/Nagri: See Sanskrit.

Nagrik: a citizen, a townsman.

The common word in north India for an old thickly populated city area is the Urdu from Persian, shahr.

NAHARI/NAHARARI *n* Urdu
An Islamic way of meat preparation, including chicken. The slow simmering, perhaps for the whole night, so that the meat just melts in the mouth. Particularly served as a breakfast dish (nahar in Persian, morning).

NAI *n* Urdu
A barber. Sometimes in village society accorded the honorific of Raja: the reason given is that only a raja can touch another man's head with  impunity. But in spite of the title, a **caste Hindu** will usually bathe following a haircut in order to remove any possible pollution from the hands of a dalit. In northern Indian village life, the barber and his wife (the nayan), at least for **brahman** families, are the traditional marriage brokers. For townsmen, newspaper advertisements perform the same service for all. The nai will assist with manicure and pedicure.

The Muslim nai (sometimes the hajjam), like the barber-surgeons of England, performs minor operations and is the traditional circumciser. To the British soldier, the barber was the nappy, probably adopted from an alternative word, from Sanskrit narpit.

As a colloquialism or banter, nai can be applied to someone alleged to be not very bright, or is thought to be not very competent at his job.

Nai/naya (Hindi): new.

Italian (Eetalian) Saloon: a term of Delhi's English speaking clerkdom. A roadside barber for whom the client may have to squat on a couple of bricks (iit in Hindi).

NAIB *n* Urdu
A deputy.

Naib Subedar: see Junior Commissioned Officers. *See also* Nawab.

NAIK/NAIYAK/NAYIK *n* Hindi
Lit. leader, hero. Military and police rank equivalent to corporal. Similarly, Lance-Naik. (In some police forces, a corporal's stripes carry the designation of Acting Head Constable.)

Hero of a story, or of a stage or film drama.

Usually in the **Sanskrit** forms, nayaka and nayika, the hero and heroine of a love poem or painting. Nayika may also refer to a skilled courtesan or procuress.

Marathi family name (spelling –

Nayak): originally a district official with the charge of ten villages.

Khalnaik - Villain

NAIR/NAYAR *n*
Member of the traditionally matrilineal (under the **Hindu Code**, matrilineal inheritance is not recognised), martial and one-time ruling racial group of what is now the state of Kerala (*see* Zamorin). Those whose family name is Menon are also of the group. Despite the present high status, it is often said that the Nairs have a **shudra** origin. The Nairs of **Malabar** must not be confused with the Nayar/Nayyars of the Punjab.

NAKHRAS *n* Urdu from Persian.
Bad manners, an air of affectation, disdain, also flirtation, pretention.

NALA/NULLA/NULLAH *n*
Urdu form of the Hindi word nadi, a stream, a small dry valley, an open drain. Nala can also mean a river, but the more usual Urdu word for a major waterway is darya from Persian.

Ganda nala: a polluted stream or foul water drain.

Often heard in north India, particularly for a man-made canal, is an Arabic word for a stream or waterway, nahr/nehar.Jawaharlal Nehru claimed that when his Kashmiri ancestors, the Kauls, (in Sanskrit, kaul–of noble birth), first came to Delhi in the service of the **Mogul** emperors (*see* Kotwali), their mansion was close to the Yamuna canal: it followed that they were known as the Nehar Kauls, later Kaul was dropped and Nehar became Nehru. (It has been pointed out that some Kauls who have never left Kashmir, also carry the name Nehru.)

NALANDA

The great university seat of Buddhist learning in Bihar. Buddhist history dates its foundation to the 3rd. century BC., but no archeological relics have been found of earlier than the 5th. century AD. It was extinguished with wholesale butchery and destruction as the result of the Muslim conquest in the 13th century AD.

NĀMA *n* Urdu

A suffix meaning a document; a report: a book, particularly a history or biography. For example, *Baburnama* – the Book of Babur. The emperor's autobiography and chronicle composed between 1528 and his death in 1530. Far more than merely a list of battles, the Baburnama is also a vivid natural history of the times. Illustrations for the book were commissioned later by Babur's grandson, Akbar. Akbar also produced his own autobiography, the *Akbarama*, with illustrations of the chase, of war and of building construction in full colour and of a liveliness matched by today's strip cartoons.

Namah (Hindi): *see* Namaskar.

NAMAK/NIMAK *n* Urdu

Salt.As with salt in Latin so namak can carry the meaning of one's livlihood.

Namak andolan: salt struggle. Name of **Mahatma** Gandhi's political march to the coast and the making of a symbolic quantity of untaxed salt from sea water. Also the all-India agitation that followed. *See* Dandi.

*Namak **halal**:* grateful, loyal.

*Namak **haram**:* ungrateful, disloyal, A traitor – one not true to his salt.

Namkin/Nimkin: saltish, tasty. (Of a person, beautiful, sexually attractive. An alternative common street word of similar meaning with reference to males is chikna, smooth, glossy. An English word could be dishy.) As a noun, namkin can mean the small nibbles, mostly salted, nuts, flour products and roasted foodgrains (also termed bhujiya); perhaps served with drinks or tea: in Britain sold under the name 'Bombay mix.'

A word for salt less often used is khara: as the Old Delhi market area, Khari **Baoli** (the brackish well).

Namak halal : As in English, faithful to one's salt.

NAMASKAR/NAMASTE *n'*
Hindi
From Sanskrit.

Words of salutation (namah: a salutation, a deferential bowing down. Kar, an action. Namaste – I bow to thee), spoken in both greeting and leave taking, to a single person  or to a group. Usually accompanied by the gesture of the hands, palms and finger-tips together, in an attitude of prayer: or with the fingers slightly arched, evoking the image of a **lotus** bud. Without words, the gesture alone is one of submission, of deference, used in an approach to God, or a salutation, or to indicate contrition and submission to authority and for calming wrath; or to render more polite a refusal of a pressed invitation. Technically, the namaskar is a samyukt mudra, a gesture using two hands: if an offering is made, perhaps a flower or petals enclosed within the slightly cupped fingers, then the name. may be anjali mudra, an act of homage to God, particularly Lord **Vishnu**. (Anjali, Sanskrit a cavity, cupped.) To indicate extremely profound feeling, the gesture may be made not at chest level but with the fingers touching the forehead, perhaps three times. At a Hindu cremation the gesture alone, without words may be offered to the body.

In Hindu tradition, a **shudra** is required to greet his superiors by bowing forward and offering the gesture of namaste. *See also* Pranam.

In the far north-western corner of India, in Ladakh, the local salutation also means a bowing down, jullay/jolay. (The tongue is Ladakhi and not, as often claimed, Tibetan.) Some aver that shaking hands is a western custom and should be discouraged, but the touching of hands between males has always been a village greeting: the stage direction of salutation "they touch hands" can be found in old Sanskrit dramas.

NAMĀZ/NAMAAZ *n* Urdu
From Persian. The word is linked to the Hindi nama, a bowing down; *see* Namaskar. In Arabic, the term is salāt. The ceremonial prayers a devout Muslim will offer five times daily: at dawn, midday, afternoon, sunset and at night. If possible, congregationally in a mosque, otherwise, in a quiet and clean area at his place of work, in the street, or wherever he may be at the due time. If there are three or more together, one should be in front to lead as **imam**. The namaz requires thirteen body positions, from standing erect facing the kiblah, Mecca, *(see* Mihrab) with the thumbs to the ear-lobes, fingers extended, palms to the front, to kneeling with the nose and forehead touching the ground: ritual phrases in Arabic have to be recited for each. Although not forbidden by canon law, women do not pray in public, neither in a mosque nor elsewhere.

Namazi: one who offers namaz regularly: a strict Muslim.

NAMBŪDIRI/NAMBOODIRIP-AD

A **Hindu** community in Kerala said to be **Aryan** (seeArya.) in origin and not **Dravidian**, whose **brahmans** are believed to have retained knowledge of ancient Vedic rituals forgotten in other parts of India and receive on this account considerable respect; there are northern temples which by tradition over the centuries are served only by Nambudiri priests.

NAMDA/NUMDAH *n* Urdu

Woollen felt cloth. In antiquity it was probably the nomads of Central Asia who first discovered the property that wet animal hairs when pounded and rolled, shrink and lock into each other to form a solid and almost waterproof fabric, suitable even for tentage (e.g., the yurt).

Namda cloth is used for rugs (usually embroidered) and in some rural areas, for weather-proof capes, for saddlecloths –and in multi-layer form, for saddles themselves. (In Britain, namda has changed into namah, and become the horse-tack expression for any cloth intended for use below a saddle.)

Namdagar: the maker of namda cloth.

NAMDHĀRI SIKHS

Three Punjab-based sects have somewhat similar names and are often confused. These are:

1.*Namdhari Sikhs*: a puritanical and vegetarian sect of Sikhism, having little contact with the parent body: members are distinguished by white turbans (*see* Puggri) worn flat against the forehead. Well known in former days for being firmly and aggressively against cow-slaughter by Muslims. Also known as kukas, since Namdharis are said to kuk (shriek) in spiritual frenzy when singing hymns: the sect is noted for its mass – and therefore economical – wedding ceremonies. A centre for Namdharis is the town of Mandi, in Himachal Pradesh.

2. *Nirankaris*: members of the Nirankari Mission, or **Mandal Sant**, founded in 1929, who believe in a Nirankar (formless Supreme Being. All Sikhs, of course, accept a nirankari deity: i.e., unlike the Gods of Hinduism, one that cannot be represented in stone or in any material way) but at the same time retain their own faiths, be they **Hindu**, Muslim, Sikh or any other. The Mission has no formal ritual, dogma or scripture: readings may be from the texts of any religion and there are no prohibitions in the matter of food or drink. One Nirankar will address another as **Sant** (spiritual being) with the greeting 'Dhan Nirankar' (Glory to Nirankar) and two great congregations, known as Sant Samagam (union of Saints: Samagam is a linked word to **sangam**) have been held annually in Delhi. The Mission claims over six

million followers, .with fifteen per cent living outside India.

3. *Nirankari Sikhs:* also known as *Nirankari Darbar* (*see* Durbar): a sect of Sikhism founded in the later years of the 19th century at Rawalpindi by one Dyal Das. Whereas orthodox Sikhs consider **Guru** Gobind Singh to have been the final Guru (save for the Guru Granth Sahib), the Nirankars address their leader as Sat Guru (True Guru). Some of the leaders of both the Nirankari Mission and the Nirankari Sikhs have the outward appearance of Sikhs and apparently are accepted as living Sikh Gurus by many of their followers: it is on this account that orthodox Sikhism from time to time clashes with the sects.

A further sect on the fringe of Sikhism is the Radha Soami Satsang Beas: Radha Soami meaning Lord of the Soul, a name chosen by the founder (Shiv Dayal Singh, born in 1818) for the Supreme Being, the godhead within mankind. Radha Soamis revere the scriptures of all religions, but particularly honour the Adi Granth (*see* Guru Granth Sahib). They are enjoined to be vegetarian and to touch no alcohol. The **dera** (encampment), as the Satsangh (*see* Sangh) call their headquarters, is a prosperous and permanent colony on the Beas river, not far from Amritsar.

NAME *n* English
Naman in **Sanskrit**, in Hindi, nām.

The vocable in some form is in almost all the Indo-European languages with the same meaning as in English.

NĀN/NAAN *n* Urdu
A leavened bread brought to India by the Muslims. White flour (maida) kneaded to a dough with curds (*see* Dahi) and allowed to stand until slightly fermented. The nan served in Moglai style eating houses is pear-shaped and sometimes seasoned, rather than circular as a **chapati**. Cooked in a **tandoor** it is intended to be eaten straight from the fire. Bakeries make nan in the shape and appearance of a bun, to be taken home. Another Muslim bread, also from Iran, is the kulcha (so-called in restaurants: a more phonetic spelling of the Urdu term would be kulche). Very similar in material and texture to the nan, but usually circular and without a garnish of poppy seeds.

Nanbai: the breadmaker.

NANDI/NANDIN *n*
Lit. the happy one. The name of a white bull. Lord Shiva's vehicle (*see* Vahan and Bhairavi), attendant and dwārpāl (door-keeper, see Kubera). Still a door-keeper, Nandi can often be seen at the threshold of a Shiv-mandir (Shiva temple), a kneeling sculptured bull sometimes larger than life-size, facing the **lingam**. Also nandi is the age-old invocation sung to a deity, particularly to Shiva

as Lord of the Dance (*see* Nataraj), seeking blessings before beginning a stage drama.

A grain trading community of Bengal.

NAR/NARI *n* Hindi from Sanskrit Man: woman. Words mostly used in a Hindu spiritual or cultural context. In everyday Hindustani, in north India, the words will be admi/aurat. (Admi is Urdu derived from Hebrew and Arabic, the name of the notional first man of the world of Judaism, Christianity and Islam). In Arabic, aurat has the meaning of a woman's due decoram, modesty, in dress and bearing. A less commonly used word for a woman in north India from Sanskrit, is stree/stri

Streeva: Womanhood, feminity. Streeshakt: woman power.

NARĀNGI *n* Urdu

A general term for the many varieties of the orange tree and fruit. From the original Persian via Arabic the source of the English name.

A recent introduction from California is the kinoo orange. Thick skinned but easily peeled and full of juice. In northern Indian winter, relatively cheaper than other oranges, since it grows well in the region.

Very popular is the santara, a small juice-filled loose-skinned orange, the tangerine, the mandarin. (The latter name is an anglicism from the loose yellow robes of a Chinese mandarin: see Mantri.) See Vidarba.

NARK *n*

This English slang word (and, using rhyming slang, its extension, nosey parker) meaning an informer, a police spy, one who 'noses' his way into another's business, derives, via Romany, from the **Sanskrit** nak/naak, the nose. (The noun – but not the English slang meaning – is the same in today's Hindi.)

NĀSBANDI *n* Hindi

Lit. closing a vein or duct in the body. Vasectomy: sterilisation of the male or female by cutting or tying the two vas deferens or the fallopian tubes. Not to be confused with nashabandi/nashbandi (closing drunkeness): prohibition.

NĀTAK *n* Hindi
Acting: the drama.

Natak Akademi: see Akademi.

Nautanki: strictly, one who takes part in a natak, an actor. But usually a reference to the theatre of travelling groups of players, often of **Banjara** origin, who, in village fairs – and sometimes on city streets – stage popular stories from **Hindu** mythology and of **rajas** and their conquests.

Nats: again, groups of itinerant players, dancers and acrobats, mostly performing in rural areas.

NĀTH *n* Hindi Lord, master, protector, husband. A frequently used suffix.

Nath: a nose ring, a jewel for a woman, of steel for a bullock.

NATIONAL HIGHWAY

Trunk road, built to central government specifications and partly paid for by the centre: the term is often abbreviated to NH (in Hindi, **Rashtra Marg**). The classification followed from the Nagpur Roads Conference of 1943, but the concept is at least as old as the **Mauryan** period (4th century BC), when specifications of royal, military and chariot roads were issued. The **Moguls** too had their state highways: *see* GT Road. The longest National highway is said to be No. 7, from Kanya Kumari (*See* Kumar) to **Varanasi**, (2338 km). From the precedent of the NH, India also has NW - National Waterways, stretches of navigable rivers, mostly on the **Ganga** and the Brahmaputra, maintained to fixed standards.

NATRAJ/NATARAJAH/ NATESA

n
Lord **Shiva** in his role as the Cosmic, or Divine, Dancer: Lord of the Dance. Worship of Shiva as Nataraj

is a cult rich in icons, so that to the world of antiques, a Nataraj means an image of the God as a dancer. Frequently a casting, either in original or a copy, of a kind made in **Tamil** Nadu of bronze since the 10th century AD (many originals from that period are still in the temples to which they were donated), depicting a four-armed Shiva in a stylised dance posture of rage with a left hand carrying fire capable of destroying the world of man (*see* Right, Hand, Left Hand) – but, simultaneously, a right hand indicates the **mudra**, or gesture, of reassurance. The dance is within a circle – or arch – of fire (prabhamandal) representing the bounds of the universe: one foot on the body of a demon dwarf.

Sometimes flames appear to be coming from the waist of a "dancing shiva" icon. These commemorate a story of south India that the devotion of a **dalit**, one Nandana, was so intense that he merged with the body of the Lord. This form of dance may be termed the tandava; the deity as **Bhairava**, the destroyer. In the south a violent frenzied dance once performed on cremation grounds. In a context away from classical dancing tandava can be a reference to any gross destruction. But in a different form, the ananda tandava is translated as the dance of eternal bliss.

NATYA/NATYAM *n* Hindi

Strictly, the classical **Hindu** theatre including music and dance drama, based on the *Natyashastra* (*see* Shastra), a treatise on stagecraft in all its aspects written in about the beginning of the Christian era. These days, except as loknatya – people's, or folk, dancing and drama – the word seems to be applied mostly to classical dancing, varying in form according to the school or centre. *See* Bharat Natyam, Kathak, Kathakali, Kuchipudi, Manipuri (*under head-words* North East India), Mudra and Oriya.

NAUTCH *n*

A dance performance. Staged dancing by women professionals (nautch girls). The word, seldom used today, is an anglicism from the Hindi naach, a dance. As a concept, the nautch was Hindustani, usually a form of **kathak**. From English writings on social life in the 18th and early 19th centuries, it appears that no wealthy Indian's entertainment for Europeans was complete without a nautch, but the guests' enjoyment as expressed to their hosts, was often politeness, for it was the rare European who could appreciate Indian music and dancing, even of the Kathak school with simple enjoyment the aim, rather than the averred spiritual uplift to the **Hindu natya**. (Nevertheless, in general, Europeans of the 18th and early decades of the 19th centuries were rather different from their suc-cessors: socially, they mixed more readily with upper class Indians, with whom many could communicate in Persian. Christianity sat lightly on their shoulders and they were ready to accept Indian culture as the custom of their hosts and had little desire to change things.)

By the 1830s, with the advent of the memsahibs and piety, Europeans tended to regard the nautch as unseemly – and sometimes, perhaps they had a point: see Dancing Girls. Senior British officials who attended nautches, even as a courteous duty, were likely to find themselves castigated in the press by the missionaries. (Nor was the then Prince of Wales, who, if nothing else, was certainly a man of the world, spared criticism after watching a suitably innocuous performance during his visit to India in 1875.)

Among the British, the word lived on to be colloquially applied to almost any musical entertainment, and in particular to a ball-room dance: a **pagal** nautch could be a fancy-dress ball.

As a term, naach has come down in the world: once covering all Indian dancing – today's names for regional styles, Bharatnatyam, **Kathakali** and so on, are of fairly recent origin it seems now to be used mostly for the somewhat crude dances staged in tents in country **melas** (fairs), but not for the classical natya performed for the elite in cities, nor even for folk or village dancing.

NAVRATNA/NAVRATHA *n* Hindi

Lit. nine jewels (pearl, diamond, coral, raby, emerald, sapphire, topaz, crystal and cow-fat – sic), which in combination are believed to possess great powers to heal disease. (Gems are associated with specific planets and are thought to contain planetary influence.)

NAVRATRI/NAURATRI *n* Hindi

Lit. nine nights. Two periods in the **Hindu** calendar of nine days and nights dedicated to the worship of the Mother Goddess, **Durga**. Periods of fasting and austerity particularly observed by women: one in the month of Chait (April) leading to the birthday of Lord **Ram** and the other preceding **Dussehra** in Asvin (September/October)

NAWĀB *n* Urdu

Strictly, the plural of **naib**, a deputy, One holding delegated authority. Originally, a governor of a province on behalf of the **Mogul** Emperor. Later, a title awarded by the emperor without necessarily territorial jurisdiction. A Muslim prince. A courtesy honorific to a major Muslim landowner.

Nawabzāda: son of a nawab.

Nawābi: the Hindustani life-style and manners of the wealthy nawabs. Often a sybarite culture which in its original form largely disappeared from India with the departure for Pakistan of its exemplars and patrons at the time of Partition (*see* Independence Day). However, the major hotels like to claim that the nawabi style is reflected in their cuisines and entertainment programmes (*see* Nautch).

In architecture, nawabi is often a reference to the ornate Muslim buildings developed in the late 18th century and continuing upto the 1850s. Particularly a style favoured by the Nawabs of **Oudh**, such buildings in their full flowering can be seen in the neighbourhoods of Lucknow and Faizabad: onion-shaped fluted domes, columns, with capitals, stucco and pottery embellishments simulating the stone of an earlier age and many other purely European features probably copied from the new merchant palaces of Calcutta. An Indian baroque. Some suggest that one reason for the change was the edict by the Emperor Aurangzeb that **Hindus** should have no part in the construction of Muslim buildings.

In Europe, the Spanish and Portuguese probably first heard the word nawab from their Muslim invaders. In Portuguese it became nababe, and in turn, in 18th century English, nabob, meaning a fabulously wealthy

Eastern prince. The English then applied it to those of their countrymen who returned from the East with large fortunes. (The way these fortunes were acquired in the late 17th and 18th centuries would be hard to justify by later standards. The **East India Company**'s officials traded imports and exports on the Company's behalf and no less tended to use their privileged position and their employers' funds to trade internally, in such commodities as rice, salt and opium to their own advantage. During the period, of course, many regarded themselves primarily as merchants and had yet to evolve into solely civil service administrators.)

NAXALITES *n*
Members of a Maoist type agrarian reform movement, particularly students. The name, journalist coined, comes from a peasant uprising in 1967 against landlords near Naxalbari (the Post Office spelling is Naksalbari), a small town on the Orissa border to West Bengal and close to the Nepal frontier, in the **terai** area of Darjeeling **district**.

By early 21st century some of these peasant groups have grown beyond the control of ill-equipped state police and can became a danger to the national body politic. It has to be admitted that in some parts of rural and forest India, groups at the very bottom of the social hierachy have a lot to be unhappy about.

NAZ'R/NAZRĀNA *n* Urdu
From Arabic, meaning a vow. A present, usually of money, from an inferior to a superior. A pledge of loyalty. As described in English historical writing on India, an offering by a visitor on being received in audience by a prince: a symbolic payment of tribute, a token of submission. The custom was–not always observed–for the recipient to touch the gift and return it. The visitor might then receive a **khillat**, a robe of honour.

Today, the naz'r operates at a much lower level of society. A 'gift' say, from a **chaprasi** to his head-clerk. From a subordinate or a supplicant to a superior with a little power: all too often with an element of bribery.

NEEM/NIM *n* Hindi
A common and valued tree particularly seen in roadside avenues all over India. *Azadirachta indica.* An old English name from Portuguese is margosa. Many traditional medical benefit are attributed to its products: recently oil made from the seeds and bark has been found to be spermicidal. In the home its dried leaves are used to keep away insects from winter woollens put aside for the summer. For murals a gum from the tree may be used to bind the powdered colours with the benefit of keeping insects away. The young twigs are used as toothbrushes (datun) everywhere. Hung over doorways the leaves will inhibit

entry by evil spirits. The tree sheds its leaves in spring to be followed almost immediately by new ones and sweet smelling white flowers. With the first monsoon showers the seeds fall and germinate in the newly soft earth.

NEHRU AWARD
Jawaharlal Nehru Memorial Award for International Understanding, instituted in 1966 by the Government of India. Recipients include President Tito, Dr. Martin Luther King, Yehudi Menuhin, Olaf Palme, Nelson Mandela and Indira Gandhi.

NEO-BUDDHISTS *n*
A reference to those members of the Scheduled Castes (*see* Dalit) who, in 1956 and later, following the example of their leader. Dr. B.R. Ambedkar, renounced Hinduism and adopted Buddhism with its casteless ideals as their religion. In practice, at least with the present generation, many of their previous social disabilities are still the lot of the neo-Buddhists.

Fifty years later, it seems that those once at the bottom of the social scale who have risen economically and educationally, prefer to adopt caste Hindu customs. See Sanskritisation.

NETAJI *n* Hindi
Neta, a leader, a guide, Plus **ji**. Frequently, a specific reference to Subhash Chandra Bose: a prominent fighter for India's freedom from British rule. Said he "Give me blood, and I will give you freedom". Evading surveillance by the Calcutta police, he escaped from India during World War II and in a series of remarkable journeys travelled to Japan: first overland to Germany, then by submarine to an Indian Ocean rendezvous with a Japanese submarine which took him to Sumatra, thence by air to Tokyo. There he became President of Azaad Hind (Free India) **Sarkar**, a government set up in Japanese-occupied South East Asia. *See also* Azaad Hind Fauj.

(Most certainly not in the case of Subhash Chandra Bose, whose memory is greatly respected, but the term neta, especially when applied to a politician, or political worker, can contain an element of irony as in the word netashahi - rule by a neta. One who considers himself above the laws that apply to ordinary people).

NEWĀRS *n*
The original inhabitants of the Kathmandu Valley. Many of them are the skilled craftsmen of Nepal.

Newar as cotton webbing: *see* Charpai.

NIGAM *n* Hindi
The **Vedas**. A city corporation (**nagar** nigam): a commercial or industrial corporation. A **kayasth** sub-caste name.

NIHANG *n* Hindi
A member of a **Sikh** military order
raised by Guru Hargobind in the
early 17th century firmly dedicated
to the faith. The name means naked,
i.e. without ties of property or family.
(The **Moguls** also had elite fighting
groups of the same name and wearing blue, in their case the word was
from Persian, meaning crocodile.)
Although representing no territory,
the Nihangs were accepted as one
of the misls, or foundation military
groups, largely cavalry, of the Sikh
state at Lahore in 1764. Thereafter,
the Nihangs supplied units of fanati-
cal fighters for the **Khalsa** armies.
Always a little larger than life and
accepting no authority other than
their own, the Nihangs sometimes
term themselves sawalakhs (1.25
lakh), a boast that one Nihang is
the equivalent of 1,25,000 other men
but at least this is not necessarily
personal braggadocio, for throughout
Sikhism it is a folk belief that a man
completely imbued with the spirit of
Guru Gobind Singh has the strength
of 'sawa lakh'. Another name, self-
given, is the Chheyanvi Kirori, a
claim that the total strength of their
force is ninety-six **crores** (960 million). Other names are the Shaheedan
(*see* Shaheed) martyrs, so called
because of their numbers killed by
the Emperor Aurangzeb. The Buddha
Dal (the veterans) and a junior wing,
the Tarang Dal (the youngsters), are
little heard of. Until the 1920s, the
Nihangs were often called **Akalis**,
but these days, an Akali is more
likely to be a member of the Akali
Dal (*see* Gurdwara), with whom the
Nihangs are ill at ease.

Today, still wearing long blue and
orange-yellow tunics and tall blue
puggris containing two or more steel
throwing quoits, probably also armed
with a polished spear and shield,
a few may be seen guarding Sikh
shrines, ensuring that visitors observe
decorum of dress and behaviour. Others follow traditional ways and wan-
der over northern India in groups on
foot and on ponies. Quixotic figures
hung about with ancient weapons,
quick to appear at any spot where
Sikh interests are believed to have
been affronted. But the fact remains
that many respectable Sikhs allege
that the Nihangs are too addicted
to intoxicants to be accepted as a
exemplars of Sikh faith and morals.
Annually, on the day after **Holi**, the
Nihangs gather at Anandpur in the
Punjab **Sivaliks**, the birthplace of
the Khalsa.

NĪKETAN *n* Hindi
A residence, an abode. A residential
area: (a modern urban Indian-English
equivalent for this last meaning could
be colony).

A Home, as in a children's or old
people's Home.

NILGAI *n* Hindi
Lit. blue cow, but referred to in

English as the blue bull. (In northern India especially in Haryana and Punjab, the name may be rojh.) A large horse-like animal, the male of grey colour with a distinctive tuft of blackish hair on the throat: closely connected to the antelope, but separate in that the horns are not ringed. A creature of scrub jungles and open plains, unique to the sub-continent. Once very common, now less so, but protected to some extent by village belief that the animal is a relative of the cow. (The villagers have a point, for as a hollow-horned antelope and not a deer, the nilgai is of the bovine family.) The protection is not absolute, for in areas where nilgai are plentiful and cause damage to crops, the **shikari** may find himself by no means unwelcome.

NIMĀNTRAN *n* Hindi
An invitation, a summons: often printed on the envelope containing an invitation card to a wedding or other function. An invitation to a high society wedding may be accompanied by a small but expensive gift.

NIMBU *n* Hindi
An Austric-Munda word (see Dravidia, Greater India) from pre-history. Used over all India for the fruit of the small lime. Some prefer the form from Punjabi, nibu.

Nimbu pani (lime water): originally an anglicism, but now, like soda, a generally acceptable Hindustani term

for a drink of nimbu juice in, usually, sweetened water or soda: the more correct northern word is shikanji/shikanjabin (lit. squeezed), or the phrase 'nibu ka sharbat'. *See* Sherbet.

Some believe that a nimbu and a hari mirch (green chilli) suspended on a string over a doorway will keep away the evil eye. *See* Toran

NIRMAL HRIDAY *n* Hindi
Pure heart. The name adopted for the homes for sick destitutes run by Mother Teresa's Missionaries of Charity in various cities of India.

NIRMĀN *n* Hindi from Sanskrit
Building construction work, a building development in a creative way.

NIRŌDH *n* Hindi
Suppression (particularly of sensual pleasure). An obstruction: a stopper, in Bengali, a cloud. Trade name for the government supplied contraceptive condom and by extension, a name for all contraceptive sheaths.

NIRVĀNA/NIRVĀN *n* Hindi
Lit. extinction: as a candle flame is blown out to leave no trace. For **Hindus**, Jains, and Buddhists, the ideal state of spiritual revelation, bliss and liberation from all earthly desires and ties: to be reached largely through **tapasya**. A release from the cycle of rebirths; normally associated

with death – but not always: Lord Mahavira (*see* Jainism) attained nirvana some thirty years before his physical death. Sometimes to add emphasis, final and complete liberation, the term used is parinirvan.

As a word nirvan is used mostly in connection with Buddhism and Jainism, Hindus prefer moksha, **samadhi** or **mukti** for a similar condition. *See also* Buddha.

NIVĀS/NIVAAS *n* Hindi
A residence, usually a fairly substantial building. Nivasi: a resident. An inhabitant, as of a mansion or a city.

Raj Nivas: state house. A name, alternative to **Raj Bhavan** for the official residence of a state governor, or perhaps, an official guest house.

NIZĀM *n* Urdu
In a **Mogul** government, one of two high officials of state, the administrator of law and order and criminal justice. The other was the **Diwan**, the administrator of revenue and civil justice. The early British in the 1770s termed the **East India Company**'s chief court of criminal justice, the Nizamat Adālat.

Part of the title of the Subedar of the **Deccan**, Asaf Jah, of Turkoman origin, appointed by the Mogul emperor in about 1713, Nizam-ul-Mulk (Administrator of the Country). In the fashion of the time, Asaf Jah later became independent of his master and his title was claimed as hereditary by his dynastic successors, Shia Muslims rulers of the **princely** state of Hyderabad (also known as The Nizam's Dominions until 1948). *See also* AP.

Nizam-e-Mustafa: see Islam.

NORTH-EAST INDIA
Since **Independence**, a number of states have been created in the mountainous north-eastern corner of India.

Arunachal Pradesh: formerly North East Frontier Agency (NEFA). A union territory bordering **Burma** and China with its capital at Itanagar. Arun, a now largely forgotten charioteer of the sun and God of the dawn, gives his name to the state (also in Hindi to the colour ruddy red), for the reason that, of all India, the rising sun is first seen there.

Manipur: earlier a **princely** state of the same name: capital at Imphal.

Manipuri – of Manipur: as used outside the state, frequently a reference to the dance style which originated with the tribes of the area. Regional language of the state.

Meghalaya: lit. home of clouds. Formed from the Khasi and Garo Hills area of Assam. Capital at Shillong:

Mizoram: before achieving statehood in 1987 the Lushai Hills District, a central government territory.

Nagaland: previously the Naga Hills area of Assam: capital at Kohima. A popular local term for the region, perhaps rather larger than the state of today, is Nagalima.

Tripura: the smallest state in India, previously a princely state: capital at Agartala.

Assam: the name of the largest state of the region, is increasingly reverting both in pronunciation and roman spelling to an earlier form, Asom – some prefer to say Ashom. The word derives from the Ahom Kings.

NŌSH *n*

This slang English food and drink word (from Yiddish) has the same meanings in Urdu (pronounced with the 'o' long, from Persian): nosh khana – to eat or drink.

NUH *n* Urdu

Islamic form of Noah. Small town some 80 km south-west of Delhi.

Toofan-i-Nuh: Noah's storm (the Flood) see Kitab.

NUMBER TWO *n*

A colloquialism for the irregular, or illegal, side of things. (the strictly legal 'all permits obtained, all taxes paid' aspects being Number One). Contraband goods or a person, or an illegal activity connected with them, may be described as Number Two. A contempt for the edicts of bureaucracy rather than physical mayhem is the mark of a Number Two man. Similar in meaning is the Hindi expression 'hera pheri'.

NUMBER TEN *n*

A reference to a person as a 'Number Ten' (das nambar admi), is an implication that he has a police record. From Section 110 of the Code of Criminal Procedure (*see* Cr. P.C.) 1898 (superseded by the Code of 1973) authorising senior police officers to obtain recognizances for good behaviour from well-known bad characters in their areas. Persons with a police record may be known as 'history-sheeters'.

355

OCTROI English and French
Municipal tax on the entry of goods
into a town. Locally known as
chungi-pathkar and toll tax. (Pathkar
can also be a head-tax on travellers).
Although still levied by most local
authorities, octroi is recognised as
a relic from the bullock cart age,
incompatible with the speedy road
transport of goods.

ŌM/AUM Hindi
A **mantra**: a mystic
syllable (or three
syllables) represent-
ing, some believe,
the glory of the sun,

also Lord **Vishnu**. *See* Har. Others
will say the sound represents the
Brahmana, the eternal creative force
which made the universe.

Says **Manu**, "**Prajapati** milked from
the three **Vedas**, the letter Ah, also the
letter Uh, and the letter Ma... All the
Vedic rites oblational and sacrificial,
pass away, but this imperishable syllable 0m is to be known as **Brahma**
and also Prajapat". This sacred sound
for the Supreme Being, lying close to

the core of Hinduism, is frequently
uttered as an invocation to God. (Of
the one thousand names for God
– sahasranama– that of Om is said to
be pre-eminent). As a formal mantra
in worship, some declare that its
resonance should be continued for
at least ten seconds: ah and uh, one
second each and then the ma sound
vibrating to silence for eight seconds.
It is said that the force behind the
voice should start from the region of
the navel (seemingly with no connection, is an English word for the navel
from Greek, omphalos). A longer
Vedic invocation is the mantra 'Hari
0m, Tat Sat' (probably mostly uttered
for the pleasure of its mystic sounds,
it could be translated as 'Oh God,
Thou Art Truth': but tat – that – can
represent the power of **Brahma**).
Written as a single **Devnagri** character, phonetically a long *u*, and over,
the chandra bindu, the moon spot,
a crescent moon lying on its back,
adding a nasal 'm' sound (under some
circumstances, the chandra bindu
imparts not ma but na), the symbol
for 0m can be seen on buildings and
is often placed at the head of a literary work, in the way Christian monks
began their manuscripts '*Laus Deo*'
and Muslims with the **Bismillah**.

Om mani padma hum (Sanskrit): the
tantric six syllables, the most common and the most sacred invocation
of Tibetan Buddhism. Said to have
been first uttered as a mantra by the
Bodhisattva (*see* Buddha) Avalok-

iteshvara (also known as the Buddha of compassion). Invariably translated as '...the jewel within the lotus' – mani has the meaning of precious stone. An esoteric interpretation of the mantra is that of the **lingam** in the **yoni**.

Om Prakash: a popular male personal name, the Light of the Vedas, or the Light of God.

Onkar/Omkar: a noun meaning the 0m mantra. Lit. the enunciation of 0m; the 0m sound.

Onkar: By Sikhs, an annunciation of their faith, Ek Onkar – One God.

Om Jai Jagdish Hare: opening words of a very popular invocatory bhajan (see Kirtan) sung as **arati**., Non-secretarian (Jagdish can be the deity of any faith), the line has been translated as O Lord of the Universe."

ONAM *n* Malayalam
The great annual festival of Kerala, celebrating the home-coming of the harvest, falling in August or September. Particularly famous are the snake boat (long canoe-like vessels, low in the bow and high in the stern, with up to one hundred paddlers) races on rivers and coastal backwaters. Also frequent during the period are **Kathakali** dances.

'ONE PEN'
A request – and sometimes even a demand – often made in English to foreigners at tourist spots by small children. Possibly a folk memory of the 1961 visit to India by the then Vice-President of the USA, Lyndon Johnson, who, as on a campaign tour, generously handed out ball-pens stamped with his name.

OPAL *n*
This gem word reached English via Latin, but its origin is the **Sanskrit** upal – a jewel stone.

OPHIR *n*
"Quinquireme of Nineveh from distant Ophir rowing home to haven in sunny Palestine, with a cargo of ivory, And apes and peacocks, Sandalwood, Cedarwood, and sweet white wine". John Masefield 1902.

(The poet has used a little licence here; the normal navigation route for goods would have been to the Gulf or a Red Sea port and then overland to the Mediterranean.)

A name in the ancient world of Greece and Rome for the source of the riches of India and popular with poets ever since. Some scholars aver that Ophir was an entreport in the Persian Gulf or in South Arabia. A modern opinion identifies it with the port later known as Sopara on the Maharashtra coast north of **Mumbai** and close to the abandoned Portuguese fortress city of Bassein.

ORCHID KINGDOM

An epithet for a natural home of orchids in India, the state of Sikkim: there are said to be more than twelve local varieties of Cymbidium alone.

ORIYA *n* and *adj* Hindi

The people and regional language with its own script of the state of Orissa; as a province of **British India** created in 1936 from the Oriya-speaking districts of the conjoint Bihar-Orissa province, itself a 1912 division from Bengal. Similarly, Odissi, but this word particularly applies to the form of **Hindu** classical dancing developed there originally, perhaps, in worship of Lord **Jagannath**. Today, the dance is performed by both men and women, often to verses from the **Gita** Govinda.

ORPIMENT *n* English

From the Latin, auripigmentum – gold colour. A metallic ore, arsenical trisulphide with about 60 per cent arsenic: also termed king's yellow and, from Arabic, realgar. (Strictly, realgar is an arsenical sulphide with a more reddish tinge than orpiment, it is also less toxic). Before chemical dyes, a source of gold and yellow colours for artists. Mixed with **indigo**, a brilliant green is obtained. In India, found in the neighbourhood of volcanic phenomena such as hot springs. Once used for colouring wall-paper and, perhaps, a source

of arsenic poisoning, but the story that Napoleon on St. Helena died from it, is now thought to be untrue. Orpiment is sold in the **bazaars** under the name **hartal** (from **Sanskrit**, harital – golden material – *see* Har) and as a depilatory. It has a role in minute quantities in homeopathy. An alternative name is murdasankh.

India yellow: Also sometimes referred to in India as orpiment, is the pigment known to European art restorers as India yellow: to a chemist it is magnesium euxanthate. Its source, for at least a millenium, is cows' urine, the cows having been fed on mango leaves. An expensive medium.

OUDH/AVADH/AWADH *n*

Oudh (to rhyme with loud) is the English pronunciation of the Hindustani name, Awadh. Traditionally, that region of present day Uttar Pradesh (*see* UP) centred round Lord **Ram**'s city, Ayodhya from which the name Awadh is derived. (As a word, Ayodhya is an example of the privative a, [*see* Ahinsa.] A-yuddh – without war, i.e., never to be attacked. During part of the **Gupta** period, historians say the city had the name Saket/ Saketa.) In **Mogul** days, a separate province with its capital at Faizabad, close to Ayodhya. From 1772, the Mogul **Subedar**, the **Nawab**, a Shia (*see* Sunni) Muslim from Iran, as the central power weakened *de* *facto* became independent from Delhi and the first of a dynasty of thirteen. In 1819 the ruling Nawab formalised the position and had himself invested, using European regal robes and a crown, as Emperor and King. The British, welcoming a diminution of Delhi's status, accepted the royal pretensions, but in official documents continued to refer to the Prince as Nawab-**Wazir**, i.e. a tributary and not a sovereign. The family badge, two curved fish, became the state emblem—the fish are said by some to symbolise the two **Hindu** deified rivers of the region, the **Ganga** and the **Yamuna**. Nawab Safdarjang (1739-56), buried in New Delhi in the last of the big garden tombs (*see* Bagh), named his citadel in Lucknow, Machhi **Bhavan** (Fish House).

In mid-19th century, the **East India Company**, after decades of using Oudh as a milch cow for money and troops – the latter to be paid for by the ruler, as a cover for their long intended action, alleged the ever-accommodating ruler to be profligate and to be mismanaging his state: by then, Lucknow had become the centre of a lively Hindustani culture. The atmosphere of the period, the tragedy of the impossibility of the nawabi culture to understand let alone counter the forces against them, is brilliantly evoked in Satyajit Ray's period film, 'Shatranj Ke Khilari' – The Chess Players. The British were naturally the villains, but of them the London film critic, Dylys Powell, said to Ray, "You have put us in our place without malice or rancour". In 1856, the King was banished to Calcutta and his dominion annexed to **British India**: the last **princely** state to be so taken over. The company claimed that they had obligations to the people that transcended any guarantees to the ruler. (A century later in the same context, Indira Gandhi echoed similar obligations.) While his domestic habits were certainly not those of the court of Queen Victoria, the Nawab was possibly more in tune with his subjects than were the straitlaced and severe Britons who followed him: the Mutiny, which broke out a year later, received more popular support in Oudh than anywhere else, thus giving some substance to Disraeli's observation in the House of Commons, that the outbreak was no mere military mutiny but a national revolt. For a few months in 1857/58, in the absence of the British, the old order was restored and a younger son of the deposed King was installed as Nawab-Wazir owing allegiance to the emperor in Delhi, his mother, Hazrat Mahal acting as Begum Regent. On the British return the family took refuge in Nepal. While another heroine and opponent of the British during the Mutiny, the Rani of Jhansi, is known to almost every school child in India, little has been heard of the Begum Regent. Of her. The *London Times* published (29 November

1858) in a report from their Calcutta correspondent before the fighting had ended: "...this woman, who, like all women who have turned up in the insurrection, has more sense and nerve than all her generals put together". With peace, the Begum refused an offer from the British government of a return to India with dignity and a pension. Of the three forces concerned, the ruler of Oudh, the Mogul Emperor and the Company, none survived the mutiny.

The case of the Begums of Oudh: Possibly because of the intriguing title, perhaps the best known of the final charges – really by Edmund Burke – in the long drawn-out (1778 to 1795) proceedings of impeachment by the House of Commons in London against Warren Hastings. The Begums were the widow and sister of the second nawab, who, as Shias, had been able to retain possession of considerable wealth. In concert with the ruling nawab, Hastings, as Governor-General, was alleged in long speeches by, amongst others, Richard Sheridan the dramatist, to have obtained a **crore** of rupees for the benefit of the Calcutta

government by unlawful coercion of the Begums. Finally, after a trial in Westminster Hall in a judgement by the peers, Hastings was acquitted on all sixteen charges: although few doubted that there was substance in the allegations, legal proof was hard to obtain from India; also the extent to which English law protected non-Europeans in India was uncertain. Verdicts the other way would have been indictments against the Company itself.

For all the indictments against Warren Hastings, it was he who began the process of turning a group of merchants interested in little but commerce and loot into administrators in the interests of India, subject to distant surveillance from London.
Awadhi: the dialect of Hindi spoken by the people of Oudh.

OUSTEE
An Indian-English neologism not to be found in standard dictionaries for one ejected from a position. Ouster for the action is accepted by the *OED*, so given time and sufficient use, oustee will no doubt be equally valid.

P

PAC/P.A.C.
Public Accounts Committee of the central parliament.

In **UP**, Provincial (now Pradeshi) Armed Constabulary, a special duties police force established in British days.

PACHOULI *n* Hindi
A small shrub of the genus *Pogostemon* cultivated in the south and in Assam its leaves yield an essential oil used as a fixative for perfumes, the patchouli of world commerce.

PADDY *n* English
From a Malay word, padi. Growing rice plants: rice grains still in the husk, for which the usual Hindi word is dhan. (Note that dhan has the meaning of wealth, property). Unhusked rice is used extensively, especially in eastern India, in **Hindu** religious ceremonies; symbolising, perhaps, plenty and nature's bounty: no doubt, the English custom of throwing rice at a wedding can be shown to be linked. In Bengal an expression has it that the food grain on a devotee's plate can be piled so high that not even a cat can jump over it.

Paddy bird: European name for a whiteish bird of marshy land and flooded paddy fields. For many, the two egrets are paddy birds. Dr. Salim Ali, the ornithologist, gave the epithet to the pond heron: a small bird, brown when standing hunched over water, but flashing white wings and tail when in flight.

Paddy-field: land carrying a rice crop, at times covered with water.

PĀDRI *n* Hindustani
A Christian priest or male missionary of any denomination. Originally from the Latin languages, the word probably entered India with the Portuguese as padre, father. Adopted by the British army as colloquially applicable to any military chaplain.

PAGAL/PAGLA *n* and *adj* Hindi
Insane, mentally retarded, a madman.

Pagal Khana: mental hospital.

Pagal Gymkhana: sports meeting with a touch of comedy, e.g., donkey and slow cycle races. *See also* Gymkhana.

PAGŌDA *n* English
European name in India for a specific type of small gold coin (half and

quarter pagodas were in silver) bearing a **Hindu** symbol; used by many rulers–even Muslim and Christian from many mints in the south from the 14th until mid-19th century AD. Pagodas struck by an **East India Company** mint in the first years of the 19th century, on one side carried the devices of a temple **gopuram** and a star. A story has it that the name pagoda was thereafter applied in English to all temples, Hindu, Buddhist and even Muslim. It is of course an English term for Buddhist buildings in **Myanmar**, China, Sri Lanka etc., such as the shrines with multi-tiered roofs developed from the simple **stupa** containing sacred relics: the word is seldom used in India today. But the fact is that the pagoda in English dates from the 16th century, at least two hundred years before the star pagoda coin. The word possibly came to English via Portuguese from dagoba, Sinhalese (*see* Singh) for a Buddhist religious building.

The exchange value of the pagoda could vary with the cost of bullion, where it had been minted and whether it was new or worn (i.e. weight). When the coin was withdrawn, in 1818, the official exchange was 100 pagodas to 43 silver Madras fanams or 350 new silver rupees.

Pagoda tree/temple tree: English names somewhat indiscriminately given to several trees of the latex-bearing *Plumeria* family often seen growing close to temples in south India – the plenitude of white flowers is no doubt useful for ceremonies – and in gardens everywhere. The tree is also called the frangipani (but to some, the true frangipani is a variety in which the flowers are red and not the usual white with a golden centre): in spite of the Indian sound, the tree is Central American and is said to have been named after the Marquise Frangepane, an Italian major-general in the French pre-revolution army who created a perfume from the flowers in the West Indies. In today's India, perfume is made from the flowers under such names as champa, champak, chameli and even jasmine (*see* Yasmin).

To shake the pagoda tree: an old European expression based on a pretence that gold pagodas grew on the tree, meaning to make money in India and probably without excessive attention to the morality of the means.

PAHĀRI/PAHĀDI *n* and *adj*
Hindi
Pahar – a mountain. Pertaining to hills or mountains, usually the **Himalaya**. A hillman. (When referring to a hillman from other than the northern ranges, the word girijan is often used – *see* Giri.)

A dialect of Hindi spoken in Himachal Pradesh and the hill districts of **Uttaranchal**.

Pahari painting: distinctive styles of miniature painting, largely representations of the Radha-**Krishna** story inspired by the poem **Gita Govinda**, which flourished under the patronage of a number of rajahs from about thirty minor states during the 18th century, in areas now part of Himachal Pradesh and particularly in Basohli, a small state near Jammu. Such court art was in the form of miniatures, often with the most beautiful coloured floral borders, with lines so delicate as sometimes to require for a brush, a single squirrel's hair: they were kept in folios. (But mural painting has always been popular in India at all levels. Probably the most famous examples are the Buddhist cave paintings dating from the 2nd century AD at Ajanta. Other cave paintings of the pre-history period of hunting scenes are remarkably similar to those of Europe.)

PAHILE AAP Urdu
Lit. – thee first. Sometimes used to mean the courtly manners, takalluf, of the Muslim nawabi aristocracy, *see* Nawab, and also of more lowly folk in a city with a largely Muslim culture, such as Lucknow or Hyderabad, where, so it was said, a deferential bow of greeting could almost touch the ground, the farshi **salaam.** Perhaps in matters of importance, the courtliness was a veneer, but even today in these cities, commerce between one man and another is less abrasive than, say, between

the drivers of Delhi in any position in society, whose philosophy is unabashedly 'pahile main' – me first. A pahile-aap situation carried to extremes, such as when neither of two gentlemen at a doorway will move because each insists that the other must precede him, is sometimes described as 'Lucknavi/'Lakhnavi' – of Lucknow, and the etiquette that led to it as tehzeeb – civilised, well-mannered.

PAIGAH *n* Urdu
Muslim nobility of the highest rank in the **princely** state of Hyderabad, as of a medieval order of knights, in support of the **Nizam.** Originally, a title granted by the second Nizam to his army commander and his family, the numbers grew so that in the later years of the state, the total of the Paigah was several hundred. Many, like the **Ranocracy** of Nepal, carried the epithet Jung **Bahadur** – Heroic in Battle – as part of their names.

PAISLEY PATTERN *n*
In the first decade of the 19th century, Kashmir shawls (*see* Pashmina) shipped to Europe by the **East India Company**, became famous for their comfort and luxury. Merchants of Paisley in Scotland, even then a 'woollen' town, reasoned that they could make a comparable article at a fraction of the cost. Not merely was the soft material copied, but into it was woven or embroidered a motif from Persia (soon to be known to

the West as the paisley pattern) to indicate an oriental origin: this was the kalanga, a stylised juniper pine, with the tip bent over by the wind. The design, particularly associated with Kashmir today, both for textiles and carpets, was not used there until about 1816, but it had been popular in India for several centuries as kairi, kalka and ambi (the **mango** bud). So thoroughly Indian is it, that some retailers will now affirm 'Paisli' to be a region of the sub-continent. Other English names for the Paisley pattern are pine, pear and flame. In connection with carpets, the motif is sometimes called simply the boteh, the design.

PĀKISTAN *n* Urdu
The theory that Indian Muslims were a people separate from Hindus and should have a homeland within India had been bandied about since the 19th century: but it was only in the 1930s that the idea and a name became active politics. The name, Pakistan, (a word from Persian with a Sanskrit suffix), See Sthan—Land of the Pure/Holy/sacred; similar in meaning to the **Sikh** Khalistan *see* Khalsa – is rather vaguely ascribed to an almost unknown and impoverished Cambridge student. A Punjabi, by name, Choudhry Rahmat Ali. He received no honour in Pakistan during his lifetime and died in Cambridge in 1948. As an acronym, Pakistan is said to represent some of the Muslim majority areas of pre-Independence India:

Punjab, Afghanistan (the Pathans of the N.W. frontier) and Kashmir.

PAKKA/PUCCA/PUKKA *adj*
Hindi
Proper, complete, confirmed, ripe, genuine. Pakka food to a **Hindu** carries the meaning of having been cooked in pure **ghee** and thus may be eaten without risk of ritual pollution.

Pakka Gana: colloquialism, classical music.

Pakka road: one metalled and sealed. All-weather.

Pakka building: a permanent building, one constructed of brick or masonry. *See also* Kachcha.

PAKŌRA *n* Hindi
Small tasty morsels of vegetables, cheese (panir), cooked egg or fish, dipped in a dal flour batter (*see* Besan) and deep fried until light brown, in the way of a fritter.

PALM SQUIRREL *n* English
Gilheri in Hindi.
Two varieties are common over all India. The five-striper largely of the north and the three striper in the south. An associate of man with noisy antics entertaining all. Not found in distant forests. Born blind in a hole in a wall or in a tree. They are easily adopted by schoolboys, living in their hosts pockets, but soon

have to be abandoned for their teeth become razor sharp. Some say the stripes are due to their having stroked by the baby Lord Krishna.

PĀN/PAAN *n* Hindi
A word from **Sanskrit**, parna, meaning a leaf (or a feather, *see* Pankha). A delicacy (but more than just  a delicacy it has an important place in culture) savoured by all throughout India: probably first introduced from south-east Asia early in the Christian era. Until recent years often also known from Sanskrit, as tambul. Those of the **Sikh** faith do not normally share the general taste for pan, although it is not actually forbidden to them, unless containing tobacco. By old custom, **Hindu** widows were not expected to enjoy pan. In traditional Hindu and Muslim society, the offering of pan by a host, together, sometimes, with a sprinkling of perfume, is an essential part of ceremonial hospitality to arriving and departing guests. The offering and acceptance of pan between parties can be said to set the final seal on an agreement or contract. Strictly, pan is the aromatic, sometimes pungent, green leaf of the betel vine (*Piper betle*: of the same family as black pepper, *see* Mirch). As a vine or climbing plant, cultivated on twine, in the manner of hops, betel is a Portuguese

corruption of the Malayalam – *see* Malabar–for a green leaf. There are two main types: desi, large green and peppery; and Banarsi (of **Varanasi**), lighter in colour and smaller and less pungent than the desi. For hygiene, before use the leaf is washed and the outer edge trimmed with scissors. In common usage, pan is not the leaf alone but the finished article: pieces of **supari** and a paste of lime, kattha, cardamom, flavoured and scented chewing tobacco – zarda, khaini – or a dash of liquid tobacco extract, kimam – or almost any other piquancy fancied, all folded into the betel leaf, and then perhaps, a covering of fine silver warq (*see* Khir), the whole pinned together with a clove: the pan ready-to-eat is sometimes termed a bira. A variety alleged to have aphrodisiac qualities, with the popular name 'palang tor' – bed breaker – is well known. For the very wealthy, a filling of crushed pearls is recommended with the same end in view. An offered pan must be placed in the mouth whole – perhaps as a quid to swell a cheek pouch to be savoured over a period – it would be against all custom for a corner to be exploratively bitten off first. In recent years, nationally advertised ready-mixed pan **masalas,** gutkha/ gutka (saada if tobacco is omitted) are being supplied to customers through pan shops and elsewhere. Such masalas may be savoured as they are from the packet without a leaf. (chewing tobacco is medically unsound and the sale of gutkha is banned in some states).

(Gutka in Hindi can be far removed from pan : a small book, particulaparticularly a respected anthology for easy reference. In Sikhism, a book of extracts from scripture or hymns, treated with great reverence.)

The red juice, staining the lips and teeth of devotees, comes partly from the kattha paste, sold to the panwala (*see below*) in the form of small solid cakes of dye made from the astringent red heartwood of a species of acacia tree (*Acacia catechu*, khair in Hindi; *see* Babul) and partly from the supari acted upon by the lime. A form of lip colour, considered sexually attractive – thence the prohibition for widows. Few actually swallow the hard pieces of supari, hence the need for frequent expectoration (pik/peek), a requirement provided for in society by the pikdaan (spittoon), or otherwise all too often by the ground or a convenient wall. The leaves and nuts of pan have a part in Hindu ritual being frequently offered to deities, both male and female – it is said there is no pan in heaven—unlike for social use, as an offering to the gods, some consider it essential that a portion of the stalk remains attached to the leaf. (The deity **Yama** is thought to reside in the stalk).

At least one famous English author has written with knowledge and understanding of the growing of the betel vine and of the qualities and ceremonial usage of pan: he also mentioned a 'tragic pan', a speciality for an enemy – containing powdered glass (E.M. Forster in an essay of 1922. Collected into Abinger Harvest).

Pandan/pandaan: a small personal box to contain the leaves and ingredients for pan. Often finely made and decorated: an old example, like a western snuffbox, may well be a collector's piece today, as may be a sarauta/sarota, a nutcracker-like instrument but with a blade for slicing the supari.

Famous from the **princely** state of Bhopal is the pan batua/batwa (batua: a cloth money purse): an embroidered round cloth bag or pouch, with the neck closed bv a tasseled drawstring. This was carried by both men and women to contain the materials and implements for making pan. Like the pandaan, nowadays such a bag can be a treasured artefact.

Panwala: the creator and seller of pan, who, sitting cross-legged on his roadside stall, has been known to achieve fame and fortune by the mastery of his art.

PANCHAGAYA *n* Hindi

A mixture of five products of the cow: milk, **ghee**, curds, dung and urine. May be ingested by a **caste Hindu** as a cleansing agent after a serious ritual sin or pollution. Also may be sprinkled for ritual cleansing purposes. A combination of five (panch, in Hindi) ingredients of another order is said by some (but not the *OED*) to indicate an anglo-Indian origin of the 17th century English drink, 'punch'. The five items being arrack (*see* Toddy), juice of the lime, spices, sugar and hot water.

PANCHAMA *n* Hindi

A fifth part: a term from Sanskrit for those outside the four castes of Hinduism, the **adivasis**, the lowest of the **dalits**, Muslims, Christians and foreigners in general. A rather nicer expression than mlechcha, also from Sanskrit with the same application: (lit. an alien barbarian, an outsider; in some ways the **Hindu** equivalent of the Islamic **kafir**. In today's Hindi, mlechcha may be used for an unclean, unwashed person. If a foreigner is regarded by the orthodox as unclean, it is not necessarily that he is thought to be unwashed nor because of his beliefs – or lack of them – but because of the 'tamas' substances he is assumed to have eaten – tamas, dark and noisome, such as the flesh of dead animals: *see* Heating Foods). A very ancient word, probably unused today, for those outside the social order, particularly the adivasis, was chandala/candala – lit. dog-eater. The English word barbarian derives from Greek, but the root is Sanskrit, barb: foreign, one whose speech is gibberish. A mlechcha.

PANCHATAVA n Sanskrit

The five elements of which a human body is composed and to which it returns on death and dissolution, as by cremation. Kshiti, earth: apah, water: tej, fire: marut/vayu, wind: vyam/akash, sky, the cosmos.

PANCHAYAT *n* Hindi

There is an ancient saying, 'Panch Parmeshwar': lit. five, is Almighty God, or more freely translated, the opinion of five persons has the authority of God. The panchayat is the group of five: the age-old council of the elders of a village (**gram** panchayat). In theory, of five members, in practice usually more, perhaps even a meeting of the whole village, but in this event, the correct title is Gram Sabha. Caste or sub-caste group council (e.g., of all the **dhobies** in an area). Another title can be 'jan sarvai' – a peoples meeting. A group of respectable citizens called by the police to witness an operation, such as the search of a suspect or of a building. The subsequent report signed by all, is termed the panchnama (*see* Nama.).

National Panchayat: the national assembly (parliament) of Nepal.

Nyaya Panchayat (law panchayat): an official court with elected members, set up since 1947 in the villages of some states, with powers to try and punish minor offenders.

Panchayati Raj: the principle of village self-government, as enjoined in the Constitution, with elected members for the councils. In practice, problems may arise between those – usually officials – who see the ideal panchayat as the village level supporter and representative of the state, and those –usually villagers – who consider that the ideal state government would support the panchayat.

In a number of states there is an official three-tier panchayat system, so that each village sends representatives to the Block Panchayat Samiti (in some regions termed the Janpad Panchayat) and the Samiti to the Zila (District) **Parishad**. Failing such a system with regular elections, a recent Constitutional amendment (the 73rd) instructs that no central funds may be released to panchayats for rural development – note that such funds must go directly to the local bodies and not be channelled via a state government. With the new (1994/5) central and state legislation requiring reservations in the panchayats for women and Backward Classes (*see* Harijan) it seems probable that the previous domination of landowners will be challenged (but women who aspire to enter public service, particularly at village level, may have to answer the age-old ques-

tion from their husbands... "and who will make the chapatis"?) In some parts of northern India, particularly where one social group is dominant over a wide area, there is also a long standing but unofficial extension of village democracy, the khap: the meeting together at irregular intervals of the elders of the panchayats of a large number of villages to discuss mutual problems or even as a court of appeal from a village judgement.

Caste panchayats exist and quite illegally can act as moral police courts and in an extreme case, will award a death sentence (see Harijan/Dalit). A more common award to an offender, individual or family, is social boycott.

Sarpanch (or simply Panch): chairman or leader of a panchayat (in some states he is known as the Pramukh).

PANCHDEV Hindi
Five gods. The five major deities of Hinduism: usually said to be **Shiva, Vishnu, Ganesh,** Surya (*see* Gayatri) and **Durga** Maa.

PANCHSHIL/PANCHSHEELA/ PANCHASILA *n* Hindi
Shil: high moral conduct, modesty, piety etc. (Sheila: a girl's name.) The traditional five precepts to be followed as the minimum moral code by one who considers himself a Buddhist. Avoidance of: stealing,

taking life, sensuality, falsity and intoxication (from drugs or alcohol). *See also* Karma.

In contemporary politics, five principles of peaceful coexistence between nations. First mentioned in the preamble to the Sino-Indian Agreement on Trade and Intercourse between Tibet and India, signed in Peking/ Beijing in 1954. The term also seems to be applied to the ten principles of friendly tolerance between nations adopted at the instance of Prime Minister Nehru by the Conference of Asian-African Nations at Bandung, Indonesia, in 1955.

PĀNDA *n* Hindi

A **brahman** particularly to be found in the **Hindu** holy places, such as Hardwar, Mathura, Nasik and **Varanasi**, keeping family records, performing religious ceremonies, and generally assisting pilgrims. The English word pander, in the sense of a go-between, normally in a wanton context, is derived from a Greek legendary leader, Pandarus.

PANDĀL *n* Hindi

Large tent, canopy, or open-sided temporary building, used for a ceremony or meeting.

PĀNDAVAS, THE

The five sons of King Pandu, whose story is to be found in the *Mahabharata* (*see* Epics). The brothers' capital city was at Indraprastha,

reputed to have been located on the site of the present Purana Quila (Old Fortress) in New Delhi.

PANDIT/PUNDIT *n* Hindi

Lit. a scholar, a learned man: as in the English derivation, pundit. A brahman guru or teacher, especially of Hinduism. A term of address to any brahman, either used alone or with his name: in writing often abbreviated to Pt. In the form Panditji – *see* Ji– affectionate respect is indicated.

A brahman subgroup or family name: in this instance the roman spelling is often Pande/Pandey.

Long-Standing Hindu families of Kashmir prefer to refer to themselves not as Hindus but as Pandits.

Pandy: used by British soldiers in 1857 (*see* First War of Independence) and for some time after, to mean an Indian soldier who had risen against British rule. The origin was the caste name of a **sepoy** of the 19th Native Infantry, Mangal Pande, who, when on parade near Calcutta on 29 March 1857, had attacked the regimental adjutant.

The Pandits: a reference perhaps to the Survey of India name for their Indian hillmen surveyors, who over a period of some twenty years from 1865, often in the guise of pilgrims, were sent into trans-Himalayan areas barred to Europeans, such as Tibet. Counting their paces using especially designed hundred-beaded rosaries and recording their observations on paper rolls inside prayer wheels, they explored and made route surveys over vast hitherto unknown regions and first established the approximate heights of many great peaks.

Panditai: scholarship, the profession of a pandit.

Panditain/Panditani : Panditain: the brahman wife of a pandit.

PANĪR/PANEER *n* Urdu
A word possibly from Central Asia, for in Turkish it is very similar. Unfermented soft cheese. Produced by curdling hot milk with lemon juice, draining the whey and compressing the solid casein residue for several hours under weights. A cheese acceptable to vegetarians. (Western type cheeses often use animal enzymes in their manufacture.)

PANJA *n* Punjabi
The hand. Showing the fingers, the election symbol of the Congress Party.

PANKHA/PUNKHA/PANKH *n* Hindi
From **Pankh**: a wing of a bird, a feather, a blade. On tall silver-mounted staves, the huge fans of peacock feathers (mayur-pankh: *see* Mor) waved above emperors.

An electric fan. A propeller, as of a ship or an aircraft.

The room pankha, first appeared in Calcutta in the 1780s; a large board with, perhaps, a small cloth fringe (as time went on the board became smaller and the cloth flap larger) suspended from the ceiling. Thanks to a human agency normally outside the room this swung slowly from side to side, pendulum fashion, making a breeze to cool the perspiring human body below. This type of pankha does not appear to have been used until introduced by the British, but *Hobson-Jobson* indicates that something similar was known to the Arabs in the 8th century AD.

Pankhawala (see Wala): the man who day and night, in homes, offices and in buildings of all kinds, kept the air in motion. Standing, sitting and, sometimes, lying on his back with one leg pulling and releasing the pankha cord tied to his foot. The job had its hazards, particularly on hot summer nights when tempers were short: it was not unknown for a drowsy puller to be violently assaulted by an irascible sleep-denied **sahib**.

Even in the late 1940s, at least thirty years after the use of the electric fan had become general in Indian cities, in some old **cantonment** barracks, electricity had replaced only the pankhawala, and soldiers were still cooled by lines of board pankhas, oscillating in unison through connection to a single motor-powered crank.

Hand pankha: a hand fan.

PANT *n*
In the singular, Hinglish (*see* Hindustani) throughout India for a pair of European type trousers.

Pant-piece: sufficient cloth with which to make a pair of trousers.

Half-pant: short trousers, shorts. (Nepalese often prefer the abbreviation of the old fashioned knickerbockers, knickers, for the same garment.)

Pant (historical Marathi, pronounced punt): a senior civil official of the Maratha state. A Maratha family name today.

PANTH *n* Hindi
Lit. a road or path: a cause. Often applied to a creed or religious order: particularly to the **Sikh** tradition and religion.

Panthshala: a **Rest House**

Panthi: a follower of a panth. A traveller.

Nanak Panth: followers of the teachings of the first Sikh Guru, (Guru Nanak, *see* Sikh) but not of the later Gurus and of modern Sikhism in general (particularly, they reject the militarism of Guru Gobind Singh). Many of the Nanak Panth are Sindhi, and may be clean shaven (sehajdhari – see Sikh): they do not use the epithet Singh as part of their names.

PAPĪTA *n* Hindi
The papaya or paw-paw, A fruit from the Americas probably introduced by the Portuguese. (Papaya as a name entered Spanish and Portuguese from the Caribbean, and what is now good Hindi, papita, could have evolved from the diminutive form, papayita – perhaps the senhors were not much impressed with the size of the fruit as first grown in India.)

From the latex of the green leaves, stems and fruit, a vegetable pepsin, papain, is prepared: this is a protein digesting enzyme used in medicine and as a meat tenderiser (for this last purpose, housewives sometimes add immature fruit to stewing meats).

To a botanist, the papita is a sexual, herbaceous perennial plant, sexually indistinguishable until flowering time—growers thus have to use irrigation and manure to raise commercially useless male plants.

PARA/PADA *n* Hindi and Bengali
A locality, an area, particularly of a town or city. In Delhi and north India the Urdu equivalent, ilāqa, is more often used. *See final paragraph,* Parikrama.

In eastern India para/pada is frequently used as a suffix to a place name.

PARAMOUNTCY

Term for the relationship between the British Crown and the ruling **princes**. Although the princes had varying degrees of independence from the **Government of India**, the Crown (in fact the British government) remained supreme until 1947. Control was exercised through the Crown Representative (the **Viceroy**) and the local Political Agent (*see* Resident).

It was Lord Mornington (later Marquess Wellesley), Governor-General from 1798 to 1805, a time when the **East India Company** held only the lower Gangetic plain and little more than the coastline elsewhere, who laid down the policy followed thereafter that since the whole subcontinent was destined to be British, the princes could be tolerated only as vassals.

PARATHA/PARANTHA *n* Hindi

A flaky layered bread of the same size and material as a **chapati**, but brushed with a little **ghee** on each side while cooking on a hot griddle. May be stuffed with a spicy vegetable filling: a popular breakfast snack, particularly of the Punjab.

In eastern India, a very similar bread may have the name luchi

PARBAT/PARVAT *n* Hindi from Sanskrit

A mountain.

Parbati/Parvati: pertaining to a mountain. The spouse of Lord **Shiva** in benign form. *See also* Girja Ghar. (Parvati is the more usual spelling for the Goddess and when used as a girl's name.) As an epithet, Parvati has the name Gauri – the golden one, the white one. On account of her later skin colour, granted as a boon by **Brahma** after Shiva taunted her for her dark complexion (the word for a European, gora, is linked).

PARGANA *n* Urdu

Originally a division of a province under a **Mogul** administration. In northern India in British days, the pargana became the tehsil, a subdivision of a **district**, covering approximately one hundred and fifty villages, the revenue officer in charge, to many villagers the embodiment of the country's government, being the tehsildar. (In some regions, the equivalent subdivision is termed a **taluk**.) *24 Parganas:* a district in West Bengal.

PARIAH *n*

This English word comes from drummers: a large **dalit** group of **Tamil** Nadu and **Malabar**. (Throughout India, those without caste have their part to play in **caste Hindu** festivals, often as drummers and musicians – only they have nothing to lose from touching the leather drumskins.) The paraiyan are now officially known as

Adi-**Dravidian**, the original Dravidians or inhabitants. Unlike the meaning of the English derivative, the lowest of the low, a social outsider, the paraiyan of south India are not at the very bottom of the hierarchy. (Parai, a drum in Tamil).
Pariah-dog: see Pi-dog.

Pariah kite: the English name (cheel, in Hindi) for the **bazaar** scavenging raptor and scourge of New Delhi's winter garden luncheon parties, the common kite-hawk; with fluffy wingtips, as with the owl, for a stealthy approach. (At a party, from high above, or perhaps from a nearby tree, the bird establishes its target, often that of a guest leaving the buffet, silently glides feet first to the chosen plate and then, with a chicken leg in its talons, zooms up and away under full power.) Amongst kites, it is unique in having a forked tail.

PARIKRAMA *n* Hindi
Parikar – a circle. The **Hindu, Sikh,** Buddhist and Jain concept of worship by walking clockwise round an object of devotion, be it a lake, a mountain peak, a temple or a **murti**. (Since the cooling water drainage channel of a shivalingam – see Lingam – should not be overstepped, for this object the circle is not completed and the parikrama is made first in one direction and then the other.) Instead of walking, some use slower and more difficult ways of progressing: such as by full-length prostration,

getting up and once again lying prone a few feet forward. A regular custom in at least one temple in the south is to make a circuit by rolling on the ground. Perhaps the longest is that of the whole River **Ganga**, from the mountains to the sea and back; a journey of more than 4830 km. Usually said to require up to two years for completion. (In 1986, a lone Briton walked the distance from the sea to the source glacier in about eight months.) A frequently used ambulatory path itself can be known as the parikrama.

Pradakshina has a meaning similar to parikrama, with the route taken known as pradakshinapath (*see* Path). In a secular use of the word, Delhi's Ring Railway calls itself in Hindi 'Parikrama Rail Sewa'.

The **Sanskrit** prefix pari, around or surrounding, the neighbourhood of, entered English via Greek as peri in perimeter and periphery.

PARISHAD *n* Hindi
An association, an assembly. Lit. from Sanskrit, seated in a circle: a round-table conference.

PARSĪ/PARSEE *n*
Lit., of Persia, A Persian/Iranian and adjectival Persian/Iranian. In Arabic (a language without a *p* sound) pronounced farsi: a word sometimes used in English to mean the Persian language. (Old Persian – i.e., pre-

Islamic – is usually referred to as Pahlavi, from the region once known as Pathia.)

An Iranian, or an Indian descendant of an immigrant from Iran, a follower of the teachings of the prophet, Zoroaster (dates varying between the 6th millenium to the 6th century BC) , whose doctrines became the state religion of pre-Muslim Persia.

With the advance of **Islam** in the 7th century AD, many Parsis, but not all, an Iranian Parsi community still exists, left their homeland in southern Persia (Pars/Fars, once a name for the whole country) and found sanctuary in western India: since when, in courtesy to their **Hindu** hosts, they have abstained from eating beef (in fact, many also avoid pork, for the reason that the angel guarding the bridge to heaven, it is believed, will not assist pork-eaters to cross the abyss).

Pre-history Persian and Vedic Indians shared a common Aryan (*see* Arya.) background, of which something still remains with their descendants today, especially a reverence for the all-purifying fire, signifying the goodness and heat of God, although neither Parsis nor Hindus actually worship fire. A Parsi religious building (agiary) is known in English as a Fire-temple: in the oldest in India, at Udwada on the Gujarat coast, the flame has burned continuously for at least 1300 years, tended by celibate

Dasturs (Chief Priests) and Mobeds (Priests). Normally, Parsis do not smoke, for smoking is regarded as disrespectful to fire. On initiation into their faith, between the seventh and eleventh year, at the Navjote ceremony, Parsi boys and girls are invested with the sacred cord (kusti), thereafter worn at all times as a girdle round the waist, and the vest (sudreh).

Following the flowering of Bombay as a great mercantile centre in the late 18th century, many Parsis left the rural areas and settled there. They accepted Western education and prospered as a people, greatly enriching their new city. Gandhiji is said to have commented of Parsis "in numbers they are beneath contempt, but in contribution, beyond compare". This was the time when some of the community adopted the Christian European custom of a family name: taking the titles of their professions (Doctor, Engineer, Contractor, **Vakil** etc. – English patronymics such as Smith, Draper, Fletcher, Baker and so on, of course came about in the same way), or using the name of the place with which they were connected (Poonawala, etc. Central European Jews who were coerced into acquiring family names at about the same period, also found the place of their residence useful as a surname). But not all names ending in **wala** are Parsi; Hindu merchants sometimes have adopted as their own, epithets given to them by the public from the commodities they deal in: e.g., Chawalwala – the riceman. Also, the use of a profession – e.g., Engineer as a final name is not unknown amongst the **Bohras**.

Generally Parsis have few restrictions with food and drink and have always been ready to socialise with Europeans. Anyone may follow Zoroastrianism as a religion, but to enter the Parsi community one must be born of Parsi parents: perhaps because of this, for many years now, the Parsis have been declining in numbers by approximately one per cent per year. In Britain, Parsis seem to prefer to describe themselves as Zoroastrians.

See also Dokma.

PARTAB/PRATAB/PERTAB/PRATAP *n* Hindi

Dignity, renown, prestige. The Urdu word iqbal has a similar meaning, but includes the quality of being consistently fortunate – birth under a lucky star. A popular **Hindu** personal name: is Rana Pratap, King of Glory.

PASHMINA *n* Urdu

A breed of goat natural to the high altitudes of Ladakh in Kashmir and the adjoining areas of Tibet and Central Asia. The animal grows a fine soft underwool as protection against the bleakness of the region and its icy winds.

Pashmina/pash/pashm: strictly, the underwool of the pashmina goat, especially suited to fine shawl making, Kashmir/Cashmere wool. But it is sometimes alleged that similar underwool from high altitude sheep and even dogs may be mixed in. The word shawl entered the English language . from Old Persian via Urdu (shal): at least since the 16th century, the Kashmir shawl has been a comfort to wealthy Indians in chilly weather. But some claim that its fame is far far older, having a mention in the *Mahabharata* (*see* Epics). In Hindi, the household name can be simply param naram – super soft. *See also* Paisley Pattern.

For males in the plains, the shawl, much folded, may be worn as no more than a decorative accessory to the **kurta dhoti** ensemble.

In India the pashmina goat is a protected animal and possesion of its wool in any form has to be registered with details of the origin. Possession otherwise is an offence.

Pashm: body hair, human and animal.

PASSAGE TO INDIA

A lengthy poem (225 lines) by Walt Whitman, printed in its final form in 1871, from which E.M.Forster obtained the title for his 1924 story of Indo-British relations." Sang Whitman: Passage to India!

"Lo, soul, seest thou not God's purpose from the first? The earth to be spann'd, connected by network,

The races, neighbours, to marry and be given in marriage,

The oceans to be cross'd, the distant to be brought near, The lands to be welded together."

After that, it is perhaps ironical that a first impression of Forster's novel can be one of rigid and irreconcilable attitudes, or antitheses.

PASSENGER TRAIN

As listed in a timetable, a train most passengers would prefer to avoid: the slow local, stopping at all halts and stations, giving way to mail trains and expresses, but often eventually covering a journey of several hundred miles. However, of all passenger services, its fares are the lowest. A feature of slow-moving rural trains, especially when jam-packed with travellers going, perhaps, to a mela or festival, is sky-class: a term for those outside on the roof, almost certainly **WT.**

Once mail trains were the fastest, in British days often prestige trains enjoying precedence over all others, carrying the foreign mails from Bombay to cities such as Calcutta, Delhi, Kalka (for **Shimla**) and Peshawar (*see* Frontier Mail). Now, new fast trains are usually termed expresses.

Janta trains are single class (second) expresses.

PATEL *n* Hindi
Village headman in western and central India.

Gujarati and Maharashtrian family name. (In **Maharashtra**, usually spelt Patil.) Its origin lies in the days of the Maratha power in western India when a group could be shareholders in the produce of a village. Such minor gentry could be addressed as Patidar (holder of a **patta** or title document) or Patel. Within the same system, slightly superior was the Desai, a person having proprietory rights over a single village or small group of villages. Superior again was the Deshmukh (*see* Desh). Today, those with the family names of Patel and Desai consider themselves more or less of a kind.

PATH *n* Hindi
Two Hindi words from separate **Sanskrit** roots, but appearing the same in roman script. With a short a: a road, a footpath. Metaphorically, as in English, a cause, or a course of action or belief, to be followed. Linked to the English path.

Pathshala: A primary school. See Rest House.

From the root, pattr, a text: a recitation, a reading, as in **Gita** Path, **Akhand** Path. Pattrika – a journal,

Pattrikar (*see* Kar) – a journalist. With the a's long: pāthshāla (lit. place of reading), a school usually primary. Pathak – a reader, particularly one reading a religious text aloud to a congregation.

PATHĀNS *n*

Pronounced P'tarn.

A Muslim, Pushtu/Pashtu -speaking people whose homeland is the mountainous and barren country on both sides of the Pakistan/Afghanistan frontier.

Pre-**Independence**, as one of the many tribes of tough fighting men of the north-west frontier, Pathans were recruited into the Indian army and irregular forces, even while their fellows were the enemy in the frontier wars – from the British side, campaigns fought not to acquire territory, but following from the use of the army as a police force, to subdue extraordinary lawlessness, such as serious tribal raids into administered areas (*see* Durand Line).

The name is derived from Paktana, a word of the **Vedas** for the country. Nowadays, Pathans tend to refer to themselves and members of other tribes of the region, as Pakhtuns, and to their land astride the Afghanistan-Pakistan border, as Pakhtunistan. Other spellings are Pashtuns and Pashtunistan. *See also* Mālik.

Pathan architecture: the Muslim style of the period of the **Sultanates** of Delhi: without, necessarily any connection with the people known today as Pathans.

PATIĀLĀ PEG *n*

From the city in the Punjab, former capital of the **princely** state of the same name ruled by a **Sikh** dynasty famed for robust living: a generous measure of spirits, the width of two fingers – the first and the fourth against a glass. Sometimes known as just a 'Patiala'. (A much repeated story, possibly apocryphal, is that even into the 20th century, going further than the medieval Popes, the Patiala Maharajahs were required in an annual ceremony to prove possession of all their faculties by a public priapic display.)

PATLIPUTRA/PATALIPUTRA

The generally accepted story is as follows: The name of the ancient city on the site of present day Patna, in Bihar. Capital of almost all India, from the 4th century BC for one thousand years as the seat of first, the Magadha kings and then the Mauryan and Gupta empires. Site of the famous Nalanda Buddhist university. A Muslim name for the city was Azimabad (Azim, an epithet for the Holy Prophet).

In the course of the Delhi **Durbar** of 1911, King George personally announced: "...we have decided upon the transfer of the seat of the government from Calcutta to the ancient capital Delhi." It is unlikely that those present thought of Patna for the new centre, but the royal speech-writer was weak in history; Delhi had certainly been the capital at times during Muslim rule and is indeed the legendary site of Indraprastha (*see* Pandavas), but had nothing like the claim of Patliputra to be the ancient all-India capital city.

It must be mentioned that late in the 20th century some distinguished historians have pointed out that the evidence for the early eminence of Patliputra/Patna is solely literary. There are no archeological remains linking the Mauryas or the Guptas to the region (If palaces there were, perhaps they were of wood). In their absence, it is claimed, history as outlined in the first paragraph above must be conjectural.

PATTA *n* Hindi
A legal deed: such as a lease or sale document, particularly a title to land.

Tamra Patta/ Patra: a deed on copper. In ancient times, edicts of a ruler, such as the authority for a grant of land, were often engraved for permanent record on thin plates of copper: if on more than one, the plates were filed on something like a large copper key ring. Nowadays, usually a copper plate presented as an award or part of an award, on which the citation is engraved.

Patwari: lit. he of the records. A government appointed village accountant and record keeper in northern India. In western India, a similar official is known by the Marathi term, Kulkarni: a word also used as a family name.

PATTI/PUTEE *n* Hindi
A bandage: whence the English word puttee, for a strip of cloth binding the leg from the ankle boot to just below the knee, as worn by men of the Himalayan regions.

PEEPAL/PEEPUL/PIPAL/ PIPIL *n* Hindi
Ficus religiosa. The most highly revered of all Indian trees: with respect going back to the Indus Valley Civilisations. To **Hindus, Shiva** and **Vishnu** are present in its branches, while Buddhists recognise it as the Bo/Bodhi tree, the tree of knowledge and understanding, under which the **Buddha** meditated and received enlightenment. (Many of both faiths believe that meditation beneath a peepal is likely to be spiritually rewarding.) Neither Hindus nor Buddhists will personally cut it down nor lop its branches, however inconvenient its growth may be. One form of worship, particularly by women, is to circle the trunk clockwise one hundred and eight times (*see* Parikrama) and in the process winding round a cotton thread. (Another reason for threads is that they are believed to be obstacles to

spirits. Some hold that the spirits of children who died young may reside in the peepal tree.)

In folklore, the peepal is considered by some to be the female of the (male) **banyan** tree. In **Sanskrit**-based Hindi, the name for the trees is ashvatth – lit. the tree under which horses shelter. In a market place, a Hindu merchant seated beneath a peepal describing his wares, generally will be accepted as speaking the truth. The peepal is one of the eighty-six members of the fig family growing in India; all have milky latex sap. Its fruit, figs little more than pea-size, is much enjoyed by birds. Like the banyan, the seeds, lodged in wall crevices, can flourish and in time, demolish buildings. The peepal is believed to be particularly cool and pleasant to sleep beneath in the hot weather and it is a fact that under certain conditions, minute droplets of water fall from the leaf tips. The old leaves are shed and new ones open in the late spring, to honour, so some believe, the Day of the Triple Blessing, the Buddha **Purnima**.

An unusual feature of the fig family is that the flower is enclosed in a button-like pouch. An insect, the gall wasp, enters the pouch by a minute hole to lay its eggs and in the process fertilises the fig seeds. It can happen that the neither the wasp nor its larvae can exit and so may be eaten by one later in the food chain, either bird, animal or human.

In the south the name is sometimes given to a flowering tree not of the fig family: this is the bhendi, a fine avenue tree with almost year-round yellow flowers. The bhendi leaves and those of the true peepal are somewhat similar.

PEG *n* English
A measure of spirits. Legally equivalent to thirty millilitres (Delhi).

Burra peg: a large drink, a 'double'. The width of three fingers against a glass.

Chhota peg: a small drink, a 'single'. The width of two fingers.

PEPSU (P.E.P.S.U).
Patiala and East Punjab States Union. After **Independence**, the first combination (1948) of a group of **princely** states. Pepsu was eventually divided and absorbed into Punjab, Haryana and Himachal Pradesh.

PERI PERI *n*
A chilli based sauce of Portuguese origin. Particularly popular in Goa and elsewhere in the world where the Portuguese settled.

PERIYAR *n* Tamil
Title of approbation accorded by the public to an elderly respected figure: equivalent perhaps, to Grand Old Man.

River and wild life sanctuary in Kerala.

PESHWA *n* Persian
Lit. guide. A minister who gives advice in front of (pesh) his enthroned ruler. The title of hereditary **brahman** prime ministers of the Maratha (*see* Maharashtra) Confederacy in **Pune**, 1707-1817. During this time, the heirs of the **kshatriya** Shivaji (*see* Chhatrapati) remained, respected but powerless, on the throne. Following the third Maratha War, the last Peshwa was exiled to Kanpur in 1818 where he lived for thirty-five years on what everyone conceded was a generous pension. The payments ceased on his death and it was his highly aggrieved adopted son, known as the Nana Sahib, who became the scourge of the British at Kanpur during the 1857 rebellion. Nana: lit. grandfather, but used in the last century by Marathas as an honorific, even if the dignity so honoured was not of grandparental years.

Living in the Nana's court – and there learning to ride like a boy, so the stories have it – was a Marathi princess, later to be known in both Indian and British history, as Laxmi Bai of Jhansi. *See* Bahen and Oudh.

PET/PETTA *n* Tamil from Sanskrit
In the south, a market-place, a suburb. A suffix to a township name. Petha in Marathi.

Belly, stomach. As a colloquilism,

pet kewaste, lit. for one's stomach; for one's livelihood, a job.

PETHA *n*
The large white pumpkin, or ash gourd. Cubed, cooked and crystallised, a sweetmeat particularly a speciality of the Agra and Mathura region.

PHAS JAYENGE *n Hindi*
A colloquial warning expression to a potential rule or law breaker. "Beware you will be caught".

PHATNA *v* Hindi
To break, to explode; the origin of the English expression, to go phut.

PHAT-PHAT/PUT-PUT *n*
Village terms for a motor-cycle. Town expression for little three-wheeled. two-seater motor-scooter taxis. (Such are the skills of **bazaar** mechanics that some of the larger six-seater models that ran on Delhi's streets until 1998 were basically American army disposals Harley-Davidson motor-cycles of World War II vintage powered by new India-made diesel engines. To replace these, jeep-like four-wheelers with the old name are running on Delhi Streets).

Phataphat: an imperative, 'very quickly'.

PHIKA *adj* Hindustani
Tasteless, without flavour. As used as an expression in connection with a cup of tea or coffee, without sugar.

PHULKARI *n* Hindi
Lit. flower work. Sometimes known as **bagh** – garden. Embroidery on homespun cloth, designs and flower patterns using silk thread. (Strictly, with bagh work, the original cloth backing should nowhere be visible.) A folk craft of Punjabi women, phulkari is used particularly to ornament shawls and bed covers. Punjabi culture has it that on the birth of a girl child, the mother should commence a phulkari work to form part of the girl's wedding trousseau.

PHULKIAN Adj
Collective name for the **Punjab-princely** states of Patiala, Jind and Nabha. The origin was the 17th century common ancestor of the **Sikh** rulers of the three states, Phul by name. (Some authorities include a fourth state, Faridkot, whose rulers descended from a collateral branch of the family.)

In the early 19th. century these states had British protection and were named the Cis Sutlej States. (Cis, Latin, this side of.)

PIAO *n* Hindi
Roadside stall or platform from which drinking water is offered free to passers-by. Frequently arranged by a wealthy person as a public service. A rather special form of piao is set up by **Sikhs** (other Punjabis also join in) in urban streets particularly on a day in May or June to mark the martyrdom of **Guru** Arjun Dev (before his death, he was tortured by thirst) and also to a lesser degree on other days also commemorating occasions in connection with the Gurus. Iced kachcha lassi (*see* Dahi), a mixture of milk, water and syrup, is distributed throughout the day by volunteers to all on the street, even those in vehicles: a most welcome gesture in the hot weather.

An Arabic/Urdu word for the piao still current in Urdu culture areas (e.g., Old Delhi or Lucknow city) is sabeel. Other Hindi terms for the same thing are paushala and pausrala.

PICE *n*
Copper coins of the British period: from the early years of the 19th century, four to an **anna**, sixty-four to a **rupee**. In later days and right up to the introduction of metric coinage in 1957, washer-like, with a hole in the middle to save metal. The word is probably an anglicism from paise – Hindi for small change money or more fully, chhote paise.

Picey: an anglicism for mean, miserly. Coins of even less value were the adhela/dhela, a half pice, (128 to the rupee) and the pie/pai worth 1/12 of an anna (192 to the rupee).

Paisa (pl. paise): the smallest unit of today's currency. In 1957 a copper coin representing - 100th of a rupee, but no longer minted. (The metal content of a hundred such coins soon became worth more than one rupee.) Paisa can be used as a term for money in general.

PICHCHAWA/PICHHVAI *n* Hindi

A form of **Kalamkari**: brightly coloured paintings on cloth originally depicting the **Krishna** stories. These days mostly produced in the Udaipur region of Rajasthan for sale to visitors – but they are also painted in Delhi. The subjects are often legends of **Rajput** chivalry. The pichchawa started as the most important of a set of Vaishnavi (*see* Vishnu) **mandir** cloth hangings intended to be used behind (pichhe) the main image: changed, perhaps, according to the season or even the hour of the day. Pichchawas and similar cloths with other names used in other parts of a mandir and in parts of India other than Rajasthan are sold commercially under the name, temple hangings.

Similar in technique to pichchawas – and often by the same artists – are the pad (story) paintings also of Rajasthan. Action-packed pictures on a cloth strip, perhaps twelve metres in length, illustrating the exploits of Rajput folk heroes. Once carried round the villages and unfolded by the wandering story-teller and minstrel, the bhopa. (Bhopa has other meanings also.) The professional family groups of bards, particularly in Rajasthan, will often refer to themselves as being of the Charan community.

PI-DOG/PYE-DOG *n* English

The country dog, the working herd-dog of India, the ubiquitous, often ownerless, dog of all villages and towns. Once distinct, now mixed with all the foreign breeds imported during the last three hundred years: but the original characteristics, the short coat, long legs and above all, the ring tail, mostly still remain. If cared for, loyal, hardy and excellent as a watch dog. The name is possibly derived from **pariah** or from the Hindi word pahi, meaning an outsider.

PIETRA DURA *n* Italian

Lit. Hard Stone. The name universally given in India to the decorative inlay of coloured stone into marble; particularly as exemplified on the Taj Mahal. The craft was practiced in Florence in the 16th century but it is uncertain whether it was imported into India, perhaps via Persia, or was developed locally. Certainly, the inlay of marble pieces into red sandstone was known before the Taj (eg. on the gateway to Akbar's tomb in 1614: of the highest quality on the tomb in Agra built by the Empress Nur Jahan for her father in the 1620s, and rather crudely in Delhi's Humayun's tomb of about 1556). This immature inlay is sometimes termed intarsia but, strictly, intarsia is wood pieces inlaid in marble. The craft is and always has been centred in Agra. thin slivers of coloured stone exactly shaped on an emery wheel are cemented into small cavities (often no more than 1mm deep) cut into marble. The whole is then polished. In Hindustani, from Persian, the name for the work is pachikari, but in Punjab, as seen in the Golden temple, the term is jaratkari.

Some of the most interesting examples of PD work are to be seen in Delhi's royal palace. Small tablets of black marble with embedded coloured inlay depicting birds and flowers: centrally over the seated Emperor's head was Orpheus seated with his lute. Probably imported from Florence by Shah Jehan. (Some dispute this, saying they are of Indian work). After the troubles of the mutiny they were sold in London by an army officer, but in 1900 Lord Curzon effected their return to Delhi.

PINDĀRIS *n*
Irregular horsemen, many, but not all, of **Pathan** and Afghan origin, in the service of the Marathas (*see* Maharashtra) who, on the break-up of that power became highly mobile robber bands terrorising all central India: no doubt, other broken armies also supplied freebooter recruits. Put down between 1817-19: but the family of at least one Pindari leader achieved

respectability, as the Afghan **Nawabs** of Tonk, the only Muslim state in the old Rajputana, now part of Rajasthan – *see* Rajput.

The origin of the name has been the subject of much controversy: plausible conjectures are the Marathi word, pendhari, meaning a brigand, and pindar, said to have been a liquor to which the horsemen were much addicted.

See also Thug.

PINJRAPOL/PINJRAPOLE *n*
Hindi
Lit. a cage. A hospital for animals and birds, particularly a sanctuary for unwanted cattle: often a Jain foundation (the Jains will accommodate vegetarian species only). Even today, long-established wholesale merchants in the old city of Delhi may levy a small semi-voluntary tax on customers, authorised by the **Mandal** (*see* Beopar) for the upkeep of a pinjrapol.

PINKY PANI *n*
An anglicism for a solution of potassium permanganate in water. This very mild oxidising agent was used by Britons in India right up to the time of **Independence** as a germicide suitable for washing vegetables etc. Earlier, it was considered a specific against the cholera vibrio and was extensively used for 'pinking' wells.

PĪSTA *n* Urdu and Persian
The edible kernel of the pistachio
nut. Pista in India is mostly imported
from Afghanistan. A general name
for nuts and dried fruit.

PLAINS, THE
A term of British days still current
to describe the relatively feature-
less land mass drained by the three
northern river systems of the subcontinent; the Indus in the west,
the **Ganga** of the centre and the
Brahmaputra in the east, between
the foothills of the **Himalaya** and
the peninsular highland. Delhi is
roughly central in the plains, about
1450 km equidistant in a straight
line from the deltas of the Indus and
the Ganga, yet the altitude is only
a little over 215m. (The continental
divide between eastern and western
drainage lies just west of the capital.) The plains were once an arm
of the sea, in geological time only
recently filled by alluvial detritus
from the hills – erosion of the Himalaya is no new phenomenon. *See
also* Dravidia and Ganga.

PLANTER'S CHAIR *n*
An easy chair for the bungalow
veranda on which a **sahib** could
put his feet up after the day's work
(memsahibs usually preferred not
to adopt the somewhat indecorous
position required) with a drink to
hand. The seat and back were of
woven cane and the arm cum leg-
rests extended for several feet, that

on the right having a circular hole
to take a glass. Sometimes, the leg
extensions could be swivelled back
when not needed.
The name, planter, is often given
to a large metal (normally, brass or
copper) bowl with ring handles, used
as a decorative outer container for a
house plant in a pot. *See* Urli.

PLEADER *n*
Prior to 1961, a lawyer on the register
of a particular High Court, and
entitled to practice only before that
court, or before a court subordinate
to it. An advocate, on the other
hand, could appear before any court
in India.

As the result of the Advocates
Act, 1961, the distinction between
advocates and pleaders has gone.
Persons on the Roll of the Bar
Council of India, are entitled to
appear before any Indian court and
all are known as advocates. A lawyer
may be designated 'Senior Advocate'
by the Supreme Court or a High
Court, in acknowledgement of his
ability and standing at the bar.

PŌL *n* Hindi
A word particularly used in north
India, especially in Rajasthan: a large
gateway, as to a palace, a fortress or a
walled city. Such names as Hathi Pol
– Elephant Gate: Vijay Pol – Victory
Gate, are common. Rajasthani cities
almost always have a Sun and a
Moon Gate.

Tripol/tripolia: a three-arched gateway.

A feature of the old city of Ahmedabad in Gujarat, was that many of the residential streets were closed off by gates (pols) manned by watchmen. In most cases, the gates and men have gone (the gateways remain), but in Ahmedabad pol has come to mean such a street itself: or residences round a courtyard.

In Delhi the old Urdu word for a large gateway to a mansion or the city wall is still in use, phatak.

POLITICALS *n*
Officers of the Indian Civil Service and Indian Army seconded to the Foreign and Political Department (renamed Indian Political Service from 1935 to the winding-up in 1947), the diplomatic service of the Crown Representative (*see* Viceroy) and of the **Government of India**. Their work was largely with the **princely** states (then called Native States, or just the States), but they also administered certain frontier areas (e.g. North West Frontier Province) and acted as diplomatic representatives in countries of special interest to India; particularly in the Persian Gulf which, until 1947, was generally seen in London through the Government of India. *See* Resident.

POLO *n*
Invariably described as hockey on horseback. Under the Persian name of chaugan -from the hooked stick used to hit the ball, certainly more like a hockey stick than the mallet of today – once played throughout central Asia: later, it spread to parts of the Middle East and to Byzantium. The chronicles say that the second **Sultan** (*see* Sultanates of Delhi) of Delhi, Qutab-u-din Aibak, died in Lahore in 1210AD from a fall on the chaugan field (similar accidents are recorded on gravestones in **European cemeteries** all over India). The British army first saw and enjoyed the game in such places as the Hindu Kush, Gilgit, Baltistan, Ladakh and also in the far north-east, in Manipur, where it had probably been received from China. In all these regions it is still a people's game. Polo or polu, is the Balti name for the ball made from the rootwood of the local willow tree.

With the caveat, probable but not proven, most authorities agree with *Hobson-jobson* that chaugan and the French word chicaner, originally meaning to win by finesse and subtlety, taking every advantage of circumstances, are the same. While chic, as style, is not so far from the original, chicanerie (and its English derivative, chicanery), has become pejorative.

Operation Polo: the code name for the military action of a few days in September 1948 whereby the Indian army entered and occupied the earlier princely state of Hyderabad. Now mostly Andhra Pradesh.

POMFRET *n*

Upright swimming marine flat fish found off India's west coast, and considered excellent eating: up to two kg. in weight. The name, sometime seen on menu cards as pomphlet, is from the Portuguese word for the fish.

PONGAL *n* Tamil

A preparation of rice, **dal**, milk and sugar or jaggery (*see* Shakkr). The equivalent in north India would be khichri (see Kedgeree). The annual four-day festival of **Tamil Nadu**, with the main day on the 14th or 15th January. The pongal, cooking in a cauldron in each household, on this day must boil over, signifying plenty following the harvest.

The festival coincides with Makara Sankranti, the beginning of the **uttarayana**, the northward journey of the sun, occurring on or about the 14th of January each year (according to the traditional, or nirayana, system of calculation. *See* Calendars).

POPPADUM/PAPAD *n* Tamil

Pappadams in the south, papads/papars (see Bangle) in the north. Round, four to eight inches across, crisp wafer-thin biscuits; made from pulses, especially urad **dal** – as words, papadam and papad have a connection with the **Sanskrit** for

urad – or rice flour, or potatoes, then sun-dried. May be seasoned or plain. Enjoyed all over the country as an accompaniment to meals – the British called them curry biscuits. Papads are bought soft in the raw state from the **bazaar** and are deep fried in the home, when they expand wondrously to crispness within seconds. They may also be dry-roasted, but in this case, the expansion is less. Finger-papads: uncooked, similar in appearance to rather large-bore macaroni pieces. Being made of rice flour, when fried these swell into crispy. cylindrical wafers. (A deep yellow colour may be due to the use of an illegal coal-tar dye.) Somewhat similar to the poppadam – also known as appalam in Tamil – is the southern appam – hoppers to the British. Rice flour pancakes made from a batter with coconut milk by the housewife, when cooked, crisp and wafer-like round the edge, but soft in the centre. Again, eaten with curries, or as a snack, say with rasam (*see* Mulligatawny). Also, sweet varieties are made in southern homes.

Papadwala: the itinerant pedlar, seller of ready-to-nibble papads. With a tall basket on his head for carrying his wares, at night topped by a guttering flame, the sign of his calling, he is a familiar bazaar and public-garden figure. In Delhi at least, it is often whispered that on request they will supply papads laced with hemp products (*see* Indian Hemp).

POSH *adj*

There is a popular anecdote that this English colloquialism, meaning elegant, of smart appearance, derives from the acronym of counsel given by old **Koi Hai's** designed to minimize the discomfort, before the days of a marine air-conditioning, of the transit of the Red Sea to and from the East: 'Port out, Starboard Home' (i.e., cabins on the northern and cooler side of the vessel). But, alas, the story is not supported by the compilers of dictionaries and glossaries of slang (*see OED*). Authenticially linked to the waterway is the term 'Red Sea Rig'. An evening wear concession to the climate for males: simply shirt, bowtie and **cummerbund,** omitting the otherwise obligatory dinner jacket.

POSH *n* Urdu

Posh; from Persian, a cover, a secret.

Safed posh: white clothes. Applied to a man, a term of respect, little used today for one who can afford to wear white clothes, a well-to-do person.

Poshteen; a knee-length sheepskin coat with the fleece on the inside, particularly worn in Central Asia.

PRABHĀKAR *n* Hindi

Lit. the sun. Title of Oriental Learning, corresponding to a pass degree, awarded by several northern Indian universities. A family name.

PRABHĀT PHERE *n* Hindi

Prabhat, Sanskrit: dawn

Lit. an early morning circular walk. Group of persons moving in a locality soon after dawn singing with musical accompaniment, mostly in a religious connection, but sometimes calling slogans in celebration of an event, or for publicity purposes (e.g., in support of an election candidate).

Phere/pheri means a circulatory progress as in sat phere, the seven rounds of the sacred fire, the climax of a Hindu wedding ceremony.

A term for a wedding.

PRABHU *n* Hindi

Lord. A respectful Hindu term of address to a deity. A personal name.

PRADESH *n* Hindi

State, as in Uttar Pradesh, the northern state.

Pradeshi: of a state.

PRADHĀN *n* Hindi

Chief, leader, chairman. Village headman. Nowadays, executive officer of the village.

Pradhan Mantri: Prime Minister (of the **Government of India**).
Family name.

PRĀJA *n* Hindi

People or subjects of a state, particularly of the erstwhile **princely** states: as in the old saying 'jaise raja, waise praja' – as the ruler (behaves) so his subjects.

*Praja **Parishad**:* people's assembly.

PRĀJAPĀTI *n* Hindi
In Hinduism, the original being existing before the foundation of the universe, whose descendants were gods, men and demons. To some, **Brahma** is Prajapati. A potter (kumhar in Hindi), especially if he models figures, can be addressed as Prajapati, for he, like Brahma, fashions men from clay: strictly, the skilled maker of images has his own title, the mrit-shilpa – the clay/earth craftsman. Nowhere in traditional **Hindu** India do women mould or turn clay on a wheel.

PRAKĀSH *n* Hindi
Light, radiance. A popular name for a boy.

Prakashak: a book publisher (one who illuminates, brings to light).

Prakashan: book publishing, a publishing firm.

PRĀN/PRĀNA *n* Hindi
To the believer, the spirit of God within man himself: man's everlasting soul. Vitality: of all the attributes of life, the pre-eminent, breath (the English word animate, i.e., to breathe life into, and pran share the same **Sanskrit** root). The life-force. The

English word psyche in the original Greek had approximately the same meaning.

Prandān: the gift of life.

PRANĀM *n* Hindi

A reverential word of salutation, used particularly within a family, from a junior to a senior member: often accompanied with the touching of the senior's feet, or a bow, and the namaste/**namaskar** gesture (to a deity the obeisance may be more profound, knees and forehead touching the ground, or a prostration). Also used in correspondence, A general word for the respectful greeting, "Ram Ram" is a pranam, so presumably, is 'Good morning' – *see* Wish. (The literal translation of "good morning" is used in Hindi. "Su prabhat".)

Some aver that the word pranam as a greeting may be used only between caste and social equals and that it would be most inappropriate if uttered by, say, a **dalit** to a brahman.

PRASĀD/PRASHĀD/ PRASHĀDAM *n* Hindi
Lit. grace. **Hindu** sacramental food, particularly honey and sweet things – said to be beloved by the gods – and fruit having been consecrated being ritually offered to a divinity. (Flesh may be considered prasad,

after having been offered to the Goddess **Kali**.) Prasad may be shared
between those assembled in the
manner of the consecrated bread of
the Christian communion service
– a parallel can be drawn, because
Hindus, like some Christians, believe
that by consuming matter a part of a
deity, that they are assimilating and
are being assimilated into that deity.
As a consecrated food, it is treated
with respect by those to whom it is
offered for example, if not eaten, it
is not simply thrown on the ground.
No less prasad are the food leavings
of a person regarded as close to God
(the food leavings of an ordinary
person are jutha, defiled and ritually
highly impure). In south India, a tika
in red or yellow paste, placed on a
worshipper's forehead by a priest,
can be termed prasad.

Traditionally, all food cooked in a
household for use by the family was
first ritually offered to the gods and
could have been considered as prasad.
Hence the extreme care taken by **caste
Hindus** to avoid pollution of the food
preparation area and of themselves
while eating. In a home, after the meal,
the spots made unclean by the used
leaf plates have to be purified.

A personal name: sometimes with
the roman spelling Pershad, a name
particularly of Bihar, God's blessing
or gift.

Kraah/kada/kurra prasad (Punjabi,

lit. blessed *halwa): prasad*: cooked in
a large iron vessel (karah) and used
in Sikh ritual. Usually **atta** or **suji**
halwa with milk ghee and sugar made
according to strict specifications
and with due reverence, consecrated
by being placed before the **Guru
Granth Sahib** and divided, or at least
touched, using a kirpan (sword) or
the khanda (*see* Khalsa).

Mahaprasad: great or special prasad.
Prasad having been offered at a
particularly important shrine, or in
some way believed to have enhanced
significance because of a special
ceremony.

Basic prasad is the batasha. Hollow
sugar buttons made in two sizes.
These may also be used by Muslims,
say, as an offering at a pir's grave: *see*
Dargah. In Delhi old city there is a
street, **Gali** Batashan.

PRAVESH *n* Hindi from Sanskrit
Griha Pravesh: an inauguration
ceremony for a new building. A
house-warming.

PRASAR BHARATI
Indian Broadcasting. Prasar,
Sanaskrit, a scattering, a diffusion.
The body to some degree indepen-
dent of the Ministery of Information
& Broadcasting, with responsibility
for official radio (AIR) and television
(DD) programmes over all India.

PRAYĀG *n* Hindi

Pra+**yagna**. Lit. an auspicious place for a sacrifice. Such as the junction of two or more rivers: the site of such convergence is thought by many **Hindus** to be particularly hallowed by the gods. The pre-Muslim name for the city now known as Allahabad (but Prayag is still used by some) at the junction of the rivers **Ganga, Yamuna,** and, so believed by many, an underground stream, the Saraswati. This spot, sacred to Hindus, also carries the names Triveni and **Sangam**. A place so sacred, said a UP government publication, that a bath at the Prayag during Magh (January/ February: *see* Kumbh), is ten million times as beneficial as a bath at any other time in any other river, and even better than giving away millions of cows as alms.

Prayag can also be used, as in a conference, for a union, or meeting, of minds.

PREPONE

A recent and felicitous Indian-English word formation: the antonym of postpone. Prepone has been accepted from the 10th edition Concise *OED*.

PRESIDENCIES

In British India, an administrative term sometimes used even today, for the provinces of Bengal, Bombay and **Madras**, deriving from the three 17th century **East India Company** factories, each in the charge of a President. The first, at Surat – in

Gujarat, was established in 1612 and moved to Bombay Island in 1687. Fort St. George in Madras became a Presidency in 1658, in the 1900s, the official name for Madras was still The Presidency of Fort St. George' – and Fort William in Calcutta in 1700. From 1805 with the intention of protecting from the Dutch the flank of the Company's trade with China, Penang (now in Malaysia) was created the fourth Presidency with a Governor and Council. But following the acquisition of Singapore, Penang became a backwater, although it remained technically part of **British India** until its absorption into the Straits Settlements and direct control from London in 1867. The 1833 Charter Act sanctioned the formation of a Presidency of Agra for the government of northern India, but this lasted for barely three years.

Following the acquisition of territories outside the factories, the title of the senior appointment to each became both Governor and President of his Council. Bengal gained an all-India authority (mainly because of eastern India's greater revenues) with a Governor-General (*see* Viceroy) and also a Lieutenant-Governor with responsibility for Bengal alone. It was then that Bengal lost its Presidency status until restoration in 1912. (Presidency Governors – often aristocrats with no Indian experience sent out from Britain – had the right to communicate direct with the home government. If, in Bengal, the Governor-General and the provincial Governor, both in Calcutta, had been reporting separately to London, friction would probably have been even greater than that which developed on this account between the Governors in distant Madras and Bombay and the Governors-General. The 1912 return to Presidency status of Bengal followed from the Viceroy's move to Delhi.)

Throughout the East India Company days and in fact until 1895 and the formation of the single Indian Army, the forces available to the Commander-in-Chief, were those of the Presidency armies. From mid-17th century the Company's navy, variously styled the Bombay Marine and the Indian Navy, was part of the Bombay establishment. By then a **GOI** service, in 1935 it became the Royal Indian Navy.

An alternative name for the early territories was Regulation Provinces, for the reason that until 1834, the legislative orders (laws) of the Governor-General and of the Governors of Bombay and Madras, were contained in three codes known as Regulations, of Bengal, Bombay and Madras. By the 1833 Charter Act of the London Parliament, laws made by the Governor-General-in-Council had the usual English style of Acts. (At the same time, the Governors-in-Council of Bombay and Madras lost their independent legislative

powers.) When the added territories under British control became too vast merely to be attached to one or other of the presidencies, new provinces were created – until the reforms of the 1920s each under the charge of a Lieutenant Governor, thereafter, in most cases a Governor. In these, the non-regulation provinces (of which the most notable was the **Punjab**), the old rules did not necessarily apply. A difference that still remains is that in the longer administered areas, the senior **district** civil officer is the **Collector**, whereas in the new, he is the Deputy Commissioner (in British days, the senior civil officers of a non-regulation province formed a Commission). Also the powers of some officials (e.g. magistrates) in today's successor states to the Presidencies (West Bengal, **Maharashtra** and **Tamil** Nadu) in some ways differ from those of their colleagues in states which more recently came under British Indian rule. Again, since the Presidency cities once had royal courts of justice administering English law, law officers' designations like Justice of the Peace and Sheriff still exist.

PRESS *n* English
A word from old English, still in Indian use for the domestic iron.

Press wala: The man whose trade is ironing—normaly not a dhobi.

PRICKLY HEAT

Skin eruption resulting from the body being constantly moist from sweat during conditions of heat and high humidity, causing a prickly sensation and intense itching. Britons sometimes referred to the affliction as the red dog. The medical term for the affliction is miliaria.

PRINCES/PRINCELY ORDER

Prior to **Independence** in 1947, and for a year or two thereafter, the hereditary rulers of about seven hundred semi-autonomous states covering two fifths of the subcontinent: most of whose predecessor feudal kings and chieftains had accepted, at least nominally, the overlordship of the **Moguls**.

Some states were huge, with their own currency, postage stamps, railways, armed forces and judicial systems – but Britons and other non-Indians when in the states were still subject to the all-India Codes. Others were little more than private country estates. To varying degrees, the princes were independent of the **Government of India**: they were a part of the British Empire in treaty relationship with the British crown, the paramount power, but their peoples, unlike those of **British India**, were not British subjects, but British Protected Persons, a fact of little consequence to most of them at the time. Travel between British India and the princely states was

unrestricted and no documents or personal papers were required from anyone crossing the borders. (Not all Rajas and Maharajas were ruling princes, some were major-landowners, particularly in **UP** – *see* Taluk – with honorary titles: they remained part of British India and enjoyed no more than magisterial powers over their tenants.)

From 1921, the rulers had a central assembly in Delhi, the Chamber of Princes, the **Viceroy** being President of the Chamber, but not being prepared to have their powers diminished within their states, encouraged by Winston Churchill, they shrank from federation as proposed in the 1935 Government of India Act. (The two major political parties of British India were also opposed to federation: had it come about the end result for the princes would probably have been unchanged, but the 1947 division of the sub-continent might conceivably have been averted. At the least, in the debates leading up to Independence they would have been part of the body politic of the nation.)

The Viceroy, as Crown Representative, through the Political Department was always informed of affairs within the states and in many ways had powers to influence rulers – in an extreme case a ruler not heeding 'advice', could be, and occasionally was, deposed. No foreign relations were permitted and until the last years even communication between one 'Native State' and another had to be through the Political Department. It was always emphasised that the princes were not sovereigns: e.g., in state emblems and on letter-paper etc., crowns had to be coronets not closed at the top: a closed crown being the prerogative of the King Emperor alone. Indian army **cantonments** in princely states (e.g., Bangalore in Mysore and Secunderabad in Hyderabad) were considered as British Indian enclaves. Against a rising tide of unfavourable Indian political opinion, Britain guaranteed the princes permanence – the map of British and Indian India differed little between 1858 and 1947 – so generally they were strong supporters of the British connection. At least some regarded its termination as a betrayal.

With Independence for British India, the princes' treaties were deemed to have lapsed – paramountcy was not transferred to the successor governments – so that, according to some, each state itself became independent and its ruler a sovereign. The position of the British Government was that while the powers of the Governor-General-in-Council could be transferred, those of the Crown Representative, paramountcy, following from treaties individually made between the princes and the sovereign, unilaterally could not: and since the Crown would have no machinery for carrying out any responsibilities fol-

lowing Independence, there could be nothing to negotiate. However, using the 1935 Government of India Act, the new Government of India quickly entered into treaty relations with the princes within their orbit (three, Junagadh, Kashmir and Hyderabad, unsuccessfully attempted to remain aloof). In the beginning, relations were very similar to those which had existed with the British Crown, but stage by stage led to the extinction of the princes: first, as rulers and, finally, as privileged persons, their princedoms being absorbed into the general administration of India so that, in most cases, the very names of their states have disappeared, or remain only as small towns or cities (exceptions are Mizoram and Tripura, in **north-east India**).

Two erstwhile princes, without territory, may still be addressed legally as "Your Highness": one is the Agha Khan (see Ismaili), the other the Prince of Arcot whose family ceased to rule through the **Doctrine** of Lapse in the time of Queen Victoria.

PRIVY PURSES *n*
Annual payments by the **Government of India** to the princes, following from guarantees contained in the Instruments of Accession signed by the rulers mostly before **Independence**, attaching their states to the Union of India. The payments were abolished by constitutional amendment in 1973.

PROCLAMATION DAY
An official holiday and a day of military parades all over India occurring annually on 21 June between 1865 and 1900, commemorating the Proclamation of Victoria as Queen in 1837 (she had come to the throne a day earlier). During the nineteen hundreds until World War II, Proclamation Day parades were held on January. 1 (Anniversary of the day in 1877 on which Queen Victoria was proclaimed not merely Queen but Empress of India: see Durbar). Yet another Proclamation Day was in November; for it was in November 1858 that it had been proclaimed that on the previous 1 September, the Queen had assumed the Government of India. "Whereas for divers weighty reasons, we have resolved to take upon ourselves the government of the territories in India heretofore administered in trust for us by the Honourable **East India Company**..." The British army serving in India, although it took part in the Proclamation Day parades, like people generally in Britain, ignored the imperial title: its officers drank to the health of The Queen or The King: only Indian service units drank to The Queen Empress or The King Emperor. (The geographical United Kingdom has never had a titular emperor or empress).

PUG/PAG/PAD *n* Hindi
A foot. Pug marks, an anglicism for animal foot prints, usually of the big cats. A word linked to the Latin pedis and the English pedal etc.

Pagdandi: a very small footpath, perhaps no more than a goat-track used as a short cut on a hillside.

Padyattra: see Yattra.
Pad as a folk art form: *See* Pichchawa.

PUGGRI/PAGRI/PAGDI/PAGH
n Hindi
A turban, a tradition-al symbol of a man's dignity: customary decorum, largely but not entirely ignored today, required that a man's head be cov-
ered in the presence of a superior. A length of cloth sometimes just loosely thrown round the head, others, like the **Sikhs**, tie theirs with meticulous care so that each fold is in its exact place – many Sikhs first put on a coloured band, the fiftis, so that when the turban is in position, there is a small triangle of colour in the centre of the forehead. In general, the style of the puggri will indicate the wearer's regional origin; hues are not normally distinctive, except when worn as uniform or livery, but some of the ruling **princes,** wthin their states, did reserve particular colours for use by members of their families.

The word turban is not understood in India by non-English speakers, being a 16th century derivation through Turkish, (tuliband, from which followed the English name for the semblance flower, the tulip) from the Persian dulband: but this actually refers to the Muslim cone-shaped skull-cap with a cloth binding. Other Persian words common in north India for a puggri are safa (particularly a white turban) and dastar (dastarbandh – a ceremony in which a turban is presented. See Kriya). The mini-puggri sometimes worn by young Sikhs, perhaps no more than a piece of cloth round the top-knot (jura), is the patka – the name also for a cloth sash, worn in the manner of a cummerbund. Another type of mini-puggri is the keski, particularly favoured in white by American ladies who have adopted Sikhism. But apart from the Sikhs, who are not fully dressed without one and by the bridegroom and a father or two at weddings, when a shade of pink is fashionable, the puggri is being worn less and less in urban India. The puggri, or any other head-dress, is equally used in or out of doors and, indeed, to enter some religious buildings, for example, a **gurdwara** in the presence of the Granth Sahib with a bare head could be a profanation.

Puggri can also mean an undercover payment: from an old custom, a sign of friendship, whereby at the conclusion of an agreement, the parties exchanged turbans, providing an opportunity for a gift from one to the other be concealed within the folds.

Puggri as a family ceremony following a death: *see* Kriya.

PŪJA *n* Hindi
Lit. adoration. Worship of a **Hindu** deity, including all the complementary rituals and offerings. While some go to a temple, for many, puja is a personal devotional activity, sometimes quite a lengthy one, carried out in the home at least once daily; the presence of flower petals, incense and fire (a small flame from a lamp) is usually considered necessary. A puja for a particular purpose in which a special favour will be requested of a deity may be termed an anusthan.

Pujari: One who worships. Usually refers to the **brahman** priest in charge of a small Hindu temple, or one who performs a religious ceremony: not necessarily a learned man, but one who at least knows the prayers and rituals by rote. In a major temple, a priest is expected to be trained in the art of karamkand, Hindu ritual.

The Pujas/Poojas: a reference to the great autumnal festival period of Bengal, the five days or so of **Durga** Puja increased by general holidays. *See also* Festival Season.

PULTAN *n* Hindustani
18th. century term for an Indian infantry regiment. Perhaps from French or Portuguese or from the English Platoon, itself from French.

PULAO/PILAO/PILAF *n* Urdu
In India, a Moglai (*see* Mogul) dish
of meats and rice, less elaborate
than the basically similar but more
banquet-worthy biryani (biriani. A
word from Persian) which is often garnished with **saffron**, fruits,
almonds, silver and gold foil (*see*
Khir) and, perhaps, sprinkled with
sweetened rose-water.

PUNE *n*
Traditional and current name for the
Maharashtrian city known in British
days as Poona. The name is said to
derive from a temple which existed
in the 13th century dedicated to a
deity with the name Punyeshwar.

Punekar: a permanent resident in
Pune.

PUNJĀB/PANJĀB
Lit. five waters (aab, water in Persian: ap in Sanskrit). The northern
Indian plain drained by the rivers
Jhelum, Chenab, Ravi, Beas and
Sutlej: all these five rivers, except
the last which rises in China, have
their sources in India and flow into
the Arabian Sea. Following a 1960
agreement with Pakistan, ' India has
unrestricted use of the waters of the
Ravi, the Beas and the Sutlej.
State of north-west India, with its
capital at Chandigarh. In area now
less that one-eighth of the province
as it was in 1900, the North-West
Frontier Province was cut off in
1901, the Delhi **district** in 1912

and the territories now the states of
Haryana and Himachal Pradesh (*see*
HP) in 1966. Punjab as it is today is
sometimes said to be divided into
three regions, the old **Mogul** province of Majha/Manjha once centred
on Lahore, but now the land between
the Beas and the Pakistan frontier,
particularly the district of Amritsar;
Malwa, south of the Sutlej; and lastly
the **Doaba**, the land between the two
rivers, Beas and Sutlej. (Also with
the name of Malwa, is the plateau in
central India immediately north of
the Vindhyas, *see* Dravidia, and east
of Gujarat and Rajasthan: part of the
state of **Madhya** Pradesh containing
such towns as Bhopal, Ujjain and
Ratlam.)

Punjabi: person from the Punjab.
The language of the Punjab, a form
of Persian-influenced Hindi written
in the **Gurmukhi** script. The script
itself. In eastern India, the long
knee-length shirt of the punjabi dress,
the **shalwar kamiz**, both male and
female wear in northern India.

Punjabi Suba: Punjabi (speaking)
province. The demand for which
largely by **Sikh** political leaders led
in 1966 to the division of the post-
Independence Punjab into Punjab,
Harayana and Himachal Pradesh.

PUO
A candid acronym of the medical services of British days – both military
and civilian – for an occasion when

accurate diagnosis was baffling. Pyrexia of unknown origin. A similar term today, but indicating technical advance, is viral fever.

PUR *n* Hindi
Also pore, or (as mostly in the south), puram; which word can also mean a huge gathering, as for a temple festival. An inhabited area: a town. Often used as a suffix to form a place name: e.g. Jabalpur – before **Independence**, Jubblepore. But probably not as often as foreign novelists with stories set in India would have their readers believe.

PURĀNAS *n* Hindi
(Really, an English plural from puraan [Hindi], meaning old stories.) In about the 4th century AD, possibly with the intention of countering the advance of Buddhism (*see* Buddha), Hindu devotees compiled in eighteen major and eighteen minor volumes, stories and beliefs common among simple people. These became scripture for a new form of Hinduism, a popular source of religious inspiration.

The Puranas (referred to by some Hindus as mythologies) accept a multiplicity of gods and accommodate almost all forms of belief then found in India: but basic doctrines, **karma**, the **dharma shastras**, the supremacy of **brahmans**, remain from Vedic Hinduism (itself a development from the original Vedic culture). While the **Gita** contains the philosophies of

Lord **Krishna**, the popular stories are to be found in the Puranas.

Puranic period: the era during which the Puranas were compiled: generally accepted to be that of the Gupta kings (300-600 AD).

PURBIYA/PURVIYA *adj.* and *n* Hindi
From the east. In northern India, the word can be a noun meaning a person from the eastern districts of the state of **UP** and adjoining Bihar, also their dialect of Hindi (properly, Bhojpuri). *See* also Deccan.

Purvanchal: eastern U.P. into Bihar.

PURDAH/PARDA *n* Urdu
A curtain, a veil. Frequently a reference to the seclusion of women, wearing of the **burkha** etc. Two Urdu words from Arabic with more or less the same meaning are hijab and hijda.

Purdanashin (women): those who observe purdah, both **Hindu** and Muslim in the north (in the south, Hindus never required strict purdah for their ladies). An associated expression with a similar meaning is char dewari: a reference to the four walls of her home within which a purdanashin is expected to remain.

PŪRI *n* Hindi
A small round disc of wheat or other

flour dough, perhaps with a little **ghee** rubbed in, deep fried until brown and puffed up. If there is a vegetable filling the name may be kachori. Similar is the Punjabi bhatura, except that this is often made with **maida** (white flour) – Today, no less a bhatura, is a bread sandwich with vegetable filling, dipped in **besan** (dal) batter and fried. Some may add a beaten egg to the puri dough, but the stuffing is usually channa dal (*see* Gram): or perhaps panir or chaat.

Pani Puri (water puri): a name largely of western India for an egg-sized hollow ball of puri material, at the moment of eating filled with a thin savoury sauce, hence the name water-puri. In the north, the name is usually gol-gappa, lit. a ball-shaped gulp or quick swallow: most often made and sold as a tasty snack by roadside vendors.

Puri: a city, as in Jagannathpuri (or just Puri), the temple and city of Lord **Jagannath** on the sea coast of Orissa.
Punjabi family name.

Bhelpuri: no connection with puri as above, but a famous snack of Mumbai. Usually sold at a roadside stall or, of an evening, by the sea on Chowpatty beach. Diced cooked vegetables, cereals especially parched rice, and chutnies (*see* Chaat) all tossed together and served in a leaf cup or on a saucer.

PURNIMA/PURNAMASHI *n*
Hindi
The day of the complete, or full, moon (a **Hindu** day runs from sunrise to sunrise). In the Hindu **calendar**, the last day of the bright fortnight of each lunar month: to the pious, a day requiring special observance, a ritual bath in a river or **tank** and perhaps, **fasting**. (Also of religious significance, is amavasya, the opposite to the purnima in the moon-cycle, the day of the moment of the change from a waning to a waxing moon and a night of darkness, the final day of the dark fortnight and of the Hindu lunar month: considered by many to be inauspicious.) A personal name.

Buddha Purnima: the full moon day of 'Triple Blessing' for Buddhists, the anniversary of the day the Buddha was born (about 560 BC), the day he received enlightenment and the day he achieved **nirvana**. Buddha Purnima falls on the full moon day of the ancient lunar month (*see* Calendars) of Vaisakh (April or May, not necessarily coincident with the solar month of which Vaisakhi/**Baisakhi** is the first day).

Kartik Purnima: the full moon day of the Hindu month of Kartik (October/November). A day when the devout bathe in a river. A dust-free time with clear skies after the rains when the moon appears exceptionally bright: an occasion for fairs and melas such as the great cattle fairs at Pushkar (*see* Tirth), Rajasthan; on the **Ganga** near Meerut and, the greatest of them all, at Sonepur in Bihar, where even elephants are bought and sold. The day is also the birthday of **Guru** Nanak, the founder of Sikhism. *See also* Kartikeya.

Poonam Specials: in Gujarat, trains which carry pilgrims and run on Poonam, or full moon, days to certain Hindu religious centres.

PUROHIT *n* Hindi
Brahman priest attached to a family; a house priest. In Vedic times, as grand or state priest (**Raj** Purohit), second in importance only to the king.

PUTI adj Sanskrit
A root sound for something rotten or excremental. Associated in English via Latin with putrid, pus, puke, purulent, pooh.

PUTTOO *n* Hindi
Homespun woollen cloth, used in the **Himalaya**, particularly in the Kangra and Kullu Valleys.

PYJAMA *n* Hindi
Lit. leg coat: in India the word is singular. Jama is Old Persian (i.e. pre-Muslim) and **Sanskrit** for a long coat. jamavar in Kashmir for a cloth length for an expensive speciman or for use as a ladies stole. Loose and comfortable cotton trousers with a draw-string (nara) at the waist: no

fly, but usually pockets. Particularly popular with Muslims, but also used as both day and night wear by many **Hindus** in northern India, As worn by ladies and historically, **Mogul** nobles, the name used may be **salwar**. With eighteenth century Europeans pyjama trousers were popular and known as long drawers. The pyjama jacket is an English invention.

Aligarh Pyjama: worn by Muslim gentlemen, narrower in the leg and ankle than the ordinary pyjama, always of sober colour and never never striped.

Churidar pyjama: tight fitting at the calves and ankles. Originally worn only by ladies at the Mogul court, in almost any material or colour: later, they became fashionable for both sexes. The name (lit. of rings), follows from the **bangle**-like folds that tend to form just above the ankles.

Dharidar pyjama: as they often are, pyjamas made using striped cloth. (Dhari – a stripe)

Farshi Pyjama: a princess' garment from the Muslim courts of the 19th century. Cut as culottes, trousers often of rich diaphanous material trailing the ground, so as to resemble a skirt. The width of leg at the bottom could be as much as 2.5m. Occasionally seen today at the weddings of old noble families.

QANUNGO/KANUNGO *n* Urdu
From the days of the **Mogul** Emperor, Akbar (16th century), to the late British period, a keeper of **District** fiscal records.

QAWALI/QAWWALI *n* Urdu
Rhymed Urdu couplets sung by a small group of leader and chorus, usually accompanied by **tabla**, harmonium and **dholak** and hand clapping to the beat. The qawali originated from the sayings – qual – of Sufi divines (*see* Bhakti) set to music and sung as a means of increasing ecstatic religious fervour, this type can still be heard in **Chisti** shrines: but on another plane, qawali songs are for popular secular entertainment, certainly romantic and possibly erotic, with repetition of well-received lines.

Masiah Qawali (*see* Isa): qawali form, vocalist and musical accompaniment, adopted for the singing of Christian hymns.

QUA'ID-I-AZAM *n* Urdu
Supreme leader, head of state. Often a reference to M.A. Jinnah, founder and first Governor-General of Pakistan. In Pakistan, a title also used for their first Head of State was Quaid-i-Millat, from Arabic: Head of the people, the nation.

Note : also a word from Arabic is quaid, a prison: qaidi, a prisoner, one in jail.

QUEEN'S (or MAHARANI'S) NECKLACE
In **Mumbai,** the view after dark from Malabar Hill, of the starry twinkling curve of Marine Drive (now officially renamed **Netaji** Subhash Road) edging the Arabian Sea from Chowpatty to Back Bay.

QUILA/KILA *n*
Urdu
Fort, Fortress.

Quiladar/Kiladar: the commandant of a fortress.

QURAYSHI/QURESHI/ KOREISHI *n* and *adj.* Urdu
Of the Quraysh, the Arab tribe to which the Prophet Mohammed belonged; claiming **Ibrahim** (Abraham) as their founder-patriarch: they were the aristocracy of Mecca and the guardians of pre-lslamic holy places. At first, hostile to Mohammed's message, they later became

his followers, descent from whom remains a mark of eminence in the Muslim world. In northern India in fairly recent years, the name has been assumed as a family one by the community of Muslim butchers (kasai) and for this reason, is now seldom used by those who consider themselves entitled to it by reason of Arab lineage. This upward social mobility is illustrated by the lines from Persian:

"Earlier I was a butcher, Afterwards I became a **Sheikh**, As grain has become cheap, this year, I have become a **Sayid**."

The word Kasai is sometimes used by those of other communities as an unfriendly reference to Muslims in general.

QUTAB *n* Arabic/Urdu
Pole Star. A book (same word as Kitab) An axis, a pivot. The highest title of sanctity for a Muslim saint, perhaps in the form Qutab-u-Din 'pivot of the faith'

In Delhi the title is always connected with the 11th century 72m high tower, the Qutab Minar, commenced by the first Muslim ruler, Qutub-u-Din Aibak in 1192 (Aibak a ruling dynasty of ancient Persia) Added to by his son-in-law and completed by Feroz Shah Tughlak in 1380.

R

RĀBI *n* Urdu

Lit. the season of spring. The main agricultural crop of the year: normally harvested in March and April; in northern India, largely of wheat, barley and **sarson** (mustard). *See also* Kharif.

RADCLIFFE LINE(S)

A name of 1947 and later, for the newly drawn frontiers within British India (Kashmir was excluded) and the Pakistan to be on the west and in Bengal. Devised by Sir Cyril Radcliffe KC, an eminent UK barrister with no previous experience of India. He was allowed 36 days for the job, using vintage survey maps indicating majority Hindu and Muslim areas and was assisted by two Muslim and two Hindu High Court Judges. He refused a salary. All his life he had been an establishment man and it now seems probable that at the last moment his award was influenced by advice from senior GOI figures: perhaps to ensure that irrigation canals were not cut off from their headworks or that a religious city like Amritsar would be viable with a hinterland. On his return to England

he destroyed all his papers relating to his work. He later became Lord Radcliffe.

Two areas received exceptional treatment. Sylhet a Muslim majority district in Assam and Baluchistan, a Muslim province in the west. In each a referendum was held in early July 1947. Both elected to join Pakistan and so they did.

RAFU *n* Urdu

Stitching (in the sense of joining), so fine as to be hard to see. Darning. *Rafugar, rafuwala:* the expert in rafu work, the best are said to come from Kashmir. Nowadays, often to be seen in dry cleaning establishments providing the service of 'invisible mending'.

RĀG/RĀGA *n* Hindi

Lit. colour. In Indian classical music, a melodic structure with a fixed sequence of notes. In vocalising, generally the voice deep from the throat is used as a musical instrument, expressing moods and emotions rather than for conveying a verbal meaning. A strictly disciplined improvisation on just seven or fewer Hindi vowel sounds flowing on and on without interval: but in some styles, notably, thumri (*see below*), words are used. The notes and form for beginnings and endings of particular ragas and some of the theme notes must be in accordance with fixed rules and it is only within these limitations that a musician is free to improvise. And improvisation there is, for traditional classical vocal music has not been notationally recorded. Each rendition is a personal spiritual pursuit by the gayak (singer). The basic instrumental scale, although far, far older, is similar to that of Europe, but with a greatly increased division of tones.

Ragas may be sung in various ways: such as **alap**, in theory an introduction to the melody used to tune the voice, but often a performance in itself of the highest standing, perhaps continued by one vocalist for several hours. There is the khayāl, an Urdu word meaning thought or whim, popularised by Muslim singers of Hindustani classical music. Also the dhrupad, a very ancient style of composition and **Hindu** devotional singing beginning, perhaps, with musical forms of the sacred syllable **Om**. Modern dhrupad originated in the Gwalior court, of which the most famous exponent was the 16th century rajgayak (court singer), Tansen: there is a saying that if the khayal comes from the lower throat, then dhrupad must come from the navel. Although dhrupad started as worship in the Hindu temple, for several hundred years many of the leading singers of the pure form have been Muslim **ustads**. But Muslim influence is most clearly noticeable in the thumri, a style favoured by the **Nawabs** of Lucknow and **Oudh**, often with an

element of the shringara **ras**. (Some say the name comes from the sound – thumak – of the stamp of a dancing girl's foot.) The range of sentiment is not wide: as a generalisation, it can be said that the themes are union, or separation, in love.

There are forms (raga and ragini), indicating male and female traits.

Almost all ragas are associated with one of the six seasons of the year and with certain periods of the day or night: performance of a particular raga except during its assigned season and time, would be against all musical tradition.

Within the two main groups of classical music, Hindustani of the north and **Carnatic** of the south, many schools of expression, known as gharānas (lit. families), have developed the rag, each in its own way.

Ragmāla (lit. rag-garland) paintings: miniatures illustrating the moods and modes of Hindustāni raga and ragini music, painted in many centres of northern India between the 16th and 19th centuries.

Ragi: a word mostly used in Punjabi, meaning a singer of religious songs, notably **kirtan**. Professional **gurdwara** singer and musician perhaps accompanying himself, or others, on the **tabla**, harmonium or **chimta** (tongs).

RAGI *n* Kannada
The name now accepted into English, for the finger, or African, millet. A nutritious coarse grain grown as a dry crop (i.e., on non-irrigated land), largely in Karnataka (*see* Carnatic) and on the **Deccan**.

RAI *n* Hindi
A variation of the word **raj**. A chief, a ruler (as Rai Pithora–chief of the clan Pithora – a title for Prithvi Raj Chauhan, the last **Hindu** king of Delhi, overthrown by the Muslim invader, Qutab-u-Din Aibak in 1193 AD). During **Mogul** times, a title of honour given to senior Hindu civilian officers: a yet higher honour was the title Rai Raiyan – Chief of Chiefs. In eastern India some of these titles remain in use having become all but Bengali family names: Rai, Roy, Ray and Ray Chaudhury – all pronounced Rai in Bengali – strictly, are variations of a title and not Bengali names. (Family names also have different forms: in particular the **brahman** group ending in 'opadhyay. It is said that the changes occurred in the 19th century because the British found the suffix hard to pronounce. In descending order of precedence: Mukhopadhyay became Mukherjee: Bandopadhyay became Bannerjee: Gangopadhyay became Ganguli and Chattopadhyay became Chatterjee. Similarly, **Thakur**, really a title, became Tagore, e.g., Rabindranath Tagore. In the south, Roy is used only as a personal name. The British

also awarded the title in the form Rai **Sahib** (*see* Bahadur). Yet another anglicised name in eastern India is Paul, derived from Pal (*see* Gopi). Pal was the family name of a line of Bengal rulers in the 9th and 10th centuries AD. From the south, Mr. Paul is likely to be a Christian.

The word rai appears at least once in English literature albeit via Romany, where it is usually taken to mean gentleman: in the 1857 book by George Borrow, The *Romany Rye*. In the final line of his work, the author/narrator expresses an intention to visit India: there is no record that he ever did so.
Rai as an oilseed: *see* Sarson.

RAIS *n* Urdu
Chief, nobleman, wealthy man. An Arabic title with a distant link to rai, and a close one to riyasat – *see* Sadar.

Raiszada: son of a rais.

RĀJ *n* Hindi
The ancient **Aryan** root syllable in the Indo-European tongues (except for classical Greek which had basileus for a king) for the state, or rule by princes (the English regal, regnant, regent, etc.).

The raj', 'the days of the raj', normally, post-**Independence** references to the period of British rule. Before 1947, Britons tended to term their 'occupation', the Empire, or the Indian Empire (*see* Durbar and Proclamation Day). But Kampani raj (*see* John Company) was a Hindustani expression for the British government of India at least upto 1858. As used today, the term is really an anglicism; in no Indian tongue can 'the Raj' refer to British rule, although a government perhaps could be mentioned using the name followed by the noun, rajya.

Raja/Rajah/Rajan: lord or king. Aryan tribal chieftain. **Hindu princely** ruler (not invariably, for some Muslim princes gave themselves the title Raja in preference to **Nawab**), his queen being the Rani. Occasionally, a ruling prince might dub a commoner Raja, as a title of honour, without power or authority. The British did the same: see Taluk.

Raj-gir: a bricklayer or mason From Persian.

Rajmata: mother of a Hindu prince, or widow of a previous ruler. The Queen Mother.

Raj Bhavan: royal residence, state house. In today's India the residence of the Raj Pal (lit. state administrator or protector), the state governor.

Rajdhani: a capital city.

Raj Marg: the way of a good ruler, his conscientious duties, his **dharma**.

In a family setting, the requirement from a member to repress his or her personal feelings and interests if there should be a conflict in order to maintain what is understood to be group prestige.

Rajiv: a **lotus**.

Maharaj: lit. great ruler. An honorific. A title sometimes assumed by Hindu religious leaders and, traditionally, the correct form of address by the humble to *brahmans*. In irony, often used to persons of lower status, particularly cooks (strictly, by tradition it is only a brahman vegetarian cook who is addressed as Maharaj). *Maharaja/Maharani:* great ruler/ great queen. Titles for the ruler and his consort of a major Hindu state. The rulers of some states had special traditional titles, such as Maharao, Maharana, Maharajrana and Mahawal. In Sind and Saurashtra (*see* Kathiawar), a few rulers carried the title of Jam. For example, the Jam **Sahib** of Nawanagar.

Maharana: the system of rule by princes, a form of government easily understood by all.

Rajniti: statecraft, the art of manipulation so as to attain a political objective.

The barber as raja, *see* Nai.
Raj, pronounced in Hindi with a short a can mean dust. Dust can be derisory

and insulting. The **dhoby** can be a rajak – one who removes dust.

RĀJAJI

In history, usually an affectionate and respectful diminutive for Chakravarti Rajagopalachari, statesman from **Madras (Tamil** Nadu): the only Indian Governor-General (1948). In his early days, also sometimes known as CR. He died in 1972. R.G. Casey, from Australia, Governor of Bengal in the 1940s, had dubbed him "the wisest man in India."

RAJDOOT *n* Hindi

Lit. Royal or State messenger. A very ancient and the current term for an ambassador.

RAJMA *n* Hindi

A popular exotic bean popular as a snack in north India. A variety of the haricot bean, introduced from central America. Considered a heating food.

RĀJPUT *n* Hindi

Lit. son of a ruler (raja). **Kshatriya** caste group of northern India and into Nepal, particularly but by no means exclusively, of Rajasthan. In the countryside, Rajputs aspire to be recognised as rajas or **thakurs** of the local squirearchy and not to cultivate land with their own hands. Traditionally rulers, yeoman land-owners and soldiers. In miniature paintings, a Rajput can usually be identified by his exuberant moustache with upturned ends.

Rajput Muslim: a Muslim either himself or his forebears converted to **Islam** from **Hindu** Rajput status. Although some Rajput Muslims are from **nawabi** families, socially they tend not to mix with other Muslims, and rarely marry outside their group. Also may be termed Rangar.

Rajputana: the name in British days for the territory, then mostly **princely** states, now termed Rajasthan, (The name of the army regiment, the Rajputana Rifles, remains unchanged.) Concerning Rajasthan and Rajputana, James Tod in his famous work *Annals and Antiquities of Rajasthan and Rajputana,* (Volume I published in 1829) wrote: "Rajasthan is the collective and classical denomination of that portion of India which is 'the abode' of (Rajput) princes. In the familiar dialect of these countries it is termed Rajwara. But by the more refined, Raethana, corrupted to Rajputana, the common denomination amongst the British to denote the Rajput principalities." Both rajwara and raethana can also be said to mean abode of rulers or chiefs.

RAJYA SABHA *n* Hindi

The Upper House of the Indian parliament. First set up in 1919 under the name Council of State (see Dyarchy).

From the 1950 Constitution of India it was intended that members of the Upper House would be permanent residents of and particularly represent the interests of their State. In the year 2000 the residential qualification was removed. The Rajya Sabh does not have the power to veto or reject a money bill (concerning taxation) sent to it by the Lok Sabha. It can, request reconsideration.

Members are elected by the lower house and the various state assemblies for a term of approximately six years. Twelve members are nominated by the President of India to represent special interests. The Rajya Sabha is never dissolved.

RAKE *n*

Railway English: originating perhaps from a northern England term for carts or animals in file. Rarely used now in Britain, but still current railway jargon in India to mean rolling stock coupled to form a train, moving or stationary, for carrying passengers or goods. A coal rake would be a whole train of coal wagons.

RAKSHA *n* Hindi

Defence, protection. A cotton thread or threads tied round the right bicep of a male **Hindu**, or the wrist, or worn round the neck: (also known as raksha kavaach – kavaach is the same word as for the carapace of a turtle, protective armour – or, when on the wrist, kalava). Propitious red in colour to avert evil or a possible calamity. Such a thread will not intentionally be removed, but will remain until it disintegrates. A black thread or threads may be worn round a part affected by an ailment (e.g., the stomach) to discourage the spirits causing the trouble. All such threads will normally be supplied by a temple **pandit**. It seems likely that the wrist bangle was once a similar protective device.

Raksha Bandhan (*see* Band) or, occasionally, saluno, but mostly, simply rakhi. A custom from **Rajput** chivalry adopted by most of the north and also western India, but not by the south. On the **purnima** (full moon) day of the month of Shravan (July/August), a sister will tie a rakhi, the coloured thread – for this occasion often of gold or silver **zari** with an attached tinsel decoration – around her brother's wrist (and at the same time usually managing to extract a small present from him), both as a symbol that she expects his lifelong protection and also to protect him (as above) from misfortune and evil influences. In some circumstances – as, for example, when both are pupils of one **guru** – a girl may make a boy her honorary brother, with all the privileges and duties of a real sibling, by presenting him with a rakhi. Folk tales abound of rajas (and even of the Great **Mogul**, Akbar) honouring the custom and of coming to the rescue of women in dire need from whom, perhaps many years before, they had received a rakhi.

*Raksha **Mantralaya**/Mantri:* Defence Ministry/Minister in the **Government of India**.

Goraksha (pronounced gauraksha): cow protection.

Sarvotam Jeevan Raksha Padak: Supreme Life Protection Medal. A gallantry award by the President of India.

Rakhi: in a historical context, protection-money. A sum of money paid by a weak ruler to one stronger to buy immunity from attack, Danegeld.

RĀKSHASA/RĀKSHAS *n* Hindi Fem. Rakshasi. One of a class of malevolent demons who can appear as men and who are really dangerous. (King Ravan of Lanka, *see* Dussehra, was a rakshasa): many are deemed to be cannibals. Less unpleasant are the common ghosties, bhoots, believed to be the spirits of men who did not receive proper funeral rites. These can be a great nuisance but are not murderous: experts (ojhas, *see* Mor) are said to be able to catch them and to shut them up in bottles. Similar are the jinns of **Islam,** a term from Arabic (variously spelt in English, djinns and geniis) generally less benign to man than the angels. A word from Persian sometimes seen equivalent to genie is peri. The really malevolent ones being the Shaitan – devils, the djinn like that from Alladin's lamp, is born of flame. (In Sanskrit, bhoot/bhuta as a term can means the five

natural elements, earth, water, fire, air and outer space).

RĀM/RĀMA/RĀMAN
Prince, later king, Ramachandra of the Raghu dynasty (hence a title, Raghu Raghupati, chief of the Raghu tribe) of Ayodhya (*see* Oudh), the capital city of  Kosala, located perhaps in today's eastern **UP**, and in time, perhaps in the 7th century BC. Actually, Lord **Vishnu** in his role of the Preserver, by his own volition born as a man in order to rid the world of a scourge of the gods and man, King Ravan of the south. Lord Ram is the hero of the epic story, the **Ramayana** and to millions of **Hindus**, the divine embodiment of all qualities desirable in a ruler.

When counting aloud, a **lala** (merchant) may use the name of Ram in place of the figure one; 'Ram, do, teen', char. (Others may use the word labh – profit – in place of the numeral one).

In addition to being the name of the God-King, as a word Ram may be identified in an abstract way with the conceptual god-head, God: as in Mahatma Gandhi's reported last words after being shot, "He Ram" –"Oh God!".

Ram Raj: the period of rule by Lord

Ram, believed to have been a time of prosperity and happiness for all, a golden age, as told in the Ramayana. As an expression, the Indian equivalent of Utopia. Today, perhaps a political assertion of the ascendency of Hindutava.

Ram-dhun: hymns sung in praise of Lord Ram. (Dhun, a tune).

Ram Lila: the story of Ram, annually acted in drama from over ten to twenty nights and days, ending one day after the festival of **Dussehra**.

Ram nam satya hai: the name of Ram is truth. Chant in a Hindu funeral group hurrying to the cremation fire. (In a traditional funeral, the body is carried shoulder high, at a pace only just short of a run: but an accompanying gong, if present, will be struck in slow time.) Usually, only males take part. But Punjabi ladies do attend the actual cremation.

Ramanavmi/Ramnaumi: birthday of Lord Ram, celebrated in March/April on the navmi, or ninth day, of the bright fortnight – *see* Calendars – of the month of Chaitra. Some will describe the day as that on which Ram became the sixth or seventh **avatar** of Lord Vishnu.

Ram Rahim: a term signifying Hindu Muslim agreement and co-existence on a particular point. (Rahim: the Merchiful, one of the Islamic names

for God). A reduction of confrontation. Hindu-Muslim unity.

Ram-Ram: a salutation between Hindus.

Sitaram: an invocation to Lord Ram and his wife Sita. Sometimes spoken in the Avadh dialect (*see* Ramayan) as Siyaram.

*Ram **Bagh**:* not necessarily a garden dedicated to the deity, for this common place name is often a derivation from pre-Muslim Persian and Sanskrit (now also Urdu) 'aram bagh', meaning a garden for ease and pleasure. The term may be used for a burial ground.

Ram Das: Personal name servant of God.

RAM/RAMAN *n* Hindi
From Sanskrit, a word for sensual enjoyment including the spiritual pleasure of being close to God. Ramarik/ramani (*adj.*): sensually attractive, beautiful (of a person). Rum Johnny: British military slang from the 18th century for a prostitute, probably from ram-jani. Hindi, a **dancing girl**.

RĀMAYĀNA/RAMAYAN *n* Hindi
Lit. **Ram**'s road/path. A **Sanskrit** epic in seven books attributed to the poet saint **Valmiki** (there are other versions also). The story of King

Ramachandra (*see* Ram) leaving his kingdom with his faithful wife, Sita, a Nepali princess, and his brother, Lakshman/Laxman: of his life in the forests, the abduction of Sita by King Ravan of Lanka and the return after fourteen years of exile to his capital Ayodhya (*see* Diwali *and* Oudh).

The Tamil poet, Kamban, in the 9th century AD used Valmiki's work to compose Ramayanam: here the southerner, Ravan, gets better treatment than in the original and later northern versions.

In north India, the popular *Ramayan*, or to give the poem its full but rarely used title, *Rama-charit-manas* (lit. the acts of Ram as a lake – lake being a metaphor for the all-embracing nature of God), is also based on Valmiki. Written by Tulsidas in the 16th century, not in Sanskrit, but in Avadhi (*see* Oudh), a form of Hindi spoken in the Lucknow area and easily understood over all north India – thus enraging the priesthood. Tulsidas produced no epic, but rather a representation of Lord Ram as an incarnate Godhead to be worshipped. From Valmiki's poem all Hindus know from childhood the finding of Sita (sometimes named Janaki) by Hanuman after her abduction by the demon king of Lanka. In the confrontation with Ravan, Hanuman's tail was set afire leading to the burning of the palaces of Lanka. Hanuman flew back to India, reported to Ram who then took an army to Lanka and personally killed Ravan with a flaming arrow from his mighty bow, an event commemorated annually today (see Dussehra and Divali).

A contemporary disciple of the poet said that the work was intended to show the beauty of God, to create enthusiasm in the hearts of the holy and to increase the joy of the good, The result was much the same as for Christianity in Europe when the Bible was published in the common tongues: Ram joined **Krishna** (both **avatars** of Lord **Vishnu**) in becoming the focus of an extreme religious devotion, particularly from humbler people, which ignored **brahman** ritual and caste barriers (*see* Shakti). Its relevance today can be gauged from the fact that when in 1988/9, the *Ramayana* was serialised on national TV for 93 Sunday mornings, for the full forty-five minutes of this programme alone, in all the urban areas of India power voltages dropped and the streets emptied. Some were of the opinion that this long serialisation was no service to the cause of secular India.

RĀNACHY *n*

A pre-1947 English colloquialism for the Rana rulers of Nepal, hereditary prime ministers from 1845 until the monarchy resumed power in 1951: this **Rajput** family originally came from the region of Udaipur, in Rajasthan. In the same vein, the extended family (A,B, or C class, according to distance from the ruling prime minister) all with names ending in Jalak Jung (Jang) Bahadur Rana (often abbreviated to JJBR) was referred to as the ranocracy.

RANGE *n*

In a police context, a relic word from the 19th century, still in use, meaning a General Police District, the senior administrative officer of which carries the rank, usually, of Inspector General of Police. A Police Range is normally larger than a civil district and may even cross State boundaries.

RANGŌLI *n* Hindi

Traditional patterns and designs on the floor, and perhaps at the entrance, of a **Hindu** home on  important religious and social occasions. Created by the ladies of the house using first, white lines normally of rice powder, then coloured powders and paints: flower petals may also be used. A more formal name for the art is rangarekhavali – making of coloured lines: in Bengal it is known as alpana and as kolam in the south. In rural areas similar words may be used for house wall ornamentation. It had to happen, plastic stick-on rangoli are now available in the bazaars.

RANIKHET

Lit. Queen's Field, or farm. A town in the **Kumaon Himalaya**. A poultry ailment, known in England as Doyle's disease or Newcastle disease.

RANN/RUNN *n* Hindi

A coastal salt desert occasionally inundated by the tide, salt marshland, particularly in Gujarat. e.g. The Rann of Kutch/Kachchh: once, the estuary of the R. Indus, now short of fresh water and people. A home for the Asiatic wild ass – *see* Kyang – and a breeding ground in the cool weather of the flamingo. In Rajasthan, the term can be applied to seasonal saline lakes, usually shallow.

RĀn/raan: lit. a thigh. Food term for leg, as in 'ran **Mirza**' – leg of **mutton** prepared in a **Mogul** style. (In establishments with little imagination, the workaday word for a leg is likely to be used, tang.)

RAS *n* Hindi

A **Sanskrit** word (rasa) often used as a prefix in Hindi – to convey meanings as wide apart as finely aesthetic appreciation and crudely sensual enjoyment in matters of art, music and poetry on one side and relish of good food and eroticism on the other. The juice of a fruit or the flavour of a dish.

Rasam: the highly seasoned vegetable drink, a soup perhaps, of the south. *See* Mulligatawny.

Rasagola: *see* Khoya.

Rasmalai: see Khoya.

Rasik/Rasika: a man of good taste, aesthete.

Nau/nav ras/rasa: the nine moods of traditional Indian literature, poetry, music and dancing. In order, these are: **kama/shringara** (sometimes said to be the rasraj, or king of passion: another epithet is adi-ras, the original ras), sensual passion, eroticism. Humour and comedy. Joy. Pathos and sadness. A longing for God. Anger and fury. Dignity, majesty, courage. Fear, awe, hate and hostility. Surprise, wonderment, anticipation. And last, peace and tranquillity.

Rasbhāri/rasberi: lit. juice-filled. Name used in northern Indian markets for the cape gooseberry (tipari in Hindi). A spring fruit of the potato family from Peru. Outside S. America, the plant seems to have been first established at the Cape of Good Hope: hence the English name. The botanical name from Greek for the genus, Physalis, a reference to the paper-like cover (the calyx) is sometimes in common use for the fruit.

Rās/Raas (Hindi): folk dance associated with the Krishna story. *See also* Lila.

Rās/Raas (Urdu, from Arabic): promontory or headland, Particularly used on the Arabian Sea coast of Pakistan.

RĀSHTRA *n* Hindi
A nation, a state.
Rashtrapati: lit. Lord of the Nation. A head of State: particularly the President of India.

*Rashtrapati **Bhavan**:* the official residence of the President of India in New Delhi.

*Rashtrapati **Nivas**:* once the Viceroy's residence in Simla (Viceregal Lodge), now the President's house in **Shimla**, since 1965 occupied by the Indian Institute for Advanced Study.

Rashtrapita: Father of the Nation. An epithet for **Mahatma** Gandhi.

RATH *n* Hindi
Strictly, a war chariot, pulled by two horses. Pas-senger car-riage, two and sometimes four-wheeled, pulled by two  or four bullocks. Also a rath is an immense replica of a **Hindu** temple on wheels in which the deity (or a duplicate) of a permanent temple is taken for an airing once or twice a year. The huge vehicle (or temple car) is dragged slowly a few feet at a time, by a multitude of devotees drawing on ropes. *See also* Jagannath *and* Car Festival.

The rath is the model for some of India's great temples: at Konarak on the Orissa coast, designed as a huge chariot in stone, the car of Surya, the Sun god (*see* Gayatri), pulled by seven stone horses.

In Himachal Pradesh, the chair borne on men's shoulders on which a village deity is taken for an excursion can also be known as a rath.

Rath is linked to the Indo-European root word for a wheel ret. Rota in Latin, leading to rotary, rotund etc. in English.

RAYALASEEMA

The southern region of Andhra Pradesh, covering the **districts** of Anantpur, Cuddapah, Chittor, Kurnool and Nellore.

RAZAI *n* Urdu

A cotton-filled quilt, a duvet, used by all for sleeping warmth and by villagers as a wrap-around cloak during the winter cold. Each autumn the razai is unquilted and the cotton carded and fluffed by the dhunkar/dhunai (dhun – a melody), often a Muslim, who calls at the home carrying what might appear to be a two metre high cello-like musical instrument: in urban northern India during the cold weather, he walks the streets advertising his services by twanging the instrument's single wire string. But this picturesque figure is now being displaced by the quicker and cheaper (the charge is based on the weight of the cotton treated) motor-driven machine in a bazaar shop: the service is still largely a Muslim one. General opinion is that the primitive dhunkar gives better results.

In England's north-eastern mining areas, a similar sleeping quilt may be called a Durham blanket. The name arose in the nineteen thirties when unemployment was rife in the area: a cotton quilt was cheaper than a woollen blanket.

REAL INDIA, THE

The phantom "**Shangi-La**" sought by visitors dissatisfied with the sight-seeing fare offered them. Also perhaps a land sought to be created by adherants to the doctrine of **Hindutva**.

REDDI/REDDY

Village headman in Andhra Pradesh. Family name.

REETHA *n* Hindi

The dried fruits of the soapnut tree (Sapindus, variants of which are found all over India), containing about ten per cent saponin. Broken pieces are soaked in hot water and the resulting suds are valued for washing woollen garments and the hair, also jewellery. Other names are aridha and **dhobi** nuts. From a belief that they strengthen and darken the hair, shikakai seed pods may be added to the reetha.

REGISTERED A. D.
Registered Acknowledgement Due,
i.e., the sender of a postal article so
despatched will receive confirmation
of delivery from the addressee.

REHRI *n* Urdu
A handcart.

Rehriwala: the man who pulls or
pushes the rehri, or who, perhaps,
sells vegetables or fruit from it: a
barrow boy.

RENONCANT *n* French
Lit. one who renounces. Generally,
in the Indian context, a **sadhu**, a
sanyasi. But in the one-time French
colonial settlements in India, the
word had and still has a particular
technical legal meaning: that of an
indigenous citizen who formally
renounced his own customary civil,
or personal, law in favour of the
French code. At the time of the de-
facto take-over of the French possessions (Chandernagore in Bengal
in 1950. Pondicherry and the other
enclaves in 1954), it was accepted
by the Government of India that the
renoncants' rights would continue.
Thus it was that in 1996 there were
approximately nine thousand Indian
citizens governed in their law relating to marriage, divorce, succession,
etc. by the Code Napoleon. As vestiges of France Outre Mer (France
Overseas), the renoncants vote to
send two deputies to the French
Senate every seventh year.

REPUBLIC DAY
26th January: celebrated annually as
the National Day of India. A major
public holiday, recalling the date
in 1950 when the Constitution Act,
in which India was declared to be
a sovereign republic, became law.
The 26th of January was chosen, as
the anniversary of the day in 1930,
announced by **Mahatma** Gandhi to
be **Independence Day**, on which all
were to pledge to work for 'purna
swaraj' – complete self-rule and
independence from Britain.

Republic Day in general is celebrated
in a larger way than the actual Independence Day: one reason, no
doubt, is that in January the weather
is usually more suitable for parades
and outdoor festivities than in the
August **monsoon** period. Also, it
could have been that in 1950 some
considered a day associated with the
Mahatma and the freedom struggle
more worthy of commemoration
than a date chosen by a Briton for no
reason other than it marked the end
of a war with Japan.

RESIDENT *n*
In British days, the representative of
the sovereign (through the **Viceroy**
and the **Political** Department) at the
Durbar of a single major **princely**
state: in practice of course, a form of
indirect rule by the British government. Small states did not have a
Resident, but were grouped together
in an Agency, in which case the

414

crown representative was known as the Political Agent (the distinction was made in common usage, but technically, both representatives were political agents). In the event that a ruler was a minor, the Resident could be required to administer the state.

Until the early years of the twentieth century, British control of many of the smaller states was exercised through the Provincial governors, not as later, direct by the Political Department at the centre.

Residency: home and office of the Resident. Held to be an enclave of British Indian territory. *See also* Politicals.

REST HOUSE *n*
The British period equivalent of the ancient **Hindu** provision for travellers, the panthshala/pathshala (lit. road-house: see also Path, Panth and Dharmshala). Government buildings providing basic European standard accommodation in rural areas for officials touring on duty. May be used by the general public with permission from the controlling authority, usually the Public Works Department.

RETIRING ROOMS *n*
Residential accommodation in major railway stations, where passengers holding upper-class tickets may stay for short periods on payment.

For second-class passengers there is dormitory accommodation, under a name, perhaps, such as Rail Yatri Nivas.

RHUBARB *n* English
A plant of the Rheum family of the **Himalaya** and into Tibet and China. Its powdered rhizomes have a use in **ayurvedic** medicine (and **allopathy** in earlier days) as a mild laxative: also as a yellow dyestuff. The variety now cultivated in European and American gardens, *R. rhaponticum,* was probably introduced early in the 19th century.

RI (R.I.)
Rigorous Imprisonment. A person sentenced to a term of RI can be required to work in jail for eight hours a day at any task allotted to him. Those sentenced to Simple Imprisonment cannot be required to work but they may do so if they wish.

RICE CORPS
In later British days a popular name for the Royal Indian Army Service Corps, both from the acronym, RIASC, and from the corps' duties – one of many – as supplier of food grains to the army.

RICKSHAW/RICKSHA/RIKSHA *n*
Small passenger-carrying two-wheeled vehicle, pulled by a man on foot: originally from Japan (jinriksha) and introduced into

India by Europeans. Nowadays, at least in northern India, more often three-wheeled and moved by pedals (the cycle rickshaw, of which the seat still slopes  downwards, sliding the passenger forward, as did that of the original jinrikshaw at rest with the shafts on the ground), or engine power (**phat-phat** or autorickshaw). The spectacle of man, as a horse, pulling another is now considered distasteful and has been banished from many municipalities.

RIGHT HAND, LEFT HAND

In Indian culture, and throughout Indo-Europe, the right side of the body is considered superior to the left. A Hindi word from **Sanskrit** for left, vaam, also means base and perverse. The right hand alone is used to convey food to the mouth and for gestures of greeting, of salutation and of pointing at a distant object. (Note that index finger-pointing at an object accorded respect, such as a person or an image of a deity, is, as in England, considered bad form. Some will say that to point to flowers or a flowering tree will cause the blossoms to fade. If the finger must be used, then it should be bent, with just the knuckle towards the indicated object.)

In performing the circulatory rite of **parikrama**, the right side remains nearest to the object of devotion. On any formal occasion, the senior guest should be to the right of the host: with two or more persons side by side traditionally, the seniormost will be on the right side of the juniors: a husband will be io the right of his wife: a brother to the right of any sister or younger male sibling: a father to the right of his son. A **sati** will lie to the left of her dead husband on the funeral pyre. In a Delhi bus, when seats are reserved for ladies, these will be on the left side facing the driver. If size permits, an object handed to anyone, should be offered and received by the right hand only or, perhaps, the left hand beneath the right. Thus is prasad always received. Extra respect is indicated if the right forearm is held by the left hand. A palmist will read the right hand of a man, but the left of a lady. According to Muslim tradition, the Prophet Mohammed ordained that men should not spit nor otherwise pollute the ground to their right " ...for there standeth the angel who recordeth your good actions". In everyday life, only the left hand is used for abdast (Persian: lit. water-hand) , washing the body after defecation.

Historically, southern culture, particularly that of Tamil Nadu, accepted a cross-caste social division into those of the right and left hands. Landowners and persons whose livelihood derived from the land, including the rajas, and the village service workers who were paid in kind, were of the superior, or right-hand group. Those of the town, the merchants and the artisans, were from the left. In practice of course, the wealth of a town merchant could give him position above that of a countryman, but man for man, he of the country, of the right hand, was accepted as superior in social status to an equivalent townsman. By the 1930s, the dichotomy had almost gone, but traces may remain even today in folk memory.

The notion of the superiority of the right, perhaps owes something to the fact that in the human daily spiritual uplift when facing the rising sun in the northern hemisphere, the solar path is to the right of the body but there must be something else, for over all mankind, to be left-handed is to be discordant. In the English language, the left is the sinister side but dexterity and adroitness (all three words from Latin) are associated with the right. A left-handed compliment is no compliment at all, or at the best, is ambiguous. A valued assistant is a right-hand man. British stage direction, the hero will enter from the right, the villain from the left. To circulate widder-shins, i.e. against the motion of the sun some consider to be inauspicious. Continental Europe – and the United States – conveys food to the mouth using a fork held in the right hand. "My

foot" in English is an exclamation of denial, of contradiction. An Indian senior civil servant in interjection to a point made by an interrogator was reported to have amplified his negative opinion by saying "my bloody left foot". (India Today, 31.5.95).
In British stage direction, the hero will enter from the right, the villain from the left. The English word meaning socially awkward, gauche, in the original French means left.

In rural Ireland a left handed woman, can be thought to be a sinistrol/sinistral, a witch.

It is generally held that when entering a building on an important occasion, the right foot should cross the threshold before the left (classical Rome had the same opinion) and when putting on trousers, it is natural for the right leg to be entered first.

RIMPOCHE/RINPOCHE n
Tibetan
Invariably translated as carrying the literal meaning of 'Precious One'. An honorific title accorded in Tibetan Buddhist countries to persons of high spiritual attainment. Also to one accepted as a reincarnation of such a person.

RISHIS n Hindi
Long long ago, **Hindu** religious teachers who lived as hermits in the mountains and in the forests. 'Spiritual beings on a higher plane

than men, who can assume a human body if they wish.' Unlike the gods who sometimes were wayward towards man, the rishis are considered to have always been benign and of high moral stature. (Perhaps, age was a reason: the gods are ever youthful, the rishis ancient and white bearded.)

Sapta Rishis: seven rishis who became the seven stars of the constellation the Great Bear/ the Dipper/the Plough. For the pole-star, *see* Dhruva.

Maharishi: a superior rishi, A name for Lord Shiva.

RISHTA *n* Hindustani from Persian

A relationship, an alliance; particularly a marriage alliance made by two families. An arranged marriage, the normal way of things, these days probably, but not necessarily, with the consent of the boy and girl. See Sarda Act.

In little used Hindi the agreement will be termed vivah or **vivahautsav**, but rishta is more generally used. For the wedding itself, again a Hindustani word, shadi, is normal. (It is said that a link can be traced between the English word marriage and the Sanskrit marya, meaning a youth in love.) See also Suhaag.

ROAST *n* English

As in 'rule the roast'. An archaic form of roost, meaning the cock-bird dominating a hen-run, or to be in control. Shakespeare: "Suffolk, the new-made duke that rules the roast." (Henry VI, Pt.ll 1) Still common in Indian English writing, but in standard English, roast in this sense has rarely been used since the 18th century. Both roost and roast derive from a word for the house-roof rafters upon which the fowls perched for the night.

RŌGHAN JŌSH *n* Urdu

Although the words are Persian (lit. butter-oil pleasure. Raughan being the Indian **ghee**) meaning cooked in butter-oil, the meat dish of this name is really Punjabi: Muslims outside the Punjab term a similar preparation, korma. **Mutton** pieces cooked in ghee (also perhaps, with **dahi**) until soft, served with a thick and seasoned brown gravy. An English term for the process can be braised. Eaten with **tandoori roti** often the tastiest meal in a roadside **dhaba**, even though the ghee is now likely to be **vanaspati**.

RŌHILLAS *n*

The people of Rohilkhand, a territory of **UP**, north of Delhi and as far east as Bareilly, its one time capital city. But the term is usually a reference to 17th and 18th century immigrant freebooters, Afghan **Pathans**, many from Roh hence their name – a highland region now covered by N.W. Pakistan and eastern Afghanistan, The most notorious was possibly Ghulam Kadir, who, from his base at Saharanpur in 1788 raided Delhi, captured the Palace (the Red Fort) and subsequently personally blinded the aged **Mogul** Emperor, Shah Alam. (The act was said to have been one of revenge, for as a youth Ghulam had been castrated by order of the Emperor.) The town of Rampur later became the capital of Rohilkhand and of a small princedom, Rampur State, with its Afghan leaders, respected **nawabs**. Even today, it is said that the Urdu of Rampur has a Pushtu flavour.

One of the few dogs with a pedigree raised in India is the Rampur hound. Bred by the Nawabs for hunting. Long legged and fast running. Hard to find today.

ROOMAL/RŪMAL *n* Urdu

From Persian, a facecloth; a pocket handkerchief: a cloth perhaps the size of a small towel, carried folded on a male shoulder. In an earlier age, the silken cloth traditionally used by **thugs** for ritually strangling their victims.

A hand embroidered cloth covering a tray of sweets, or any other small object, being sent as a gift.

Chamba rumal: a speciality of Chamba district (once a **princely** state) in Himachal Pradesh (*see.* HP). A cloth approximately two feet square, (but examples much larger are known) folk embroidered, usually a depiction of a scene from the **Krishna** story. Often said to be the embroidery equivalent of a **pahari** painting.

Rumali: a **chapati** so soft and thin as to be like a very large round headscarf. A wrestler's breech-clout.

ROORKHI CHAIR *n*

A folding camp chair; a wooden frame, canvas for seat and backrest and two wide leather straps for armrests. Designed, perhaps, in the civil or military engineering centre of the **UP** town, in the 19th century.

RŌTI *n* Hindi

Indian style bread, the **chapati**. As with bread in English, so in Hindi the word is used figuratively to mean a livelihood.

Double-roti: this old hybrid is the widely used Hindustani (*see* Khari Boli) term for European bread. Possibly originally an anglicism from dabba-roti, meaning box-like bread, or bread made in a box. In eastern and western India this bread may be known as pau/paon roti (lit. footbread) from an early belief that bare feet were used to knead the dough.

Makki ki roti: maize flour bread from Indian corn – the English adjective of course, refers to North America. A Punjabi speciality.

Roti-gong: a British army expression for the Good Conduct and Long Service Medal: for the reason that it did not have to be won but 'came up with the rations' after eighteen years of more or less, trouble-free service.

Missi roti: lit. mixed bread: **Besan** (gram flour) with perhaps some white flour also, well seasoned, small **chapati** size: cooked on a tawa (griddle) and deep fried.

Tandoori roti: bread cooked in a **tandoor** (a type of oven) and not on a hot griddle as a chapati. *See also* Chapati, Nan, Paratha, Puri *and* Roomal.

ROXB./ROXBURGH

Either of the above forms following the botanical name for an Indian plant is a reference to its classification by Dr. William Roxburgh, Superintendent of the Calcutta Botanic Garden, 1793-1813, then called the Company Bagh (*see* John Company. It later became the Royal Botanic Garden, and today, still going strong, is the Indian Botanic Garden). Kolkata's Garden Reach, on the Hooghly, in the early 18th century an attractive stretch of the river leaving the city to the south and the sea, derived its name both from the botanical garden on the west bank and on the eastern, from the gardens of palatial houses down to the water's edge. Dr. Roxburgh's classifications were collected into three volumes, Flora Indica, published in 1832. An earlier volume,

Hortus Bengalensis, (Garden of Bengal), cataloguing the plants of Roxburgh's Garden was compiled and published by Dr. William Carey of the Danish enclave of Serampore (originally Srirampore).

RŌZA *n* Urdu

A fast (*see* Fasting). The Fast; the Persian and Urdu colloquial name for the ninth month of the Islamic year (*see* Calendars). Otherwise known as Ramzan/Ramadan. (From Arabic, sometimes Saum.) Often referred to as Ramzan Sharif – noble Ramzan – or Ramzan Mubarak – auspicious Ramzan – to honour the month on the first day of which the Holy **Kor'an** was made known to the Prophet Mohammed. A month of day-long fasting and abstention from sensual pleasures for all Muslims (even cinema takings drop during the month). Between dawn and the evening darkness, no food nor liquid should pass the lips, nor even the consolation of tobacco smoke. (Tobacco, of course, is not mentioned in scripture, but Muslims agree that, as a sensual pleasure, it must be given up during the day for the month of the roza: an added reason, is that in Arabic, and in Urdu, the verb to smoke is the same as to drink.) There is Kor'anic exemption for those who are sick or on a journey, when rigid observance could be a danger to health, but they too should fast for the number of days missed as soon as they are in a position to do so: the strict will even refuse a medical injection during daylight hours.

Following each dav's sunset, the first meal, iftar, is somewhat formal in a family setting: the early morning meal which must be completed before dawn, has the name, sehri.

The month of Roza begins and ends with the sighting of the evening new moon, Since the Islamic Calendar is lunar, by the Gregorian Calendar the month of Roza begins eleven days earlier each year with the sighting of the evening setting new moon. but if, due to cloud, the moon is not visible when theoretically possible. then the thirtieth day is the last (*see* Calendars). Following the end of Roza is the major festival day of the Muslim year. **Id**-ul-Fittr, when all celebrate, put on new clothes, go to the mosque or ldgah and friends greet one another.

Ramzan is not like the wholly austere period of the Christian Lent (but in an Indian Christian context, the word roza is normally applied to the days of Lent), for the nights are convivial, with **bazaars** in Muslim areas crowded, shops and eating houses ablaze with lights until dawn. Four weeks, when Muslims – although not all fully observe the fast. – especially rejoice in their faith and their togetherness.

Rozadar: one who observes the fast. Roza (more correctly rauza) can also mean the garden tomb of a respected person, for example, an Urdu speaker may mention the Roza **Taj Bibi** at Agra.

RSS/R.S.S.
Rashtriya Swayaimsewak Sangh, National Voluntary Service Organisation. A largely **Hindu** semimilitant organisation with its not always obedient political wing, the Bharatiya Janta Party (BJP). A drill, or meeting, of members is known as shakha: lit: branch (of a tree). The ruling council of the Sangh has the name, Kendriya Karyakari Mandal.

The volunteer workers of the RSS are termed swayam sewaks.

RŪBIA *n* Hindustani
Originally, a double twisted cotton thread voile textile: nowadays synthetic fibres mav be used. Often chosen for summer clothing, such as **kurtas, saris** and shirtings. The name is a fairly recent one, coined from the red dye plant, maddar, *Rubia tinctorium*, the leaf pattern of which, the weave is said to resemble. In the 19th century a red pigment made in Turkey from the madder root was used in Manchester to colour cheap cotton textiles, a bulk export named Turkey Red to the Indian and African markets. Later the dye became chemical but the name for the red cloth continued.

RUDRĀKSH/RUDRAKSHA/RUDRAKI *n* Hindi
Dark brown, much grooved, turb-

ercled seeds from the tree. *Elaceo-carpas ganitras*, largely growing in Nepal, but also in parts of India: there is some import of the seeds from Indonesia. According to popular opinion, the test for a genuine seed is that it must sink in water. Cleaned, polished and sometimes stained, they are strung together as beads for necklaces and rosaries for use by Shaivites (*see* Shiva). As a rosary. the beads may be fingered inside a sock-like bag called a gaomukh (cow's mouth) to shield them from evil influence. The name rudraksh follows from a belief that the seeds represent the tears of Rudra (or Shiva) and when in a rosary the fifty characters (aksha) of the **Sanskrit (Devnagri)** alphabet. Many **Hindus** wear a rudraksh **mala** (necklace) from a conviction that it possesses supernatural medical powers and that. in particular, it is a specific against high blood pressure. Dried immature fruit of the bael tree (bel. in Indian English) are also connected with Shaivite worship – the trifoliate leaves replicate the **trisul** –they may be interspersed in a rudraksh mala. (When ripe, the citrus bel fruit is about the size of a large orange the peel may be almost two centimetres thick, astringent, and is said to be valuable as a cooling agent [*see* Heating Foods], and under the name Bengal quince, was earlier considered a remedy for dysentery and even cholera. To the botanist it is *Aegle marmelos*.)

A connection can be demonstrated between rudh – red colour in Sanskrit – through the Germanic tongues to the English, red, ruddy, blood etc.

RUMBLE-TUMBLE
Scrambled eggs. An army British officers' mess term: seemingly of no great age, since it is not mentioned in *Hobson-Jobson*. Understood by elderly cooks who have served British masters.

Similar in origin and use hurry-scurry understood to mean French toast.

RUNNING ROOM
A rest room at major railway junctions or stations for use by travelling railway staff.

RUPEE *n*
English, from rupiya, Hindi for a silver piece: the Indian unit of currency. Rupiya coins of indeterminate weight were in circulation even before the 12th century AD. (The **Gupta** kings issued silver coins known as rupaka) but the rupee of 180 grains Troy (175 grains pure silver), was first introduced by Sher Shah in 1542 (Sher Shah Suri an able administrator, occupied the Delhi throne during a break in Humayun's rule). It continued as the standard coin with little theoretical variation until both its metallic debasement and partial replacement by paper money during World War II: but there are still huge

hoards of these old coins, which form a major source of silver bullion for the jewellers (the price per hundred pieces is quoted on the commodity pages of the newspapers – in 2006, just about Rs. 22,000). Being practically equivalent to sterling silver, unlike pure silver which is too soft, the metal from old coins is ready for immediate use. The coin of today is made from cupro-nickel. In a **lala**'s home or in a family business where **Lakshmi** is particularly worshipped, especially at **Divali** time, it is the old silver coins, perhaps by the trayful, that are displayed in rites to solicit the blessings of the goddess. A number of countries with a past Indian connection also term their currency unit the rupee (or rupia): these include Indonesia, Mauritius, Nepal, Pakistan and Sri Lanka. Colloquially in English, the rupee is often referred to as a chip. An Urdu word sometimes used in conjunction with rupees is sicca/sikka, meaning a coin whose purity could be tested by ringing against a stone as opposed to a currency note. (The English sequin, is derived from the Arabic original of sikka which first had the meaning of a coining die.)

In 1941, there was an idea to issue a silver coin with the face value of Rupees $2^1/_2$, to be called a dollar. A few pattern coins were made by the Calcutta mint, but with the war, the price of silver rose and the dollars never went into production. *See also* Anna, Pice.

The one rupee note (printing ceased in 1992) and the one rupee and five rupees coins are actual money, issued by the Finance Ministry of the **GOI**. Paper currency of other face values is issued by the Reserve Bank and each piece is no more than a promissory note. The reason for the distinction is historical and has no practical meaning today: it dates from a time when coinage had not only a face value but also an intrinsic worth as bullion. For a sum of less than Rs. 2.00, the correct abbreviation is Re.

RYOT *n* Urdu
Lit. protected. A cultivator: either of his own land, or else as a tenant who cannot normally be dispossessed.

Ryotwari: a revenue term of British days, meaning the system whereby each actual cultivator, even of a small plot, was assessed separately for land tax. A form of **settlement** found mostly in southern and central India. On the other hand, in the zamindari system of Bengal, a local influential person collected and paid the tax on behalf, sometimes, of whole villages, and eventually became recognised as the freehold owner, the **zamindar**. In a ryotwari village there was little common land.

S

etables. *See also* Indian Hemp. Hindi equivalents are bhaji and bhujiya: these can also mean a dish of cooked vegetables, greens. Bhujiya as a name can also be applied to saltish snacks, namkin (*see* Namak) or, as Punjabis enjoy them, a mixture of salty and sweet nibbles.

Sabziwala: vegetable seller.

Sabzimandi: vegetable market (normally also selling fruit).

SACHIVĀLAYA *n* Hindi
Lit. the abode of the sachiv (secretary). Secretariat.

SADAR/SADIR/SUDDER *n* Urdu
Premier, chief, important. In Urdu, the normal way of referring to the President of India is Sad'r-i-Riyasat – Chief of State. This was also a title of the ruler of the **princely** state of Jammu & Kashmir, and of the former Maharaja while Governor of the state within the Union of India.

*Sadar **Bazaar**:* the main bazaar in a city or town.

SĀDHANA *n* Hindi
In Hinduism, a course of spiritual, and to a lesser degree, physical, self-discipline, with the intention of gaining a greater realisation of oneself and God, leading perhaps to the state of **samadhi**. Any discipline for training the mind for a worthy purpose, or of acquiring a technical

SAAG/SĀG *n* Hindi
Lit. any cooked vegetable, but the word usually refers to spinach-like cooked leaves of green vegetables, particularly of the mustard plant (**sarson**). A popular saag is palak, similar in taste to the European spinach but with differently shaped leaves from a different plant. Palak comes from the common beetroot (Beta vulgaris) of which several varieties are grown.

Spinach in English derives from a Persian and Arabic original.

SABHA *n* Hindi
A parliament, an assembly, an association. An audience, particularly of classical music or dancing. The word dates from Vedic days, then meaning a body of tribal chiefs in consultation with their ruler. *See also* Samaj.

Shok Sabha: a condolence meeting. A commemorative meeting following a death. See Ashok.

SABZI/SABJI *n* Urdu
Lit. greenery, verdure. Fresh veg-

skill such as classical music. The sad-hak is the person practising sadhana. (No less a sadhak is a disciple, as of a **guru** or master in an **ashram**) *See also* Tapasya.

SĀDHU *n* Hindi
Lit. A virtuous man. **Hindu** religious ascetic who, in following his chosen path has renounced all family ties: one may be a member of an order or sect (sampraday), living a community life in an **ashram** or some great **math**, or perhaps walking from village to village, with particular rules of behaviour and dress – or, perhaps, of no dress at all (nang-dharang. The Sanskrit root sound for naked, nang, is connected to Latin and English). Another may be alone, remaining, say, beneath the same tree year after year, his food being supplied by respectful villagers who seek his counsel. Some, usually devotees of Lord **Shiva**, practise extreme asceticism or perhaps mutilate or cripple their bodies. Today, some Christian monks and priests also term themselves sadhus.

A word from Hindi sometimes used in English to describe Hindu religious itinerants is vairāgis/bairāgis (from viraag renunciation). Strictly, vairagi should be applied only to a Vaishnavite (*see* Vishnu) sadhu, while a Shaivite (*see* Shiva) is a go-sain. *See also* Aghori and Akhara.

It has been estimated that there are three million sadhus in India: some are saints, some are rogues, but most, as with people generally, are some-where in between. A group of sadhus, perhaps accompanied by an elephant, demanding food and alms from villagers, to Western eyes may appear to have a relation with locusts, but the well-fed mendicants will receive courtesy and their needs will be met.

Sadhu derives from **sadhana**, and means one who has achieved knowledge. Sadhu-sant: *see* Sant.

Sadhvi: in the original Sanskrit, devout and chaste woman: in today's Hindi, a woman sadhu.

SAFFLOWER *n* English
Kardi, in Hindi. A small thistle-like shrub with orange-yellow flowers (which, powdered, may be used as an adulterant of the highly expensive **saffron**): cultivated mostly for its oil-seeds. The oil has industrial uses, particularly for soaps and paints and is valued as an edible oil/cooking medium on account of what are claimed to be low cholesterol inducing properties. A dye-stuff can be made from the flower petals.

SAFFRON *n*
An anglicism, derived from the Arabic (and Urdu) zafran. Deep yellow powder used for flavouring and colouring food-stuffs. Made from the three orange-red stigma of the purple flower of the saffron crocus (Crocus

sativus): native from southern Europe across to Iran – a saffron crocus has been shown on a vase of the Minoan civilisation, dated, perhaps, 1500 BC and certainly has been cultivated in Kashmir since antiquity. The dried petals are often sold under the name **Kusum**. It is said that a quarter of a million flowers are required to make just one pound weight of saffron: with a flowering period of just over two weeks in autumn, naturally an expensive spice with a retail sale price in Delhi (1996) of Rs. 5,000 for one hundred grams of Kashmiri saffron. It is sometimes alleged that Indian, or **country**, saffron powder, **haldi** (turmeric), is used to adulterate the genuine Kashmir saffron.

Following from the Hindi word for saffron – kesar is the adjective for saffron and yellow-red ochre colour, kesri, the colour associated with Hinduism since Vedic days. Other names for the colour are gerua and bhagwa (*see* Bhagwan): an association, perhaps, with the sun. Certainly from the sun is the Vedic colour, arun, the orange of the golden dawn. To wear saffron robes is a claim to be a Hindu or Buddhist religious. Muslims do not wear saffron (except those with the **Bauls**), nor do Sikhs for religious reasons (but Sikh **Nihangs** may wear some yellow, and the mast, the Nishan Sahib, is covered in kesri cloth. *See* Gurdwara). In Rajput chivalry, to put on kesri had the meaning that one was entering a last-ditch fight,

when honour could not permit surrender and that one was ready to become a martyr (*see* Jauhar). To wear kesri today, be it only a puggri, the actual shade of which may be anything from red, through orange, to yellow, can be a proclamation that one is ready to die for a political cause. As a noun, the kesri can be the ochre flag or pennant used by Hindu rajas, flown over Hindu temples and carried on staves by sadhus. It is, of course, the topmost band of colour on the tiranga (tricolour), the national flag.

As a recent journalistic term, saffron may be a reference to those thought to be discordantly Hindu, the Kesariya brigade.

SAGAI/SAGAN *n* Hindi/Punjabi
Following the marriage settlement between the two families, the betrothal, the engagement. Sometimes celebrated by a grand party for families and friends.

Presents of money or sweets will be exchanged between relations of both parties.

SĀGAR *n* Hindi
The sea. A name often given to large lakes, e.g. the Gobind Sagar, the sheet of water above the Bhakra Dam in Himachal Pradesh.

Mahasagar: an ocean. The Hind Mahasagar, the Indian Ocean.

Sagar Matha (Nepali): lit. Mother of the Sea, i.e., the place from which the sea draws its sustenance. The Nepali name for Mount Everest.

Sagar Samrat: Emperor of the Ocean. Name of a moveable drilling platform employed on the **Bombay High.**

Himsagar Express (The Snow to the Ocean Express): a name coined for the train with the longest run in India: from Jammu, in the foothills of the Himalaya in the state of Jammu and Kashmir to the Southern most mainland tip, Kanyakumari (See Kumar), a distance of about 3,750 km. covered in just over sixty-seven hours.

Sagar, a word from Sanskrit, was used in the title of an early Hindi dictionary.

SĀHARA *n*
Urdu from Arabic a desert. Hindi – support, aid, succour. In building, a prop.

SAHIB *n* Urdu
In the original Arabic, a Sahibi, a Lord, was a companion (*see* Qurayshi), an associate of the Prophet Mohammed, or at the very least, a Muslim who had seen him personally. It has been estimated that the number of Ashab (Arabic plural of Sahibi) at the time of the death of the Prophet was about 1,44,000. Sahib, or Sahiban – the modern Urdu plural

– is a term of respect offered both to people and objects. In the form 'bhai sahib' (brother sahib), with its assumption of equality, a polite and conciliatory way of address to anyone humbler, or not too obviously the superior of the speaker. As a respectful spoken form of address, or in a reference to a person, Sahib/Saab is widely used, but as a suffix to a man's name, there is a tendency now to replace it with the Hindi equivalent, **ji.**

Often used by **Sikhs** to show respect to a historic **gurdwara**, particularly for one with which a **Guru** was personally connected (Harmandir Sahib – *see* Amrit: Anandpur Sahib – *see* Khalsa, and others), and also, of course to their sacred scripture, the Guru Granth Sahib.

The Sahibs (or the sahib-log): during the British period, at least according to British novelists, the Hindustani collective term for Europeans (but *see also* Bandar).

Memsahib: the female of the species. A hybrid word from early British days, a contraction of Madam Sahib.

Burra Sahib/Burra Memsahib/ Burra Mem: expressions used just as much in English circles as by Indian servants: the great sahib, the number one in an organisation and his wife, the senior lady, often a formidable memsahib indeed. (Within an organisation, the memsahib tended to acquire – and to exercise – rank and authority equal to that of her husband. It was said that the collective term for a group of burra mems was an umbrage. At a formal party, a guest wishing to leave early was expected to ask permission from the burra mem before that of the hostess.) Social mores from home continued. In 1857 an officer's wife, for reasons of advanced pregnancy, was in the British camp outside the walls of Delhi (*see* First War of Independence) where she delivered a son (the boy, Stanley, Delhi Field-Force, Tytler, lived until 1948.) In her memoirs written fifty years after, she claimed that she had been the only lady present at the siege of the city. Later she mentions that she had been attended by her French maid, Marie. Her home, a covered bullock cart and a small armoury - a bell of arms. (Twenty years later, Harriet returned to almost the same site but in a very different style, as a guest at the 1877 Imperial Durbar at which Queen Victoria was proclaimed Empress of India.)

Brown Sahibs: a modern usage of the phrase coined by Lord Macaulay in a different context in the 19th century, 'brown Englishmen'. Indians who since **Independence**, are thought by some to have adopted the outlook and manners of the departed British rulers – some are even alleged to re-

fer to a trip to Britain as home-leave. *See also* Box Wala. A Brindian, on the other hand, was a British term of approval in the 1920s for one of the new young Indian army officers who so successfully adapted to his environment that the British saw an image of themselves, and liked what they saw. A down-to-earth **bazaar** term with the same meaning is Kala Angrez – black Englishman. In South India an equivalent word for sahib is dorai and in Myanmer (Burma) thakin (words without an Islamic connection).

SAHITYA AKADEMI *n*
Sahitya, **Sanskrit**, a literary work. A national organisation set up in Delhi in 1954, for the promotion of Indian letters. The Akademi makes annual awards to Indian authors of outstanding books published in Indian languages (including English), and compiles the national bibliography.

SAINIK SCHOOL *n*
Sainik (Hindi): a soldier. A residential school with a strong military bias, established by the Defence Ministry for boys in the age group 9-18. *See* Vahini.

SĀL *n* Hindi
A valuable hardwood tree, *Shorea robusta,* the timber so heavy that it sinks in water. Grows best on the higher levels of the Indo-Gangetic plain. Following chemical treatment, the seeds, winged to aid wind

disposal, yield a useful edible oil resembling cocoa butter.

SĀLA *n* Hindi

A man's wife's brother. Also a term of abuse to someone who is not the speaker's wife's brother: the insult lies in the implication that the sister of the person abused is available to the speaker as a wife.

Sali a man's wife's sister.

In Roman script, at least two Hindi words pronounced shala, are frequently written as sala: one has the meaning of a place, usually as a compound word: e.g., the hill town in Himachal Pradesh, Dharamsala. The other is from architecture, meaning a rounded, or barrel roof: the most common example being the summit of a temple **gopuram** of the south. A rectangular building with a rounded roof may itself be referred to as a sala.

Sala/Salar (Urdu): a leader, as in the title (and personal name) Salarjang.

SĀLĀM/SĀLAAM *n* Urdu

A word of salutation in greeting and leave-taking. From assalam, an Arabic word with a number of meanings (submission, prosperity and 'the Peaceful One' – an attribute of God [*see* Allah]). World-wide, one Muslim will greet another with the Arabic blessing 'Assalam walai kum', to which the normal response is 'Walai kum, assalam' – 'Peace be upon

you': 'Upon you, be peace'. Mohammed taught that the person of higher degree should salute first on meeting one junior to him. In Hebrew, the same salutation appears as 'Shalom'. The name Solomon is from the same word.

Lal Salaam: a red salute. The political left-wing salute using the clenched fist.

Salamkabool: words of a particularly respectful salutation, as from a junior to a senior – a boy to his grandfather – a humble person to a superior. A free translation could be 'accept my submission'.

Salaam can also mean a reception or audience where respects are paid to an important personage: a **durbar**.

Salami: a salute, and colloquially, a bribe.

An alternative word of salutation, particularly popular in Lucknow and the **nawabi** culture of **Oudh**, is the Persian adāb, (or in full, adab-e-arz), also meaning respectful submission. The gesture of the right hand, palm inwards moving several times to the forehead often accompanies the expression. Unlike salam, or for example, the **Hindu** courtesy **Ram**

Ram, adab has no religious connection; it can therefore be a greeting between, say, Hindu and Muslim, to which neither can take exception.

Historically, to the **Sultans** the salutation was the kornish, placing the right palm on the forehead and bowing the head. Some of the **Moguls** (not Aurangzeb) required the sijda/sajda, a gesture as in the mosque at prayer: the knees and the forehead touching the ground.

SALAMANDER *n* English

Apart from its natural history application – the salamander is a newt-like amphibian, once believed to have the ability to live in fire – to the British in India the word had the meaning of a light open-air boiler for warming bathwater. Usually made of galvanised iron, for quick heating the flue from the fire below passed through the centre of the water-tank, in the manner of a samovar.

In an earlier age, also a salamander was an iron plate, heated to redness and held over a cooked dish for the purpose of browning the top.

SALIGRAM/SALAGRAM/ SHALIGRAM SHILA *n* Hindi

(Shila: a rock or stone). An ammonite, a fossilised, marine mollusc petrified in the shape of a curled ram's horn. Found in sub-Himalayan river beds and revered by **Hindus** as a symbol of Lord **Vishnu**. The term

and association are also applied to spherical or ovoid stones, particularly if apparently containing an ammonite or with unusual markings or colours. In this case, the symbolism is of Shiva and not Vishnu. *See* Lingam.

A Hindu personal name; usually in the form Saligram.

Shaligrama: the Sanskrit form of the word.

SAMĀDHI *n* Hindi

For **Hindus**, Buddhists and Jains, the deep trance of the highest state of meditation (dhyan in Hindi): intense concentration of thought, causing a temporary withdrawal from the world. Also the final and irrevocable withdrawal, reunion of the soul with the godhead, **moksha**, death: perhaps a voluntary act, as by self-starvation. (Although a technical suicide and a crime under the Western-introduced **IPC**, such an action by a spiritually minded person would be unlikely to be hindered by associates and could only earn respect under the age-old Indian culture. *See* Fasting.)

The place where a Hindu soul attains moksha. The tomb or platform built to mark a grave or place of human cremation. Samadhishal.

The death of a person considered to be on a particularly high spiritual plane, may be termed mahasamadhi.

SAMĀJ *n* Hindi
Society, or association, of people with a similar interest. A word with the same meaning, but particularly used in eastern India, is samiti/samity. (In the original **Sanskrit**, samiti referred to a people's assembly under the ruler. As mentioned in the Rig **Veda**, the samiti could be said to have been a lower house, with the **sabha**, the upper.)

SAMMĒLAN *n* Hindi
A conference. An assembly of persons with like interests, e.g., kavi-sammelan, a gathering of poets: sangeet-sammelan, a meeting of musicians and other performing artistes. **Shikhar** sammelan: a political summit meeting.

SAMŌSA *n* Urdu
A plump three-cornered patty made from **maida** (white flour) or **atta**, with a filling of spiced  vegetables or meats: cooked in hot fat. Seemingly similar, but circular in shape is the kachori. In eastern India, the samosa is usually termed a **singara**. With Tibetans, a patty not unlike the samosa but with a chopped meat filling, is the momo, often sold in a little restaurant with the words Tashi Delek (welcome) over the threshold.

SANAD *n* Urdu
Charter or grant. A formal certificate or deed.

SANĀTAN DHARMA/DHARM Hindi
The strict orthodox **Hindu** way of life. (Sanatan: eternal, time-honoured.) Some claim that this phrase, the eternal way of life, and not Hinduism should be the name for the majority religion of India.

SANDALWOOD *n* English from Arabic from Sanskrit In commerce, the scented heartwood of the timber and roots (especially the roots) of a particular species (Santalum alba: white Sandalwood) of the sandal family: a tree which begins life as a parasite on the roots of other bushes and trees on the uplands (530m and above) of peninsular India, principally in Karnataka (*see* Carnatic) and **Tamil** Nadu.

The wood (known in Hindi as chandan or, particularly when used in a medical or spiritual context, shrikhand) is very close grained, almost like ivory and is unrivalled for delicate carving: its fragrance lasts for many years. An essential oil distilled from the powdered timber and roots (the roots are especially rich in oil, to obtain which it is necessary to uproot the tree when it is about thirty years old, traditionally, by using a trained elephant). It has been pre-eminent as a perfume base for at least 2,000 years and world demand is still strong. Also from the powder is made the paste for the **tika** and marks of religious significance on-

Vaishnavi (*see* Vishnu) foreheads: the age-old way of making the powder for sāndal paste is by rubbing a stick of the wood on stone. (Followers of Lord **Shiva** use **ash** rather than sandal paste on their bodies.) The paste has a medical use for soothing skin irritation.

Sandal is the traditional wood for the cremation pyre of the wealthy, but this extravagance must be rare when its value is such that the retail price (Delhi 1996) for low grade wood is about Rs. 60 per kilogram. Nevertheless, token pieces are often used. (High quality wood suitable for carving is sold at approximately Rs. 500 per kilogram.)

Red sandalwood (or red sanders, lal chandan, dyewood, Pterocarpus santalinus), unrelated to the true sandalwood and without fragrance. A heavy close-grained wood; as powder and oil with uses in traditional medicine. A tree of the **Coromandel** coast: as a source of blood-red dye, once a valuable export. (In 1980, billets of the wood with still recoverable dye were salvaged from a Swedish vessel which sank off the Orkney Islands in 1740.) From powder an auspicious paste is made in the home for **Hindu** body marks, such as the **tika**.

SANGAM *n* Hindi
Union of two or more things or persons, such as the junction of two rivers (triveni sangam for the conflu-

ence of three). Usually a reference to the meeting of the rivers **Ganga** and **Yamuna** at **Prayag** (Allahabad): a third, the Saraswati, is believed by many **Hindus** to join unseen at the same place. A club or society, particularly in the south, where 'Tamil Sangam' by the year 1000 BC is thought to have carried the meaning of a meeting of literary academics.

Colloquially, a sexual conjunction.

SANGEET *n* Hindi
Term covering the inter-connected arts of classical dancing (**natya**), vocal (**geet**) and instrumental music (**gandharv**).

Sangeet Natak Akademi: a national organisation, set up in New Delhi to foster the development of dance, drama, music and folk arts. Annual awards are conferred on distinguished artists.

Rabindra Sangeet: the music and songs of Rabindranath Tagore, with an emotional impact on the heartstrings of every Bengali.

SANGH *n* Hindi
Society, association, organisation.

Sangha: collective term for the Buddhist orders of monkhood (*see* Buddha).

Sangh Parivar: lit. the Sangh family. A journalistic collective name for the various groups of the orthodox **Hindutva** movement associated with the political Bharat Janta Party. (Once, the Jan Sangh party).

Sangat/Sanghat: to **Sikhs**, a congregation in a **gurdwara**, or the whole Brotherhood of Sikhs. An association or union of people. A commercial company. A musical accompaniment.

Sangharsh: a group struggle, particularly of a political nature.

Satsangh/Satsang: lit. an assembly of good, true and pious men. A fellowship with a spiritual purpose. A meeting for a **Hindu** religious discourse.

Sanghathan: a group of people with a common interest, a union.

SANSAD *n* Hindi
Parliament, pertaining to parliament.

**S A N S K Ā R / S A N S K Ā R A /
SAMSKĀRA** *n* Hindi
Hindu socio-religious ceremonies concerning an individual, such as the **mundan**, the upanayana (*see* Janeu), marriage and the **shraddh**: a rite of passage. A sacrament. Also a mental impression, moulded by one's family and cultural heritage. One's fate or destiny. The rites of passage: generally only the concern of Hindu males.

Bharatiya Sanskar: the basic cultural heritage common to all Hindu India. The concept and term is no less part of Tibetan Buddhism.

SANSKRIT/SANSCRIT *n*
Sanskrit
Lit. purified, refined. The classical language of learning and of Hinduism (sometimes described as devavani – the speech of God), with a relationship to almost all the European languages (the connection with Latvian and Lithuanian is said to be particularly close), The Finnish-Ugaric people from Central Europe are thought to have migrated to the Baltic area in about 5000-4000 BC bringing with them words from an Indo-Vedic culture, some still preserved in the Baltic region. Baltistan is still a region in Kashmir. Every visitor realises for himself a connection with English on learning that the Hindi for father and mother is pita (in Sanskrit, pittri, also meaning forebears) and mata. (Daughter is linked to the Sanskrit duhita). The relationship to the Indic group (the north Indian languages. Old Persian, Romany, and Nepali) is, of course, far closer. (Another word from Sanskrit for father is Janak. Often in the sense of originator, rather than paternity of a child.) *See also.*

Varnmala: Devnagri characters strung together to represent a spoken sound. A knowledge of which begins Sanskrit and Hindi scholarship.

Vedic Sanskrit (*see* Vedas), the language of at least some of the almost pre-history linguistically **Aryan** tribes invading from approximately the region of today's Iran, remained in use by the priests (their sacred hymns, memorised generation after generation, were preserved almost unchanged). But for others, with the course of time and influence of local tongues, the language became prakrit, or natural. The speech of the people.

In about the 4th century BC, a grammarian, Panini, scientifically codified classical Sanskrit, formulating over four thousand rules: from this time onwards, the name Sanskrit (the purified or perfected, language) appeared and for several hundred years it was used not only by the priesthood but also by the governing and educated classes in the Indo-Gangetic plain and over much of the rest of India (in fact, the language of the elite, the English of the time), even becoming partly accepted in many of the **Dravidian** tongues. Later, once again the prakrits asserted themselves amongst the educated, eventually becoming the Hindi and Hindi-associated languages of today, but above all, Sanskrit remained, as it still is, the language of brahmanical Hinduism. Some profess that a Hindu is born in Sanskrit, marries in Sanskrit and will die in Sanskrit. Its influence, of course, is evident in the languages of South-East Asia, including Indonesia

(*see* Greater India). One Prakrit, still studied in India, Sri Lanka and South East Asia, is Pali, the language of the canons of Buddhism. For some, Sanskrit is a living language, with the addition of neologisms able to cope with modern affairs: indeed All India Radio carries a daily news bulletin in Sanskrit. But it is said that the number of persons capable of fluent conversation in Sanskrit (as distinct from those having memorised texts) decreases year by year.

Vedic Sanskrit was not written: the earliest examples of writing so far deciphered (*see* Indus Valley Civilisation) are in the Prakrit languages and date from the **Mauryan** period, using a scientific and phonetic script, read from left to right, known as Brahmi. Brahmi evolved into Nagari (urban), now more often called Devnagri (*see* Dev), used today for writing Sanskrit, Hindi, Marathi and also Nepali. Specimens of printed Sanskrit, dating from the 9th century AD, have been found in central Asian desert caves.

Sanskriti: cultural, relating to cultural affairs.

Sanskritisation: a current sociology term for the process by which those at the lower end of the social scale (e.g., tribals – *see* Adivasi and dalit) endeavour to achieve **caste Hindu** acceptance by abandoning their own earlier ways of life and adopting

434

Hindu customs such as vegetarianism. No less, with the almost universal access to national TV, even caste Hindu unorthodox practices in remote areas, such as public buffalo sacrifice, are likely to diminish and pass away.

SANT *n* Hindi from Sanskrit
An honorific bestowed by devotees on one who is believed to have acquired knowledge of deep spiritual truths: not quite the same meaning as the English 'saint', although saintliness may well be an attribute of many sants. Vaishnavi musician-poets of the **bhakti** tradition often received the title and in Hinduism and Sikhism still do. Alternatively, sant can be said to derive from sadhu-sant, lit. one who has renounced the world.

Santni: the female form of the word.

Sant Samāgam: a meeting of sants, a term for a **Hindu** or **Sikh** religious congregation.

SANTŌSH *n* Hindi
Satisfaction, contentment. A term often used for a commercial establishment or product.

SANYĀSI/SANNYĀSI *n* Hindi
A **Hindu** who has accepted sanyas: the renunciation of all worldly ties, including those of caste family and possessions in favour of a simple

religious subsistence. One who after a long period of penance and abstinence has reached a high spiritual plane. Enjoined as the ideal fourth and final stage of a complete **brahman** life – but having with everything else, renounced **dharma**, a brahman turned sanyasi cannot act in any ritual priestly capacity: in the uncommon event of his re-entry to the world and marriage, the children of such a marriage would be considered to be of the **shudra** caste. After death, the body of a respected sanyasi may be buried in a seated position and not cremated as is the usual Hindu practice.

Fem. Sanyasini.

SAR/SIR *n* Hindi
The head, a frequent prefix meaning chief, headman. From **Sanskrit** and Old Persian the word is linked to the Latin word cerebrum, the brain.

SARAK/SADAK *n* Hindi
Road or street. In eastern India, the word becomes sarani and in Tamil, salai.

Sarak-chaap: A man of the streets. A pejorative and colloquial expression for one perhaps with an educated background but no settled employment who is thought to pass a lot of him time in occupations of low probity in the bazaar streets.

Sarak-e-Azaam: see G.T, Road.

SARANGI *n* Hindi
A box-shaped, violin-type musical
instrument, with sometimes as many
as forty strings, of which, perhaps
not more than three are touched by
the bow – the others vibrate in sym-
pathy. Usually played as an accompaniment to a vocalist or a **kathak**
dancer. The sarangi is particularly
suited to slow time and the mournful
music associated with death.

The name is said to be derived from
saurangi, one hundred colours: from
the instrument's claimed ability to
reproduce one hundred tones from
the human voice.

SARASWATI
The patroness God-
dess of learning and
the arts: reputedly
the inventor of the
veena and normally
portrayed dressed in
white holding a simi-

lar musical instrument. She is the
consort of **Brahma** and her vehicle
(*see* Vahan) a hansa (*see* Hans), in
English usually termed a swan. She
may be worshipped daily, especially
by students (*see* Vandana) but her
annual festival is the day of **Basant**
Panchami.

The Goddess is personified in the
river named after her; in Vedic times
a mighty waterway superior even to
Mother **Ganga**, flowing westward
through Rajasthan so that her name

is sometimes coupled with the **Indus** Valley Civilisation. But, alas,
no longer visible, to the faithful she
joins the Ganga, underground, at Allahabad (*see* Prayag, Sangam).

A book falling to the ground, a child
may be told, is an insult to Saraswati. On picking it up it should be
touched to the forehead as a gesture
of apology.

Saraswati Brahmans : a Sect of Brahmans generally regarded as being of
high attainment and status. Almost
prehistory residing on the banks of
the R. Saraswati. Now dispersed over
all India, usually with Saraswat as a
family name.

SARDA/SHARDA ACT
Popular title for the Child Marriage
Restraint Act of 1929, introduced by
Dewan **Bahadur** Sarda, appointing
fourteen years (raised in 1978 to eighteen) as the minimum marriage age
for girls and eighteen (now twenty-
one) for boys. For a long period the
Act was largely ignored particularly
in villages where prepubertal marriages are still common: but since the
1970s, the all-India mean marriage
age has been rising and in the 1990s
is probably over eighteen years for
girls and twenty-three for boys. When
registration of marriages becomes the
practice, observance of the law in this
field is likely to become normal social
custom. (In England, it was only in
1929 that the minimum age for mar-

riage – not the same thing as the age of consent – was raised from twelve to sixteen years.) The usual roman spelling of the measure is not phonetic; in Hindi the Dewan's (*see* Bahadur) name is pronounced Sharda.

A child marriage is illegal, but if performed, not invalid: so that should the boy die, the child wife is culturally a widow, with all the social disabilities, possibly for the rest of her life.

SARDĀR *n* Urdu

Lit. Sir-dar (Persian): the holder of the office at the head (*see* Zamindar). A chief, a commander. Title occasionally used by Muslims, but given to all followers of the **Khalsa** (**Sikhs**) by **Guru** Gobind Singh. (A Sikh should not be addressed by the honorific alone, without also using **Sahib**, or **ji**, or his personal name: e.g., Sardar Sahib: Sardarji: or, say, Sardar Hukum **Singh**.)

In Rajasthan, even today a member of a once princely family, an erstwhile noble, may use Sardar as a title.

Sardarni: the feminine form of the word (Sikhs only).

Sirdar/Sardar: a foreman, particularly in eastern India: a leader, e.g., **Sherpa** Sirdar. Even a street gang leader can be the Sardar.

SĀRI/SĀREE *n* Hindi

A piece of cloth approximately 5.5m long and about 1.2m in width, used as the outer garment by most Indian women, although many in the north prefer the **salwar** kamiz. (There is an old tradition still sometimes followed, that a woman visiting her husband's parents should wear an extra long sari, say of 8.5m.) First, one end round the hips over a petticoat, pleated on the left side, then the other round the waist, up across the bosom and **choli** and finally, normally to fall to the back over the left shoulder, but with the decorative border (palla/pallu) it may be used to cover the head or, in certain circumstances, the face. There are regional differences in the mode of wear, it is said that there are more than eight hundred ways of draping a sari – as an echo of their equestrian forebears, Marathi (*see* Maharashtra) ladies take one end between their legs to be tucked in at the back – and a sari may cost anything from a few rupees to thousands for just one, say, auspicious for a wedding, red silk brocaded with gold thread. Something more simple for everyday wear and plain white for a widow. A large red circle at the back on a Rajasthani peasant woman's sari proclaims her pride at being a mother of a son.

In all but well-to-do homes, as an expensive item, perhaps an heirloom, the sari is reserved for special occasions: the more ordinary piece of printed cotton used for household work and local shopping – perhaps with keys and small change knotted into one corner – being often referred to as a **dhoti**.

Judging by extant art relics, the draped sari is of no great age: it was first seen in about the 11th century AD.

Sari fall: Hinglish (*see* Hindustani) term of the **bazaar** draper for a relatively inexpensive border designed to be attached on the inside of a sari at the bottom edge to take the wear of the actual contact with the ground.

SARISTADĀR/SHERISTADĀR *n* Urdu from Persian

Lit. Keeper of the string: one who has responsibility for bundling the records of a superior court of law. The court administrator. As a term, now archaic. See also granth, under Guru Granth Sahib.

SARKĀR *n* Hindi and Old Persian

Lit. Head of work: (the man) the head of affairs of business. Used in this sense by the humble as a term of respect to the head of an organisation, or of a family, or when addressing any supposed important person. In Sher Shah Suri's India (about 1540 AD, *See* Rupee), sarkar had the meaning of an administrative area, roughly equivalent to a **district**: today, it can mean the government – 'Bharat Sarkar', the **Government of India**.

In Bengal in the 19th century, the sarkar/sirkar could have been an accountant employed as finance manager of a large household or business. The word lives on as a Bengali family name. *See also* Circars.

SARSŌN *n* Hindi

Together with rai, a member of the mustard and rape oil seeds group of the large brassica (cabbage) family: the seeds are crushed (*see* Ghee) to produce mustard oil, used for cooking and application to the body, an oil bath. (from Sanskrit, abhyangam.) By traditional medicine regarded as highly beneficial to the body (coconut oil is also used: see Maleesh.) To Victorian Britain, mustard oil was colza or rape oil. The leaves of the plant are eaten as spinach (sarson ka **saag**).

English mustard is the cleaned, dried and powdered seed, particularly of the variety known as white mustard, with wheat flour added to absorb the oil, also sometimes turmeric (*see* Haldi) for the same purpose and to give colour. India has the largest area under mustard in the world, but with other spicy condiments available, table mustard has no customary use.

SARUS *n* Hindi
The red-headed grey crane, at upto one and a half metres in height, probably India's tallest bird – but not the  largest, the great Indian bustard, Rajasthan's state bird, at 18 kg, a bird of grasslands, can be double the weight of the sarus. Usually seen in pairs, either wading or near water. Popularly believed to mate for life, thus often spoken of as an example of conjugal devotion.

SARVŌDAYA *n* Hindi
Lit. universal uplift (daya, compassion in Sanskrit). The Gandhian ideal of emphasis on traditional **Hindu** village values, loosely organised into a movement by J.P. Narayan and Vinoba'Bhave (*see* Fasting). The aim was to raise the cultural, moral and material standards of the peasant. Sarvodaya as a word was an inspiration by Gandhiji: during his South Africa days he had been greatly influenced by John Ruskin's essays of 1860 advocating non-violence and social justice for all–highly controversial when written–with the collective title of *Unto This Last*. The **Mahatma** made a paraphrase and published them as a longish pamphlet in Gujarati in 1908. The heading he gave was Sarvodaya. (In somewhat similar fashion, Gandhi acquired another term of the Freedom Struggle, 'Civil Disobedience'. He read and was impressed by the words of a lecture of this title delivered by Henry David Thoreau in 1848 after having been imprisoned for one day for non-payment of poll-tax – Thoreau had been protesting against slavery.)

Sarvodaya Express: the train running between Delhi and Ahmedabad. Gandhi had close connections with the latter city.

SATI/SUTTEE Hindi
Lit. a virtuous woman: if married, a faithful wife devoted to her husband. The root word, sat, has the meaning of truth. Sati (also known as Uma–light) was the wife of Lord **Shiva**: for the reason that her father had slighted her husband, she burnt herself to death on a sacrificial fire before all the gods: she was later reborn as Parvati. The goddess gave her name to the anglicism for the practice of self-immolation by a **caste Hindu** widow on her late husband's cremation fire. (The Hindi word applies to the lady, not to her action.) In Indian terms, 'widow' is inappropriate for a sati-to-be, for immediately as she announced her intention, she would have been treated as a deity only temporarily separated from her lord and so escaping the odium attached to the status of widowhood.

Another Hindi word for the sati is sahagamani – the happy state of a woman accompanying her husband. (Not only wives could be expected to die with their husbands; in the case of a noble or **princely** family, concubines and even maid-servants sometimes joined their lord on the pyre. There was also the custom of **Rajput** chivalry, the **jauhar** – death before a dishonourable surrender to an enemy, in battle for the men, self-sacrifice by fire for all the women.) In society, a sati brought considerable prestige to her family; there was, therefore, at least one strong motive for relatives to use pressure on a widow to take to the pyre. At the gate or door of old palaces and mansions, particularly in Rajasthan, one or more bangled wrists may be depicted in red paint or in stone. Each originated from a sati on her last journey leaving a palm print near the door, and proclaims the honour done to the house.(some will aver that only a Rajput can become a true sati).

In 1812, the British sought to reduce the large number of satis in Bengal and district authorities were instructed not to allow other than clearly voluntary self-immolation (cases had been reported of struggling women being tied to heavy logs) and that those insisting must not be drugged, must have reached puberty, and must not have infant children. By 1829, the Government was ready to challenge **Hindu** tradition and by Regulation (*see* Presidencies) the encouragement and abetment of a sati (both by fire or by burying alive) was made a criminal offence in Bengal: the rest of

British India followed later. By the Indian Penal Code of 1860 (*see* IPC), attempted suicide and abetment and encouragement of suicide became a criminal offence in all British India. This Act is still the law today. By the 1870s, sati had all but died out in the whole of the subcontinent: but not in Nepal where it was banned only in 1927. Since **Independence**, occasional cases have been reported from rural Rajasthan, where social sanction for this climactic act of the cult of pati-**bhakti** (husband-worship) is still strong, particularly amongst the Rajputs. In a recent sati of 1987, both the young widow's parents and the villagers will tell with pride of the glory brought to the family and to the community. It could be that an echo of this prestige lurks in the Indian female psyche, for of the methods of suicide, a painful death by fire is that frequently chosen.

It might have been that awareness of the life awaiting a bereaved wife influenced some to take the extreme step. In traditional Hindu society even today, a widow can be stigmatised as a woman of ill-omen and, even if never voiced, of bearing responsibility for her husband's death. Her lot can be an unhappy one, not only from the trauma of having lost her husband, but from the mores of those around her, relieved to some extent if she has a young male child to look after. Re-marriage, or any social life is usually unthinkable (in a village she can become a widow at a very early age). Her dress and comportment are expected to be such as to make her unattractive to men. If ignorant and subject to pressure from family and community she may be unable to claim her legal right for a share for herself from her late husband's property. As personifying ill-fortune, she can be shunned and unwelcome at any family or community celebration. Her life can be one of continuous drudgery at subsistence level with religion her only consolation.

Sati savitri: an epithet for a faithful wife. From a story that Savitri by her devotion to her husband, so moved **Yama** who had come to collect his soul, that the God of Death relented and allowed him to live.

Asati: a wife considered to be other than virtuous : see Ahinsa.

Satisthal: the site of a sati. In spite of official disapproval, perhaps a place of worship as a shrine.

SAT SRI AKĀL Hindi
Lit. the Timeless/Everlasting One (i.e. Almighty God) is Truth: *see* Shri and Akali. Greeting to, or between, **Sikhs** The war-cry of the old Sikh armies.

SATTA *n* Hindi
Speculation. The illegal numbers game. A popular form of gambling in the major cities, particularly in Mumbai, where it is known as matka (a clay water-pot. *See* Chagul). Payments are accepted by street corner agents and winnings are paid to daily draws of lucky numbers (from a matka).

*Satta **Bazaar:*** the Stock Exchange, and also the area of street dealing in shares. Satta can also mean power, authority.

SATURDAY *n* English
Sanichar in Hindi.

In India, as with the classical Romans, a day under the ascendancy of Saturn: the planet deified by **Hindus** and given the name Shani or more respectfully, Shani Maharaj. His vehicle (see Vahan) is a vulture: he is also associated with cats, so this animal may not be a welcome guest in a Hindu home. (But the cat is not without friends, for she is the vehicle of Shasti, a form of the deity Durga, who helps barren women conceive.) Shani is considered to have a malefic influence (paap in Hindi. Paap also means sin in general), to avert which believers make offerings (Shanidan) of coins to the God represented by horrific black and red sheet-iron cut-outs (iron, even a nail or a horseshoe, will keep him away). These images, with some flower petals, a burning wick, a bowl with some oil for the money (the wrath of Shani is appeased by mustard oil) and an attendant – perhaps with a blackened face – are to be found in busy **bazaar** streets of northern India only on Saturdays. Traditionally, the attendant is a Dakaut, a **brahman** sub-group whose duty it is to take on themselves on behalf of the community, the evil influence of Shani. But these days, many **dalits** also perform the service and one person may have the charge of a number of scattered 'shanidan' bowls, which, although containing coins, can be left on the street, unattended, but safe. Other practitioners, carrying small images of Shani, visit housewives at their homes, to receive money or, perhaps, mustard oil. Iron articles and mustard oil are not bought and some housewives will not cook black **dal** on Saturdays, neither will the orthodox have their hair cut nor finger nails. On this day, many Hindus worship **Hanuman**.

SATYA *n* Hindi
From Sanskrit, sat, that which is Truth, righteousness in accordance with **dharma**.

Satyagrah: from **Sanskrit**, grasping truth, insistence on truth. A phrase used by **Mahatma** Gandhi in South Africa, to mean. he said, a moral protest: passive resistance to authority, non-cooperation in order to set right a wrong. He employed the practice as his main weapon to embarrass the British during the freedom struggle: today, it may be termed courting arrest.

Satyagrahi: one who practices satyagrah.

Satyameva Jayate: the **Sanskrit** motto in Devnagri (*see* Dev) below the crest, the emblem, of the Union of India, the **Ashok** Capital (*see* Chakra); officially translated as 'Truth Alone Triumphs'. The words are a quotation from the **Upanishads**, 'Satyameva jayate nanritan'–'Truth alone triumphs, not falsehood'.

SAUNF *n* Hindi
The aromatic seed of the fennel plant, used as food flavouring and often served after meals as an aid to digestion. Very similar in use and taste to the aniseed known in Hindi as **bilaiti** saunf.

SAYID/SAYEED/SYED *n* Urdu
A Muslim claiming descent from the family of the Arab Holy Prophet through his daughter, Fatima, and the sons of her husband, Ali, who became the fourth Caliph (*see* Khilafat), and in the Islamic world entitled to respect on that account: in Delhi society, respect superior perhaps to that accorded to the descendants of the **Moguls**, by comparison, only recent converts to the faith. The plural of Sayid is Sadat: when used as a personal name, the meaning is 'of the family of the Prophet'. Mainly used by Shias (*see* Sunnis), a similar pedigree is indicated by the final name Alvi, denoting a claim to descent from Ali (but in India, many

of those with the name Alvi are in fact Sunnis).

SBI (S.B.I.)

State Bank of India. After **Independence**, the first essay of the **Government of India** into nationalisation. Prior to July 1955, the SBI was the privately owned Imperial Bank of India, itself in 1921 an amalgamation of **Presidency** banks doing government business.

SCINDIA/SINDIA

A British corruption of the Maratha (*see* Maharashtra) family name, Shinde, one of the minor chieftains who became the senior commanders of the Maratha Confederacy and the de facto rulers of all northern India following the weakening of the Delhi emperors and before the rise of British power in the north. By the late 19th century, the Scindia territory had shrunk to the twenty-one gun (*see* Gun Salutes) state of Gwalior, (earlier their city had been Ujjain) with the prince, in the pattern of the **Nizam** of Hyderabad, known simply as The Scindia.

SCREW GUNS *n*

By World War II, 3.7" gun Howitzers (in Kipling's day, they were smaller), the weapons of the Mountain Artillery of the British Indian Army. Carried dismantled on the backs of mules (eight mules to a team), the component parts had to be assembled – for the barrel, two parts needed to be screwed together – before the piece was ready for action: with a trained team, a process requiring something less than three minutes, for most circumstances, each team of a troop and each mule of a team, knew its position for tactical deployment. The mountain Artillery have a no less valuable role in the Indian Army of today, artillery pieces suitable for transportation by helicopter.

SDM (S.D.M.)

Sub-divisional Magistrate. The officer responsible in the first instance for judicial administration in a subdivision of a district. Earlier, now less frequently, the office was combined with that of SDO.

SDO (S.D.O.)

Sub-divisional Officer in charge of a sub-division of a **district**, usually, the first appointment of a newly joined IAS officer. (**ICS** officers passed their first year or so as 'Assistants' before being **gazetted** SDOs, being known to the junior office staff as the 'stunt/'stant Sahibs.)

SECTION 93 PROVINCE

The Government of India Act, 1935, gave full authority to the elected Provincial governments, ending **dyarchy**, but Section 93 of the Act authorised a Governor, if he considered it unavoidable, to assume to himself all or any of the powers of government. This section was invoked during the early days of World War II, when Congress Ministries resigned (although the party held majorities in the legislature), so that seven out of eleven Provinces of **British India** became 'Section 93 Provinces'.

Today, similar powers fall to the President under Article 356 of the Constitution, permitting him if considered unavoidable, to suspend a state government and/or legislature, thus introducing 'President's Rule'. (In practice, rule by the Central Government, and since the President is constitutionally bound to accept the advice of his Council of Ministers, it is in fact the **Government of India** which has the power to dismiss a state government.) In the state of Jammu & Kashmir, Governor's and not President's Rule had to be imposed: but this purely titular exception was removed in September 1987. Although a state legislature may have been suspended under President's Rule, it is not the case that the democratic voice is totally stifled, for the state's members of Parliament contin-ue to sit in the Central Legislature.

SECTION 144

When said to be enforced, normally a reference to a local instruction forbidding the assembly of five or more persons together in a public place within a designated area. Also termed Prohibitory Orders, such instructions under the authority of Section 144 of the Code of Criminal Procedure (*see* Cr. PC.), may be issued by a senior magistrate on apprehension of riot or public disorder. If a violent disturbance actually arises, control may be restored though a curfew: streets are closed and all persons living within the area are prohibited from leaving their homes without permission. In media English, a curfew having been ordered is often said to have been 'clamped'.

To show potential law-breakers that force is available to suppress disorder, at this time an armed military unit may be ordered to stage a 'flag-march' through the streets. A showing of the flag, although these days it is unlikely that an actual flag will be carried and the 'marchers' may well be in vehicles.

SEERSUCKER *n* English

A term from Persian meaning perhaps, blistered. A cotton or linen textile exported to Europe by the East India Company. The fabric had a puckered, dimpled surface woven into it and was popular as a dress material (the blisters in today's seersucker may be due to treatment with chemicals.)

SEHRA *n* Hindi

A **Hindu** ceremonial wedding head-dress for the bridegroom: also used by Muslims. In the sehrabandi ceremony, before the **barat** leaves for the place of the wedding, a close relative places the sehra on the boy's head and veils his face with strings of flowers.

A topical poem, perhaps commissioned from a professional eulogising the happy couple their relations and friends read aloud with copies distributed to the wedding guests.

A heavy garland, made perhaps of gold and silver tinsel, velvet embroidered tassels and large flowers. Much grander than the simple gendamala (garland of French marigold flowers: *see* Mala).

SELECTION GRADE

A term used in government and semi-government service, apparently without strict definition. An employee, having reached the maximum permissible number of annual pay increments in a particular grade, if thereafter allowed 'selection grade', will be eligible for consideration for promotion 'by selection'.

SEPOY/SIPAHI *n* Urdu

A foot soldier or constable. A private soldier .i.e., of the lowest rank.

Sepoy Revolt: A British term for the rebellion of 1857 (*see* First War of Independence).

Spahi: meaning a cavalryman of

colonial French North Africa is from the same Turki/Persian root.

SEMI-

This English prefix is connected via Latin and Greek (Hemi) with the Sanskrit sami – partly, half.

SERĀNG *n* Urdu

Boatswain in charge of a group of seamen.

SERIOUS

In Indian English, a state of illhealth. Such as in a newspaper notice "Vicki, Mother serious, come immediately".

SERVICE *n* English

A particularly Indian-English use of the word is of employment. To be in service is to be in a full-time job.

SETH *n* Hindi

Pronounced as the English sate. A wealthy **Hindu** merchant or industrialist. Moneylender. In Western India, a wealthy Muslim, particularly if a contractor, may also be addressed as Seth.

Sethani: his wife.

The presence of 'sethis', i.e. professional financiers of rulers and of commerce, has been noticed as early as the first millenium BC.

SETTLEMENT *n* English

The process of computing the

445

amount of tax a piece of cultivated land should pay annually to government revenue for a stated period of years. The amount of tax, the land revenue, due from a given piece of land. The system followed from the **Hindu** and Muslim concept that all land belonged to the ruler. The sums collected are really a ground rent, for while remission in full or in part can be granted to an area in the event of widespread crop failure, generally payment has to be made whether or not cultivation has given the proprietor any profit. Over the length and breadth of the country, each and every field is measured and mapped with such details recorded as the quality of the soil, sources of irrigation, the owner, the actual cultivator and the estimated income.

Permanent Settlement: in 1793, Lord Cornwallis, as Governor-General, ordered that the amount of land tax, then on the high side, paid by **zamindars** in Bengal (at that time also covering parts of today's Bihar, Orissa, and Bangladesh), would remain unchanged forever – a measure of the confidence in the stability of the currency – in the expectation of creating a contented landed gentry on the English pattern who would use at least part of their increased income to improve agriculture and the position of their cultivator tenants. In the years that followed, the landlords in general did benefit (but in times of poor harvests too many

were dispossessed for non-payment of the settlement, ιo be replaced by absentee financiers from the cities), but little was gained by agriculture and even less by the cultivators. The permanent settlement was finally abrogated in the 1950s, but not without appeals (rejected) to the Supreme Court by those affected. But the fact is, that land tax, once the major source of government revenue, is now insignificant; so that some states have abolished it altogether.

SETU *n* Hindi
A bridge. The Urdu equivalent, 'pul', is more commonly used in northern India.

SEVA/SEWA *n* Hindi
Service, assistance.

Sewadar/Sewak: strictly, a servant. But the words are often applied to those such as social workers, who receive little pay. Also to one who offers his labour in a purely voluntary capacity.

Such English words as service and servitude, via Sanskrit and Latin, are linked.

Kar-seva: see Kar.

SGPC (S.G.P.C.)
Shiromani Gurdwara Prabandak Committee. Set up in 1920 as a movement for **Sikh Gurdwara** reform. Since a 1925 Act of the **Punjab**

Government (then in control of a much larger territory than the State of Punjab today), the Committee, democratically elected by the votes of all adult Sikhs, has had the legal responsibility for the major and historic gurdwaras and also for Sikh schools and colleges of northern India and consequently, control of vast resources. The SGPC, together with its political wing, the Shiromani **Akali Dal**, until the troubles of the 1980s, was the major representative organisation of the Sikh community and in the Punjab, was said to rival in power the state government.

The title of the committee can be translated as Chief Gurdwara Management Committee. (Delhi State now has its own Gurdwara Committee.)

SHABĀSH Urdu
An exclamatory 'Well done'.

SHAB-I-BARAT Urdu
Persian for the middle day (the 15th) of the Islamic month of Shaban – the month preceding Ramadan (*see* Roza). A day of fasting for Muslims. On the night before, it is said that God reviews the actions of man during the previous twelve months and decides who will be punished for sinning and who rewarded for good deeds: who will live and who will die during the forthcoming year. Muslims should remain awake during the whole night and midnight prayers are usually held in mosques. During the night, in India there is a custom to eat **halwa**.

SHĀH *n* Urdu
King; of country, chess and cards – but for cards, the term badshah is more usual, with **begum** (*see* Beg) for the queen.

Shahenshah: king of kings, emperor.

Shahi: regal, majestic, royal, or simply as in the village expression, **gora-shahi,** white rule.

Shahzada/Shahzadi: son/daughter of a king or ruling prince.

Shahji: north Indian honorific form of address to a respectable man, be he ever so humble.

Shah mat (Old Persian): An exclamatory 'the king is dead/defeated'. In the game of chess, transliterated to English from Old French (eschec mat) as 'checkmate'. Similarly, a link can be traced to the game through French for words concerning a design of squares, check, chequered. Since computation of accounts in England was once assisted by moving counters on a squared cloth, some words connected with money are also related, cheque/check and exchequer; the Chequers, a name for a pub. An English word for the castle in chess, rook, also derives from Persian, rukh.

Shah and its associated words (e.g. badshah, badshaw, paṣna, padishah, all meaning a ruler, a commander of some degree, usually in an Islamic context) derive from an Old Persian word kin to the **Sanskrit** origin of the current Hindi, **kshatriya**.

SHAGUN *n* Hindi
A gift of money or sweets to mark an auspicious moment or event. Particularly as claimed as a due by **hijras**.

SHAHEED/SHAHEEDI/SHAHID *n* Urdu
Specifically, a Muslim who dies in **Jehad**, for the cause of **Islam**.

A martyr: title accorded by popular acclaim as a posthumous honorific to one who is considered to have died for his beliefs, be they religious or political. *See also* Nihangs.

SHAHTŪSH *n* Urdu
Lit. king's wool. A shawl fabric made in Kashmir since **Mogul** days, from the silky underhair of the Tibetan antelope (chiru) to obtain which the animals are killed. (Since 1977 sale of the hair has been banned and possession of an unregistered shawl, even if a family heirloom, is a legal offence.) Claimed to be amongst the world's finest and warmest woollen materials.

In the trade, the wool is simply known as toosh. (see also Pashmina).

SHAITĀN *n* Urdu
The Devil. The Unholy Ghost of **Islam**, Judaism and Christianity: the tempter of Eve in the scriptures of all three theologies. (Satan and Shaitan are, of course, kin words.)

Used in abuse and equally, a tongue-in-cheek noun for a naughty child.

See also Saturday

SHAKKR *n* Sanskrit
The root word of all European names for sugar, indicating from where the Western world first learned of the sweet juices of certain grasses. (In the 4th century BC, Alexander's soldiers – *see* Sikander – remarked on honey made without bees: but sugar in some shape was known in India at least a thousand years earlier. It is said that the original home of the sugar grasses is the island of New Guinea in the Pacific, but how they travelled to Asia in those prehistoric times is not known.)

In India, sugar takes a number of forms:

Gur (the name comes from an ancient kingdom in Bengal, now usually written, **Gaur**), or jaggery, is unrefined village-made sugar. (Strictly, jaggery, as a word from Portuguese India, refers to palm sugar only, but in common usage, the word covers all crude sugars.) The larger portion of India's cane is crushed almost where it is grown, to make gur, using bullock-powered crushers (kolhus, inefficient in terms of juice extraction). Cane-juice, also the sap of the date palm tree in Bengal and in the south, is boiled in open pans, heated usually by burning the **bagasse** (the cane stalk after the juice has been extracted), to remove much of the water; a certain amount of clarification may be carried out before the semi-solid hot mass is formed on a flat surface to set in round golden cakes about ten inches across.

Shakkar: a slight refinement on gur in that the colour is changed by chemicals from a brown to a pale yellow or white and solids are reduced to a powder: if the powder is very fine, the name is boora/bura. Shakkar/boora is used mainly by confectioners.

Khandsari: further refined again; the juice is still concentrated in open pans, but after clarification it is centrifuged to separate the thicker molasses, resulting in a crystalline product only a little inferior to mill sugar, particularly if a simple form of sulphitation is employed. The state of **UP** is the centre of the khandsari industry.

Chini: crystalline sugar produced by the vacuum process in a modern mill, plantation sugar.

Misri: Arabic.

lit. from Egypt. Sugar candy, large crystals formed on a string. (The English word candy, has a relation to the **Sanskrit** khanda, meaning a division or a piece, a sugar lump.)

Ganna: today's Hindi for a sugarcane.

Ganna-ras: cane juice often extracted and sold on the roadside. A tasty and cooling drink, although a form of filtration would sometimes be an advantage. A highly regarded folk medicament in case of jaundice.

SHAKTI/SAKTI *n* Hindi
Power: mechanical or animal strength. (*Vidyut shakti:* electric energy.) Also power in the sense of authority.

Divine power personified in the female consort of Lord **Shiva**, without which the potency of her husband is incomplete. Mahashakti, the Mother Goddess, sometimes benevolent, sometimes terrible: under such names as Ambika, Bhairavi, **Bhowani**, Devi, Durga, Gouri/Gauri, Mahadevi, Parvati, **Sati**, Shaktidevi and Uma. In the south, a term may be Ammar. The original Mother Goddess of them all was Aditi mentioned very vaguely in the Rig **Veda** as the eternal mother of all creation, including many of the gods themselves. Her name was given to the great exhibitions of Indian art and culture held in the USA and in Europe in the 1980s.

As a carved or moulded icon, an image of a Mother Goddess, possibly with a child on her hip, may be termed a matrika/ matrka (as in the English matrilineal, matri is a Hindi prefix meaning motherhood). An age-old form of woman power, still daily worshipped in folk culture, is Dharti Maa/ Matri: the Earth Mother; she who gives food and shelter to all. She has no formal image but many field workers throughout India will salute her before starting the day's work by raising a clod of earth to their foreheads. As for thousands of years in Europe, so in a drinking group, from the first glass a small quantity of liquor may be poured on the ground as a libation to the Earth Mother.

Worship exclusively of shakti is known as tantrism, **tantra**, or 'of the left hand', from the tradition that a **Hindu** wife, or a Goddess in stone, will stand or sit on her spouse's left, indicating that she is contributing stree shakti, the power of a married woman, to her husband. *See* Right Hand, Left Hand.

Shakta: a worshipper of Lord Shiva through shakti. A tantric initiate. Although rarely used in this sense in everyday speech, a shakta may also refer to a weapon in the hand of sculptured deity, particularly a short sword or a spear.

SHĀLIMĀR/SHĀLAMĀR Hindi Lit. Shala-Mar: abode of Mar (Mara,

a name for Kamadev, the **Hindu** Cupid. *See* Kama). A site on the Dal Lake in Kashmir, first of a garden house built in the 6th century AD: later of a garden commenced by the **Mogul** Emperor Jehangir in about 1620: additions were made by his son who reigned as Shahjehan. The Muslims named the garden Farah Baksh (freshness, happiness-giving): Shahjehan preferred to continue the old Hindi word and was so entranced that he used the name (Shalimar **Bagh**) for the gardens he constructed at Lahore (1642) and in Delhi in 1650. (The Delhi garden was first named after a concubine.)

A good portion of the British public knew the gardens to be an eastern river, or at least a lake, from the first line of a popular song of 1908, 'Pale hands I loved beside the Shalimar'. Set to music from a collection published in 1901, *The Gardens of Kama and Other Love Lyrics from India*, by Lawrence Hope, actually the wife of an Indian army officer, Lt. General Nicholson. (After his death in 1904, she killed herself.)

A much earlier introduction for .Europeans was a long fantasy poem *Lalla Rookh* (approximately 5,500 lines with interspersed prose passages) by an Irishman, Thomas Moore, who had never visited India. Lalla Rookh is the name of a fictitious daughter of the Emperor Aurangzeb: betrothed to a young king living amidst the 'splendid domes and saloons' of the Shalimar palace in Kashmir, the princess sets out in a cavalcade on her way to the mountains from Delhi. To while away the tedium, a youth in the party, improbably, is instructed to recite to her. Not unnaturally, the princess is enraptured both by the romantic verses and the versifier and on arrival in Kashmir is desolate at having to leave him. It is only in the ultimate poem and prose sections that the bloom of the Vale is actually mentioned and in the final lines it is revealed that the royal groom is none other than the poet. First published in 1817, the work was vastly popular right through the century and in all is said to have sold a total of 83,500 copies.

Today's storytellers in Srinagar claim that Lalla Rookh did not live in the Shalimar Palace but in another mountain garden, Darogha Bagh, on Manasbal Lake.

SHĀLWĀR/SĀLWĀR KAMIZ
n Urdu

Nowadays, usually a reference to the colourful dress adopted by girl students all over India, changing frequently in detail according to fashion: but originally, the Muslim costume worn by the artisan and similar classes of the pre-Independence **Punjab, Hindu** and Muslim, male and female.

The salwar is the loose trousers probably derived from the Turki trousers of Central Asia, tied with a drawstring and roughly contoured to the leg. Often, there is quite a distance between one leg and the other (in the design favoured by elderly ladies, this may be several feet) producing a puckered effect below the waist when worn. In spite of the roman spelling, the usual pronunciation is shalwār.

The shirt-like upper garment, worn outside the salwar, with short slits at the side, is the kamiz. For girls and women a flimsy **dupatta** completes the ensemble. As a Hindustani word for shirt, kamiz perhaps was brought by the Portuguese, but in the north its entry into the vocabulary seems more likely from the Arabic Kamis. Camise/Chemise in European languages derives from Latin.

SHAMĪANA *n* Urdu

An awning, a decorative cloth canopy, with or without cloth side-walls (kanats/qanats). Erected on poles so as to create a temporary but rarely water-proof shelter for open air functions. The shamiana is formed of brightly coloured pieces of cloth sewn together, or to a backing cloth, so as to make an attractive pattern. A number of shamiana combined to form one large unit may be termed a **pandal**.

The shamiana came to India as the portable travelling palaces of the **Moguls**, derived perhaps, from the tents of their **Mongol** forbears in central Asia, sometimes so vast that several weeks were required for their construction.

SHĀNTI/SHAANTI/SĀNTI *n*
Hindi
Peace: particularly tranquillity to the mind and of the soul. A girl's name. In **Hindu** and Buddhist philosophy, shanti is more than merely absence of physical strife: it denotes a serenity of mind realised through tolerance, moderation and absence of desire. (But Buddhists are warned against excessive enthusiasm for enforcing shanti on themselves or on others, such is not the shantipath, the road to peace.) T.S.Eliot ended his poem *The Waste Land* in the manner of a closing **mantra** or prayer of an **Upanishad, 'Om** Shantih Shantih Shantih'. But he himself translated the line as 'The peace which passes understanding. (from St Paul's phrase 'The peace of God which passeth understanding'). The triple invocation of peace, "Om Shanti, Shanti, Shanti" is a common bidding prayer to complete congregational worship.

The word in Urdu from Arabic for peace, tranquillity, is a man.

Santiniketan: abode of peace (in eastern India, when spelling shanti in roman script, the h is omitted). The village in West Bengal in which Rabindranath Tagore established his school, **Brahmacharya Ashram** (lit.

the student, the celibate, stage of life, ashram): much later to become in 1951, the Viswa Bharati University of today. Unusually, but following **Brahmo-Samaj** practice, the weekly holy and rest day for the university is Wednesday.

Shanti Path: the road of peace. There is also the meaning of a ceremony in a bereaved family held some days after the cremation. (Note that path is now a reading, see Path). A reading from scripture invoking peace for the departed spirit.

Shanti Vana: a forest, or grove, of peace. The place on the bank of the R. **Yamuna** in Delhi where the body of Prime Minister Nehru was cremated in 1964: now a national shrine and a wooded public park.

SHARĀB *n* Urdu
In the original Arabic, any drinkable fluid: in Hindustani it has become a general word for all potable alcohols. As shrub, in the 18th and early 19th centuries the word travelled to England to mean wine, or a cordial of fruit juice and spirits. *See also* Sherbet.

On the streets of Delhi, the popular word for liquor (also Hindustani) is dāru, Urdu from Persian.

Sharabi: pejorative for a drinker.

Kachchi Sharab: see **Kachcha.**

SHARIAH/SHARIAT *n* Arabic
Lit. the pathway to water (i.e. to a
desert Arab, to life). The code of laws
binding Muslims in religious, civil and
criminal affairs and, no less, the little
things of daily personal life within the
home and family. Based on the Holy
Kor'an, the Hadis/Hadith (the recorded
sayings of Mohammed and Sunni
custom and tradition), the Shari'ah
has been formed by generations of
Muslim scholars (*see* Ulema). When
the Prophet spoke of spiritual matters, his words are held to have been
inspired by God and to be immutable:
on other subjects some discrimination
is allowed. Since the Shari'ah has
been put together by men, much of
it by scholars working in the early
centuries to fit the local needs of their
time, in theory it can evolve to some
extent to meet new circumstances, but
in practice any change on other than a
regional basis is very difficult. **Islam**
is not a hierarchical church with a single secretariat and after the abolition
of the **Khilafat** in 1923, there is no
obvious head. While doubts may arise
over particular points, the Shari'ah is
accepted by most Muslims as being of
divine origin, as relevant today as it
was to the inhabitants of 7th century
AD tribal Arabia. In India, any suggestion for amendment, particularly if
made by a non-Muslim, is likely to be
rejected as an attack on Islam.

Nevertheless, the Prophet could be
practical. There is a story that he had
once instructed certain date palm
growers on a detail of their craft. They
complied but the results were not
fruitful. A Hadith then has it that the
growers were told "continue doing as
you used to, since you know the matters of the world better than I".

SHĀSTRAS/SĀSTRAS *n* Hindi
In common usage, all ancient **Hindu**
treatises considered to have authority, are referred to as shastras. Many
subjects are covered, examples being
dharma shastra detailing the correct
behaviour and duties for both ruler
and citizen in religious, state and
domestic affairs: temple architecture (shilpa/silpa shastra): medicine
(chikitsa shastra); statecraft (artha-
shastra, see Chanakya) and poetry
(kavishastra).

The true shastras were composed
during the **Gupta** period in **Sanskrit**
verse, amplifying and building on the
early **Vedic** prose shruti (heard), directly received texts and therefore of
the highest sanctity and authority.

Of somewhat lesser authority from
the 'heard' shastras, are those which
were **smriti** – remembered, before
being written down in Sanskrit verse.
The **Epics** come into this class, also
the laws of **Manu**. Also smriti are
the sutras (lit. threads in Sanskrit. Via
Latin, suture is an English collateral),
short aphorisms in prose or verse.
The collection probably best known
in the West in English translation
is the 'Aphorisms of Love' (**Kama**

Sutra), by Vatsyayana, a set of about twelve hundred and fifty shloks/slokas (metrical stanzas – sometimes couplets – employed in Sanskrit poetry). Instructions to the wealthy man-about-town of, perhaps, the 4th century AD, on how to manage his household affairs in the sensual context. As published for the coffee tables of the West, its sexual content is frequently heightened by reproductions of relatively modern erotic paintings completely irrelevant to the text. But the sutras do indeed provide a valuable commentary on Indian upper class domestic life of the period.

Shastr: a weapon, a tool. Shastr puja, the worship of his arms by a soldier, his tools by an artisan – as on Vijayadashami (*see* Dussehra).

Shok shastr: condolence salute. A gesture of respect, and tribute. The firing of weapons at a military funeral.

Shastra Police: armed police.

Salami Shastr: the military command 'Present Arms'.

At one time, in roman script, 'sha' could be represented by *c* cedilla, so that in books of the turn of the 20th century, ºhastra can be seen as Sastra.

SHĀSTRY/SHĀSTRI/SĀSTRI *n* Hindi

A **pandit** well-versed in the study of the **shastras**. A title, equivalent to a First Degree in oriental studies, awarded by the Varanaseya Sanskrit Vishvavidyalaya, of **Varanasi**; Benaras **Hindu** University and a few other universities. A family name.

SHAT *n* Hindi
(A more phonetic spelling would be 'shut'.) The previously rarely heard **Sanskrit** word, meaning one hundred, has recently acquired prominence in Hindi as part of the names of a number of super-fast trains introduced in 1988, preceding the actual centenary year (1989)of the birth of Jawaharlal Nehru, the Shatabdi Expresses, the Centenary Expresses. The best known is probably that running non-stop between Delhi and Agra and then on to Bhopal. The universally used Hindi word for one hundred is the Prakrit (*see* Sanskrit) form of shat, sau. In Urdu from Arabic the word for a century is sadi.

Pratishat: per cent. Shat pratishat: one hundred per cent.

The word for one hundred is of some significance for ethnologists. At a stage in pre-history possibly from the lower Danube basin, some speakers of satam, meaning one hundred, migrated westward: with them, satam became centam and philogians interested in the Indo-European tongues have noted the two divisions of speech from that period, those of the centam and satam users. The centam group includes Latin, Greek, and the Germanic and Celtic tongues. The satam group, generally to the north and east, includes Sanskrit, Old Persian and the Slavonic and Baltic languages (these last includes Lettish, spoken by Latvians, who can still identify Sanskrit words in their speech).

SHAURYA *n* Sanskrit
Heroism.
Shaurya Divas: an expression used by journalists and politicians. A day of heroes or of heroic action.

SHEESHAM/SHISHAM *n* Hindi
A valuable hardwood forest tree of the Dalbergia family: particularly used for furniture. May also be known as Indian or Bombay rosewood or sissoo. Like teak immune to attack by white ants.

SHEIKH *n* Urdu
Lit. an old man: an elder in a Muslim community. A title sometimes accorded to a convert to **Islam**. A Muslim personal name, with an implied claim to Arab descent.

SHENAI/SHAHNAI *n* Urdu
Wind instrument of the oboe family introduced by the Muslims. Two reeds and eight or nine holes, seven of which are played on. Traditionally, the shenai is particularly used for open air ceremonial processions, but in recent years, expert players (**ustads**)

have brought it to the concert platform. It is a little exercise on the shenai that is the tuning signal before the beginning of each transmission of All India Radio.

Some find a connection between the shenai and the medieval European double-reed instrument, the shawm.

It was a piece on the shenai, played by Ustad Bismillah Khan, that in the Delhi Parliament house at midnight on 14/15 August 1947 distinguished the midnight hour and India's "tryst with destiny" in the words of Jawaharlal Nehru.

SHĒR *n* Urdu
A lion. An unofficial title, as for example, Sher-e-**Pun-**  **jab**, Lion of the Punjab, given to the great Ranjit Singh, the **Sikh** king in the early 19th century. An alternative meaning, also Urdu, is a poetical couplet.

A personal name.
Both lions (**singh** in Hindi) and tigers are immigrants to the subcontinent: the tiger from the far north, perhaps Siberia, and the lion from West Asia. Today, the Asiatic, or Persian, lion can only be found in one sanctuary, the Gir forest in **Kathiawar**.

A little used Urdu word (from Arabic)

for lion is asad. An example is the Asad Burji on the river side of Delhi's Red Fort.

SHERBET *n* English
Derived from the Arabic word **sharab**, a drink – any drink, even water. (Syrup and the European culinary word, sorbet, come from the same source: in English dictionaries, sharab can be found as the archaic shrub.) But in India, sharab has come to mean solely an alcoholic drink. The Urdu sharbat is used for a flavoured sweet drink without alcohol: an orange squash, say, would be a sharbat, or, more traditionally, an essence from roses. (*See* Attar). In English, syrup is a linked word.

SHERPA *n* Tibetan
Lit. people from the east. Fem. sherpani. A member of a Buddhist tribe of Tibetan origin living at approximately 3,050m altitude in the valley of the Sapt Kosi river below Mount Everest in Nepal. Although personally having little interest in mountaineering other than as a profession in a hungry environment, they have become famous first as porters and then as climbers, with **Himalaya** expeditions. Now, Sherpas also assist, and a few organise, the gentler trekking tours. Tensing Norgay, one of the first two men to reach the summit of Everest, was a Sherpa.

Sherpa Sirdar: leader of a team of Sherpas.

Sherpa Tiger: title and award from the Himalayan Club to Sherpas who have accompanied expeditions to heights above 7860m.

High Altitude Sherpas: those skilled and experienced to assist expeditions at heights in excess of 6400m.

SHIKĀR Urdu
The literal meaning of the word in the original Persian was a victim, a human or animal target: but to the **Moguls** and Anglo-India the sense was of shooting and fishing for sport, as it still is in those circles in which these activities remain popular. A self-imposed code, such as 'sundown, gun-down' was rigid. Except perhaps within the princely order shikar was repugnant to orthodox Hindus.

The highly organised shoot (a word of British times for a hunting expedition) is a thing of the past. Some indeed were highly organised: many princes had a department of state, supported by the manpower of the royal army as beaters, for the sole purpose of managing shoots for themselves and important guests. Now, only the occasional tiger, officially proscribed as a man-eater, may legally be killed, or, perhaps, anaesthetised by a dart and then placed in a zoo. Legacies of the princely hunting grounds are many of the national parks and animal sanctuaries of today. In 1947 the tiger population was estimated to have been about 70,000. In 2001, from 800 to 2000.

Shikari: a person who goes on, shikar. Also a professional assistant, tracker, a ghillie.

Shikara: a light boat, paddled and not rowed: used on the Kashmir lakes. The passenger variety is cushioned and partly covered with a reed thatch roof.

See also Machan.

SHIKHARA/SIKHAR *n* Hindi

Lit. summit, pinnacle. Term for the tower(s) of a Hindu temple, typically built over the central shrine: in northern India, usually curvilinear in shape. In the south, the tower over the main shrine is the vimana, normally with square angles and in the form of a stepped pyramid (*see* also Gopuram): there, only the topmost part is the shikhara.

The crest of a peacock is shikandi. (From the **Mahabharat,** shikandi can mean an effeminate man.)

Shikhara Choti: see Choti.

Shikhar Sanmelan: summit meeting in a political sense.

SHIKSHA *n* Hindi Education.

Shiksha Mantri: Education Minister in the Government of India.

SHIMLA

The current official name and the way the hill people have always spoken of the Himachal Pradesh (*see* HP) town known to the British as Simla. The word comes from a **Hindu** temple in the area, certainly older than the British discovery of the site of the hill station (*see* Hills) in the early 19th century, dedicated to Shyamala Devi, the Mother Goddess (*see* Shakti) in a local form.

Further to the west in the same state, the erstwhile Kulu town and valley are now recognised as Kullu.

SHISHYA *n* Hindi

A student: a disciple, *see* Guru.

SHĪT/SHEET Hindi

Cold: coolth.

Shital: cool. Absence of sexual passion. Although the Hindi word derives from **Sanskrit**, Arabic also has shita, meaning cold – or the winter season. An example of early Aryan Persian travelling both east and west.

Shital Jal: Chilled water, normally for drinking.

Shitala/Sheetla: **Hindu** Goddess portrayed in red garb and riding a donkey. In her hand a bundle of stinging nettles; a touch from these and smallpox will result. Shitala has temples dedicated to her in which prayers for deliverance from the nettles are offered but if the present cautious hopes of the World Health Organisation are justified, then her scourge has been put away for ever.

SHIVA/SIVA/SHIV

Rudra, a powerful Vedic deity, sometimes terrible, sometimes benign, was often addressed by such propitiatory terms as gracious or auspicious – shiva in **Sanskrit**. In the course of time, the attributes became the epithet and Rudra merged into Shiva (but lives on in **rudraksh**): the destroyer and the creator. Lord of the dance as **Nataraj**; Mahadev (the great God); Shankar; Nilkanth (the blue-throated one. The similarly adorned and colourful roller bird or blue jay, in Hindi also Nilkanth, is greatly respected by **Hindus** on this account); Shishndev (Lord of the penis); Vishvanath (Lord of the World) and so many other names. Shiva is particularly connected with south India and indeed one school of thought holds the opinion that millenia before the Vedas were heard in India, the deity was the object of monotheistic worship in the south. Unlike **Vishnu**, he has no **avatar** but has many aspects.

Associated with Lord Shiva are **Nandi**, the white bull; snakes; the **lingam**; and as a weapon, the trident (**trisul**). On images made in the south, one of the Lord's four hands will often be holding a leaping deer, and another, a stylised battle-axe (charri): probably, the earrings will not be a pair.

As the great **yogi** (Maha Yogi), Lord Shiva is believed by many to sit, **ash**-covered, in permanent meditation on Mount **Kailas**. His coiled hair spans the firmament, entwining the crescent moon: from the same hair springs to earth the sacred River **Ganga**. Hence a name for the Lord, Gangadhara (Ganga bearing). To the European, with an 'either or mind, the God exhibits in abundance the uncertainties of Hinduism: he is the great ascetic, a devoted family man and yet the lusty exponent of eroticism: the creator of life and the peaceful teacher: yet the wearer of skulls and the frequenter of cremation grounds: he personifies masculinity, but it is recognised that his power, his **shakti,** is incomplete without a female component so one aspect of the Lord is Ardhanarishwara, with both ' male and female features in the one body (the right half is the male half). As Nataraj, the youthful and comely cosmic dancer, he wears a large ring in his left ear to denote femininity (*See* Right Hand, Left Hand).

Shaivite/Shivite: a devotee of Lord Shiva, also adjectival.

Shivabooti: cannabis (*see* **Indian** Hemp).

Shivratri (or, more correctly Ma-hashivratri): festival in February/ March commemorating the occasion of Lord Shiva saving the gods, the human race and all the creatures on earth by drinking deadly poison produced before the **amrit** at the churning of the ocean. The Lord's neck turned blue and he remained senseless the whole day, recovering only at midnight, the moment signalled in all Shiv **mandirs** with **conches** and, perhaps, fireworks. For others, the midnight hour following the day of Shivratri is the moment of the Lord's birth. (Some hold that Shiva has no physical form and so was never born.) To some Shaivites, Mahashivratri is the chief purely religious festival of the year, for it is also said that on this day those who worship the Lord in lingam form will receive countless blessings. The cannabis plant is particularly associated with Shiva and on Shivratri many devotees will drink bhang or smoke ganja: or eat the fresh green leaves of shivabooti which will be on sale in city **bazaars** : (*see* Indian Hemp).

Shivalingam: a symbolic phallus, representing Lord Shiva, the creator. *See* Lingam.

Shivala: a Shiv mandir, a temple dedicated to Lord Shiva. A Sanskrit name for the Lord is Ishwar, so a temple name ending in 'ishwar/es-hwar e.g. Mukteshwar, will be a Shivala: the name, perhaps, will also cover the village or town.

SHIV SENA *n* Hindi
Lit. Shiva's army. (Originally a reference to Shivaji, the 17th century Maratha hero: see Chhatrapati.) A political party based in Maharashtra.

SHLŌKA/SLŌKA/SLŌK *n* Hindi
Strictly, a stanza of **Sanskrit** poetry, particularly one from the **Epics**, having the form of four quarters of equal length and, usually, eight syllables to the quarter. Loosely used for any couplet from Sanskrit scriptural poetry.

SHO (S.H.O.)
Station House Officer. The officer in charge of a police station. *See also* Thanedar.

SHOE *n*
Of the major parts of the human body (head, trunk, arms and feet), in India the head is considered the most worthy of respect, the feet, the least. (As an act of submission and self-abasement, a suppliant may grasp the ankles, or place his hands on the feet, of the one being begged for a favour.) Before sleeping, many ensure that their feet will not be pointing towards scripture or a devotional object – a Muslim may take care that he will not be lying feet first in the direction of Mecca. By association and to a **Hindu**, intrinsically if

made of leather, shoes are regarded as unclean, to be removed before entering any place requiring special respect such as a religious building or a home (particularly the kitchen area, both because of the possibility of food pollution and of the age-old respect due to the fire in the hearth (*see* Havan). Shoes should never be worn when lying on a bed, nor placed on a table nor, in the opinions of some, near a book (*see* Kor'an). Even in a home where shoes are normally worn, on the occasion of a death in the family, with the body in the house, all will be expected to be barefoot. Traditionally, a son formally approaching his parents should first remove his shoes and, at least up to the early years of the 19th century, a junior in rank on approaching someone very senior, would do so barefoot. (Europeans looked for the same deference from Indian visitors.) While a Hindu will always leave his shoes outside a temple he intends to enter, a Muslim on going into a mosque may carry them in his hand: during his devotions, he will place them on the ground by him on their sides, sole to sole. The concession under which a foreigner could enter some Islamic revered areas, shod but wearing canvas overshoes, is now on the way out, but the anguish of winter cold and summer heat on marble can be reduced for stockinged feet are generally - but not always – tolerated. In a Gurdwara, if an exception is made for medical reasons, a clean pair of socks to be donned at the threshold may be insisted on.

In October 1987, the Delhi press reported that in order to garland – *see* Mala – a public statue in Agra, it had been necessary for the State Chief Minister to mount a ladder attached to the sculpture: while doing so, he omitted to remove his shoes. It was held by local political leaders that to correct the impropriety, the statue had to be washed with **Ganga** and **Yamuna** waters and milk. Purification – shuddikaran.

Shoe Beating: to be beaten with a shoe is far more degrading although probably less painful than to be beaten with a stick. Similarly, to kick someone is not merely an assault but because of the use of the foot a gross insult and dishonouring humiliation.

Shoe Garland: as an act of public execration, a garland of shoes may be placed round the neck of someone particularly disliked or, more likely, around the neck of his effigy in his absence. By way of an unwelcoming and umbrageous gesture, a visiting dignitary, in addition to the more usual black flags, may find he is passing below a line of shoes suspended from an archway (*see* Toran) put up over his path.

A stylised representation of a shoe

(in fact, often an Arabian Nights type of slipper) is frequently painted at the front and rear of a commercial vehicle. Its purpose is to so disgust the Evil One that he does not interfere with the vehicle's safe passage. (The parallel with the English custom of a shoe on the back of a wedding car, or in the form of a charm, is obvious.) For similar protection, in village India a shoe may be hung by a sleeping child. Also designed to discourage the evil eye is the practice, particularly favoured by taxi and **rickshaw** drivers, of hanging girls' black hair braids – chutila– from the rear of their vehicles.

In 1961, a **Sikh** leader vowed to fast to death unless certain political demands were met; he was ignored but he failed to become a martyr. The penance awarded by his community elders for breaking the vow, was that for five days he was to clean the shoes of those who entered the Golden Temple in Amritsar (*see* Amrit) and to clean utensils. Again, in 1988, a Sikh ex-Chief Minister of **Punjab** accepted from the elders that he was to clean shoes in public while carrying a small board announcing that he had sinned (the sins were political). Amongst rural folk, like burning feathers in Victorian England, so the inside of a shoe may be held to the nose of an unconscious person as an aid to resuscitation.

Electricians, tend to refer to a two or three-pin power plug (i.e., excluding the socket) as a shoe.

SHRĀDDH/SHRĀDDHA *n* Hindi
Faith, homage, respect, veneration. A word from **Sanskrit** particularly applied to ceremonies originating in Vedic times relating to the propitiation of the souls of the recently dead and of family ancestors: especially pinda dān (offerings of rice balls). Those able to take part, members of the extended family group having a common ancestor, being known as sapinda. An annual two-week period (shraddh paksh – see Calendars – or pitri paksh, ancestors fortnight) just before **Dussehra** is set apart in the **Hindu** calendar for shraddh ceremonies. At this time, the devout will practise austerities and even the less traditionally minded will often abstain from alcohol and, if normally non-vegetarian, meat.

A death anniversary may be termed (from **Sanskrit**) punyatithi with the first being barsi.

SHRAMDĀN *n* Hindi
Lit. donation of labour (i.e., the gift of work for a charitable or social purpose). Voluntary work, often, but not necessarily, physical work for the good of a community as, for example, for village road making, or constructing a needed school building. *See also* Kar.

SHRI/SRI *n* Hindi from Sanskrit

A feminine word, attributes (radiance, splendour, wealth) of the Goddess **Lakshmi**, sometimes used as her name (usually, in roman spelling, Sri or Sridevi): the Devnagri (*see* Sanskrit and Dev) character for Shri is her symbol.

Used before a personal name, Shri (sometimes expanded to Shriman) is a **Hindu** male title of respect given to a person of position: nowadays, by Government encouragement, applicable to all. The equivalent of Mr. Title of respect preceding the name of something devoted to God: a book, a temple, a school. Exceptionally, with the sacred book, the **Gita**, Shri becomes Shrimad. A woman also can be Shri, provided she is venerated as a religious personage. **Sikhs** may refer to their holy city as Shri Amritsar (*see* Amrit). But Shri is not used when addressing a Sikh.

In the Hindu Kingdom of Nepal, it is common in correspondence to use Shri three times when addressing someone known personally: the King himself, has Shri repeated five times before his other titles and is often known as the Shri Panch. In India, certain religious leaders claim one hundred and eight Shrees in front of their names (the figure has some significance in Buddhism and Hinduism, as that of the one hundred and eight holy books of Buddhism): others claim 1001.

Sarvashri: Messrs/Messieurs

Shrimati: form of address to a married woman, abbreviated on paper to Smt., Mrs. In writing to a woman whose marital status is unknown, Sushshri may be used before the name. To indicate additional affectionate respect, ji will be added as a suffix to Shrimati and Shriman. When addressing a couple, it is customary to mention the lady first–Shrimati and Shriman so-and-so; Radha-Krishna.

Sri Lanka: since **Vedic** days, the Indian name for the island at the south-eastern tip of the subcontinent has been Lanka (although Silan or Eelan/llam in **Tamil** – had locally been in use and which in time became Ceylon). Some years after the 1948 **Independence** from Britain, the Sinhalese (*see* Singh) adopted the Vedic name for their country, adding Sri as a title of honour.

Srinagar: the city of Sri (Lakshmi). The ancient Hindu name of the chief city of Kashmir. During the time of Muslim rule, the city itself was known as Kashmir (or Kashmir Shahr). On coming under the Sikhs (1819), the original name was restored.

Srinagar once the capital of the Garhwal region of Uttaranchal State.

Srinath: the Lord of Sri. An epithet for Lord **Vishnu** (husband of Lakshmi), either as himself or, frequently, as Lord **Krishna**.

Implying a recognition of superior birth or education is the term from Sanskrit, mahashay (nobility) used before a person's name: in some ways equivalent to the use in Urdu of sharif or esquire in English.

SHRINGAR/SHRINGARA *n*
Hindi
Sexual passion, desire, emotion: especially in connection with the arts. And in everyday life, elegance, smartness (of appearance), personal adornment, and make-up; so that a shringari **otsav** will not normally be a festival of overt sensuality, but one of grace and style for the well-dressed, the haute monde. *See* Ras. Of recent coinage is Kar Shringar — car beauty.

SHRIVĀTS/SHRIVĀTSA/SRIVĀTS *n* Hindi
Like the **swastika**, an auspicious sign: an indication of superhuman qualities. A brilliant jewel (by name Kasturba), produced at the Churning of the Ocean (*see* Amrit), flower petals, on the chest of Lord **Vishnu**, especially on his images made in the south. It is said that the shrivats is a symbol of his consort, Sri, or **Lakshmi**, dwelling within him at that point.

On Jain images, the shrivats may be no more than a slightly etched mark (sometimes, like two S's back to back) on the bare upper body of a tirthankara (Jain saint), usually over the central breastbone, but, occasionally, again when from the south, well to the right of the body, almost on the shoulder. While Lord Vishnu is usually identifiable, it may be difficult for the non-expert to distinguish between images of Jain and Buddhist origin. The shrivats on an unclothed image indicates **Jainism**, but from its absence the reverse cannot be safely inferred, for Jain sculptors of eastern India did not include it. A representation, possibly unique, in which the **Buddha** does carry the shrivats on his chest, may be seen on a mural in the Aural Stein Central Asian collection in the National Museum, New Delhi. Convention required that the singularity of the Buddha himself be indicated by such devices as a protuberance or hair-bun on his head, the ushnisa, an ancient symbol of a ruler, and a fighting man – it has been suggested that a Sikh's top-knot has the same origin. The usual word for a hair-bun or top-knot is jura.

SHROFF *n*
The word is an anglicism from saraf, Arabic and Urdu for a money-changer; the traditional appraiser of bullion and specie. Shroff has been adopted into Hindi and is used as a **Parsi** and **Hindu** family name. The meaning today is of a banker or money-changer in a big way, a dealer in jewels or in precious stones. When applied to a goldsmith, the more traditional roman spelling, saraf, is often used,

SHUBH *adj* Hindi
Auspicious: good. A person may ask another's 'shubh nam', as in formal English, his good name.

SHŪDDH *adj* Hindi
Pure, unadulterated, sacred. Shuddh Hindi: pure Hindi, based on Sanskrit roots.

SHŪDRA/SUDRA *n* Hindi
Of the four great divisions within **Hindu** society (*see* Caste Hindus), the lowest in status: the manual workers, the menials, yet whose hereditary occupations are not so polluting as to cause them to be outcaste. Probably the descendants of local people assimilated by the invading Aryans (*see* Arya.). Although within the Hindu fold – according to **Manu**, the sudra has been formed from the feet (*see* Shoe) of **Brahma** – traditionally, he was not permitted to study, nor even to hear, Vedic scripture. The line between the shudra and the acchut (untouchable) is not sharply defined.

SIDHA *adj.* Hindi
Of a direction, straight: or metaphorically, a path of rectitude, uprightness. By some of a man, simplicity, naivety.

SIDDHA *n* Hindi
An ancient **Hindu** system of herbal medicine, still practised, especially in south India. One who is believed to have occult powers, particularly of a **tantric** nature. Siddhi: supernatural powers, given to some at birth, received by others after long study and **tapasya**. A person who has attained spiritual perfection. One who has successfully accomplished a planned course of spiritual or yogic training. In a general way, the word may be applied to one who is usually successful in what he sets out to do. A master of his craft. A statement that a person attained siddhi on a certain date may be a euphemism regarding his death.

Siddhidatta: see Ganesh.

Sidi-See Habsh

SIFĀRISH *n* Urdu
Lit. recommendation. Frequently a reference to a belief that employment is obtained not on merit, but through influence or 'pull'.

SIKH *n*
The word is derived from the **Sanskrit** shishya, a student, a disciple: cognate, is the Hindi verb, sikhana – to teach. In pronunciation,  the *i* is short (seekh has another meaning, see Kababs). Sikhism as a word is an anglicism: a Sikh will describe his faith as Gurmat – observance of the code of the Gurus. A male (fem. also Sikh, but sometimes, Sardarni. A bazaar word, Sikhni is

not acceptable to the community). An adherent to the monotheistic sect founded in the **Punjab** by Guru Nanak in the 16th century (but not all followers of the first Guru are Sikhs, *see* Panth, and although the Guru used the term to describe his disciples, it only came into general use with the raising of the **Khalsa** by the tenth Guru, Gobind Singh, to whom modern Sikhism owes much of its outward form and observances). Of the population of India, the number of Sikhs is small; 1.94%. (2001 census) is usually quoted, but in their now truncated homeland, the State of the Punjab, the proportion is more than sixty.

The centre of Sikhism is the Golden Temple at Amritsar (*see* Amrit), together with the building close by, the Akal Takht (lit. Throne of God), the official seat of authority of the elders of the community, an edict from whom on matters of Sikh faith or behaviour (hukamnama, lit. order-document, *see* Nama) is binding, on pain of excommunication or a lesser punishment (tankha). Sikhism was intended, perhaps, as a protestant movement against some features of Hindusim (such as the **caste** system and image worship) and perhaps again, as a bridge between **Islam** and Hinduism; there is a tradition that Guru Nanak, no doubt because of his interest in **Sufism**, visited Mecca, receiving divine help to enter the city normally barred to non-Muslims: his

conclusion was said to have been that neither Islam nor Hinduism was the answer to his vision of service to God and man. Islamic influence, like the absence of a priesthood and simple temples (*see* Gurdwara) devoid of images, still remain – but for some, pictures of the Gurus, forbidden in the early days, do appear to serve the purpose of icons. The work ethic is emphasised: a man should prosper for himself and his family. The renunciation of the things of this world and reliance upon others for sustenance is not a virtue in Sikhism. The Hindu doctrine of the transmigration of the soul with the ultimate object of merging with the Godhead is there in Sikhism together with the theory of **karma** – as a man sows, so he shall reap.

The visible signs of a keshdhari Sikh (lit. one who observes the Sikh hairstyle, i.e., an orthodox Sikh: but a more likely term for one strong in his faith is amritdhari Sikh – *see* Amrit) are the five kakkars, or K's: kesh (uncut hair and beard, the sign of a warrior), a wooden kangha (comb), katchha (under-shorts), kara/kadda (steel **bangle** worn on the right wrist, signifying restraint, a curb on the senses or on a desire to infringe on any of the rules of the Khalsa) and kirpan (sword – as a word, kirpan derives from Sanskrit, kripa/kripan mercy, compassion as well as a weapon. A sword used with mercy can relieve oppression. Since in modern living, to wear a full-length sword in an office, say, could be a little inconvenient, a Sikh to comply with the rule, will usually carry either a curved dagger, with a blade of about seven inches, in a scabbard hanging from the shoulder; or else, a purely token piece of no more than two or three inches in size, but whatever its shape or blade length, it will be referred to as a kirpan, The right of a Sikh to carry a kirpan is included in Article 25 of the Constitution of India. The general word for a Sikh who has cut his hair and shaved his beard is mõna/mõnas: lit. clean-shaven. A harsher word is patit – fallen, depraved. Sehajdhari can also mean a clean-shaven Sikh (or at least, without the Sikh-style beard and full-length hair), but the definition is more precise. The tenth Guru, who made the five K's mandatory for his soldiers and for those who aspired to leadership, also allowed a form of associate membership of the community: sehajdhari (the easy/comfortable one). Of the sons of a Punjabi family, perhaps only one would be a keshdhari Sikh. A sehajdhari must be able to recite certain Sikh prayers, must perform rites, must abjure tobacco and Muslim **halal** meat and must not have been a renegade from keshdhari status. Such an individual can be considered a Sikh and provided he is on the rolls of a **gurdwara**, is legally entitled to vote in **SGPC** elections. (Today, orthodox Sikhs are objecting to this clause in the SGPC Act of

1925, saying that no male without the regular hair style can be considered a Sikh). Until reforms in the 1920s, most gurdwaras were controlled by sehajdharis, many hardly distinguishable from **Hindus**. In general, those of the Nanak **Panth** are sehajdhari. These days, many keshdharis will not accept anyone with trimmed hair and no Sikh-style beard as a member of the community. One who has dyed his beard (black, for cosmetic effect) may be held to have lapsed from strict orthodoxy.

All Sikhs use the title **Singh** (lion) before their family name, a **Rajput** custom adopted by Guru Gobind Singh (born Gobind Rai, but in some contexts he is referred to as Gobind Das). In addition, the Guru ordered that his followers should wear no hat other than their distinguishing dastaar (Punjabi for **puggri**). But whatever the canonical justification, wherever in the world Sikhs happen to be, the wearing of the turban in public is a proclamation of faith, a personal 'nishan-sahib' (*see* Gurdwara) and they strongly contest any suggestion that in this matter they should'be as other men; even when greater head protection seems desirable, as when riding a motor-cycle. Other proscriptions, probably once intended to safeguard the health of Sikhs as fighting men, are alcohol, intoxicating drugs and the use, cultivation or commerce of tobacco in any form. A Sikh should not eat the meat of an animal killed in the Muslim fashion (*see* Halal and Jhatka). Beef is not specifically forbidden, but because, no doubt, of their close connections with Hindus in the past, few Sikhs will actually eat it. While the great majority of Sikhs abjure tobacco, it has to be admitted that the prohibition of alcohol and drugs is not so strictly observed. Today, orthodox Sikhism regards tobacco not merely as a health hazard but with all the revulsion felt by **Islam** for pork or Hinduism for beef, a contaminating and polluting substance. A packet of cigarettes carried into a gurdwara can be held to have desecrated the place of worship. A cigarette offered to a Sikh can be taken as an insulting suggestion that he is lax in matters of his religion. As far as possible, a Sikh should offer prayers (ardas), standing, at least four times a day; on rising before dawn at home, then congregationally as a liturgy in the gurdwara; then again at home at sunset and before going to bed.

Although Hargobind (1606-44) raised and used military forces against the **Moguls,** (Sikhs say he girded two swords, one spiritual one temporal), it was Guru Gobind Singh and oppression by the Emperor Aurangzeb – the Guru's father and four sons accepted execution rather than embrace Islam – who changed the gentle followers of Guru Nanak into almost a military order (said the later Guru, for the true Sikh, his weapons are his jewels'), leading to the Sikh kingdom based on Lahore. A period of some eighty years between the decline of Moguls and the arrival of British power in the Punjab, looked back upon with nostalgia by many Sikhs today. A time when the British referred to the Sikh nation. (The Persian word from Arabic, quaum, that the Sikhs applied to themselves, can mean either nation or community; but it is the British translation which in the 1980s bedeviled relations between some Sikhs and the Government of India.) The Sikh state, formed by the coalescence of a number of Sikh chieftains and the overrunning of the territories of non-Sikh others, seems to have had no formal specific name other than that of the Khalsa Raj or Khalsa **Sarkar,** the Singh Sarkar (the last also a title for Ranjit Singh) and Lahore Durbar. The coinage carried the image of Guru Nanak and not that of the founder and ruler, Maharaja Ranjit Singh, who died in 1839 leaving no capable heir or successor.

Struggles for power followed leading to a breakdown of civil administration. So that the eight years of peace after the annexation of the kingdom to **British India** in 1849, after two hard-fought 'Sikh Wars', so impressed the robust peasantry that in general they sided with the British in the **Hindustan** uprising of 1857. While the prospects of revenge and of looting their old Muslim masters of Delhi may have been an added inducement, the Sikhs at that time were not necessarily anti-Muslim: in their two wars against the British, particularly the first, many of their best gunners, including the artillery commander, were Muslims. Earlier, some of Ranjit Singh's most loyal and trusted advisers were also Muslims. But certainly there was no feeling of community with the soldiers from the Gangetic plains who had risen against the British, men who some years earlier had helped the Europeans to annex the Punjab.

While naturally tending to follow his father's faith, a Sikh is not born as such, but has to enter the community through the pahul/pahal (gateway) ceremony receiving amrit from exactly five Sikhs, as did the tenth Guru. In an unusual ceremony, he personally admitted his first five followers (panch pyare) and then he in turn was initiated by them. It was then that he changed his name from Guru Gobind Rai to Gobind Singh. In many Punjabi families until quite recently, the tradition was that some of the siblings would be Sikh and some Hindu: intermarriage between Sikh and Hindu was also common. Nowadays, with many Sikhs striving to project a separate religious, social and political identity for their faith, such intercommunion is becoming rarer.

With the object of raising the status of women, the tenth Guru instructed that the final name of all Sardarnis

should be Kaur – princess – a word connected with **kanwar**, a prince.

Not all of the community accepted the measures of Guru Gobind Singh, so of one period historians can refer to Sikhs (the traditionalists) and to Singhs (followers of the last living Guru). By the time of Ranjit Singh as ruler (1800-1839) the distinction had gone, all were Singhs and were described as Sikhs. *But see also* Panth.

What is known of Guru Nanak is largely based on Janam sakis (lit. life-stories), a series of tracts produced in the 16th century. Accepted by many as literal truth, gospel, and so expounded by preachers, by others, some controversial historians among them, as mostly fiction, composed for political purposes.

Sikhs suffered much at the hands of Muslim rulers, but the community is not anti-Islamic. Sikh scripture and the Punjabi language contain many Persian terms; their religious buildings, even those reconstructed today, contain many Muslim architectural features, the foundation stone of the Golden Temple in Amritsar was laid by a Muslim, and in a prominent New Delhi gurdwara in 1999, as part of the tercentenary celebrations of the forming of the **Khalsa** in accordance with tradition, Muslim professional musicians from Pakistan sang the holy Sikh **kirtan**.

Bhapa Sikh: one whose original homeland was the north-western region of the pre-**Independence** Punjab, now the Rawalpindi district of Pakistan. At least these days, most are urban with interests in commerce and industry rather than agriculture.

Jat Sikh: probably a farmer, tough, hard working and strong in his faith.

See also: Akali, Amrit, Gurdwara, Guru, Guru Granth Sahib, Khalsa, Langar, Mazhabi Sikhs, Nihangs, Panth, Piao, Singh.

SIMKIN *n*
Said to have been the pronunciation by Indian servants of the word champagne: later adopted by their British masters.

SINDHI *n* and *adj*
In the Indian context, a **Hindu** who, or whose family, comes from Sind, the country at the mouth of the River Indus (now in Pakistan): Sindhi family names often end in 'ani', e.g. Advani, Durani, Mirchandani. The language of the province of Sind.

SINDOOR/SINDUR *n* Hindi
Lit. the colour vermillion: an auspicious colour in India, particularly to **Hindus**. The red line of powder on the first few inches of the parting of a Hindu woman's hair sometimes termed the rekha. (Almost universal in eastern India but rarely seen in the south and seldom on those of the **Sikh** faith), proclaiming her married status: the first application, the sindoor dan, by the bridegroom, sometimes immediately follows the wedding ceremony.

Reddish paint to assist worship, applied to images of the deities **Ganesh** and **Hanuman**, and in village areas, to stones or holes in large tree trunks, or any other such place deemed to represent a local godling.

SINGĀRA/SINGHĀRA *n* Hindi
Trapa bispinosa: the water chestnut. Sometimes called the Jesuit's nut and a single nut has been termed a caltrop. The autumnal green seed of a floating water-plant cultivated in ponds and tanks throughout India. The white starchy kernel is eaten both raw and cooked or, after drying, may be ground into a flour for **Hindu** use on a particularly religious or auspicious occasion. One species, T. natans, has four horn-like projections, two at each end, and the more common bispinosa two in all. (In Hindi, a horn is 'sing' as in **barasingha**.) The caltrop was a medieval weapon, a small ball with four spikes: left on the ground, one always was uppermost in a position to injure a horse or a lightly shod man (reintroduced in World War II to puncture vehicle tyres).

In eastern India, the singara is not the chestnut, but the Bengali equivalent of the somewhat similarly shaped

samosa patty. (There, the bazaar term for the chestnut is the Hindustani, paniphal – water fruit.)

SINGH *n* Hindi

Lit. lion. Adopted by **kshatriyas**, particularly **Rajputs** and some **Jats**, as a caste title: also used by all male **Sikhs** as a part of their names, following the lead of **Guru** Gobind Singh, who so addressed his first five followers, they who formed the original **Khalsa**. Meaning that they would be as lions, doughty fighters for their faith. Nowadays, some Sikh women are also using the title. Like the word Sikh, Singh is to be found in the Pali (*see* Sanskrit) scriptures of Buddhism, where lion' is intended to imply an energetic human seeker after truth.

In Bihar, Singh takes the form Sinha, and in the south, the original **Sanskrit** Simha/Simhan – e.g. Narsimhan' (*see* Vishnu). The zodiac sign of Leo is also known as Simhan,

The **Aryans** who colonised Lanka in, perhaps the 5th century BC, called themselves lions (sinha): hence the current word for the majority community and of the language (now part Dravidian) of Sri Lanka, Sinhala, with English forms Sinhalese/Singhalese.

The name of the now independent island of Singapore, travelled from India (*see* Greater India) as the name

of a settlement, Sinhapura (meaning lion city), centuries before the British arrived there.

Sinhasan/Simhasan (*see* Yoga): lit. lion seat. Hindi from Sanskrit for the throne of a ruler or high religious dignity.

SIRŌPA/SARŌPA *n* Hindi

Lit. head to toe. Originally, a full-length robe of honour presented by a **Hindu** ruler (the Muslim equivalent was the **khilat**). The name and the custom carries on in the Punjab as a gift to a visiting dignitary by the Chief Granthi (*see* Guru Granth Sahib) of a major **gurdwara**, usually of a sword, or a **puggri** or a shawl.

SITĀR *n* Urdu

Musical instrument, something like a guitar, with a hollow dried gourd as sound-box. Five to seven strings: all the fingers may be used with the main strokes applied by a plectum (mizrab) on the right hand index finger – so much so that it soon becomes calloused. Nineteen to twenty notes.

Bin-sitar: sitar with a gourd at each end, or one at an end and one just off-centre, to increase the resonance. Generally, the sitar is an instrument of northern Hindustani music (it is in fact a 13th century combination of the Persian sehtar – three strings – and the classical Indian **veena**, to which the south remains faithful). Similar, but smaller, is the sarōd: the plectrum for which is often a piece of coconut shell.

SKAND *n* Sanskrit
To jump, to leap about. In English through Latin the word to jump about with the eyes, to scan.

SMRÎTI *n* Hindi
Memory, remembered. Certain Hindu religious texts are known as smriti – those which are remembered (*see* Vedas).

Brahmans, mostly from the south, who closely follow the codes of the Smriti texts, are known as Smartas. In worship, the Smartas make little distinction between the major Hindu deities. Smriti is from the **Sanskrit** root smer, rememberance, memory, with links to Latin and Greek and so to the English memory words, commemoration, memorial etc. A link can also be seen to martyr.

Gandhi Smriti: the name of the mansion (Remembrance of Gandhi) in New Delhi – formerly, Birla House – in the grounds of which the Mahatma was assassinated in 1948.

SNĀN *n* Hindi
A bath: an obliga-
tion for **Hindus**
before perform-
ing any religious
ritual and for most
Indians a duty before the first meal of the day and again in the evening. As

a word, snan is direct from **Sanskrit** and tends to be used more for bathing for reasons of purification rather than routine hygiene. Dropping the s, in everyday Hindi to take a bath is nahana. (Soon after the beginning of the British period, returning nabobs – *see* Nawab – carried the custom of daily bathing home with them to a largely unwashed England and the age of the European domestic bathroom was born.) If possible, flowing and not still water as in a tub, '...like a buffalo's wallow' must be used. It is this aversion to still water that partly accounts for the frequent absence of a stopper in a wash-basin: the well-equipped Westernised traveller outside the ambience of five-star hotels carries his own. For hand-washing, the traditional method for the wealthy was for one servant to hold a basin below while another poured scented water; a third could be holding a towel.

Antim snan: the last bath. A ritual whereby, if possible, a body is immersed in flowing water, or in a tank, several times before cremation.

Ardh snan: a half bath. A colloquial term for a bath without wetting or washing the hair: another term for a similar sketchy bath is kak snan, a crow's bath. In universal use in India is the word sabun for soap, Urdu from Arabic

Islam requires bodily cleanliness

before an approach to God. A Muslim is instructed to wash his hands, arms, face and feet before prayer and to take a full bath (*see* Ghusl) after certain pollutions. Dispensation is given to those in a desert where water may be short, in such circumstances, the body may be rubbed with fine sand.

SNEEZING *v*

It is a **Hindu** folk belief that to hear a sneeze (chhink, in Hindi) is inauspicious, an evil portent: cause enough for the superstitious to abandon for the day an intended important project. This is particularly the case if, on setting out, the sound is heard from behind. Within the hearing of others therefore, it is accepted good manners to stifle an incipient sneeze rather than to let it rip. In medieval Europe, the sneeze also had unpleasant associations, but there it was he who sneezed that was in for trouble, hence the English hearer's invocatory response 'May God bless you'. A riposte to a sneeze is also an Arab custom, 'God be praised': the Prophet Mohammed is reputed to have declared that while God is not unhappy with a sneeze, it is the yawn – denoting idleness – that is anathema.

The chinkara (lit. the sneezer), the Indian gazelle, a graceful creature of dry scrubland, is so named from its alarm call, a sound remarkably similar to a sneeze.

SOLAR/SOLA TOPI *n*

The solar topi and the sola topi are not necessarily the same article; the solar topi is the genus, the sun hat. For at least one hundred years until the middle of World War II, winter and summer, mandatory wearing for Britons in India as protection from the sun's rays, then considered lethal on the uncovered European head. (E.M. Forster, in a 1957 short story, wrote: "...the sun in those far-off days was a mighty power and hostile of the Ruling Race".) By 1944, military medical opinion finally agreed with the locals that, on the whole, the sun was benign, that sunstroke and the lesser 'touch of the sun' – as distinct from heatstroke, which could be deadly to Indian and European alike – described no actual ailments and that, while a shady hat in hot sun was a comfort, the protective helmet could be declared redundant. Sola in sola topi, strictly, refers not to the sun but to the substance from which this type of sun hat is made: light pith from a marshland plant, particularly, but not solely of Bengal: in Hindi, sola/shola. (But shola in the south can be an anglicism meaning a dense thicket of evergreen rainforest – from solai, the **Tamil** equivalent.) To make the hat, the sola pith is built up in strips, so that the thickness of the final cloth covered pith helmet is several centimeters. The sola topi was the usual European daywear, for male and female, child and adult: and for others, perhaps a token of Western civilisation.

The Bombay bowler was the sun helmet issued to the British armed forces, modelled possibly from a cavalry casque. Much thinner than the sola topi, with high crown, wide forepeak and deep neck cover. Towards the end of the Raj, as military millinery, it was not considered attractive. In mid-Victorian times, a forerunner of the topi was the havelock, so called from General Havelock who was said to have popularised it: a cloth cover for the military cap, with a lengthy flap at the back designed to protect the neck from the sun.

Many dictionaries condemn 'solar topi' as a solecism, alleging that 'sola topi' is the correct form: but since by no means all sun helmets were or are made of the sola pith (the Bombay bowler for example), as an anglicism it seems no greater enormity than other hybrids generally accepted. (Although pith is the universal term for the material from the two varieties of the sola plant used for sun helmets, botanists aver that in fact it is not a pith but an ultra-light timber similar to the balsa wood of Central America.)

Additional protection against the sun was the spinepad, available until at least the 1930s: a quilted pad worn from the shoulders to almost the waist. A refinement was a model to be worn outside the coat at the back with small knobs on the inside so as to allow circulation of air. Also hindering body-heat loss was the warm flannel cholera belt, or belly-band, until the germ theory causes of stomach disorders became accepted in the late 1880s. A more useful specific against cholera once it had broken out was for the troops to be marched to a temporary camp; some medical opinion had it that the direction had to be to the north – or the south – to be effective. The fact was, of course, that the source of infection was left behind.

SŌMA *n* Hindi
Vedic deity, personifying the sacred plant and liquor of the same name. In the Rig Veda (*see* Vedas), soma is hailed as the drink of the gods, those who received it enjoyed immortal life. Also referred to as the juice of the moon-vine; alas, under either name, it is no longer identifiable. (An English botanist has claimed that the soma plant was a hallucinatory mushroom.) Since Vedic times, the moon has been associated with soma and today, the Hindi word for Monday (moonday), is Somavar (*see* Calendars). But an even earlier moon deity was Chandra and the word in Hindi for the moon is still chānd. Soma or som ras can be colloquialisms for any alcoholic drink.

Lord Shiva is linked with both the moon and soma and is particularly worshipped on Mondays.

SOOP/SUP *n* Hindi
From **Sanskrit**: a broth, cooked food. Other words for soup are jhol,

shurua and shorba from Persian (lit. a saltish drink).

A flattish tray made of fine cane for winnowing grain, once a must for every kitchen but now used mainly in village India.

SŌWAR/SAWĀR *n* Urdu
An animal rider. A cavalryman (horse, camel, and nowadays, armour) in the rank of private soldier: trooper would be the British army equivalent. A mounted police-constable. A linked word is sawari, meaning a passenger in a conveyance – in American English, a vehicle passenger may well be a rider. Although generally considered to be Urdu from Persian, sowar is older than **Islam** and the ultimate source is probably ashvavara, **Sanskrit** for a horse-rider.

SP (S.P.)
Superintendent of Police. The chief police officer in a district administration. (Unlike in the famous trial episode in Forster's Passage to India, it was no part of an SP'S duty to act as prosecutor in court.)

Dy SP: Deputy Superintendent of Police. (For an officer of the IPS in British days, the equivalent rank was designated Assistant Superintendent of Police – ASP.)

SPEED MONEY
A modern colloquialism used as in the following hypothetical situation. A citizen wishes to pursue a course of action for which official permission is a legal necessity. The low-level clerk receiving the application hints that a payment of 'speed-money' will ensure prompt attention. The unstated implication being that failing such a payment, the papers may take a considerable time to process.

STAR OF INDIA *n*
In the later British period, a five-pointed star adopted as an emblem of the country. Although many rulers claimed descent from the sun or the moon, a single five-pointed star had no particular connection with either feudalism or religion. During the **Sultanate** period, a six-pointed star, a hexagram, was frequently a prominent decorative feature of mosque and tomb buildings, but this owed nothing to **Islam**. It was a cultural symbol from the ancient middle-east imported by the Seljuk Turks from Anatolia. In the West, now termed the Star, or Shield, of David, also Solomon's seal. In Hinduism, the hexagram – shat/sat kon in Hindi, six corners – as a **tantric** yantra, one triangle imposed on another, is a symbol for Lord **Shiva** and his **Shakti**, each having equal powers: the downward pointing triangle represents the lady and today in red is the sign of the government sponsored family planning organisation.

The British first used a star – then,

of eight points in the badge of the Indian Order of Merit (1813): again, in the Order of British India (1837) and, by now a five-pointer, as part of the badge of the heraldic Order of the Star of India in 1861 (the main feature, a cameo of Queen Victoria, was pendant from a rather insignificant star). The Star and the motto of the Order, 'Heaven's Light our Guide', formed a device in the centre of the Union Jack as the British Indian flag (likewise, on the flys of the Indian Red and Blue ensigns). In New Delhi, the Star may still be seen in stone on the empty (2005) Lutyens' plinth by India Gate once occupied by a statue of the King-Emperor, George V, and ornamenting the high points of the gates and of the iron railings to the forecourt at Rashtrapati **Bhavan**. (But in the same place, to make it three-dimensional, Lutyens had to give six points to the Star, whimsically pirouetting atop his Jaipur Column, above a bronze **lotus** and a stone cosmic egg – *see* Lingam.) the five-pointed star continues as the badge of the Board of Control for Cricket.

STATION *n*

A word current amongst Europeans in government service before **Independence** meaning the place to which they were posted for their work. In this sense, the term is probably only used today by the defence services and establishments of other specialist groups, such as the airlines.

As a British term, applied to an up-country (*see* Mofussil) town, say a **district** headquarters, the station also had a collective meaning of the **gazetted** officers and their families living there, plus perhaps an honorary member or two, such as a European bank manager or other high status professional: sub-divisions, if defence service officers were present, would have been civil and military. 'To dine the station', had the meaning of an invitation from one in European society to all the other socially eligible Europeans (and in later days, Indians also, if members of the **convenanted** services) to an evening meal, either together, or in turn over a period.

The Week: in British days in a station of any pretensions, for both Europeans and locals an annual period of festivity and social entertainment lasting perhaps for three days or even ten graced by the provincial Governor. Race meeting, horse and cattle shows, a gymkhana, flower and vegetable shows, polo.

Hill station: see Hills.

Out of Station/Outstation: away from the place where one lives. Particularly the term is used in banking, for cheques from accounts outside a local clearing area. Also the railway phrase, Outstation Agency, meaning an office handling railway goods traffic in a place where there is no railway (combined road/rail conveyance on one consignment note).

STEPNEY *n*
A spare wheel for a vehicle. The term, dating from at least 1904, is still in everyday garage use in India and is a reference to a firm, 'The Stepney Spare Motor Wheel Co. Ltd,', who patented a rim complete with inflated tyre, which could be temporarily attached to a punctured car wheel: a great convenience for the Edwardian motorist. The name followed from the maker's location Stepney Street in Llanelly, South Wales: in 1990, the town's main shopping precinct. (The Stepneys were a local iron-master family prominent towards the end of the 19th century.) Honouring the invention of the spare wheel within its municipal limits, in 1913 the Llanelly Borough Council was permitted to include a representation of the stepney on its corporate heraldic badge. In heraldry, a badge is usually a less complicated identifying device than a full coat of arms: these days Llanelly appears to have forgotten its badge and to use for its blazon, only the less industrial and rather grander coat of arms.

Among Delhi office staffs, an easy-going colleague not always of great assistance, but of some help in an emergency, may be referred to as a stepney. Another English word used with a Hindustani meaning in the vehicle repair business is 'bubbling'. Vibration in a steering wheel perhaps from a wobble in the front wheels from which the word probably derives.

STHĀN *n* Hindi
Also sthali. **Sanskrit** (and Old Persian, whence into Urdu, see Abad) for a place, locality. The Sanskrit root stha connected with immovable, appears in English in such words as stand, station, status, statue, etc. May be used as a suffix as in Rajasthan – land of kings. Place in a competition, e.g., pehla sthan – the first place (in a race).

STHAPĀTI *n* Hindi
An architect: a sculptor, particularly one from south India, creating deities in stone, or metal using the lost wax process. In northern India, the word shilpi is more often used.

STICK *n* English
The unit of sale of cigarettes from the normal retail outlet for most buyers, the corner **pan** shop, will be the glossy packet, but for some customers it is a single cigarette, universally known as a stick.

STŪPA *n* Hindi
Lit. a mound. Buddhist burial mound, originally of earth, later of brick with a rounded dome-like top, containing the bones or relics of a revered person. (Not invariably, the famous stupa at Sanchi in Central India – see

chakra – is a solid monument and never contained any relics). Worship can be offered by circling the rotunda in a clockwise direction (*see* Parikrama). In **Burma** and China, the stupa developed into the **pagoda**. *See also* Tope.

The Hindi architectural term (as distinct from the Urdu **gumbad**) for a dome (in Sanskrit, the dome or crown of the human head). In New Delhi, Lutyens' dome over **Rashtrapati Bhavan** to some extent replicates a Buddhist stupa, particularly that at Sanchi, of the 2nd century AD, complete with the vedika, the encircling boundary post and rail fence in stone. Of all Indian architectural features Lutyens especially admired the vedika. A modern vedika in the traditional form can be seen in New Delhi's **Buddha Jayanti** Park.

SU Particle Hindi
A **Sanskrit** prefix implying high quality, excellence. Eg. gandh – odour, smell: su-gandh – perfume. Sunabh – a beautiful navel. (Nabh, the navel, possibly a link to the English word from Latin, abdomen.) Su-manas – pleasure to the mind, a flower, a good friend (personal name) both male and female.

Ku: the opposite particle to su. Eg. putr, a son: kuputr, a son who is a wastrel, a bad lot.

SUBALTERN'S PHEASANT *n*

Otherwise known as the crow pheasant, although it is neither a crow nor a pheasant, but of the cuckoo family. Ornithologists term it the coucal. A crow-sized bird conspicuous with chestnut-red wings and a glossy dark blue body and tail: more fond of hopping about in undergrowth than flying. The English derisory name came from an allegation that a **griffin** Second Lieutenant on his first shoot would pot one in the belief that he had bagged a pheasant. Unlike most cuckoos the coucal builds its own nest.

SUBEDĀR *n* Urdu
A satrap (this English word comes from old Persian through Greek). Under a Muslim administration, the officer in charge of a subah or **district** (in some cases, a province). As a military rank, see Junior Commissioned Officers.

SUDDEN DEATH *n*
A European epithet of the later British period for the spatchcock; the chicken, the main course of the standard short-notice meal served at such places as **Rest Houses** and small railway refreshment rooms. The bird was alleged to have been despatched subsequent to the ordering of the meal and in consequence, its meat was not always tender. Also part of the legend was that the second course of the meal was invariably caramel custard. (The First Class railway refreshment room in a

small town, particularly where there was no European club, had a social importance now hard to imagine: it was probably the only place where a Western type meal and a drink could be obtained on payment. It was also neutral ground, where the occasional Briton and Indian could entertain one another.)

No less important in a small town was its role as a supplier of ice, brought in daily by train from a larger town having an ice factory.

SŪFI *n* and *adj* Urdu
A follower of, or pertaining to, a system of Islamic philosophy with roots older than **Islam** itself and, perhaps, owing something to early Hinduism. The Sufiyan (plural) would appear to be greatly at variance with mainstream Muslim thought and practice, yet, in general, have been tolerated since the days of Mohammed. The name is said to derive from suf, wool in Arabic, a reference to the rough single often woollen, garment worn by **dervishes** and fakirs. To Sufi thought, all actions, good and bad, are inspired by God and all religions, excepting that Islam is pre-eminent. Likewise, to be in a state of religious fervour and ecstasy (*see* Shakti) is to be close to God and to this end music, poetry, dancing and all the senses may be legitimately employed. The final objective, similar to the nirvana of Hinduism, is the merging of the soul with the deity. The Sufiyan are

divided into numerous sects (silsila), of which the **Chistis** are probably the most. widely known in India: their annual urs (festivals) attract vast crowds. *See* also Baul, Bhakti, Chisti, Dargah, Dervish, Urs.

SUHAAG : *n* Hindi
The essential and auspicious condtion of a Hindu woman's life. The state of marriage following the suhaag rat. The night of consumation. See Sindoor.

SŪJI *n* Hindi
A coarse wheat graded fine to coarse using only the central portion of the grain, semolina: particularly used for making halwa and the **Sikh** karah **prasad**. Also known as rava.

A salty suji porridge, served with karipatta (see curry) and rice and vegetables, has the name from the south, upma, Available with variable trimmings over much of India.

SULAIMĀN
The Islamic form of the name, Solomon.

SULTĀN *n* Urdu
In the original Arabic, might or authority, a Muslim ruler, either male or female: e.g. a ruling princess (there were two) of the state of Bhopal was styled in English 'Her Royal Highness **Nawab** Sultan, **Begum** of Bhopal'. Non-ruling ladies of a **princely** family, by custom, some-

478

times did, and indeed do today, use the style. As a title it is said to have been invented by an ambassador of the Caliph (*see* Khilafat) of Baghdad and conferred on the Central Asian Turk, Mahmoud, who had established himself in Ghazni, Afghanistan: it was Mahmoud who, in the 11th century AD, led the first Muslim invasion into Northern India (*see* Islam).

Sultana: the style used by Razia, the daughter of the Sultan, on gaining the Delhi masnad – throne, *see* Gaddi – in her own right following the death of her father. Sultan Iltutmish, in 1236 (the Sultan had pronounced her more fit to rule than any of her brothers; she lasted three years. The next woman ruler of India was, nominally, Queen Victoria and then Indira Gandhi in 1966). Since then the designation seems to have been only for a Muslim queen consort, the principal wife of a male Sultan. In Muslim families today, a girl's name.

Salatin: plural of Sultan. Sometimes applied to mean the extended families of Muslim rulers. In the case of the last **Mogul**, the King of Delhi, by the time of the British takeover in 1857, a group of more than a thousand 'princes', living in squalor in the palace (the Red Fort).

SULTANATES OF DELHI

It is not always realised that before the first enthroned **Mogul**, there had already been some three hundred years of permanent Muslim rule in northern India and in the **Deccan**: a period marked for us by its many impressive monuments still in existence, often styled Afghan or **Pathan**, the octagonal tomb being distinctive and typical of the later **Sultans**. Strictly, all Muslim monarchs are **Sultans**, but as used by historians, the phrase, the Delhi Sultanates, usually means the governments of a line of thirty rulers, including one woman (Razia Sultana), of five dynasties from about 1193 AD: the cause for succession all too often being death in battle or murder. That year, the last **Hindu** King of Delhi and Ajmer was executed by Qutab-ud-Din Aibak, Viceroy of Sultan Mohammed bin Sam of Ghor (a region near Herat in today's Afghanistan: although the Sultan died, in 1206, on the banks of the River Indus, some claim that his body was later brought to Delhi and is buried within the Qutab complex), Qutab-ud-Din became the next Sultan. With the death of the last, Ibrahim Lodi, in 1526 at the hands of Babur, the Afghan period ended and that of the Moguls began. (But Humayun's reign was interrupted by a Sultan, Sher Shah Suri, for 15 years from 1540.)

For a period of nearly one hundred years until 1290, more or less one dynasty, the early Sultans are sometimes referred to in English as the Slave Kings or Mamlukes. See Ghulam and Minar.

SUNNI Urdu
Those who follow the Sunna (*see* Kor'an),, the traditionalists. The larger of the two great divisions within **Islam**, followed by about ninety-five per cent of Indian Muslims: the other being Shia, but in the city of Lucknow, the proportion of Sunnis is much less, little more than parity with the Shias, perhaps a consequence of the Kings of **Oudh** themselves being Shia. In Arabic, the pronunciation is Shia but in the Urdu speech of India, the term is often Shea. The major difference between the sects concerns the legitimacy of the early Caliphs (*see* Khilafat), but doctrinal dissensions exist as well. One in particular is the opinion held by Shias that laymen need experts (clergy, ayatollahs) between themselves and God: Sunnis accept teachers, but do not recognise intermediaries.

Shias hold that the Khilafat must remain within the descendants of Mohammed, or at least, with the **Quraysh**, and do not recognise as legitimate even Abu Bakr, the first Caliph following the Holy Prophet, maintaining that the succession should have gone to Ali, cousin of Mohammed and husband of his daughter, Fatima. Ali, in fact became the fourth Caliph of the Sunnis.

In matters of succession, Shias are more generous to women than are the Sunnis. In Shia personal custom, in the absence of a son, property and rank can pass to a daughter in circumstances where the Sunnis would seek a collateral male. In general, to Shia divines, music, even when in praise of God, is anathema. Over the centuries, Shia Muslims have had little political success, but in recent years, with the Ayatollahs (**Imams**) in power in Iran and with their brothers in West Asia a force to be reckoned with, they are tending to hold their heads a bit higher. *See also* Muharram.

SUPĀRI *n* Hindi
The so-called betel nut: the seed of the fruit of the areca palm, in appearance like a largish nutmeg, grown as a plantation crop in the coastal areas of south India. Half nuts of supari, sometimes raw dried, sometimes first cooked and then dried, are sliced into small pieces, and chewed by almost all throughout India (also throughout South East Asia) as part of the delicacy, **pan**. The supari itself can vary in taste from astringency to near sweetness. Supari is used in **puja** (**Hindu** ritual) to represent both the Goddess **Lakshmi** and **Ganesh**.

As a cant word in the underworld of Mumbai, supari can refer to a contract killing. The offering and acceptance of the supari being to seal the contract as with a pan.

SVARN *n* Adj. Hindi from Sanskrit.
Gold, golden. Often seen as a

personal name in roman script as Swaran.

SWADĒSH *n* Hindi
Lit. one's own country. *See* Desh.

Swadeshi: of one's country, usually a reference to goods manufactured in India. That Indians should buy swadeshi goods only, was one of **Mahatma** Gandhi's points in his campaign against British rule (for the British, this was history repeating itself, for 150 years earlier, the North American colonists had adopted similar tactics). In India, the term and concept had been used in 1905 as a protest against Lord Curzon's partition of Bengal. *See* Independence Day.

Swadeshi andolan: the freedom struggle of the 1920s and 1930s for independence from Britain.

SWĀGAT/SWĀGATAM *n* Hindi
First syllable pronounced long. Welcome.

SWĀMI/SWĀMY *n* Hindi
From **Sanskrit**: Unbeholden to anyone. Owner, master, lord. In north India, mostly a title of respect and, in the form Swamiji (*see* Ji) of affection, for a male **Hindu** religious: in the south, a title to a deity (e.g., Swaminarayan – Lord Narayan, *see* Vishnu), or to an owner of property, or as a personal name, often as a suffix (e.g., Goswami, Lord of the Cow). Following ancient tradition, many a wife will not refer to her husband by his personal name, instead she may well use as a paraphrase, a title such as Swami/ Swamiji.

SWĀRĀJ *n* Hindi
Self-rule; independence for a country. As a political slogan, perhaps first used by the Marathas against the **Mogul** rule of Aurangzeb. Arising from the resentment following the partition of Bengal in 1905 (*see* Independence Day), Swaraj became a call for freedom from Britain. (Buying **swadeshi** goods began as a form of political protest at the same time.)

Purna-swaraj: full self-rule. In the latter days of the **raj**, a slogan opposed to acceptance of British offers of conditional and limited self-government.

In the early years of the twentieth century, a nationalist Maharashtrian in opposition to foreign rule, Gangadhar Tilak, electrified India with his unequivocal "Swaraj is my birthright, and I will have it". In later decades, British opinion declared of liberty "...it is a blessing that must be earned before it can be enjoyed" and placed the aphorism in letters of gold over the entrance to the north block of the New Delhi Secretariat. where it can still be seen.

Mahatma Gandhi extended the usual meaning of swaraj to a personal level, a control over one's own body, particularly at the sensual level.

SWĀSTIKA *n* Hindi
The two-dimensional limbed cross with the English name fylfot. A Hindu yantra (*see* Jantar Mantar). A symbol of good omen found in many parts of the world with, seemingly, no Indian connection: e.g. in Central America and even on Easter Island. The root of the name, svast/su-asti, literally meaning it is well, is generally understood as representing prosperity, well-being, good health; may be spoken aloud in ritual as a **mantra**, particularly following the sound **Om**. or as a blessing, a benediction, to a person.

In Hinduism, the swastika has been found decorating pottery shards dating from approximately 100 BC and is particularly as a symbol of **Ganesh**, beloved of the Vaisiya (merchant) caste, with whom it will often be seen finger painted in red (**sindoor**) either on or near the cash box with, perhaps the word labh (profit). It is also a symbol of the sun on its auspicious northward journey (*see* Uttarayana) and of Lord **Vishnu**. To be effective, normally the swastika is drawn so that at the top of the vertical line, the arm is to the right and at the bottom, to the left. The other way round is considered the feminine form used, especially in Bengal, when dedicated to a god-

dess, or in connection with worship by ladies: in this form it can represent the sun during its less auspicious path to the south. Contrary to popular contemporary belief, for its state aryan symbol, Nazi Germany used the swastika of Ganesha. Until he felt it had been degraded by Hitlerite Germany, Rudyard Kipling used the symbol as a personal talisman on all his published books. Some say that the symbol is not complete without four **bindu**/bindi (dots) within the arms.

In connection with **Jainism**, the swastika is the symbol of the tirthankara, Suparsvanatha/Supasa, number seven in the line of twenty-four.
In Bengal, another auspicious symbol is also termed a swastika: a stick man, again finger-painted in red. Mostly used indoors.

The Swastika was used in Europe by medieval christians, the Nestorians or Cathars, with a middle eastern background (regarded as heretical by the orthodox) adopted it as a cross and it may be seem to this day on the walls of some French churches.

SWEEPER *n* English
A person, whatever his actual occupation, within the **Hindu** order of life, an untouchable, a **dalit**, whose divinely ordained destiny it is, or so some Hindus believe, as retribution for sins in a past life, to clean for, but keep separate from **caste** Hindus.

Also known by the abuse word, bhangi, from, as a class, an alleged addiction to bhang (*see* Indian Hemp), **mehtar, jemadar**, and jharoowala (broom man). In government services, a sweeper is now officially designated as safai **karamchari**, cleaning employee.

The connection with hemp is not accepted by all, some relate bhangi with a Sanskrit root meaning separate, divided, rejected.

A humble person of any religion who cleans streets, houses, buildings, a remover of night-soil and food rubbish: tasks considered ritually polluting by caste Hindus.

Dry sweeper: one employed to clean rooms etc., but not latrines nor bathrooms.

It may be noted that not all bhangis are or were at the bottom of society. Historically in the Punjab, the Bhangis were one of the honoured and leading fighting misls (*see* Nihang) of the old Sikh loose confederation: with territory largely that of Lahore and Amritsar. The name arose from the attachment of their founder to bhang. The famous cannon of Kim's Lahore, Zam Zama, captured from the Afghans, was also known as Bhangion ki tõp. (The gun remains where it was but the museum was rebuilt soon after Kipling's father left in 1893).

SYCE/SICE *n*
An anglicism from the Urdu, sais: a man who looks after horses, a groom, a stableman. Car syce: a 20th century extension of the meaning of the word (more commonly used in what is now Malaysia and Singapore than in India). The man who looks after, and perhaps drives as an employee, the car. In a car park, he will be expected to place it in a section reserved for 'Driver Driven Vehicles'.

SYIEM *n* A local chieftain in the Khasi Hills of north eastern India.

T

TABLA *n* Urdu
Pair of small drums, one for each hand, played with the ball or
heel, and fingers of the left hand and the fingers and flat palm of the right: normally used as an accompaniment, or with a vocalist, a dialogue in Hindustani music. (When played solo, the percussion may be described as a dialogue between two hands). The equivalent in **Carnatic** music is provided by the single drum, the mridangam, with a skin at each end. The tabla, developed from the mridangam was the creation of a 13th century genius of many parts, Amir Khusro.

While the pair is generally known as the tabla, strictly only the drum played with the right hand (on which the black composition patch for percussion is central) carries the name; the bass drum for the left hand is the dagga or bayan (left). On this the patch is off-centre. The tabla is normally made of wood and the dagga of metal. Tabālchi, tabibya,

tablawarak: words meaning a player on the tabla.

TACCĀVI/TĀQAVI/TAKĀVI *n* Urdu
An advance of money to a farmer, usually by the government often following some calamity, such as a flood, for the purchase of seeds, bullocks, implements, etc.

TAFFETA *n* English
A word from India for a silk, or a similar material with a sheen. From the Persian, tafta, meaning a silk woven from a twisted yarn. The fabric was exported to Europe by the **East India Company** during its commercial period.

TAHZIB *adj.* Urdu from Arabic
Applied to a man, impressively refined, cultured.

TĀJ *n* Urdu
Almost any form of formal bejewelled or be-tasselled helmet or headgear worn as regalia by a prince (or, indeed, by a **dervish**). The usual translation word, crown, meaning a European circlet crown, is inadequate. As with crown in English, so taj – especially in its full form, sertaj (head-crown), may be used metaphorically. A wife may refer to her husband as her sertaj. **Mahatma** Gandhi could be referred to in Urdu by the public as the betaj badshah (the crownless king, *see* Shah).

Taj Mahal: the most famous mausoleum anywhere. Wrote Edward Lear after a visit to Agra in the 1870s "... let the inhabitants of the world be divided into two classes – them as has seen the Taj Mahal, and them as hasn't."

Those, of course, aspiring to the first category providing the well-being of many, many of Agra's citizens.

With the monument, Taj can refer not only to a crown but also to a rendering of a short form – almost a pet name – of the title Mumtaz Mahal, given by Shah Jehan to his queen (her childhood name was Arjumand), Mumtaz, a word from Arabic, can be translated as eminent or distinguished : so the title was really the 'Distinguished one of the Palace'. (See Mahal). Taj, widely used today, is really a corruption of the queen's familiar name. Villagers call the grand tomb, 'Taz Bibi ka Rauza' the garden mausoleum of Lady Taz (rauza, in Arabic, a garden). Alternatively, since in a noble Muslim family 'of the palace' came to be synonymous with wife (as it still is in a courtly city like Hyderabad), Mumtaz Mahal also had the meaning of the Distinguished Wife.

Taj Mahal of the Raj: or the Raj Taj: present-day epithets for the Victoria Memorial Museum in Kolkata.

TAKHT *n* Urdu

Throne; a small wooden platform. Takht ya Takhta: throne or funeral bier. A saying of Muslim days of alternatives for the rurlers' sons. In Sikhism, five major **Gurdwaras** are honoured as takhts: a pronouncement on the **Sikh** religion from any one of them is considered to have great authority.

Takht-i-Taus: the Peacock' Throne of the **Mogul** Emperors ; (*see* Mor).

TAKA *n* Bengali

The **rupee**. The unit of currency in Bangladesh. In the column on all Indian currency notes of the face value in thirteen regional languages, takka is used in Assamese, Bengali and **Oriya**. (Hindi and English are used in the text on the notes, making a total of fifteen languages in all.)

Historically, the taka was a copper coin of the sultanates period.

TĀL *n* Hindi

A **Sanskrit** term for a lake: common in the **Uttaranchal Himalaya**, e.g., Naini Tal (lit. the Lake of the Eye; an anglicism from the local name, Nayani Tal, from a belief that Parvati – Lord **Shiva**'s wife – lost an eye in the waters). From the same root as tal is the Avadh (*see* Oudh) word, also meaning lake or **tank**, talab/**talao**.

Tairan tal: a swimming pool.
In music, tal means the rhythmic beat.

TALAK *n* Arabic
The word, spoken or written (a bill of divorcement) repeated three times over a period or four months (to ensure that the woman is not pregnant) by which a Muslim husband may anul his wedding contract. Say the holy books (but not the **Koran** in which the action is not mentioned) "the thing which is lawful but disliked by God, is divorce... put them away with generousity".

An Act of the Indian Parliament of 1939 gave Muslim women the right to seek divorce under certain conditions, but litigation will probably be necessary for a woman to obtain a just settlement and is beyond the means of most. The subject of Muslim personal law in India is too complicated to be addressed here.

Within the Indian Muslim community, at least some today (2005) are of the opinion that the practice of the oral triple talak is inappropriate and should be banned.

TALUK/TALUQ *n* Urdu
A tract of country.
Talukdar: a major landowner. In some princely territories, e.g., Hyderabad, a district officer, the equivalent of.the **Collector** of British India. Some talukdari estates were so vast, particularly in the United Provinces, as to earn their proprietors both **Hindu** and Muslims, honorary titles of Raja or Maharaja, although never the style 'His Highness', and without the powers over their tenants of the semi-independent ruling **princes**; many were **Rajputs** able to trace their lineage far preceding the Muslim conquest.

TAMARIND *n*
An anglicism, probably received through Portuguese, of the Arabic and Persian, tamar-i-Hind, date of India. (Some are of the opinion that the Arabic should be Thamar-i-Hind, fruit of India. In spite of the name, the tree is from tropical Africa.) Imli in Hindi.

In the north, no more than a graceful shade tree, but in the south, where it flowers and fruits, it is the provider of a sour pulpy seed pod much valued all over the country for flavouring – an exported extract is an ingredient of **Worcester** sauce. For the **bazaar**, tamarind seed pulp is compressed into a brown sticky mass, not unlike a block of dates. So acidic is the pulp that it has a secondary use as a household metal polish, a cleaner of brass articles. Yet another use for it is as a vegetable glue.

Fish tamarind: black in colour, the astringent smoked peel of a fruit not of the tamarind tree. Popular in Kerala as a seasoning with fish, where it is known by the **Malayalam** name, kodampoli.

The northern equivalent of the tamarind, a relish for year-round acidity as flavouring for food, is amchur, sun-dried slices, or powder, of unripe mangoes.

The timber is hard and resilient and is particularly used for making mallets.

TAMĀSHA *n* Urdu
A spectacle for public amusement: a celebration in a light-hearted way. A simple entertainment, with a touch of buffoonery perhaps, particularly for the less sophisticated.

In Maharashtra, tamasha is the professional folk theatre, originating with religious themes performed in temples. Also folk entertainment in Maharashtra is lavani. A programme of earthy satire, music, dancing and comedy, sometimes of such a bawdy nature that lavani troupes get banned from city stages.

TAMIL *n*
The oldest **Dravidian** language of south India and probably the only one wilh an adequate vocabulary of non-**Sanskrit** origin words – but in everyday Tamil, words from the north are common. The centre of the Tamil country is Madurai, south of Chenai.

Tamil /Tamilian: a Dravidian natural Tamil speaker.

Tamil Nadu/Tamil Nad: the country of the Tamils. As spoken by many southerners, a more phonetic spelling of the Tamil word nadu would be natu. By those from outside the region, particularly by those of the north, the pronunciation may well be nara: for in the Hindi spelling, the *d* sound is a combination of *da* and *ra* – *see* Bangle. The name adopted in 1969 for the state formed from the Tamil speaking region of the British **Madras Presidency**.

Tamil Sangam: the cluh for cultural and social activities set up wherever a group of Tamils find themselves outside their own state. It is said that the first Tamil Sangam was a meeting of Tamil scholars as far back as 1000 BC.

TANDOOR *n* Urdu
A corruption of the Arabic word tanoor, an oven. The usual form in an eating house (*see* Dhaba) is of earthernware,  rather like a large flower pot with a fairly wide opening at its base, inverted over a smokeless fire. The food to be cooked (tandoori), is either slapped on the hot inside wall (**roti**–bread), or hung inside on rods (meats and chicken, usually first marinated). A dry form of roasting, since all moisture escapes from the top. The tandoor came to India from Persia in Mogul times as an oven for breads, but the now ubiquitous tandoori chicken

only arrived after 1947, brought by refugees from the north-west frontier, by then a part of Pakistan.

TANK *n*

In India, an artificial pond, reservoir or lake. Experts differ on the origin of the word in the sense of reservoir. The *OED*, a little hesitantly perhaps; suggests **Sanskrit**: others offer Portuguese from Latin and then to India. Certainly, for a long time, tank has been considered a vernacular word, particularly in western India. An Urdu term with the same meaning (equally, it can be applied to the domestic sink) is hauz: commemorated in Delhi place names such as Hauz Khas (*see* Khalsa) and **Kazi** Hauz in the old city. In eastern India, a tank is a dighi.

TANKA/THANG-KA *n* Tibetan

Temple banner. Tibetan' Buddhist (*see* Buddha) sacred pictures or designs, painted to strict rules on treated cotton or silk cloth: thereafter placed on walls or ceilings, or rolled into scrolls. With bright colours and images of deities and divine **lamas**, thang-ka are intended as aids to meditation, but for this use they require to be first consecrated.

Tanka (Urdu): Persian silver coin introduced into India during the **Sultanate** period, but Sher Shah Suri adopted the **rupee** and the tanka depreciated to copper. Term used today for wages (tankha).

TANTPUR SANDSTONE

A name sometimes used to describe the red sandstones of various hues used for building and cladding in the Delhi region for at least fifteen hundred years and from much earlier for the Mathura carvings of the Kushan period (*see* Greeks). Tantpur is a quarrying and stone-distributing centre to the south-west of Fatehpur Sikri which has given its name to reddish stone blocks cut from many quarries in the Agra neighbourhood: Mathura, Bharatpur and Fatehpur Sikri. To geologists, the material, including the much lighter coloured stone (really a creamy-white) from Dholpur, south of Agra, is Vindhyan sandstone.

TANTRA *n* Hindi

(A more phonetic spelling would be tantr.) Strictly, a system of philosophy, particularly one of **Hindu** or Buddhist worship of deities, both male and female. (Although the **Buddha** never suggested that his followers should worship deities, the practice became widespread after his death.)

Today, probably a reference either to attempts to acquire supernatural powers, or to worship of the Mother Goddess (or a combination of the two) in one of her many forms by initiates (*see* Shakti), through secret and mystical practices, **mantras**, and diagrams (yantra) thought to make the mind receptive to cosmic influence; also talismans and amulets. Some of the rites are far removed from normal Hindu religious and social observance, but are not dissimilar to those of fertility cults and for propitiating the Mother Goddess the world over: known in India as varm-marg, or the left hand path (*see* Right Hand, Left Hand). While regarded with revulsion by many **brahmans**, tantric practices have always had adherents in eastern India. From time to time allegations appear in the press that tantric practices to the far left of God such as child sacrifice, still continue.

Tantric: pertaining to tantra.

Tantric/tantrika: an initiate to tantra. One who practises tantra.

Loktantra: people's system, democracy.

Panchatantra: five lines (systems) of conduct in one book of fables; written in **Sanskrit** at the latest by 500 AD and probably very much earlier. Designed to educate young princes in the ways of the world, the stories are similar in form to Aesop's, and include such animal characters as the fox, the lion, the crow and a pair of jackals.

Swatantra: the system of being independent, of being in control of one's own way of life. Parliamentary democracy.

Swatantra Divas: **Independence Day**.

Gantantra: a republic form of government, a republic. (Gan – a community, a group.)

Gantantra Divas: Republic Day.

TAPĀS/TAPĀSYA *n* Hindi
Lit. heat, i.e., generation of God-like power or heat (tepid in English, has a link to the same Sanskrit root). Austerities practised on one's own body with a view to being rewarded by the gift of an exceptional favour by a deity: such as spiritual insight or supernatural power. Perhaps penance for a transgression. In a Gandhian sense, self sacrifice, extreme self-discipline, especially celibacy.

Tapasvi: one who practices tapas (fem. tapasvin). An ascetic. Also a word from Sanskrit for an ascetic is tyag/thyegi, as with the Telegu composer, Thyagaraj (King of Renunciation. See Carnatic).

TĀR *n* Hindustani from Persian. Wire. A telegram. *See also* Toddy.

TARĀKSHI *n*
An ornamental inlay of brass wire and small brass pieces on furniture. An ancient craft particularly of Saharanpur in western U.P.

TASAR/TASSAR *n* Hindi

A species of wild and semi-cultivated silk moth and its product, a coarse brown silk (tussore, in English). Unlike that of the other common wild silk moth, the **eri**, a tasar cocoon is a single continuous filament.

TAXI *n* English and Hindustani
Colloquialism used in the appropriate urban circles for a prostitute who operates at a place required by her clients: a call-girl.

TEAK *n*
A valuable hardwood tree (Tectona grandis) with large leaves. Native to the peninsula (*see* Dravidia),, but it probably grows best in the higher areas of central India. The English name derives from the **Telugu** teeku (or from theka in Malayalam: see Malabar). In Hindi the timber is called sagwān. It is of little use as a shade tree, for in the heat of summer until the arrival of the monsoon, the branches are generally bare.

As an example of its longevity as a material, a ship built in Bombay of Malabar teak for the Royal Navy in 1816, the Trincomalee, is still in commission in Portsmouth (England) harbour.

TEEJ/TIJ *n* Hindi
Lit. third. A festival of the monsoon on the third day of the first fortnight of the month of Shravan. Particularly celebrated by woman and girls in honour of Parvati (see Shakti). A time when swings are put on the trees of north India.

TEEPOI/TEAPOY *n* Urdu
Teen pai – three legs. A small table, a bedside table – even if it has four legs. (By a quirk, in Britain the name teapoy, with its Indian sound, has been applied to the antique tea caddy, a word from Malay, kāti – once used to safeguard under lock and key the **East India Company**'s new product for the wealthy – which actually came from China.)

TEHELKA/TAHALKA *n* Urdu
Excitement, sensation, A word from Persian from Arabic, now known to all India. As Tehelka dot com, a private channel web site, over a period of some three months, sponsors of an investigation by two of their staff carrying hidden sound and video transmitting devices of a fairly basic nature while posing as agents of a fictitious overseas military suppliers firm. Seemingly, clear evidence of acceptance by military and civilian officers (also political parties) of undercover cash payments was obtained and exposed to the nation in March 2001, rocking the government and leading to the temporary resignation of the Defence Minister.

TEJPAT/TEJPATTA *n* Hindi
As a condiment, the sun-dried aromatic leaf of a laurel tree of the large cassia family: a tree with

cinnamon bark is related(darchini). Mostly growing on the lower slopes of Himalayan north-east India, Equivalent in use to the English bay-leaf, especially in **pulao:** Like cinnamon, carried to Europe by the Arabs under the name malabathrum. (In north India, cinnamon is termed dal-chini).

TELUGU/TELUGO *n*
The language of the **Deccan** plateau, particularly the southern part of the state of Andhra **Pradesh** (*see* AP): but in the state capital itself, Hyderabad, Urdu (*see* Khari Boli) speakers predominate. Dravidian based, with its own script Telugu has been much influenced by **Sanskrit.**

Telengana: Telugu speaking districts of the original **princely** state of Hyderabad, centred round the city of the same name, prior to its reorganisation including the Telugu areas of the then **Madras** state.

TEMPO *n* English and Hindustani
Originally a proprietory trade name for a particular model of a three-wheeled light vehicle chassis with either a goods or passenger body, in which the engine drives the single front wheel through a chain. Now, also a generally accepted name for a light delivery vehicle, with either three or four wheels, not being a form of scooter **rickshaw.**

Another proprietory name for a light

van or open pick-up has also become that of the genus, Matador: a somewhat bizarre choice in the Indian context. Literally (from Spanish) it means the killer (of bulls).

TENT & LIGHT HOUSE *n*
Much social entertaining in India, in both humble and wealthy homes, requires equipment beyond the capacity of the residence. The tent house exists to supply on hire the deficiencies: tentage (**shamiana** – large enough to cover a football pitch if needed); decorative lights for the house and gas lamps for a **baraat**; a wedding band and high volume amplifiers for the latest film songs; archways over the road to welcome the guests; a quiet horse and a sword for a bridegroom; tables and chinaware for a banquet; for a public meeting, a stage and loud – very loud – speakers. All can be arranged at short notice by the gentlemen of the Tent & Light House.

TERAI/TARAI *n* Hindi
Lit. wet land (tar – moist). A belt of thick and swampy jungle between the **Himalaya** foothills and the cultivated plains of **UP** and Bihar: a region that once might have been described in English as a piedmont. Earlier an area of the most virulent malaria (terai fever), Since **Independence** much of the belt has been cleared and drained for agriculture. In north-eastern India, similar terrain is duar (anglicised into The Duars):

the word really means gateway, the gateway to Bhutan and the hills. Duar/dwar is **Sanskrit** via the Indo-Germanic tongues the English word door, meaning the same thing, is cognate. In **Uttaranchal** particularly the foothills country immediately above the Terai was given the name Bhabar.

Terai Hat: a felt hat with a wide flat brim.

Double-terai: two such hats sewn one inside the other to give extra stiffness: as worn by the Indian army **Gorkha** regiments thus also known as Gorkha hats (in addition to the Gorkhas, a number of other regiments of hillmen – e.g., the **Garhwalis** – also wear the double-terai as uniform). In the 1920s and 1930s the double-terai was sometimes blocked into the shape of a civilian trilby hat.

THĀKUR *n* Hindi
A local chieftain of the warrior **caste**, especially in Rajasthan and **UP**.

Landed genry: as **kshatriyas, Singh** is either the last or the next to last of their names. (But in Bengal and eastern India, a Thakur can be a **brahman**, the most famous example being the man of letters, Rabindranath Tagore – see Gita. Tagore is an anglicised form of an old family title, Thakur: in the Bengali language, Thakur is still the preferred name. *See also* Rai.)

In roman script, Thakur as a personal title may be abbreviated to Th.

Thakurwad/Thakuniad: the traditional living style of thakurs, feudalism. A style now under threat from those below.

THĀLI *n* Hindi
A metal tray on which food for one person is served. Dry items such as rice and **chapatis** are in the middle, while foods in a sauce such as **curry** vegetables are in small bowls (katori) round the rim. The thali is also used for carrying gifts of sweets or fruits or for offerings to a temple deity. If the tray is very large – it can have a diameter of at least a metre– thal will be the more appropriate name.

On a restaurant menu thali is a complete meal served on a tray usually at a fixed price. In south Indian languages the thali is the marriage necklace the equivalent of the northern mangalsutra (*see* Tuesday).

THAMBI/THUMBI *n* Tamil
Younger brother. As used by the army or in north India, a friendly term for a man from the south.

THĀNA *n* Hindi
A police sub-district. The chief police station of that sub-district: any police station: a municipal ward. The word derives from **sthan, Sanskrit**, a place, a post (of . duty). A town and river near Bombay.

Thanedar: the police officer in charge of a thana; A position of considerable local influence and prestige, particularly in the countryside. 'May your son become a Thanedar' has long been a rural benediction. *See* SHO.

THANKA *n* Urdu from Persian
A silver coin introduced into India during the **Sultanates** period, but Sher Shah Suri adopted the **Rupee** and the tankha depreciated to copper. Term used today for wages, salary.

THEKA/TICCA/TIKKA *n* Hindi
A contract. A person or thing engaged for a particular job: e.g., (in the 19th century), a tikka **gharry**, a hired vehicle. Since the right to sell liquor by retail is auctioned annually by state governments to contractors (thekedars), theka can be an epithet for country spirit: English theka – whisky, gin, etc. *See* Wine.

THEOSOPHY *n*
Lit. wisdom concerning God. In an Indian context, normally a reference to the practice of members of the Theosophical Society, founded in the U.S.A. in the late 19th century: but in 1882 the headquarters was set up in Adyar (where it still is), then a suburb of Chennai, in the belief that India is the spiritual teacher of the world. The society's most famous leader was Dr. Annie Besant (1847-1935), an Englishwoman who also took a major part in the political movement to obtain self-government for India. Theosophists are non-sectarian and endeavour to establish the universal brotherhood of man. In particular, they are interested in the study of India's ancient religions.

THĪK *adj.* and *adv* Hindi
Either a statement or a question. Correct, right, true, in good order. Amplifying slightly by using the verb, to be.'thik hai' – everything is OK etc., a basic expression for the newcomer: the British soldier, as with bon and a Frenchman, could conduct a lengthy conversation with no larger Indian vocabulary than 'thik' and 'no thik'.

THIRU/THEERU/TIRU *n* Tamil
Respect: the attribute of divinity to a person, place or thing. Used in the manner of **Shri** as an honorific before a man's name. Appears in many south Indian place names: e.g. Tiruchchirrappali (*see* Cheroot), Thiruvananthapuram, earlier known as Trivandrum, and the great temple town in **AP**, Tirupati.

In south India the occasional ceremonial journey on a **rath** of a deity through a temple town can be known as thiru.

THUG/THAG *n* Hindi
An imposter, cheat, deceiver. (The Indo-European of the Hindi word, meaning to cover up, is the same as for the English thatch – to cover a

building.) In the early 19th century, the British applied thug (in Hindi, the th is pronounced as in Thames) to the newly discovered phansigars (lit. noose-workers), thought to be secret followers of an ancient all-India cult originally, perhaps, devoted to appeasement of the Mother Goddess, **Kali**/Bhowani, but by the time the British authorities came to learn about them, thug groups, both Muslims and **Hindu**, worked in gangs travelling the roads of India, but always at a distance from their homes, so that they were unlikely to be recognised.

Victims were first befriended; then, with the sudden use of the **roomal**, were ritually throttled as sacrifices to the deity: in the process, considerable booty accrued to the thugs. The code required that male travellers only were to be murdered, but this rule was often ignored. Europeans were never attacked. The gangs were mostly broken up by the 1850s, largely through the lifetime perseverance of one officer, who died at sea in 1856, Major-General Sir William Sleeman, K.C.B. A subsequent estimate of the toll was that of approximately forty thousand strangulations a year over a period of three centuries. In about 1840, the people of a small village in the heart of the thagi country, renamed their home, Sleemanabad. In 1989, it is still the name of the same village, now in the state of Madhya Pradesh.

Thagi/thugee: the practice of a thug. Deceit.

The immutable last word in history is rarely reached and some historians now say that while undoubtedly highway robbery and violence were widespread during the early years of the 19th century, they have been unable to find any unquestionable evidence of an all-India organised thugee cult as alleged by supporters of General Sleeman. They believe that the British stories of just such a demonology were based on reports by prisoner **approvers** providing the type of information sought by their captors. A lengthy and detailed novel *Confessions of a Thug* by Meadows Taylor, first published in 1839, both fascinated and horrified Victorian Britain, including the Queen. It is still in print (RUPA). It purports to be the life story of a father and son, jemadars of a thug group over many years. There is a chapter or two on the **Pindaris**.

The leader of a gang of thugs usually caried the title of Jemadar.

THUK/THOOK *n Hindi*
Sometimes called the great Indian spit.

THUNDER BOX *n*
A commode. Normal furniture in any western-type bathroom before the introduction of the flush system. The flush was rarely found outside

the major cities earlier than the 1960s. The removable white enamel receptacle inside the commode, from its shape, had the colloquial name in British circles of the top hat. For emptying by the **sweeper**, for reasons of delicacy, the top hat was usually conveyed in a large round basket, of the type now sometimes chosen by foreign ladies for their **bazaar** shopping.

TIFFIN *n* English
A vestigial word still in current use in India from a short-lived slang expression of 18th century England – but by the 1800s, its meaning had to be explained to newcomers. A light midday meal, luncheon.

Tiffin-carrier: almost a Hindustani term, part of the vocabulary of most of middle-class India. A nest of several circular metal containers in which the courses of a meal can be carried on a journey or to the office. A refinement is a tray at the bottom in which burning charcoal keeps the whole warm. In **Mumbai** there is the professional dibba/dabbawala (container-man) who each morning collects filled standard-sized tiffin-carriers from suburban housewives and, through a most complicated but efficient organisation of some two thousand others, arranges for the containers to be delivered in time for lunch, each to the correct husband at the correct office table in the city centre. The 'empties' are later returned.

Nowadays, the tiffin-carrier is likely to be at least in north India – little more than pocket-size, with just two compartments.

In 2005 two dabbawalas from Mumbai earned world publicity as invited guests to Prince Charles' wedding in Windsor, U.K.

TĪKA/TILAK *n* Hindi
A mark on the centre of a **Hindu** forehead (correctly, tika for women, tilak for men: nowadays, a tika may be applied to either sex, but a tilak almost always only to a man), either self-applied, or as a sign of recognition or blessing, by another, using the thumb of the right hand moving upwards. Vaccination and inoculation, for both sexes, tika only. A facial mole can be referred to as a til or tilak.

The circular dot on a woman's forehead is known as a bindi (but tilak in Sanskrit). *See* Bindu. It derives, perhaps, from the blood smear once ceremoniously offered from a sacrificed animal to a bride entering her new home. (In places such as **Garhwal** and **Kumaon** where animal sacrifice as Hindu ceremony – but not for weddings – continues, the blood tika for those taking part is still usual.)

Following a visit to a Hindu temple both men and women may receive a mark, or, after prayers at home, apply one to themselves, perhaps of **sandalwood** paste or **sindoor** (vermilion).

Within the family, as a gesture of blessing, a parent will put the tika/tilak on his children, and on certain occasions (e.g. Bhai duj, the second day following **Divali**), sisters on their brothers.

In confirmation of a wedding engagement, the boy may receive the tilak from the father of the bride-to-be, signifying acceptance, and at the same time a present (once a gold sovereign, today a substantial gift, may well contravene the anti-**dowry** legislation). With a wealthy family, perhaps the occasion for a grand party. During the installation ceremony of a Hindu prince, a tilak on the royal forehead (the raj tilak) from the chief priest had the same symbolism as the placing of a crown in a similar Western situation.

At a wedding, at the close of the ritual and immediately before the saptapadi, also known as saat phere, seven circuits are said to represent for the couple a life of happy companionship with mutual respect and friendship. Following the actual sacred and legal ceremony of union, the seven steps of bride and groom together circling the fire (*see* Havan), the priest will place a tika on the forehead of each.

Tikka – a piece. As a culinary term,

cut into small pieces: e.g. mutton tikka: normally boneless and roasted as in a tandoor.

In **princely** and major landowning families, the Tikka **Sahib** will be the eldest son, the heir.

Ticca – see Theka..

TĪKHANA/TEHKHANA *n* Urdu
Although often written tikhana, the pronounciation should be teh-**khana**. Teh – Persian for below, underneath. A cellar, a basement. Underground living accommodation in a large traditional house, often Muslim, designed for coolness in hot weather especially for afternoon resting.

Thikhana (Hindi): as with the Urdu word above, sometimes unphonetically written as tikhana. A large residence, or estate, particularly one of a feudal type in Rajasthan.

TIL *n* Hindi
Sesame, or gingelly, oil, pressed from the seeds of the sesamum plant. Although said to have originated in East Africa, the til seed is one of the most ancient crops cultivated in India and was certainly known to the **Indus** Valley civilisation. In commercial references to the plant, a mention is often made to a similar East African oil seed, niger.

Since the presence of til oil is detectable by a simple chemical test, in order to check the adulteration of milk **ghee** with the vegetable product, by law a small quantity of til oil must be added to all manufactured vanaspatis.

Til: a .body mole, a beauty spot: the pupil of the eye. A word popular with poets.

Tīla: see Tope.

TINDAL *n*
A word of the sea and the coast originally from Malay: thence into **Tamil** and Malayalam and the anglicism, tindal. The boatswain of a coasting vessel or, if very small, the master. Ashore, a foreman in charge of a group of labourers. *See also* Lascar and Serang.

TIN CUTTER *n*
Making the metal the noun instead of the container, the Indian English equivalent of the tin-opener.

TIPU/TIPOO SULTAN
The Tiger **Sultan**: the Tiger of Mysore (tipu meaning tiger in Kannada, *see* Carnatic). Epithet for the second ruler of a dynasty of just two which effectively controlled Mysore for a period of about fifty years (Tipu's father, Haider Ali – haider from Arabic, a lion – a Punjabi, began in the ranks of the Mysore army, became its commander and, finally, took over the **Hindu** kingdom). During most of this period, the royal family, the

Wodeyars, although in obscurity, remained the titular ruling house.

Tipu Sultan and his father collided several times with the British (the four Mysore Wars of the history books), largely because of a refusal to come to terms with the power of the **East India Company**, itself fearful of Indian designs by the young Napoleon (28 years): from whom Tipu did in fact receive some assistance and, of course, until Nelson's naval victory of the Nile in August 1798, a French army was firmly established in Egypt. Today, Tipu's refusal is seen by many as a patriotic desire to retain independence in the face of British imperialism – no easy matter when the Governor-General (Lord Mornington) was inspired by a vision that the whole subcontinent was destined to come under British hegemony. The subsequent ending of the Fourth Mysore War in the storming and sacking of the then Mysore capital, the fortress of Seringapatnam (in today's Karnataka, Shrirangapatana), in May 1799, was considered a memorable feat of British arms (Lord Mornington thereafter became the Marquess Wellesley). Tipu himself died in the fighting and Colonel Arthur Wellesley – brother to the Governor-General – the future Duke of Wellington, was present commanding a brigade.

A surprise weapon used by Tipu's forces to great morale effect was the rocket. The British were so impressed that specimens were sent to Woolwich Arsenal near London: there developed they became a new armament against the French, particularly in maritime use, the Congreve rocket. (Another piece of ordnance developed in the same region but much later was the Bangalore torpedo in 1913: five feet lengths of steel piping which couldbe screwed together and stuffed with explosive. Used in World War I to cut a way through barbed wire entanglement. In World War II they were used to explode a safe passage through a minefield.)

Until recently, Tipu has been accepted as a hero of Indian nationalism, but today's **Hindutva** historians are giving more prominence to his undoubted anti-Hindu actions, such as temple destruction.

It was a princess descendent of Tipu Sultan who in World War II as a British agent in France won the George Cross and the Croix de Guerre. She was betrayed by a one-time friend and shot by the Germans.

TIRPĀL *n*
Acceptable Hindustani for a waterproof canvas sheet as used, say, for a truck cover: from the English word tarpaulin. (Writers in the past have sometimes mentioned a 'tirpaulia' in connection with a fort or palace. This is the same word as tripolia,

see Pol, three openings as of doors, gateways or arches.)

TIRTH/TIRTHA *n* Hindi
A **Hindu** sacred place, particularly one by the waters of a river or lake, a ford. A place for pilgrimage, where heaven and earth meet. The blessing itself and absolution of sins a pilgrim may receive from a sacred place. See dham.

Tirthraj: of sacred places, the king, the pre-eminent place for pilgrimage. By many Hindus this is considered to be the **Sangam** at **Prayag** (Allahabad). But for some, other sites merit the title, such as the lake at Pushkar near Ajmer in Rajasthan at the time of Kartik **Purnima**.

Tirthyatra: a pilgrimage. A group of villagers seen travelling together and wearing yellow coloured clothes, will probably be on tirthyatra. Once, they would have journeyed on foot or by rail, now, as likely as not, a coach complete with a video screen will be hired. *See* Yatra.

Tirththankara: see Jainism.

TŌDAS *n*
Small community of cattlemen, only several hundred in all, living in the Nilgiri Hills of south India. They are non-**Hindu**, but the object of their worship is their buffaloes and milk.

TODDY *n*

An anglicism (or perhaps a Scoticism) from tarri (taar/taal, a palm tree), Hindi for the fermented sap of the date, coconut and other palms, obtained by cutting into the young flowering branches at the crown; with alcohol content of about four per cent. If fermentation continues for more than twenty-four hours, an undrinkable vinegar is produced: this can be clarified and matured into a table vinegar. Distilled toddy produces arrack, sometimes known to the earlier British as rack (*see* Country Liquor). As a drink in the fresh or unfermented state, palm sap has the name nira/neera. In Britain, and in particular, Scotland, toddy has come to mean a drink of spiced or flavoured spirits with hot water and sugar.

Toddy cat: the so-called civet cat (it is a civet, but not a cat). Named from the fact that the animal has been seen to climb palm trees in order to drink from the clay pots which toddy tappers fix at their crowns to collect the sweetish sap. Other English names are palm civet and paradoxure: like all civets, it is fiercely, but not exclusively, carnivorous.

TOM-TOM *n* English
With no further precision most authorities ascribe an Indian origin to this onomatopoeic expression: it comes perhaps from tam-tam, a  bazaar term for the drumming that may accompany a town-crier. Also a tam-tam (in this case probably a corruption of the English tandem) is a light, open horse-drawn carriage or two-wheeled 'dog-cart' and, until they were abolished, at least in Delhi, a tram, a street-car.

TONGA/TANGA *n* Hindi
An anglicism from the Hindi, tanga: a light two-wheeled horse-drawn vehicle designed for four passengers (in fact, of course, many more are often carried). The seat for two facing the rear is the prestige one. In action, at one and the same time the driver clucks to encourage his pony and loudly addresses other road users slow to move out of his way in such terms as – a mild example this 'Eh, charas pine-wala', (*see* Indian Hemp), 'Oh, drinker/ smoker of hash': the while, if the front seat is occupied, balancing himself on the off-side shaft.

TONIC *n* English
Under the name of Jesuits' bark, from Central America, the prophylactic value of quinine as a specific in combating aches and fevers had been known in Europe since at least the 17th century - it was said that the Puritan Lord Protector of England, Oliver Crowell. had died of malaria since he would not accept a physic savouring of the papacy. But it was only in the late 19th century that the sahibs in India turned their attention to

499

making palatable the evil-tasting daily dose. Their answer was to dissolve the five grains in soda-water and Indian Tonic water was born, to be taken each evening at sundown (when mosquitoes become active) with just a trace, shall we say, of gin to help the medicine go down. (The military often favoured sherry. Kipling mentioned 30 grains in sherry.) Thus giving protection to the bloodstream against the malaria parasite for several hours, after which the sahib was expected to be safe within his mosquito net for the night. (For the public, the Government sold small packets of quinine—made up in jails—from Post offices.)

The connection between the anopheles mosquito and malaria was discovered in India in 1897 by western medicine, but it has been claimed that West Africans had been aware of it much earlier.

The Government of India quietly sponsored an expedition to Equador and Peru to collect and to smuggle out (no other phrase is appropriate) seeds and plants of the 'fever-tree' (cinchona) for growing in India. The expedition achieved its object and cinchona was grown in India, but quinine was never produced of the same quality and quantity as by the Dutch in the East Indies.

Although David Livingstone visited Bombay at least twice, there is no record that his own remedy against malaria was popular in India. Well known in Africa under the name 'Livingstone rousers', the Doctor compounded his pills in about 1850 using quinine, rhubarb, calomel, cardamom and ginger.

Much of the 'tonic' water sold in the bazaars today has little therapeutic value for the quinine has been replaced by the equally sharp-tasting citric acid.

TOOFĀN/TŪFĀN *n* Urdu
A storm with strong winds: anything from an inland local squall to a disastrous tropical hurricane hitting the sea coast. In its Arabic original, almost certainly the origin of the word typhoon. In English, a typhoon is. necessarily associated with a tropical ocean and nearby shores, but the Urdu toofan can be much less serious in its effect and can occur anywhere. In the Indian Ocean and neighbouring seas a toofan or hurricane may well be termed a cyclone. It has to be said that for India cyclones develop far more often in the Bay of Bengal than in the Arabian Sea. In Chinese tufan is said to mean 'great wind'.

Toofan Express: a train linking Delhi and Kolkatta in each direction.

TOPE *n*
An anglicised form of the **Tamil** word toppu, used by pre-**Independence** Europeans all over the country to mean a grove, an orchard –especially

one of mango trees – but not known in any north Indian language: a Hindi equivalent for a pleasing grove of trees is kunj. Tope, even in the 1990s, is still in the vocabularies of southern writers in English. In an earlier century another purely European use of the word was for a Buddhist **stupa** (some guide books refer to this as a current usage). In this instance, perhaps the derivation is from toba, Punjabi from the northwest, now Pakistan, where there are many stupas, for a mound or hillock. (An ancient and current Hindi term for the same feature is tila.) Alexander Cunningham, a military engineer later to be Major-General Sir Alexander, first Archaeological Surveyor-General of India, gave an imprimatur for the use of tope with his book *The Bilsa Topes*, published in 1853. An account of the Buddhist monuments at Sanchi in central India.

Top: Urdu from Persian. A cannon, an artillery piece.

TŌPI/TŌPEE *n* Hindi
A hat. In northern India, correctly, a hat without a brim (a type mandatory for Muslims at prayer, since a brim would prevent the forehead from coming in contact with the ground and it would be disrespectful to worship God with the head uncovered), such as, for example, the now rarely seen Muslim fez, the tarboosh, the Turki/Turkey topi.

Gandhi Topi: white cotton forage cap

as supplied, it has been suggested, to prisoners in South African jails (in India, the spelling is never gaol), where no doubt, it was seen by **Mahatma** Gandhi. But in fact, there are a number of traditional Indian caps almost similar to the present day design. When first adopted by the Congress Party as a uniform headgear using **khadi** cloth in 1918, the cap was somewhat taller than it is today with the sidebands almost twice the present width. Although never illegal all over India, the **Raj** tended to regard the Gandhi cap as a sign of disaffection and its wear a 'disloyal' act: throughout the 1920s and 1930s it was therefore occasionally locally proscribed. It seems improbable that the Mahatma himself ever wore for any length of time the cap named after him: and probably never after 1921 when he vowed to wear no more than the simplest essential clothing. The white cap is sometimes termed a 'neta topi' – a leader's hat.

Jinnah Topi/Cap: a popular warm cap of Afghanistan and north-west Pakistan, traditionally using the curled fleece of the Asian, or caracul/kurakul, sheep, similar to astrakhan. Although associated with Mohd. Ali Jinnah, Muslim leader and first Governor-General of Pakistan, in India wearing the Jinnah cap has never been considered an overt political declaration but simply a matter of comfort in cold weather.

Topi-walas: the hat people. An Indian

term for the British, for, of course, until the 1940s all Europeans wore a hat out of doors most of the time. See also Sola Topi.

TOPPER *n*
Indian English for one who 'tops the list', that is, comes first in an examination.

TORĀN *n* Hindi
An ornamental archway over a road, usually temporary, in honour of a visiting dignity or an event. Of carved stone in Buddhist days, as over the great entrances to the stupa at Sanchi. An ornamented cloth round the sides and over the top of the door to a village dwelling, in one time North American, a lambrequin perhaps a festoon of mango leaves or of **mirch** and **nimbu** together also over the door to avert the evil eye. Linked to the Sanskrit root is the German tor, a gateway.

TŌSHAKHĀNA/TOSHKHĀNA *n* Urdu
The government storeroom to which presents given to officers in the course of their official duties (e.g. when on a visit to a foreign state) are handed in. Such 'presents' may be recovered on payment. Any room designed for the keeping of jewellery or valuables: a prince's treasury.
The word was originally from Persia, where it had the meaning of a storeroom in a palace for valuable furniture or robes.

TOTA *n* Hindi
Always translated into English as parrot, but in fact the bird known elsewhere as the parrot is not to be found in India in the wild state. Strictly, the tota is the parakeet, to be seen everywhere and popular in the home as a caged pet. A bird of the parrot order, seed and fruit eating, smaller than the real parrot but with a long tail.

TOUCHSTONE *n*
A black river-polished stone from a mountain stream. When rubbed with gold or gold alloy the colour of the mark on the stone will indicate to an expert the purity of the gold which caused it. Touchstones are on sale in the streets of the bullion markets in Delhi city under the Hindi name kasauti.

TRAFFIC SIGNAL *n* English
A small leafed branch torn from a tree or bush at the rear of a roadside stationary vehicle is a signal to passing drivers that the vehicle is a non-runner.

TRISŪL/TRISHŪL *n* Hindi
From Sanskrit, lit. three spear or pike points. A trident: associated with Lord **Shiva** and to be seen as his symbol on all Shiva temples (those dedicated to Mahadev), usually as the finial above the **shikhara** (tower). Carried

by Shaivite **sadhus**. The emblem has been found on seals discovered at the archaeological sites of the **Indus Valley Civilisation**.

In recent years, in the context of strife between one religious group and another, a custom has arisen of Hindus carrying the trisul as a battle weapon, and, often in minature form, a symbol of militancy.

A mountain in the **Garhwal Himalaya** with three peaks (the highest of 7193m. In the English Lake District, a hilltop also may be likened to a pike).

TROPICS
At latitude 23° 28' N, in India the Tropic of Cancer crosses the country roughly on the line Ahmedabad, Jabalpur, Ranchi. Kolkatta is within the tropics by about 160 km and **Mumbai** by 500 km. Delhi lies about 500 km. north: where at midsummer midday the sun is at an angle of just over 5° from the vertical. (There is a Delhi legend that the tower of the Qutab **Minar** at this moment will cast no shadow: the plausible explanation – on most days of the year–usually given is that the angle of taper of the minar is also 5°. Unfortunately for the story, at midsummer local mid-day – about 1221 p.m. **IST** – the 72.5m high Qutab does cast a shadow, albeit a small one of about 0.76m, for the 12th century architect in fact made the taper not 5° but about 4.5°.)

TSAMBA/TSAMPA *n* Tibetan
Roasted and ground barley, staple food grain of Tibet, said to resemble sawdust in appearance.

TSO *n* Tibetan
A lake: a word used in the Tibetan-speaking northern frontier areas.

TUESDAY
In Hindi, Mangalwar: a day dedicated to Lord **Hanuman** and associated with the planet Mars, a particularly auspicious day for **Hindus**, but also having something of the ethos of a Protestant Sunday. While the strict may pray at the temple daily, be vegetarian and touch no alcohol, many Hindus who do not accept these austerities totally, at least on Tuesdays will abstain from meat and drinks and will go to a temple (usually one dedicated to Hanuman.) But in fact there is no religious obligation for the devout to visit a public temple daily, or even at all: almost every Hindu home will contain the domestic equivalent, a small shrine with icons). Haircutting and perhaps shaving, will be avoided if possible on Tuesdays – the day on which **bazaar** barbers and barber shops normally have their weekly holiday. Some Hindus eat no food for the whole day – *see* Fasting. A Tuesday party invitation, welcome on another day, may be refused. The reason for the weekly mortification is respect for Hanuman, who has the reputation of being an austere ascetic and no voluptuary.

In eastern India, an aspect of the **Mother Goddess**, under the name Mangala, is worshipped on Tuesdays, particularly by women.

TULADAN *n* Hindi
Tula, a balance, a pair of scales. An ancient Hindu practice, adopted by Muslim rulers, of an eminent person, perhaps as a birthday celebration, having himself weighed against valuables, such as bullion, diamonds, food grains or even sweetmeats, to be gifted to charity. The ceremony is not unknown today.

TULSI/TULASHI *n* Hindi
Basil, the royal plant, of the mint family containing an aromatic oil. Held in great veneration by **Hindus** as representing the Goddess Tulsivrinda, or Tulsi Mata (Mother Tulsi) and very frequently grown in temples and homes: hence the botanical name, *Ocymum sanctus* – Holy Basil. In the home, it is in the special care of the ladies. Tulsi leaves are used in the worship of Lord Vishnu and are added by some to sanctify cooked food, especially during an eclipse, in addition to being a pleasing potherb. Together with **Ganga** Jal (Ganga water), the leaves may be placed on the lips of a dying man.

The root wood is used particularly by Vaishnavites to make the hundred and eight beads of the Hindu rosary, and for the beads of the small throat necklace (kanthi) and others, worn by Vaishnavite religious orders.

TUT/TUTI *n* Hindustani, perhaps from Persian
The mulberry: a common tree of India from China, giving shade to roadsides and the leaves, food to silkworms. The catkin fruit is much enjoyed by children and birds.

TWO *n* English
In general, the sounds for the numeral digits in the Indo-European languages are linked through Latin, Greek or the Germanic tongues to the same numbers in Sanskrit. In English, particularly recognizable is the Sanskrit du/dwi for the numeral two (do/doh in Hindi), in such words as dual, duet, duo, diarchy, dichotomy, dodeca (two plus ten) and double.

No less linked are the words and prefixes for the numeral three. In Hindi/Sanskrit tray, tri, tir. (eg. tiranga, three colours, the Union flag of India) and the English suffixes tre and tri. For some, three is an inauspicious number, so, particularly in eastern India, three of one item should not be gifted.Some will not serve three chapatis on one plate.

Triratna: the three jewels of Buddhism, the **Buddha,** the **Dharma** and the **Sangha.**

ŪDIPI/ŪDUPI
Town on the west coast of South Kanara districts in Karnataka (see Carnatic), whose cooks, having started in the kitchens of the great **Krishna** temple there, are said to excel in their craft. An establishment named an Udipi/Udupi Hotel (in 1975, the name of the town was changed from Udipi to Udupi) is advertising a claim to provide high quality south Indian vegetarian food. Udupians have a story that when the first-ever climbers reached the summit of Everest, they were greeted by an Udupi coffeewala with an enquiry whether **idli** or masala **dosa** were required.

Udupi is less well-known as the centre of a regional folk theatre, by name Yakshagana.

UDYŌG *n* Hindi
Industry.

ULĒMA *n* Urdu from Arabic

The body of Muslim theologians: expounders of Islamic law. The word is the plural of alim, a wise and learned man.

Maulvi Alim: a degree in Islamic studies.

Jamiat-ul-Ulema (Association of Ulema): the authority in India on matters of **Sunni** Islamic law and faith. Located at the Dar-ul-Ulim (House, or Seminary, of Islamic Studies) at Deoband, near Meerut in **UP**. A **fatwa** issued by the Jamiat, is accepted as the highest Sunni Muslim learned opinion in the country.

The Jamiat also supervises all Sunni Muslim education in India. Politically, the Jamiat has usually supported the Congress Party, and is by no means the most fundamentalist of Muslim groups. But, nevertheless, the Deobandis generally do not approve of customs and celebrations not authorised by the **Kor'an** or the Hadith. (The other large section of UP Muslims, the Barelvies or Brelvis those of Bareilly – on the other hand are alleged by the Deobandis to be innovative, to regard their religious leaders almost as priests and, for example, to celebrate the various **Urs** in ways that owe something to **Sufism**.

ULLĀS *n* Hindi from Sanskrit.
Joy, delight; when raising a convivial glass in good company the equivalent of "Cheers".

ULLŪ *n* Hindi
An owl. The English word is linked to the Sanskrit original, uluk. Colloquially, a word for one thought to be not very bright.

UMEED *n* Urdu
Hope, expectation.

Umeedwar: one who is hopeful. A candidate for election to an office or for selection for an appointment.

UNDERTRIAL *n*
The generally used term for one who in England would be a remand prisoner. Probably once a lawyers' colloquialism for a person in the position described in the Prisons Act of 1894 – still the effective Act – as an 'unconvicted criminal (*sic*) prisoner': a person in custody but against whom legal proceedings have yet to be completed.

UNION TERRITORY *n*
An area administered by the Government of India, but, with varying responsibilities, each also has a local legislature. Examples are Chandigarh, Pondicherry (wef 2006 Puducherry), and its associated enclaves, Lakshadweep.

UP *n* Hindi from Sanskrit
Pronounced oop. A prefix with a number of meanings: in the vicinity of, subordination, a secondary character, deputy, assistant as in Up **Mantri** – Deputy Minister.

UPANISHAD n Hindi
Often written in English as the Upanishads (in Hindi pronunciation, the first 'a' is all but silent). The literal meaning is sitting at the feet of a teacher (shad,

Sanskrit to sit, linked via Latin to such English words as sedentary, saddle etc.). A series of philosophical texts of the later Vedic period (approximately 1000 to 700 BC), regarded as revealed scripture by **Hindus**. Also known as Vedanta (anta, the end), the heart or a final exposition of the **Vedas**. Upanishad teaching relies solely on intellect, rejecting ritual and sacrifice, and was not intended for the masses who, in fact, were not allowed access to Vedic scripture. From the same Sanskrit root, in the vicinity of, there is the Bengal and eastern Uttar Pradeshi Brahman family name, Upadhyay (in the vicinity of learning), often taken to mean a teacher specialising in a part of the Veda without the wide coverage expected of an **acharya.**

UPASI
Acronym of United Planters' Association of Southern India.

UP TRAINS AND DOWN TRAINS
On an all-India basis, not a great deal of system about these: in the timetables of the railways concerned, trains tend to run Up to their HQ stations: but for the historical reason that Bombay was the first terminus in India, with one exception, all railways run their trains Up to that city. On the Southern Railway, all trains run up to **Chennai**, so in the SR time-table, the Mumbai Mail, for example, leaves Chennai as the 10 Down, but arrives

in Bombay (in the time-tables of the Central Railway, HQ Mumbai) as the 10 Up. Confusion is averted by numbering the train in the reverse direction as the 9 Up or Down. All trains entering Kolkata are Down and those leaving Delhi (except for Kolkata) are Up.

Towards the end of 1989, all train identity numbers became of four digits. The first refers to the zone, the second to the railway division looking after the coaches and the last two are special to the train as above.

URLI/URALI *n* Malayalam
A large shallow cooking vessel, in diameter from 30cms to 3 metres the depth of even the largest size being little more than 60 cms, usually cast in bell metal or brass: there is no cover. A big one may require the labour of six men to lift. Used in **Kerala** and the south mostly for sweet dishes that need constant stirring; also for **ayurvedic** medicine that may have to be kept simmering for seventy-two hours continuously. Often seen in prosperous northern homes as planters, decorative containers for flowers or potted plants.

URS *n* Urdu
Ceremonies observed on the death anniversary of an Islamic pir (saint, *see* Dargah) particularly within the **Sufi** tradition, in a place connected with his life.

USTAD *n* Urdu

Fem. Ustani. An expert in any skill who is also a teacher. The Muslim equivalent of the **Hindu guru**: particularly when the ustad is a respected musician, the reverence he receives from his pupils is that enjoined as the correct relationship between **chela**, or **shishya** and guru. Of course, a maestro only reaches eminence after many many hours in daily riaz (Arabic: toil, exercise, practice).

UTKAL
The ancient name for the territory which today is the northern portion of the state of Orissa (the southern part was known as Kalinga). *See also* Oriya.

UTSAV/UTSAVA *n* Hindi
A celebration.

Mahotsav: a major, or grand, celebration.

Vana Mahotsav: lit, forest celebration. An annual period during the **monsoon** when the value of forests and of tree planting is brought to public notice.

Also Hindi words for a festival or celebration are parv and samaroh.

UTTAR PRADESH/UP
The north state. Before 2000, north Gangetic India and the hill territory to the Chinese (Tibet) frontier. The region taken by the British from the Marathas following the 1803 war and first given the name 'The Conquered

and Ceded Provinces of Bengal'. Excluding **Oudh**, it then became 'The Upper Provinces'or 'The Western Provinces of Bengal'. In 1834, the Agra **Presidency** was authorised by London, but this was never set up and two years later the name changed to The North Western Provinces, administered from Agra. (Between 1856 and 1877 the Oudh territory was governed independently by a Chief Commissioner.) In 1902, to avoid confusion with Curzon's new North Western Frontier Province, the name became 'The United Provinces of Agra and Oudh'. The final change was in 1950 to Uttar Pradesh. In November 2000 the hill territory of **Garhwal** and **Kumaon** was detached to become the new state of **Uttaranchal**.

UTTARANCHAL Hindi
Lit. the northern frontier. The name of the state formed in November 2000 when the hill, or Himalayan, region was separated from UP: **Garhwal** and Kumaon. The capital town, perhaps to be changed later, is Dehra Dun.

The traditional name for the region is Uttarakhand/Uttarkhand, the territory under the protection of the consort of Lord Shiva, personified as the twin peaks of Nanda Devi (7117m).Uttarakhand became the official name in 2006.

UTTARAYANA *n* Hindi

The northern path. The period of the northward journey of the sun from the Tropic of Capricorn to the Tropic of Cancer and of returning heat to northern India: an auspicious six months for **Hindus**, compared with the Dakshinayana, or southward journey, during the other half year. The festival of Makara Sankranti (the entering by the sun into the zodiacal house of Makara, a mythical beast seemingly owing something to a crocodile – but, in fact, the Indian equivalent of Capricorn, the goat) marks the commence-ment of the period. This falls on 14 – but occasionally on 13 January of each year. The time is exactly calculated and be it, say, 1.14 a.m., that is the moment large numbers of the devout will immerse themselves in rivers or **tanks**, braving the near ice cold of the northern winter. The evening before is celebrated, particularly by Punjabis, as Lohri: open-air fires are lit, often in the streets and with rural robust merriment and gaiety, people enjoy the warmth. The days following this sankrant (*see* Calendars) are considered to be particularly of happy omen and so are very popular for Hindu weddings. According to Western astronomy and astrology (tropical calculations – sayana in Hindi – true to the solstice), the sun touches Capricorn on 22 December, but in the traditional Indian calculations (sidereal – nirayana, without the solstice), each zodiacal house is now entered some twenty-three days later. *See* Calendars, Kumbh and Pongal.

VĀHAN/VĀHANA *n* Hindi

A carrier, a vehicle. In Hinduism, the animal steed of a deity. For example, **Kali/Durga** rides a lion or an attendant tiger: **Shiva**, a bull (by name - **Nandi**): **Indra**, an elephant: **Vishnu**, a part human-eagle (garuda; adopted by Indonesia as its national emblem, see Greater India): **Kartikeya**, a peacock (*see* Mor): **Ganesh**, a musk-shrew: **Lakshmi**, an owl: and Shani (*see* Saturday), a vulture. In **Hindu** iconography, the vahan is a pointer to a deity's identity – and no less so for the images of the Jain tirthankara. (Some Christian saints also have animal companions, a winged bull for St. Luke, an eagle for St. James, the winged lion of St. Mark, the lamb of St. John the Baptist and St. Theodore on his pillar in Venice is accompanied by a crocodile.) As in heraldry, the English term cognisance, is sometimes used for these identifying devices.

Another word for a vehicle of the gods, a sort of car in which they crossed the heavens, is viman/vimana; in today's Hindi, it means an aircraft. (A second meaning in **Sanskrit** of viman/vimana is a tower: in the

south, it is applied to the main shrine building of a temple complex.)

The root word of vahan is the Sanskrit vah, to carry or draw in the sense of pulling, in Latin it appears as vehere, to carry; thence to English as vehicle, wagon and wain.

Parvihan: transport

VAHINI/BAHINI *n* Hindi

An army. As bahini, a word particularly used in eastern India, but more often applied to political action groups than to the military forces. Sena, also from **Sanskrit**, is commonly used to mean the army (Senapati: Commander-in-Chief). The words for the defence services are: sena, the army; nau-sena, the navy (na/nau in Sanskrit can mean water, the sound has come to English via Latin as in naval, navigator, and through Greek, nausea); and vayu-sena, the air-force. In British days, from Urdu, fauj, was the normal word for the army.

Senik (but more often in the form sainik): military.

VAISIYA/VAISHYA *n* Hindi

The trader/merchant caste in **Hindu** society: but in the **Punjab**, the caste – largely **Sikh** – is usually known as Khatri, or Arora (*see* kshatriya).. The equivalent of **Bania**/vania. Going back far enough into almost prehistory, vaisiya had the meaning of settler, a farmer. In English speech or writing the group may be referred to as the Vaish community.

VAKĀR *n* Hindi
The name of the character in the devnagri (*see* Dev) Hindi alphabet representing sounds equivalent to the roman *v* and *w* – also sometimes *o*. So place names written as **Varanasi** and, in Delhi, Vasant Vihar, by a Hindi speaker will be pronounced Waranasi and Wasant Wihar. Dev (God) is usually pronounced Deo. With words such as rajiv (**lotus**) and sajiv (vivacious) the final roman *v* represents the usual speech form. In Bengal and eastern India the problem does not arise since *v* and *w* is written and pronounced as *ba*. With Urdu, like in Arabic, there is no *v* sound, the letter named *wao* is always a *w* sound, as in **wala**.

VAKIL/WAKIL *n* Urdu
Lawyer, agent, representative. Gujarati, **Hindu** and **Parsi** family name.

(Legal terminology in India is largely unchanged from British days: Latin, English and Urdu words remain in daily use in the courts. The British inherited **Urdu** from the Moguls.)

The Hindi equivalent is adhivakta, but this is very seltom used. It is said that there are in excess of eight lakhs vakils in India.

VALMIKI
Said to have been India's first poet, the adi-**kavi**: the author in **Sanskrit** of the **Ramayana**, a one-time bandit (so say some) who became a **rishi**. He acquired his name, meaning an ant-hill, from an occasion when seated deep in contemplation, ants built over him, as around a forest tree trunk.

Valmiki/Balmiki: a sweeper subgroup. Although a very old claim by some, the now firm conviction of all valmiki sweepers that the author of the Ramayana was of their clan is of fairly recent origin. In the last century most Punjabi sweepers (**Hindu/Sikh/** Muslim) accepted Valmiki as an ancestral godling, believed to live in a jand tree (*Prosopis spiegera*). Now the image of the minor deity and poet has merged and sweeper leaders tend to contest the possibility that the poet was ever a bandit. Also, many of those who previously had the derogatory word bhangi (*see* Sweeper) as their group and family name, have now adopted Valmiki.

VANASPĀTI *n* Hindi
Lit. Lord of the Forest. A **Sanskrit** term from ancient scripture for trees thought to bear fruit without first having to flower. Borrowed in the 1920s by the importers as a generic name useful to advertise the natural vegetable origin of their hitherto unknown product, a cheap substitute for **ghee**–cooking medium made from hydrogenised oils. Also known as vegetable ghee. *See also* Til. (European edible oil manufacturers in the 1880s likewise used a classical dictionary when naming their new butter substitute; they found the Greek word margaron – a pearl – and coined margarine. Some

give margaron a Sanskrit link, manju – beautiful.)

VANDANA *n* Hindi from Sanskrit
Obeisance, devotion, worship. A sung eulogy to a person or a deity. The touching of a revered person's feet.

Saraswati vandana: particularly in a school, a song of praise to **Saraswati** before the day's work. A girl's name.

VANDE MATERAM *n* Sanskrit
India's national song. Adoration, salutation, homage to the Motherland. A poem from a novel "Anandmath" by Bankim Chandra Chatterjee. Set to music by Rabindranath Tagore it was sung at the Congress party session of 1896 and was soon adopted as India's National Song (distinct from the National anthem) which it still is today. In the 1930's Muslims objected to verses invocating the deity, Durga Maa. The Congress Party lead by Subhas Chandra Bose, in 1938 declared that only the first two verses which are secular- would be used when sung as the National Song.

VANILLA *n*
The plant is a vine of the orchid family originating in Central America, now grown throughout the tropical world including a small quantity in South India (in 2005 said to be about eight tonnes annually). The world-wide name, including India, is vanilla. After a lengthy process of sun curing the beans extending to several months, the flavouring is produced and is normally sold here in essence form.

VARANĀSI
Claimed to be the oldest continuously inhabited city in the world and **Hindu** religious centre situated on a curve on the left bank of the river **Ganga**: to the British, known as Benares. (Used as an adjective, or meaning a person from the place, the word remains Banarasi – or sometimes, just Banarsi.) In the 19th century, under Muslim rule, the official name was Mohammedabad: but to orthodox Hindu India, the city dedicated to the worship of Lord **Shiva** is, and always has been, Kashi/Kasi (Shining) or in full, Kashi Vishvanath. *See also* Jyoti.

VARŪNA
The all powerful early Vedic God of the firmament the sky, the universe. Later, just the deity of the waters, the ocean. Closely associated with Mittra (see Vedas). A translation of a few lines from the Rig Veda concerning Varuna reads: "This earth is his, to him belong those vast and boundless skies. Both seas within him rest, and yet in that small pool he lies". Also known as Jalapati, Lord of the Waters. As Varun, a male personal name.

VĀSTU *n* Hindi
In full, Vastu Shilpa **Shastra**. Texts expounding the principles of building and sculpture so as to be in beneficial consonance with the elemental forces inherent in the portion of the earth occupied. (Vās, Sanskrit, A prefix syl-

lable with many meanings, but generally of something having substantial reality, such as wealth, a monument or a dwelling. The name for the Roman votaries of the domestic hearth, the vestal virgins has a link.)

In practice at its most basic, using classical traditional concepts, the design of a building including, if possible, the choice of a site, the external and internal dimensions, the facing direction, particularly that of the main entrance, so as to enhance the well–being of particular occupants.

VĀSUDEV/VĀSUDEVA

An early Vedic deity, associated, or perhaps identical with, Lord **Vishnu**. A name for Lord **Krishna**, himself Vishnu incarnate, derived from his putative father, a Vasudev of the **Yadava** tribe living in the Mathura district of **UP**.

VEDAS *n* English plural

A collection of four books each known in Hindi as Ved/Vaid, (knowledge but the Sanskrit root is vid, seeing, as in the English word vision). Some refer to the *Mahabharata – see* Epics – as the panchamveda, the fifth Veda accepted by **Hindus** as inspired by God himself and received by the early Aryan (*see* Arya) settlers in the Punjab (second millennium BC). Of the four, the Rig Veda (rig – verse), 1028 hymns – strictly 1017 since eleven recur unchanged – to the Vedic deities, is the oldest literature in the Indo-European languages. The Vedas were not written (in **Sanskrit**)

until many centuries after their composition, but were passed from generation to generation by careful memorising of the texts, **smriti**. Other texts accepted as being spoken directly by the authors and so of greater authenticity than the smritis are termed shruti – heard.

A dvivedi/dwivedi could recite two books, a trivedi/tripathi/ tripati three, a chaturvedi all four: these are **brahman** family names today but for some, Dvivedi has become Dube/ Dubey and Chaturvedi, Chaube/Chaubey. Said **Manu**, "As a eunuch is unproductive with women... so a brahman who knows not the (Vedic) verses is useless". It has been claimed that if every existing copy of the Vedas was to be destroyed, even today they could still be set down from men's memories word for word as the originals. (It is perhaps, this tradition as background that at some levels causes a schoolmaster of today to accept as evidence of scholarship a pupil's ability to repeat verbatim a text on a subject.)

Until recent times, **dharma** restricted the reading and hearing of the Vedas to male **caste Hindus** (Manu said that a woman should hear no Vedic verses other than the **mantras** at her own marriage ceremony), and only brahmans were permitted to expound on them. (For many centuries. Catholic Europe considered that to allow simple people free access to the Bible would be to subvert the social order.)

Vedanta: Lit. the end (i.e. the object)

of the Vedas. That view of the Vedas revealed in the **Upanishads**. Also the system of monistic philosophy which holds that the formless **Brahma** uniquely represents the universe, eternal and omnipresent in all thought and matter.

The major Vedic gods (goddesses are little mentioned, except for the shadowy Aditi, the first Mother Goddess of all, *see* Shakti, and Prithvi, the earth personified: Prithvi is now largely a male name and Usha, the Goddess of the Dawn, the counterpart of the Roman Aurora) can be referred to as the Adityas – sons of Aditi – and are identified with the elements. Dyaspita/Devapita/ Divapita, **Indra**, Lord of the firmament and of storms (Jupiter to the Romans, Zeus to the Greeks): Agni or fire (whose **vahan** is a ram), to whom oblation were and are made (*see* Havan): Surya/ Savitra of the sun (*see* Gayatri),, still the focus of countless brahmanical early morning prayers and libations of water (Surya **Pranam**): also addressed as Bhaskara – the Creator of the Sun. Another Vedic deity, Mittra/Mitra (known to Europe through the Mithraism of the Roman soldiers, the 'Light of the World', also a solar deity, the strong competitor of early Christianity), is seldom heard of today, except as a **kayasth** family name and in the Hindi word meaning friend as in the personal name Soumitra/Sumitra – name given to Lakshman, the brother of Lord **Ram**. In some cases as a family name, Mittra has been anglicised to Mitter it is possible that the English word, mate meaning a friendly companion has a link to mitra.

VEENA/VINA/BEENA *n* Hindi
Stringed musical instrument with a sound box at each end. The strings are plucked as with a lute. Particularly used by the **Carnatic** musicians of the south. Also popular in the home, where it is usually played by the ladies. Because of an association with Lord **Shiva**, the instrument is sometimes known as the Rudra-Veena. The deity **Saraswati** is usually depicted holding a veena, so she has the epithet Veena-pani, she with the veena in her hand. (Pani in **Sanskrit** means hand: in Hindustani, of course, it is water.) A popular name for a girl.

VERANDA *n* English
While all authorities agree that this word, meaning an open, roofed gallery on one side of a building, entered English from India, its origin in uncertain. There is the Hindustani varanda, with a similar meaning and also, in Persian, buraamda, a projection or a jutting-out from a building, but both these may have been acquired from a very similar word in Portuguese. *Hobson-Jobson* mentions that in their very early reports home, the Portuguese used veranda not as from India, but as a word needing no explanation. The wide verandas of the typical bungalow of the British period (*see* Bangla) not only provided agreeable and much used extra living space, but assisted

to keep the interior rooms cool by shading the main structural walls from direct sunlight.

VERNACULAR

The normal English expression during the British period for Indian languages in general. Rarely used today, perhaps because of its origin, the Latin for a second or later generation slave. In its place is a Hindi equivalent from Sanskrit, particularly for a spoken or literary work in a regional language, bhasha.

VICEROY OF INDIA

A descriptive title, not to be found in any statutory enactment, for each of a succession of twenty statesmen administrators (there were also a few temporary incumbents) between 1858 and 1947 as ceremonial representative of his sovereign. The official designation for the grandest summit of power in the Empire was Governor-General of India (Governor-General of Fort William in Bengal, until 1834): first held by Warren Hastings in 1774 and titularly ending with C.R. Rajagopalchari's (see Rajaji) retirement in 1950 and the appointment of India's first President. Lord Mountbatten thought it simply 'the greatest office in the world'. Hastings held an opinion, unlike most of his contempories, that India had been civilised for many hundreds of years.

The title was not unknown in India before (nor in the Empire, there was also a Viceregal Court in Ireland:

only there, the administrative burden and the personal responsibility of the holder, officially the Lord Lieutenant, was far less), but it became the normal way of referring to the head of the Government of India only in 1858 after Queen Victoria in a proclamation styled Lord Canning as her Viceroy – the occasion was the assumption by the Crown and United Kingdom government of full responsibility for the administration of India. When the sovereign came in person, as in 1911/12, the title was not used.

Viceroys were political appointees by the home government, usually aristocrats not quite of the highest rank, without previous Indian experience. (One surprising translation to the Viceregal throne was in 1916: that of Lord Chelmsford, while serving as a Territorial Army Captain in the Simla Hills. But before the war he had been twice a Governor of an Australian state.) Only one Governor-General was appointed more than once, Lord Cornwallis in 1786 and in 1805 – he died ten weeks into his second term. Only two came from the civil service. Sir John Shore (later Lord Teignmouth) in 1793 and Lord John Lawrence in 1864, but a number of civil servants acted to fill temporary vacancies. Although not limited by statute, the normal period in office was five years. (Exceptions in the 20th century were Lord Curzon, six years; Lord Chelmsford, five years six months; Lord Linlithgow, seven years; Lord Wavell, three and a half years; and Lord Mountbatten, five months as Viceroy.

The work was on several planes: from 1858 to 1947, as personal representative of the sovereign (with the title of Crown Representative from 1935). In theory it was possible for this office to be held by a person other than the Governor-General, but in fact never was: with the '**Politicals**' as his executives, the Crown Representative was responsible for relations with the Princes. The monarch was kept informed and was often keenly interested, but instructions for action could only come from the Secretary of State in London.

At least in later days, the crown representation with its ceremonial protocol was chiefly the reason for the regal splendour in which the Viceroy lived. In the manner of royalty, he had his personal cypher, formed from the initial letter of his title embroidered on staff liveries, printed on his house cigarettes and so on. He had a bodyguard of splendidly uniformed and mounted lancers. For travel he had his own white-painted eleven-coach train and in Calcutta, a personal river-launch (some questioned its necessity, for surely the Lord-**Sahib** could walk on water?) He was referred to as 'His Excellency – as were the Commanders-in-Chief and the provincial Governors. As Govemor-General-in-Council, i.e., President of his Executive Council, the Viceroy was charged with the superintendence,

direction and control of the civil and military administration. The Council members, until 1935, were appointed from London (the first Indian, G.K. Gokhale, being nominated in 1909): but whatever views he or his Council might have, he was also expected to be the executant of the policy of the home government. A second Lord Curzon. of whom as Viceroy it was said that he regarded himself as the head of a power independent of, and not always friendly to, Britain would not have been accepted. Curzon expressed an opinion that since the Secretary of State in London was paid by India, he should be representing the interests of India and not those of the British government. By no means the whole story, but the immediate cause of his resignation as Viceroy in 1905, was that of London overriding his objection to a particular officer being appointed Military Supplies Member of his council. So it was, for instance, that Viceroys who wished to protect Indian industry soon had to realise that the ultimate sanction lay with the members of the House of Commons whose constituents required the promotion of British exports. Thus it followed that in 1947 all the bicycles in India still came from Birmingham or Nottingham. The position of the last Viceroy, Lord Mountbatten, with the single and popular task of arranging the British withdrawal and allowed a freedom of action denied to his predecessors, was unique. From 1833, the Governor-General, as the executive authority, had the assistance of a Legislative Council: this advanced by slow stages from a single member (the Legislation Member, Lord Macaulay) through the Indian Councils Act of the British Parliament of 1892 authorising a handful of Indian members (the Imperial Legislative Council) to become the Central Legislature of 1919 with two Chambers and a total membership of 205, the majority elected. Well on the way to parliamentary democracy for its powers were considerable and, in matters of finance particularly, able to embarrass – but not, of course, to remove – the executive. This was roughly the position at the centre until the eve of **Independence**. The Interim Cabinet, formed in 1946 with Jawaharlal Nehru as 'Prime Minister', technically was the Viceroy's Executive Council of which Nehru was Lord Wavell's Vice-Chairman of the Council. (Drawing on his military experience, the Viceroy ungallantly likened forming his Council of Hindu and Muslim members to loading recalcitrant mules into a railway truck. Wavell earlier had been Commander in Chief South Asia.)

To project the legislative story. In 1946 the Legislative Assembly was dissolved and later in the year a Constituent Assembly (ie. for the purpose of devising a constitution for an undivided independent India) was elected by a limited franchise from each Province and princely state: a total of 392 members in all. The first meeting was inaugurated by Lord Wavell in 1946, but due to the demand for partition, the Assembly was not able to fulfil its stated purpose until after August 1947 when a separate Constituent Assembly was set up for Pakistan (9 August). In India, the Assembly, by then down to 299 members, de facto became the Indian Parliament and as such it continued until its dissolution in 1952 and India's first general election.

Vicereine: an India-given unofficial title for the wife of the Viceroy. The lady did not represent the Queen Consort and the courtesies she received, such as being addressed as 'Your Excellency' and in ceremonial durbar, a throne to the left of the Viceroy, derived solely from her husband.

Viceroy and Captain-General of the Indies of the East: English translation of the original title of the Portuguese representative of his sovereign (who was styled 'Lord of the Conquest, Navigation and Commerce of Ethiopia, Arabia, Persia and India'), with headquarters at Goa, originally governing, nominally at least, the Estado da India – the State of India - and all the Portuguese toe-holds in Asia and East Africa, from Macao to Mombassa: in 1572 his responsibilities were limited to the lands between the Red Sea and Burma. (In 1857 a limited resurgence of Portuguese suzerainty followed from recognition by the Pope of the King of Portugal as the 'Royal Protector of the Catholic Church in the East'. So that church authorities in Goa claimed religious jurisdiction over all Roman Catholics in the subcontinent. It was only in 1886, after protests by Britain, that the Papacy resumed direct control over most of their flock in British India, but pockets of Portuguese domination remained in the south until 1929.)

A Portuguese still (2004) remembered as a man of principle with a New Delhi street name, was the 16th century Alphonso Albuquerque.

VIDESH *n* Hindi
A foreign country.

Videsh **Mantri**: the Minister of External Affairs in the **Government of India**.

Videshi: foreign, a foreigner. The antonym to **swadeshi.**

VIDHĀN *n* Hindi
Law, legislation.

Vidhan **Parishad***:* the upper house in a state bicameral parliament.

Vidhan **Sabha***:* the lower (but more powerful) house in a state bicameral parliament, or the single house if the state has only a one-chamber legislature.

VIDHĀRBA Hindi
A region of central India now especially known for orange growing, with two crops a year, July and December. In later British days the Maratha speaking area of the Central Provinces; after Independence

transferred to Bombay and now in Maharashtra. In early times known as Varadh, corrupted in English to Berar, once part of the Nizam's Dominions (Hyderabad State) most unwillingly leased to British India. With the movement for smaller states, there is now a demand for a Vidharba State with its capital at Nagpur.

Vidharba is known to anthropologists as a region of iron-age megalithic burial sites.

VIDYA/VIDDYA *n* Hindi
Knowledge, learning. 'Vidya', said an ancient sage, '...is the highest ornament a man possesses... to be carefully guarded, for it gains food, glory and blessing.' The **Sanskrit** root is in English in such words as wit, wisdom and witness.

Vidyapeeth /Vidyapith: lit. a seat of learning. A university. Vidyalaya: lit. place of knowledge, a school.

Navodaya Vidyalaya: With the object of improving education outside the larger towns, a pace-setting or lead school controlled by the Central Government, with a standard higher than the average. The present target being one such school for each predominantly rural district in the country.

Vidyarthi: student.

Vishvamdyalaya/Visvamdyalaya: university (lit. school of the world or universe).

Vidwan/Vidhwan: a man of learning, a distinguished scholar. Particularly in **Carnatic** music, a maestro.

VIGYĀN *n* Hindi
Science. The **Sanskrit** root can have a meaning of wisdom as distinct from mere knowledge.

Vigyanik/vigyanveta: a scientist.

VIHĀRA *n* Hindi
Originally, a Buddhist dwelling place: more recently, a Buddhist monastery or place of retreat. Nowadays, in the form vihar, often just a residential area. Modern Bihar (the roman spelling Behar was usual prior to 1912) derives its name from that part of the state south of the River **Ganga**, called Vihar by the 11th century Muslim invaders, from the number of ancient Buddhist vihars (vihara) they found there. In eastern India, the northern *va* sound often becomes ba in pronunciation, and, of course, Bihar is now accepted all over India as the name of the state. But a Bihari is not necessarily a person from Bihar: in both Bangladesh and Pakistan, Bihari can be a somewhat pejorative term for a migrant Muslim from any part of India – to describe whom the neutral word (linked to **hajj**) would be muhajir/ mohajir: Arabic for a refugee. The muhajirun (plural) who accompanied the Holy Prophet on his departure from Mecca (*see* Hijra under Calendars) were honoured on that account. On Delhi's streets, the word Bihari again can be derisory, meaning a dehati (see Gaon), a villager, a simpleton rustic.

Bodh Vihara: traditionally, a place enclosing a revered bodhi tree (see Peepal). Providing a clean space for worship and circumambulation by Buddists.

VIJAY/VIJAYA *n* Hindi
Victory, Conquerer.

Digvijay: conquerer of many lands. Vijaya : feminine form of Vijay. Name for Durga. see Dussehra. Vijaya–the conquerer – may be used as a title for Arjuna, See Gita.

Vijay Ghat: Victory **Ghat**, in particular the public park in Delhi made at the place on the bank of the River Yamuna where Prime Minister Lal **Bahadur** Shastry was cremated after his death in Tashkent, U.S.S.R., in 1966, following the war with Pakistan.

A **Hindu** male personal name.

VILLAGE DAUGHTER *n*
English
Translation of the expression used to distinguish girls born in a particular village from those who entered by marriage. The former do not cover their faces before local men, the latter may be expected to.

V I N D A L O O / V I N D A L U / BINDALOO *n*
Generally, English food preparation has little local acceptance in India, but Portuguese style via Goa has found favour. An example is the dish with the original name of

"vinhas de alhos", meaning rich in garlic. In Goa it changed character and became known all over India: vegetables (especially potatoes – **alu** in Hindi), alone or with meat, with which the **curry** sauce is thin and made somewhat sour with vinegar or lime. In the south, **tamarind** is an essential ingredient. Pork vindaloo is particularly popular with non-vegetarians.

VĪR *n* Hindi
From **Sanskrit**: semen. A prefix denoting maleness, heroism etc. The English word virile, received via Latin, of course has the same root. It may be of some psychiatric significence that a Sanskrit word for gold also has the meaning of semen, hiran.

VISHNU
In Hinduism, to their separate devotees (Vaish-navites and Shaivites), Lord  Vishnu and Lord **Shiva**, each is the one universal God, of whom all other deities are merely alternative forms. Each has Vedic origin. Unlike Shiva, Vishnu is wholly benign, the fighter for good against evil, the protector of the world. He is portrayed as blue in colour and, usually, as having four arms. His symbols are the cobra (by name, Ananta-eternity, with no beginning or Sheesha, also Sheesh Nag, on which the Lord sleepas. Some believe that a priceless jewel, Nagmani, is secreted in the snake's

hood.) Other symbols are the boar, a golden mace; a quoit (used as a mighty weapon and named Sudar-shan **Chakra**); a **conch** shell and the **lotus**: his vehicle (*see* Vahan), the eagle, the king of birds with a human face, Garuda/Garur. (Some identify Garuda with the brahminy kite). His wife is **Lakshmi**. The conjoint name for the pair, as with an icon, being Lakshmi Narayan.

Vaishnavites consider Lord **Ram**, **Krishna**, and some, the **Buddha**, to be incarnations of Vishnu (in fact, a Vaishnavite is far more likely to worship Ram or Krishna than Vishnu as himself). A more recent **avatar**, some believe, was the 16th century Bengali bhakti saint, Chaitanya: now, perhaps, regarded by those of the Hare Krishna movement as their preceptor. Many accept that the present age of sin and sorrow, the kaliyug, will only end when Lord Vishnu returns yet again: this time under the name Kalka/Kalkin, riding a white horse, sword in hand to destroy all that now exists, but then to establish righteousness on earth. In Jaipur, built by the city-founder (18th century) is a temple dedicated to Kalkin and is complete with a white horse. Closed to the public it awaits the Lord's arrival.

It is sometimes said that Vishnu appeared on earth in nine or ten avatar forms (incarnations), but in fact it is hard to be precise, for there is no general agreement as to which of these was the Lord himself under a different name, or as a completely different being. Vishnu is thought to have a thousand names: (sahasranama – some say 1008): a few of the more often used are: Hari (*see* Har); Narayan/Narain (*also* Daridra-narayan – Lord, or Protector of the Poor. Used in a Gandhian way as a generic term for the poor themselves): Madhava; Keshav and Mukand. He is the deity of some of the great temples of India, e.g., as **Jagannath** in Puri and as Venkateshwara (or Balaji) at Tirupati in Andhra **Pradesh**. On one occasion, the Lord assumed the form of a half-lion half-man (Narasimhan) in order to rid the world of a troublesome demon king. The Nepalese regard their sovereign as an incarnation of Lord Vishnu. The name, Narayan (he of the waters, the ocean), enunciating slowly all three syllables, may be used as a **mantra** and pronounced as a blessing. In verse, Narayan may be a reference to **Krishna.**

Unlike some Shaivite forms of worship, Vishnu requires no animal sacrifice, and Vaishnavites themselves are usually vegetarians. (However, Lord Krishna did once assume the form of the Goddess Kali, an occasion celebrated annually in the far from vegetarian temple in Kolkata).

VIVIDH BHARATI *n* Hindi
Lit. the diversity of India. The name given to the light or popular programme channel of All India Radio: carries commercial advertisements.

VOMITORY *n* English
(In abbreviation: VOM), How this rarely used word from ancient Roman gluttony came to be occasionally employed in modern Kolkata in its Latin sense of a passage of exit (and entrance) from a public auditorium or stadium is obscure. It seems probable that the usage is solely of the 20th century, for *Hobson-Jobson* has no notice of it; introduced perhaps as a drollery by a classically minded Briton, or one trained in a seminary of the Roman Church. Alternatively, it could be native-born, with a derivation far older than the Caesars, for vam in **Sanskrit** has the meaning of vomit or something ejected, or something base. (Also the left side, so that a circulatory walk round a revered object is clockwise. Curiously, two other vomit words in English, spew and sputum, also have Indo-European roots.)

WĀLĀ/WALLA/VĀLA/WĀLI*n*
Urdu and Hindustani
From wali, in the original Arabic, proximity: e.g., a madman, one believed to be close to God, may be termed an **Allah**-wali. Plural: auliya – see Chisti. In Urdu, a multi-use suffix adding to a word (noun, verb or adjective) the meaning of a person or thing associated with that word. Some examples: carwala – driver or owner of a car: sabziwala – vegetable seller: Poonawala – one whose home is Poona (now **Pune**): janewala one who is going, or is about to leave: lalwala – the red one (person or thing): gaonwala—villager: gharwala – man living in the house referred to; an expression meaning that he is of the family; or, as used by a wife, since by custom she will not mention him by name, the man of the house – her husband.

Occasionally in the **Punjab** and quite frequently in the Dehra **Dun** district, villages named from a person will include the suffix 'wala', e.g. Raiwala. If the person or object is feminine, wala becomes wali. (Wali can also mean a Muslim prince or governor, e.g., the famous Wali of Swat – now in Pakistan. The crown prince, the heir apparent, being the Walidad.) see also Box Wala.

WAQF/WAKF *n* Urdu
A Muslim endowment or trust for a charitable or pious purpose. Strictly, in Muslim law, ownership of the property vests in God. The trustee or guardian in charge being termed the mutwali (sometimes nazim).

Auqf., plural of waqf.

WASHP/VASHP *n* Hindi from Sanskrit
Vapour. With links to words in Indo-European languages, including English, with the same meaning.

WATER HYACINTH n English
A floating scourge of water bodies throughout India originating from tropical America. A quick growing floating plant, said to be able to double its coverage of an area within two weeks. Large leaves and attractive blue flowers. Although full of nutrients it is not palatable to cattle. After fermentation it can have a use as a soil fertiliser and for growing mushrooms.

Little controlled in India, mechanical and chemical methods are too expensive to be used on a large scale.

WATT'S

When quoted as an authority, almost certainly a reference to the monumental work A *Dictionary of the Economic Products of India* in six volumes, compiled by George Watt and published in 1889; reprinted in 1972. Its successor is the Wealth of India, Raw Materials, published in eleven volumes by the Council of Scientific & Industrial Research (CSIR) in the 1970s. An encyclopaedia of the animal, vegetable and mineral products of the country used in commerce.

WAZĪR/VAZĪR *n* Urdu

Adviser to a head of state: a Minister. Direct from Arabic; in English the title became Vizier.

Wazir-i-Azam: Chief or Prime Minister.

"WHITE MAN'S BURDEN"
An often repeated quotation from a set of verses by Rudyard Kipling: a message that it is the duty of the European "to serve your captives' need" by taking law and civilisation to those less privileged, without thought of reward, thanks or even acknowledgement. Many Britons were satisfied that this sentiment reflected their role and mission in India.

In fact, Kipling addressed his words "Take up the white man's burden" in 1899 to the United States, which, as the result of a short war with Spain

and payment of $ 20m (to Spain) suddenly became a colonial power. (The Philippines was the largest of several acquisitions.) While received by Governor (of New York) Theodore Roosevelt as politically useful, there is no evidence that Americans in general were grateful for the exhortation.

A line often associated with "the white man's burden", "Or lesser breeds without the law" is part of another Kipling work, *Recessional*, written earlier than the 'burden'. Who the lesser breeds' might be is not clear, nor did the author ever explain his words.

Somerset Maugham has been quoted as saying that the main burden of the East was the white man.

WIDOW *n* English
An Indo-European word—linked to the **Sanskrit** widh/vidh, meaning lacking, bereft, alone. Social death. In today's Hindi, a widow is widhwa. In Urdu from Persian the word is bewah.

Also from Sanskrit meaning widow is rand, but in the language of the streets today, perhaps in the form randi, the word means prostitute.

WINE *n*
In Indian English, a catch-all for alcoholic drinks. A translation from the Hindi, sura – alcohol. (Sura as a word and a drink has **Sanskrit**, Vedic, and

Old Persian antecedents. It is also an **ayurvedic** medicine of today: a herbal tincture which can be taken pharmaceutically, as a medical comfort, by those to whom a glass of spirits would be anathema.) A generic word for spirits is daru or madd/madh.

Wine shop: a. retail outlet by the bottle exclusively of, almost certainly, except, perhaps, in the major cities, beer and spirits. An establishment advertising itself as an 'English Wine Shop' is implying that **country**, or inferior liquor will not be available and that what is sold is India Made Foreign Liquor, or IMFL. A legal term meaning exotic spirits (whisky, gin, brandy, etc.) distilled in India, and beer. It was coined in the 19th century when controls were imposed on the sale of spirits and it became necessary to distinguish local from imported brands.

Pava/Pawa: a quarter. The name for the popular bottle size of 250 ml. spirits.

WISH *n*

As a verb, one use little heard in standard English is,common in India; as in '... the Director wished me', meaning that the Director was good enough to notice me and to say 'Good Morning'. Even such a careful stylist in English as Nirad C. Chaudhuri has written, deploring pre-**independence** British manners, "...in the case of unavoidable meetings, an abrupt business-like termination without even wishing back to an Indian's wish" (The Continent of Circe). India, like other parts of English influenced Asia, is very literal in defining the time of day: in Europe, morning lasts up to lunch, in India at 1201 hours, one may well be wished a good afternoon, or just a good noon.

WORCESTER SAUCE *n*

This seemingly very English table accessory is said to be a copy of a **chutney** from Bengal, made up in Worcester by a local **compounder** from a recipe taken home by an 18th century nobleman, Lord Sandys. The story adds that a Mr. Lea was the nobleman's butler and a Mr. Perrin the chemist. An important ingredient was essence of tamarind.

WORDY MAJOR *n*

An anglicism, adopted by Indian troops, for the adjutant of an Indian cavalry regiment: perhaps derived from vardi, a uniform.

Adjutant Stork. So called from its measured stately walk. A bird of north-eastern India of just over a metre in height. Distinguished by a red naked pouch pendant from below the beak: related to the marabou of north western Africa. Frequently municipally protected on account of its usefulness as a scavenger.

WRITER *n*

The junior-most in rank of the **East**

India Company's covenanted servants (in the very early days boys were sent out as apprentices, only becoming Writers after some years service) : as were the cadets of the Company's army, they were often so young when appointed, that for the voyage out they had to be warned that unless made extra large, ere they disembarked, they would have grown out of their clothing. Senior to writer, in ascending order, were, factor, junior merchant and senior merchant: until replaced by a Governor appointed from London in the 18th century, each of the three major settlements was in the charge of a President (*see* Presidencies). The four junior designations were abolished together with the Company's commercial business in 1833.

Writers' Building: once the collegiate-type residence of the Company's writers in Calcutta. Erected in 1780 probably by Thomas Lyon (*see* Dalal).. Later, offices for the Company and now the Secretariat of the Government of West Bengal. (In England, 'building' as part of a proper name is usually plural: in India, singular.)

WT

To travel WT is to use public transport 'without ticket'. The antibody to the disorder, produced by the authorities, being the TTE (Travelling Ticket Examiner).

XEN *n*

Abbreviation for Executive Engineer, as of the Public Works Department.

DEN: Divisional/District Engineer.

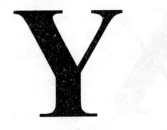

Y

YAAR/YĀR *n* Urdu

Beloved, a close friend. A bazaar term of address from male to female in the Hindustani courtesan culture as of 18th century Lucknow. Now, perhaps due to use in Mumbai films, a colloquial word of endearment between males without, necessarily, any sensual content; but the original Lucknavi application can still be heard.

Yaraana: to those who would use the term yaar, close friendship, buddyship.

YĀDAV/YĀDAVA

Now mostly of the state of **UP**, the almost tribal community of the Yadava trace their ancestry to Yadu, 'a prince of the period when history and mythology merge; the parents of Lord **Krishna** were Yadavas. Although their traditional occupation has been cattle keeping, by **caste** they are **kshatriya** and their lineage is from rulers. (In medieval India a major Yadava kingdom of the northern **Deccan** was centred on Deogiri – Mountain of God. This great **Hindu** fortress was captured by the Muslim **Sultan** of Delhi in 1318 and some years later, under Mohammed Tughlak, renamed Daulatabad – City of Wealth – for a decade, the capital of India. Now Daulatabad is no more than a spectacular halt for visitors on their way to the Ajanta Caves.) Today, in UP at least, even though some are wealthy landowners, the Yadava may not be considered the social equals of the **Rajputs**, the **Thakurs**. However, their numbers are such that in the often stormy rural politics of their state, they are a force to be reckoned with, with a militant wing, the Srikrishna Sena.

YAGNA/YUGNA/YOGYA *n Hindi*

Lit. ritual sacrifice.

An ancient Vedic rite of worship which included animal sacritice by the sacred fire (*see* Havan). An offering to a deity through the medium of fire. Still takes place occasionally, but nowadays more likely to refer to a continuous reading of Vedic scripture, with the object of intercession with the gods for some social purpose. Performed round the yagna-**kund** by relays of **brahmans**, sometimes night and day continuously for a period of weeks, thus becoming a **maha-yagna. But this has become unusual and a family yagna will run only from sunset to dawn. As an offering or**

oblation to a deity is made, as instructed in the very beginning by **Prajapati**, the word Svaha will be repeated several times.

YAHYA
Islamic form of the name, John.

YAK *n English*
From the Tibetan, yag, male of the Bos grunniens, the all-purpose bovine animal of Tibet: the female – the source of the milk for the rancid butter mentioned by all foreign writers about the country – should be called a dri. Within India, the yak is found in the wild only in one small region of Ladakh, in the state of Jammu & Kashmir. The bushy white tail, mounted in a handle and waved ceremoniously, and accorded dignity from Mongol Central Asia, has long been a symbol of Indian royalty: in Hindi it is known as chauri. It may be used in this way in a Gurudwara over the holy Granth. These days, yak hair finds a market in the wig making trade and in Britain, if not exactly royal, it is at least used in the proximity of royalty, for it is to be seen in the plumes of the full-dress helmets of the sovereign's Household Cavalry. Yak hybrids, crossed with domestic cattle, are called zo/dzo if horned and zum if without horns.

YAKUB
Islamic form of the Biblical name, Jacob.

YALE
Elihu Yale was born of English parents in 1649 in Boston, Massachussetts. He went to London and entering the **East India Company**'s service was appointed to **Madras** in 1672 as a **Writer** on a yearly salary of £10. Over the years he became wealthy, but even for an age when many combined Company and private business he was thought to shake the **pagoda** tree rather too vigorously. Nevertheless, in 1687 he became President of the Madras Council and Governor of Fort St. George (i.e., Governor of the **Presidency**), but five years later, following an enquiry into allegations that he was unduly favouring his private trading ventures, he was required to step down: he returned to England with a large fortune. But none of this is the reason his name is known the world over. From England, Elihu sent gifts of books and money to help 'The Collegiate School' of Brandford, near New Haven, Connecticut. In gratitude, the trustees changed the name to 'Yale College', now Yale University.

YALLI/YAALI *n* Tamil
In Southern Indian tradition an animal with the body of a lion and the trunk and tusks of an elephant. Strangely, such a piece has recently been added to St. Georges Chapal at Windsor Castle in England as a sculptured corbell by a Tamil **Sthapati.**

In 1994 it was reported that the 46m tall teak flagmast at Fort St. George was beyond repair and was to be replaced. It is said the Union flag (then of England and Scotland alone) was first hoisted on this mast by Governor Yale in 1687.

YĀMA

The Vedic god of the realm of the dead, the collector of souls and producer of evidence of an individual's good and bad behaviour before the judgement seat of the Supreme God. He is depicted carrying a club and often riding a black bull buffalo, Mahish in Sanskrit and Hindi, a personification of unknown darkness. Yama is also called Dharmaraj (an epithet given to one who speaks the truth fearlessly).

Yamadoot/Yamdoot: messenger of Yama (some see a lone black crow as filling this role, a harbinger of death).

YAMUNA/JUMUNA *n* Hindi

Current and ancient name for the northern Indian river known in British days as the Jumna. Believed by some to be the goddess Yami, sister of **Yama**, the God of Death. In iconography, she is usually seen standing on the back of a turtle: See Vahan. Rising in the **Himalaya**, the river flows through the plains to join her sister deity, Ganga Mai (Mother **Ganga**), at the **Sangam** at Allahabad. The western and northern limits of the

river's watershed may be said to be the sub-continental divide, for further to the north and west, drainage is not to the east to the Bay of Bengal, but west to the Indus and the Arabian Sea. The Yamuna and Ganga alluvial tract, the Indo-Gangetic plain, is reported to be home to 10% of the world's population.

The banks of the Kalindi, an alternative name from scripture for the river, particularly in the Braj region (*see* Janmashtami), in the Vrindaban, the forest country near Mathura (Muttra in the British period), are known to all **Hindus** as the place where the child **Krishna** played and where later he dallied with his village love, Radha.

Yamuna Pār: the other side the far side. In Delhi the way those of the west bank (New Delhi) refer to the left bank (also trans-Yamuna).

YASMIN *n* Urdu

The Persian generic name for the many varieties (said to number at least two hundred) of the climbing shrubs of the Asian jasmine family. (The English word, of course, is derived from the Persian.) Generally known in Hindi as chameli/chambeli/ champa. Almost all have white flowers and a scent which is believed to be stronger after dark. A jasmine summer evening pleasure garden was a feature of many palaces. The flowers yield a perfume oil and are valued in Hindu worship: also for making garlands and decorative evening chaplets for ladies' hair. (For **puja** – worship – Hindus say sweet smelling flowers are best liked by the gods: flowers from a poisonous plant. such as the oleander, should not be used. But see also Dhatura.)

Yasmin is a popular Muslim name for girls and is sometimes favoured by the **Parsi** community.

YATRA/JATRA *n* Hindi
A journey, travel, especially a pilgrimage. A festival; a stage performance.

Folk theatre: especially in Bengal and in eastern India. Travelling companies of players enacting stories, usually of **Hindu** mythology, in song, dance and dialogue in villages and small towns. Theatre in the round, for their stage is just a cleared circle on the ground, or a platform in the centre of their audience. Recently, there has been a revival of interest in jatra (the usual spelling in eastern India), the form has been modernised and the term can now be said to mean the living theatre of Bengal, both amateur and professional, urban and rural.

Yatrik/Yatri: a traveller, a passenger, a pilgrim.

Dolyatra: see Holi.

Padyatra: a journey on foot. The term is sometimes used for a lengthy

march with a political purpose, or to draw attention to a grievance.

Shobh(a) yatra: a procession, often a parade of decorated vehicles, each carrying a tableau on a religious theme, normally Hindu or Jain.

Tirthyatra: a pilgrimage. Also a dharmyatra. See Tirth.

YEHŪDI *n* Arabic/Urdu
Jew or Jewish.

YŌGA *n* Hindi
Lit. total, a combination, a union: the English 'yoke' is linked to the **Sanskrit** *root word.* An ancient system of self-discipline and concentration of the mind pursued with the intention of uniting one's soul with the infinite, or the supreme soul, or the universal order (such freely used terms are rarely defined), or of acquiring supernatural power. A branch of **Hindu philosophy. Yoga as an aspect of physical culture is of fairly recent origin from the west.**

Yoga takes many forms: some of the best known are: **bhakti**-yoga: jnana-yoga (study and knowledge, see Gym): **mantra**-yoga: hatha-yoga (control of the body – sometimes even of the systems known to **allopathic** medicine as involuntary). For some, the object of hatha-yoga is the awakening of kundalini (from the root word, **kund**, a reservoir), a Hindu tantric (*see* tantra) belief of a store of energy, likened to a personal goddess, normally unrealised, in the form of a coiled and dormant snake within the perineum of each human being. Kundalini, or hatha-yoga is a discipline designed to awaken the goddess and to cause her to uncoil through the body to reach the skull. Super-human power is thought to be available to the yogi whose kundalini has risen up the spinal cord to his head.

Yogi/Jogi (Fem. Yogini/Jogin): one who practises yoga. Hindu ascetic, religious mendicant; one on the path to self-realisation. (Yogin/Jogin can also mean a woman – sometimes even a very young girl – notionally married to a deity as the **devadasi** but not confined to a temple and, in fact, living a life of prostitution. South India, and, in particular, the Telengana region of Andhra Pradesh, is alleged to be the centre of this practice.)

Yogiraj (King of Yogis): a great yogi. A name sometimes applied to Lord **Shiva**.

Yogasan (asan – a posture): the postures of the body enjoined by hatha-yoga, leading to control of breathing and the senses, and ultimately perhaps, to **samadhi**. Asan can also be a formal sitting place, as the strictly personal piece of carpet or deer or tiger skin on which a yogi sits in meditation (as sits the Mahayogi, Lord Shiva, **ash**-covered, on Mount **Kailash**), although in this case, the more appropriate word would be devasan, *see* Dev.

Sinhasan: see Singh.

YŌJANA *n Hindi*
A plan, e.g. Panch varshiya yojana – five-year plan: parivar niyojan yojana – family planning. An ancient measure of length, equivalent to four kos: between twelve to fourteen kms.

Yojana Bhavan: the building in Delhi housing the Planning Commission of the **Government of India**.

YŌNI *n Hindi*
A vaginal symbol. The symbolic form normally used in association with the equally symbolic Shivalingam *(see* Shakti and Lingam): usually only marginally more explicit than the down-turned horsehoe seen over cottage doors in the West. In Hinduism, also a term for rebirth.

YŪNUS Urdu
Islamic form of the Old Testament name, Jonah.

YŪSUF Urdu
Islamic form of Joseph.

YŪV/YUVA *adj Hindi*
Youth, young.

Yuvraj: young prince, the heir apparent to a throne.

Z

ZAMINDĀR/ZEMINDĀR *n*
Urdu

A major land owner (zamin—land). In earlier days, a person who was assessed for land revenue (*see* Settlement): but in northern India, a really great land-owner, proprietor of many villages covering a considerable tract of country, could have been termed a talukdar (*see* Taluk).

Another Urdu word for landowner/ landlord, not used in the north, but current in **Tamil** Nadu even now and since the days of the Muslim rulers (e.g., the **Nawab** of Arcot: *see* Carnatic) is mirāsdar (mirās, Arabic to inherit).

Zamindari: the estate of a major landowner. The system adopted in Bengal in early British days, whereby the individual responsible for collecting and paying to the government the revenue from a tract of land (normally, a locally influential person) became recognised as the freehold owner. (The suffix 'dar', as in zamindar, from Persian, meaning owner or possessor of a thing material, or of an office, is much employed in Urdu.

While the parallel is not exact, in English a suffix 'ar', 'er' or 'or' can serve the same purpose.)

ZAMORIN
The English for, through Portuguese, the **Malayalam** titles Samuri – in Hindi this would be Samudri, King of the Sea – and Tamurin, of the **Nair rajas** of Kozhikode (of which Calicut was a corruption): a medieval minor princedom on the **Malabar** coast. The chief trading post in India of the Arabs (*see* Monsoon and Mappila): after the landfall there of Vasco da Gama in 1498, the colourful title of the rulers became quite well known in Europe and their city gave the English name to Indian cotton cloth, calico.

Hyder Ali of Mysore (*see* Tipu Sultan), overran the Zamorin's little state in the 18th century and following the end of the Third Mysore War in 1792, the British annexed it to the Company's India, first to become part of Bombay **Presidency** and then of **Madras**. The territory is now in Kerala State.

ZĀR *n* Urdu from Persian
Gold, golden, golden yellow,

Zarda: a sweetened rice flavoured and coloured with **saffron**, served on special occasions. (Zarda as scented tobacco, *see* Pan).

Zari: metallic thread, silver or gold,

or gold-plated silver, wound on silk or cotton.

Zardozi: A traditional Muslim craft; embroidery using fine zari thread on garments, kurtas and bedcovers. Heavier thread on velvet. Golden finery particularly appropriate for weddings. Rather similar is gota, gold or silver thread lace in the form of a tape. Also zardozi is embroidery using small coloured beads.

Zarijoota: slipper of traditional Muslim pattern, richly embroidered in gold or silver. Tested zari: a trade term for brass or copper thread gilded so as to resemble precious metal.

ZĒBU *n* English
A word coined by the French naturalist, Buffon, for the Bos indicus, the original domestic ox of India, distinguished by its hump. Most of the animals, with some exceptions, are of no specific breed and carry the generic name of scrub cattle.

ZENĀNA *n* Urdu
Relating to women (zan, Persian for a woman). When used with reference to a male, a meaning of an effeminate one, an impotent one, a transvestite (*see* Hijra.).

Zenana Khana (often, just zenana): portion of a house set apart for women and children. (The part reserved for men is the mardana. In New Delhi's social world, 'a zenana-mardana party' means a gathering at which the sexes spontaneously separate into exclusive groups.) Coupled sometimes with zenana is the Hindi word deorhi, in the context of a mansion or palace, the area where begums and ladies could receive visitors (feminine). (*see* Kothi and Haram).

ZERO *n*
While conclusive proof has yet to be found, it is almost certain that the great contribution to world progress in numeration using nine digits and a zero symbol, was invented in India early in the Christian era: later taken to the Muslim Middle-East and Europe with the name, Arabic numerals. In the European dark ages (500-1100 AD), Andalusia, Islamic Southern Spain, was a centre of world science. **Aryabhata**, the **Hindu** mathematician of the 5th century AD, seems to have been aware of the system. So far, there is no memorial to the unknown mathematician-inventor save the universal use of his inspiration. Extended today by the binary system of notation.

In ancient India, as today in Hindi, zero was called shunya/ sunya, and also **bindu** – the spot. (*see* Tika. Originally, the symbol was just a dot, as it still is in Arabic and Urdu. 13th century Europe surrounded the dot with a circle to make it a similar size to the other numerals: later, the dot was left out. The modern Hindi zero is a small circle). Shunya became sifa in Arabic – and in Urdu – which became both cipher and zero in English. (For some, shunya—nothing, infinite space – can represent the supreme Godhead.) Poetically, shunya can be an emptiness, as of a desert: a void. Road distances from Delhi on the 'milestones' are measured in kilometres with the zero point at Rajghat, the **samadhi** of **Mahatma** Gandhi.

Altitudes are calculated from the Survey of India average of Mean Sea Level, established over many years' readings at some fourteen port stations on the east and west coasts.

In the European dark ages (500-1100AD) Andalusia, Islamic Sourthern Spain (the name derives from the Vandals) was the centre of world science. Christian Europe's reaction was to eject the Muslims and an action giving the greatest satisfaction to the Church, the destruction by fire of Islam's – and Europe's – treasure, the library of Granada. Centuries earlier the no less celebrated library of Alexandria had been destroyed by Islam.

ZIMMI *n* Urdu
From Arabic. Strictly, a non-Muslim,

but being a Christian or **Jew**, a person of the Book, see Kitab, permitted to live and to receive protection as a citizen, in a Muslim state. But in India, the term can be applied to, say, a **Hindu** living in a Muslim dominated village.

ZINDĀBAD interjection Urdu
Used as a slogan following the name of a person, or of a people, or of a nation, meaning 'Long Live...' The converse is '...Murdabad', 'Death to...' 'Down with...'

ZOOLUM/ZULAM *n* Urdu, from Arabic
Tyranny, oppression. Also mayhem and hooliganism.

ZONAL COUNCIL *n*
High level advisory body providing a forum for discussion of matters affecting areas larger than states: e.g., Haryana, Himachal Pradesh,Jammu &: Kashmir, Punjab and Delhi send delegates to the northern zone council. But it has to be admitted that these councils are far from active today (1996).

Index of words from the text not being Headwords

Ajanta Caves	Yadav	Ambedkar, Dr. B.R.	Mahars
Ajlaf	Mohur		Neo-Buddhists
Ajwain	Ajvan	Ambi	Diwan
Akal Takht	Sikh		Paisley Pattern
Akbar	A'in-Allah-	Ambika	Shakti
	Akbar	Ambrosia	Amrit
Akbarnama	A'in-i-Akbari	Amchur	Mango
	Nama		Tamarind
Akhil	Akhand	Ameer	Amir
Aksha	Rudraksh	Amhurst, Lord	Hills,The
Al	Allah	Amir Khusro	Tabla
Alaka	Kailas	Amma	Abba
Alams	Muharram	Ammar	Shakti
Albuquerque	Viceroy	Ammonite	Saligram
Alexander	Greeks, The	Amulet	Bismillah
	Sikander		Cummerbund
Ali	Hijra		Koh-i-Noor
Aligarh	AMU		Raksha
	Koil	Anandpur Sahib	Khalsa
	Pyjama		Nihang
Alishan	Maha	Ananta	Vishnu
Allahabad	Abad	Anar/Anarkali	Baluster Pillar
	Prayag	Anchal	Bazaar
	Sangam	Anchor	Langar
Aloe	Agarbatti	Andalusia	Zero
Alpana	Rangoli	Andaman Islands	Kala
Alta	Henna	Andhra Pradesh	A.P.
Alvi	Sayid	Andolan	Namak
Am/Ambi	Diwan		Swadesh
Amah	Ayah	Andrews C.F.	Din
Amalaka	Amla	Andropogan	
Aman	Shanti	muricatus	Khus
Amar Jyoti	Jyoti	Angan	Bal
Amar Sonar Bangla	Jana Gana		Bangla
	Mana	Angarkha	Kurta
Amavasya	Calendars	Angkor Wat	Banyan
	Purnima		Greater India
Ambar	Charkha	Angrez	Sahib
Ambassador	High Commi-	Angutha	Chhap
	ssioner	- ani	Sindhi
	Rajdoot	Aniline	Indigo

534

Animate, to	Pran	Arogya	Ayurveda
Aniseed	Saunf	Arora	Vaisya
Anjanakal	Kajal	Ar'q/Arrack	Country
Anjali	Namaskar		Liquor
Ankush	Mahout		Panchagaya
Anna DMK	DMK		Toddy
Annapurna	Kali	Arsenical trisulphide	Orpiment
Anta	Upanishad	Arthasastra	Chanakya
Antelope	Nilgai		Shastras
Antim	Snan	Artocarpus integra	Jackfruit
Antimacassar	Kusum	Arun/Arunachal	North-East
Antimony	Kajal	Pradesh	India
Anustan	Puja		Saffron
Aonla	Amla	Arvind	Lotus
Ap (Skt.)	Punjab	Aryan	Arya
Aparajita	Durga	Asad	Sher
Apothecary	Compounder	Asafoetida	Hing
	IMS	Asan	Chowk
Appalam/Appam	Poppadum		Lotus
Apple Juice	Cider		Yoga
Aquarius	Kumbh	Asati	Sati
Arabesque	Masjid	Ascetic	Tapas
Arakan	Mugg	Ashab	Sahib
Aram	Ram	Ash gourd	Petha
Arang	Gaddi	Ashok	Ahinsa
Aravali	Lakshadweep		Mauryan
Arcot	Carnatic		Period
Ardas	Sikh	Ashok Capital	Chakra
Ardhanarishwara	Shiva	Ashok Chakra	Defence
Ardh Kumbh	Kumbh		Services
Areca	Pan		Awards
	Supari	Ashrafi	Mohur
Argentum	Gita	Ashura	Muharram
Arhar Dal	Dal	Ashvatth	Peepal
	Idli	Ashvavara	Sowar
Aridha	Reetha	Asian	Anglo-Indian
Aril	Jaiphal	ASP	SP
Arjuna	Arjuna Awards	Assalam	Salaam
	Dharma	Assam Mirch	Mirch
	East India Co.	Astami	Janmastami
	Gita	Astrology	Jyotish

	Uttarayana	Azadari	Muharram
Asura (Hindi)	Kumbh	Azam	G.T. Road
Asura (Urdu)	Muharram		Moguls
Aswin	Dussehra		Wazir
Ataturk, Kemal	Khilafat	Azimabad	Patliputra
Atithi	Guest	Aztec	Curry
Ati Vishist Sewa	Defence		Mirch
Medal	Services	Baag / Baghi	Bargadar
	Awards		Bagh
Atlas of India	GTS		Dacoit
Aubergine	Brinjal		
Auchinleck, Field	Azad Hind	Baajuband	Cummerbund
Marshal	Fauj		Koh-i-Noor
Aul	Baul	Babblers	Bhai
Auliya	Chisti		Brain Fever
Aum	Om		Bird
Auqf	Waqf	Babur	Moguls
Aurang	Gaddi		Sultanates of
Aurangabad	Moguls		Delhi
	Gaddi	Baburnama	Nama
Aurat	Nar	Backward Classes	Harijan/Dalit
Aurora	Vedas	Bactria	Greeks, The
Auspicious	Shiva	Badhai	Hijras
	Swastika	Badralok	Bhaddralok
Austric	Adivasis	Badshah	Shah
	Dravidia		Taj
	Greater India	Bael	Rudraksh
Autar	Avatar	Bagan	Bagh
Avadh	Oudh		IST
Avalokiteshvara	Om	Bahadur Shah Zafar	Moguls
Avdhoot	Anand	Bahangi	Dak
Avla	Amla	Bahini	Vahini
Axis Deer	Chital	Bahujan	Harijan/Dalit
Ayacut	Anicut	Bai	Bahen
Ayana	Calendars	Baig/Baigmat	Beg
	Uttarayana	Baiji	Bahen
Ayatollah	Sunni		Dancing Girls
Ayodhya	Divali	Baingan	Brinjal
	Oudh	Bairagi	Sadhu
	Ram	Bairam	Id
	Ramayana	Bajrang	Hanuman

536

Baker, Sir Herbert	High Commissioner		Panchama
		Barbel	Mahseer
Baking Powder	Bicarbonate of soda	Barbet	Coppersmith
		Bard	Baul
Bak'r Id	Id		Pichchawa
Bakriwals	Gaddis	Barelvi/Brelvi	Ulema
Balak	Bai	Bargad	Banyan
Balakrishna	Bal Krishna	Bargi	Bargadar
Bali	Greater India	Bari	Bal
Balidan	Dussehra		Kali
Bālkan	Bal		Rag
Balmiki	Valmiki	Bark	Tonic
Balsa Wood	Sola	Barley	Jau
Balti	Curry	Baroda	Gaekwar
Balvadi	Bal	Barnshoot	Bahen
Ban	Charpai	Barsi	Shraddh
Banarsi	Vakar	Bartan wala	Kabari
	Varanasi	Barua	Mugg
Banbas	Ashram	Basil	Tulsi
Bandana	Band	Basileus	Raj
Bandar Log	Log	Basilisk	Gecko
Bandhini	Band	Basin	Besan
Bandgala	Jodhpurs	Basohli	Pahari
Bandung Conference	Panshil	Bas-relief	Chittr
Banerji, Hemchandra	Bande Materam	Bassein	Ophir
		Bat	Banyan
Banga Bhanga	Independence Day	Batakh	Hip
		Batasha	Prasad
Bangan	Brinjal	Batata	Alu
Banged Up	Indian Hemp	Bangalore Torpedo	Tipu Sultan
Bangri	Bangle	Batua	Pan
Bangy-dak	Dak	Bayan	Tabla
Banns	Bhan	Bawa	Baba
Banta	Kanchiwala Botal	Bawari	Baoli
		Bari	Baoli
Bansari/Bansi	Krishna	Bayadere	Devadasi
Bapre bap	Bapu	Bayleaf	Tejpat
Bara	Idli	Bayram	Id
Baradari	Biradari	Beas R.	Greeks, The
Baramasa	Calendars	Beebi	Bibi
Barbarian	Jungle	Beecham's Pills	Gol

Beena	Veena	Bhapa	Sikh
Begum	Beg	Bharal	Mutton
Begum of Bhopal	Sultan	Bharat Milap	Dussehra
Be-halal	Halal	Bharatiya Jnanpith	Gyan
Behan	Bahen	Bharatpur	Jat
Bekar	Kar	Bhaskara	Vedas
	Garib	Bhasha	Ahinsa
Bekti	Bhetki		Vernacular
Bel	Mistri	Bhasma	Ash
	Rudraksh	Bhat	Dal
Bengal Cat	Bangla	Bhatijavad	Bhai
Bengal Light	Bangla	Bhatts	Dharna
Bengal Mud	Bangla	Bhatura	Puri
Ben Oil	Drumsticks	Bhed/Bher	Mutton
Beni Israel	Jews	Bhelpuri	Puri
Bentinck, Lord	Durbar	Bhendi	Peepal
Beriberi	Kwashiorkor	Bhik	Baksheesh
Besant, Dr. Annie	Jana Gana Mana	Bhils	Adivasi
	Theosophy	Bhindi	Ladies'
Betel	Pan		Fingers
Bewick's Swans	Kailas	Bhisti	Bihisti
Bhabar	Terai	Bhoi	Boy
Bhabhuti	Ash	Bholanath	Kanwar
Bhadra Jan	Bhadralok	Bhonsle	Chhatrapati
Bhadramahila	Bhadralok	Bhoodan/Bhudan	Bhumi
Bhadon	Janmastami	Bhoot	Rakshasa
Bhagat	Bhakti	Bhopa	Pichchawa
Bhagavati	Bhagwan	Bhopal	Bhumi
	Dev		Madhya
Bhagirathi R.	Ganga		Pradesh
Bhagwa	Bhagwan		Pan
	Saffron		Shat
Bhai Duj	Divali		Sultan
Bhairon	Bhairavi	Bhrata	Bhai
Bhajan	Kirtan	Bhujiya	Namak
Bhaji	Sabzi	Bhukamp	Bhumi
Bhakra Dam	Sagar	Bhumidar	Bhumi
Bhandara	Langar	Bhumiputra	Bhumi
Bhang	Indian Hemp	Bhushan	Civilian Awards
Bhangi	Sweeper	Bhutan	Dragon
	Valmiki		Kingdom

Bhuta	Rakshasa	Body	Jism
Bibhuti	Ash	Bodo/Boro	Eri
Bidonville	JJ Colony	Bokhara	Alu
Bihar	Oriya		Imam
	Vihara	Bombay	Mumbai
Bijli	Ghat	Bombay Bowler	Sola Topi
Bijoya Dashami	Duga Puja	Bombay Marine	East Indiamen
	Dussehra		Presidencies
Bikku	Bhikshu	Bombay Mix	Namak
Bilsa	Tope	Bommelo	Bombay Duck
Binaula	Kapok	Bonded Labour	Begar
Bindaloo	Vindaloo	Bone	Asth
Bindas	Mast	Bone Setter	Akhara
Bindi	Bindu	Bong	Bangla
Bin Sitar	Sitar	Bonnet Monkey	Bandar
Biogas	Gobar		Hanuman
Bir	Guru Granth	Bon Vivant	Bhog
	Sahib	Book	Daftar
Bira	Pan		Guru Granth
Bird Chillies	Mirch		Sahib
Biri	Bidi		Kitab
Birla House	Smriti	Boondi	Hanuman
Biryani	Pulao	Boora	Shakkr
Bishnoi	Chipko	Boro (Crop)	Aman
Bison	Gaur	Borrow, George	Rai
Bitora	Gobar	Bose, Subash	Azad Hind Fauj
BJP	RSS	Chandra	
Black Buck	Cheetah	Bos grunniens	Yak
Black Cotton Soil	Deccan	Bos indicus	Zebu
Black Gold	Green Whisky	Botanic Garden	Roxb.
Black Market	Kala	Boteh	Paisley Pattern
Black Town	Civil Lines	Bo Tree	Peepal
Blighty	Bilait	Braces	Galis
Blochmann H.	A'in-i-Akbari	Bracelet	Bangle
Blue Bull/Cow	Nilgai	Brahmana	Vedas
	Shiva	Brahmanda	Lingam
Blue Jay	Indigo	Brahmaputra	Bangla
Blue Pottery	Multani Mitti		Brahma
Bobbery Bob	Bapu	Brahmi	Dev
Bodh	Buddha		Sanskrit
	Vihara	Brahmrandhr	Brahma

539

Braised Meat	Roghan Josh	Byamshala	Akhara
Braj	Janmastami		
Brassica	Sarson	Cafila	Caravan
Breakfast	Hazri	Caffre	Kafir
Bribe	Hafta	Cagots	Harijan/Dalit
	Nazrana	Caju	Kaju
Brick	Nai	Cakravartin	Chakrabarty
Brihan	Mumbai	Caladium	Arvi
Brindian	Sahib	Calcutta	Kali
Brinjarries	Banjaras		Viceroy
British German	European	Calico/Calicut	Zamorin
Legion	Cemeteries	Calimore, Point	Coromandel
British Indians	Anglo-Indians	Caliph	Khilafat
Brocade	Kimkhob	Calligraphy	Masjid
	Zari	Caltrop	Singara
Brother	Bhai	Campani Bagh	John Company
Brown Flour	Atta	Camphire	Henna
Buck	Bakwas	Campion Hall,	Delhi Order
Buckshi	Baksheesh	Oxford	
Buddh/Buddhu	Buddha	Canal	Nala
Buddha Purnima	Buddha	Canarese	Carnatic
	Purnima	Candala	Panchama
Budhwar	Buddha	Candy	Kandy
Buffalo Chips	Gobar	Candy (sugar)	Shakkr
Buffon	Zebu	Cannabis	Indian Hemp
Buggy	Carrying		Shiva
	Chairs	Canning, Lady	Lady Kenny
Bundar	Bandar	Canning, Lord	Viceroy of India
Bundobust	Bandobast	Cantt.	Cantonment
Bungalow	Bangla	Cape Comorin	Kumari
Bura	Shakkr	Cape Gooseberry	Ras
Burqa	Burkha	Capricorn	Uttarayana
Burra/Bara	Peg	Capsicum	Mirch
	Sahib	Caracal	Cheetah
Burton, Sir Richard	Kama	Caracul Sheep	Topi
Bustard, Great Indian	Sarus	Carapace	Raksha
Butea frondosa	Flame of the	Carat	Bazaar Weights
	Forest	Cardamom	Elaichi
Butter	Krishna	Cardinal Points	Deccan
Buttocks	Hip	Carnauba	Lac
Buxar	East India Co.	Carob	Bazaar Weights

Cashew	Kaju
Cassia fistula	Amaltas
Castor	Musk
Catholikos	Mar
Cats	Saturday
Cauvery	Kaveri
Cawnpur	Kanpur
Cayenne Pepper	Mirch
Celibacy	Brahmacharya
	Hanuman
Centem	Shat
Central Provinces	Madhya Pradesh
	Maharastra
	Vidharba
Ceylon	British India
Ch.	Chaudhri
	Chiranjivi
Chach	Dahi
Chaddi/Chudies	Underwear
Chador	Chaddar
Chai	Char
Chaitanya	Vishnu
Chakkar	Chukka
Chakkliya	Chamars
Chamach	Chamcha
Chamba Roomal	Roomal
Chamber of Princes	Princes
Chambhars	Chamars
Chameli/Champa	Pagoda
	Yasmin
Champagne	Simkin
Champi	Maleesh
Chamra	Chamar
Chand	Soma
Chandan	Haldi
Chandela	Manu
	Panchama
Chandi/Chandni	Chand Kali
Chandragupta	Mauryan

	Period
	Chanakya
Chandu	Madak
Chank	Conch
Channa	Dal
Chaoni	Cantonment
Chapkan	Achkan
Chaplain	Metropolitan
	Padri
Character	Charitr
Charan	Dahi
	Pichchawa
Charas	Indian Hemp
Char Bagh	Bagh
Char Dewari	Purdah
Charch	Dahi
Charisma	Karishma
Charit	Ramayana
Charri	Shiva
Char Sau Bis	Four Twenty
Chatti	Chagul
Chatni	Chaat
Chattak	Bazaar Weights
Chatterjee/Chattopadhya	Rai
Chaturvarn	Caste Hindus
Chaturvedi	Vedas
Chaube	Vedas
	HIP
Chaudhri, Nirad C.	Wish
Chaugan	Polo
Chauki	Chowk
Chauri/Chowri	Guru Granth Sahib
	Yak
Cheel	Pariah
Cheers	Ullas
Chela	Guru
Chelum	Munarrum
Chelmsford, Lord	Dyarchy
	Viceroy

Chennai	Madras	Chitral	Great Game, The
Cheque/Check	Shah	Chittr	Kathak
Chess	Shah	Chlorodyne	Indian Hemp
Chetak	Mewar	Cholera	European
Chettinad	Chettiyars		Cemetaries
Chettri	Kshatriya		Pinky Pani
Chhakka	Hijras		Solar Topi
Chhana	Burfi	Choori	Bangle
	Dahi	Chop	Chhap
	Khoya	Chor	Bazaar
Chhink	Sneezing	Chosgyal	Chogyal
Chhipkali	Chipko	Chotu	Chokra
	Gecko	Chotanagpur	Jharkhand
Chhota/Chota	Dhaba	Chuchunder	Ganesh
	Hazri	Chuckler	Chamar
	Peg	Chudiyan	Bangle
	Pice	Chungi	Octroi
Chhotolok	Bhaddralok	Chunni/Chunri	Dupatta
Chicanery	Polo	Chupati	Chapati
Chick Pea	Dal	Churas	Maza
Chicle	Chiku		Mazabi Sikhs
Chiefs	Gun Salutes	Churchill, Winston	Princes
Chikitsa	Shastras	Churidar Pyjama	Pyjama
Chikna	Namak	Churki	Choti
Child Marriage	Sarda Act	Churning of the	Amrit
Restraint Act		Ocean	Lakshmi
Chilli	Curry		Shiva
	Mirch	Chutila	Shoe
Chillum	Hookah	Chutney	Chaat
Chilman	Chicks	Cid	Habshi
China Orange	Kumquat	Cinchona	Tonic
Chinese Parsley	Dhania	Cinnamon	Tejpat
Chini	Shakkr	Cipher	Zero
Chini Ghas	China Grass	Citric acid	Tonic
Chinkara	Chital	City of Light	Jyoti
	Sneezing	Civet Cat	Toddy
Chinnamasta	Kali	Civil/Civilian	Indian Civil
Chintz	Cheetah		Service
Chip	Rupee	Civil Surgeon	District
Chiragh/Chiraagh	Diya		IMS
Chiranjiv	Kama	Clive, Robert Lord	Ava

	East India Co.	Confederacy	Maharashtra
	Flame of the	Congreve Rocket	Tipu Sultan
	Forest	Conjee	Kanji
Closepet	Charnokite	Connaught Rangers	European
Clove	Laung		Cemeteries
CNSL	Kaju	Connolly,	Great Game, The
Coastline	Bazaar	Capt.	Author
Cobra	Vishnu	Constantinople	Islam
Coccidea	Lac	Constitution of	Harijan/Dalit
Cochin	Jews	India, 1950	Mahar
Cochineal	Lac		Section 93
Cockatrice	Gecko		Province
Cock up	Bhekti		Sikh
Coconut	Hookah	Constituent	Dyarchy
Coconut Oil	Sarson	Assembly	
Code Napoleon	Renoncant	Continental Divide	Plains, The
Coffee	Kahwa		Yamuna
Coffle	Caravan	Contour Bunding	Bund
Coffre/Caffree	Kafir	Cooking Medium	Vanaspati
Cognisance	Vahan	Coolie	Mazdoor
Cognizable Offence	Cr. PC	Cooling Foods	Heating Foods
Cola	Chola	Copal	Lac
Coldstream Guards	Chowk	Copra	Coir
Colic	Solar Topi	Corbett National	Mugger
Colocaria esculenta	Arvi	Park	
Colony	Niketan	Coriander	Dhania
Colza Oil	Sarson	Coriaria nepalensis	Mansuri
Commander of	Momin	Cornwallis, Lord	Settlement
the Faithful		Cornucopia	Kumbh
Commiphora	Agarbatti	Corruption	Bhrastata
Comorin, Cape	Kumar	Corundum	Carborundum
Companions	Qurayshi	Cosmic Egg	Lingam
	Sahib		Star of India
Company, The	Bagh	Coss	Koss
	East India Co.	Costus	Kuth
	John Co.	Cot	Charpai
Company Art	John Co.	Coucal	Subaltern's
Compassion,	Om		Pheasant
Buddha of		Council of India	Hobson-Jobson
Comprador	Bania	Council of States	Rajya Sabha
Condom	Nirodh	Country Liquorice	Bazaar Weights

Courtesan of Lucknow	Hindustan	Crow Pheasant	Subaltern's Pheasant
Cousin-brother	Bhai	Crown	CRP
Covelong	Coromandel	Representative	Paramountcy
Cow/Cattle	Cowdust-time		Princes
	Gaekwar		Viceroy of India
	Ganga	Cryer	Azaan
	Gaur	CT	Criminal
	Gobar		Tribes
	Gopi	Cuddalore	Coromandal
	Goshala	Cumin	Dhania
	Gotra	Cunningham, General	Tope
	Gous	Sir Alexander	
	Nandi	Cuon	Dhole
	Nilgai	Cupid	Kama
	Raksha		Shalimar
	Yadava	Curcuma	Haldi
	Zebu	Curd	Dahi
Cow-belt	Hindustan	Curfew	Section 144
Cowrie	Kourie	Currency Notes	Rupee
C.R.	Rajaji		Takka
Cranny	Anglo-Indian	Curtain	Purdah
Creamy Layer	Harijan-Dalit	Curzon, Lord	Bande
Cremation	Ghat		Mataram
Crescent Moon	Islam		Dandi
Crew	Kar		Durbar
Crim Con	Criminal Tribes		Independence
Crimean War	European		Day
	Cemeteries		Viceroy of India
Criminal Proceedure	Cr. PC	Cuscuta	Akash
Code		Cushy	Khush
Crims	Criminal Tribes	Custard Apple	Chiku
Crimson Lake	Lac	Cutch	Mangrove
Cripps, Sir Stafford	Dyarchy	Cutchery	Kutchery
Crocodile	Ganga	Cyamopsis	Gaur
	Mugger	Cyclone	Toofan
	Nihang	Cymbals	Kirtan
Crocus sativus	Saffron		
Croissants	Islam	Dabba Wala	Tiffin
Crossing over	Fasting	Dacca/Daccai	Flame of the Forest

	Jamdani	Daru	Sharab
	Mugg		Wine
Daffadar	Havildar	Dar ul Ulum	Ulema
Dagga	Tabla	Darzi	Durzi
Dagoba	Pagoda	Dasa/Dasi/Dasyus	Adivasi
Dagshai	European		Bharat
	Cemeteries		Devadasi
Daivika	Gandharv	Dasain	Dussehra
Dakait	Dacoit	Dasami Dar	Brahma
Dakaut	Saturday	Dasam Granth	Guru Granth
Dakhma	Dokma		Sahib
Dakia	Dak	Dasiatam	Bharat
Dakshin/	Deccan	Das Nambar Admi	Number Ten
Dakshinapath		Dastaar	Puggri
Dakshinayana	Uttarayana		Sikh
Daku	Dacoit	Dastakar/Dastakhat	Kar
Dalan	Masjid	Dastur	Parsi
Dalchini	Tejpat	Datoon	Akhrot
Dalhousie, Lord	Doctrine of		Neem
	Lapse	Datura	Dhatura
	Koh-i-noor	Daughter	Sanskrit
Dalia	Harijan/Dalit	Daulatabad	Yadav
Dalit	Harijan/Dalit	DAV	Arya
Dalip Singh,	Koh-i-noor	David	Daud
Maharaja		Dawk	Dak
Daly, James	European	Dawn	Gayatri
	Cemeteries		Vedas
Dam/Damn	Cash	Dawoodi Bohra	Bohra
Damascene	Bidri	Day	IST
	Jauhar	Daya	Sarvodaya
Damma	Dharma	Day of Triple	Peepal
Dan	Da	Blessing	Purnima
Dandi	Carrying Chairs	Dayabhaga	Mitakshara
Danger	Khatra	Dayanand Saraswati	Arya
Danphe	Impeyan	Death	Amrit
	Pheasant		Mar
'dar as suffix	Zamindar	Deedar	Darshan
Darbar	Durbar	Deeg	Jat
Darchini	Tejpat	Deen	Din
Daridranarayan	Vishnu	Deep/Deepak/	Diva
Darjeeling	Dorje	Deepam	

545

Deepavali	Divali	Dharmaraj	Yama
Deh	Jism	Dhanush	Inder
Dehati	Gaon	Dhari	Pyjama
Dehra Dun	Dun	Dharti Maa	Shakti
	Gorkha	Dhat	Vir
	Uttaranchal	Dhela	Pice
Delonix regia	Gul Mohur	Dhoban	Dhobi
Demchok	Kailas	Dholavira	Indus Valley
DEN	XEN		Civ.
Denmark	Coromandel	Dhooli	Carrying Chairs
Denotified Tribe	Criminal Tribes	Dhoop	Agarbati
Deoband	Ulema	Dhri	Dharma
Deogiri	Yadav	Dhrupad	Rag
Deolali/Devlali	Doolaly	Dhulandi	Holi
Deorhi	Zenana	Dhun	Rag
Depressed Classes	Harijan		Razai
Dera	Bhog	Dhunai/Dhunkar	Razai
	Camp	Dhurrie	Duree
	Gurdwara	Dhvaja/Dvaja	Chakra
	Namdhari Sikhs		Lat
Desai	Patel	Dhyan	Samadhi
Desert Cooler	Khus	Diarchy	Dyarchy
Desi	Desh	Dibbawala	Tiffin
Devaki	Krishna	Diclofenac	Dokma
	Janmastami	Digambar	Jainism
Devavani	Sanskrit	Dighi	Tank
Devil's Wind	First War of	Digvijay	Vijay
	Indepen-	Diksha	Janeu
	dence	Dinesh	Gayatri
Devnagri	Dev	Dipper (constellation)	Rishi
	Sanskrit	Disaster	Jyotish
Dewan	Diwan	Disha	Dhruv
Dexter	Deccan	District Magistrate	Collector
DFO	District Forest	Ditchers	Mulligatawny
	Officer	Divine Dancer	Nataraj
Dhak/a	Flame of the	Divorce	Talaq
	Forest	Dixie	Degshi
	Mugg	Dixit	Diksha
Dhan	Divali	Djinn	Rakshasa
	Paddy	Dodder	Akash
Dhanteras	Divali	Doi	Dahi

Doka	Carrying Chairs	Dvip/Dwip	Bharat
Doli/Dooli	Carrying Chairs	Dwarka	Krishna
Dolly	Dali		Math
Dollar	Rupees	Dwarpal	Kubera
Dolphin	Ganga		Nandi
Dolyatra	Holi	Dwivedi	Vedas
Doomba	Hobson-Jobson	Dyer, Brig. General	Jallianwala Bagh
Doonga	Houseboat	Dyewood	Sandalwood
Door	Duree	Dzo	Yak
	Gurdwara	Earth (soil)	Multani Mitti
	Har	Earth (planet)	Vedas
	Terai	Earth Mother	Shakti
Doordarshan	Akash	Easter	Calendars
Dopatta	Dupatta	East Indian	Anglo-Indian
Dopehar	Calendars	Eaves	Chajja
Dorai	Sahir	Ebony	Bidri
Double Roti	Roti	Eclipse	Gayatri
Doyle's Disease	Ranikhet	Eed	Id
Dri	Yak	Eelam	Shri
Driver	Syce	Egg Plant	Brinjal
Drukpa/Druk Yul	Dragon Kingdom	Eire	Arya
		Ekadashi	Fasting
Drum (Architecture)	Gumbaz	Ekalaviya	East India Co.
Duars	Terai	Ektara	Baul
Dubashi	Bania	Elaceocarpas ganitrus	Rudraksh
Dube(y)	Vedas	Electricity	Shakti
Ducks	Bombay Duck	Elephant	Mahout
Dufferin, Lord	Ava	Elephant's Ears	Arvi
Duggi	Baul	Eliot, T.S.	Shanti
Duhita	Sanskrit	Ellenborough, Lord	East India Co.
Duj	Divali	Embilica officinalis	Amla
Dulband	Puggri	Emir	Amir
Dumb Doll	Gungi Gudiya	Encampment	Camp
Dumru	Damaru		Cantonment
Durani	Sindhi	Endi	Eri
Durham Blanket	Razai	Engagement	Sagai
Dussehra	Dashain	Entrails	Antar
Dustak	Kar	Eshwar	Isa
Dutch East India Co.	Coromandel		Shiva
		Essence	Attar
Duvet	Razai	Eunuchs	Hijras

	Khoja	Fil	Mahout
Eurasian	Anglo-Indian	Filmigeet	Geet
	Chi-Chi	Finger Millet	Ragi
	Country-Made	Finnish Ugaric	Sanscrit
Eve	Muharram	Fire, respect for	Havan
Everest	Chomolungma	Fire Temple	Parsi
	Sagar	Flag March	Section 144
	Sherpa	Flamboyant	Gul Mohur
Exchequer	Shah	Flame Tree	Gul Mohur
		Flamingo	Hans
Factor	Factory		Rann
	Writer	Flattery	Chamcha
Fagin, Mrs	Koh-i-Noor		Malish
Fakir/Faqir	Dervish	Flatus	Dal
Faluda	Kulfi	Flute	Krishna
Family Planning	Star of India	Flip-flops	Chappals
Faridkot	Phulkian States	Flora Indica	Roxb.
Fanam	Pagoda	Flood, The	Nuh
Farshi Salaam	Pahile Aap	Fontanelle	Brahma
Farzi	Parsi		Choti
Father	Sanskrit	Foreign Liquor	Wine
Fatima	Sunni	Foreign & Political	Politicals
Fauj/Fouj	Azad Hind Fauj	Service	
FCs	Harijan	Forest	Jungle
Federation (GOI	Princes	Forster, E.M.	Ganga
Act, 1935)			Pan
Feet	Baithak		Passage to India
	Kor'an		SP.
	Pug	Fort St. David	Coromandel
	Shoes	Fort St. George	Madras
	Shudra		Yale
Feni	Kaju	Frangipane /	Pagoda
Fennel	Saunf	Frangipani	
Fenugreek	Methi	Frank	Feringi
Ferula	Hing	Freedom Fighter	Bagh
Fez	Topi		First War of
Ficus benghalensis	Banyan		Independence
Ficus elastica	India	French Marigolds	Mala
Ficus krishnae	Krishna	Friday	Masjid
Ficus religiosa	Peepal	Fuller's Earth	Multani Mitti
Fiftis	Puggri	Fylfot	Swastika

		Gargoyle	Gali
Gabriel	Kor'an	Gari	Gharry
Gadi	Gharry	Garland	Mala
Gaj	Mahout		Rag
Gajar	Halwa	Garlic	Lahsan
Gajendra	Mahout	Garuda	Vahan
Gajra	Mala		Vishnu
Gala	Gali	Gauche	Right hand
	Jodhpurs		Left hand
Galena	Kajal	Gauhati	Guwahati
Gamcha	Dhoti	Gauri/Gouri	Parbat
Gamete	Gaman		Shakti
Gantantra	Tantra	Gavaksha	Chaitya
Gana(pati)	Ganesh	Gavial/Garial	Mugger
Ganda Nala	Nal	Gayak	Rag
Gandhi, Indira	Charnokite	Gayal	Gaur
	Emergency, The	Gazal	Ghazal
Gandhi, Mahatma	Bapu	Gazelle	Chital
	Dandi	Geeta	Gita
	Harijan	Gelatine	Babul
	Jallianwala Bagh		Halal
	Khadi	Gemini	Maithuna
	Khilafat	Gendamala	Mala
	Mahatma		Sehra
	Republic Day	Genii	Rakshasa
	Sarvodaya	Genitals	Jan
	Satya	Gentoo	Hindu Code
	Topi	George V. King	Dandi
Ganga Dhara	Shiva	Emperor	Durbar
Ganges R.	Ganga		Patliputra
Gangetic Dolphin	Ganga	German Legion	European
Gangotri	Ganga		Cemeteries
Ganikaa	Dancing Girls	Gerua	Saffron
Ganja	Indian Hemp	Ghalughara	Blue Star
Ganji	Bania	Ghara	Chagul
Ganna	Shakkr		Mugger
Gaomukh	Ganga	Gharana	Rag
	Rudraksh	Gharial	Mugger
Garbagriha	Mandir	Gharwala	Wala
Garden Reach	Roxb.	Ghaut	Ghat
Gargle	Gali	Ghazipur	Madak

Ghiaspur	Chisti		Krishna
Ghoos	Bandicoot	Gold Colour	Orpiment
Ghora/i	Gora	Golden Shower	Amaltas
Ghoti	Bangla	Golden Temple	Amrit
Ghulam Kadir	Rohillas		Durbar
Ghunghat	Dupatta		Frontier Mail
Ghungroo	Kathak		Sikh
Ghus	Bandicoot		Shoe
(a bribe)	Hafta	Gold Mohur	Gul Mohur
Gian	Gyan		Mohur
Gilheri	Palm Squirrel	Golgappa	Puri
Gingelly Oil	Til	Goli	Gol
Ginger	Adrak	Gomateshwara	Jainism
	Barasingha	Gondh	Babul
	Haldi	Gonds/	Adivasis
Gippy Tummy	Delhi Belly	Gondwanaland	Deccan
Gir Forest	Kathiawar	Goo	Gu
Girijan	Harijan/Dalit	Good Morning	Pranam
	Pahari		Wish
Giriraj	Himalaya	Goose	Hans
Gitanjali	Gita	Gooseberry	Amla
Gitpit	Angrez		Ras
Glendoveer	Gandharv	Gopal	Gopi
Glucoside	Curry	Gope Ratna	Krishi
Goa	Anglo-Indian	Gopi Chandran	Caste Marks
	Kaju	Goraksha	Raksha
	Viceroy	Gorkhaholic	Gorkha
	Vindaloo	Gosadan	Goshala
Goad	Mahout	Gosain	Sadhu
Goat	Chagul	Gosht	Haram
Goat-meat	Mutton	Goswami	Swami
Gobind Sagar	Sagar	Got/Gota	Zar
Godaam	Godown	Governor-General	Rajaji
Godavari	Dravidia		Viceroy
	Ganga	Govinda	Gita
Godhuli	Cow Dust Time	Grahan	Gayatri
Goglet	Chagul	Gram (Pulse)	Besan
Gogra R. .	Ganga		Dal
GOI	Government	Grand Trunk Road	GT Road
Gokul	Holi	Granth (i)	Guru Granth
	Janmastami		Sahib

Great Bear (Constellation)	Rishi		Mazabi Sikhs Sikh
Greatcoat	Brandicoat	Guru Hargobind	Sikh
Great Trigonometrical Survey	GTS	Guru Ram Das Gutka	Guru Pan
Green	Haj	Gyalwa Rimpoche	Dalai Lama
Griha Lakshmi	Lakshmi	Gypsies	Banjaras
Grihastha	Ashram		Doms
Grille	Darshan	Haar	Har
Groundnut	Mungphalli		Lakh
Gudaliya Lohars	Gadis		Mala
Gudiya	Gungi/Gudiya	Habitual Criminal	Criminal Tribes
Guggal	Agarbati	Hackery	Chakra
Guides, The	Khaki	Hadith/Hadis	Kor'an
Gujjia	Indian Hemp	Hadji	Haj
Gulab	Attar	Hahnemann Shop	Allopathic Medicine
Gulab-Jamun	Lady Kenny		
Gulam	Ghulam	Haider/Hyder Ali	Tipu Sultan
Gulel	Gulal	Hajjam	Nai
Gules	Gulal	Halaku	Chengis Khan
Gum Arabic	Babul	Haldia	Caldia
	Flame of the Forest	Halhead	Hindu Code
		Handa	Degchi
Gunfire	Hazri	Hand Cooler	Lingam
Gunga Din	Bihisti	Handloom	Khadi
Gur	Shakkr	Hangul	Barasingha
Gurubani	Guru	Hans Raj	Arya
Gurguri	Hookah	Hansa	Hans
Gurj	Kesri	Hanu	Hanuman
Gurkha	Gorkha	Harappa	Indus Valley Civilisation
	Khud		
	Kukri	Hardwar	Har
	Line Boys	Hari	Har
Gurmat	Sikh	Haricot	Rajma
Gursikh	Guru	Harkara	Dak
Guru Amar Das	Langar	Harmandar Sahib	Amrit
Guru Gobind Singh	Akali	Hasan	Muharram
	Baisakhi	Hashish	Indian Hemp
	Guru Granth Sahib	Hasta	Mudra
		Hastings, Warren	Impeyan Pheasant

	Oudh	History Sheeter	Number Ten
	Viceroy	Hog Deer	Chital
Hat	Bazaar	Hom	Havan
Hatha Yoga	Yoga	Homeopathy	Allopathic
Hathi	Mahout		Medicine
Hauz	Tank	Honesty	Money Plant
Havelock	Solar Topi	Honey	Mead
Hawai	Chappals	Honey Wagon	Conservancy
Hawk Cuckoo	Brainfever Bird	Hong Kong	Government
Hawa	Muharram	Hooghly	Ganga
Hayat Baksh	Hayat		Roxb.
Hazrat Mahal	Oudh	Hooligan	Goonda
Head Constable	Havildar	Hope, Lawrence	Shalimar
Heart's Ease	Dil	Hoppers	Poppadum
HEICS	East India Co.	Horde	Khari Boli
	Indian Civil	Horn	Barasingha
	Service		Singhara
Hera Pheri	Number Two	Horoscope	Jyotish
Hepta	Hafta		Uttarayana
Henhouse	Gymkhana	Hortus bengalensis	Roxb.
Hexagram	Star of India	Houri	Hur
Hibiscus suculens	Ladies' Fingers	Housey-Housey	Jildi
Hijab	Burkha	Hriday	Nirmal
	Purdah	Hubble-Bubble	Hookah
Hijda	Hijra	Hukamnama	Sikh
	Purdah	Hulugu	Chengis Khan
Hijri	Ansar	Hunger Strike	Dharma
	Calendars	Huns/Hunas	Gupta Period
Hillock	Tope	Hunting Leopard	Cheetah
Himachal Pradesh	H.P.	Hurriana Light	Haryana
Himalayan Cedar	Deodar	Infantry	
Himsagar Express	Sagar	Hurricane	Toofan
Hinayana	Bhikku	Hussain	Sunnis
	Buddha		Muharrum
Hindi	Dev	Hu-tu-tu	Kabaddi
	Hindustan	Huxley, Aldous	Moksha
	Khari Boli	Hyderabad	AP
Hind Mahasagar	Sagar		Nizam
Hindustani	Hindustan		Pahile Aap
	Khari Boli		Paigah
Hinglish	Hindustani		Princes

Jagatguru	Math	Janma Bhumi	Bhumi
Jaggery	Shakkr	Jan Jagran	Jagrata
Jagmohan	Mandir	Janpad	Panchayat
Jagran	Jagrata	Janpad	Panchayat
Jail Bharo	Chukka	Jan Sarvai	Panchayat
Jaimala	Mala	Janta	Jan
Ja'i-namaz/Janamaz	Mihrab	Jap	Mantra
Jaipur	Jai	Jaratkari	Pietra Dura
	Jantar Mantar	Jariya	Kundan
Jai Singh	Jantar Mantar	Jasmine	Pagoda
Jal	Akash		Yasmin
	Jali	Jata (hair)	Jat
Jalapati	Varuna	Jatamansi	Agarbatti
Jaldi	Jildi	Jathedar	Jatha
Jalousie	Chicks	Jatni	Jat
Jalpan	Hazri	Jatra	Gita
Jam (wine)	Mushaira		Yattra
Jam (conserve)	Murabba	Javeri	Jauhar
Jam (stoppage)	Chukka	Javittr	Jaiphal
Jam Sahib	Raj	Jawahar	Jauhar
Jama	Cummerband	Jawala Mukhi	Akhand
	Pyjama	Jay, Blue	Indigo
Jamaat	Id		Shiva
Jamaat Khana	Ismailis	Jayadev	Baul
Jama Masjid	Masjid		Gita
Jamavar	Pyjama	Jeera	Dhania
Jambudvip	Bharat	Jehan	John Company
Jamiat-ul-Ulema	Ulema	Jelabi	Jalebi
Jamin	Zamindar	Jelly	Babul
Jampan	Carrying Chairs		Halal
Jamshed Navroz	Calendars	Jequirity	Bazaar Weights
Jamun	Lady Kenny	Jesuits' bark	Tonic
Jan	Begum	Jesuits' nut	Singara
Janaka	Maithila	Jesus Christ	Ahmedis
Janam Patri	Jyotish		Isa
Jand	Babul	Jewel in the Crown	Durbar
	Valmiki	Jhampani	Carrying Chairs
Jangal/Jangli Kutta	Dhole	Jhanki	Janmastami
Janghiya	Kachcha	Jhansi, Rani of	Bahen
Jang-i-Lat Sahib	Lat		Oudh
Jangli	Jungle	Jharoka	Darshan

Jharoowala	Sweeper	Julay	Namaskar
Jhil	Jheel	Julep	Attar
Jhilmil/Jillmil	Chicks	Jullundur	Jalandhar
Jhol	Soop	Juma	Masjid
Jhopad	JJ Colony	Jumna	Yamuna
Jhonpri	JJ Colony	Jung	Paigah
Jhotu	Jute	Jungli	Jungle
Jhuggi	JJ Colony	Junior Merchant	Writer
Jhula	Jhoola	Jura	Puggri
JIFS	HIFS		Shrivats
Jihad	Jehad	Jurisdiction Bill	Ilbert Bill
Jimson Weed	Dhatura	Ka'aba	Haj
Jina	Jainism		Mihrab
Jind	Phulkian States	Kaavach/Kavach	Raksha
Jinnah, Mohd. Ali	Khoja	Kabool	Salaam
	Qua'id-i-Azam	Kabuja/Kabuza	Musk
	Partition	Kachchhe	Rann
	Topi	Kachori/Kachauri	Puri
Jinriksha	Rickshaw		Samosa
Jira	Dhania	Kadir Cup	Khadar
Jiv	Atman	Kafila	Caravan
Jnana	Gyan	Kaftan	Caftan
	Yoga	Kaghazi Akhrot	Akhrot
JJBR	Ranachy	Kahar	Carrying Chairs
Job	Ayub		Kanwar
Jogini	Devdasi	Kaisar-i-Hind	Durbar
John	Yahya	Kak	Snan
Johnson, Lyndon	'One pen'	Kake	Kaka
Jolay	Namaskar	Kakkar's, the five	Sikh
Jomu	Gompa	Kalaingar/kalanyar/	Kala
Jooming	Jhuming	Kalakar	
Joota	Zar	Kalamdan	Kabristan
Jopad	JJ Colony	Kalangar	Paisley Pattern
Joseph	Yusuf	Kalava	Raksha
Joss Sticks	Agarbatti	Kalidasa	Calendars
Jot/Joth	La	Kalindi	Krishna
Judas Tree	Jacaranda		Yamuna
Judgement Day	Kitab	Kalinga	Utkal
Juggernaut	Jagannath	Kali	Indian Hemp
Jujube	Ber	Kali Puja	Divali
Julaha	Momin	Kalka/Kalkin	Vishnu

Kalma	Islam		Coir
Kamadev	Kama	Kapha	Dosha
	Shalimar	Kapur / Kapuri	Camphor
Kamal	Lotus	Kara/Kada	Bangle
Kamandal	Chagul		Sikh
Kamarband	Cummerbund	Karakul Sheep	Topi
Kama Sutra	Kama	Karamkand	Puja
	Shastras	Karbala	Muharrum
Kamban	Ramayana	Karchhi	Chamcha
Kambuja	Greater India	Kardi	Safflower
Kamdhenu	Amrit	Kari	Curry
Kamiz	Salwar Kamiz	Karigar	Kar
Kamkhwab	Kimkhob	Karim/Prince	Ismaili
Kamla	Lakshmi	Karkhana	Kar
	Lotus	Karma Bhumi	Karma
Kampani	Raj	Karmik	Kar
Kampong	Compound	Karnali R.	Kailash
Kanarese	Carnatic	Karnataka/Karnatic	Carnatic
Kan/Khan (Inn)	Khana	Karunda	Carborundum
Kanat	Shamiana	Karvan	Caravan
Kan Bhedi	Ear Cleaner	Karveh	Kahwa
Kanchi	Math	Kasai	Quraysh
Kandahar	Gandhara	Kasauti	Touchstone
Kandy	Carrying Chairs	Kashi/Kasi	Varanasi
Kandahar	Gandhara	Kashmir	Dogra
Kangha	Sikh		Princes
Kanhaiya	Krishna	Kashya	Cash
Kanishka	Greeks, The	Kasturba	Shrivats
Kanji	Lotus	Kasturi	Musk
Kan Mailiya	Ear Cleaner	Katcha	Kachcha
Kannada/	Carnatic	Kathal	Jack Fruit
Kannadiga		Kathmandu	Mandap
Kannauj	Attar		Gorkha
Kansa	Krishna	Kati	Teepoi
Kanthi	Khus	Katle-am	Blue Star
	Tulsi	Katori	Krishna
Kanungo	Qanungo		Thali
Kanwal	Lotus	Katra	Basti
Kanwaris	Kanwar	Katta/Katti	Country-made
Kanyakumari	Kumar	Kattha	Babul
Kapala	Aghori		Pan

Kattir	Brahman	Uttar
Kaul	Nala	Amrit
Kaur	Sikh	Khanda (weapon)
Kautilya	Chanakya	Khalsa
Kavaach	Raksha	Khandsari	Shakkr
Kaval Towns	Kabal Towns	Khanqah	Madrasa
Kavi (raj)	Ayurveda	Khanum/am	Khan
	Mushaira	Khap	Panchayat
Kavi Sammelan	Mushaira	Khari/kara	Namak
Kavishashtra	Shastras	Khas	Diwan
Kawaria	Kanwar		Khalsa
Kayasth	Kshatriya	Khas Khas	Khus
Kebabs	Kababs	Khat	Charpai
Kedarkhand/	Garhwal	Khatri	Bedi
Kedarnath		Khazanchi	Kshatriya
Keekar	Babul	Khel	Munim
Keema	Kofta	Khesari	Malik
Kelly, Sir George	Durbar	Khichri/Khichdi	Dal
Kendriya	Kendra		Kedgeree
Kendriya Karyakari	RSS	Khoi	Pongal
Mandal		Khopra	Bagasse
Kendu	Bidi	Khunki	Coir
Kerala	Malabar	Khush	Khedah
	Zamorin		Abad
Kermes	Lac		Cushy
Kes	Sikh	Khuswant Singh,	Dil
Kesar/Kesri	Saffron	Sardar	Hindustan
Keshav	Vishnu	Khwaja	Chisti
Keshdhari	Sikh	Kiang	Kyang
Keski	Puggri	Kibla	Mihrab
Ketchup	Chat	Kikar	Babul
Khaak	Khaki	Killick	Langar
Khad	Khud	Kila	Quila
Khadi Boli	Khari Boli	Kilta	Kandy
Khagan	Chengis Khan	Kimam	Pan
Khaini	Pan	Kinari	Bazaar
Khalifat	Khilafat	Kinkob	Kimkhob
Khalistan	Khalsa	King of Delhi	Moguls
Khan/Kan	Khana	Kings Yellow	Orpiment
Khand/a	Akhand	Kintar	Bazaar Weights
	Shakkr	Kiosk	Chhatri

557

Kipling, Rudyard	Army in India	Korma	Roghan Josh
	Ava	Kornish	Salaam
	Bihisti	Kosala	Ram
	Caravan	Kotha Sahib	Gurdwara
	Dhole	Kotla	Kotwal
	European	Kovil	Mandir
	Cemeteries	Kozhikode	Zamorin
	GT Road	Kraah/Karah Prasad	Prasad
	Hobson-Jobson	Krishna (black)	Kala
	Kalighat Art	Kriti	Kar
	Lakh	Kriya	Kar
	Mangas		Kirya
	Swastika	Krore	Crore
Kiraani	Anglo-Indian	Ku	Su
Kirpan	Prasad	Kubla Khan	Chengis Khan
	Sikh	Kucha	Chelan
Kirti Chakra	Defence Ser-		Gali
	vices Awards	Kukas	Namdhari
			Sikhs
Kistna R.	Carnatic	Kul	Gurukul
Kite Hawk	Pariah	Kulu/Kullu	Shimla
Knickers	Pant	Kulcha/e	Nan
Knot	Guru Granth	Kulhar	Char
	Sahib	Kuli	Coolie
Kochi	Jews	Kulkarni	Patta
Kodagu/Kodavi	Coorgi	Kulthi	Dal
Kodampoli	Tamarind	Kumari	Kumar
Kohl	Kajal	Kumbhar/Kumbhkar	Kumbh
Kohlu	Ghani	Kumhar	Kumbh
	Shakkr		Prajapati
Koila/Koyla	Kachcha	Kundalini	Yoga
Kokila	Koel	Kunj	Tope
Kolam	Rangoli	Kunwar	Kanwar
Kolhapur	Chappals	Kurakul	Tope
	Chhatrapati	Kurbani	Id
Kolhar	Char	Kurra Prasad	Prasad
Koli	Kali	Kurukshetra	Epics
Kolkata	Kali		Gita
Konarak	Rath	Kushan Empire	Greeks, The
Koodiyattam	Kathakali	Kushk	Kotwali
Koreishi	Qurayshi	Kushti	Akhara

Kutch	Marwari	sativa	
	Rann	Latvia	Shat
Kutcha	Kachcha		Sanskrit
Kutiyattam	Kathakali	Laudanum	Madak
Labh	Swastika	Lavani	Tamasha
Laburnum	Amaltas	Lawrence, Lord Sir	Koh-i-Noor
Laccadive Islands	Lakshadweep	John	Viceroy
Laddoo	Luddoo	Laws of Manu	Manu
Lafanga	Badmash	Lawsonia	Henna
Lagna	Jyotish	Lawyer	Vakil
Lahoo	Khun	Laxman	Lakshman
Lahore Durbar	Koh-i-noor		Ramayana
	Sikh	Lea & Perrin	Worcester
Lahoria	Gorkha		Sauce
Lake, General Lord	Ava	Lead Sulphide	Kajal
Lakhauti	Gaur	League of Nations	Dyarchy
Lakme	Dhatura		Madak
	Lakshmi	Ledikeni	Lady Kenny
Lakshman Jhoola	Jhoola	Lee-Metford	Dum Dum
Lal	Wala	Left Hand Way	Right Hand,
Lala/Lalla	Bania		Left Hand
Laladika	Bania		Shakti
Lal Bazaar	Bazaar		Vomitory
Lal Chandan	Sandalwood	Lehnga	Dupatta
Lalit	Kala	Leishmaniasis	Kala
Lalla Rookh	Shalimar	Lemon/Lime	Nimbu
Lalluhan Baisakhi	Jallianwala Bagh	Lent	Roza
Lambrequin	Toran	Lentils	Dal
Land Revenue	Settlement	Leo	Singh
Langot	Hanuman	Leopard	Cheetah
Langur	Bandar	Lepchas	Dragon
	Hanuman		Kingdom
Lascari Khana	Kababs	Levant	Khana
Lashkar	Laskar	Levee	Durbar
Lassi	Dahi	Leviticus	Kafir
	Piao	Light House	Tent House
Laswari	Ava	Lilac	Indigo
Lata Mangeshkar	Devadasi	Lime	Chuna
Laterite	Kankar		Pan
Lathi	Lat	Lingayat	Lingam
Lathyrism/Lathyrus	Dal	Lion	Kathiawar

Lion Capital	Chakra		Viceroy
Liquorice	Mulethi	Mace (weapon)	Charri
Litmus	Haldi	Mace (condiment)	Jaiphal
Lithuania	Sanskrit	Madan	Kama
Litters	Carrying Chairs	Machiavelli	Chanakya
Livingstone, David	Tonic	Madder	Rubia
Liwan	Masjid	Madhava	Vishnu
Lizard	Gecko	Madhu/Madira	Mead
Llanelly	Stepney	Madrasa	Madras
Lobh	Love	Madrasi	Dravidia
Lock Hospital	Bazaar	Madurai	Tamil
Lohars	Gadi Lohars	Magadha	Jainism
Lohri	Uttarayana		Patliputra
Loktantra	Tantra	Magar	Mugger
Long Drawers	Pyjama	Magh (month)	Kumbh
Longi	Mirch		Purnima
Long Peppers	Mirch	Magh (people)	Mugg
Lotiya	Lota	Magrib	Masjid
Loyal Toast	Proclamation	Mahabharata	Epics
	Day	Mahadev	Har
Luchi	Paratha		Murti
Lucknavi	Pahile Aap		Shiva
	Yaar	Mahadevi	Durga Puja
Luffa	Loofah		Shakti
Luke, St.	Vahan	Mahakali	Kali
Luso-Indian	Anglo-Indian	Mahan	Maha
Lustration	Dahi	Mahapalika	Nagar
	Lingam	Mahapparinravena	Calendars
Lutera/Lutna	Loot	Maharajah/	Raj
Lutyens, Sir Edwin	Bagh	Maharana/	
	Lingam	Maharao/	
	Star of India	Mahawal	
	Stupa	Mahasagar	Sagar
Lyon, Thomas	Lyon's Range	Mahashakti	Shakti
	Dalal	Mahashay	Shri
Lytton, Lord	Durbar	Mahavir	Hanuman
Maa-Bap	Mai Bap	Mahavira	Calendars
Macaque	Bandar		Divali
Macassar	Kusum		Jainism
Macaulay, Lord	IPC	Maha Vir Chakra	Defence
	Sahib		Services

560

	Awards	Manava	Manu
Mahayagna	Yagna	Manchester	Kanpur
Mahayana	Buddha	Mandalis	Dussehra
	Lama	Mandarin	Mantralaya
Mahesh	Murti		Narangi
Mahindra	Indira	Mandor	Marwari
Mahi Seem	Oudh	Maneka	Mala
Mahish	Yama	Mangala/Mangal	Mangal
Mahishsura	Durga Puja	Sutra	
Mahmud of Ghazni	Sultan	Mani	Mani Stones
Mahotsav	Otsav		Om Vishnu
Mahr/Mehr	Dowry	Manipur	North East
Mahratha	Maratha		India
Maida	Nan	Mansab	Jagir
Maidservant	Ayah	Mantri	Mantralaya
Maitra	Ganga		Shiksha
Maitreya	Buddha	Maqbara	Kabristan
Majha	Punjab	Mara	Shalimar
Majun	Indian Hemp	Marabou	Wordy Major
Makara Sankranti	Pongal	Marasmus	Kwashiorkor
	Uttarayana	Maratha	Chhatrapati
Makbara	Kabristan		Maharashtra
Makhan	Krishna		Peshwar
Makki-ki-roti	Roti		Pindaris
Makhana	Lotus	Maratha Ditch	Bargadar
Maktab	Madrasi		Mulligatawny
Malabathrum	Teipat	Marathwada/	Maharashtra
Makna	Ganesh	Marathwara	
Malai	Janmastami	Mardana	Zenana
Malaria	Tonic	Margarine	Vanaspati
Malayalam	Malabar	Margi	Marg
Malka/Malika/Malkin	Malik	Margosa	Neem
Mallet	Tamarind	Marigolds	Mala
Malwa	Punjab	Marijuana	Agarbatti
Mamluk	Ghulam		Indian Hemp
	Minar	Mark Twain	Anglo-Indian
	Sultanates of	Marriage	Dowry
	Delhi		Nimantran
Manas/Manasarovar	Hans		Rishta
	Kailas		Suhaag
	Su	Marriage Restraint	Sarda Act
		Act	

Mars	Mangal	Maund	Bazaar Weights
	Tuesday	Maur	Morha
Marseillaise	Bande	Mausam	Monsoon
	Mataram	Mawa/Mava	Khoya
Martyr	Smriti	Mayhem	Zoolum
Maruti	Hanuman	Mayo, Lord	Bazaar Weights
Mascara	Kajal	Mayur	Kartikeya
Masefield, John	Ophir		Mor
Mashal	Masalchi	Mazaar	Dargah
Mashuk	Ghazal		Kabristan
Masih	Isa	Meadows Taylor	Thug
	Qawali	Mean Sea Level	Zero
Masnad	Gaddi	Medieval India	Gupta Period
Masoor	Dal	Meeri	Gurdwara
Massage	Maleesh	Meerut	European
Mastan	Mast		Cemeteries
Master	Durzi		First War of
Mast Tree	Ashok		Independence
Masturbation	HP		Khadir
	Maithuna		Moguls
Mata	Sanskrit	Meetha	Khatta
		Meetha Neem	Curry
Matador	Tempo	Meghalaya	North East
Matam	Muharram		India
Mate	Vedas	Mehat	Maha
Matha Tekna	Gurdwara	Mehman	Guest
Matheran	Carrying Chairs	Mehndi	Henna
	Hills, The	Mehrbani	Dhanya
Mathur	Kayasth	Mehta, Narasimhan	Harijan
Mathura	Greeks, The	Memory	Smriti
	Holi	Memsahib	Sahib
	Jantar Mantar	Mensuration	Mer
	Krishna	Merchant	Writer
	Madhuban	Meru	Kailas
	Panda	MES	Inspection
	Yamuna		Bungalow
Matka	Chagul	Mesha	Baisakhi
	Kanwar		Calendars
	Satta	Mesquite	Babul
Matribhumi	Bhumi	Messiah	Isa
Matrika	Shakti	Messrs	Shri

Metre Gauge	Broad Gauge
	Hobson-Jobson
Metrication	Bazaar Weights
Mewat	Machery
Midday	IST
Middle Path	Buddha
Mikdar	Meh
Milad	Id
Milaria	Priekly Heat
Military Hotel	Hotel
Millat	Quaid-i-Azam
Millets	Bajra
	Jowar
	Ragi
Milo	Jowar
Milton, John	Banyan
Mina/Minakari/	Meena
Minakshi	
Minah	Brahma
Mincemeat	Kofta
Mir	Amir
Mirasdar	Zamindar
Mirasi	Hijra
Mirror work	Mochi
Mirza, Ghulam Ahmed	Ahmedis
Mishti Doi	Dahi
Misl	Nihangs
Misri	Shakkr
Missi	Roti
Mistan	Burfi
Mithun	Gaur
Mithuna	Maithuna
Mitti	Multani Mitti
Mizoram	North East India
	Princes
Mlechha	Manu
	Panchama
Mobed	Parsi
Mocha	Kahwa
Moda	Mohra
Moderator	Metropolitan
Mohajir	Vihara

Mohammed, the	Allah
Holy Prophet	Ansar
	Ghusl
	Haj
	Id
	Islam
	Khilafat
	Kor'an
	Masjid
	Mimbar
	Muharrum
	Qurayshi
	Sahib
	Sayid
	Shariah
	Sunni
Mohenjodaro	Indus Valley
	Civilisation
Mohinder	Indra
Mohiniattam	Kathakali
Moira	Halwa
Mole (facial)	Caste Marks
	Til
Molugutunni	Mulligatawny
Momo	Samosa
Mona	Sikh
	Jallianwala Bagh
Monal	Impeyan
	Pheasant
Monday	Soma
Mongol	Chengis Khan
	Moguls
Mongoose	Mangas
Monkey-cap	Bandar
Monkeyman	Damaru
Montezuma's	Delhi Belly
Revenge	
Montford Reforms	Dyarchy
Moonshi	Munshi
Moore, Thomas	Shalimar
Moorat	Mahurat

Moorum	Kankar	Muhajir	Vihara
Moplah	Mappila	Muhammedabad	Varanasi
Morchal	Mor	Mujahid	Jehad
Moringa	Drumsticks	Mujra	Dancing Girls
Morni	Mor	Mukherjee	Ji
Morning Song of	Jana Gana Mana		Rai
India		Mukhopadhyaya	Rai
Mornington, Lord	Tipu Sultan	Mukhya Mantri	Mantralaya
	Paramountcy	Mukta	Moksha
Moses	Musa	Mukund	Vishnu
Mosque	Masjid	Mulberry	Tut
Mother	Sanskrit	Muli	Moolah
Mother Goddess	Bhowani	Mulk/Mulki	Nizam
	Durga Puja	Mulls	Mulligatawny
	Dussehra	Mulnivasi	Adivasis
	Kali	Mumtaz/j	Taj
	Shakti	Munda	Adivasis
	Tantra		Greater India
Motherland	Bhumi		Nimbu
Mother Teresa	Nirmal Hriday	Mung	Dal
Moulvi	Maulvi	Mundu	Lungi
Mount Abu	Lakshadweep	Muram	Kankar
	Malabar	Murdabad	Zindabad
Mountain Artillery	Screw Guns	Murdasankh	Orpiment
Mountbatten, Lord	Ava	Murex snail	Indigo
	Burma	Murgi Khana	Gymkhana
	Independence		Khana
	Day	Murraya koeniga	Curry
	Viceroy	Murugan	Kartikeya
Mouse	Musa	Musafir	Caravan
Mozzy-net	Machardani	Mushak	Bihisti
Mridangan	Tabla	Musk-shrew	Ganesh
Mrit (clay)	Prajapatti	Muslim/Moslem	Islam
Mrit (death)	Amrit	Muslin	Jamdani
Muazzin	Azaan	Mussoorie	Hills, The
	Masjid		Mansuri
	Minar	Must	Mast
Mubarak	Id	Mustafa	Islam
Muga Silk	Tasar	Mustanga	Khampas
Mugdar	Akhara	Mustard	Sarson
Mughal	Moguls	Mutiny, The	First War of

	Independence		Namda
Mutiny Memorial	Hobson-Jobson	Naman	Caste Marks
Muttra	Yamuna	Namaz	Azaan
Mutwali	Wakf		Masjid
Myanmar	Burma	Namibia	Cheetah
Myrhh	Agarbatti	Namkin	Namak
Myrobalan	Amla	Nanak (title),	Guru
Mysore	Carnatic	Nanak Guru	Panth
	Dussehra		Sikh
	Tipu Sultan	Nanakshahi	Calendars
Mystery	Mistri	Nanda Devi	Uttaranchal
Naar	Minar	Nana Peshwar	Peshwa
Naba Barsha	Baisakhi	Nandana	Natraj
Nabh	Su	Nang-dharang	Sadhu
Nabha	Phulkian States	Napoleon	Tipu Sultan
Nabi	Id	Nappy	Nai
Nabob	Nawab	Narakasura	Divali
Nadi	Nala	Narasimhan	Vishnu
Nadir Shah	Koh-i-Noor	Narayan J.P.	Sarvodaya
Nag	Vishnu	Narcissus	Kofta
Nagaland/Nagalima	North East India	Nargi/Narghile	Hookah
Nagara	Nagar	Nargis	Kofta
Nagari	Sanskrit	Narpit	Nai
Nagarathars	Chettiyars	Narrow Gauge	Broad Gauge
Nag Mani	Vishun	Nashta	Hazri
Nagpur	Vidarba	Nashtalique	Khari Boli
Nagpur Plan	National Highways	Nates	Hip
Nahana	Snan	National Animal	Bagh
Nahar	Nala	National Bird	Mor
Naib Subedar	Junior Commissioned Officers	Native	Anglo-Indian
		Native States	Politicals
			Princes
Naini Tal	Tal	Natya Shastra	Bharat Natyam
Najul	Khalsa	Naujawan	Jawan
Nak/Naak	Nark	Naukrani	Ayah
Naka	Chowk	Naulakhaar	Lakh
Naked	Jainism	Nauratri/Navratri	Dussehra
	Sadhu	Nautanki	Natak
Nalini	Lotus	Navjote	Parsi
Namah	Namaskar	Navodaya Vidyalaya	Vidya
		Nav/nau sena	Vahini

Nav Chhidra	Brahma	Nil/Nilam	Indigo
Nayak	Naik	Nilgiri	Giri
Nayaṇ	Nai	Nilkanth	Indigo
Nayer	Nair		Shiva
Naxalbari	Naxalites	Nimkin	Namak
Nazam	Mushaira	Nine Gates	City of
Nazarene	Isa		Nine Gates
Nazim	Waqf	Nira	Toddy
Nazul	Khalsa	Niraj	Lotus
NCE	Followers	Nirankari Sikhs	Namdhari
Neaten	Hazri		Sikhs
Neechi Jati	Jat	Nirayans	Calendars
Neel	Indigo		Uttarayana
Neemuch/Neemach	Madak	Nishada	Adivasi
Neera	Toddy	Nishan Sahib	Gurdwara
NEFA	North East	Niskham	Kama
	India	Nitamb	Hip
Negapatam	Coromandel	Nizamuddin	Chisti
Nehar	Nala	Nizaris	Ismaili
Nehru, Jawaharlal	Achkan	Nobel Prize	Gita
	Jodhpurs	Nomad	Gujars
	Jyoti		Moor
	Khadi	Non-Regulation	Presidency
	Kotwali	Province	
	Nala	Non-violence Silk	Eri
	Shat	North Western	U.P.
Nelumbo nucifera	Lotus	Province	
Nephellium	Lichi	Nosey-Parker	Nark
Nepotism	Bhai	Nritta/Mritya	Abhinaya
Netashahi	Netaji	Numerals	Zero
Neta-topi	Topi	Nutmeg	Jaiphal
Newal	Mangas	NW/National	National
Newar	Charpai	Waterway	Highway
Newcastle Disease	Ranikhet	NWFP	Jirga
NH	National	Nyaya	Panchayat
	Highway	Nymphaea	Lotus
Nibbles	Bhujiya	OBC	Harijan / Dalit
Nibu	Nimbu	Ocymum sanctus	Tulsi
Niger	Til	Odhni/Odhini	Dupatta
Nikah	Kazi	Odissi	Oriya
Nikerdhari	Pant	O'Dyer, Sir Michael	Jallianwala Bagh

Ogedai	Chengis Khan
Ohja	Mor
Oil Bath	Maleesh
	Sarson
	Rakshasha
Okra	Ladies' Fingers
Oleander	Yasmin
Omar Khayyam	Ghazal
Ombudsman	Lok
Omphalos	Om
Omrah	Amir
Onkar/Omkar	Om
Ootacamund	Hills, The
Opium	Green Whisky
	Kuth
	Madak
Orhni	Dupatta
Oriel Window	Darshan
Orpheus	Pietra Dura
Ostend Co.	Coromandel
Otto	Attar
Ottoman	Diwan
	Khilafat
Outer Line	Inner Line
	McMahon Line
Outram, General	First War of
Sir-James	Independence
Outstation	Station
Ozymandias	Durbar
Paap	Saturday
Pachami	Deccan
Pachikari	Pietra Dura
Pad (foot)	Pug
Pad (tale)	Pichawa
Pada	Para
Padam	Lotus
Padishah	Shah
Padma	Lakshmi
	Lotus
Padma Bhushan/	Civilian Awards

Vibhushan/Shri	
Padmini	Lakshmi
	Lotus
Padyatra	Bhumi
	Yatra
Pag/Pagdandi	Pug
Pagdi/Pagri	Puggri
Pahardi	Pahari
Pahi	Pi-dog
Pahlavi	Parsi
Pahlwan	Akhara
Pahul	Amrit
	Sikh
Paigam	Kharita
Paise	Pice
Pajama	Pyjama
Pakhal	Bihisti
Pakhtoon/Pakhtun	Pathans
Paksh	Calendars
	Shraddh
Pal	Gopi
	Krishi
	Lok
	Raj
Palak	Saag
Palampore/Palang	Kalam
Posh	
Palang	Charpai
	Kalam
Palang Char	Hazri
Palang Tor	Pan
Palanquin	Bearer
	Carrying Chairs
Palas	Flame of the
	Forest
Pali	Sanskrit
Palika	Nahar
Palki	Carrying Chairs
Pall	Chaddar
Pala	Ghunghat
	Sari

Pallavaran Gneiss	Charnockite	Paradise Lost	Banyan
Palm Sugar	Country Liquor	Paradoxure	Toddy
	Shakkr	Parakeet	Kama
Pampas Grass	Kans		Madhuban
Pancasila	Panchshil	Param Narm	Pashmina
Panch	Panchayat	Parampara	Guru
	Yojana	Param Vir Chakra/	Defence Ser-
Panchamrit	Amrit	Vishist Medal	vices Awards
Panchang	Calendars	Parbhrit	Koel
Panchatantra	Tantra	Parboiled Rice	Basmati
Panchnama	Panchayat	Parda	Purdah
Pande/Pandey	Pandit	Pardesh	Desh
Pander	Panda	Parikar	Parikrama
Pandi-Kokku	Bandicoot	Parinirvan	Nirvana
Paneer	Panir	Parivar	Yojana
P&O Express	Frontier Mail	Parlok	Lok
Pangat	Langar	Parna	Pan
Pani	Billait	Parmeshwar	Panch
	Chowk	Pars	Parsi
	Jau	Parson	Kal
	Nimbu	Parsvanathan	Jainism
	Pinky-Pani	Partition	Independence
	Veena		Day
Panini	Sanskrit	Parv	Kumbh
Paniphal	Singara		Utsav
Panipatya	Kala	Parvati/Parbati	Girja Ghar
Panjab	Punjab		Kailas
Pankaj	Lotus		Shakti
Panther	Cheetah	Pasha	Shah
	Dalit	Pashm	Pashmina
Panthshala	Dak	Pashtun	Pathans
Pantua	Lady Kenny	Pataliputra/Patna	Patliputra
Papads	Poppadum	Patal Lok	Lok
Papain/Papaya	Papita	Patchouli	Pachouli
Paprika	Mirch	Pathak/Pathi	Akhand
Par	Yamuna	Pathkar	Octroi
Para (Deer)	Chital	Patna Rice	Basmati
Paradise	Ghazi	Pathshala	Dak
	First War of		Rest House
	Independence	Patidar	Patel
Paradise Garden	Bagh	Patience Nuts	Chilgoza

Patil	Patel	Peon	Chaprasi
Patit	Sikh	People of the Book	Kitab
Patka	Cummerbund	Pepperwater	Mulligatawny
	Puggri	Peri	Rakshasha
Patra	Patta	Permanent	Settlement
Patri	Bazaar	Settlement	
Patta (Textiles)	Dupatta	Perron, General	Koil
Patwari	Patta (document)	Peshkash	Khilat
Pauri	Har	Phad	Pichhawa
Paushala	Piao	Phali	Drumsticks
Pavan Sut	Hanuman	Phansigar	Thug
Pawnee	Bilait	Phatak	Pol
Paw Paw	Papita	Phatuhi	Bania
Payal	Kathak	Phera	FERA
Peace	Shanti	Phera/i	Prabat Phere
Peacock	Kartikeya	Pheran	Kangra
	Mor	Phillipines	White Man's
	National Bird		Burden
	Takht	Phulka	Chapati
	Vahan	Phut	Phatna
Peacock Flower	Gul Mohur	Physalis	Ras
Peacock Throne	Koh-i-Noor	Picey/Pie	Pice
	Mor	Pichkari	Holi
	Takht	Piedmont	Terai
Peanuts	Mung Phalli	Pig-sticking	Khadar
Pearl Millet	Bajra	Pik/Peek	Pan
Pedal	Pug	Pil	Mahout
Peeri	Gurdwara	Pilaf	Pulao
Peeth	Vidya	Pine apple	Anana
Pehar	Calendars	Pinda	Shraddh
Pehlwan	Akhara	Pine Nuts	Chilgoza
Penang	Presidencies	Pipal	Peepal
Peninsular India	Deccan	Piper betle	Pan
	Dravidia	Piper nigrum	Mirch
	Ghat	Pipii	Mirch
Penis	Aagey Wala	Pir	Dargah
	Inder	Pisces	Meena
	Lingam	Pishpash	Kedgeree
	Shiva	Piston	Kedgeree
Pen-name	Moguls	Pita	Sanskrit
Pennisetum	Bajra	Pith	Sola Topi

Pitri	Shraddh	Potter	Prajapati
Pitta	Dosha	Poverty Line	Antyodya
Pittri	Sanskrit	Powell, Dylys	Oudh
Planning Commission	Yojana	Prabhamandal	Natraj
Plantago ovate	Isabgol	Pradakshina	Parikrama
Planter	Indigo	Pradhan Mantri	Mantralaya
	Planter's Chair	Prakrit/i	Maithuna
	Urli		Sanskrit
Plassey	East India Co.	Pramukh	Panchayat
	Flame of the	Prapti	Ganga
	Forest	Prasar Bharti	AIR
Plato	Akademi	Pratima	Durga Puja
Playback Singer	Devadasi		Murti
Pliny	Kajal	Prati Shat	Shat
Plough (constellation)	Rishi	Prayer Wheel	Chakra
Plumeria	Pagoda	Prayer Rug	Mihrab
Poda	Jhuming	Prayopasan	Fasting
Poetry	Mushaira	President's Rule	Section 93
Pogostemon	Pachouli		Province
POK	Azaadi	Prithvi	Lok
Pole Star	Dhruv		Vedas
Political Agent	Resident	Prithvi Raj Chauhan	Rai
Polo, Marco and	Chengis Khan	Privative Particles	Ahinsa
Nicole	Hobson-Jobson	Privet	Henna
	Kumar	Prize Fund	Loot
Polyalthia longifolia	Ashok	Probashi	Bangla
Pomegranate	Baluster	Proclamation Day	Durbar
Pondicherry/	Coromandel	Prohibitory Orders	Section 144
Ponducherry	Renoncant	Prosopis	Babul
	Union	Protected Area	Inner Line
	Territory	Protection Money	Raksha
Pond Heron	Paddy	Proutist Bloc	Anand
Pony	Tattu	Provinces	Presidencies
Poona	Pune		Section 93
	Wala		Province
Poonam	Purnima	Psyllium	Isabgol
Poppy Seed	Khus	Pt.	Pandit
Potassium	Pinky Pani	Pterocarpus	Sandalwood
permanganate		sanatalium	
Potato	Alu	Ptolemy	Krishna
Pothos aureus	Money Plant	Pucca	Pakka

Rajasik	Heating Foods	Rasta	Chukka
Rajasthan/Rajputana	Rajput	Rat/Rut/Rati	Kama
Rajgayak	Rag		Kali
Rajghat	Zero	Ratna	Lotus
Rajhans	Hans	Ratti	Bazaar Weights
Rajiv	Lotus	Raughan	Roghan Josh
Rakh	Ash	Rauza	Roza
Rakhi	Raksha		Taj
Ramadan	Roza	Rava	Suji
Rambutan	Lichi	Ravan	Dussehra
Ram Das, Guru	Amrit		Hanuman
Ramdaspura	Amrit		Ramayana
Ramgopal	Bharat	Ravi Das	Chamars
Ramie	China Grass	Ray	Rai
Ramjani	Ram	Razia Sultana	Sultan
Ram Lila	Dussehra		Sultanates of
Rampur	Rohillas		Delhi
Ramzan	Islam	Realgar	Orpiment
	Roza	Recessional	White Man's
Rana Pratap	Mewar		Burden
Ranchi	Jharkhand	Red Dog	Prickly Heat
Rand/Randi	Widow	Red Fort	Moguls
Rangar	Rajput		Rohillas
Rangarekhavali	Rangoli		Sultan
Rangoon Runs	Delhi Belly	Red Sea Rig	Posh
Rani	Raj	Refulgence	Dev
Ranjit Singh, Raja	Degchi	Registan	Abad
	Koh-i-Noor	Regulation	Presidencies
	Sher	Provinces	
	Sikh	Rekha	Lakshman
Rape Oil	Sarson		Sindoor
Rasagola	Khoya	Remie	China Grass
Rasam	Mulligatawny	Restricted Area	Inner Line
Rasbhari	Ras	Rhesus Monkey	Bandar
Rashi	Calendars		Hanuman
Rashtra Marg	National	RIASC	Rice Corps
	Highway	Riaz/j	Ustad
Rasik	Ras	Rice	Basmati
Rasm	Kriya		Paddy
Rasmalai	Khoya		Parsi
Rasoi	Khana		Pulao

572

Rice Christians/	Indian Christians	Dr. William	
Rice Soldiers		Roy	Rai
Riki Tiki Tavi	Mangas	Roy, Ram Mohan	Brahma Samaj
Riksha	Rickshaw	Rubai	Ghazal
Ripon, Lord	Ilbert Bill	Rubber Plant	India
Risaldar	Junior Comm-	Rubia tinctorum	Rubia
	issioned	Rubicon	Lakshman Rekha
	Officers	Rudra	Murti
Rishwat	Hafta		Rudraksh
Rita	Reetha		Shiva
Rites of Passage	Sanskar	Rudraveena	Veena
Ritu	Basant	Ruffian	Badmash
	Calendars		Goonda
	Monsoon	Rukmini	Krishna
Ritumala	Mala	Rumal	Roomal
Rituraj	Basant	Rumjohnny	Ram
Riyasat	Sardar	Rupak	Rupee
Robe of Honour	Siropa	Ruskin, John	Sarvodaya
Roberts, Lord	Hills, The	Ruswa, Mirza	Hindustan
Rohilkhand	Rohillas	Rut	Kama
Rojh	Nilgai	Saab	Sahib
Roller Bird	Indigo	Saada	Pan
Roman Urdu	Khari Boli	Sabeel	Piao
Romany	Banjaras	Sabun	Snan
	Dom	Sacharum	Kans
	Rai	spontaneum	
	Sanskrit	Sachha Badshah	Guru Granth
Rooh/Ruh	Attar		Sahib
Roosevelt, Theodore	White Man's	Sacred Thread	Janeu
	Burden	Sacrifice	Dussehra
Rosary	Mala		Id
	Rudraksh		Mithun
	Tulsi	Sadak	Sarak
Rose, Sir Hugh	Ava	Sadan	Bhavan
Roseapple	Lady Kenny	Sadhak	Sadhana
Roshogola	Khoya	Sadhusant	Sant
Rosin	Lac	Sadhvi	Jainism
Rowlatt Acts	Dyarchy		Sadhu
	Jallianwala Bagh	Sadi	Shat
	MISA	Sadir	Bharat
Roxburgh	Roxb.	Safa	Puggri

Safai Karamchari	Sweeper	Samanya Sewa	Defence Ser-
Safai Mazdoor	Mazdoor	Medal	vices Awards
Safari	Caravan	Samargam Sant	Namdhari Sikhs
Safdar Jang, Nawab	Oudh	Samaroh	Utsav
Safed	Bandar	Sambar	Idli
	Posh	Sambha	Durga Puja
Saga Bhai	Bhai	Samiti	Samaj
Sagamatha	Chomolungma	Sampradai	Sadhu
Sagwan	Teak	Samrat	Sagar
Sahagamani	Sati	Samskara	Sanskar
Sahasranama	Om	Samvat Vikram	Calendars
	Vishnu	Samyukt Mudra	Namaskar
Sahayak	Bearer	Sandas	Gu
Sahukar	Bania	Sanatoria	Cherrapunji
Sainik	Vahini		Hills, The
Sais	Syce	Sanchi	Buddha
Saivite	Shiva		Stupa
Sajda	Salaam		Tope
Sajiv	Vakar	Sanda	Gecko
Saka	Calendars	Sanders Wood	Sandalwood
Saket / Saketa	Oudh	Sandesh	Burfi
Saki	Mushaira	Sandys, Lord	Worcester
Sakora	Char		Sauce
Sakra	Indra	Sangat	Khalsa
Sakti	Shakti		Sangh
Sakyamuni	Muni	Sangha	Buddha
Salai	Sarak		Sangh
Salary	Thanka	Sangharsh	Sangh
Salat	Islam	Sanichar	Hafta
	Namaz		Saturday
Salatin	Sultan	Sanidan	Saturday
Saliva	Havan	Sankara	Math
	Mirch	Sankh	Conch
Salmalia	Kapok	Sankirtan	Kirtan
Salt	Namak	Sankranti	Baisakhi
Saltpetre	Bangla		Calendars
Salt Tax	Dandi		Pongal
Saluno	Raksha		Uttarayana
Salute States	Gun Salutes	Sansar	Ghar
Salwar	Shalwar	Santalum alba	Sandalwood
Saman	Khansama	Santala/Santhala	Adivasis

574

Santyals	Jharkhand	Sathi-Bhai/Sathin	Gorkha
Santara (orange)	Narangi	Satrap	Subedar
Santara/Santharan	Fasting	Satsangh	Sangh
Santi	Shanti	Sattvik	Heating Foods
Santiniketan	Archarya	Sau	Shat
	Shanti		Vedas
Sapindra	Shraddh	Saubhagyawati	Devadasi
Sapodilla/sapota	Chiku	Saudagar	Bania
Saptah	Hafta	Saum	Fasting
Saptapada	Tika		Id
Saracen	Moor		Islam
Saraf	Shroff		Roza
Sarai	Caravan	Saurashtra	Kathiawar
Sarak-e-Azam	G.T. Road	Saussurea lappa	Kuth
Sarani	Sarak	Savarn	Caste Hindus
Saraswati	Basant		Harijan/Dalit
	Brahma	Savitra	Gayatri
	Dev	Savitri	Sati
	Indus Valley	Sawa/Sawai	Jantar Mantar
	Civilisation		Nihang
	Lakshmi	Sawalakh	Nihang
Prayag	Sangam	Sawar/Sawari	Sowar
Sarauta/Sarota	Pan	Sayana	Uttarayana
Sardeshmukh	Desh	Sayya	Charpai
Sarnath	Chakra	Scale Insects	Lac
	Mahabodh	Scheduled Areas/	Adivasis
	Society	Tribes	
Sarod	Sitar	Scheduled Castes	Harijan/Dalit
Saroj	Lotus	Schleichera oleosa	Kusum
Saropa	Siropa	Scimitar	Bahadur
Sarovar	Amrit	Scindapsus aureus	Money Plant
Sarpanch	Panchayat	Scopolamine	Dhatura
Sarvashri	Shri	Scotch Eggs	Kofta
Sarvottam Jeevan	Padak	Scott, Paul	Anglo-Indian
Raksha	Raksha	Scrambled Eggs	Rumble-Tumble
Sat	Ram	Scrub Cattle	Zebu
	Sangh	Seasons	Calendars
	Sat Sri Akal	Seat	Arsan
Satam	Shat		Upanishad
Satan	Shaitan	Secretary of State	Covenanted
Satara	Chhatrapati	(London)	Services

	Dyarchy	Shahadah	Islam
	East India Co.	Shaheeds	Nihangs
	Indian Civil	Shahi	Imam
	Service		Shah
	Viceroy	Shah Jehan	Baluster
Sect Marks	Caste Marks		Taj
Secunderabad	Greeks, The	Shahzada	Shah
Seditionists	First War of In-	Shaitan	Rakshasha
	dependence	Shaivite	Shiva
Seekh	Kababs	Shakarkhand	Alu
	Sikh	Shalom	Salaam
Seer	Bazaar Weights	Shama	Mushaira
Seerath	Kor'an	Shaman	Mor
Sehajdhari	Sikh	Shampoo	Maleesh
Sehri	Roza	Shamshan Ghat	Ghat
Sela	Basmati	Shamsher	Bahadur
Seljuk Turks	Star of India	Shangri La	La
Semen	Dhat	Shani	Saturday
	Vir	Shanipriya	Indigo
Semolina	Suji	Shankar	Shiva
Sena/Senapati	Vahini	Shankaracharya	Math
Senior Advocate	Pleader		Maya
Senior Merchant	Writer	Shankh	Conch
Senna	Amaltas	Sharab	Kachcha
Sequin	Rupee		Sherbet
Serai	Caravan	Sharif	Kor'an
Serampore	Roxb.		Mohur
Sergeant	Havildar	Sharifa	Chiku
Seringapatnam	Tipu Sultan	Sharda Act	Sarda Act
Sesamum	Til	Shashlik	Kababs
Seven Brothers/	Bhai	Shat/Sat Kona	Star of India
Sisters		Shatranj (i)	Duree
Sewak/Sewaka	Gram	Shawl	Pashmina
	Lok	Shawm	Shenai
	Sewa	Shawwal	Id
Sex Ratio	Dowry	Sheesha/Sheesh Nag	Vishnu
Shaal	Pashmina	Sheeshadari	Mochi
Shabad/Shabd	Kirtan	Shellac	Lac
Shabnam	Dupatta	Shelley P.B.	Durbar
Shadi	Nimantran	Sheriff	Presidencies
Shagird	Chela	Shertha	Mirch

Sherwani	Achkan	Sidi	Habshi
	Jodhpurs	Sif'a	Zero
Shia	Sunni	Sigri	Kangri
Shi:el/a	Panchshil	Sijda	Salaam
Shikakai	Reetha	Sikander	Greeks, The
Shikandi	Shikara	Sikhana	Sikhs
Shikanji	Nimbu	Sikka	Rupee
Shila	Saligram	Sikkim	Chogyal
Shilpa/Silpa	Mandir	Silk	Eri
	Prajapati	Silk Cotton Tree	Kapok
	Shashtras	Silladar	Bargadar
Shinde	Scindia	Silsila	Sufi
Shit (excrement)	Gu	Silver Fish	Oudh
Shitala (Goddess)	Shit	Simha/Simhan	Singh
Shivaji	Chhatrapati	Simla	Shimla
	Shiv Sena	Simla Convention	McMahon Line
Shobh(a)yattra	Yattra	Simla Mirch	Mirch
Shok	Shastras	Simple Imprisonment	RI
Shola	Solar Topi	Simples	Ayurveda
Shoot	Shikar	Simul	Kapok
Shorba	Soop	Sindhu	Hindu
Shore, Sir John	Viceroy		India
Shorea robusta	Sal	Singh (horn)	Singara
Shravan	Kanwar	Sindia	Scindia
Shravana Belgola	Jainism	Singh, Khuswant	Hindustan
Shrew Rat	Ganesh	Singing Girl	Dancing Girls
Shrikhand	Dahi	Sinhasan	Singh
	Sandalwood	Sinha/Sinhalese	Singh
Shrub	Sherbet	Sinister	Right Hand,
Shruti	Vedas		Left Hand
Shuddikaran	Shoe	Sirdar	Sardar
Shufti	Dekko	Sita	Divali
Shukla	Calendars		Hanuman
Shukriya	Dhanya		Ramayana
Shunya	Zero	Sita Ashok	Ashok
Shurua	Soop	Sitaphal	Chiku
Shuruttu	Cheroot	Siva	Shiva
Shyam	Krishna	Sivaliks	Dun
Shyama	Kali		Garhwal
Sicca/Sikka	Rupee	Siyaram	Ram
Siddha	Durga Puja	Skanda	Kartikeya

Skirt	Ghagra	Spahi	Sepoy
Skull	Aghori	Spikenard	Agarbati
	Coir	Spinach	Palak
Sky Clad	Jainism		Saag
Sky Class	Passenger Train	Spinepads	Solar Topi
Slash and Burn Cultivation	Jhuming	Spittoon	Pan
		Spoon	Chamcha
Slav	Habshi	Spring	Basant
Slave	Ghulam	Springing Tigers	Azad Hind Fauj
Slave Kings	Sultanates of Delhi	Sravan	Krishna
		Sri	Lakshmi
Sleeman, Sir William	Thug		Shri
Sloka	Shastras	Sri Krishna Sena	Yadav
	Shloka	Sri Lanka	British India
Sloth Bear	Madari		Rupee
Smack	Madak		Singh
Smallpox	Shit	Srinagar	Shri
Smt.	Shri	Sringara	Shringar
Snake Boat	Onam	Sringeri	Math
Snake Charmers	Been	Srnga	Barasingha
Soap	Snan	St. Mathew	Dal
Soapnuts	Reetha	St. Theodore	Vahan
Soda Water	Bilait	St. Thomas	Mar
Sodhi, Ram Das, Guru	Guru	Stable	Istibil
Solomon	Sulaiman	Stabilising Agent	Babul
	Indigo		Guar
Solomon's Seal	Star of India	Stant Sahibs	SDO
Somnath/Somanatha	Islam	Star of David	Star of India
Sonar Bangla	Bangla	States, The	Politicals
Sonepur	Purnima	Statutory Civil Service	Indian Civil Service
Sopara	Ophir	Steel Frame	Indian Civil Service
Sorbet	Sherbet		
Sorghum	Jowar	Step Well	Baoli
Soup	Soop	Stevens, Thomas	East India Co.
Soumitra/Sumitra	Su	Sthali	Sthan
	Vedas	Stole	Pyjama
Southpaw	Right Hand, Left Hand	Stramonium	Dhatura
		Stree/Stri	Nar
Sowkar	Bania	Streedhan	Dowry
Spatchcock	Sudden Death	Street Car	Tam Tam

Stubbs, George	Cheetah		Factory
Stuti	Ganesh	Suri, Sher Shah	Rupee
Subha	Subedar		Tankha
Subash Chandra	Azad Hind Fauj	Surinder	Indra
Bose,	Netaji	Surma	Kajal
Subedar (Military)	Junior Com-	Survey of India	GTS
	missioned		Pandit
	Officers	Surya	Gayatri
Subramanium	Kartikeya		Rath
Suchak	Dhruv		Vedas
Sudarshan	Vishnu	Surya Siddhanta	Calendars
Sudder	Sadar	Sursarita	Ganga
Sudra	Shudra	Sushri	Ganga
Sudreh	Parsi	Sutlej R.	Punjab
Sufi	Bhakti	Suttra/Sutra	Janeu
Sugar	Shakkr		Shastras
Sugriv	Hanuman	Suttee	Sati
Sujani	Madhuban	Suture	Shastras
Sukh	Anand	Svaha	Yagna
Suleiman the	Islam	Svetambar/	Jainism
Magnificent		Swetamba	
Sultana	Sultan	Swadharm	Dharma
Sun	Gayatri	Swarg	Himalaya
Sunday	Gayatri	Swat	Wala
Sunderbans	Mangrove	Swatantra	Rajaji
Sunga/Shunga	Mauryan		Tantra
	Period	Swayambhu	Lingam
Sunna	Kor'an	Swayam Sewak	RSS
	Shariat	Sweet Potato	Alu
Sunnat	Islam	Swetchhatri	Chhatrapati
Sunstroke	Solar Topi	Swidden	Jhuming
Sunya	Zero	Syed	Sayid
Sup	Soop	Syedna	Bohra
Supervisor	Collector	Syphilis	Firang
Suprabhat	Pranam	Syrian Church	Mar
Supreme Court	Harijan/Dalit		Metropolitan
Sura	Wine	Taar/Taal	Toddy
Surah	Kor'an	Taaviz	Bismillah
Surahi	Chagul	Tabalchi	Tabla
Suraj	Gayatri	Tabasco	Mirch
Surat	East India Co.	Tabernacle	Gurdwara

Tagete patula	Mala	Tarang	Jal Tarang
Tagore, Rabindranath	Akash	Tarangambadi	Coromandel
	Babu	Tarboosh	Topi
	Bande	Tares	Dal
	Mataram	Tari	Curry
	Bangla	Taro	Arvi
	Gita	Tarri	Toddy
	Guru	Tartar	Moguls
	Jana Gana Mana	Tarzias	Muharram
	Rai	Tat	Brahma
	Sangeet		Gunny
	Shanti		Om
	Thakur	Tatti	Khus
	Indian	Tau	Chacha
Tagore,	India Civil	Taus	Mor
Satyendranath	Service		Takht
		Tavern	Maikhana
Takalluf	Pahile Aap	Tavernier, Jean	Banjaras
Takallus	Moguls	Baptiste	Koh-i-Noor
Takbir	Allah	Tawa	Chapati
Taksaal	Gurdwara	Tawaef/Tawaif	Dancing Girls
Takshashila	Gandhara	Taxila	Gandhara
Tal/Taal	Toddy	Taylor, Meadows	Thug
Talao/Talab	Tal	Tazia	Muharram
Tamas(ik)	Heating Foods	Tea	Char
	Panchama	Tectona grandis	Teak
Tambul	Pan	Teekha	Mirch
Tamil Sangam	Sangam	Teen Murti	Murti
Tamjharm	Carrying Chairs	Tegh	Degchi
Tamra Patra/Patta	Patta		Khalsa
Tam-tam	Tom-Tom	Tehband/Tehmad	Lungi
Tandava	Natraj	Tehbazaari	Bazaar
Tang	Rann	Tehkhana	Tikhana
Tangerine	Narangi	Tehsil/Tehsildar	Parganah
Tanjavur	Chola	Tehzib/Tehzeeb	Hindustan
Tankhiya	Sikh		Pahile Aap
Tansen	Rag	Teignmouth, Lord	Viceroy
Tap	Doolally	Tej	Akash
Taqavi	Taccavi	Tekka	Theka
Tar (tree)	Toddy	Tel	Maleesh
Tar (wire)	Dak	Telengana	A.P.

	Telegu	Thyagaraj	Carnatic
	Yoga	Tibb/Tibbia	Hakim
Teli	Ghani	Ticca/Tika/Tikka	Theka
Telicheri/Tellicherry	Kahwa	Tidal Forest	Mangrove
	Mirch	Tie and dye	Band
Temple Hangings	Pichchawa	Tiger	Bagh
Temple of Bread	Langar		Machan
Temple Tree	Pagoda	Tik-Tiki	Gecko
Tendu	Biri	Tikli	Charka
Tendua	Cheetah	Tila	Tope
Tensing Norgay	Sherpa	Tilak	Tika
Tent Club	Khadar	Tilak, Gangadhar	Swaraj
Tepid	Tapas	Time-waster	Kal
Terahwan	Kriya	Timur	Beg
Tested Zari	Zari		Chengis Khan
Testicle	Gol		Gumbaz
Tesu	Flame of the		Mcguls
	Forest	Timur Ruby	Koh-i-Noor
Tetrahydrocannabinol	Indian Hemp	Tinned Food	Heating Foods
Tezpur	Mirch	Tip	Baksheesh
Thag	Thug	Tipari	Ras
Thakin	Sahib	Tir	Two
Thalasserry	Kahwa	Tirhut	Maithila
Thanda Pani	Chowk	Tirthankara	Jainism
Chowkidars		Tiruchchirrappali	Cheroot
Thandai	Green Whisky		Thiru
	Indian Hemp	Toady/Todi	Chamcha
Thangka	Tanka	Toba	Tope
Thank-you	Dhanya	Tod, James	Rajput
Tharra	Country	Tola	Bazaar Weights
	Liquor	Toli	Hijra
Theka (Timber)	Teak	Toll tax	Octroi
Theravada	Buddha	Tom Raw	Griffin
Thermantidote	Khus	Tonjon	Carrying Chairs
Thikhana	Tikhana	Tonk	Pindari
Thiruvananthapuram	Thiru	Tonsil	Multani Mitti
Thoreau H.D.	Sarvodaya	Toosh	Shahtoosh
Thorn Apple	Dhatura	Top	Topi
Three	Two	Top Hat	Thunder Box
Thumri	Rag	Toran	Ganesh
Thunderbolt	Dorji	Tota	Kama

	Madhuban	Turani	Moor
Tour	Camp	Turban	Puggri
Tower of Silence	Dokma	Turk	Moor
Town	Nagar	Turki	Khari Boli
	Nigam	Turkey-Red	Rubia
	Pur	Turkey Trots	Delhi Belly
	Shahr	Turki Topi	Topi
Town Cryer	Dhandhorichi	Turkish Bath	Hammam
Trabeate	Arch	Turmeric	Haldi
Tranquebar	Coromandel	Tussore	Tasar
Transferred Subjects	Dyarchy	Twice-born	Caste Hindus
Transvestites	Hijras		Janeu
Trapa bipinosa	Singara	Tyagi/Thyagi	Tapas
Tribals	Adivasi	Typhoon	Monsoon
Trichinopoly	Cheroot		Toofan
Tricolour	Saffron	Tyre (Milk)	Dahi
Trident	Shiva	Tyre/Tire	Stepney
	Trisul	Tytler, Harriet	Sahib
Triennale	Lalit Kala	Udam Singh	Jallianwala Bagh
	Akademi	Udagamandalam	Hills, The
Trilok	Lok	Uddyan	Bagh
Trimmings	Bazaar	Udupi	Udipi
Trimurthi	Murthi	Udyan Pandit	Krishi
Trincomalee HMS	Teak	UGC	Hindu Code
Tripathi	Vedas	Ujjain	Calendars
Tripolia	Pol		IST
	Tri		Jantar Mantar
Tripundr	Caste marks		Kumbh
Tripura	North East India	Ulan Bator	Bahadur
Trivandrum	Thiru	Uma	Sati
Trivedi	Vedas		Shakti
Triveni	Prayag	Umbrella	Chatrapati
	Sangam		Chhatri
Tsangpo	Kailas	Ummah/Ummat	Islam
Tsar	Durbar	Umrah	Haj
TTE	WT	Unani	Hakim
Tufan	Toofan	Underwear	Kachcha
Tulashi	Tulsi	United Provinces	U.P.
Tuliband/Tulip	Puggri	Unsweetened	Phika
Tulsidas	Ramayana	Unto this last	Sarvodaya
Tundra Swans	Kailas	Untouchable	Harijan
		Upadhyay	Up

Upal	Opal	Vaivaswata	Manu
Upanayana	Janeu	Vajra	Dorji
	Sanskar		Indra
Upari/Upori	Hafta	Vajrayana	Buddha
Up country	Hindustan	Vaju	Ghusl
	Mofusil	Valentia, Lord	Anglo-Indian
Upjat	Caste Hindu	Vam	Vomitory
Upla	Gobar	Van	Garland
Upma	Suji	Vana Mahotsav	Utsav
Up Mantri	Mantralaya	Vanars	Hanuman
Upper Provinces	U.P.	Van Mala	Devnagri
Upvan	Bagh	Vande Mataram	Bande
Upvas	Fasting		Mataram
Urd/Urad	Gram	Vanaprastha	Ashram
	Poppadam	Vang	Bangla
Urdu	Camp	Vanvas(i)	Adivasis
	Khari Boli		Ashram
Urumastix	Gecko	Vapour	Washp
Ushnisa/Usnisa	Shrivats	Varadh	Vidharba
Ustani	Ustad	Varaq	Khir
Uthala/Uthaoni/	Kriya	Vardi	Wordy Major
Utharna		Varna	Caste Hindus
Utopia	Ram	Varsha	Barsaat
Uttar	Deccan		Monsoon
Uttar Pradesh	U.P.		Yojana
Uzbeks	Abad	Varun	Varuna
	Moguls	Vasant	Basant
		Vasco da Gama	Zamorin
Vaam/Varm Marg	Right Hand,	Vasudev	Krishna
	Left Hand	Vat	Banyan
	Tantra	Vata	Dosha
Vada	Dahi	Vatika	Bagh
	Idli	Vatodar	Gaekwar
Vadi	Bal	Vatsyayana	Kama
Vadodara	Gaekwar		Shastra
Vaid	Ayurveda	Vav	Baoli
Vaikunth	Himalaya	Vayu	Akash
Vairagi	Sadhu		Hanuman
Vaisakh	Baisakhi	Vayu-Sena	Vahini
	Purnima	Vazir	Wazir
Vaishnavite	Vishnu	VCO	Junior Comm-

583

	issioned Officers
Vedacharya	Acharya
Vedanta	Upanishads
Vedaranyam	Dandi
Vedi	Bedi
Vedika	Stupa
Vegetable Ghee	Vanaspati
Vehicle	Gharry / Vahan
Veni	Mala
Venkateshwara	Vishnu
Venu	Krishna
Verger	Church Bearer
Verma	Kayashth
Vermilion	Hind / Hanuman / Sindoor / Tika
Veshti	Lungi
Vestal Virgins	Vaastu
Vetiver	Khus
Vibhag	Caste Hindus
Vice-Chancellor	Kulpati / Lady Kenny
Vicereine	Viceroy of India
Viceroy Commissioned Officer	Jemadar / Junior Commissioned Officers
Victoria, Queen	Army in India / East India Co. / European Cemeteries / Hafiz / Hind / Koh-i-Noor / Proclamation Day / Viceroy
Videsh	Desh

Vidh/Widhwa	Widow
Vidhwan	Vidya
Vidyut	Shakti
Vijayadashami	Divali / Dussehra
Vilas	Lakshmi
Villain	Naik
Vimana (aircraft)	Vahan
Vimana (architecture)	Shikara
Vina	Veena
Vinayak	Ganesh
Vindhyachal	Dravidia
Vindhyan Sandstone	Tantpur
Vindhyas	Deccan / Dravidia
Vinoba Bhave	Bhumi / Fasting / Sarvodaya
Vir Chakra	Defence Services Awards
Visarjan	Durga Puja
Vishist Seva Medal	Defence Services Awards
Vishnugupta	Chanakya
Vishvakarma	Divali
Vishvanath	Mandir / Shiva
Vishva Bharat University	Acharya
Vishvavidyalaya	Shastry / Shanti / Vidya
Vitamin R	Hafta
Vithi	Marg
Vivah/a	Rishta
Vizier	Wazir
Vow	Maun
Vraj	Janmastami
Vrata	Maun

Upal	Opal
Upanayana	Janeu
	Sanskar
Upari/Upori	Hafta
Up country	Hindustan
	Mofusil
Upjat	Caste Hindu
Upla	Gobar
Upma	Suji
Up Mantri	Mantralaya
Upper Provinces	U.P.
Upvan	Bagh
Upvas	Fasting
Urd/Urad	Gram
	Poppadam
Urdu	Camp
	Khari Boli
Urumastix	Gecko
Ushnisa/Usnisa	Shrivats
Ustani	Ustad
Uthala/Uthaoni/	Kriya
Utharna	
Utopia	Ram
Uttar	Deccan
Uttar Pradesh	U.P.
Uzbeks	Abad
	Moguls
Vaam/Varm Marg	Right Hand,
	Left Hand
	Tantra
Vada	Dahi
	Idli
Vadi	Bal
Vadodara	Gaekwar
Vaid	Ayurveda
Vaikunth	Himalaya
Vairagi	Sadhu
Vaisakh	Baisakhi
	Purnima
Vaishnavite	Vishnu

Vaivaswata	Manu
Vajra	Dorji
	Indra
Vajrayana	Buddha
Vaju	Ghusl
Valentia, Lord	Anglo-Indian
Vam	Vomitory
Van	Garland
Vana Mahotsav	Utsav
Vanars	Hanuman
Van Mala	Devnagri
Vande Mataram	Bande
	Mataram
Vanaprastha	Ashram
Vang	Bangla
Vanvas(i)	Adivasis
	Ashram
Vapour	Washp
Varadh	Vidharba
Varaq	Khir
Vardi	Wordy Major
Varna	Caste Hindus
Varsha	Barsaat
	Monsoon
	Yojana
Varun	Varuna
Vasant	Basant
Vasco da Gama	Zamorin
Vasudev	Krishna
Vat	Banyan
Vata	Dosha
Vatika	Bagh
Vatodar	Gaekwar
Vatsyayana	Kama
	Shastra
Vav	Baoli
Vayu	Akash
	Hanuman
Vayu-Sena	Vahini
Vazir	Wazir
VCO	Junior Comm-

	issioned	Vidh/Widhwa	Widow
	Officers	Vidhwan	Vidya
Vedacharya	Acharya	Vidyut	Shakti
Vedanta	Upanishads	Vijayadashami	Divali
Vedaranyam	Dandi		Dussehra
Vedi	Bedi	Vilas	Lakshmi
Vedika	Stupa	Villain	Naik
Vegetable Ghee	Vanaspati	Vimana (aircraft)	Vahan
Vehicle	Gharry	Vimana (architecture)	Shikara
	Vahan	Vina	Veena
Veni	Mala	Vinayak	Ganesh
Venkateshwara	Vishnu	Vindhyachal	Dravidia
Venu	Krishna	Vindhyan Sandstone	Tantpur
Verger	Church Bearer	Vindhyas	Deccan
Verma	Kayashth		Dravidia
Vermilion	Hind	Vinoba Bhave	Bhumi
	Hanuman		Fasting
	Sindoor		Sarvodaya
	Tika	Vir Chakra	Defence
Veshti	Lungi		Services
Vestal Virgins	Vaastu		Awards
Vetiver	Khus	Visarjan	Durga Puja
Vibhag	Caste Hindus	Vishist Seva Medal	Defence
Vice-Chancellor	Kulpati		Services
	Lady Kenny		Awards
Vicereine	Viceroy of India	Vishnugupta	Chanakya
Viceroy Commi-	Jemadar	Vishvakarma	Divali
ssioned	Junior Comm-	Vishvanath	Mandir
Officer	issioned		Shiva
	Officers	Vishva Bharat	Acharya
Victoria, Queen	Army in India	University	
	East India Co.	Vishvavidyalaya	Shastry
	European		Shanti
	Cemeteries		Vidya
	Hafiz	Vitamin R	Hafta
	Hind	Vithi	Marg
	Koh-i-Noor	Vivah/a	Rishta
	Proclamation	Vizier	Wazir
	Day	Vow	Maun
	Viceroy	Vraj	Janmastami
Videsh	Desh	Vrata	Maun

Vrindaban	Krishna	Wheel	Chakra
	Yamuna		Rath
Vulture	Dokma	White Cheeseboard	Alstonia
	Saturday		scholaris
	Vahan	White Embroidery	Chikan
Vyaghra	Bagh	Whore	Hur
Vyamshala	Akhara	Widdershins	Right Hand,
Vyopar	Beopar		Left Hand
Wada/Wara	Bal	Widhwa	Widow
Wah/Wahi	Guru	Windsor Castle	Yalli
	Mushaira	Winter Line	Hills, The
Waju/Vaju	Ghusl	Wild Ass	Kyang
Wakil	Vakil		Rann
Warq/Wark	Khir	Wrestling	Akhara
	Pan		Charri
Washerman	Dhobi		Dangal
	Harijan	Yag	Yak
Wat	Banyan	Yakshagana	Udipi
Water Music	Jal Tarang	Yakshini	Apsara
Water Chestnut	Singhara		Kubera
Watering	Jauhar	Yami	Yamuna
Water Nymphs	Apsaras	Yangon	Burma
Waterpots	Chagul	Yantra	Jantar Mantar
	Kumbh		Mandal
Wattle	Babul		Tantra
Wavell, Lord	Viceroy	Yantrashala	Jantar Mantar
Wazu	Ghusl	Yard (measure)	Gaz
Wealth of India	Watts	Yavana	Greeks, The
Wearunders	Kachcha		
Weather Time	IST	Yeats, W.B.	Gita
Wedding	Havan	Yehudi	Jews
	Kund	Yellow Clothing	Tirth
	Nimantran	Yesudas	Adivasi
	Suhaag	Yogi/Yogini	Yoga
	Rishta	Yogin	Devadasi
Week, The	Station	Yoghurt	Dahi
Welcome	Samosa	Yoke	Yoga
Wellesley, Sir Arthur	Ava	Yuddh	Dharma
	Banjaras	Yule, Sir Henry	Hobson-Jobson
	Tipu Sultan	Yurt	Namda
Wellesley, Marquess	Paramountcy		

Zaban	Khari Boli	Ziarat	Dargah
Zafar	Moguls	Zila	District
Zakat	Id	Zil-Haj	Haj
	Islam		Id
Zam Zama	Sweeper	Ziziphus mauritiana	Ber
Zan	Zenana	Zizya	Jizya
Zarda/Zardozi	Pan	Zo	Yak
	Zar	Zopad	JJ Colony
Zaveri	Jauhar	Zoroaster	Parsi
Zenanas	Hijras	Zum	Yak